SCHOOL ENGLISH THESAURUS

Abbreviations used in this book

adj	adjective
adv	adverb
Amer	American
conj	conjunction
fml	formal
inf	informal
n	noun
npl	plural noun
prep	preposition
vb	verb

Published 2009 by Geddes & Grosset,
David Dale House, New Lanark, ML11 9DJ, Scotland

ISBN 978 1 84205 681 3

Printed and bound in UK

Introduction

This book consists of an English thesaurus with related phrases and idioms for many entries, and a guide to letter-writing.

The thesaurus provides an alphabetical listing of words with their related synonyms. For example, if you want to say that a story or joke is funny, the thesaurus will tell you that you could use 'amusing', 'comical', 'humorous', 'hilarious', 'entertaining', or a number of other words instead.

Many words have more than one meaning. 'Funny', for example, does not only apply to things that make you laugh. It can also be applies to things or people that are rather odd, and under this meaning the thesaurus lists 'odd', 'peculiar', 'queer', 'weird', 'bizarre', and so on.

In this book, you will find that those words that have more than one meaning have more than one list of words and that these are numbered **1**, **2**, and so on. Thus, 'funny' meaning 'amusing' is under **1** and 'funny' meaning 'odd' is under **2**. Some words have quite a few different lists depending on the number of meanings attached to them.

To help you find out which list of meanings you are looking for, an example sentence or phrase showing how the particular word is used is placed in brackets after the part of speech and the number. Thus, the entry for 'funny' has **funny** *adj* **1** (*They laughed at his funny stories*) followed by a list of appropriate alternatives.

Throughout the text you will also find some common phrases which are related to some of the headwords. These phrases appear after the the main entry for the headword (as indicated by the symbol ▼). They are followed by the meaning of the phrase and a sentence showing how the phrase is used, and sometimes the origin of the phrase is also indicated. For example, after the main entry for **dust** you will find:

> **not see (someone) for dust** not to see (someone) because he or she has run away (*When it is discovered that he has stolen the money, you won't see him for dust*) <refers to clouds of dust left behind by horses or vehicles moving fast>.

Though some may question the need to write letters nowadays, most of us will need to write letters at some time. Writing a letter allows you to consider carefully what you want to say, to express your feelings, to put things in logical order, to revise and fine tune, and so to produce an impressive and effective result. The guide to letter-writing in this book gives practical advice on how to create the right impression whether you are writing to a prospective employer or composing a thank-you letter. As well as examples of standard letters, there is also information on tools and equipment and on presentation and layout.

Contents

foreigner, non-native. **2** (*aliens from another planet*) extraterrestrial, (*inf*) little green man.

alight *vb* **1** (*alight from the bus*) get off, dismount, descend. **2** (*butterflies alighting on leaves*) land, come down, come to rest, settle, touch down.

alike *adj* (*sisters who are very much alike*) like, similar, the same, identical, indistinguishable.

alive *adj* **1** (*soldiers wounded but still alive*) living, live, breathing, (*inf*) in the land of the living. **2** (*streets alive with shoppers*) crowded, packed, teeming, swarming, overflowing, thronged, (*inf*) crawling.

allegation *n* (*deny their allegations that he was a thief*) claim, charge, accusation, declaration, assertion, statement.

allergic *adj* (*allergic to cows' milk*) hypersensitive, sensitive.

alley *n* (*attacked in a dark alley leading off the high street*) alleyway, lane, passage, passageway, backstreet. ▼

---

blind alley an action or situation that cannot be of advantage to one (*His present job is just a blind alley—he has no hope of promotion*) <Literally a 'blind alley' is a lane that is blocked off at one end so that no exit is possible>.

---

alliance *n* (*foreign countries forming an alliance against the enemy*) union, association, league, coalition, federation, partnership, affiliation.

allot *vb* (*allot work to each of the students/allot grants of money to those in need*) allocate, distribute, give out, share out, dispense, apportion.

allow *vb* **1** (*allow them to use her swimming pool*) let, permit, give permission to, authorize, (*inf*) give the go-ahead to. **2** (*allow half a roll of wastepaper for wastage*) plan for, make provision for, provide for, take into account, take into consideration.

allowance *n* (*a dress allowance*) money, payment, remittance, contribution, grant, subsidy. ▼

---

make allowances for someone *or* **something** to expect a less high standard from someone because of special circumstances (*You must make allowances for his wife—she is not usually so short-tempered but she is still upset about her mother's death*).

---

allude *vb* (*He alluded to the history of the town in his speech*) refer to, mention, mention in passing, touch upon, make an allusion to.

alluring *adj* (*a woman of alluring beauty*) attractive, fascinating, charming, enchanting, captivating, bewitching, beguiling, tempting.

ally *n* (*their allies in the war*) confederate, associate, collaborator, partner, friend.

almost *adv* (*almost four o'clock/almost two miles long*) nearly, close to, just about, around, not quite, practically, approximately.

alone *adj* **1** (*go to the party alone*) by oneself, unaccompanied, unescorted, companionless. **2** (*left all alone by her father's death*) solitary, lonely, isolated, desolate, deserted, forlorn. **3** (*He alone can answer the questions*) only, solely, just.

aloof *adj* (*People who are aloof do not have many friends*) distant, remote, unresponsive, unapproachable, standoffish, unsociable, unfriendly, cold.

aloud *adv* (*cry aloud*) out loud, audibly, clearly, distinctly.

also *adv* **1** (*buy a bed and a wardrobe also*) too, as well, besides, in addition, into the bargain. **2** (*He's poor; also he's ill*) furthermore, besides, moreover, in addition. ▼

---

also-ran *n* an unsuccessful person (*She was not one of the leading competitors—she was just an also-ran/He will never gain promotion—he is an also-ran*) <A horse-racing term for a horse that is not one of the first three horses in a race>.

---

alter *vb* **1** (*alter the dress*) change, adjust, modify, convert, reshape, remodel, vary, transform. **2** (*The village has scarcely altered*) change, become different, vary.

alteration *n* **1** (*make alterations to the dress/make alterations to the letter*) change, adjustment, modification, amendment, revision, variation. **2** (*the alteration of his appearance after his illness*) change, difference, variation, transformation, metamorphosis.

alternative *n* (*offer an alternative on the menu for vegetarians*) choice, option, possibility, preference.

altitude *n* (*the altitude of the ski-resort*) height, elevation.

altogether *adv* **1** (*six of us altogether*) in all, all told, in total. **2** (*not altogether sure*) completely, quite, entirely, totally, thoroughly, absolutely, fully, perfectly. ▼

---

in the altogether is a humorous informal way of saying naked or nude (*You don't expect me to answer the door in the altogether, do you?*)

---

always *adv* **1** (*We always shop there*) regularly, invariably, consistently, unfailingly, repeatedly, without exception. **2** (*She's always cheerful*) continually, continuously, constantly, incessantly, perpetually. **3** (*promise to love her always*) forever, forever and ever, evermore, eternally, endlessly, everlastingly.

amaze *vb* (*His sheer stupidity amazed us*) astonish, astound, surprise, dumbfound, flabbergast, daze, shock, stun, (*inf*) stagger, nonplus.

amazing *adj* (*have an amazing memory*) exceptional, extraordinary, remarkable, phenomenal.

ambiguous *adj* (*Her message was ambiguous*) unclear, uncertain, doubtful, dubious, vague, obscure, puzzling, perplexing, enigmatic, abstruse.

ambition *n* **1** (*young members of the firm full of ambition*) aspiration, drive, striving, force, enterprise, enthusiasm. **2** (*Her ambition is to go on the stage*) aim, goal, objective, purpose, intent, dream, hope.

ambitious *adj* (*ambitious people seeking promotion*) aspiring, forceful, purposeful, enterprising, go-ahead, assertive.

ambush *n* **1** (*terrorists waiting in ambush for the soldiers*) hiding, concealment, cover. **2** (*lay an ambush for the enemy soldiers*) trap, snare, pitfall.

amiable *adj* (*in the company of amiable people*) friendly, pleasant, agreeable, charming, good-natured, sociable, genial.

amnesty *n* (*declare an amnesty for all political prisoners*) general pardon, pardon, reprieve, forgiveness, absolution.

among/amongst *prep* **1** (*a house among the trees/live among enemies*) in the midst of, amid, amidst, surrounded by, in the thick of. **2** (*divide it among you*) between, to each of.

amount *n* (*a small amount of wood/a large amount of attention*) quantity, mass, measure, volume, extent.

amount *vb* (*The bill amounted to hundreds of pounds*) add up to, total, come to, run to.

ample *adj* **1** (*ample food for everyone*) enough, sufficient, plenty, adequate, more than enough. **2** (*an ample supply of money*) plentiful, abundant, copious, liberal, generous, lavish. **3** (*her ample bosom*) large, big, substantial.

amplify *vb* **1** (*amplify the sound level*) make louder, increase, boost, augment. **2** (*amplify your suggestion*) expand, enlarge on, elaborate on, develop.

amputate *vb* (*The surgeon had to amputate his leg after the accident*) cut off, remove, sever, excise.

amuse *vb* **1** (*try to amuse the children on a cold, rainy day*) entertain, occupy, interest, divert. **2** (*The comedian's jokes amused everyone*) make laugh, entertain, cheer up, delight.

amusement *n* **1** (*various forms of amusement in the holiday resort*) entertainment, diversion, fun, interest, pastime, hobby, recreation. **2** (*smile with amusement at the comedian's jokes*) laughter, mirth, hilarity, pleasure, enjoyment.

amusing *adj* (*an amusing story*) funny, humorous, comical, entertaining, hilarious.

analyse *vb* (*analyse the election results*) examine, study, investigate, enquire into, dissect.

anarchy *n* **1** (*The fall of the government was followed by a period of anarchy*) absence of government, lawlessness, revolution. **2** (*anarchy on the streets when the police went on strike*) lawlessness, disorder, chaos, confusion, mayhem.

ancestor *n* (*trace his ancestors back to the time of Queen Anne*) forbear, forefather, progenitor, forerunner, predecessor.

ancestry *n* (*She is of royal ancestry*) descent, extraction, origin, derivation, parentage, blood, family tree.

ancient *adj* **1** (*ancient customs*) very old, age-old, time-worn. **2** (*in ancient times*) earliest, early, primeval, prehistoric. **3** (*His ideas on fashion are ancient*) antiquated, old-fashioned, out-of-date, outdated, outmoded, obsolete.

and *conj* (*my family and I*) along with, with, together with, as well, in addition to, plus.

angel *n* **1** (*angels in heaven*) seraph, cherub, archangel, guardian angel. **2** (*My kind neighbour is an absolute angel*) saint, gem, dear, darling. ▼

---

on the side of the angels supporting or agreeing with what is regarded by most people as being the good or the right side (*The teacher has to pretend to be on the side of the angels and support his colleagues although he has a lot of sympathy for the pupils' complaints*).

---

anger *n* (*feelings of anger at cruelty to animals*) annoyance, rage, fury, indignation, wrath, irritation, ire.

anger *vb* (*They were angered by his

rudeness) annoy, infuriate, enrage, irritate, incense, madden, provoke, rile.

angry *adj* (*angry mothers scolding their children*) annoyed, cross, furious, infuriated, indignant, irate, livid, enraged, wrathful, incensed, (*inf*) mad.

anguish *n* (*The children were in anguish when their pet died*) agony, suffering, pain, torment, torture, distress, misery.

animated *adj* (*an animated discussion*) lively, spirited, excited, enthusiastic, passionate, fiery, dynamic, energetic.

annexe *n* (*add an annexe to the house*) extension, wing.

annihilate *vb* (*annihilate the enemy army*) destroy, wipe out, exterminate, eliminate, obliterate, eradicate.

announce *vb* (*announce that the president was dead*) make known, make public, proclaim, publish, broadcast, report, state, declare, reveal, disclose.

announcement *n* (*an announcement of the president's death*) report, statement, notice, proclamation, declaration, bulletin, communiqué, intimation.

announcer *n* (*a BBC announcer*) commentator, presenter, newsreader, newscaster, broadcaster, reporter.

annoy *vb* **1** (*Her attitude annoyed her parents*) anger, infuriate, enrage, irritate, incense, madden, provoke, rile. **2** (*Don't annoy your mother while she is working/children annoying the dog*) bother, disturb, pester, worry, torment, tease.

annul *vb* (*annul the marriage/annul the agreement*) declare null and void, nullify, invalidate, cancel, rescind, revoke.

anomaly *n* (*anomalies in the tax system*) abnormality, irregularity, deviation, aberration, oddity, peculiarity, inconsistency.

anonymous *adj* (*The money for the charity was from an anonymous donor*) unnamed, nameless, unknown, unidentified, incognito.

another *adj* **1** (*another cup of tea*) additional, second, further. **2** (*go another time/get another car*) different, some other.

answer *vb* **1** (*answer the question*) reply to, give a response to, respond to, retort. **2** (*answer our requirements*) meet, satisfy, fulfil, fill, serve. **3** (*a man answering the description issued by the police*) fit, match, correspond to, be like.

answer *n* **1** (*receive no answer to his question/waiting for an answer to his letter*) reply, response, acknowledge, retort, rejoinder. **2** (*the answer to the puzzle*) solution, explanation. ▼

---

know all the answers to have all the information that is required to deal successfully with a situation, especially when one is conceited about this (*She never listens to any advice from other people—she always acts as if she knows all the answers*).

---

antagonism *n* (*a great deal of antagonism between the two sides*) hostility, opposition, animosity, antipathy, enmity, dissension, conflict, friction.

anthology *n* (*an anthology of poetry*) collection, selection, miscellany, compendium.

anticipate *vb* **1** (*The organizers are anticipating a large audience for the concert*) expect, foresee, predict, forecast, look for, await. **2** (*anticipate his opponent's move*) forestall, intercept, prevent, (*inf*) beat someone to it.

anticipation *n* **1** (*buy champagne in anticipation of victory*) expectation, prediction. **2** (*girls full of anticipation before the dance*) expectancy, hopefulness, hope.

anticlimax *n* (*After all the fun of planning the actual holiday was rather an anticlimax*) disappointment, let-down, disillusionment.

antiquated *adj* (*children thinking that their parents have antiquated ideas/an antiquated television set*) out-of-date, old-fashioned, outmoded, outworn, obsolete, archaic, passé.

antique *adj* (*antique furniture*) old, antiquarian, vintage, early.

antisocial *adj* **1** (*antisocial people who dislike parties*) unsociable, reserved, aloof, withdrawn, retiring, uncommunicative, unfriendly. **2** (*Playing loud music late at night is an example of unsocial behaviour*) disruptive, disorderly, lawless, unruly, obstreperous.

antithesis *n* (*The antithesis of good is bad*) opposite, reverse, converse, inverse, other extreme.

anxiety *n* (*full of anxiety about the lateness of her husband*) worry, concern, uneasiness, disquiet, nervousness, apprehension, tenseness.

anxious *adj* **1** (*anxious parents out looking for their children*) worried, concerned, uneasy, nervous, apprehensive, fearful, tense. **2** (*anxious to learn*) eager, keen, longing, avid.

apart *adv* **1** (*blow the place apart*) to pieces, in pieces, to bits, asunder. **2** (*a couple living apart*) separated, separately, divorced. **3** (*a man standing apart at the party*) to one side, aside, separately, by oneself. ▼

---

be poles *or* **worlds apart** to be completely different (*The two girls are sisters but their attitudes to work and money are poles apart/The two parts of the city are close together but they are worlds apart—one has expensive houses and the other has slums*).

---

apathy *n* (*Because of apathy many people did not vote*) lack of interest, indifference, unresponsiveness, unconcern, lethargy.

apex *n* **1** (*the apex of the triangle*) top, tip, pinnacle, vertex, peak. **2** (*the apex of his career*) peak, summit, top, zenith, acme, apogee.

apologetic *adj* (*feel apologetic for the trouble which they caused*) sorry, regretful, contrite, remorseful, repentant, penitent, rueful.

apologize *vb* (*apologize for his error*) say one is sorry, express regret, ask forgiveness, (*inf*) eat humble pie.

apology *n* (*accept his apology for his wrongdoing*) regret, regrets. ▼

---

an apology for (*inf*) a very poor example of (*The cafe served us up an apology for a meal/The tradesman we employed was an apology for a joiner*).

---

appalling *adj* **1** (*an appalling accident*) shocking, frightful, horrifying, terrible, dreadful, awful, ghastly. **2** (*a piece of work that is quite appalling/appalling behaviour*) very bad, unacceptable, unsatisfactory, intolerable.

apparent *adj* **1** (*It was apparent that she was unwell/problems* *that were apparent from the start*) obvious, clear, plain, evident, discernible, perceptible, manifest. 2 (*He eventually saw through her apparent sincerity*) seeming, ostensible, outward, superficial.

apparition *n* (*They thought they saw an apparition in the graveyard*) ghost, spectre, phantom, spirit, wraith, (*inf*) spook.

appeal *n* **1** (*make an appeal for help*) request, call, plea, entreaty, supplication. **2** (*a possibility that holds little appeal for her*) attraction, attractiveness, charm, allure, interest. **3** (*He has been convicted of the crime but the case is going to appeal*) review, reconsideration, re- examination.

appear *vb* **1** (*A figure appeared out of the mist*) come into view, come into sight, emerge, materialize, surface. **2** (*The visitors were very late but they finally appeared*) come, arrive, make an appearance, turn up, (*inf*) show up. **3** (*She appeared rather thoughtful*) seem, look, have the appearance of, have the air of, give the impression of. **4** (*He once appeared in a production of 'Hamlet'*) act, perform, play, take part.

appearance *n* **1** (*the sudden appearance of the police*) arrival, advent, materialization, surfacing. **2** (*having an appearance of sadness*) look, air, expression, impression, manner. **3** (*His statement had the appearance of truth but it was a lie*) semblance, outward appearance, guise, show, pretence. ▼

---

keep up appearances to behave in public in such a way as to hide what is going on in private (*He has lost his job but he tries to keep up appearances by leaving the house at his usual time each morning*).

---

appease *vb* (*try to appease his angry wife by giving her flowers*) calm down, placate, make peace with, pacify, soothe, conciliate, mollify, propitiate.

appetizer *n* (*serve smoked salmon as an appetizer*) starter, hors d'oeuvre, antipasto.

appetizing *adj* **1** (*an appetizing dish*) tasty, mouth-watering, flavoursome, delicious. **2** (*appetizing smells coming from the kitchen*) tempting, inviting, enticing, alluring.

applaud *vb* **1** (*The audience applauded*) clap, give a standing ovation to, (*inf*) to give a big hand to. **2** (*Everyone applauded his courage*) praise, admire, compliment on, commend, acclaim, extol, laud.

appliance *n* (*electrical appliances in the kitchen*) gadget, tool, implement, apparatus, device, machine.

applicant *n* (*applicants for the job*) candidate, entrant, competitor, interviewee.

apply *vb* **1** (*apply for a job*) put in an application for, ask, put in for, try for. **2** (*apply ointment to the sore*) put on, rub in, cover with, spread, smear. **3** (*have to apply force to open the box*) use, employ, administer, utilize, exercise, bring to bear. **4** (*These regulations do not apply*) be applicable, be relevant, be pertinent, be apposite, be appropriate.

appoint *vb* (*appoint a new manager*) name, select, choose, pick, elect, designate, nominate.

appointment *n* **1** (*have a business appointment this afternoon/a dinner appointment*) meeting, engagement, date, rendezvous, assignation. **2** (*take up his new appointment as manager*) job, post, position, situation, place.

appreciate *vb* **1** (*appreciate offers of help*) be grateful for, be thankful for, be appreciative of, give thanks for. **2** (*appreciate the urgency of the situation*) recognize, acknowledge, realize, know, be aware of, be conscious of, understand. **3** (*appreciate good wine*) value, prize, treasure, respect, hold in high regard, think highly of, enjoy, take pleasure in. **4** (*a house that has appreciated in value over the years*) increase, gain, grow, rise.

apprehensive *adj* (*apprehensive at the thought of going into hospital*) frightened, fearful, scared, nervous, anxious, worried, uneasy, concerned.

apprentice *n* (*find work as an apprentice in the garage*) trainee, learner, beginner, probationer, novice.

approach 1 *vb* (*visitors approaching the house*) come/go near, draw near, move towards, advance towards. **2** (*beggars approaching strangers to ask for money*) go up to, speak to, talk to, engage in conversation, address, hail. **3** (*approach the task with energy*) set about, tackle, begin, start, commence, embark on, make a start on. **4** (*temperatures approaching freezing point*) come close to, come near to, approximate.

approach *n* **1** (*the approach to the house*) driveway, drive, access, entrance, entry, way in. **2** (*a new approach to education*) method, system, technique, procedure, style, mode, way. **3** (*make approaches to the government for money*) application, appeal, advances, overtures.

appropriate *adj* (*an appropriate time/an appropriate reply*) suitable, fitting, proper, right, apt, apposite, opportune.

approval *n* **1** (*The audience showed its approval by applauding*) favour, liking, admiration, appreciation, approbation, regard. **2** (*The committee gave its approval to their plans*) acceptance, agreement, consent, assent, sanction, authorization, (*inf*) the go-ahead, the green light, (*inf*) the OK. ▼

---

on approval an expression used of goods that a customer takes home to try on or try out and that can be returned to the shop if the goods are not suitable or if the customer is not satisfied (*The young lady took several ball gowns home on approval*).

---

approve *vb* **1** (*unable to approve of their actions*) think well of, think highly of, think favourably of, look upon with favour, like, admire, hold in high regard. **2** (*The committee approved her plans*) accept, pass, agree to, consent to, assent to, sanction, authorize, (*inf*) give the go-ahead to, give the green light to.

approximately *adv* (*a distance of approximately five miles*) about, just about, around, roughly, nearly, close to, almost, more or less, in the neighbourhood of, in the region of, circa.

apron *n* pinafore, overall, (*inf*) pinny. ▼

---

tied to someone's apron strings completely dependent on a woman, especially one's mother or wife (*He is so tied to his wife's apron strings that he never goes out with his friends*).

---

apt *adj* **1** (*apt to lose his temper*) inclined, given, likely, liable, ready, disposed, prone. **2** (*an apt comment*) appropriate, suitable, fitting, applicable, relevant, apposite. **3** (*an apt pupil*) clever, bright, intelligent, quick, able.

aptitude *n* (*have an aptitude for word games*) talent, gift, flair, skill, ability, capability, bent, knack.

arbitrary *adj* **1** (*a purely arbitrary decision/The choice of players seemed arbitrary*) personal, subjective, discretionary, unreasoned, unsupported, random, chance, whimsical, capricious, erratic. **2** (*an arbitrary ruler*) despotic, tyrannical, absolute, autocratic, dictatorial, domineering.

arbitrate *vb* (*asked to arbitrate in the dispute between union and management*) adjudicate, judge, adjudge, umpire, referee.

arc *n* (*the arc of a rainbow*) curve, bow, arch, bend, crescent, semicircle.

arch *vb* (*a cat arching its back*) curve, bend, bow, arc.

archaic *adj* (*archaic language/archaic attitudes*) old, out-of-date, old-fashioned, outmoded, antiquated, passé, obsolete, (*inf*) old-hat.

architect *n* **1** (*the architect of the new church*) designer, planner, building consultant. **2** (*the architect of the new scheme*) author, originator, planner, creator, founder, instigator, prime mover.

archives *npl* (*study the archives of the firm*) records, annals, chronicles, register, documents.

arctic *adj* (*arctic temperatures*) freezing, frozen, frigid, icy, glacial, frosty, chilly, cold.

ardent *adj* (*an ardent supporter of the local football team*) passionate, avid, fervent, zealous, eager, enthusiastic, keen.

arduous *adj* (*an arduous task*) difficult, hard, taxing, laborious, strenuous, tough, onerous, burdensome, tiring, exhausting, gruelling, Herculean.

area *n* **1** (*live in a pleasant area of the city*) district, part, region, quarter, neighbourhood, locality, sector, zone, territory. **2** (*a specialist in the area of computing*) field, sphere, department, discipline, realm, sector. **3** (*measure the area of the room*) dimensions, extent, size, expanse. **4** (*the changing area of the swimming pool*) section, part, portion, space.

arena *n* (the sports *arena*) ground, field, stadium, ring. ▼

---

arena is Latin in origin meaning 'sand'. The central area of Roman amphitheatres, where the gladiators fought, was covered in sand to soak up the blood from the wounded or dead contestants. In time, the word was used for the central area itself and then for any enclosed area used for contests.

---

argue *vb* **1** (*Brother and sister are always arguing*) quarrel, disagree, bicker, squabble, wrangle, fight, dispute, (*inf*) fall out. **2** (*He argued that his method was the best*) assert, declare, maintain, hold, claim, contend.

argument *n* **1** (*children having an argument over toys*) quarrel, disagreement, squabble, wrangle, fight, dispute. **2** (*the argument* *against the new scheme*) reasoning, line of reasoning, reasons, grounds, case, defence, evidence, proof.

argumentative *adj* (*argumentative people/an argumentative mood*) quarrelsome, belligerent, disputatious, contentious, combative, litigious.

arid *adj* **1** (*arid areas of the world*) dry, dried up, desert, waterless, parched, barren. **2** (*an arid discussion*) uninspiring, uninteresting, dull, dreary, dry, colourless, lifeless, boring, monotonous, tedious.

arise *vb* **1** (*deal with any problems that arise*) appear, make an appearance, come to light, crop up, turn up, emerge, occur. **2** (*matters arising from our discussion*) result, proceed, follow, stem, originate, emanate, ensue. ▼

---

arise in its original meaning of 'get up' or 'stand up', as in 'They arose at dawn', 'He arose slowly from his chair', is not used in modern English and is now considered an old or literary use.

---

aristocracy *n* (*a member of the British aristocracy*) nobility, peerage, gentry, upper class, high society, (*inf*) upper crust.

arm *n* **1** (*have an arm amputated*) upper limb. **2** (*an arm of the civil service*) branch, offshoot, section, department, division, sector. ▼

---

the long arm of the law the power or authority of the police (*The crook thought that he had got away with the bank robbery, but the long arm of the law caught up with him as he tried to leave the country*).

---

arm *vb* (*arm oneself with a gun/arm oneself with a stick to protect oneself against attack*) provide, supply, equip, furnish.

armaments *npl* (*a military armaments store*) arms, weapons, firearms, munitions.

armistice *n* (*the armistice that ended the war*) truce, ceasefire, peace.

armour *n* (*knights wearing armour*) armour plate, chain-mail, coat of mail, mail, protective covering. ▼

---

a chink in someone's armour a weak or vulnerable spot in someone who is otherwise very strong and difficult to get through to attack (*The old man is very stern but his little granddaughter has found a chink in his armour/The opposition are always trying to find a chink in the government's armour*).

---

arms *npl* **1** (*soldiers laying down their arms*) weapons, firearms, guns, armaments. **2** (*the family arms*) coat of arms, emblem, crest, insignia, heraldic device.

army *n* **1** (*the invading army*) military force, troops, soldiers. **2** (*armies of tourists on the island in the summer*) horde, crowd, host, multitude, swarm, throng, mob.

aroma *n* (*the aroma of freshly baked bread*) smell, scent, fragrance, perfume, odour, bouquet.

aromatic *adj* (*aromatic spices*) fragrant, sweet-smelling, scented, perfumed, piquant, spicy, pungent.

around *adv* **1** (*turn around*) in the opposite direction, in reverse. **2** (*around nine o'clock/around five miles away*) approximately, roughly, close to, near to, nearly, circa. 3 (*flowers planted around the tree*) about, on all sides of, on every side of, surrounding, circling, encircling. 4 (*newspapers scattered around the room*) about, here and there in, all over, everywhere in, in all parts of. ▼

---

to have been around 1 (*inf*) to have had a lot of experience of life (*She is unlikely to be deceived by him—she's been around a bit*). 2 to have been alive (*The old man said that he had been around so long that he could remember Queen Victoria*).

---

arouse *vb* **1** (*The noise aroused the neighbours*) rouse, awaken, waken, wake, wake up. **2** (*behaviour arousing suspicion/actions arousing panic*) cause, induce, stir up, provoke, call forth, whip up.

arrange *vb* **1** (*arrange the books*) put in order, set out, order, sort, organize, group, classify, categorize. **2** (*arrange a meeting*) fix, fix up, organize, settle on, plan, schedule.

arrangement *n* (*make an arrangement to meet tomorrow*) preparations, plans, provisions, agreement, deal, contract.

arrest *vb* **1** (*Police arrested the thieves*) take into custody, take prisoner, detain, seize, capture, catch, (*inf*) run in, nick. **2** (*try to arrest the spread of the disease*) stop, halt, bring to a halt, end, check, nip in the bud.

arresting *adj* (*her arresting appearance*) striking, noticeable, conspicuous, impressive, remarkable, extraordinary, unusual.

arrival *n* **1** (*the arrival of winter*) coming, advent, appearance, occurrence. **2** (*several new arrivals in the village*) newcomer, incomer, immigrant.

arrive *vb* **1** (*arrive at their destination*) reach, come to, attain. **2** (*when mother arrives*) come, get here, appear, put in an appearance, turn up, come on the scene, (*inf*) show up.

arrogant *adj* (*a very arrogant young woman/have a very arrogant manner*) haughty, proud, conceited, vain, self-important, egotistic, overbearing, condescending, disdainful, snobbish, supercilious, imperious, presumptions, bumptious, boastful, (*inf*) cocky, (*inf*) stuck up.

art *n* **1** (*studying art at college*) painting, drawing, visual arts. **2** (*the art of conversation*) skill, craft, aptitude, knack, technique, facility, talent, flair, gift.

artful *adj* (*get his own way by artful means*) cunning, crafty, wily, sly, deceitful, scheming, shrewd, ingenious, clever.

article *n* **1** (*a range of articles going on sale*) thing, object, item, commodity. **2** (*an article in the newspaper on violence*) item, piece, story, feature, report, account, write-up.

artificial *adj* (*artificial flowers/an artificial beard*) manmade, synthetic, imitation, simulated, ersatz, mock, sham, fake, bogus, counterfeit, (*inf*) phoney.

ashamed *adj* (*She was obviously ashamed of what she had done*) sorry, shame-faced, abashed, repentant, penitent, remorseful, sheepish.

ask *vb* **1** (*We asked where they were going*) inquire. **2** (*They asked a favour from her/You should ask for more money*) request, demand, apply for, beg for, plead for. **3** (*The police asked him about his movements on the night of the murder*) question, interrogate, cross-examine, give the third degree to, pump, (*inf*) grill.

assault *vb* (*They assaulted the old man to get his wallet*) attack, set upon, strike, hit, (*inf*) mug.

assemble *vb* **1** (*The children assembled in the school hall to hear the news*) gather, come together, congregate, convene. **2** (*He is assembling the evidence for the prosecution*) get together, gather together, collect, accumulate, amass. **3** (*You buy the furniture in a flat pack and have to assemble it yourself*) put together, fit together, construct, build, erect.

assist *vb* (*He assisted the doctor to care for the accident victims*) help, aid, give assistance to, lend a hand to, support.

associate *vb* **1** (*She associates home with security*) connect, link, relate. **2** (*The clubs are associated in some way*) connect, link, join, attach, affiliate. **3** (*He associates with crooks*) mix, keep company with, socialize, fraternize.

astonish *vb* **1** (*Their boldness astonished us*) amaze, astound, dumbfound, stun, surprise.

attach *vb* **1** (*They should attach luggage labels to their suitcases*) fasten, tie, secure, stick, affix. **2** (*We attach no importance to that*) place, lay, put, apply, ascribe.

attend *vb* **1** (*He is unable to attend the meeting*) be at, be present at, put in an appearance at, be there/here. **2** (*She promised to attend to the matter immediately*) deal with, see to, cope with, handle. **3** (*You should attend to what your teacher says*) pay attention to, pay heed to, heed, listen to, take note of.

attitude *n* **1** (*I don't like her attitude to people from other countries*) view, point of view, opinion, outlook, thoughts, ideas. **2** (*She stood in an attitude of thought*) stance, pose, position.

attractive *adj* **1** (*She is a very attractive girl*) good-looking, pretty, beautiful, handsome. **2** (*That is an attractive idea*) appealing, pleasing, tempting.

authentic *adj* (*He is the authentic heir to the estate*) real, genuine, rightful, lawful, legal, valid.

authority *n* **1** (*He does not have the authority to stop us going*) power, right, control, force, influence. **2** (*We have the authority of the king to be present*) permission, sanction, authorization, (*inf*) say-so. **3** (*He is an authority on local history*) expert, specialist, pundit.

available *adj* **1** (*have to make do with the material that is available*) obtainable, handy, to hand, accessible, ready. **2** (*There are still tickets available*) free.

average *adj* **1** (*She was of average height for her age*) normal, typical, ordinary, common. **2** (*Her work was just average*) run-of-the mill, mediocre, unexceptional.

awful *adj* **1** (*She has an awful cold*) dreadful, nasty, unpleasant, troublesome, bad. **2** (*in the awful presence of God*) awesome, awe-inspiring.

awkward *adj* **1** (*They arrived at an awkward time*) inconvenient, difficult, problematic. **2** (*She is a very awkward child and keeps bumping into things*) clumsy, ungainly, inelegant, gauche. **3** (*It is an awkward piece of furniture*) clumsy, unwieldy.

B

baby *n* (*babies in their prams*) infant, child, toddler. ▼

throw out the baby with the bath water accidentally to get rid of something valuable or wanted in the process of getting rid of something worthless or unwanted.

babyish *adj* (*older children acting in a babyish way*) childish, immature, infantile, juvenile.

back *n* **1** (*the back of the building*) rear, far end. **2** (*the back of the envelope*) reverse, other side. **3** (*break his back in the accident*) spine, backbone.

back *adv* (*without looking back*) backwards, behind, to the rear.

back *vb* **1** (*back the plan*) support, give support to, help, assist, encourage, favour. **2** (*look for someone to back the theatrical production*) finance, subsidize, sponsor. **3** (*back the horse*) bet on, place a bet on, gamble on. **4** (*back the car out of the garage*) reverse, drive backwards.

backer *n* (*the backers of the theatrical production*) sponsor, promoter, financier, benefactor, (*inf*) angel.

background *n* **1** (*people from a wealthy background*) upbringing, family circumstances, environment, experience. **2** (*photographed against a white background*) setting, backdrop, scene. **3** (*in the background of the photograph*) rear, distance.

backlog *n* (*a backlog of work*) accumulation, stockpile, arrears, (*inf*) mountain.

backward *adj* **1** (*a backward look*) to the rear, rearward. **2** (*a backward area of the world*) underdeveloped, slow, retarded, unprogressive. ▼

know something backwards to know a great deal about something (*She knows Shakespeare's plays backwards*).

bacteria *npl* (*bacteria from rotting food*) germs, micro-organisms, (*inf*) bugs.

bad *adj* **1** (*bad people*) wicked, evil, immoral, wrong, sinful, dishonest, dishonourable, criminal, (*inf*) crooked, naughty, mischievous. **2** (*a bad accident*) serious, severe, terrible, shocking, appalling. **3** (*a bad performance*) poor, unsatisfactory, inadequate, inferior, substandard, defective, shoddy, (*inf*) lousy. **4** (*Smoking is a bad habit*) harmful, damaging, dangerous, unhealthy. **5** (*bad food/food gone bad*) rotten, decayed, mouldy, tainted, putrid, (*inf*) off. **6** (*bad weather*) unpleasant, nasty, dreadful, terrible, disagreeable. **7** (*feel bad about hurting her*) sorry, regretful, apologetic, guilty, sad. **8** (*an invalid feeling bad today*) ill, unwell, sick, poorly, under the weather, (*inf*) below par. ▼

hit a bad patch to experience difficulties or a difficult or unsuccessful period (*The team *were playing well but they have now hit a bad patch*).

---

badge *n* (*wear the club badge on their blazers*) crest, emblem, symbol.

badly *adv* 1 (*do the work badly*) poorly, unsatisfactorily, inadequately, shoddily. 2 (*Things worked out badly*) unsuccessfully, unfortunately, unfavourably, unluckily, unhappily. 3 (*want something badly*) greatly, very much, enormously, to a great degree. 4 (*behave badly*) wrongly, naughtily, improperly, wickedly, immorally, sinfully, criminally.

baffle *vb* (*police baffled by the crime/students baffled by the exam question*) puzzle, perplex, mystify, nonplus, stump, flummox, bamboozle, bewilder.

baggage *n* (*collect one's baggage at the airport*) luggage, bags, suitcases, things, belongings, gear, paraphernalia. ▼

---

bag and baggage absolutely all one's belongings (*We had to move out of the flat bag and baggage when the new tenants arrived*).

---

baggy *adj* (*wear baggy clothes*) loose, slack, roomy, floppy, ballooning.

bake *vb* 1 (*bake cakes*) cook. 2 (*earth baked by the sun*) scorch, burn, parch, dry, harden.

balance *n* 1 (*weigh the substance on a balance*) scales, weighing machine. 2 (*trip and lose one's balance*) steadiness, stability, equilibrium. 3 (*pay the balance of the account*) remainder, rest, residue, difference, surplus, excess.

bald *adj* 1 (*men going bald*) baldheaded, hairless, (*inf*) thin on top. 2 (*a bald statement*) direct, forthright, blunt, plain, unadorned.

ball *n* 1 (*a glass ball*) sphere, globe, orb. 2 (*be invited to a ball*) dance, formal dance. ▼

---

drop the ball to make a mistake or fail to do something (*The export manager said that the French firm would definitely place an order with us, but he dropped the ball during the negotiations and the deal is off*).

have the ball at one's feet to be in a position to be successful (*When he left university he thought that he had the ball at his feet but he could not find a job*) <From football.>

---

ballot *n* (*choose the new leader by ballot*) vote, poll, election.

ban *vb* (*ban smoking in the hall*) prohibit, forbid, debar, bar, veto, make illegal.

ban *n* (*impose a ban on smoking*) prohibition, veto, embargo, interdict.

band *n* 1 (*the jazz band playing at the wedding celebrations*) group, ensemble, orchestra. 2 (*a band of thieves*) group, troop, company, gang, pack, bunch, mob, team. 3 (*a metal band/a rubber band*) binding, cord, tie, link, ring, hoop, ligature. 4 (*a band of blue on the white sweater*) strip, stripe, steak, line, bar. 5 (*a band round her hair*) ribbon, braid.

bang *n* 1 (*a loud bang when the bomb went off*) boom, crash, blast, explosion, report. 2 (*get a bang on the head*) blow, knock, bump, hit, smack.

bang *vb* 1 (*the door banged shut*) slam, crash. 2 (*bang the table with his fist*) strike, hit, beat, thump, rap, whack, (*inf*) bash. ▼

---

bang one's head against a brick wall to do something, usually to keep doing something, in vain (*You are banging your head against a brick wall if you try to persuade him to change his mind*).

---

bang *adv* (*bang in the middle of his speech*) right, exactly, precisely, absolutely, directly, (*inf*) smack.

banish *vb* **1** (*banish them from their native land*) exile, deport, cast out, send away, expel. **2** (*banish the child's fears*) drive away, dispel, dismiss, get rid of, cast out.

bank *n* **1** (*borrow money from the bank*) financial institution, high-street bank. **2** (*a child's bank*) piggy bank, savings bank, cash box. **3** (*a bank of information*) store, stock, reserve, reservoir, repository. **4** (*children sliding down grassy banks*) slope, rise, incline, hillock. **5** (*the river bank*) edge, side, shore. ▼

---

bank on (*bank on their help*) rely on, count on, depend on, pin one's hopes on.

---

bankrupt *adj* (*bankrupt after the failure of his business*) ruined, insolvent, penniless, impecunious, (*inf*) in the red, (*inf*) on the rocks, (*inf*) broke.

banner *n* (*banners flying for the king's coronation*) flag, standard, pennant, streamer.

banquet *n* feast, dinner, dinner party, (*inf*) spread.

baptize *vb* (*baptize a baby*) christen, name.

bar *n* **1** (*an iron bar*) rod, pole, rail, girder. **2** (*a bar of soap*) block, cake, lump, wedge. **3** (*getting drunk in bars*) pub, public house.

bar *vb* **1** (*bar the door*) bolt, lock, padlock, fasten, secure. **2** (*bar them from joining the club*) debar, prohibit, forbid, preclude, ban. **3** (*fallen trees barring their way*) block, hinder, impede, obstruct.

bare *adj* **1** (*sunbathing bare*) nude, naked, stark naked, undressed, unclothed, without clothes, unclad. **2** (*a bare room*) empty, vacant, unfurnished, unadorned. **3** (*a bare landscape*) barren, bleak, desolate.

barely *adv* (*barely enough food*) hardly, scarcely, only just, just.

bargain *n* **1** (*make a bargain not to quarrel*) agreement, pact, contract, deal. **2** (*get a bargain at the sales*) good buy, (*inf*) snip. ▼

---

drive a hard bargain (*drive a hard bargain for carpets in the market*) haggle, argue, negotiate.

---

barge *vb* **1** (*people barging into each other in the crowded shops*) bump, collide, cannon, crash. **2** (*barge into a private meeting*) interrupt, intrude on, burst in on, (*inf*) butt in on.

barn *n* outbuilding, outhouse, shed, byre.

barrel *n* (*a barrel of beer*) cask, keg, vat. ▼

---

have someone over a barrel to get someone into such a position that one can get him or her to do anything that one wants (*They owe him a lot of money and so he has them over a barrel*).

---

barren *adj* **1** (*barren fields*) infertile, unproductive, arid, desert, waste. **2** (*barren women*) infertile, sterile, childless. **3** (*barren discussions*) fruitless, worthless, useless, valueless, purposeless.

barricade *n* (*barricades keeping back the crowds*) barrier, blockade, obstacle, bar.

barrier *n* (*a barrier to keep the spectators off the football pitch*) barricade, bar, fence, railing, blockade.

base *n* **1** (*the base of the statue*) foundation, support, prop, foot. **2** (*paints with an oil base*) basis, essence, source. **3** (*climbers setting up a base*) headquarters, depot, centre, camp, starting-point.

base *vb* **1** (*base his statement on the facts available*) found, build, establish, ground. **2** (*base the novel on his childhood memories*) locate, situate, station.

bashful *adj* shy, reserved, diffident, retiring, modest, self-conscious.

basic *adj* (*the basic facts/the basic principles*) fundamental, elementary, rudimentary, primary, essential, chief.

basin *n* (*a pudding basin*) bowl, dish, container, receptacle.

basis *n* **1** (*the basis for his conclusions*) grounds, foundation, base. **2** (*issues that form the basis of the discussion*) starting-point, foundation, base.

batch *n* (*a batch of new pupils/a batch of old magazines*) group, quantity, collection, set.

bathe *vb* **1** (*bathe the wound*) clean, cleanse, wash. **2** (*bathe in the sea*) swim, go swimming, (*inf*) take a dip.

batter *vb* (*batter the door*) bang, beat, strike, knock, pound, thump.

battle *n* (*a battle to prevent the enemy army invading*) conflict, fight, clash, skirmish, engagement, encounter, struggle, contest.

bawl *vb* (*bawl in order to attract attention*) shout, cry out, yell, roar, bellow, scream.

bay *n* (*ships anchored in the bay*) inlet, cove, gulf, basin, bight.

bay *vb* howl, bark, yell, cry, growl.

bazaar *n* (*tourists at an eastern bazaar*) market, market-place, souk.

beach *n* (*pull the boat on to the beach*) seaside, coast, shore, sands.

beam *n* **1** (*roof beams*) board, timber, plank, joist, rafter, support. **2** (*a beam of light*) ray, shaft, steam, streak, flash, gleam, glint.

bear *vb* **1** (*bearing gifts*) carry, bring, take, convey. **2** (*bear the weight*) carry, support, hold up, sustain. **3** (*unable to bear the pain*) put up with, stand, suffer, endure, tolerate. **4** (*bear a son*) give birth to, produce. **5** (*bear a grudge*) have, hold, harbour. ▼

---

bear up to keep cheerful or strong under strain or stress (*She is in a great deal of pain but she somehow succeeds in bearing up*).

---

bearded *adj* (*a bearded man*) unshaven, whiskered, stubbly, hirsute.

bearings *npl* (*lose our bearings on the mountain*) location, position, whereabouts, way, course, direction.

beast *n* **1** (*the beasts of the jungle*) animal, creature, mammal. **2** (*He was an absolute beast*) brute, monster, savage, pig, ogre.

beat *vb* **1** (*beat the drum*) bang, hit, strike, pound. **2** (*with hearts beating*) throb, pound, thump, pulsate, pulse, palpitate. **3** (*They beat their children*) hit, strike, batter, thump, wallop, thrash, slap. **4** (*birds with their wings beating*) flap, flutter, vibrate, **5** (*beat the butter and sugar*) mix, blend, whisk, stir. **6** (*beat the opposition*) defeat, conquer, vanquish, rout, trounce, crush, overwhelm, (*inf*) lick. **7** (*beat the record*) outdo, surpass, exceed, excel, transcend. ▼

---

beat about the bush to approach something in a very indirect way (*He was beating about the bush instead of telling her frankly that her work was not good enough*) <In game-bird hunting bushes are beaten to make the birds appear>.

---

beat *n* **1** (*the beat of the music*) rhythm, time, measure, pulse, throb. **2** (*the policeman's beat*) round, circuit, course, route.

beautiful *adj* **1** (*a beautiful woman*) lovely, pretty, attractive, handsome, glamorous, gorgeous. **2** (*a beautiful view*) lovely, attractive, picturesque, charming, delightful, magnificent, splendid.

beauty *n* **1** (*a woman of great beauty*) loveliness, prettiness, attractiveness, handsomeness, glamour. **2** (*the beauty of the scheme*) advantage, benefit, asset. ▼

---

beauty is only skin deep people have more important qualities than how they look. <*She is not pretty but she is very interesting and amusing. After all, beauty is only skin deep*>.

---

becoming *adj* **1** (*a becoming dress*) flattering, attractive, elegant. **2** (*behaviour that was hardly becoming*) fitting, suitable, appropriate, apt, proper, seemly, decorous.

before *adv* (*We had met before*) previously, earlier, formerly, in the past.

beg *vb* **1** (*homeless people begging in the streets*) ask for money, cadge, scrounge. **2** (*beg for mercy*) ask for, require, plead for, entreat, beseech, implore. ▼

---

beg the question in an argument or debate, to take for granted the very point that requires to be proved.

---

beggar *n* vagrant, down-and-out, tramp, mendicant.

begin *vb* **1** (*begin work*) start, commence, set about, embark on. **2** (*when the trouble begins*) start, commence, get going, arise.

beginning *n* **1** (*the beginning of he relationship*) start, starting-point, commencement, outset, onset, inception. **2** (*the beginning of the book*) start, commencement, first part, introduction, opening, preface.

begrudge *vb* (*begrudge him his success*) grudge, envy, be envious of, resent, be jealous of.

behave *vb* (*behave in a responsible way*) act, conduct oneself.

behaviour *n* (*criticize the behaviour of the football crowd*) actions, conduct, manners.

being *n* **1** (*the reason for our being*) existence, life, living. **2** (*beings from another planet*) creature, living thing, individual.

belief *n* **1** (*It is her belief that he is still alive*) opinion, feeling, impression, view, viewpoint, way of thinking, theory. **2** (*religious beliefs*) faith, creed, doctrine, credo. **3** (*have no belief in their ability*) faith, trust, reliance.

belligerent *adj* (*a belligerent fellow who started a fight*) aggressive,

aid *vb* **1** (*aid the rescue workers*) assist, help, support, lend a hand. **2** (*medicine to aid his recovery*) assist, help, speed up, hasten, expedite, facilitate. ▼

---

aid and abet *vb* to provide help and encouragement in some bad or illegal activity (*She was arrested for aiding and abetting the bank robber by hiding him from the police*).

---

aid *n* **1** (*stop to give aid to a motorist who had broken down*) assistance, help, support, a helping hand. **2** (*give aid to poor countries*) assistance, help, contributions, subsidy, gift, donation. **3** (*a hospital aid*) helper, assistant, girl/man Friday.

ailment *n* illness, complaint, disease, disorder.

aim *vb* **1** (*aim a gun at*) point, direct, train, level. **2** (*aim to get there before dark*) plan, intend, propose, try.

aim *n* (*their aims in life/Their aim is to make a lot of money*) goal, ambition, objective, object, target, purpose, intention, plan, aspiration, design, desire.

aimless *adj* **1** (*lead an aimless life*) pointless, purposeless, futile, undirected. **2** (*aimless young people wandering the streets*) unambitious, drifting, wandering.

air *n* **1** (*fly through the air*) atmosphere, sky. **2** (*an air of loneliness about her*) impression, appearance, atmosphere, mood, quality, look, feeling. **3** (*playing a sad air on the piano*) tune, melody, song, theme. ▼

---

be up in the air to be undecided, yet to be decided (*We were going on holiday tomorrow but our plans are up in the air now since our daughter has got chickenpox*).

---

air *vb* **1** (*air clothes/air a room*) ventilate, freshen. **2** (*air one's views*) make known, make public, publicize, voice, express, vent, communicate, reveal.

aisle *n* (*the aisles in planes/trains*) gangway, passageway, passage, corridor.

alarm *vb* (*alarmed by a loud bang in the night*) frighten, scare, startle, terrify, unnerve, disturb, upset.

alarm *n* **1** (*a burglar alarm/a fire alarm*) alarm signal, alarm bell, danger signal, siren, warning. **2** (*a burglar causing alarm in the neighbourhood*) fear, fright, apprehension, terror, panic, disturbance, anxiety, upset, disquiet. ▼

---

alarums *or* **alarms and excursions** confused and noisy activity (*There were alarums and excursions in the middle of the night when we thought we heard a burglar downstairs*) <In Shakespeare's history plays, the expression 'alarums and excursions' was used as a stage direction calling for activity typical of the scene at the edge of a battle>.

---

alert *adj* (*stay alert when on sentry duty*) awake, wide awake, aware, attentive, watchful, wary, observant, vigilant.

alien *adj* **1** (*alien lands*) foreign, overseas. **2** (*find themselves in an alien environment*) strange, unfamiliar, unknown.

alien *n* **1** (*aliens deported from the country at the start of the war*) seniority, advancing years. 2 (*in the Elizabethan age*) era, period, epoch, time.

agency *n* (*an advertising agency*) organization, business, firm, company, office, bureau.

agenda *n* (*on the agenda for tonight's meeting*) programme, schedule, timetable, list. ▼

---

hidden agenda intentions or a motive that is deliberately hidden by another activity: *Deirdre seemed to act like Anthea's new best friend, but she had a hidden agenda—she was after Anthea's boyfriend.*

---

agent *n* 1 (*an insurance agent/a travel agent*) representative, negotiator, operator, (*inf*) rep. 2 (*an enemy agent*) spy, (*inf*) mole, (*inf*) spook.

aggravate *vb* 1 (*aggravate the situation/aggravate the illness*) make worse, worsen, exacerbate, intensify, increase. 2 (*inf*) (*children aggravating their mother with their noise*) annoy, irritate, anger, exasperate, provoke, get on someone's nerves.

aggravate should be used in the meaning of 'annoy' only in informal situations, such as in speech or personal letters between friends. Many people regard this as a wrong use of the word and it should be avoided in formal writing, such as essays.

aggressive *adj* 1 (*people getting aggressive when they get drunk*) quarrelsome, argumentative, belligerent, pugnacious. 2 (*aggressive salesmen/aggressive young workers seeking rapid promotion*) assertive, forceful, dynamic, thrusting, (*inf*) pushy.

aghast *adj* (*aghast at the decision to close the local steelworks*) horrified, appalled, astounded, amazed, shocked, flabbergasted.

agile *adj* (*old people still agile/agile young gymnasts*) active, nimble, lithe, supple, sprightly.

agitate *vb* 1 (*The news agitated her*) upset, work up, fluster, perturb, ruffle, disconcert, flurry, excite. 2 (*demonstrators agitating for more nursery schools*) campaign, argue.

agonizing *adj* (*an agonizing pain*) excruciating, painful, unbearable, insufferable, piercing.

agony *n* (*accident victims in agony*) suffering, pain, torture, torment, distress, anguish. ▼

---

agony aunt *n* a woman who replies, in an agony column, to personal problems sent in by readers to a magazine or newspaper.

---

agree *vb* 1 (*agree with your suggestions*) concur, comply, accord. 2 (*agree to your demands*) consent to, accept, assent to, acquiesce in. 3 (*accounts of the accident that do not agree with each other*) match, accord, correspond, coincide, tally, (*inf*) square.

agreeable *adj* 1 (*We are agreeable to your coming with us*) willing, amenable, compliant, consenting, assenting, accommodating. 2 (*an agreeable occasion*) pleasant, delightful, enjoyable, pleasurable. 3 (*an agreeable young man*) pleasant, likable, amiable, friendly, nice, affable.

agreement *n* 1 (*all in complete agreement*) accord, assent, concurrence, harmony, unity. 2 (*sign an agreement to purchase*) contract, compact, covenant, pact, pledge, deal.

administrator *n* (*business administrators*) manager, director, executive, controller.

admire *vb* **1** (*admire her hat/admire the view*) express admiration of, approve of, like, compliment, praise. **2** (*admire their courage*) approve of, respect, think highly of, appreciate, applaud, praise, esteem.

admit *vb* **1** (*admit his guilt/admit that she could be wrong*) acknowledge, confess, own up, reveal, make known, declare, disclose, divulge. **2** (*a ticket that admits only one person*) let in, allow in, allow entry, permit entry.

admittance *n* (*no admittance to the private building*) entry, right of entry, entrance, access.

adolescence *n* (*a young person just reaching adolescence*) teenage years, (*inf*) teens, growing up.

adopt *vb* **1** (*adopt a child*) take as one's own, take in, take care of, be adoptive parents to. **2** (*adopt a parliamentary candidate*) select, choose, pick, vote for. **3** (*adopt modern customs/adopt a foreign style of dress*) assume, take on, take over, affect, embrace, espouse.

adorable *adj* (*an adorable little baby*) lovable, sweet, dear, darling, delightful, appealing, charming, enchanting, winsome.

adore *vb* **1** (*They adore their children*) love dearly, be devoted to, dote on, cherish, idolize. **2** (*adore ice cream*) like very much, love, be fond of, enjoy, relish. **3** (*adore God*) worship, praise, glorify, revere, venerate.

adorn *vb* (*flowers adorning the room/adorn the Christmas tree with lights*) decorate, embellish, ornament, beautify.

adroit *adj* (*her adroit handling of the situation*) skilful, skilled, deft, expert, clever, able, adept.

adult *adj* **1** (*adult people*) grown-up, (*fml*) of age. **2** (*adult trees*) mature, fully grown, developed.

advance *vb* (*The armies advance*) move forward, go forward, proceed, press on, forge ahead, make progress.

advance *adj* **1** (*the advance party*) leading, first, in front. **2** (*advance warning*) early, previous, prior, beforehand.

advanced *adj* **1** (*advanced technology*) progressive, modern, up-to date, ultra-modern, sophisticated, avant-garde. **2** (*advanced studies/schoolwork that is more advanced*) higher-level, complicated, difficult.

advantage *n* **1** (*one of the advantages of being tall*) benefit, asset, good point, blessing, boon. **2** (*have an advantage over his rivals*) superiority, ascendancy, supremacy, upper hand. **3** (*There is little advantage in going into business with her*) benefit, profit, gain, good. ▼

---

take advantage of someone or something to make use of someone or something in such a way as to be of benefit to oneself (*People take advantage of her generosity and are always borrowing money from her/Her neighbours take advantage of the kind old lady and use her as an unpaid babysitter*).

---

advantageous *adj* **1** (*an advantageous position*) favourable, helpful, beneficial, useful. **2** (*advantageous to his hopes of promotion*) of benefit, beneficial, of assistance, useful, valuable.

adventure *n* **1** (*tell her grandchildren of her adventures at sea*) exploit, escapade, deed, feat, experience. **2** (*a journey full of adventure*) risk, precariousness, danger, hazard, peril, uncertainty.

adventurous *adj* (*an adventurous life*) risky, precarious, dangerous, hazardous, perilous.

adversary *n* (*their adversaries in the battle/her adversary in the tournament*) opponent, enemy, foe, antagonist, rival.

adversity *n* **1** (*a homeless person leading a life of adversity*) misfortune, ill-luck, bad luck, trouble, hardship, distress, misery. **2** (*many adversities in his life*) misfortune, mishap, setback, trial, disaster, catastrophe, calamity.

advertise *vb* (*advertise a new product*) promote, give publicity to, publicize, (*inf*) push, (*inf*) plug.

advice *n* (*give careers advice/get advice on a personal problem*) guidance, counselling, counsel, help, suggestions, hints, tips.

advisable *adj* (*Such action is not advisable*) desirable, wise, sensible, prudent, suitable, appropriate, recommended.

advise *vb* **1** (*advise them on future careers*) give advice to. give guidance on, guide, counsel, give recommendations, offer suggestions, give hints. **2** (*advise carefulness*) recommend, suggest, urge, commend, advocate.

advocate *vb* (*advocate spending less money*) advise, recommend, suggest, urge, press for, favour, support.

affable *adj* (*an affable neighbour/in an affable mood*) friendly, amiable, genial, cordial, pleasant, agreeable, good-natured, sociable, courteous.

affair *n* **1** (*It's my affair*) concern, business, matter, responsibility. **2** (*The sacking of the boss was an unfortunate affair*) event, happening, occurrence, incident, episode, state of affairs.

affect *vb* **1** (*a tragedy which affected all of us*) have an effect on, influence, have an influence on, act on, work on, change, alter. **2** (*a disease affecting his stomach*) attack, infect. **3** (*We were deeply affected by the orphan's sad story*) move, touch, upset, disturb, trouble, stir.

affected *adj* (*an affected way of speaking*) pretentious, artificial, false, pretended, unnatural, assumed.

affection *n* (*feel affection for his children*) love, fondness, caring, devotion, liking, warmth.

affectionate *adj* (*an affectionate farewell*) loving, fond, devoted, tender, warm.

afflict *vb* (*people afflicted by a terrible disease*) trouble, distress, trouble, torment, plague.

affliction *n* (*the afflictions associated with old age*) trouble, disorder, disease, ailment, pain, suffering, hardship.

affluent *adj* (*affluent people living in expensive houses*) wealthy, rich, well-off, prosperous, well-to-do, (*inf*) well-heeled.

afford *vb* (*unable to afford a new car*) buy, purchase, pay for, pay the price of, meet the expense of.

affront *n* (*sexist remarks that are an affront to women*) insult, offence, slight, snub, indignity.

afraid *adj* **1** (*afraid of the wild animal/afraid to enter the haunted house*) frightened, scared, nervous, terrified, apprehensive, fearful. **2** (*I'm afraid that I cannot help you*) sorry, regretful, apologetic, unhappy.

age *n* **1** (*the wisdom that comes with age*) old age, maturity, quarrelsome, argumentative, pugnacious.

belong *vb* **1** (*The car belongs to me*) be owned by, be the property of. **2** (*She belongs to the tennis club*) be a member of, be associated with.

belongings *npl* (*lose all her belongings*) possessions, things, property, personal effects.

beloved *adj* (*her beloved husband*) dearest, darling, loved, adored.

beloved *n* (*wish to marry her beloved*) sweetheart, boyfriend/girlfriend, fiancé/fiancée.

belt *n* **1** (*wear a plastic belt round her waist*) girdle, sash, strap, cummerbund. **2** (*a belt of green fields between the towns*) area, region, tract, zone. **3** (*a belt of blue across the white walls*) strip, stripe, streak, line, band. ▼

---

tighten one's belt to reduce the amount of money which one spends (*Since their father now earns less money the family will have to tighten their belts*) <Belts have to be tightened if one loses weight—in this case because less money will be spent on food>.

---

bench *n* **1** (*pupils sitting on a bench*) form, seat. **2** (*a carpenter's bench*) work-bench, work-table, table, counter.

bend *vb* **1** (*try to bend the iron band*) curve, flex, loop, arch, twist, contort, warp. **2** (*The road bends to the left*) curve, turn, twist, swerve, veer, incline. **3** (*She bent down to pick up the letter*) stoop, crouch down, lean down, bow down. ▼

---

on bended knees very humbly or earnestly (*She asked him to forgive her on bended knees*).

---

bend *n* (*a bend in the road*) curve, turn, twist, corner, angle.

beneficial *adj* (*a climate beneficial to her health*) of benefit, advantageous, favourable, helpful.

benefit *n* **1** (*one of the benefits of living near the sea*) advantage, gain, good point, asset, boon. **2** (*things that are of benefit to all*) advantage, good, profit, use, value, help, service.

benevolent *adj* **1** (*a benevolent old man*) kind, kindly, kind-hearted, generous, helpful. **2** (*benevolent institutions*) charitable, non-profit-making.

bent *adj* **1** (*a bent iron rod*) curved, crooked, angled, twisted, contorted, warped. **2** (*with bent backs*) bowed, arched, stooped, hunched.

bent *n* (*of a musical bent*) inclination, leaning, tendency, predisposition, talent, aptitude, flair.

bequest *n* (*receive a bequest in her employer's will*) legacy, inheritance.

bereavement *n* (*Their grandfather has died—we must sympathize with them on their bereavement*) loss, death, decease.

bereft *adj* (*bereft of speech*) deprived of, robbed of, devoid of, lacking.

berserk *adj* (*He went berserk when he saw the damage to his car*) mad, insane, frenzied, out of one's mind, wild, enraged, raging, amok, (*inf*) ape, (*inf*) bananas.

besides *adv* (*I do not want to go—besides it is too late*) also, in addition, additionally, moreover, furthermore.

besides *prep* (*four people besides us*) as well as, apart from, in addition to, not counting.

besiege *vb* (*a city besieged by the*

enemy) lay siege to, blockade, surround, encircle, beleaguer.

best *adj* **1** (*the best player*) top, foremost, leading, finest. **2** (*the best thing to do*) right, correct, most suitable, most fitting.

bet *vb* (*bet £100 on a horse*) gamble, wager, stake, risk, venture.

bet *n* **1** (*place a bet on a horse*) wager, stake. **2** (*one's best bet*) choice, option, alternative, course of action. ▼

---

hedge one's bets to try to protect oneself from possible loss, failure, disappointment, etc (*We decided to hedge our bets and book seats for both performances*) <From betting the same amount on each side to make sure of not losing>.

---

betray *vb* **1** (*betray his friend to the police*) be disloyal to, break faith with, inform on, double-cross, (*inf*) blow the whistle on, sell down the river. **2** (*betray her secret*) reveal, disclose, divulge, let slip, give away.

beware *vb* (*advised to beware of thieves*) be careful, be wary, be on one's guard, guard against, watch out.

bewilder *vb* (*bewildered by all the traffic signs*) confuse, muddle, puzzle, perplex, baffle, nonplus, bamboozle, bemuse.

bewitch *vb* **1** (*bewitched by the pianist's performance*) captivate, enchant, entrance, beguile, charm. **2** (*The wizard bewitched the prince*) put a spell on, cast a spell over, enchant.

biased *adj* (*accuse the referee of being biased/a biased attitude*) prejudiced, one-sided, influenced, partial, bigoted, unfair, unjust.

bid *vb* **1** (*bid £100 for the vase at the auction*) offer, tender, proffer, put forward. **2** (*bid them farewell*) wish, greet, tell, say.

big *adj* **1** (*a big house/a big car*) large, sizeable, great, substantial, huge, enormous, vast, colossal, gigantic. **2** (*a big man*) large, tall, heavy, burly, thickset. **3** (*a big decision*) important, significant, major, serious, grave, weighty. ▼

---

a big fish in a small pond a person who seems better, more important, etc, than he or she is because he or she works or lives in a small, limited area (*He did well in the village school where he was a big fish in a small pond but when he went to a large city school he was just average*).

---

bigotry *n* (*religious bigotry*) prejudice, intolerance, bias, partiality, narrow-mindedness, fanaticism.

bilious *adj* **1** sick, nauseated, queasy. **2** (*walls of a bilious colour*) garish, violent, nauseating.

bill *n* **1** (*send them the bill for the work/pay the restaurant bill*) account, invoice, (*inf*) tab. **2** (*post bills to advertise the show*) poster, advertisement, notice, circular.

bin *n* (*a rubbish bin/a bin for corn*) container, receptacle, box, can.

bind *vb* **1** (*bind the sheaves of corn together*) tie, tie up, fasten, secure, attach, truss. **2** (*bind the wound*) bandage, dress, cover. **3** (*bind the seams*) edge trim, hem, finish.

birth *n* **1** (*present at the birth*) delivery, childbirth, confinement. **2** (*of humble birth*) origin, descent, family, parentage, extraction, ancestry. **3** (*the birth of civilization*) origin, beginning, start, creation.

bit *n* (*a bit of chocolate/a bit of cheese*) piece, section, segment, lump, chunk, scrap, sliver, morsel, grain, speck, particle.

bite *vb* **1** (*bite into the apple/biting her nails*) chew, munch, crunch, nibble at, gnaw at, eat. **2** (*The dog bit the postman*) sink one's teeth into, snap at, nip. **3** (*bitten by mosquitoes*) sting, puncture.

bite *n* **1** (*a bite of the apple/a bite of food*) mouthful, piece, morsel, bit. **2** (*The dog gave her a bite*) snap, nip. **3** (*insect bites*) sting, prick, puncture. **4** (*food with a bite*) sharpness, spiciness, piquancy, pungency.

bitter *adj* **1** (*a bitter taste*) acid, tart, sour, acrid, harsh, pungent, vinegary. **2** (*a bitter old man*) embittered, resentful, sour, acrimonious, spiteful, vindictive. **3** (*a bitter wind*) biting, sharp, raw, penetrating, stinging, freezing. **4** (*from bitter experience*) painful, distressing, unhappy, sad, tragic.

black *adj* **1** (*black clothes/black horses*) jet-black, pitch-black, inky, sable, dusky. **2** (*black nights*) dark, pitch-black, inky, murky, unlit, starless. **3** (*in a black mood*) depressed, gloomy, pessimistic, melancholy, sad. ▼

---

in black and white in writing or in print (*We had a conversation and agreed to work together but our lawyer says we should put the details in black and white*) <From black print on white paper>.

---

blame *vb* **1** (*blame her for the crime*) hold responsible, hold accountable, accuse, charge, find guilty, condemn. **2** (*blame the crime on her*) attribute, ascribe, lay at the door of, (*inf*) pin on.

blame *n* (*put the blame for the crime on her*) responsibility, accountability, liability, fault, accusation, guilt, condemnation (*inf*) rap.

bland *adj* **1** (*bland food*) tasteless, flavourless, insipid, mild. **2** (*a bland manner*) smooth, suave, urbane, gracious.

blank *adj* **1** (*a blank piece of paper*) empty, unfilled, unwritten on, unmarked, bare. **2** (*a blank tape*) clean, empty, unfilled, unused. **3** (*a blank face*) expressionless, vacant, empty, deadpan, impassive.

blast *n* **1** (*hear the blast several streets away*) explosion, bang, report, eruption. **2** (*a blast of cold air*) gust, rush, draught, wind, gale. **3** (*a blast of loud music*) blare, boom, roar.

blatant *adj* (*a blatant crime*) glaring, flagrant, obvious, conspicuous, unmistakable, brazen.

blaze *n* **1** (*old people killed in the blaze*) fire, flames, conflagration, inferno. **2** (*a sudden blaze of light*) flash, flare, beam, streak.

blaze *vb* **1** (*logs blazing in the fire*) burn, be ablaze, flame. **2** (*lights blazing*) shine, beam, flash, flare.

bleak *adj* **1** (*a bleak countryside*) bare, barren, desolate, dismal, exposed. **2** (*a bleak future*) gloomy, depressing, miserable, dismal, grim, dark.

blemish *n* **1** (*blemishes on the fruit*) mark, spot, blotch, bruise, imperfection. **2** (*a blemish in his character*) flaw, fault, defect. **3** (*a blemish on her reputation*) stain, blot.

blend *vb* (*blend the ingredients for the pudding*) mix, combine, mingle.

blessing *n* **1** (*The minister said a blessing*) benediction, grace, prayer, dedication. **2** (*The rain is *a blessing for the dried-out gardens*) boon, advantage, benefit, asset, help. **3** (*give the scheme his blessing*) approval, support, sanction, endorsement. ▼

---

a blessing in disguise something that turns out to be an advantage after at first seeming unfortunate (*Being declared redundant was a blessing in disguise. She got a much more interesting job*).

---

blind *adj* **1** (*a blind person with a guide dog*) unsighted, sightless, unseeing, visually impaired, visually challenged. **2** (*blind to the problems*) unmindful of, heedless of, oblivious to, indifferent to, unaware of, unconscious of, ignorant of.

blind *n* **1** (*The blind kept out the sunlight*) screen, shade, shutters, curtain. **2** (*His shop was a blind for drug-pushing*) front, screen, smoke screen, camouflage, cloak, disguise.

blink *vb* **1** (*people blinking in the bright light*) screw up one's eyes, wink, squint. **2** (*with eyelids blinking*) flicker, wink, bat. **3** (*Christmas trees blinking*) flicker, twinkle, wink, glimmer, glitter.

bliss *n* (*the bliss of being in love*) ecstasy, elation, euphoria, joy, rapture, happiness, delight.

block *n* **1** (*a block of chocolate*) bar, cake, brick, slab, chunk, lump, hunk, wedge. **2** (*a block in the waste pipe*) blockage, obstruction, stoppage. **3** (*the science block of the university*) building, complex.

block *vb* **1** (*leaves blocking the drains*) clog, choke, stop up, obstruct, (*inf*) bung up. **2** (*fallen trees blocking the flow of traffic*) bar, halt, obstruct, hinder, impede, hold back.

bloodshed *n* (*a battle which resulted in great bloodshed*) killing, murder, slaughter, massacre, carnage.

bloom *vb* **1** (*flowers which bloom in the summer*) flower, be in flower, come into flower, blossom. **2** (*children blooming in their new environment*) flourish, thrive, blossom, get on well, prosper, succeed.

blot *n* **1** (*ink blots/blots of grease*) blotch, spot, smudge, splodge, smear. **2** (*a blot on her character*) stain, blemish, flaw, fault, defect, taint.

blot *vb* **1** (*paper blotted with ink spots*) spot, smudge, blotch, smear, mark. **2** (*blot their reputation*) sully, blacken, stain, tarnish, besmirch. **3** (*blot out memories of the past*) wipe out, rub out, erase, obliterate, destroy.

blow *n* **1** (*a blow on the head*) hit, knock, bang, thump, smack, slap, rap, (*inf*) clout. **2** (*It was a blow when her friend went away*) shock, upset, jolt, setback, disappointment, misfortune, disaster, catastrophe.

blue *adj* **1** (*blue skies*) azure, indigo, sapphire, ultramarine, navy, navy blue, sky-blue, powder-blue, royal blue. **2** (*feeling blue*) depressed, gloomy, miserable, downcast, glum, sad, unhappy, melancholy. **3** (*blue jokes*) obscene, indecent, improper, dirty, smutty. ▼

---

blue-eyed boy a male who is someone's favourite (*He certainly will not lose his job. He is the manager's blue-eyed boy*). **out of the blue** without any warning (*The news of his death came out of the blue*).

---

bluff *n* (*He said that he would report her but it was only a bluff*) pretence, sham, fake, deception, subterfuge, hoax.

bluff *adj* (*The policeman had a very bluff manner*) outspoken, plain-spoken, blunt, direct, frank, candid.

blunder *n* (*It was important not to make a blunder in the calculations*) mistake, error, slip, inaccuracy, (*inf*) slip-up, (*inf*) boob, (*inf*) clanger.

blunder *vb* **1** (*discover that someone had blundered and had forgotten to book the hall*) make a mistake, err, (*inf*) slip up, screw up. **2** (*During the power failure, he was blundering about in the dark without a torch*) stumble, lurch, stagger, flounder.

blunt *adj* **1** (*A blunt knife will not cut cleanly*) dull, dulled, unsharpened. **2** (*a blunt statement*) abrupt, curt, brusque, outspoken, plainspoken, direct, frank, straightforward, candid.

blur *vb* **1** (*Tears blurred her vision*) obscure, dim, make hazy, make misty, make fuzzy, cloud. **2** (*Grease blurred the windscreen*) smear, smudge. **3** (*Time had blurred her memory*) dim, make hazy, make vague, dull, confuse.

blur *n* (*When she did not have her glasses on everything was just a blur*) haze, mist.

blurred *adj* (*She had a headache and blurred vision*) hazy, misty, fuzzy, indistinct, unclear.

blush *vb* (*She blushed with embarrassment*) redden, go red, turn red, go scarlet, go crimson, flush, colour.

board *n* **1** (*a bridge made of wooden boards*) plank, slat, beam. **2** (*charge her for her board*) food, meals.

board *vb* **1** (*board the plane*) get on, enter, go on board, mount, embark. **2** (*board up the windows*) cover up, shut up, seal. **3** (*He boards with a friend of his mother*) lodge, live, have rooms. ▼

---

go by the board to be abandoned (*His dreams of going to university have gone by the board since he failed his exams*) <The board here is a ship's board or side—'to go by the board' literally was to vanish overboard>.

---

boast *vb* (*She was always boasting about how well she could sing*) brag, crow, blow one's own trumpet, show off, swagger, (*inf*) swank.

boastful *adj* (*a boastful person always telling people about her fine house*) bragging, swaggering, conceited, vain, (*inf*) big-headed, (*inf*) swanking.

boat *n* vessel, craft, dinghy, yacht, ship, rowing-boat. ▼

---

miss the boat to fail to take advantage of an opportunity (*She meant to apply for the job but she missed the boat. She posted the application letter too late*).

rock the boat to do something to spoil or put at risk a happy or comfortable situation (*It was a happy neighbourhood until came along and rocked the boat by complaining about everything*).

---

body *n* **1** (*healthy bodies*) physique. **2** (*pains in his body and in his limbs*) trunk, torso. **3** (*bodies in the mortuary*) dead body, corpse, carcass, cadaver. **4** (*the ruling body in the organization*) group, party, band, company, bloc. **5** (*a large body of water*) mass, expanse, extent.

bodyguard *n* (*the president's bodyguard*) guard, protector, defender.

bog *n* (*The walkers got stuck in the bog*) marsh, marshland, swamp, mire, quagmire.

bogus *adj* **1** (*The man in the hospital turned out to be a bogus doctor*) fraudulent, fake, sham, (*inf*) phoney. **2** (*pay for the goods with bogus £10 notes*) counterfeit, forged, fake, fraudulent, sham, (*inf*) phoney.

boil *vb* (*soup boiling on the stove*) bubble, cook, simmer.

boisterous *adj* **1** (*boisterous children*) lively, active, spirited, noisy, loud, rowdy, unruly. **2** (*a boisterous wind*) blustery, gusting, stormy, wild.

bold *adj* **1** (*a bold adventurer*) brave, courageous, valiant, gallant, daring, adventurous, intrepid, fearless, heroic. **2** (*a bold young woman/so bold as to invite themselves to the party*) brazen, impudent, forward, audacious. **3** (*bold colours*) striking, bright, vivid, eye-catching, showy.

bolt *n* **1** (*bolts on the door*) bar, catch, latch, fastener, lock. **2** (*nuts and bolts*) rivet, pin, peg. **3** (*make a bolt for it*) dash, run, sprint, dart, rush. ▼

---

a bolt from the blue something very sudden and unexpected (*His decision to leave was a bolt from the blue*).

---

bolt *vb* **1** (*They bolted the door*) bar, lock, fasten, secure. **2** (*bolt from the room in fear*) dash, run, sprint, dart, rush, hurtle, flee. **3** (*The children bolted their food*) gulp, gobble, wolf, guzzle.

bomb *n* (*a building blown up by a bomb*) incendiary device, incendiary, explosive, shell.

bombard *vb* **1** (*The enemy bombarded the military stores*) bomb, shell, torpedo, blitz, attack. **2** (*bombard them with questions*) assail, attack, besiege, subject to.

bond *n* **1** (*the bond between mother and child*) tie, link, connection, attachment. **2** (*prisoners escaping from their bonds*) chains, fetters, shackles, rope.

bonus *n* **1** (*The good food on holiday was a welcome bonus*) extra, addition, (*inf*) plus, benefit, gain, boon. **2** (*staff getting a Christmas bonus*) gift, tip, gratuity, (*inf*) perk, reward.

bony *adj* angular, scraggy, gaunt, skinny, skeletal.

book *vb* (*book theatre seats/book hotel rooms*) reserve, make reservations for.

book *n* (*borrow a book from the library*) volume, tome, publication. ▼

---

bring someone to book to make someone explain or be punished for his or her actions (*The boys who stole the car were soon brought to book*). <Perhaps a reference to the book in which a police officer keeps a note of crimes>. **read someone like a book** to understand someone completely, not to be deceived by someone (*I knew that he was lying—I can read him like a book*).

---

bookish *adj* (*She is rather a bookish child*) studious, scholarly, academic, intellectual, learned, highbrow.

boom *vb* **1** (*hear guns booming*) bang, banging, blast, roar, rumble. **2** (*a boom in the number of tourists*) increase, growth, upsurge, upswing, upturn, boost.

boor *n* (*boors with bad manners*) lout, oaf, (*inf*) yob, (*inf*) yobbo.

boost *vb* (*boost the morale of the troops*) raise, increase, heighten, improve, encourage, help, assist.

booth *n* **1** (*a market booth*) stall, stand, counter. **2** (*a telephone booth*) cubicle, compartment.

booty *n* (*the booty hidden by the burglars*) loot, spoils, plunder, haul, (*inf*) swag.

border *n* **1** (*sew a colourful border on the skirt*) edging, edge, fringe, trimming. **2** (*a flower border*) bed. **3** (*the borders of the lake*) edge, verge, perimeter, margin. **4** (*show one's passport at the border*) frontier, boundary.

bore *vb* **1** (*bore into the wood/bore a hole in the wood*) drill, pierce, perforate, penetrate, puncture. **2** (*an audience bored by the comedian*) weary, tire, fatigue, be tedious to, bore to tears, bore to death.

boring *adj* (*a boring speech*) dull, tedious, monotonous, unexciting, uninteresting, wearisome, tiring.

borrow *vb* (*borrow money from someone/borrow someone's pen*) ask for the loan of, take as a loan, use temporarily, (*inf*) scrounge, (*inf*) cadge.

boss *n* (*The workers asked the boss for a wage rise*) employer, manager, director, owner, (*inf*) honcho.

bossy *adj* domineering, bullying, overbearing, dominating, dictatorial.

bother *vb* **1** (*The children were told not to bother their mother when she was resting*) disturb, trouble, worry, pester, annoy, harass, (*inf*) hassle. **2** (*Please don't bother to wait for me*) take the trouble, trouble oneself, inconvenience oneself, make the effort. **3** (*It bothers me that she is not here yet*) concern, worry, trouble, upset.

bother *n* **1** (*Please don't go to any bother over dinner*) trouble, inconvenience, effort, fuss. **2** (*There was a bit of bother at the football match*) trouble, disturbance, commotion, disorder, fighting.

bottle *n* **1** (*a bottle of milk/a bottle of wine*) container, flask, carafe. **2** (*not have the bottle to climb the high tree*) courage, bravery, daring, nerve, boldness. ▼

---

crack a bottle to open a bottle (*Let us celebrate by cracking a bottle of champagne*).

---

bottom *n* **1** (*at the bottom of the hill*) foot, base. **2** (*the bottom of the sea*) floor, bed, depths. **3** (*the bottom of the garden*) the far end, the farthest point. ▼

---

bottom drawer a collection of articles for the home which young women used to gather together before marriage (*She had sheets and towels in her bottom drawer*).

---

bound *vb* (*bound into the room/bound over the fence*) leap, jump, spring, vault, spring.

bound *adj* (*She thought that she was bound to win*) certain, sure, very likely, destined.

boundary *n* **1** (*the boundary between the countries*) border, frontier, dividing line. **2** (*the boundary of the estate*) bounds, border, perimeter, periphery, confines, limits, margin.

bouquet *n* (*the bride's bouquet/a bouquet of roses*) bunch of flowers, bunch, spray, posy.

bout *n* 1 (*a boxing bout*) combat, contest, match, round, fight. 2 (*a bout of coughing*) fit, attack, turn, spell.

bow *vb* (*bow his head*) incline, bend, nod, stoop.

bowl *n* (*a bowl of cereal*) dish, basin, container.

bowl *vb* (*bowl a ball*) pitch, throw, fling, hurl, toss.

box *n* container, receptacle, carton, case, pack, chest, bin, crate.

box *vb* 1 (*He used to box for England*) fight. 2 (*box the child on the ears*) strike, hit, cuff, slap, smack, wallop, (*inf*) belt.

boy *n* (*when he was a boy*) youth, lad.

boycott *vb* 1 (*boycott goods from that country*) bar, ban, black, blacklist, embargo, place an embargo on, prohibit. 2 (*boycott their company*) shun, avoid, spurn, send to Coventry, eschew.

boyfriend *n* (*She has a new boyfriend*) sweetheart, young man, lover, partner.

bracing *adj* (*a bracing climate*) invigorating, refreshing, stimulating, exhilarating, reviving, health-giving.

brag *vb* (*He brags about having a lot of money*) boast, crow, blow one's own trumpet, show off, (*inf*) talk big.

brain *n* (*have a good brain*) intellect, mind, intelligence, powers of reasoning, head. ▼

---

pick someone's brains to find out someone's ideas and knowledge about a subject so that one can put them to one's own use.

---

branch *n* 1 (*the branch of a tree*) bough, limb. 2 (*the local branch of the business*) division, subdivision, section, department, part.

brand *n* 1 (*a brand of breakfast cereal*) make, kind, variety, type, sort, line, label, trade name, trademark. 2 (*her brand of wit*) kind, variety, type, sort, style.

brandish *vb* (*a criminal brandishing a knife*) wave, flourish, swing, wield, shake.

brash *adj* (*a brash young man*) bold, cocky, self-confident, self-assertive, insolent, impudent, cheeky, brazen.

brave *adj* courageous, valiant, intrepid, fearless, plucky, gallant, heroic, bold, daring.

brawl *n* (*a brawl in a public house*) fight, affray, wrangle, rumpus, row, quarrel, argument, squabble, free-for-all, scrap.

brawny *adj* (*brawny hammer-throwers*) burly, muscular, hefty, powerful, strong, strapping.

bray *vb* (*donkeys braying*) whinny, neigh, hee-haw.

brazen *adj* (*It was brazen of her to kiss a complete stranger on the lips*) bold, audacious, forward, brash, impudent, insolent, impertinent, immodest, shameless.

breach *n* 1 (*a breach in the sea wall*) break, split, crack, gap, hole, opening. 2 (*a breach of the legal agreement*) breaking, violation, infringement.

breadth *n* 1 (*measure the breadth of the room*) width, wideness, broadness, span. 2 (*discover the breadth of her knowledge of the subject*) extent, range, scope, scale, degree.

break *vb* 1 (*break a cup*) smash, shatter, crack. 2 (*break the handle of the bag*) snap, split, tear. 3 (*The machine broke*) break down, become damaged, stop working, cease to operate, (*inf*) go kaput. **4** (*break the law*) violate, contravene, breach, infringe, disobey, disregard, defy. **5** (*break his arm*) fracture, crack. **6** (*break the news*) tell, impart, announce, communicate, reveal, disclose. ▼

---

break even to have one's losses balanced by one's gains, to make neither a loss nor a profit (*We did not make any money on our investment but at least we broke even*).

---

break *n* **1** (*a break in the water pipe*) crack, hole, gash, split, fracture, chink, tear. **2** (*a break in her career to look after her children*) interruption, discontinuation, pause, hiatus. **3** (*have a cup of tea during her break*) rest period, interval, intermission, breathing-space. **4** (*take a weekend break*) holiday, vacation, time off.

breakthrough *n* (*a breakthrough in cancer research*) advance, step forward, development.

breathe *vb* **1** (*breathe in/breathe out*) inhale/exhale, inspire/expire, puff, pant. **2** (*as long as he breathes*) be alive, live, have life. ▼

---

breathe down someone's neck 1 to be very close behind someone (*He was in the lead in the race but there were several other runners breathing down his neck*). **2** to be waiting impatiently for something from someone (*The boss is breathing down her neck for those letters which she is typing*).

---

breathless *adj* (*breathless after running for the bus*) out of breath, gasping, panting, puffing.

breed *n* (*a breed of cattle*) variety, kind, strain.

breed *vb* **1** (*Rabbits breed very rapidly*) reproduce, multiply, give birth. **2** (*He breeds horses*) raise, rear. **3** (*poverty which can breed crime and violence*) cause, bring about, give rise to, create, produce, stir up.

breeze *n* (*a cool breeze on a hot day*) puff of wind, gust of wind, current of air, draught, zephyr.

bribe *vb* (*try to bribe a member of the jury*) buy off, corrupt, give an inducement to, (*inf*) grease the palm of, (*inf*) give a backhander to, (*inf*) give a sweetener to.

bridge *n* (*a bridge over the motorway*) overpass, flyover, viaduct, suspension bridge. ▼

---

cross a bridge when one comes to it to worry about something or attempt to deal with something only when it actually happens instead of worrying about it beforehand (*She is worrying about losing her job although she might not. She should learn to cross a bridge when she comes to it*).

---

brief *adj* **1** (*a brief statement*) short, concise, succinct, to the point, compact, terse. **2** (*a brief friendship*) short, short-lived, fleeting, passing, transient, transitory, ephemeral.

brief *vb* (*brief a lawyer*) instruct, give instructions to, direct, give directions to, inform, give information to, prime.

bright *adj* **1** (*a bright light*) shining, brilliant, dazzling, blazing, gleaming, radiant. **2** (*bright colours*) vivid, brilliant, intense, glowing, bold, rich. **3** (*bright children*) clever, intelligent, sharp, quick,

quick-witted, (*inf*) smart, brilliant, (*inf*) brainy, gifted, talented. **4** (*a bright future*) promising, favourable, hopeful, optimistic, encouraging, fortunate, good. ▼

---

bright-eyed and bushy-tailed very lively and cheerful (*She is always bright-eyed and bushy-tailed early in the morning but her sister is sleepy and bad-tempered*) <From squirrels who have bright eyes and bushy tails>.

---

brilliant *adj* **1** (*a brilliant light*) bright, shining, dazzling, gleaming, radiant. **2** (*brilliant children*) bright, clever, intelligent, sharp, quick, quick-witted, (*inf*) smart, (*inf*) brainy, gifted, talented.

brim *n* (*glasses full to the brim*) rim, lip, top, edge.

brim *vb* (*glasses brimming with wine/eyes brimming with tears*) be full, be filled with, overflow, run over.

bring *vb* **1** (*bring food home*) carry, take, convey, transport, fetch. **2** (*famine which brought disease*) cause, produce, create, result in, give rise to.

brink *n* **1** (*on the brink of the lake*) edge, verge, boundary, border, margin. **2** (*on the brink of the disaster*) edge, verge, threshold, point.

brisk *adj* **1** (*walk at a brisk speed*) quick, fast, rapid, swift, speedy, energetic, lively. **2** (*Business was brisk*) busy, active, hectic.

brittle *adj* (*Toffee is a brittle substance*) hard, crisp, breakable, splintery.

broad *adj* **1** (*a broad street*) wide. **2** (*a broad range of subjects*) wide, wide-ranging, broad-ranging, general, comprehensive. **3** (*a broad statement of their plans*) general, non-detailed, imprecise, vague. ▼

---

have broad shoulders to be able to accept a great deal of responsibility, criticism, etc (*He never minds being blamed when things go wrong. He says that he has broad shoulders*).

---

brochure *n* (*an advertising brochure*) booklet, leaflet, pamphlet, circular, notice, bill.

brooch *n* (*She wears a silver brooch on her lapel*) pin, clip.

brow *n* **1** (*wipe the sweat from his brow*) forehead, temple. **2** (*the brow of the hill*) top, summit, crown, peak.

brown *adj* (*go brown in the summer*) tanned, sun-tanned, bronze, bronzed. ▼

---

in a brown study deep in thought (*She did not hear anything he said. She was in a brown study*).

---

brush *vb* **1** (*brush the back yard*) sweep, clean. **2** (*brush her hair*) groom, tidy. **3** (*brush her cheek with his lips*) touch, flick, glance. ▼

---

brush up on something to refresh one's knowledge of something (*brushing up on their French before going on holiday*).

---

brusque *adj* (*a brusque reply*) abrupt, blunt, curt, sharp, gruff, rude.

brutal *adj* (*a brutal attack*) savage, cruel, vicious, callous, ruthless.

bubble *vb* **1** (*champagne bubbling*) fizz, effervesce, sparkle, foam, froth. **2** (*a sauce bubbling on the stove*) boil, simmer.

bucket *n* (*need a bucket of water to wash the floor*) pail, container. ▼

---

a drop in the bucket a very small part of what is needed (*We collected a lot of money for the famine relief fund but it is just a drop in the bucket*). **kick the bucket** (*inf*) to die (*He hoped to be left a lot of money when the old man kicked the bucket*) <'bucket' here is perhaps a beam from which pigs were hung after being killed>.

---

buckle *n* (*the buckle of the belt*) clasp, catch, fastener, fastening, clip.

bug *n* **1** (*bitten by bugs when sitting on the grass*) insect, mite, (*inf*) creepy-crawly. **2** (*He caught a bug and is off work*) infection, virus, germ, bacterium, micro-organism.

build *vb* **1** (*build a new school*) construct, put up, erect. **2** (*build model planes*) make, construct, assemble, put together. **3** (*build his own business*) found, set up, establish, start, begin, develop, institute. ▼

---

build castles in Spain to have dreams or hopes that are very unlikely to be realized.

---

building *n* (*old buildings which are tourist attractions*) edifice, structure.

bulge *n* (*The bag of sweets made a bulge in her pocket*) swelling, bump, lump, protuberance.

bulk *n* **1** (*The wardrobe was difficult to move because of its sheer bulk*) size, mass, extent, largeness, hugeness. **2** (*The bulk of the people voted against the proposal*) majority, most, preponderance, mass.

bulky *adj* (*bulky furniture*) large, big, massive, substantial, heavy, unwieldy, cumbersome, awkward.

bully *vb* (*older boys bullying the younger ones*) browbeat, domineer, intimidate, threaten, persecute, torment, tyrannize, (*inf*) push around.

bump *vb* (*the car that bumped into ours*) knock, hit, strike, crash into, bang, collide with, ram.

bump *n* **1** (*The child fell out of the tree with a bump*) thud, thump, bang, jolt, crash. **2** (*He has a bump on the head from the accident*) lump, swelling, bulge.

bumpy *adj* (*bumpy roads*) uneven, rough, rutted, pitted, potholed.

bunch *n* **1** (*a bunch of flowers*) bouquet, spray, posy, sheaf. **2** (*a bunch of grapes*) cluster, clump. **3** (*a friendly bunch of people*) group, band, crowd, gang.

bundle *n* (*a bundle of old clothes*) pile, heap, stack, bale.

burden *n* **1** (*the pony's burden*) load, pack. **2** (*the burden of being head of the family*) responsibility, obligation, onus, worry, weight, strain. ▼

---

the burden of proof the responsibility for proving something (*The burden of proof lies with the accusers*) <A legal term>.

---

burglar *n* (*catch a burglar breaking into the house*) housebreaker, cat burglar, thief, robber.

burglary *n* (*He was sent to prison on a charge of burglary*) house-breaking, breaking and entering, forced entry, theft, robbery, larceny.

burly *adj* (*the burly figure of the hammer-thrower*) muscular, powerful, thickset, strapping, hefty, beefy, stout.

burn *vb* **1** (*The house was burning*) be on fire, be ablaze, blaze. **2** (*burn the rubbish*) set on fire, set alight, ignite. **3** (*burn the shirt with the iron*) scorch, singe, sear. ▼

the burning question a question that is of great interest to many people (*The burning question is which of the men will she marry*).

burst *vb* **1** (*The water pipes have burst*) crack, split, fracture, rupture. **2** (*They burst into the room*) push one's way, barge. **3** (*burst into tears*) break out, explode, erupt, begin suddenly.

bury *vb* **1** (*bury the corpse*) inter, lay to rest. **2** (*bury her head in her hands*) hide, conceal, cover, put, submerge.

business *n* **1** (*She owns her own business*) company, firm, concern, organization, establishment. **2** (*We don't know what business he is in*) occupation, line, work, profession, job, career. **3** (*People employed in business*) commerce, industry, private enterprise, e-commerce. **4** (*It was none of their business*) concern, affair, problem, responsibility. **5** (*an odd business*) affair, situation, matter, circumstance, thing. ▼

mean business to be determined to do something, to be serious about something (*He was smiling when he said that we had too many members of staff but I think he means business*).
mind one's own business to occupy oneself with the things that concern oneself and not to interfere in those that concern others.

busy *adj* **1** (*Don't disturb your mother—she's busy*) occupied, engaged, working, at work. **2** (*have a busy day*) active, energetic, full, hectic.

buy *vb* (*buy a new house*) purchase, make a purchase of, pay for, invest in.

bypass *n* (*the city bypass*) ring road, detour, alternative route.

C

café *n* (*They stopped for a snack at a café*) coffee bar, coffee shop, cafeteria, snack bar, tea-room, tea shop, restaurant, wine bar, bistro.

cajole *vb* (*Try to cajole him into coming with us*) wheedle, coax, inveigle, persuade.

cagey *adj* (*They seemed rather cagey about where they were going*) secretive, guarded, non-committal.

cake *n* **1** (*have some cake and coffee*) gateau. **2** (*a cake of soap*) bar, block, slab, lump. ▼

---

a piece of cake something that is very easy to do (*Winning the race was a piece of cake*). **a slice of the cake** a share of something that is desirable, profitable or valuable (*You should invest some money in your brother's firm and get a slice of the cake*). **have one's cake and eat it, eat one's cake and have it** to have the advantage of two things or two situations when doing, possessing, etc, one of them would normally make doing, possessing, etc the other one impossible (*He's engaged to one of the sisters but he would like to eat his cake and have it and go out with the other one too*).

---

calculate *vb* (*calculate the cost*) work out, count, estimate, gauge, figure out, reckon.

call *vb* **1** (*She called out in fear*) cry, shout, yell, scream. **2** (*They called their son Peter*) name, christen. **3** (*The vegetables are called courgettes/That is called wind-surfing*) name, style, designate, term, describe, dub, label. **4** (*She called you from a public telephone box*) telephone, phone, ring. **5** (*He will call tomorrow to do his aunt's shopping*) pay a call, pay a visit, stop by, drop in. **6** (*If the child is ill you had better call a doctor*) send for, ask for, summon. **7** (*They called a meeting of the committee*) call together, convene, summon. **8** (*I call it shocking that he got away with the crime*) think, consider, regard, judge. ▼

---

call off to cancel (*They were to be married next week but she suddenly called off the wedding*). **call a spade a spade** to speak bluntly and in a forthright manner (*I don't think you should try to break the bad news to her gently. She would much rather that you called a spade a spade*).

---

calm *adj* **1** (*She remains calm even in an emergency*) cool, composed, self-possessed, unruffled, tranquil, quiet, relayed, (*inf*) laid-back. **2** (*The sea was calm when the boat set out*) still, smooth. **3** (*It was a calm day for their trip to the seaside*) still, windless, mild.

camouflage *n* (*The polar bear's coat is a camouflage in the snow*) protective colouring, disguise, cover, screen, concealment.

camp *n* **1** (*the soldier's camp*) encampment, campsite, camping ground. **2** (*He is in the left-wing camp of the party*) group, set, faction, clique. ▼

have a foot in both camps to have associations with two groups who have opposing and conflicting views and attitudes (*He is one of the workers but he has shares in the firm and so he has a foot in both camps*).

can *n* (*a can of soup*) tin, container. ▼

carry the can to be given the blame or responsibility for something, usually for something that someone else has been involved in (*Several of the pupils were responsible for breaking into the school but Jack was the one that was caught and he had to carry the can*). **in the can** (*inf*) certain, agreed or decided upon (*He had a good interview and he thinks the job's in the can*) <A reference to a completed cinema film that is stored in large metal containers or cans>.

cancel *vb* **1** (*They had to cancel the meeting because of bad weather*) put off, call off. **2** (*They cancelled the order because it was late*) call off, retract, declare void, declare null and void, revoke.

candid *adj* (*He was quite candid with them about his reasons for leaving*) frank, open, honest, direct, forthright, blunt, plain-spoken.

cap *n* **1** (*He wore a cap to hide his baldness*) hat, bonnet. **2** (*I can't get the cap off the bottle*) top, lid, stopper, cork. ▼

put on one's thinking cap to begin to think very carefully about something (*If you put on your thinking cap I am sure that you will come up with a solution to the problem*). **to cap it all** on top of everything else, usually everything else that has already gone wrong (*I was late and to cap it all the car would not start*). **cap in hand** very humbly, usually when asking for something (*Although he had quarrelled with his father he had to go cap in hand to ask for a loan to pay the rent*).

capable *adj* **1** (*She is a very capable person*) able, competent, efficient, effective. **2** (*He is quite capable of cheating*) likely to, liable to.

capital *n* **1** (*Edinburgh is the capital of Scotland*) first city, chief city, seat of administration. **2** (*He does not have enough capital to buy the company*) money, finance, funds, cash, means, resources, wherewithal, assets. **3** (*write the title in capitals*) capital letter, upper case letter, (*inf*) cap. ▼

make capital out of (something) to make use of (something), usually something that is in some way disadvantageous to someone else, for one's own advantage (*In the court case the counsel for the defence made capital out of the fact that the witness for the prosecution was very nervous*).

capsize *vb* **1** (*The boat capsized in heavy seas*) overturn, turn over, up-end, keel over, turn turtle. **2**

(*The child capsized the bucket of water*) upset, overturn, up-end.

captivity *n* (*enjoy freedom after months in captivity*) imprisonment, custody, confinement, incarceration.

capture *vb* (*The police have captured the escaped prisoners*) catch, take prisoner, take captive, take into custody, arrest, apprehend, seize.

card *n* **1** (*She sent a card to her mother on her birthday*) greetings card, postcard. **2** (*The salesman handed them his card*) business card, identification, ID. **3** (*He was asked to deal the cards*) playing card. ▼

---

be on the cards to be very likely (*The firm is losing money and so the closure of the factory is on the cards*) <A reference to reading the cards in fortune-telling>. **have a card up one's sleeve** to have an idea, plan of action, etc, in reserve to be used if necessary to get what one wants (*The person who wants to build the new flats thinks that he has won but I have a feeling that the protesters have a card up their sleeve*) <A reference to cheating at cards>. **play one's cards close to one's chest** to be secretive or non-communicative about one's plans or intentions (*I think that they are moving overseas but they are playing their cards close to their chest*) <From holding one's cards close to one in card-playing so that one's opponents will not see them>.

---

care *n* **1** (*The children were told to cross the road with care*) carefulness, caution, heed, heedfulness, wariness, attention, vigilance, prudence. **2** (*She iced the cake with care*) carefulness, conscientiousness, accuracy, meticulousness, punctiliousness. **3** (*The child is in the care of the local authorities*) protection, charge, keeping, custody, supervision. **4** (*They show no care for other people*) concern, regard, interest, solicitude, sympathy. **5** (*She looked older than she was after a life full of care*) worry, anxiety, trouble, distress, hardship, stress.

careful *adj* **1** (*The children were told to be careful crossing the road*) cautious, heedful, wary, attentive, vigilant, prudent. **2** (*You must be careful of your belongings at the airport*) mindful, heedful, protective. **3** (*You must be careful what you say to the lawyer*) mindful, attentive, heedful, thoughtful. **4** (*They are all careful workers*) conscientious, painstaking, accurate, meticulous, punctilious. **5** (*They do not earn much and so they have to be very careful with money*) thrifty, economic, frugal, cautious, canny.

careless *adj* **1** (*a careless pedestrian who walked out in front of the moving car*) unthinking, inattentive, thoughtless, forgetful, remiss, negligent. **2** (*The pupil's exercise is very careless*) inaccurate, slapdash, disorganized, (*inf*) sloppy.

carpet *n* **1** (*They laid a new carpet in the hall*) rug, floor covering, mat. **2** (*a carpet of autumn leaves on the grass*) covering, layer. ▼

---

be on the carpet to be scolded or punished by someone in authority (*She will be on the carpet* *when the boss finds out she's late*) <A reference to the piece of carpet in front of a desk where someone might stand to be scolded by a head teacher, etc>. **sweep (something) under the carpet** to try to hide or forget about (something unpleasant) (*They try to sweep under the carpet the fact that their son steals money from them*).

---

carry *vb* **1** (*She was asked to carry the shopping home*) bring, take, transport, convey, lug. **2** (*Will the bridge carry the weight of the car?*) take, support, bear, sustain. **3** (*The shop carries a wide range of goods*) sell, stock, offer. ▼

---

carry coals to Newcastle to do something that is completely unnecessary, especially to take something to a place where there is already a great deal of it (*Taking a cake to her was like carrying coals to Newcastle. She spends most of her time baking*) <Newcastle in England used to be a large coal-mining centre>.

---

case *n* **1** (*put the cases in the boot of the car*) suitcase, brief case, piece of luggage. **2** (*a silver cigarette case*) container, box, receptacle. **3** (*a display case for ornaments*) cabinet, cupboard. **4** (*It was the case that she had been ill*) situation, position, circumstance. **5** (*They decided that it had been a case of misunderstanding*) instance, occurrence, occasion, example. **6** (*He has been accused of murder and the case comes up next week*) lawsuit, trial, legal proceedings. **7** (*the heart cases in the ward*) patient, sufferer, victim, invalid.

cash *n* **1** (*He earns quite a lot but he never seems to have any cash when we go out*) money, wherewithal, funds, (*inf*) dough, (*inf*) the ready. **2** (*They want us to pay in cash but we have only credit cards*) money, ready money.

cast *vb* **1** (*snakes casting their coats*) shed, slough, discard, throw off. **2** (*The street lamps cast a yellow light*) give off, send out, shed, emit, radiate. **3** (*The children were casting stones in the river*) throw, fling, pitch, toss, hurl, heave. **4** (*She cast him a glance of contempt*) send, throw, bestow. ▼

---

cast pearls before swine to offer something valuable, desirable, enjoyable, to someone who does not appreciate it (*Taking her to the opera would be a case of casting pearls before swine*) <A biblical reference to Matthew 7:6>.

---

casual *adj* **1** (*She wears casual clothes at the weekend*) informal, leisure. **2** (*He is a casual acquaintance not a close friend*) slight, superficial. **3** (*casual hotel work in the summer*) irregular, temporary, part-time. **4** (*He just made a casual remark about the state of the business*) spontaneous, offhand, impromptu. **5** (*They have a very casual attitude to the dangers of the journey*) unconcerned, nonchalant, blasé, indifferent. **6** (*I did not arrange to meet her—it was just a casual meeting*) chance, accidental, unintentional, unforeseen, unexpected.

catch *vb* **1** (*He failed to catch the ball*) get hold of, grasp, grab, seize, snatch, grip. **2** (*The police are determined to catch the escaped prisoner*) capture, take captive, seize, apprehend, arrest. **3** (*Did you catch what he said?*) get, understand, follow, grasp, make out, comprehend, fathom. **4** (*Something bright caught his attention*) attract, draw, capture. **5** (*The child has caught a cold*) contract, develop, get, become infected with, come down with. ▼

---

catch it to be scolded or punished (*He will catch it when his father sees what he has done to the car*). **catch (someone) with his** *or* **her pants** *or* **trousers down** to surprise (someone) when he or she is unprepared or is doing something wrong (*When the boss came into his office he was sitting snoozing with his feet on the desk. He was certainly caught with his trousers down*).

---

catch *n* **1** (*The catch of the bag is broken*) lock, fastener, fastening, clasp. **2** (*There is no catch on the door*) lock, snib, latch, bolt. ▼

Catch 22 a situation in which one can never win or from which one can never escape, being constantly hindered by a rule or restriction that itself changes to block any changes in one's plans; a difficulty that prevents one from an unpleasant or dangerous situation (*You can get money from the social security department if you have somewhere to live but you cannot get anywhere to live without money. It's a Catch 22 situation*) <From the title of a novel by Joseph Heller>.

---

cause *n* **1** (*What was the cause of the accident?*) origin, source, root, agent. **2** (*The patient's condition gives cause for concern*) reason, justification, grounds, call. **3** (*the cause of animals' rights*) ideal, principle, belief.

cautious *adj* (*be cautious about trusting strangers*) careful, wary, watchful, guarded, chary, heedful, attentive, alert, vigilant.

cease *vb* (*The firm has ceased to operate/It ceased operating*) stop, halt, finish, leave off, suspend, quit, desist from.

celebrated *adj* (*the celebrated painter*) famous, renowned, well-known, notable, noted, distinguished, eminent, illustrious.

central *adj* **1** (*occupying a central position in the town*) middle. **2** (*central London*) middle, inner. **3** (*That is the central issue of the discussion*) main, chief, principal, key, core, focal.

centre *n* **1** (*The town hall is in the centre of the town*) middle, heart. **2** (*at the centre of the quarrel*) middle, hub, core, focus, focal point, hub, kernel.

certain *adj* **1** (*They are certain that he will arrive*) sure, positive, confident, assured. **2** (*Failure is certain*) sure, assured, inevitable, inescapable, (*inf*) in the bag. **3** (*It is certain that they have already left*) sure, definite, unquestionable, beyond question, indubitable, undeniable, incontrovertible. **4** (*There is no certain remedy for the disease*) sure, definite, definite, unfailing, dependable, reliable, foolproof, (*inf*) sure-fire. **5** (*There were certain people who did not believe him*) particular, specific.

chain *n* (*a chain of events*) series, succession, string, sequence, train, progression.

chance *n* **1** (*They took a chance when they crossed the bridge—it is very rickety*) risk, gamble, hazard. **2** (*There is a good chance that we will get there on time*) prospect, possibility, probability, likelihood. **3** (*You will not get another chance like that again*) opportunity, opening. **4** (*We haven't been in touch for years—we met again quite by chance*) accident, coincidence, luck, fortuity. ▼

---

chance it to take a risk (*I don't think I'll take an umbrella—I'll chance it*). **have a sporting chance** to have a reasonable chance of success (*A great many people have applied for the job but with his qualifications he must have a sporting chance*).

---

change *vb* **1** (*We have had to change the arrangements for the meeting*) alter, modify, vary, reorganize, transform. **2** (*She has changed completely since I last saw her*) alter, be transformed, metamorphose. **3** (*She has changed jobs*) switch. ▼

---

change one's tune to change one's attitude or intention (*He disagreed with me completely on the issue but he changed his tune when he heard the facts*). **change horses in mid-stream** to change one's opinion, plans, sides, etc, in the middle of something (*At the beginning of the campaign he was in favour of the new road but he changed horses in mid-stream and joined the protesters*).

---

character *n* **1** (*He seems to have changed in character since I first knew him/The character of the seaside village has altered*) nature, disposition, temperament, temper, personality, make-up, ethos. **2** (*We need a person of character in the job*) strength, backbone, integrity, uprightness, honesty. **3** (*His former teacher gave him a letter saying he was of good character/The incident damaged his character*) reputation, name, standing. **4** (*one of the characters in Shakespeare's 'Hamlet'*) role, part, persona. **5** (*one of the village's characters*) eccentric, individual, (*inf*) card.

characteristic *adj* (*He treated the occasion with characteristic arrogance*) typical, distinguishing, individual, particular.

charge *vb* **1** (*The accused has been charged with murder*) accuse, indict. **2** (*The French forces charged the enemy army*) attack, rush, assault, storm. **3** (*The soldier charged the cannon*) load, fill. **4** (*What did they charge for the car?*) ask, levy. **5** (*Tell them to charge it to my account*) debit, put down to, bill.

charge *n* **1** (*The charge was one of murder*) accusation, indictment, arraignment. **2** (*He has charge of the accounts*) responsibility, care, protection, custody. **3** (*What is the charge for hiring the boat?*) cost, price, fee, rate, amount, payment.

charm *n* **1** (*She had a great deal of charm/They were taken with the charm of the village*) attractiveness, attraction, appeal, allure, fascination. **2** (*She has a tiny horseshoe as a lucky charm*) amulet, talisman. **3** (*She has a bracelet with charms on it*) trinket, ornament. **4** (*the sorcerer's charm*) spell, magic. ▼

lead a charmed life regularly to have good fortune and to avoid misfortune, harm or danger (*The racing driver seems to lead a charmed life. He has been in many serious accidents but has never been badly injured*) <It is as though someone has cast a spell on him or her to ensure protection>. **work like a charm** to be very effective, to work very well (*His efforts to get the old woman to like him worked like a charm*) <It is as though a sorcerer has cast a spell>.

---

chart *n* (*record the information in the form of charts*) table, graph, diagram.

chase *vb* **1** (*The hounds were chasing the fox*) run after, pursue, follow. **2** (*They chased away the burglar*) put to flight, drive away. ▼

---

chase (after) rainbows to spend time and effort in thinking about, or in trying to obtain, things that it is quite impossible for one to achieve (*He is always applying for jobs that are away beyond his qualifications. He should concentrate on finding a job which he can do and stop chasing rainbows*).

---

cheap *adj* **1** (*Fruit is very cheap in the summer there*) inexpensive, low-cost, low-priced, reasonable, economical. **2** (*She wears cheap and gaudy jewellery*) inferior, shoddy, tawdry, trashy, tatty, cheapjack, (*inf*) tacky.

cheat *vb* **1** (*He cheated the old lady into giving him her savings*) deceive, trick, swindle, dupe, hoodwink. **2** (*His brother cheated him out of his inheritance*) deprive of, deny, thwart, prevent from.

check *vb* **1** (*The police checked the car's tyres*) examine, inspect, look at, scrutinize, test. **2** (*You must check that the door is locked*) confirm, make sure, verify. **3** (*They had to find some way to check the vehicle's progress*) stop, halt, slow down, delay, obstruct, impede.

cheeky *adj* (*He was scolded for being cheeky to the teacher*) impertinent, impudent, insolent, disrespectful, forward .

cheer *vb* **1** (*The crowds began to cheer*) applaud, shout hurrah, hurrah. **2** (*The arrival of her friends cheered her*) brighten up, buoy up, perk up, enliven, hearten, exhilarate, gladden, elate.

cheerful *adj* **1** (*They were in a cheerful mood when the sun shone*) happy, merry, bright, glad, lighthearted, carefree, joyful. **2** (*She was wearing a dress in cheerful colours*) bright.

cherish *vb* **1** (*She cherishes memories of her father*) treasure, prize, hold dear, revere. **2** (*The children cherish their pets*) look after, care for, tend, protect. **3** (*They cherish hopes of success*) have, entertain, cling to, harbour.

chest *n* **1** (*He was wounded in the chest*) breast, sternum.**2** (*The miser kept his treasure in a chest*) box, trunk, casket, coffer, container, receptacle. ▼

---

get (something) off one's chest to tell (someone) about (something) that is upsetting, worrying, or annoying one (*If you know something about the* *accident you must get it off your chest and tell the police*).

---

chew *vb* (*children told to chew their food thoroughly*) munch, crunch, champ, masticate. ▼

---

chew the cud to think deeply about something (*You will have to chew the cud before coming to a decision on such an important issue*) <A reference to cows literally chewing the cud>.

---

chief *adj* **1** (*the chief man of the tribe*) head, leading, foremost, principal. **2** (*We must discuss the chief points in the report*) main, principal, most important, essential, prime, key, central.

child *n* **1** (*when he was a child*) young one, little one, youngster, young person, (*inf*) kid. **2** (*parents and their child*) offspring, progeny, son/daughter. ▼

---

child's play something that is very easy to do (*With your experience you will find the work child's play*).

---

choice *n* **1** (*You have some choice in the matter—the meeting is not compulsory*) option, selection, preference. **2** (*There is a wide choice of fruit and vegetables in the supermarket*) selection, range, variety. **3** (*We have little choice but to go*) option, alternative, possibility. ▼

Hobson's choice no choice at all; a choice between accepting what is offered or having nothing at all (*The hotel has only one room available for tonight. It's Hobson's choice, I'm afraid*).

---

choke *vb* **1** (*The murderer choked her to death*) strangle, throttle. **2** (*He choked to death on the smoke from the fire*) suffocate, smother, stifle, asphyxiate. **3** (*The drains are choked and had to be cleared*) block, clog, obstruct.

choose *vb* **1** (*The child chose some sweets from the shop's selection*) pick, select, settle on, opt for, decide on. **2** (*He always does just as he chooses*) like, wish, want, prefer, fancy, desire.

chop *vb* **1** (*They began to chop the old trees down*) cut down, fell, hew, hack down. **2** (*They chopped up the vegetables for the soup*) cut up, dice, cube. ▼

---

chop and change to keep altering (something), to keep changing (something) (*I am supposed to be going on holiday with them but they keep chopping and changing the arrangements*). **get the chop** (*inf*) **1** to be dismissed or discontinued (*Both he and his research project got the chop when the budget was cut*). **2** to be killed (*The gang made sure that their enemy got the chop*).

---

chronic *adj* **1** (*She suffers from a chronic illness*) long-standing, long-term, persistent, lingering. **2** (*They are chronic liars*) habitual, hardened, inveterate.

circle *n* **1** (*The children were asked to draw a circle*) ring, round, ball, globe, sphere, orb, loop, disc. **2** (*She has a large circle of friends*) group, set, crowd, ring, clique.

circuit *n* (*They had to run three*

circuits of the track) round, lap, turn, loop, ambit.

circulate *vb* **1** (*They circulated information to the club members*) spread, distribute, issue, give out, disseminate, advertise. **2** (*blood constantly circulating*) flow, move round, go round, revolve, rotate.

circumstances *npl* (*The family lives in poverty-stricken circumstances*) state, situation, conditions.

civil *adj* **1** (*There had been a civil war in the country*) internal, domestic, home. **2** (*The army were in control but there is now a civil government*) civilian, non-military. **3** (*She might have asked in a more civil way/They are very civil people*) polite, courteous, mannerly, well-mannered, refined, civilized, cultured.

civilized *adj* **1** (*peoples of the world who were not then civilized*) enlightened, educated, socialized. **2** (*She is a very civilized person*) cultivated, cultured, educated, sophisticated, refined, polished.

claim *vb* **1** (*He wrote in to claim his prize*) lay claim to, request, ask for, demand. **2** (*They claim that they had nothing to do with the crime*) assert, declare, maintain, profess, allege.

clash *vb* **1** (*The child clashed the cymbals*) strike, bang, clang, clatter, clank. **2** (*I have another appointment which clashes with my proposed meeting with you*) coincide, conflict. **3** (*One group of the committee clashed with the other*) be in conflict. have a disagreement, argue, quarrel, fight. **4** (*The curtains clashed horribly with the carpet*) jar, be incompatible, be discordant, (*inf*) scream.

class *n* **1** (*what appeals to the middle classes*) social division. **2** (*The awards are divided into four classes*) grade, rank, level, classification, category, set, group. **3** (*a lot consisting of one class of objects*) category, group, set, order, sort, type, variety, order, species, genre, genus. **4** (*The two pupils are in the same class*) study group. ▼

---

in a class by oneself, itself, *etc*, **in a class of its,** *etc*, **own** far better than other people or things of the same type, without equal (*No one ever beats her at the tennis club. She is in a class by herself*).

---

clean *adj* **1** (*The children had no clean clothes*) unsoiled, spotless, laundered. **2** (*The village is in need of a clean water supply*) pure, clear, unpolluted, untainted, uncontaminated. **3** (*The pupil asked for a clean piece of paper*) unused, blank. **4** (*people who live clean lives*) good, virtuous, upright, honourable, righteous. ▼

---

a clean slate a record free of any discredit, an opportunity to make a fresh start (*He has paid the penalty for his crime and now that he is out of prison he hopes to start again with a clean slate*). **come clean** to tell the truth about something, especially after lying about it (*He finally decided to come clean and tell the police about his part in the crime*).

---

clear *adj* **1** (*It was clear that she was ill*) obvious, evident, plain, apparent, unmistakable. **2** (*You must try to give a clear account of what happened*) plain, explicit, lucid, coherent, intelligible. **3** (*We had a clear day for our flight*) bright, fair, fine, cloudless. **4** (*a door made of clear glass*) transparent. **5** (*You have to stay five clear days*) whole, complete, entire. ▼

---

as clear as crystal extremely easy to gasp or understand (*It was as clear as crystal that she was lying*). **be in the clear** to be free from suspicion (*The police suspected him of the crime but they have now discovered that he is in the clear*). **the coast is clear** the danger or difficulty is now over (*She has quarrelled with her father and does not want to go into the house while he is still there. Could you tell her when he has gone out and the coast is clear?*).

---

clever *adj* **1** (*He is a very clever pupil*) intelligent, bright, smart, gifted. **2** (*It was clever of them to open a new restaurant at that time*) smart, shrewd, astute, ingenious. **3** (*They are not very academic but they are clever with their hands*) skilful, deft, handy, dexterous.

climate *n* **1** (*a cold climate*) weather, weather pattern. **2** (*an unstable political climate*) atmosphere, feeling, mood, spirit.

climb *vb* (*The boy climbed the ladder*) go up, ascend, mount, scale, clamber up.

cling *vb* **1** (*She began to cling to her mother's hand*) hold on to, grip, clutch, grasp, clasp. **2** (*They tried to change her mind but she clings to her old beliefs*) stick to, hold to, stand by, adhere to.

clip *vb* (*She clipped her son's hair*) cut, trim, snip, crop, shear, prune. ▼

---

clip (someone's) wings to limit the freedom, power, or influence of (someone) (*She used to go out every night but her wings have been clipped since she has had a baby*) <A reference to the practice of clipping the wings of a bird to prevent it from flying>.

---

cloak *n* **1** (*She wore a black evening cloak*) cape, mantle, shawl, wrap. **2** (*There was a cloak of secrecy surrounding the whole affair*) cover, screen, mask, mantle, veil, shield. ▼

---

cloak-and-dagger involving or relating to a great deal of plotting and scheming (*There was lot of cloak and dagger stuff surrounding the sacking of the chairman*) <The combination of a cloak and dagger suggests conspiracy>.

---

clog *vb* **1** (*They thought that it was leaves that were clogging up the drains*) block, obstruct, stop up. **2** (*The sheer volume of correspondence has clogged up the system*) obstruct, impede, hinder, hamper.

close *vb* **1** (*They were asked to close the gate*) shut, fasten, secure, lock, bolt. **2** (*They closed the meeting with the chairman's speech*) end, bring to an end, conclude, finish, wind up. **3** (*The gap between the two runners closed*) narrow, lessen, grow less, dwindle. **4** (*They finally closed the bargain*) conclude, complete, settle, seal, clinch.

close *adj* **1** (*The cottages were very close to each other*) near. **2** (*They have been close friends for years*) intimate, devoted, close-knit, bosom. **3** (*You must pay close attention to what she says*) careful, attentive, intense, assiduous. **4** (*She was able to give a close description of the man who attacked her*) exact, precise, accurate. **5** (*The weather was very close*) humid, muggy, stuffy, airless, oppressive. **6** (*The whole family is extremely close with money*) mean, miserly, parsimonious, stingy. ▼

---

too close for comfort so near that one feels uncomfortable, worried, etc (*That car behind us is a bit close for comfort*). **a close shave** something that was only just avoided, especially an escape from danger, failure, etc (*He had a close shave when his car skidded and hit a wall*).

---

clothing *n* (*They washed all their clothing*) clothes, garments, attire, apparel.

cloudy *adj* **1** (*under cloudy skies*) overcast, hazy, grey, leaden, heavy. **2** (*The liquid in the glass was cloudy*) opaque, milky, murky, muddy. **3** (*Her vision is rather cloudy*) unclear, blurred, hazy.

clumsy *adj* **1** (*The antique wardrobe is a clumsy piece of furniture*) awkward, unwieldy, hulking, heavy, solid. **2** (*The child is clumsy and is always bumping into things*) awkward, ungainly, uncoordinated, blundering, maladroit, like a bull in a china shop.

coarse *adj* **1** (*The coat was made of a very coarse fabric*) rough, bristly, hairy, shaggy. **2** (*She prefers to bake with a coarse flour*) unrefined, unprocessed, crude. **3** (*They all have rather coarse features*) heavy, rugged. **4** (*He tells coarse jokes*) crude, vulgar, smutty, blue, dirty, bawdy, earthy, obscene, pornographic.

cold *adj* **1** (*It was a cold winter's day*) chilly, cool, freezing, icy, raw, frosty, glacial. **2** (*The children were feeling cold*) chilly, freezing, frozen, frozen to the marrow, shivery. **3** (*She seems rather a cold woman/She received them with rather a cold manner*) frigid, unresponsive, unemotional, indifferent, apathetic, distant, remote, reserved, detached. ▼

---

come in from the cold to be allowed to take part in some activity from which one was excluded before (*After months of not being selected for the team he has come in from the cold and has been offered a game this week*). **leave (someone) cold** to fail to impress or excite (someone) (*The comedian was meant to be very funny but he left the audience cold*).

---

collect *vb* **1** (*The children were collecting firewood for a bonfire*) gather, accumulate, amass, pile up, stockpile, store, hoard. **2** (*They are collecting money for a children's charity*) gather, raise. **3** (*She collected the shoes from the repair shop*) fetch, call for, go and get. **4** (*A crowd collected round the speaker*) gather, assemble, converge, congregate.

collide *vb* (*The cars collided*) crash, smash, bump.

colour *n* **1** (*She has sweaters in several colours*) shade, hue, tint, tone. **2** (*people of different colour*) skin-colouring, skin-tone, complexion, colouring. **3** (*The children were told to add a bit of colour to their stories*) vividness, life, animation. ▼

---

change colour to become either very pale or very flushed through fear, distress, embarrassment, anger, etc (*She changed colour when she realized that her crime had been discovered*).

show oneself in one's true colours to reveal what one is really like after pretending to be otherwise (*She pretended to be his friend but she showed herself in her true colours by reporting him to the boss*) <A reference to a ship raising its colours or flag to indicate which country or side it was supporting>.

---

combine *vb* **1** (*They combined the ingredients*) mix, blend, amalgamate, bind. **2** (*They have combined their resources to open a restaurant*) join, put together, unite, pool, merge. **3** (*They have combined to form one team*) get together, join forces, team up, club together, cooperate, associate, amalgamate, merge.

comfort *n* **1** (*They were poor but they now live in comfort*) ease, cosiness, snugness, well-being, affluence. **2** (*They tried to bring some comfort to the widow*) solace, consolation, condolence, sympathy, support. **3** (*The children were a comfort to their mother*) solace, help, support. ▼

---

cold comfort no consolation at all (*When one suffers misfortune it is cold comfort to be told that there are many people who are worse off than oneself*).

---

comic *adj* (*It was a comic situation*) funny, amusing, entertaining, diverting, droll, hilarious, farcical.

command *vb* **1** (*The king commanded them to go*) order, direct, instruct, bid. **2** (*He commands the force*) be in command of, be in charge of, control, rule, govern, direct, preside over, head, lead, manage.

comment *n* (*He passed comments on how ill she was looking*) remark, observation, statement, view.

commercial *adj* **1** (*He has undertaken a commercial training*) business, trade, marketing. **2** (*The seaside village is becoming too commercial*) money-orientated, profit-orientated, mercenary, materialistic. **3** (*His business idea was not a commercial one*) profit-making, profitable.

commitment *n* **1** (*She has a great deal of commitment to her job*) dedication, devotion, involvement. **2** (*He had many financial commitments*) responsibility, obligation, undertaking, duty, liability.

common *adj* **1** (*Fighting in the street is common there*) usual, ordinary, everyday, regular, frequent, customary, habitual, standard, routine, commonplace, run-of-the-mill, traditional. **2** (*There is a common *belief that the place is haunted*) widespread, universal, general, prevalent, popular. **3** (*things that appeal to the common people*) ordinary, normal, average, typical, run-of-the-mill. **4** (*It was a very common type of watch*) ordinary, commonplace, common-or-garden, unexceptional, undistinguished. **5** (*The politicians said that they were working for the common good*) communal, collective, public. **6** (*They regard her as a very common girl*) vulgar, coarse, uncouth, low. ▼

---

common-or-garden completely ordinary (*I'm not going to wear anything special to the ceremony. I'll just put on a common-or-garden skirt and top*).
the common touch the ability to get on well with ordinary people (*He is a wealthy prince but most of his friends are ordinary students. He has the common touch*).

---

communicate *vb* **1** (*They were unable to communicate the information back to headquarters*) pass on, convey, make known, impart, report, relay. **2** (*We do not communicate with them any more*) be in touch, be in contact, have dealings with. **3** (*In order to get a job in some industries it is important to be able to communicate*) be articulate, be fluent, be coherent, be eloquent.

compatible *adj* **1** (*The couple are just not compatible*) suited, well-suited, like-minded, in tune, having rapport. **2** (*The two accounts of the incident are not at all compatible*) in agreement, consistent, in keeping.

compel *vb* (*They plan to compel him to go*) force, make, coerce, oblige, dragoon, pressurize, pressure.

compete *vb* **1** (*Will they all compete in the race?*) take part, participate, go in for, be a competitor, be a contestant. **2** (*The two brothers are competing against each other in the final*) vie, contend.

competent *adj* (*They are very competent workers*) capable, able, proficient, efficient, skilful.

complaint *n* **1** (*They made a complaint about the standard of the food*) protest, criticism, grievance. **2** (*Nothing ever pleases them—they are full of complaints*) grumble, (*inf*) grouse, (*inf*) gripe. **3** (*He has a stomach complaint*) illness, disease, disorder, ailment.

complete *vb* (*They failed to complete the job on time*) bring to completion, finish, conclude, accomplish, fulfil, achieve, execute, perform.

complete *adj* **1** (*He has the complete set of books*) whole, entire, full, total, intact, unbroken. **2** (*They think that she is a complete fool*) absolute, utter, thorough, thoroughgoing, total, out-and-out.

complicated *adj* (*It is a very complicated problem*) difficult, involved, complex, puzzling, perplexing.

compose *vb* **1** (*The children were asked to compose a poem*) make up, think up, create, concoct, invent, produce. **2** (*She was upset but tried to compose herself*) calm, calm down, quieten, control.

comprehend *vb* **1** (*unable to comprehend the scientific information*) understand, grasp, fathom, take in. **2** (*We cannot comprehend how they could behave like *that*) understand, imagine, conceive, fathom, perceive, get to the bottom of.

comprehensive *adj* (*His knowledge of the subject is quite comprehensive*) inclusive, thorough, extensive, exhaustive, full, broad, widespread.

compulsory *adj* (*Attendance at school assembly is compulsory*) obligatory, mandatory, forced, essential, de rigueur.

conceal *vb* **1** (*She concealed the papers under her mattress*) hide, keep hidden, cover up, secrete, tuck away. **2** (*They tried to conceal their fears*) hide, cover up, disguise, mask.

conceited *adj* (*She is so conceited that she spends ages looking in the mirror*) vain, proud, arrogant, haughty, immodest, egotistical. (*inf*) big-headed.

concern *n* **1** (*We were full of concern for the safety of the missing children*) worry, anxiety, distress, apprehension. **2** (*The news was of concern to all parents*) interest, importance, relevance. **3** (*They were told that it was none of their concern*) business, affair, interest, responsibility, job, duty. **4** (*They are partners in a manufacturing concern*) business, firm, company, establishment.

concise *adj* (*a concise report that gave all the main points*) brief, short, succinct, terse, crisp, to the point.

conclude *vb* **1** (*We concluded the talks at midnight*) finish, end, close. **2** (*We were unable to conclude an agreement with the other side*) negotiate, bring about, pull off, clinch. **3** (*We were forced to conclude that he was lying*) come to the conclusion, deduce, gather, assume, suppose.

condemn *vb* **1** (*We condemned them for injuring children*) blame, censure, criticize, disapprove of, upbraid. **2** (*The murderer was condemned to death*) sentence.

condition *n* **1** (*housing conditions*) state, situation, circumstances, position. **2** (*The horses were in good condition*) form, shape, order, fitness, health. **3** (*They were allowed to rent the land but with certain conditions*) restriction, proviso, provision, stipulation, prerequisite, stipulation. **4** (*The old lady has a heart condition*) complaint, disorder, disease, illness, ailment, problem.

conduct *n* **1** (*The teacher reported the child's conduct to his parents*) behaviour, actions. **2** (*Their conduct of the economy was criticized*) direction, organization, management, control.

confess *vb* **1** (*She confessed when she heard that her friend was being blamed for the crime*) own up, admit guilt, plead guilty, accept blame, make a clean breast of it. **2** (*I must confess that I know nothing about it*) admit, acknowledge, concede, allow, grant.

confidence *n* **1** (*The people have no confidence in the government*) trust, faith, reliance. **2** (*competitors full of confidence*) self-confidence, self-assurance, poise, aplomb. **3** (*The girls exchanged confidences*) secret, private affair. ▼

---

confidence trick the act of a swindler who gains the trust of someone and then persuades him or her to hand over money or something valuable (*She thought she was giving money to charity but the collector was playing a confidence trick on* *her and kept the money for himself*).

---

conflict *n* **1** (*There has been conflict between the neighbours for years*) disagreement, discord, dissension, friction, strife, hostility, ill will. **2** (*the conflict between love and duty*) clash, friction. **3** (*There were many killed in the military conflict*) battle, fight, war, clash.

confuse *vb* **1** (*All the questions confused the child*) bewilder, puzzle, perplex, muddle. **2** (*His remarks just confused the situation*) muddle, mix up, jumble, obscure, make unclear. **3** (*The old man became confused in old age*) muddle, disorientate, befuddle. **4** (*She confused the two books which looked alike*) mix up, mistake.

congratulate *vb* (*We congratulated them on the birth of their son*) wish joy to, offer good wishes to, compliment, felicitate.

connect *vb* **1** (*The gardener connected the garden hose to the tap*) attach, fasten, join, secure, clamp, couple. **2** (*Only a path connects the two mountain villages*) link, join, unite. **3** (*The child connects his mother with security*) associate, link, equate, identify.

connection *n* **1** (*There is no connection between the crimes*) relationship, link, association, correspondence. **2** (*They had a meeting in connection with staff redundancies*) reference, relation. **3** (*one of her husband's connections*) relative, relation, kindred.

conscientious *adj* (*conscientious workers*) careful, diligent, painstaking, hard-working, assiduous, meticulous, punctilious.

consequence *n* **1** (*unable to foresee the consequences of their actions*) result, effect, upshot, outcome, repercussion. **2** (*It was a matter of no consequence*) importance, significance, note.

considerate *adj* (*She has very considerate children*) thoughtful, attentive, concerned, solicitous, obliging, kind, sympathetic.

consistent *adj* (*keep the room at a consistent temperature*) uniform, steady, constant, unchanging.

conspicuous *adj* **1** (*There had been conspicuous alterations to the city*) obvious, clear, noticeable, evident, apparent, discernible, visible. **2** (*Her clothes were conspicuous by their bright colours*) obvious, striking, obtrusive, blatant, showy.

constant *adj* **1** (*keep it at a constant temperature*) uniform, even, regular, steady, stable, unchanging, invariable. **2** (*We have had a constant stream of enquiries*) continuous, uninterrupted, unbroken. **3** (*tired of her constant complaints*) never-ending, non-stop, endless, unending, incessant, continual, perpetual, interminable. **4** (*He was constant in his love for her*) faithful, devoted, staunch, loyal, true.

contact *vb* (*They tried to contact her parents*) get in touch with, communicate with, be in communication with.

container *n* (*containers to transport the food*) receptacle, vessel.

content *adj* (*He is quite content with his life*) contented, satisfied, pleased, happy, comfortable.

contest *n* (*the competitors in the contest*) competition, tournament, match, game.

continual *adj* **1** (*tired of their continual questions*) frequent, regular, repeated, recurrent, persistent, habitual. **2** (*There was continual* *noise from their flat*) continuous, endless, non-stop, incessant, constant, interminable.

continue *vb* **1** (*The road continues beyond the village*) go on, extend, keep on, carry on. **2** (*He may continue as chairman*) go on, carry on, stay, remain, persist. **3** (*We continued the search all night*) maintain, sustain, prolong, protract. **4** (*They continued looking for the ring*) go on, carry on, keep on, persist in, persevere in. **5** (*They stopped the search overnight but continued it at dawn*) resume, renew, recommence, carry on with.

continuous *adj* (*They have a continuous supply of fuel/upset by the continuous traffic noise*) constant, uninterrupted, unbroken, non-stop, endless, perpetual, incessant, unceasing, interminable, unremitting.

contract *n* (*a business contract*) agreement, arrangement, deal, settlement, pact, bargain, transaction.

contrast *n* **1** (*the contrast between the two styles of government*) difference, dissimilarity, distinction, disparity. **2** (*He is a complete contrast to his father*) opposite, antithesis.

contribute *vb* **1** (*They were all asked to contribute to the charity*) give, give a contribution, donate, give a donation to, subscribe to, help, give assistance to, assist, aid, support. **2** (*His leadership contributed to the success of the company*) add to, help, assist, have a hand in, be conducive to, be instrumental in.

control *vb* **1** (*It is she who controls the budget of the company*) be in control of, be in charge of, manage, administrate, direct, govern, head. **2** (*The fire fighters could not control the fire*) contain, keep in check, curb, limit.

convenient *adj* **1** (*select a time convenient for both of us*) suitable, appropriate, fitting, favourable, advantageous. **2** (*houses convenient for schools*) handy, within reach, within easy reach, accessible.

convert *vb* **1** (*We converted the attic into another bedroom*) alter, adapt, make into, turn into, change into, transform. **2** (*convert pounds into dollars*) change, exchange. **3** (*The missionary converted the tribesmen to Christianity*) cause to change beliefs, reform, convince of. ▼

---

preach to the converted to speak enthusiastically in favour of something to people who are already convinced of its good points and are in favour of it (*You are preaching to the converted by singing the praises of that make of car to us. We have had one for years*) <A reference to someone trying to convert someone else to a religion which the person already believes in>.

---

convict *n* (*The convict escaped*) prisoner, jailbird, criminal, felon, (*inf*) crook.

convincing *adj* **1** (*Her argument seemed very convincing*) persuasive, plausible, credible, cogent, powerful. **2** (*Our team had a convincing victory*) decisive, conclusive.

cool *adj* **1** (*The weather was rather cool*) cold, coldish, chilly, fresh. **2** (*They wanted a cool drink*) cold, refreshing. **3** (*people who can remain cool in an emergency*) calm, composed, self-possessed, unexcited, unruffled, unperturbed, **4** (*She was rather cool when we went to see her*) aloof, distant, remote, offhand, unfriendly, chilly, unwelcoming, unresponsive, apathetic. **5** (*They were amazed at the cool way she stole the goods from the shop*) bold, audacious, brazen, impudent. ▼

---

as cool as a cucumber extremely calm and unexcited (*Everyone else was agitated when the fire started but she remained as cool as a cucumber*). **cool, calm and collected** completely calm, in full control of one's emotions (*Even when her car broke down on the motorway she remained cool, calm, and collected*). **cool one's heels** to be kept waiting (*They were late for the meeting and I was left cooling my heels in the hall*).

---

cope *vb* **1** (*He found it difficult to cope when his wife died*) manage, carry on, get by, get along. **2** (*He had to cope with the money problems*) deal with, handle, contend with, manage.

copy *n* **1** (*give out copies of the report at the meeting*) duplicate, facsimile, photocopy, Xerox (trademark), Photostat (trademark). **2** (*It was not the original vase but a clever copy*) reproduction, replica, fake, sham, counterfeit. **3** (*buy several copies of the newspaper*) issue, example. ▼

---

carbon copy a person or thing that is extremely like another (*Her new boyfriend seems like a carbon copy of her previous one*) <A reference to carbon paper used in copying documents>. **blot one's copybook** to spoil a previously good record of behaviour, achievement, etc, by doing something wrong (*The teacher had just said how much his behaviour had improved when he blotted his copybook by getting involved in a fight*) <'Copybook' was formerly the name given to a book in which a child was learning to write>.

---

correct *adj* **1** (*That is not the correct answer*) right, accurate, true, precise, exact, (*inf*) spot on. **2** (*What is the correct behaviour on such an occasion?*) proper, suitable, fitting, seemly, appropriate, apt, accepted, usual.

cost *vb* **1** (*How much does a car like that cost?*) be priced at, sell for, come to, fetch. **2** (*You should get the mechanic to cost the repairs for you*) price, put a price on, estimate, evaluate. ▼

---

cost the earth to cost a great deal of money (*The meal at that restaurant costs the earth*). **at all costs** no matter what must be done, given, suffered, etc, whatever happens (*You must stop her finding out at all costs*).

---

cosy *adj* (*a cosy room*) snug, comfortable, homely, home-like, secure.

count *vb* **1** (*pupils asked to count the row of numbers*) count up, add up, total, calculate, compute. **2** (*Could you count the people as they enter the hall?*) keep a count of, keep a tally of, enumerate. **3** (*What he thinks does not count*) matter, be important, be of account, mean anything. **4** (*They *counted themselves fortunate to have somewhere to live*) consider, regard, think, judge.▼

---

out for the count unconscious or deeply asleep (*The children were so tired after their long walk that they are still out for the count*) <A reference to boxing when a boxer who has been knocked down by his opponent has to get up again before the referee counts to ten in order to stay in the match>. **count one's chickens before they are hatched** to make plans which depend on something that is still uncertain (*You should not give up this job before you get the offer for the other one in writing. Don't count your chickens before they are hatched*). **count the cost** to consider the risks, difficulties and possible losses involved in doing something (*He did not stop to count the cost before he drove without a licence. Now that he has been charged by the police he is counting the cost*).

---

counterfeit *adj* (*counterfeit bank notes*) fake, forged, fraudulent, sham, bogus, (*inf*) phoney.

country *n* **1** (*all the countries of the world*) nation, state, realm. **2** (*He would do anything for his country*) native land, homeland, fatherland, mother country. **3** (*They left the city to live in the country*) countryside, rural area. **4** (*The government should listen to what the country thinks*) public, general public, people, nation, population. **5** (*The country around there is very flat*) land, terrain, territory. ▼

---

country cousin a person from the country, considered unsophisticated by a town or city dweller (*They regard her as a country cousin because she has never been to a pop concert*). **go to the country** to hold a general election (*When the government was defeated on the bill the prime minister decided to go to the country*).

---

courage *n* (*the courage of the soldiers in battle*) bravery, valour, gallantry, heroism, boldness, daring. ▼

Dutch courage courage that is not real courage but brought on by drinking alcohol (*He went out for a drink at lunch time. He needed some Dutch courage before he asked the boss for an increase in salary*).

---

course *n* **1** (*in the course of a varied career*) progress, progression, development. **2** (*The ship was a bit off course*) route, way, track, direction, path, tack, orbit. **3** (*You should try a different course of action*) method, procedure, process, system, technique. **4** (*The car disappeared in the course of a few minutes*) duration, passage, lapse, period, interval, span. **5** (*The race was cancelled as the course was flooded*) track, circuit. ▼

---

run its course to continue to its natural end, to develop naturally (*Your child will recover soon. The infection just has to run its course*). **stay the course** to continue to the end or completion of (something) (*She has started on a new diet but we* *don't think that she will stay the course*).

---

courtesy *n* (*She showed a lack of courtesy towards elderly people*) politeness, civility, good manners, respect, deference.

cover *n* **1** (*There was a cover of snow over the ground*) covering, layer, coat, blanket, carpet, mantle, film. **2** (*They sought cover from the storm*) shelter, protection, refuge, sanctuary. **3** (*His business is just a cover for his drug-dealing*) cover-up, concealment, disguise, pretext, front, camouflage, screen, mask, cloak, veil. **4** (*The insurance policy provides cover against fire and theft*) insurance, protection, compensation. **5** (*the design on the cover of the book*) jacket, dust jacket, wrapper. **6** (*pull up the covers over the sleeping child*) bedcover, bedclothes, blankets, duvet.

cowardly *adj* (*He is too cowardly to complain*) timid, timorous, fearful, faint-hearted, lily-livered, (*inf*) yellow, (*inf*) chicken.

crack *n* **1** (*There is a crack in this cup*) chip, chink. **2** (*There are several cracks in the wall*) fracture, split, crevice, slit. **3** (*The crack on the head made him pass out*) blow, knock, bump, smack, whack, thump, wallop. **3** (*They heard the crack of a pistol*) report, bang. ▼

---

get cracking to start moving, working, etc, quickly (*You had better get cracking or you'll miss the train*). **have a crack at something** (*inf*) to have try at (something) (*You won't know if you are good at tennis unless you have a crack at it*). **not all it's cracked up to be** (*inf*) not to be as good as it is said to be (*This holiday resort gets a good reputation but in our opinion it's not all it's cracked up to be*).

---

crash *vb* **1** (*The cymbals crashed*) clash, clang, clank, clatter, bang. **2** (*The car crashed into the wall*) bang into, bump into, hit, collide with. **3** (*His son crashed his car*) smash, wreck, write off. **4** (*The chimney crashed on to the pavement*) topple, fall, plunge, tumble. **5** (*They listened to the sea crashing against the ship*) dash, batter, smash, break. **6** (*Their business crashed*) fail, collapse, fold, go under, go to the wall.

credit *n* **1** (*He received little credit for a fine performance*) praise, commendation, acclaim, tribute, applause, recognition. **2** (*The famous artist was regarded as being a credit to the town*) honour, asset, glory. **3** (*His credit is not good*) financial standing, solvency.

creep *vb* **1** (*creatures that creep along the ground*) crawl, slither, wriggle. **2** (*They began creeping up on the burglar*) steal, sneak, slink, tiptoe. ▼

---

give (someone) the creeps to arouse dislike, disgust or fear in (someone) (*This house is so dark and damp. It gives me the creeps*).

---

crime *n* **1** (*He was convicted of the crime of theft*) offence, misdeed, wrong, misdemeanour, felony. **2** (*Crime is on the increase*) lawbreaking, wrongdoing, felony, evil, vice.

criticize *vb* (*She is always criticizing him*) find fault with, blame, censure, pick holes in, (*inf*) slam, (*inf*) nit-pick.

crooked *adj* **1** (*a crooked stick*) bent, curved, twisted. **2** (*The old man had a crooked back*) deformed, misshapen. **3** (*That picture is crooked*) tilted, at an angle, askew, slanted, sloping. **4** (*They think that he is a crooked salesman*) dishonest, dishonourable, unscrupulous, fraudulent.

cross *adj* **1** (*Their mother was cross at the children's naughtiness*) angry, annoyed, irritated, vexed. **2** (*She is a cross old woman who is always shouting at the neighbourhood children*) irritable, short-tempered, bad-tempered, ill-humoured, disagreeable, surly, crotchety, cantankerous.

crush *vb* **1** (*The workers crushed the grapes*) squash, squeeze, compress. **2** (*They crushed the stones*) break up, smash, pulverize, ground, pound. **3** (*Sitting so long had crushed her dress*) crease, crumple, rumple, wrinkle, crinkle. **3** (*The army crushed the rebellion*) quell, quash, suppress, subdue, put down, stamp out, overpower.

cry *vb* **1** (*The children began to cry for their mothers*) weep, shed tears, sob, wail. **2** (*She cried out in pain*) call out, shout out, yell, scream. ▼

---

a far cry from (something) a long way from (something), very different from (something) (*His present wealthy lifestyle is a far cry from his poverty-stricken childhood*). **be crying out for (something)** to be badly in need of (something) or to be badly in need of (something) being done (*The house is crying out for a coat of paint*).

---

cure *n* (*trying to find a cure for cancer*) remedy, treatment, panacea.

curious *adj* **1** (*We are curious to hear what happens at the meeting*) interested. **2** (*She is always curious about the affairs of her neighbours*) inquisitive, prying, meddlesome, snooping, (*inf*) nosy. **3** (*It was a curious sight*) odd, strange, unusual, peculiar, queer, weird, bizarre, mysterious.

current *adj* **1** (*the current fashion for pale-coloured clothes*) present, present-day, contemporary, existing, modern. **2** (*Those traditions are no longer current*) around, prevalent, common, general, popular.

curved *adj* (*a curved stick/a curved back*) bent, arched, bowed, crooked, rounded, humped.

custom *n* **1** (*The local customs are dying out*) tradition, practice, convention, ritual. **2** (*It was his custom to go for a walk before breakfast*) habit, practice, routine, wont, way. **3** (*He is grateful for their custom*) trade, business, patronage.

customer *n* (*shops trying to attract new customers*) client, patron, buyer, shopper, consumer.

cut *vb* **1** (*cut the meat into cubes*) cut up, chop, divide, carve, slice. **2** (*He cut his finger with a razor blade*) wound, gash, slash, pierce. **3** (*She cut her son's hair*) trim, clip, crop, snip, prune, shear. **4** (*The firm must cut its expenditure*) cut back on, reduce, decrease, curtail, slash. **5** (*The essay is too long—you must cut it*) shorten, abridge, condense, abbreviate. **6** (*She cut some paragraphs from the article*) cut out, delete, excise. **7** (*The driver cut the engine*) switch off, turn off. ▼

a cut above (someone *or* **something)** superior to (someone or something) (*The office workers think that they are a cut above the factory workers*). **cut it out** to stop doing (something) (*The children were teasing the cat and I had to tell them to cut it out*). **cut up** upset (*She was very cut up about the death of her dog*). **not cut out for (something)** not naturally suited to (something) (*He was not cut out for the army*).

cynical *adj* (*She is cynical about our chances of success/They are very cynical people*) pessimistic, sceptical, doubting, distrustful, suspicious.

D

dagger *n* (*He killed his enemy with his dagger*) stiletto, poniard, dirk, knife.▼

---

at daggers drawn feeling or showing great hostility towards each other (*The neighbours have been at daggers drawn ever since they quarrelled over repairs to the dividing wall*).
look daggers at (someone) to look with great dislike or hostility at (someone) (*When she won the prize her fellow contestants looked daggers at her*).

---

dainty *adj* **1** (*a dainty little girl*) petite, neat, graceful. **2** (*dainty china cups*) delicate, fine, exquisite.

damage *n* **1** (*There was a great deal of damage to his car*) harm, destruction, accident, ruin, impairment. **2** (*The incident caused damage to his reputation*) harm, injury, hurt, detriment, loss, suffering. ▼

---

what's the damage? (*inf*) how much is it?, what does it cost? (*'What's the damage?' the diners asked the waiter*).

---

damp *adj* **1** (*They hung up their damp clothes to dry*) wet, soaking, sopping. **2** (*The ground was damp*) wet, soggy. **3** (*It was a damp day*) wet, rainy, drizzly, humid, muggy. ▼

---

a damp squib something which is expected to be exciting, effective, etc, but which fails to live up to its expectations (*Everyone looked forward to the party, but it turned out to be a damp squib*) <A reference to a wet firework that fails to go off>.

---

danger *n* **1** (*There was an element of danger in the job*) peril, jeopardy, risk, hazard. **2** (*Pollution is a danger to lives*) risk, menace, threat, peril.

dangerous *adj* **1** (*They were in a dangerous situation*) risky, perilous, hazardous, precarious, insecure. **2** (*The police say that he is dangerous*) threatening, menacing, alarming, nasty.

dare *vb* **1** (*He did not dare climb the high tree*) have the courage, pluck up courage, have the nerve, risk, venture. **2** (*His friends dared him to jump from the high wall*) challenge, throw down the gauntlet. **3** (*They dared their father's anger to go to the nightclub*) defy, brave, face, confront.

daring *adj* (*a daring deed*) bold, adventurous, brave, courageous, plucky, reckless, rash.

dark *adj* **1** (*It was a very dark night*) black, pitch-dark, pitch-black, inky, dim, murky, unlit. **2** (*She has dark hair*) dark brown, black, jet-black, sable. **3** (*They lived in the dark ages*) unenlightened, ignorant, uneducated, uncultivated, uncultured. **4** (*dark, dingy rooms*) gloomy, dismal, drab, dim, dingy, bleak, dreary, cheerless. **5** (*She *was in a dark mood*) gloomy, depressed, morose. ▼

a shot in the dark an attempt or guess based on very little information (*We don't know his address but it's worth taking a shot in the dark and trying the telephone directory*). **keep (someone) in the dark** to keep (someone) unaware or ignorant of (something) (*They kept their parents in the dark about their marriage*).

dawdle *n* (*They dawdled on their way to school*) dally, loiter, linger, delay, tarry.

day *n* **1** (*She doesn't mind driving during the day*) daylight, daytime. **2** (*in this modern day*) time, age, era, epoch. ▼

have had one's day to be past the most successful part of one's or its life (*I thought the cinema had had its day when television came in but it is flourishing now*). **make (someone's) day** to make (someone) very pleased or happy) (*He really made his mother's day by sending her flowers*).

dead *adj* **1** (*Her father is dead/a dead man*) deceased, departed, lifeless, gone. **2** (*dead village traditions*) extinct, gone, perished. **3** (*dead matter*) without life, lifeless, inanimate. **4** (*Her fingers were dead with cold*) numb, benumbed, without feeling. **5** (*The small town is dead at night*) boring, dull, uneventful, unexciting. ▼

a dead duck a person or thing that is very unlikely to survive or continue (*The proposed new traffic scheme is a dead duck. The council does not have the money for it*). **as dead as a dodo** completely dead or extinct, no longer popular or fashionable (*They are trying to revive village traditions that have been as dead as a dodo for years*) <A reference to a flightless bird that has been extinct since 1700>. **over my dead body** in the face of fierce opposition from me (*The council will pull my house down over my dead body*).

deadly *adj* **1** (*He drank a deadly poison*) fatal, lethal, toxic, poisonous. **2** (*He was struck a deadly blow*) fatal, mortal, lethal, dangerous, death-dealing, terminal. **3** (*They were deadly enemies*) fierce, hostile, grim, hated.

deaf *adj* **1** (*The accident left him deaf*) with impaired hearing, stone deaf, as deaf as a post. **2** (*They were deaf to her pleas*) indifferent, unmoved by, oblivious to, heedless of.▼

turn a deaf ear to (something) to refuse to listen to (something), to take no notice of (something) (*He turned a deaf ear to her pleas for help*). **fall on deaf ears** to go unnoticed or unheeded, not to be listened to (*There is no point in offering her any advice. It will only fall on deaf ears*).

deal *vb* **1** (*She was unable to deal with the problem*) cope with, handle, attend to, sort out, tackle, manage. **2** (*They need a book that deals with the early history of the town*) be about, have to do with, concern, discuss. **3** (*He does not *know how to deal with children*) act towards, behave towards, cope with, manage. **4** (*He was asked to deal the cards*) distribute, give out, share out, divide out, dole out. **5** (*They dealt him a fatal blow*) give, deliver, administer.

deal *n* **1** (*a business deal*) arrangement, agreement, transaction, contract, pact. **2** (*He did not get a fair deal*) treatment, usage. ▼

---

a good deal *or* **a great deal of (something)** a great amount of (something) (*He is in a great deal of danger*). **a raw deal** unfair treatment (*The younger son got a raw deal when his father's estate was divided*).

---

dear *adj* **1** (*He lost his dear wife*) beloved, loved, darling, cherished. **2** (*She was a dear child*) sweet, adorable, lovable, darling, attractive, winning, enchanting. **3** (*It was a dear car*) expensive, costly, high-priced, valuable, exorbitant.

death *n* **1** (*Death was caused by strangling*) dying, demise, decease, loss of life, passing away, killing, murder, slaughter. **2** (*There were many deaths in the flu epidemic*) fatality, dead people. **3** (*The close of the firm marked the death of his hopes*) end, finish, cessation, destruction, ruin, annihilation. ▼

---

at death's door extremely ill, dying (*She seemed to be at death's door but she has made a complete recovery*). **be in at the death** to be present at the end or final stages of something (*The factory closed today. It was sad to be in at the death*) <Refers originally to being present at the death of the prey in a hunt>.

---

decay *vb* **1** (*The food had begun to decay*) go bad, rot, decompose, putrefy, spoil. **2** (*The Roman empire decayed*) decline, degenerate, deteriorate, wane, ebb.

deceitful *adj* **1** (*She is a very deceitful child*) lying, untruthful, dishonest, false, insincere, untrustworthy, underhand. **2** (*He got into the house by deceitful means*) underhand, fraudulent, crooked, dishonest, cheating, crafty, sneaky.

deceive *vb* (*His friends did not realize that he was deceiving them*) delude, mislead, take in, hoodwink, pull the wool over (someone's) eyes, swindle, dupe.

decent *adj* **1** (*He seemed a decent enough fellow*) honest, honourable, trustworthy, worthy, civil. **2** (*Her behaviour was not considered decent*) seemly, proper, appropriate, decorous, pure. **3** (*He earns a decent salary*) reasonable, ample, good, adequate, sufficient.

decide *vb* **1** (*They decided to stay*) come to a decision, reach a decision, make up one's mind, resolve, commit oneself. **2** (*That decided the matter*) settle, resolve, determine. **3** (*The judge will decide the case*) judge, make a judgement on, make a ruling on, give a verdict.

decision *n* **1** (*They finally reached a decision*) resolution, conclusion, determination, settlement. **2** (*The judge will announce his decision*) judgement, verdict, ruling. **3** (*He is a man of decision*) decisiveness, determination, resolution, resolve, firmness.

decisive *adj* **1** (*Her personality was*

the decisive factor in her getting the job) deciding, determining, conclusive, critical, crucial. **2** (*They need someone decisive in charge of the firm*) determined, resolute, firm, forceful.

decline *vb* **1** (*They declined the invitation*) turn down, refuse, say no to. **2** (*The influence of the leader has declined*) get less, lessen, decrease, diminish, dwindle, fade. **3** (*The Roman empire was declining then*) deteriorate, degenerate.

decorate *vb* **1** (*They decorated the Christmas tree*) adorn, ornament, embellish, trim. **2** (*They have begun to decorate the house*) paint, paper, renovate, (*inf*) do up. **3** (*The soldier was decorated for bravery*) honour, give a medal to, cite.

decrease *vb* **1** (*The number of the pupils at the school is decreasing*) grow less, lessen, diminish, dwindle, drop, fall off, decline. **2** (*They have decreased the number of places available at the school*) reduce, lower, lessen, cut back, curtail. **3** (*The storm finally decreased*) die down, abate, subside.

deed *n* **1** (*a dishonest deed*) act, action, feat, exploit, undertaking, enterprise. **2** (*The deeds to the house*) document, contract, title deed.

deep *adj* **1** (*They dug a deep hole in the garden*) yawning, cavernous. **2** (*They have a deep affection for each other*) intense, fervent, ardent, heart-felt. **3** (*He has a deep distrust of doctors*) profound, extreme, intense, great. **4** (*He has a very deep voice*) low, low-pitched, bass, booming, resonant. **5** (*She always wears clothes in deep colours*) rich, strong, vivid, intense, dark. ▼

---

be thrown in at the deep end to be put suddenly into a difficult situation of which one has no experience (*The trainee journalist was thrown in at the deep end and set out on a story on his first morning on the newspaper*) <A reference to the deep end of a swimming pool>. **go off at the deep end** to lose one's temper (*His father went off at the deep end when he saw the wrecked car*) <A reference to the deep end of a swimming pool>.

---

defeat *vb* **1** (*The army finally defeated the enemy*) beat, conquer, vanquish, win a victory over, get the better of, overcome, rout. **2** (*The parliamentary motion was defeated*) reject, overthrow, throw out, outvote.

defect *n* **1** (*a defect in the material*) fault, flaw, imperfection, blemish. **2** (*They tried to find the defects in the system*) deficiency, weakness, shortcoming, failing, inadequacy, snag.

defence *n* **1** (*Walls built as a defence for the house*) protection, safeguard, guard, security, cover, fortification, barricade. **2** (*a report in defence of the system*) justification, vindication, argument, apology, exoneration.

defer *vb* (*They had to defer the date of the meeting*) put off, postpone, delay, hold over, adjourn.

deficiency *n* **1** (*She suffers from vitamin deficiency*) lack, want, shortage, dearth, insufficiency, scarcity, deficit. **2** (*It was the only deficiency in the system*) defect, flaw, fault, imperfection, failing, shortcoming, drawback, snag.

definite *adj* **1** (*They have no definite plans*) clear-cut, fixed, established, precise, specific, particular. **2** (*It is not definite that he is leaving*) certain, sure, settled, decided, fixed.

defy *vb* **1** (*They decided to defy their parents and go to the cinema*) disobey, disregard, ignore. **2** (*The army defied the enemy*) withstand, resist, stand up to, brave, confront.

degree *n* **1** (*There was a marked degree of improvement in her work*) extent, amount, level, measure. **2** (*The dancers reached a high degree of expertise*) level, stage, grade, point. ▼

---

be one degree under to feel slightly unwell (*She is not at work—she is feeling one degree under*). **give (someone) the third degree** to subject (someone) to intense questioning, especially by using severe or harsh methods (*The enemy officers gave the captured soldiers the third degree*).

---

dejected *adj* (*She was feeling dejected after her friends left*) miserable, wretched, downcast, depressed, sad, despondent.

delay *vb* **1** (*We have had to delay our holiday*) postpone, put off, put back, defer, adjourn, put on ice. **2** (*They were delayed by heavy traffic*) hold up, hold back, detain, hinder, impede, hamper, obstruct.

deliberate *adj* (*His murder was quite deliberate*) intentional, on purpose, planned, calculated, prearranged, premeditated.

delicate *adj* **1** (*She was very delicate as a child*) weak, frail, sickly, unwell, infirm. **2** (*cups made of delicate china*) fine, exquisite, fragile, thin. **3** (*It was a very delicate matter*) difficult, sensitive, tricky. **4** (*The situation required delicate handling*) careful, tactful, discreet, diplomatic.

delicious *adj* (*They serve delicious food at the restaurant*) tasty, flavoursome, appetizing, luscious, (*inf*) scrumptious.

delight *n* (*She was filled with delight at seeing her friend again*) joy, pleasure, gladness, happiness.

delightful *adj* **1** (*We had a delightful evening at the theatre*) pleasant, enjoyable, entertaining, amusing, diverting. **2** (*She is a delightful person*) charming, engaging, attractive, nice.

deliver *vb* **1** (*He delivers morning newspapers*) distribute, bring, take round. **2** (*They delivered the little girl to her mother*) hand over, convey, present. **3** (*She delivered a moving speech/deliver a sigh of relief*) give, give voice to, utter, speak, express, pronounce. **4** (*They were able to deliver the prisoners*) free, set free, liberate, release.

demand *vb* **1** (*The workers demanded a wage rise*) call for, ask for, request, press for, insist on, clamour for. **2** (*The work demanded patience*) call for, require, need, take, involve.

demanding *adj* (*They have very demanding jobs*) difficult, taxing, exacting, hard, tough.

demolish *vb* (*They began to demolish the old buildings*) knock down, tear down, pull down, level, flatten, raze, dismantle.

demonstrate *vb* **1** (*She demonstrated how to change an electric plug*) show, illustrate, teach, explain. **2** (*Her expression demonstrated how she was feeling*) show, indicate, display, exhibit, manifest. **3** (*The documents demonstrated that she was telling the truth*) show, establish, prove, confirm, verify. **4** (*They planned to demonstrate against the new road*) protest, stage a protest.

dense *adj* **1** (*They were lost in a dense forest*) thick, close-packed, impenetrable. **2** (*He was too dense to follow the instructions*) stupid, thick, dim, slow.

deny *vb* **1** (*He began to deny that he had said it*) contradict, refute, retract, negate, disagree with. **2** (*The committee might deny their request*) refuse, reject, turn down, decline, dismiss.

depart *vb* **1** (*We have to depart at dawn*) leave, go, take one's leave, take oneself off, set out, start out, (*inf*) make tracks. **2** (*results that depart from the norm*) deviate, diverge, differ, vary.

depend *vb* **1** (*The firm depends on him to look after the place*) rely on, count on, bank on, lean on, put one's faith in. **2** (*The success of the business will depend on the order*) be dependent on, hinge on, turn on, hang on, rest on, revolve around.

deport *vb* (*They decided to deport the refugees*) banish, expel, exile, evict, transport, extradite, expatriate.

depreciate *vb* (*The houses have depreciated in value*) decrease, lessen, lower.

depressed *adj* (*He was feeling depressed having lost his job*) miserable, downcast, low in spirits, melancholy, gloomy, glum, dejected, sad, unhappy.

depth *n* **1** (*measure the depth of the water*) deepness. **2** (*It was a book of great depth*) profoundness, profundity, wisdom, insight, understanding, weight, importance. ▼

---

be out of one's depth to be in a situation which one cannot cope with (*The child is out of depth in that class. The work is too hard for him*) <Refers literally to being in water deeper than one can stand up in or swim easily in>. **in depth** thoroughly (*The committee must study the problem in depth before coming to a decision*). **plumb the depths of (something)** to reach the lowest level of unhappiness, misfortune, etc (*He plumbed the depths of misery when his wife died*).

---

deprived *adj* (*deprived children brought up in poverty*) poor, needy, in want, disadvantaged.

derelict *adj* (*derelict farmhouses*) dilapidated, tumbledown, rundown, ramshackle, broken-down, abandoned, forsaken.

descend *vb* **1** (*She descended the stairs gracefully*) come down, go down, climb down. **2** (*The hot air balloon descended*) go down, come down, drop, fall, sink, plummet. **3** (*They descended from the train with their luggage*) get off, get down, alight, dismount.

describe *vb* **1** (*He was asked to describe the incident*) give a description of, give an account of, give details of, recount, relate, report, explain, tell about, narrate. **2** (*They have described her as beautiful*) call, label, designate.

desert *vb* **1** (*a man who had deserted his family*) abandon, forsake, leave, turn one's back on, leave in the lurch, throw over. **2** (*The army are looking for the soldiers who deserted*) abscond, run away, quit, defect.

deserve *vb* (*He deserves reward*)

merit, be worthy of, warrant, rate, be entitled to, have a claim on.

design *n* **1** (*The architect showed the committee the designs for the new building*) plan, blueprint, sketch, drawing, outline. **2** (*The fabric designs are very modern*) pattern, motif, style. **3** (*It was a cunning design to break into the building*) plan, scheme, plot, stratagem, aim. **4** (*They did it with the design of stealing money*) aim, intention, goal, objective, purpose.▼

---

have designs on (someone *or* **something)** to wish to possess (someone or something), usually belonging to someone else (*I think he has designs on my job*).

---

desire *vb* **1** (*She desires some comfort in her old age*) wish, want, long for, yearn for, crave, covet, hanker after, (*inf*) have a yen for. **2** (*They desire to leave at once*) wish, want, feel like.

desolate *adj* **1** (*on the edge of a desolate moor*) bare, barren, bleak, wild. **2** (*an area full of desolate farms*) deserted, forsaken, solitary, lonely, isolated. **3** (*She was desolate when he went away*) miserable, wretched, sad, unhappy, dejected, forlorn, lonely.

despair *vb* (*He has despaired of ever getting a job*) lose hope, give up hope, lose heart, be discouraged, give up, throw in the towel.

desperate *adj* **1** (*It was a desperate attempt to save the town*) daring, risky, hazardous, wild, reckless, rash, imprudent. **2** (*Some desperate criminals have escaped*) wild, violent, lawless, reckless. **3** (*They are in desperate need of more food*) urgent, pressing, critical, crucial, serious, dire, great. **4** (*They are desperate for money*) in great need of, in want of. **5** (*The family is in a desperate state*) dreadful, shocking, appalling, deplorable, intolerable. **6** (*help required for desperate people*) despairing, hope-less, despairing, distressed, wretched.

despise *vb* (*She despises people who tell lies*) scorn, look down on, shun, disdain, sneer at, mock, hate, loathe.

despondent *adj* (*The pupil was despondent when she heard that she had failed the exam*) downcast, cast down, low in spirits, disheartened, discouraged, disappointed, gloomy, melancholy, wretched, miserable.

destroy *vb* (*The bridge was destroyed in the war*) demolish, knock down, pull down, tear down, wreck, smash, shatter, blow up, wipe out.

detach *vb* **1** (*She detached the hood from her coat*) unfasten, remove, separate, uncouple, free. **2** (*She detached herself from her group to join us*) move away from, separate, dissociate.

detail *n* **1** (*The police try to notice every detail at the scene of the crime*) particular, point, circumstance, feature, aspect. **2** (*draw up a general plan and not bother with the details*) particular, fine point, minutiae.

detect *vb* **1** (*They thought that they detected a smell of gas*) notice, note, make out, spot, identify, distinguish, sense, observe. **2** (*The police were detecting the crime*) investigate, probe.

deter *vb* (*They hope the stiff sentence will deter others from committing such a crime*) put off, prevent, stop, discourage, restrain, scare off.

determined *adj* **1** (*He is a very determined person and will probably win*) firm, resolute, tenacious, single-minded, strong-willed, dogged, persistent, stubborn, inflexible. **2** (*They are determined to leave*) set on, intent on, bent on.

detest *vb* (*The rivals detest each other*) hate, loathe, abhor, feel aversion to, feel hostility to.

detrimental *adj* (*The incident was detrimental to his reputation*) injurious, harmful, damaging, hurtful, disadvantageous, destructive.

develop *vb* **1** (*children quickly developing into adults*) grow, turn, mature. **2** (*modern cities developing rapidly*) grow, expand, enlarge, spread, progress, evolve. **3** (*They are trying to develop a scheme for expansion*) originate, set in motion, establish, form, institute. **4** (*They have the beginnings of a plan but they have to develop it*) elaborate, work out, enlarge on, amplify, flesh out. **5** (*The child has developed a cough*) acquire, get, contract. **6** (*A quarrel developed between the two women*) begin, start, commence, happen, come about, break out.

device *n* **1** (*a handy device for use in the kitchen*) gadget, appliance, utensil, implement, tool, apparatus, contrivance, contraption. **2** (*They thought of a cunning device to get into the building*) ploy, ruse, trick, stratagem, scheme, dodge, plan.

devil *n* **1** (*a story about the devil and hell*) Satan, Beelzebub. **2** (*She dreamt that she was being pursued by devils*) demon, evil spirit, fiend. **3** (*The slave's master was a devil*) brute, savage, monster, beast, fiend, scoundrel, villain. **4** (*The child is a little devil*) scamp, rascal, rogue. ▼

---

be between the devil and the deep blue sea to be faced with two possible courses of action each of which is as unacceptable, difficult, dangerous, etc, as the other (*He is between the devil and the deep blue sea. If he stays in his present job he will have to take a big cut in salary. If he leaves he will have to move to the other side of the country to get a job*). **speak of the devil** here is the very person that we have just been speaking about or referred to (*Speak of the devil! Here is Jim and we were just talking about him playing in the match tomorrow*). **there will be the devil to pay** there will be serious trouble (*There will be the devil to pay when father sees the broken window*) <From legends in which bargains are struck with the devil by which one could have immediate worldly success, happiness and riches, if one gave him one's soul at a later date when he asked for it>.

---

devious *adj* (*They are very devious people/They will get what they want only by devious means*) underhand, cunning, sly, crafty, wily, deceitful.

devoted *adj* **1** (*the king's devoted followers*) loyal, faithful, true, staunch, dedicated, committed, constant. **2** (*time devoted to hobbies*) set aside, allocated, assigned, allotted.

devout *adj* **1** (*devout churchgoers*) pious, religious, godly, holy, churchgoing. **2** (*It was their devout hope* *that he would be present*) sincere, deep, profound, earnest, heart-felt, fervent, genuine.

diagnose *vb* (*The doctor diagnosed mumps*) identify, recognize, distinguish, detect, pronounce.

dialogue *n* (*a dialogue between the presidents*) conversation, talk, exchange of views, discussion, conference, tête à tête.

die *vb* **1** (*The doctors think that he is going to die*) pass away, breathe one's last, lose one's life, meet one's end, (*inf*) give up the ghost, (*inf*) kick the bucket, expire. **2** (*All hope died when they heard the news*) end, come to an end, vanish, disappear, pass, fade. **3** (*The car's engine died*) stop, fail, break down, peter out. ▼

---

die hard to take a long time to disappear or become extinct (*He is trying to give up smoking but old habits die hard*). **die with one's boots on** to die while one is still working (*He did not want to retire. He would have wanted to die with his boots on*). **never say die** never give up hope (*It is going to be difficult to pass the exam but never say die—just work as hard as you can*).

---

differ *vb* **1** (*Their tastes differ completely*) be different, be dissimilar, be unlike, vary, diverge. **2** (*The two sides still differ on the best course of action*) disagree, dissent, be at variance, be in dispute, be in conflict, clash, argue, quarrel. **3** (*The scientist's results differ from the norm*) vary, diverge, deviate, depart from, contradict.▼

---

agree to differ to agree not to argue about something any more since neither party is likely to change his or her opinion (*Having spent many hours arguing about what is the right course of action they finally decided that it was a waste of time and agreed to differ*).

---

difference *n* **1** (*There was marked difference between the two sisters*) dissimilarity, distinction, variation, contrast, disparity, incongruity. **2** (*They have had several differences over the years*) difference of opinion, disagreement, dispute, clash, argument, quarrel, row, altercation. ▼

---

bury one's differences to forget about past disagreements (*The two members of the board hold different views but in the interests of the company they decided to bury their differences*). **split the difference** to agree on an amount of money halfway between two amounts, especially between the amount that one person wants to charge for something and the amount of money that someone else is willing to pay for it (*If he is asking £200 for the table and you only want to pay £100 why don't you split the difference and offer him £150?*).

---

different *adj* **1** (*Their tastes in clothes are very different*) dissimilar, unlike, at variance, contrasting. **2** (*With her new hairstyle she looks completely different*) changed, altered, transformed. **3** (*She wears a different sweater every day*) another, fresh. **4** (*The dress is available in different colours*) various, several, varied, assorted. **5** (*She was looking for something a bit different to wear to the wedding*) unusual, out of the ordinary, uncommon, distinctive, special, singular, extraordinary, rare. ▼

---

a different kettle of fish a completely different set of circumstances (*I know that we turned down his first suggestion, but this one is a completely different kettle of fish*). **as different as chalk from cheese** completely different (*The two girls are sisters but they are as different as chalk from cheese*).

---

difficult *adj* **1** (*Working on the building site was very difficult work*) hard, strenuous, arduous, demanding, taxing, laborious, tiring. **2** (*It is a difficult problem to solve*) hard, complicated, complex, involved, intricate, problematic, tough. **3** (*I felt that we had arrived at a difficult time*) inconvenient, ill-timed, unfavourable. **4** (*The family has gone through a difficult period*) hard, tough, distressing, grim. **5** (*She has always been a difficult child*) troublesome, unmanageable, recalcitrant, intractable.

dig *vb* **1** (*dig the earth before planting potatoes*) break up, work, turn over, loosen. **2** (*The prisoners dug a tunnel to try to escape*) dig out, excavate, hollow out, gouge out, scoop out, burrow, mine. **3** (*She dug her friend in the ribs at the lecture to wake him up*) prod, jab, poke, push, elbow. **4** (*The newspaper reporter is trying to dig up facts about the politician's private life*) search, probe, investigate, research, delve. ▼

---

dig one's heels in to show great determination, especially in order to get one's own wishes carried out (*There's no point in trying to persuade him to attend the meeting. He's digging his heels in and refusing to go*). **dig one's own grave** to be the cause of one's own misfortune or ruin (*It is a pity that he lost his job but in fact he dug his own grave. He kept taking days off and was hardly ever there*).

---

dignity *n* **1** (*She was anxious not to lose her dignity in front of people*) pride, self-esteem, self-respect. **2** (*the dignity of the royal procession*) stateliness, ceremoniousness, formality, decorum, majesty, grandeur, nobility.

dilapidated *adj* (*an area full of dilapidated houses*) run-down, tumble-down, broken-down, ramshackle, crumbling, in disrepair, decaying, neglected.

diligent *adj* (*diligent pupils studying hard*) conscientious, industrious, hard-working, assiduous, painstaking, studious, zealous.

dim *adj* **1** (*The light from the street lamps was dim*) faint, feeble, weak. **2** (*people frightened to walk along the dim corridors*) dark, gloomy, badly lit, dingy. **3** (*They saw a dim shape in the mist*) vague, indefinite, ill-defined, blurred, shadowy, fuzzy. **4** (*They have only a dim recollection of the incident*) vague, indistinct, hazy, blurred, confused. **5** (*He failed to understand because he is a bit dim*) stupid, dense, thick, dull, slow-witted. **6** (*His prospects of getting a job are rather dim*) gloomy, unpromising, depressing, discouraging. ▼

---

take a dim view of (something) to look with disapproval on (something) (*The boss takes a dim view of people making private telephone calls from the firm's phones*).

---

dingy *adj* (*They live in run-down dingy houses*) dim, dark, gloomy, dull, drab, murky, dirty, discoloured, shabby.

direct *adj* **1** (*the direct route to the city*) straight, shortest, uncircuitous. **2** (*a very direct manner/a direct statement*) frank, straightforward, blunt, forthright, clear, plain, candid, open.

direction *n* **1** (*They complained about his direction of the project*) administration, management, government, leadership, supervision, conduct, handling, control, guidance. **2** (*You must obey the teacher's directions*) order, command, instruction, directive, bidding. **3** (*The climbers have gone in the wrong direction*) route, way, course, path.

dirt *n* **1** (*They cleaned the dirt from their boots*) grime, mud, muck, filth, dust. **2** (*piles of dirt in the garden*) soil, earth, loam. **3** (*She complained about the dirt in some of the videos*) filth, obscenity, indecency, smut, pornography, bawdiness, lewdness, ribaldry. **4** (*She is given to spreading dirt about her neighbours*) scandal, slander, gossip.▼

---

treat (someone) like dirt to treat (someone) with contempt, to treat (someone) very badly (*The head of production treats his staff like dirt*).

---

dirty *adj* **1** (*Their boots were dirty*) unclean, soiled, grubby, grimy, muddy, mucky, filthy, dusty, messy, stained, polluted. **2** (*He embarrassed her by telling dirty jokes*) filthy, obscene, indecent, blue, smutty, pornographic, bawdy, lewd, ribald **3** (*That was a dirty trick*) nasty, unfair, dishonest, dishonourable, deceitful, underhand, fraudulent. ▼

---

do (someone's) dirty work to do something wrong or unpleasant on behalf of someone else (*The manager has asked his deputy to do his dirty work and sack some of the workers*).

do the dirty on (someone) to treat (someone) in an unfair, dishonest or disloyal way (*He did the dirty on his friend by going out with his girlfriend*).

---

disability *n* (*help for people with some form of disability*) incapacity, learning difficulty, learning disability, infirmity, handicap.

disadvantage *n* **1** (*discover the disadvantages of the system*) drawback, snag, weak spot, weakness, flaw, defect, fault, handicap, obstacle, minus. **2** (*children who suffer from financial disadvantage*) deprivation, hardship. **3** (*The incident turned out to be to their disadvantage*) detriment, disservice, harm, damage, injury, hurt, loss.

disadvantageous *adj* (*The circumstances were disadvantageous to them*) unfavourable, adverse, unfortunate, detrimental, prejudicial, deleterious, damaging, injurious.

disagree *vb* **1** (*The two sides had talks but they still disagreed*) differ, diverge, be at variance, be at odds. **2** (*The police said that the stories of the witnesses disagreed*) differ, be dissimilar, be unlike, be different, vary, clash, conflict, diverge. **3** (*The children were always disagreeing*) argue, quarrel, bicker, wrangle.

disagreeable *adj* **1** (*It was a very disagreeable experience*) unpleasant, nasty, horrible, foul, dreadful, revolting. **2** (*He is a disagreeable old man*) bad-tempered, ill-natured, cross, irritable, surly, churlish, rude, nasty, unpleasant.

disappear *vb* **1** (*The sun disappeared behind the cloud*) vanish, recede, fade, retire, retreat. **2** (*traditions which have now disappeared*) die out, be no more, end, pass, fade, perish, become extinct.

disappoint *vb* **1** (*We hated to disappoint the children by cancelling the picnic*) let down, dishearten, upset, sadden. **2** (*We had to disappoint their hopes*) thwart, frustrate, baulk, foil, baffle, hinder, obstruct, hamper, impede.

disapprove *vb* (*She disapproves of the young people's behaviour*) find unacceptable, dislike, be against, be displeased by, frown on, blame.

disaster *n* **1** (*earthquakes and other natural disasters*) catastrophe, calamity, tragedy, mishap, setback, reversal. **2** (*The play was a disaster*) failure, flop.

discard *vb* (*discard old newspapers*) throw away, throw out, dispose of, jettison, scrap, dump.

discharge *vb* **1** (*The pipe was discharging a foul-smelling liquid*) give off, send out, emit, exude, excrete, ooze, leak. **2** (*Several workers were discharged*) dismiss, sack, get rid of, declare redundant, (*inf*) fire, (*inf*) axe. **3** (*She did not discharge her duties*) carry out, do, perform, execute. **4** (*He discharged a firearm*) let off, fire, shoot. **5** (*The prisoner has been discharged*) set free, free, release, let go, acquit, clear, reprieve.

disclose *vb* (*She finally disclosed her reasons for leaving*) make known, reveal, divulge, tell, communicate, impart.

discomfort *n* **1** (*She experiences some discomfort in her eye*) ache, pain, soreness, twinge, irritation, throbbing. **2** (*the discomfort of travelling long journeys in a very small car*) inconvenience, difficulty, trouble, bother, drawback.

discordant *adj* (*She has a discordant voice/discordant sounds*) harsh, strident, shrill, grating, jarring.

discourage *vb* **1** (*The young man was discouraged by failing his driving test*) dishearten, dispirit, deject, depress, disappoint, demoralize. **2** (*They tried to discourage the girl from applying for the job*) deter, dissuade, talk out of, advises against, restrain.

discover *vb* **1** (*The police discovered a new clue*) uncover, find, come across, bring to light, turn up, unearth. **2** (*The scientists have discovered a new cancer drug*) invent, devise, originate. **3** (*We discovered that he was very ill*) learn, find out, come to realize.

discreet *adj* (*behaviour that was far from being discreet/a few discreet remarks*) careful, cautious, prudent, tactful, diplomatic, wise.

discriminate *vb* **1** (*Children should be taught to discriminate between right and wrong*) distinguish, differentiate, separate. **2** (*She said that her employers discriminated against women*) show prejudice towards, show bias towards, be biased towards.

discuss *vb* (*The committee discussed the problem*) talk about, confer about, debate, consider, deliberate.

disease *n* (*The old man is suffering from a brain disease*) illness, disorder, complaint, condition, malady, ailment.

disgrace *n* **1** (*He found it difficult to endure the disgrace of being in prison*) shame, humiliation, dishonour, degradation, ignominy. **2** (*The pupil is in disgrace for playing truant*) disfavour, discredit, disrepute.

disgraceful *adj* **1** (*Their behaviour was disgraceful*) shameful, shameless, dishonourable, shocking, outrageous, unseemly, improper. **2** (*The pupil's work is disgraceful*) very bad, appalling, dreadful, terrible, shocking.

disguise *vb* **1** (*They disguised themselves as police officers*) dress up, camouflage. **2** (*He tried to disguise the scar on his face*) conceal, hide, cover up, mask, screen.

disgust *vb* **1** (*The thought of eating snails disgusts them*) revolt, repel, put off, sicken, nauseate, (*inf*) turn off. **2** (*They were disgusted by the behaviour of the teenagers*) scandalize, shock, appal, outrage, offend.

dishevelled *adj* (*They felt dishevelled after their long journey*) untidy, unkempt, bedraggled, messy, tousled.

disinterested *adj* **1** (*The judges of the competition must be disinterested*) unbiased, unprejudiced, impartial, detached, objective, neutral, fair. **2** (*They were completely disinterested in the subject*) uninterested, bored, indifferent, apathetic.

dismal *adj* **1** (*feeling dismal because he was ill and had to stay in bed*) miserable, wretched, despondent, gloomy, sad, unhappy. **2** (*They plan to redecorate the dismal room*) dark, dim, dull, dingy, drab, dreary, bleak, cheerless.

dismiss *vb* (*He was dismissed from his job*) sack, give notice to, discharge, lay off, declare redundant, (*inf*) fire.

disobey *vb* (*They disobeyed the rules*) defy, disregard, flout, contravene, infringe, violate.

disorderly *adj* **1** (*They tried to tidy the disorderly office*) untidy, messy, cluttered, disorganized, out of order, chaotic. **2** (*The police tried to control the disorderly crowds*) unruly, rowdy, boisterous, rough, wild, lawless, rebellious.

display *vb* **1** (*They displayed the goods in the shop window*) exhibit, put on show, show, present, set out. **2** (*The young gymnasts displayed their expertise*) demonstrate, exhibit, show, show off, flaunt. **3** (*The accused displayed no emotion as he was sentenced by the judge*) show, exhibit, indicate, manifest, show evidence of, demonstrate.

dispose:— dispose of *vb* (*They disposed of the rubbish by burying it*) get rid of, throw away, throw out, discard, jettison, scrap, dump.

dispute *n* (*The two friends had a dispute over money*) argument, quarrel, row, wrangle, clash, altercation, feud.

disrupt *n* (*The protesters disrupted the meaning*) disturb, interrupt, interfere with, obstruct, impede, hamper.

dissolve *vb* **1** (*Salt dissolves in water*) liquefy, melt. **2** (*They both dissolved in tears*) break into, be overcome by. 3 (*They have decided to dissolve their partnership*) end, terminate, break up, discontinue, wind up. 4 (*The crowds dissolved when the police arrived*) break up, split up, disband, separate, go their separate ways.

distance *n* 1 (*measure the distance between the two trees*) space, gap, interval, span, stretch. 2 (*They were concerned about the distance of the house from the town*) remoteness. ▼

---

go the distance to complete something successfully, to last until the end of something (*It was such a long university course that we thought that he would not go the distance, but he got his degree last week*) <A reference to a racehorse finishing the course>. **keep one's distance from (someone** *or* **something)** not to come too close to (someone or something), not to be too friendly with (someone) (*It is advisable for teachers to keep their distance from pupils*). **within striking distance of (something)** reasonably close to, or very close to (something) (*He was within striking distance of the town when he collapsed*).

---

distant *adj* 1 (*The children like to hear stories of distant places*) far-off, remote, out of the way, outlying, far-flung. 2 (*in distant times*) long ago, far-off. 3 (*The two villages are ten miles distant from each other*) away, apart, separate. 3 (*I have only a distant recollection of what happened*) dim, vague, faint, hazy, indistinct. 4 (*She is rather a distant person*) aloof, detached, remote, reserved, unfriendly, unsociable, uncommunicative, stand-offish, unapproachable.

distinct *adj* 1 (*There was a distinct resemblance between the two crimes*) clear, clear-cut, plain, obvious, marked, definite, unmistakable, manifest. 2 (*There are two distinct issues to be discussed*) separate, individual, different, disparate.

distinguish *vb* 1 (*He found it difficult to distinguish some colours from others*) tell apart, tell the difference between, differentiate, discriminate. 2 (*They thought that they could distinguish a dim shape in the mist*) make out, detect, discern, notice, see, observe. 3 (*The soldier distinguished himself in the battle*) make famous, bring fame to, bestow honour on.

distress *n* 1 (*the child's distress on being separated from her parents*) suffering, pain, agony, misery, wretchedness, heartache, sorrow, sadness. 2 (*homeless people in distress*) hardship, adversity, misfortune, need, want, poverty, deprivation.

distribute *vb* 1 (*They distributed advertising leaflets on the street*) issue, pass out, pass round, circulate. 2 (*The teacher distributed books to the children*) give out, hand out. allocate, issue, allot, dispense.

district *n* (*They live in a district at the edge of the city*) area, region, place, locality, neighbourhood, sector.

disturb *vb* 1 (*They don't like being disturbed when they are at work*) interrupt, distract, bother, trouble, pester, intrude on, interfere with, harass, (*inf*) hassle. **2** (*The cleaner was asked not to disturb the documents on the desk*) disarrange, disorganize, muddle, confuse. **3** (*The news of the closure of the school disturbed them*) concern, worry, upset, fluster, perturb.

dive *vb* (*He dived into the water to save the drowning child*) jump, leap, drop, nose-dive.

diverge *vb* (*The roads diverge at the end of the village*) separate, divide, split, part, fork, branch off.

divide *vb* **1** (*You should divide the rope in two*) sever, cut, split, separate. **2** (*The road divides suddenly*) diverge, separate, divide, split, part, fork, branch off. **3** (*They divided the cake out among the children*) distribute, deal out, share out, allocate, allot, apportion.

divine *adj* **1** (*divine beings*) godly, heavenly, celestial, holy. **2** (*Taking part in divine worship*) religious, holy, spiritual. **3** (*The bride looked divine*) lovely, beautiful, charming, wonderful, marvellous.

doctor *n* (*They called a doctor when the child was ill*) medical practitioner, general practitioner, GP, hospital doctor, consultant, specialist. ▼

---

just what the doctor ordered exactly what is required at the time (*When they arrived back hot and thirsty a cold drink was just what the doctor ordered*).

---

document *n* (*the documents relating to the business deal*) paper, official paper, certificate, record, deed.

dogged *adj* (*They admired her dogged determination*) determined, resolute, stubborn, obstinate, tenacious.

dominant *adj* **1** (*He is the dominant member of the group*) supreme, controlling, influential, authoritative, domineering. **2** (*It was the dominant issue on the agenda*) chief, main, principal, leading, predominant.

domineering *adj* (*He is so domineering that everyone is afraid of him*) overbearing, arrogant, dictatorial, masterful, tyrannical, bullying, (*inf*) bossy.

doom *n* (*people who are always predicting doom*) catastrophe, disaster, destruction, ruin, downfall.

door *n* (*stand at the door of the block of flats*) doorway, entrance, entry. ▼

---

darken (someone's) door to go into (someone's) house (*He told his son never to darken his door again*). **on (someone's) doorstep** very close to where (someone) lives (*Naturally they do not wish a motorway built on their doorstep*). **show (someone) the door** to make (someone) leave one's house or premises (*Some of the guests at the party were causing such a disturbance that he was forced to show them the door*).

---

doting *adj* (*doting parents*) indulgent, adoring, devoted, fond.

double *adj* **1** (*They parked on a double yellow line*) duplicate, twofold, in pairs. **2** (*a double thickness of cloth*) twofold, folded, two-ply. **3** (*His words had a double meaning*) dual, ambiguous, ambivalent, two-edged. ▼

at the double extremely quickly (*We are very late—we had better get there at the double*) <A military term, literally at twice the normal marching speed>. **double Dutch** unintelligible words or language (*I had no idea what the lecturer was talking about—he seemed to be talking double Dutch*).

---

doubt *n* **1** (*They are having doubts about his efficiency as a leader*) misgiving, mistrust, distrust, reservations. **2** (*They are full of doubts about what they ought to do*) uncertainty, indecision, hesitation, irresolution.

doubtful *adj* **1** (*It is doubtful that he will be present*) uncertain, in doubt, unsure. **2** (*The genuineness of the signature is doubtful*) open to question, questionable, uncertain, dubious, debatable, disputable, inconclusive. **3** (*The meaning of the word is doubtful*) dubious, unclear, ambiguous, obscure. **4** (*His parents thought that he was associating with doubtful people*) dubious, questionable, suspicious, suspect.

down *adj* **1** (*They were feeling down at the end of the holidays*) downcast, dejected, depressed, gloomy, miserable, sad, unhappy. **2** (*The computer system is down*) malfunctioning, inoperative, not working. ▼

---

down the drain completely wasted (*Something went wrong with the computer and I lost all my material. It was a day's work down the drain*). **down under** Australia or New Zealand (*He has many relatives down under*). **get down to (something)** to begin to work at (something) in earnest (*The exams are coming up and we'll have to get down to some studying*). **have a down on (someone** *or* **something)** to be very hostile or opposed to (someone or something) (*The teacher seems to have a down on the new pupil*).

---

downright *adv* (*She was downright rude*) utterly, completely, totally, absolutely, thoroughly, positively.

drab *adj* (*They live in very drab surroundings*) dingy, dull, dismal, dreary, gloomy, cheerless, dim, dark.

drag *vb* **1** (*They dragged the fallen trees from the forest*) haul, pull, draw, tug, yank, tow. **2** (*Time dragged*) move slowly, crawl.

drastic *adj* (*a drastic remedy*) extreme, severe, rigorous, harsh, radical, dire .

draw *vb* **1** (*draw a house*) sketch, make a picture of, make a diagram of, portray, depict, design. **2** (*draw a chair up to the table*) pull, drag, haul, tow, tug, yank. **3** (*He drew a sword from its sheath*) take out, bring out, withdraw, extract, produce . **4** (*Her hat drew a lot of attention*) attract, catch, captivate. **5** (*draw the curtains*) pull, close, shut. **6** (*They drew level with the other car*) move, go, proceed.

dreadful *adj* **1** (*It was a dreadful accident*) terrible, frightful, horrible, grim, awful, shocking, appalling, ghastly, gruesome. **2** (*What a dreadful man!*) nasty, unpleasant, disagreeable, horrible, frightful, odious.

dream *vb* **1** (*The child seems to dream every night*) have dreams, have nightmares. **2** (*He said that he saw a ghost but he must have *been dreaming*) see things, hallucinate, imagine things. **3** (*She was dreaming instead of concentrating on her work*) daydream, be in a reverie, be lost in thought, be in a brown study. **4** (*He would not dream of upsetting her*) think, consider.

dreary *adj* (*They live in dreary surroundings*) dismal, drab, dingy, dull, gloomy, cheerless, gloomy, dark.

dress *vb* **1** (*They were all dressed in black*) clothe, attire, array, garb. **2** (*She was late and had to dress quickly*) get dressed, put on clothes. **3** (*The nurse dressed the wound*) cover, bandage, bind up. **4** (*The children dressed the Christmas tree*) decorate, adorn, ornament, trim, deck. ▼

---

be dressed to kill, to be dressed up to the nines to be dressed in one's smartest and most eye-catching clothes so as to attract attention (*She was dressed to kill when she went to the party*).

---

drink *vb* (*She drank the water quickly*) swallow, gulp down, partake of, quaff, (*inf*) swig.

drip *vb* (*Water began to drip from the tap*) trickle, dribble, plop, leak, splash, ooze, exude.

drive *vb* **1** (*young people learning to drive a car*) operate, steer, handle, direct, manage. **2** (*They came by train but we drove here*) go by car, come by car, travel by car, motor. **3** (*They drove the cattle to the milking parlour*) press, urge, push, prod, goad, spur. **4** (*Poverty drove them to steal*) force, compel, oblige, make, pressure, coerce. **5** (*They began to drive posts into the ground to make a fence*) hammer, ram, bang, plunge, sink. ▼

---

be driving at (something) to be suggesting or trying to say (something) (*We weren't sure what he was driving at but we thought that he might be suggesting that we were lying*). **drive a coach and horses through (something)** to destroy (an argument, etc) completely by detecting and making use of the weak points in it (*The defence lawyer was able to drive a coach and horses through the prosecution's case against his client*) <A reference to the fact that the defects or holes in the argument are so large that one could drive a coach and horses through them>.

---

drop *vb* **1** (*The hot air balloon dropped out of the sky*) drop down, descend, fall, plummet, plunge. **2** (*Water dropped from the branches*) fall, drip, trickle, dribble, plop. **3** (*She dropped her luggage and fell into a chair*) let fall, let go. **4** (*He has decided to drop piano lessons*) give up, stop, abandon, discontinue, cease, end, finish. **5** (*She has dropped her latest boyfriend*) leave, forsake, abandon, jilt. **6** (*House prices have dropped*) fall, lessen, decrease, decline, dwindle, plummet, plunge. ▼

---

drop off to fall asleep (*Grandfather usually drops off in his chair after dinner*). **drop out** to withdraw from school, university, etc or from society (*After his first year at college he decided to drop out/He reacted against his wealthy parents'* *lifestyle and decided to drop out and live rough*). **let (something) drop, let it drop** to let (something) be known by accident, or supposedly by accident (*Her father found out that her boyfriend was married but felt that he shouldn't let it drop to his daughter*).

---

drowsy *adj* (*People often feel drowsy after a heavy meal*) sleepy, tired, weary, lethargic, sluggish.

drug *n* **1** (*Medical scientists have discovered a new cancer drug*) medical drug, medicine, medication, medicament, cure, remedy. **2** (*concern over young people who are addicted to drugs*) addictive drug, narcotic, opiate, barbiturate, (*inf*) dope.

drunk *adj* (*drunk people staggering down the road*) intoxicated, inebriated, under the influence, tipsy.

dry *adj* **1** (*the dry regions of the world*) arid, parched, scorched, dehydrated, desiccated. **2** (*dry autumn leaves*) withered, shrivelled, wilted, desiccated. **3** (*The cheese has grown very dry*) dried out, hard, stale. **4** (*The lecture was very dry and the audience was bored*) boring, dull, uninteresting, tedious, monotonous, tiresome. ▼

---

a dry run a practice attempt, a rehearsal (*The headmaster wanted to have a dry run of the next day's prize-giving*). **as dry as dust** extremely dull and boring (*The pupils thought that the play which they had to read was as dry as dust*). **dry up** to forget what one was going to say (*The bride's father started to give a speech at the wedding and then dried up*).

---

dual *adj* (*He plays a dual role in the firm*) double, duplicate.

dubious *adj* **1** (*He is dubious about going to the meeting*) doubtful, unsure, uncertain, hesitant, irresolute, wavering. **2** (*The result is still dubious*) doubtful, uncertain, unsure, unsettled, up in the air. **3** (*He seems rather a dubious character*) suspicious, suspect, questionable, untrustworthy.

dull *adj* **1** (*It was a dull day*) overcast, cloudy, dark, gloomy, dismal, bleak. **2** (*She always wore dull colours*) drab, dreary, dark, sombre. **3** (*We heard the dull thud of something falling*) muffled, muted, indistinct. **4** (*The lecturer gave a very dull talk*) boring, uninteresting, dry, tedious, monotonous.

dumb *adj* **1** (*He has been dumb since birth*) without speech, mute. **2** (*They were struck dumb at the beauty of the view*) speechless, silent, wordless, mute, inarticulate, at a loss for words. **3** (*He is so dumb that he did not get the job*) stupid, unintelligent, dense, thick, slow-witted.

duplicate *vb* **1** (*She was asked to duplicate the documents*) copy, photocopy, reproduce, Photostat. **2** (*There does not seem to be work around and workers are duplicating tasks*) repeat, do over again.

duplicity *n* (*his duplicity in swindling the old lady*) deceit, deceitfulness, double-dealing, trickery, guile, dishonesty.

durable *adj* **1** (*the durable effects of the drug*) long-lasting, lasting, persisting, permanent, **2** (*The boots must be durable*) long-lasting, lasting, hard-wearing, sturdy, strong, tough.

dust *vb* **1** (*dust the furniture*) wipe,

brush, clean, mop. **2** (*She dusted the cake with icing sugar*) sprinkle, dredge, scatter. ▼

---

not see (someone) for dust not to see (someone) because he or she has run away (*When it has been discovered that he has stolen the money you won't see him for dust*) <Refers to clouds of dust left behind by horses or vehicles moving fast>. **throw dust in (someone's) eyes** to attempt to confuse or deceive (someone) (*They threw dust in the policeman's eyes by saying that they had seen an intruder in the garden but this was just to give the real burglar time to get away*) <Dust temporarily blinds people if it gets into their eyes>.

---

duty *n* **1** (*He has a sense of duty towards his parents*) responsibility, obligation. **2** (*He failed to carry out his duties and was sacked*) job, task, chore, assignment. **3** (*They had to pay duty on the goods which they brought into the country*) tax, levy, tariff, excise.

dwindle *vb* (*Their hopes are dwindling as time goes on*) grow less, lessen, decrease, diminish, fade.

E

eager *adj* **1** (*eager students*) keen, enthusiastic, avid, earnest, zealous, fervent. **2** (*people eager to learn/eager for information*) avid, anxious, longing for, yearning for, desirous of. ▼

---

eager beaver a very enthusiastic and hard-working person (*The new student is a real eager beaver who works late into the night*) <Beavers are small animals that build dams with great speed and skill and are traditionally thought of as being very hard-working>.

---

early *adv* **1** (*get up early*) at dawn, at daybreak, with the lark, at cockcrow. **2** (*visitors who arrived early*) too soon, ahead of time, prematurely. **3** (*It is very important that you arrive early for your interview*) in good time, ahead of schedule.

early *adj* **1** (*an early reply*) prompt, speedy, quick, rapid, fast, without delay. **2** (*an early crop*) advanced, forward, premature, precocious. **3** (*early man*) primitive, prehistoric, primeval.▼

---

the early bird catches the worm a person who arrives early or acts promptly is in a position to gain an advantage over others who are later or slower to act.

---

earn *vb* **1** (*earn an extremely high salary*) make, get, receive, obtain, draw, clear, take home. **2** (*earn the respect of his colleagues*) gain, win, attain, secure, merit, deserve.

earnest *adj* **1** (*an earnest young man who studies hard*) serious, solemn, grave, intense, staid, studious, diligent. **2** (*make an earnest plea for mercy*) fervent, ardent, passionate, intense, heartfelt, sincere, urgent.

earnest:— in earnest *adj* **1** (*They were in earnest about walking all the way home*) serious, sincere, not joking. **2** (*They set to work in earnest*) zealously, wholeheartedly, with a will, with commitment, determinedly.

earnings *npl* (*She tries to save part of her earnings*) income, salary, wages, pay.

earth *n* **1** (*earth, moon and stars*) globe, world, planet. **2** (*the earth and the sky*) land, ground. **3** (*children getting covered in earth from playing in the garden*) soil, dirt.▼

---

bring (someone) back down to earth to make (someone) aware of the practical nature of life or a situation and so stop dreaming or imagining (*She was daydreaming about a holiday in the sun when the sight of the pouring rain brought her back down to earth*).

---

earthenware *n* (*a shop selling local earthenware to the tourists*) pottery, crockery, stoneware, ceramics.

earthly *adj* **1** (*a book about creatures that were not earthly*) terrestrial. **2** (*earthly pleasures*) worldly, non-spiritual, secular, temporal, material, fleshly, carnal. **3** (*They have no earthly chance of success*) feasible, possible, conceivable, likely, realistic.

earthy *adj* **1** (*the earthy smell of a newly dug garden*) soil-like, dirt-like. **2** (*tell jokes which were rather earthy*) bawdy, crude, coarse, ribald, indecent, blue.

ease *n* **1** (*wealthy people leading a life of ease*) comfort, contentment, affluence, wealth, prosperity, luxury. **2** (*do the job with ease*) effortlessness, facility, no difficulty, deftness, adroitness. **3** (*Ease of manner is important in his job*) naturalness, relaxedness, composure, affability.

ease *vb* **1** (*receive some pills to ease the pain*) lessen, reduce, diminish, relieve, soothe, alleviate, mitigate. **2** (*The storm finally eased*) lessen, grow less, abate, moderate, slacken off. **3** (*A letter would ease his mother's mind*) comfort, give comfort to, calm, soothe, give solace to. **4** (*try to ease the part of the machine into the right position*) guide, manoeuvre, inch, edge, steer, slide.

easy *adj* **1** (*an easy task*) simple, effortless, uncomplicated, straightforward, undemanding. **2** (*She had an easy mind when she knew her family were safe*) at ease, untroubled, unworried, at peace, calm, tranquil, composed. **3** (*an easy manner*) natural, relaxed, easygoing, composed, unreserved, affable, (*inf*) laid-back. ▼

---

as easy as falling off a log extremely easy (*She was worried about having to use the computer but she discovered that it was as easy as falling off a log*).

---

easygoing *adj* (*He is too easygoing to get upset about anything*) even-tempered, relaxed, placid, happy-go-lucky, tolerant, understanding, undemanding, patient, (*inf*) laid-back.

eat *vb* **1** (*eat sweets*) consume, devour, chew, swallow, gulp down, bolt, wolf, (*inf*) tuck into, scoff. **2** (*What time do you eat?*) have a meal, take food. **3** (*Acid had eaten away the material*) erode, corrode, wear away, rot. ▼

---

have (someone) eating out of one's hand to have (someone) doing everything that one wishes, because he or she likes or admires one or is trying to flatter us (*That class is meant to be very wild but the teacher has them eating out of her hand*) <From an animal that is so tame that it will take food from one's hand>.

---

eavesdrop *vb* (*The child tried to eavesdrop on her parents' conversation*) listen in on, overhear.

ebb *vb* **1** (*when the tide ebbed*) go out, flow back, retreat, draw back, recede. **2** (*The popularity of the president ebbed*) decline, lessen, decrease, dwindle, fade away, peter out.

eccentric *adj* (*The villagers think he is eccentric/She has an eccentric way of dressing*) strange, peculiar, odd, queer, weird, outlandish, bizarre, zany, freakish, unconventional, (*inf*) off-beat, (*inf*) way-out.

echo *vb* **1** (*The sound echoed round the hall*) resound, reverberate, ring. **2** (*She simply echoed what her father said*) repeat, reiterate, reproduce, copy, imitate, parrot.

economical *adj* **1** (*have to be economical with fuel so that it will last the winter*) sparing, thrifty, careful, frugal. **2** (*an economical form of transport*) inexpensive, reasonable, low-cost, low-price, cheap. ▼

---

be economical with the truth not to tell the whole truth, or to lie (*We did not believe the figures which the politician quoted—we thought that he was being economical with the truth*).

---

economize *vb* (*Since prices have gone up we will have to economize*) cut back, spend less, cut expenditure, tighten one's belt, draw in one's horns.

ecstasy *n* (*Her idea of ecstasy was to lie on a beach all day*) bliss, rapture, joy, elation, delight, happiness, pleasure.

ecstatic *adj* (*They were ecstatic when their team won the championship*) elated, exultant, in raptures, overjoyed, joyful, jubilant, jumping for joy, on cloud nine, in seventh heaven.

edge *n* **1** (*the edge of the road*) side, verge. **2** (*the edge of the town*) border, boundary, perimeter. ▼

---

have the edge on (someone or something) to have an advantage over (someone or something), to be superior to (someone or something) (*He has the edge over the other basket ball players as he is so tall/This washing machine definitely has the edge over the other one*). **take the edge off (something)** to make (something) less sharp, to reduce (something) (*An apple took the edge off our appetite/Her smile took the edge off her criticism*).

---

edgy *adj* (*feel edgy when her children were late home*) on edge, anxious, nervous, tense, uneasy, worried, (*inf*) nervy, (*inf*) uptight.

edible *adj* (*food that is scarcely edible*) eatable, consumable, digestible, palatable.

edict *n* (*by edict of the emperor/obey the official edicts*) order, decree, command, law, rule, act, statute.

edit *vb* **1** (*They edited the manuscript which he had written*) revise, correct, alter, adapt, emend. **2** (*He edits the daily newspaper*) be the editor of, be in charge of, direct.

edition *n* (*last week's edition of the magazine*) issue, number, publication.

educate *vb* (*children who were educated at the little local school*) teach, instruct, school, train.

educated *adj* (*the kind of books that educated people might read*) well-read, knowledgeable, literate, cultivated, cultured.

education *n* (*receive a good education*) schooling, teaching, instruction, training, tuition.

eerie *adj* (*hear an eerie noise in the middle of the night*) strange, unnatural, uncanny, ghostly, frightening, (*inf*) scary.

effect *n* **1** (*It is difficult to say what the effect of the changes will be*) result, consequences, outcome, influence, impact. **2** (*I like the general effect of the colour scheme*) impression, impact.

effect, take effect *vb* **1** (*new regulations taking effect from next week*) come into force, come into operation, begin, become law, become valid. **2** (*when the sleeping pills take effect*) work, be effective.

effective *adj* **1** (*an effective government*) successful, competent, capable, efficient, productive. **2** (*an effective colour scheme*) striking, impressive, attractive. **3** (*rules which will be effective from next year*) valid, in force, in operation, operative.

effects *npl* (*her personal effects*) belongings, possessions, goods, things, luggage.

effervescent *adj* (*effervescent soft drinks*) sparkling, fizzy, bubbly, carbonated.

efficient *adj* **1** (*a very efficient worker*) capable, competent, able, effective, productive, skilful, organized. **2** (*an efficient system*) effective, well-organized, well-run, streamlined.

effigy *n* (*effigies of ancient kings*) likeness, image, statue, bust.

effort *n* **1** (*work requiring a great deal of effort*) exertion, power, energy, work, force, application, struggle, strain, (*inf*) elbow grease. **2** (*She passed the driving test at her second effort*) attempt, try, endeavour, (*inf*) shot, (*inf*) go.

effortless *adj* (*He made lifting the heavy weights seem effortless*) easy, simple, uncomplicated, trouble-free, unexacting, undemanding.

effrontery *n* (*She had the effrontery to go straight to the top of the queue*) impudence, impertinence, cheek, audacity, temerity, (*inf*) nerve, (*inf*) brass neck.

effusive *adj* (*When she pays people compliments she is so effusive*) gushing, fulsome, demonstrative, extravagant, lavish, (*inf*) over the top.

egg, egg on *vb* (*His friends egged him on to steal the apples*) encourage, urge, spur, goad, prod, prompt. ▼

---

be left with egg on one's face to be left looking foolish (*She boasted that she would win easily but she lost and was left with egg on her face*) <From having forgotten to wipe one's face after having got one's breakfast egg smeared on it>.

try to teach one's grandmother to suck eggs to try to tell someone else how to do something when that person is much more experienced and has been doing such a job for years (*He has only just learned to drive and he was giving my father advice. I told him not to try to teach his grandmother to suck eggs*).

---

eject *vb* **1** (*He was ejected from the club for trying to start a fight*) throw out, remove, banish, evict, (*inf*) kick out, (*inf*) turf out, (*inf*) chuck out. **2** (*She was ejected from the plane*) thrust out, throw out, propel.

eke:—**eke out** *vb* **1** (*eke out the lamb stew by adding a lot of vegetables*) stretch out, increase, supplement. **2** (*We must try to eke out our fuel supplies*) be economical with, be sparing with, economize on. **3** (*The poor peasants eke out a living from the soil*) scrape, scratch.

elaborate *adj* **1** (*elaborate carvings/elaborate patterns*) detailed, intricate, complex, ornate, fancy, showy, fussy, (*inf*) flashy. **2** (*draw *up an elaborate plan*) complicated, detailed, complex, involved, intricate.

elaborate *vb* (*asked to elaborate on his suggestion*) expand, enlarge, amplify, flesh out.

elapse *vb* (*A long time elapsed before they met again*) pass, go by, roll by, slip by.

elastic *adj* **1** (*elastic materials*) stretchy, springy, pliant, flexible, rubbery. **2** (*Our holiday plans are elastic*) flexible, fluid, adaptable, adjustable.

elated *adj* (*They were elated at their victory*) overjoyed, jubilant, jumping for joy, joyful, delighted, gleeful, ecstatic, euphoric, over the moon, on cloud nine, in seventh heaven.

elation *n* (*their elation at their victory*) jubilation, joy, joyfulness, delight, glee, ecstasy.

elbow *vb* (*elbow him out of the way to get to the front of the crowd*) push, jostle, shoulder, knock, bump. ▼

---

elbow grease hard physical work (*New polishes are all very well but it will take elbow grease to get a good shine on that furniture*). **give (someone) the elbow** (*inf*) to get rid of (someone), to dismiss (someone) from a job or to end a relationship with (someone) (*He has given his girlfriend the elbow and is going out with someone else*).

---

elderly *adj* (*the elderly couple next door*) oldish, old, advanced in years.

elderly:—**the elderly** *npl* elderly people, older people, senior citizens, old-age pensioners, pensioners, OAPs, retired people (*be kind to the elderly*).

elect *vb* **1** (*elect a team captain*) choose, select, pick, opt for, appoint, decide on. **2** (*elect an MP*) vote for, choose.

election *n* (*vote in an election for a new leader*) ballot, poll.

electrify *vb* (*He electrified the audience with his performance*) excite, thrill, rouse, stir, move, fire.

elegance *n* (*admire the elegance of the model*) stylishness, style, grace, gracefulness, fashion, fashionableness.

elegant *adj* (*the elegant women at the wedding reception*) stylish, graceful, fashionable, tasteful, artistic.

elegy *n* (*an elegy for his friend's death*) funeral poem, funeral song, lament, dirge, requiem.

element *n* **1** (*the main elements of the project*) component, ingredient, constituent, factor, feature, detail. **2** (*the natural element of the lion*) environment, habitat, milieu, sphere. ▼

---

in one's element in a situation in which one is very happy or at one's best (*She is in her element when she is organizing something*) <A reference to the four elements of medieval science—fire, earth, air and water>.

---

elementary *adj* **1** (*He said that the problem was elementary*) easy, simple, uncomplicated, straightforward. **2** (*students taking a course in elementary mathematics*) basic, fundamental, rudimentary, primary.

elements *npl* (*climbers braving the elements*) weather, climate, atmospheric conditions.

elicit *vb* (*try to elicit the information from them*) draw out, extract, obtain, get.

eligible *adj* (*not eligible for the post/ not eligible to take part in the race*) qualified, suitable, acceptable, authorized.

eliminate *vb* **1** (*She was eliminated from the team*) drop, leave out, exclude, omit, reject. **2** (*a gunman hired to eliminate the members of the other gang*) get rid of, dispose of, destroy, put an end to, kill.

elocution *n* (*take lessons in elocution*) speech, diction, enunciation, articulation, voice production, delivery.

eloquent *adj* (*an eloquent speech*) articulate, expressive, fluent, persuasive, forceful.

elude *vb* (*try to elude the police*) avoid, dodge, evade, escape from, get away from.

emaciated *adj* (*emaciated children in the famine region*) skeletal, gaunt, wasted, scrawny, skinny, scraggy, thin as a rake.

embargo *n* (*place an embargo on trade with that country*) ban, bar, prohibition, interdict.

embark *vb* **1** (*Passengers were asked to embark early*) board ship, board a plane, go on board. **2** (*someone embarking on a new career*) set out on, begin, start, commence, enter on, set about.

embarrassed *adj* (*feel embarrassed when she forgot the words of her speech*) awkward, uncomfortable, self-conscious, upset, disconcerted, discomfited, flustered, confused, abashed, ashamed, mortified.

embarrassment *n* (*overcome with embarrassment when she forgot the words of her speech*) awkwardness, discomfort, self-consciousness, discomfiture, confusion, shame, mortification.

embezzle *vb* (*embezzle money from his company*) steal, rob, thieve, pilfer, filch, appropriate, (*inf*) nick.

emblem *n* (*the emblem of the society*) crest, badge, symbol, sign, device.

embrace *vb* (*He embraced his daughter as she got on the train*) hug, cuddle, clasp, cling to, squeeze.

emerge *vb* **1** (*They stood around the pool as the swimmers emerged*) come out, come into view, appear, surface, become visible. **2** (*waiting for the facts to emerge*) come out, become known, come to the fore.

emergency *n* (*emergencies such as fires*) crisis, danger, accident, extremity.

emigrate *vb* (*people emigrating to find work*) move overseas, move abroad, migrate, relocate.

eminent *adj* (*an eminent writer*) famous, well-known, distinguished, renowned, notable, noteworthy, great, important, prominent.

emit *vb* **1** (*chimneys emitting smoke*) give out, pour out, issue, send forth, discharge, issue. **2** (*emit a scream for help*) utter, express, voice.

emotion *n* (*in a voice in which there was no emotion*) feeling, sentiment, passion.

emotional *adj* **1** (*an emotional person*) passionate, ardent, demonstrative, excitable. **2** (*an emotional moment*) moving, touching, affecting, poignant, emotive.

emphasis *n* **1** (*As far as the interviews were concerned the emphasis was on qualifications*) stress, priority, importance, weight, urgency. **2** (*put the emphasis on the first syllable*) stress, accent, accentuation.

emphasize *vb* **1** (*emphasize the

importance of working hard) stress, accentuate, underline, highlight, spotlight, point up. **2** (*emphasize the first syllable*) stress, put the stress on, accentuate.

emphatic *adj* (*He issued an emphatic denial*) definite, decided, firm, positive, absolute.

employ *vb* **1** (*He wishes to employ three more people in his office*) engage, hire, take on, sign on. **2** (*His work employs all his time*) take up, occupy, fill, use up. **3** (*employ modern methods in their factory*) use, make use of, apply.

employment *n* (*He is looking for employment in the computing industry*) work, occupation, job.

empty *adj* **1** (*an empty house*) vacant, unoccupied, uninhabited, unfilled. **2** (*an empty page*) blank, unused, clean. **3** (*empty threats*) meaningless, futile, ineffective, idle, insubstantial. ▼

---

empty vessels make most noise the most foolish or least informed people are most likely to voice their opinions (*They know nothing whatsoever about the new scheme but they are protesting about them—empty vessels make most noise*).

---

enchant *vb* (*The children were enchanted by the ballet*) captivate, fascinate, entrance, bewitch, charm, delight.

enclosure *n* (*the enclosure for the animals at the dog show*) compound, ring, arena, paddock, fold.

encounter *vb* **1** (*She encountered an old friend in the shopping centre*) meet, run into, run across, come upon, (*inf*) bump into. **2** (*encounter problems*) meet, be faced with, face, confront.

encourage *vb* **1** (*encourage those who had given up hope*) inspire, hearten, stimulate, motivate, incite, prompt. **2** (*a plan to encourage exports*) boost, promote, help, assist, aid.

end *n* **1** (*the far end of the lake*) edge, border, boundary, extremity, tip. **2** (*the end of the film*) ending, conclusion, close, finish, culmination, denouement. **3** (*the end of the train*) rear, back. **4** (*their end in mind*) aim, objective, intention, purpose. **5** (*meet a peaceful end*) death, demise.

end *vb* **1** (*when his membership of the club ends*) come to an end, finish, come to a stop, stop, cease, conclude. **2** (*The incident ended their friendship*) bring to an end, bring to a close, finish, stop, discontinue, wind up.▼

---

at the end of one's tether at the end of one's patience, tolerance, etc (*She is at the end of her tether looking after two small children*). **make ends meet** to live within the limits of one's means (*They have a large family and find it difficult to make ends meet*) <The ends referred to are the start and finish of one's annual financial accounts>.

---

endanger *vb* (*things which endanger the species*) put in danger, expose to danger, put at risk, risk, jeopardize.

endearing *adj* (*one of her endearing features*) charming, attractive, loveable, adorable, engaging, sweet.

endeavour *vb* (*endeavour to do better*) attempt, try, exert oneself, make an effort, strive.

ending *n* (*a happy ending to the*

novel) end, finish, close, conclusion.

endless *adj* **1** (*endless patience*) unending, without end, unlimited, infinite, everlasting, boundless. **2** (*an endless chain*) continuous, unbroken, uninterrupted, unbroken.

endorse *vb* (*endorse their course of action*) approve, support, back, champion, uphold, subscribe to.

endow *vb* (*She was endowed with good looks*) give, provide, supply, gift, confer.

endure *vb* **1** (*unable to endure the traffic noise any longer*) put up with, stand, bear, tolerate, abide. **2** (*hope that their love would endure*) last, continue, remain, live on, persist.

enemy *n* (*the army of the enemy/regard his former friend as an enemy*) foe, opponent, adversary, rival.

energetic *adj* (*not feeling energetic enough to go for a walk*) active, lively, sprightly, vigorous, animated, enthusiastic.

energy *n* (*lacking in energy after her illness*) strength, stamina, vigour, power, force, liveliness, vitality, animation, (*inf*) get-up-and-go.

enforce *vb* **1** (*enforce the law*) apply, carry out, administer, implement, impose. **2** (*enforce silence on the group*) force, compel, insist on.

engage *vb* **1** (*engage a new nanny*) employ, hire, appoint, take on. **2** (*engage in a game of chess/ be engaged in a bitter argument*) take part in, join in, participate in, enter into. **3** (*an attempt to engage their attention*) attract, catch, draw, gain, capture.

engaged *adj* **1** (*The manager is engaged*) busy, occupied, unavailable, (*inf*) tied up. **2** (*The toilet is engaged*) occupied, in use. **3** (*engaged couples*) going to be married, betrothed, affianced.

engaging *n* (*an engaging smile*) charming, attractive, appealing, winning, pleasing, sweet.

engineer *vb* (*engineer a secret meeting between them*) bring about, cause, contrive, devise, (*inf*) wangle.

engrave *vb* **1** (*engrave their initials on the tree*) carve, etch, inscribe, cut. **2** (*Her words are engraved on his heart*) fix, set, imprint, stamp.

engross *vb* (*The book engrossed me*) occupy, absorb, preoccupy, engage, rivet.

engulf *vb* (*a town engulfed by a tidal wave*) flood, inundate, swamp, swallow, swamp, submerge.

enjoy *vb* (*enjoy a trip to the seaside*) like, love, be entertained by, take pleasure in, delight in.

enjoy:— enjoy oneself *vb* have a good time, have fun, (*inf*) have a ball (*The children are enjoying themselves at the funfair*).

enjoyable *adj* (*an enjoyable occasion*) entertaining, amusing, delightful, pleasant, nice.

enlarge *vb* (*enlarge the garden*) expand, extend, add to, amplify.

enormous *adj* (*an enormous creature/an enormous load*) huge, immense, massive, vast, colossal, gigantic, mammoth.

enough *adj* (*We have enough food*) sufficient, adequate, ample, abundant. ▼

---

enough is as good as a feast if one has enough of something for one's needs that is all that matters and large quantities are not necessary (*We had only a* *little bread and cheese for a snack on our walk but it stopped us from being hungry—enough is as good as a feast*). **have had enough of (someone or something)** to be unable to put up with (someone or something) any longer (*I have had enough of listening to her complaining*).

---

enrol *vb* **1** (*enrol for a French course*) register, sign up, enter, volunteer. **2** (*We enrolled several new recruits in the society*) register, sign up, take on, admit, accept.

ensue *vb* (*the argument and the fight that ensued*) follow, come after, result, arise.

ensure *vb* (*You must try to ensure that he will be present*) make sure, make certain, guarantee, certify.

enter *vb* **1** (*enter the hall*) come into, go into, pass into, move into. **2** (*a bullet entered his chest*) go into, pierce, penetrate. **3** (*enter a competition*) go in for, take part in, participate in. **4** (*enter one's name on the form*) put down, register, record, mark down, note.

enterprise *n* **1** (*The festival is an annual enterprise*) project, undertaking, operation, venture. **2** (*The wool firm is a private enterprise*) business, industry, firm, establishment. **3** (*young people showing some enterprise*) resourcefulness, initiative, drive, imagination, spirit, enthusiasm, boldness, (*inf*) get-up-and-go.

enterprising *adj* (*an enterprising member of staff*) resourceful, go-ahead, imaginative, spirited, enthusiastic.

entertain *vb* (*He entertained the children with conjuring tricks*) amuse, divert, please, delight, interest.

entertainment *n* **1** (*several forms of entertainment for non-working hours*) amusement, fun, recreation, diversion, distraction. **2** (*sing for the entertainment of the children*) amusement, enjoyment, diversion, pleasure, delight, interest. **3** (*the entertainment at the club that evening*) show, performance.

enthralling *adj* (*The acrobats gave an enthralling performance*) fascinating, gripping, riveting, spellbinding, enchanting, captivating, entrancing.

enthusiastic *adj* (*enthusiastic members of the flying club*) eager, keen, ardent, zealous, passionate, wholehearted, devoted, earnest, fanatical.

entice *vb* (*try to entice customers into his shop*) lure, tempt, attract, coax, decoy.

entire *adj* **1** (*his entire collection of records*) whole, total, complete, full. **2** (*not an entire success*) total, absolute, unqualified, thorough, outright.

entirely *adv* (*not entirely true*) absolutely, completely, totally, wholly, altogether.

entitle *vb* **1** (*Your pass entitles you to go to three matches*) allow, permit, enable, qualify, give the right to. **2** (*His novel is entitled "Lost Dreams"*) call, name.

entrance *n* **1** (*the entrance to the office block*) way in, entry, doorway, gateway, lobby, porch, foyer. **2** (*gain entrance to the building*) entry, access, admission, admittance. **3** (*the entrance of the headmaster*) entry, arrival, appearance.

entrance *vb* (*We were entranced by

their graceful dancing) hold spellbound, fascinate, captivate, enchant, enthral.

entrant *n* (*count the number of entrants for the competition*) competitor, contestant, participant, candidate, applicant.

entreat *vb* (*She entreated us to go with her*) beg, implore, beseech, plead with, appeal to.

entrenched *adj* (*entrenched political ideas*) deep-rooted, well-established, fixed, set, firm, unshakeable, dyed-in-the wool.

entry *n* **1** (*the entry to the block of flats*) entrance, doorway, gateway, lobby, porch, foyer. **2** (*gain entry to theoffice building*) entrance, access, admission, admittance. **3** (*the entry of the ballet dancers*) entrance, arrival, appearance. **4** (*an entry in her diary*) statement, item, record, note, listing.

envelop *vb* (*mountain tops enveloped in mist*) cover, blanket, surround, engulf, swathe.

enviable *adj* (*He has an enviable collection ofCDs*) desirable, tempting, impressive, excellent.

envious *adj* (*She was envious when she saw her friend's new car*) jealous, covetous, green, begrudging, resentful.

environment *n* (*Children need a loving environment/the ideal environment for tigers*) surroundings, habitat, background, situation, conditions, circumstances, atmos- phere, milieu.

envy *n* (*her envy of her neighbour's garden*) enviousness, covetousness, jealousy, resentment.

envy *vb* (*She envies her friend her new car*) be envious of, be jealous of, covet, be covetous, begrudge, grudge, resent.

ephemeral *adj* (*the ephemeral life of the mayfly*) short-lived, fleeting, transitory, brief, passing, temporary.

episode *n* **1** (*the second episode of the TV serial*) part, instalment, section. **2** (*an unhappy episode in their lives*) incident, event, occurrence, happening, experience.

equal *adj* **1** (*children of equal ability*) the same, identical, like, comparable. **2** (*an equal contest*) even, evenly matched, level. **3** (*not feeling equal to the task*) up to, fit for, ready for, capable of. ▼

---

all things being equal if all other facts when taken into consideration make no difference (*She is much younger than her husband and should, all things being equal, live longer than he will*).

---

equal *vb* **1** (*six plus six equals twelve*) be equal to, come to, amount to, add up to, make, total. **2** (*The runner equalled the record for the race*) match, be level with, reach.

equate *vb* (*They equate money with happiness*) associate, bracket, link, connect.

equip *vb* **1** (*equip the children for their skiing trip*) fit out, kit out, rig out, dress. **2** (*equip the hall with gymnastic apparatus*) fit out, furnish, supply, stock.

equipment *n* (*the equipment needed to do the job*) tools, gear, apparatus, materials, things, paraphernalia.

equivalent *adj* (*ask the shop to exchange the item for something of equivalent value*) equal, the same, identical, similar, like, comparable, corresponding, matching.

equivalent *n* (*the equivalent of our Chancellor of the Exchequer in* *their country*) counterpart, opposite number, equal.

era *n* (*furniture from the Jacobean era*) age, period, time, days, aeon, epoch.

eradicate *vb* (*try to eradicate the weed from his garden/A government tries to eradicate tax avoidance*) get rid of, do away with, root out, wipe out, eliminate, extirpate.

erase *vb* (*erase the incorrect passage from the report*) remove, rub out, wipe out, delete, cancel, expunge.

erect *adj* (*Human beings stand erect*) upright, vertical, straight.

erect *vb* **1** (*erect a tent*) put up, set up, set upright, pitch, assemble. **2** (*erect a block of flats*) build, construct, put up, raise.

erode *vb* (*cliffs eroded by the sea*) wear away, wear down, eat away, corrode.

err *vb* **1** (*They erred when they accused him of theft*) be in error, be wrong, be incorrect, make a mistake, be mistaken, get it wrong, miscalculate, (*inf*) slip up. **2** (*ministers who urge the members of their congregation not to err*) do wrong, sin, behave badly, misbehave, transgress. ▼

---

err on the side of (something) to be guilty of what might be seen as a fault in order to avoid an opposite and even greater fault (*He tended to err on the side of leniency when punishing children*). **to err is human** it is part of human nature to do wrong or sin at some point.

---

errand *n* task, job, chore, assignment, mission.▼

---

a fool's errand a journey or task that turns out to have been a waste of time, a pointless or useless journey or task (*They sent us on a fool's errand to the bank—it was closed on Saturdays*).

---

erratic *adj* **1** (*worried about her erratic behaviour*) inconsistent, irregular, variable, unstable, unpredictable, unreliable, capricious. **2** (*a driver steering an erratic course*) wandering, meandering, wavering.

erroneous *adj* (*an erroneous statement*) wrong, incorrect, inaccurate, untrue, false, mistaken.

error *n* **1** (*an error in their calculation of the building costs*) mistake, inaccuracy, miscalculation, blunder, fault, oversight, (*inf*) slip-up. **2** (*see the error of his ways*) wrongdoing, sin, evil, misbehaviour, misconduct. ▼

---

trial and error the trying out of various methods or approaches of doing something until one finds the right one (*They found a cure for her allergy by trial and error*).

---

erupt *vb* **1** (*A flow of lava erupted from the volcano*) to be discharged, gush, pour out, issue, belch. **2** (*violence erupted between the two gangs of football supporters*) break out, flare up, blow up, burst forth.

eruption *n* **1** (*an eruption of violence*) outburst, outbreak, flare-up. **2** (*an eruption on her face*) rash, inflammation, outbreak.

escalate *vb* **1** (*The violence has escalated/The war escalated*) increase, intensify, heighten, accelerate, be stepped up, mushroom. **2** (*Prices have escalated*) go up, mount, climb, soar.

escapade *n* (*The children were punished for their escapades*) adventure, prank, stunt, trick, (*inf*) lark.

escape *vb* **1** (*The prisoners escaped from the jail*) get away, run away, abscond, bolt, break free, make one's getaway, (*inf*) do a runner, (*inf*) do a bunk. **2** (*succeed in escaping punishment*) avoid, evade, dodge, elude, steer clear of, sidestep. **3** (*gas escaping*) leak, seep out, discharge, spurt, gush.

escort *n* (*require an escort for the dance*) partner, companion, attendant, (*inf*) date.

especially *adv* **1** (*The products sell well, especially in the summer*) particularly, above all, chiefly, mainly, principally. **2** (*designed especially for her*) specially, specifically, expressly, particularly, exclusively.

espionage *n* (*a novel about espionage*) spying, intelligence, undercover work.

essay *n* (*asked to write an essay on a favourite author*) composition, dissertation, paper, article, thesis, discourse.

essence *n* **1** (*the essence of good speech*) essential part, main ingredient, nature, kernel, quintessence. **2** (*vanilla essence*) extract, concentrate, distillate. ▼

---

of the essence of the greatest importance (*Speed is of the essence if we are to reach the hospital in time*).

---

essential *adj* **1** (*essential equipment/It is essential to arrive early*) necessary, vital, indispensable, crucial, important. **2** (*the essential theme of the novel*) basic, fundamental, inherent, principal.

establish *vb* **1** (*establish a computing firm*) set up, form, found, institute, create, inaugurate. **2** (*try to establish his innocence*) prove, show, demonstrate, verify, certify.

estate *n* **1** (*He owns a town house and a country estate*) property, land property, lands, land-holding. **2** (*His estate at his death amounted to nearly a million pounds*) assets, resources, effects, possessions, belongings, wealth. **3** (*a housing estate*) area, development.

esteem *n* (*hold the writer in great esteem*) regard, respect, admiration, honour, reverence, appreciation.

estimate *vb* (*estimate the cost of repairs*) work out, calculate, assess, gauge, reckon, guess, (*inf*) guesstimate.

estimation *n* **1** (*In our estimation he is the best player*) opinion, view, judgement, consideration, way of thinking, feeling. **2** (*When she lied she went down in our estimation*) good opinion, regard, respect, admiration, approval, favour.

estuary *n* (*boats in the estuary*) river mouth, inlet, cove, bay.

eternal *adj* **1** (*life eternal*) everlasting, endless, without end, never-ending, perpetual, immortal, infinite. **2** (*We are tired of their eternal quarrelling*) endless, never-ending, incessant, ceaseless, non-stop, constant, continuous, continual, interminable, unremitting. ▼

---

eternal rest death (*The old man has gone to his eternal rest after enduring much pain*). **the eternal triangle** a relationship involving one man and two women or one woman and two men (*He sometimes lives with *his wife and sometimes with his girlfriend—a definite case of the eternal triangle*). **The Eternal City** Rome.

ethical *adj* (*not an ethical thing to do*) moral, honourable, virtuous, good, decent, honest.

ethnic *adj* (*ethnic restaurants/ ethnic customs*) racial, cultural, national.

etiquette *n* (*wedding etiquette*) rules of conduct, accepted behaviour, protocol, custom, convention.

eulogy *n* (*a eulogy about their team's performance*) praise, accolade, acclamation, applause, tribute, paean, panegyric.

evacuate *vb* **1** (*people asked to evacuate areas likely to be bombed by the enemy*) leave, vacate, quit, abandon, retreat from, (*inf*) pull out. **2** (*The police evacuated everyone from the area*) move out, clear.

evade *vb* **1** (*try to evade her responsibilities*) avoid, escape from, dodge, shirk, side-step, (*inf*) duck. **2** (*succeed in evading the enemy*) avoid, escape from, elude, shake off, give the slip to, keep out of the way of, steer clear of.

even *adj* **1** (*even ground*) level, flat, smooth, uniform. **2** (*The temperature of the room must remain even*) constant, uniform, steady, stable, unchanging. **3** (*We gave the children even amounts of money*) equal, the same, identical, like, similar, comparable. **4** (*The score was even at half-time*) level, equal, all square, tied, drawn, (*inf*) even steven. **5** (*people of an even disposition*) even-tempered, calm, placid, serene, composed, unexcitable, unperturbable. ▼

break even to have one's losses balanced by one's gains or profit (*We did not make much money from the restaurant in its first year but at least we broke even*). **get even with (someone)** to be revenged on (someone), to do something bad to (someone) who has done something bad to one (*When they deliberately damaged his car he vowed to get even with them*). **get on an even keel** to get into a steady or stable situation with no sudden changes (*We would be all right if we could just get our finances on an even keel*).

event *n* **1** (*The sad and happy events in their lives*) happening, occurrence, occasion, episode, incident, experience. **2** (*the track events in the Olympic Games*) contest, competition, match. ▼

in the event as it happened, as it turned out (*We thought our team would lose but in the event they won easily*). **in the event of (something)** if something should happen (*You will get your money back in the event of the goods being faulty*).

eventually *adv* (*She took her driving test several times and eventually passed*) in the end, finally, at last, ultimately.

everlasting *adj* **1** (*everlasting life*) eternal, endless, without end, never-ending, perpetual, abiding, immortal, infinite. **2** (*their everlasting complaints*) endless, never-ending, non-stop, incessant, ceaseless, continuous, continual.

evict *adj* (*get evicted from their*

house for not paying the rent/get evicted from the club for being under age) throw out, put out, turn out, eject, remove, oust, (*inf*) chuck out, kick out, turf out.

evidence *n* **1** (*They will have to produce evidence of his guilt*) proof, confirmation, verification, corroboration. **2** (*There was evidence of a struggle at the scene of the murder*) sign, indication, mark. ▼

---

in evidence easily seen (*The police were very much in evidence at the protest match*). **turn Queen's/King's evidence** to give evidence against a fellow criminal in order to have one's own sentence reduced (*The accused bank robber turned Queen's evidence and gave the police information about his friend who killed the guard*).

---

evident *adj* (*It was evident that he was unwell/an evident improvement*) obvious, clear, apparent, plain, noticeable, conspicuous, perceptible, visible.

evil *adj* (*appalled at his evil deeds*) wicked, bad, wrong, sinful, immoral, villainous. ▼

---

put off the evil hour to keep postponing something unpleasant (*He knows that he should make an appointment with the dentist but he is putting off the evil hour*).

---

exacerbate *vb* (*His remarks exacerbated the situation*) make worse, worsen, aggravate, intensify, add fuel to the fire.

exact *adj* **1** (*an exact description*) precise, accurate, close, faithful, true. **2** (*the exact time*) precise, accurate, right.

exacting *adj* (*an exacting task*) demanding, difficult, hard, arduous, tough, laborious, taxing, onerous.

exactly *adv* **1** (*His estimate was exactly right*) precisely, absolutely, just, quite, (*inf*) on the nail, (*inf*) bang on, (*inf*) spot on. **2** (*repeat the information exactly*) word for word, verbatim, literally, to the letter, closely, faithfully.

exaggerate *vb* **1** (*exaggerate the length of time the journey took*) overstate, overemphasize, overstress, overestimate. **2** (*It's not that expensive—you're exaggerating*) overstate, embroider, embellish, overdraw, add colour, over-elaborate, make a mountain out of a molehill, (*inf*) lay it on with a trowel, (*inf*) lay it on thick.

examine *vb* **1** (*It is necessary to examine the facts*) look at, study, inspect, survey, analyse, review, observe, check out, weigh up. **2** (*examine a patient*) look at, check over, give a check-up, assess.

example *n* **1** (*buy an example of the artist's early work*) sample, specimen, instance, illustration. **2** (*follow his brother's example*) model, pattern, standard. **3** (*punish some pupils as an example to the others*) warning, caution, lesson.

exasperate *vb* (*She was exasperated by their objections*) annoy, irritate, anger, infuriate, incense, enrage.

excavate *vb* **1** (*excavate a trench*) dig, dig out, hollow out, scoop out. **2** (*excavate an ancient Roman settlement*) unearth, dig up, uncover, disinter.

exceed *vb* **1** (*His talent as a musician exceeds that of his brother*) be greater than, be more than, be superior to, surpass, outstrip, outshine, overshadow, top, cap. **2** (*exceed the speed limit*) go beyond, go over, do more than, overstep. **3** (*at a price not exceeding £5000*) be greater than, be more than, go beyond, top.

exceedingly *adv* (*She was exceedingly beautiful*) extremely, exceptionally, extraordinarily, tremendously, enormously, vastly, greatly, highly, hugely.

excellent *adj* (*an excellent player*) very good, first-rate, first-class, great, fine, distinguished, superb, outstanding, marvellous, brilliant, (*inf*) Al, (*inf*) top-notch.

exception *n* **1** (*the whole school will go with the exception of the first class*) exclusion, omission. **2** (*Their case is an exception*) special case, anomaly, deviation, irregularity, oddity, freak.▼

---

the exception that proves the rule the fact that an exception has to be made for a particular example of something proves that the general rule is valid (*All the family have black hair. The youngest member is the exception that proves the rule*). **take exception to (something)** to take offence at (something) (*She took exception to his remarks about her outfit*).

---

exceptional *adj* **1** (*exceptional weather for the time of year*) unusual, uncommon, abnormal, out of the ordinary, extraordinary, atypical, rare. **2** (*people of exceptional talent*) excellent, extraordinary, remarkable, outstanding, phenomenal.

excerpt *n* (*read an excerpt from one of Shakespeare's plays*) extract, passage, quotation, quote, piece, section.

excessive *n* **1** (*an excessive amount of water*) too much, extravagant, immoderate, undue, inordinate, (*inf*) over the top. **2** (*The prices seem excessive*) exorbitant, outrageous, unreasonable.

exchange *vb* (*The children agreed to exchange toys*) swap, trade, barter.

excite *vb* **1** (*the thought of the party excited the children*) thrill, stimulate, rouse, animate, (*inf*) turn on. **2** (*excite feelings of anger in the crowd*) cause, bring about, rouse, arouse, incite, provoke, kindle, stir up.

exclamation *n* (*He gave an exclamation of surprise*) cry, call, shout, yell, shriek.

exclude *vb* **1** (*She was excluded from their talks*) leave out, keep out, debar, bar, ban. **2** (*They cannot exclude the possibility of murder*) rule out, set aside, preclude, eliminate.

exclusive *adj* **1** (*an exclusive club*) select, private, fashionable, chic. **2** (*gave them her exclusive attention*) complete, undivided, full, absolute, entire, total. **3** (*the price exclusive of drinks*) excluding, not including, omitting, not counting, excepting.

excruciating *adj* (*an excruciating pain in her stomach*) agonizing, acute, severe, intense, extreme.

excursion *n* (*go on an excursion to the seaside*) trip, expedition, jaunt, outing, journey.

excuse *vb* **1** (*impossible to excuse their crime*) forgive, pardon, condone, justify, defend. **2** (*ask to be excused from the gymnastics class*) let off, exempt, release.

excuse *n* **1** (*their excuse for not arriving on time*) defence, justification, reason, grounds, vindication. **2** (*His supposed illness was just an excuse for staying off school*) pretext, cover-up, front, pretence.

execute *vb* **1** (*Murderers used to be executed*) put to death, kill, hang. **2** (*execute a plan*), carry out, perform, accomplish, fulfil, put into effect, implement.

exercise *vb* **1** (*The women were exercising in order to keep fit*) do exercises, work out, train. **2** (*try to exercise a little patience*) use, employ, apply, exert.

exercise *n* **1** (*do exercises every morning to keep fit*) physical training, work-out, drill. **2** (*Some exercise is necessary to keep healthy*) activity, physical exertion, physical effort. **3** (*pupils given an English exercise*) task, piece of work, problem.

exert *vb* **1** (*They could finish the job in time if they exerted themselves*) make an effort, spare no effort, put oneself out, try hard, do one's best, strive, struggle, strain, labour. **2** (*It was necessary to exercise some pressure*) employ, use, apply, wield.

exhaust *vb* **1** (*The long walk exhausted her*) tire, tire out, wear out, fatigue, weary, (*inf*) poop, (*inf*) knacker. **2** (*We have exhausted our supplies of food*) use up, consume, finish, deplete, expend.

exhaustive *adj* (*The police made an exhaustive search*) intensive, all-out, comprehensive, extensive, thorough.

exhibit *vb* **1** (*The firm exhibited their latest works*) put on show, show, put on display, display, put on view, demonstrate, present. **2** (*exhibit patience/exhibit signs of improvement*) show, indicate, reveal, demonstrate, express.

exhibition *n* **1** (*a book exhibition*) show, display, demonstration, presentation, fair, exposition. **2** (*an exhibition of bad temper*) display, show, expression, indication, demonstration.▼

---

make an exhibition of oneself to behave embarrassingly in public.

---

exile *vb* (*exiled from their native land*) banish, expatriate, deport, expel, outlaw.

exile *n* **1** (*sent into exile*) banishment, expatriation, deportation. **2** (*exiles from their native land*) expatriate, deportee, outlaw, refugee, displaced person.

exist *vb* **1** (*children believing that fairies exist*) be, have being, have existence, live, be living. **2** (*difficult to exist on such a low income*) live, stay alive, survive.

exit *n* (*the exit from the cinema*) way out, egress.

expand *vb* **1** (*substances that expand when heated*) grow larger, get larger, increase in size, swell, distend. **2** (*expand the business*) make larger, make bigger, increase, amplify, add to, extend.

expanse *n* (*an expanse of blue water*) stretch, area, extent, tract, sweep.

expect *vb* **1** (*I expect that they will arrive soon*) believe, think, assume, suppose, imagine, presume, surmise. **2** (*I am expecting a parcel from them*) await, wait for, look for, anticipate, hope for.

expedite *vb* (*try to expedite the process*) speed up, hasten, hurry, accelerate, step up.

expedition *n* **1** (*an expedition to the

centre of the jungle) journey, exploration, safari, undertaking, quest. **2** (*a shopping expedition*) trip, outing, excursion, jaunt. **3** (*the members of the expedition to climb Everest*) group, team, party, company.

expel *vb* **1** (*expel him from school/ expel him from the club*) throw out, oust, drum out, bar, ban, blackball. **2** (*expel them from their native land*) banish, exile, drive out, cast out, expatriate, deport.

expense *n* **1** (*victory in the war at the expense of many lives*) cost, sacrifice. **2** (*go to a great deal of expense to buy her a present*) outlay, cost, spending. ▼

---

at the expense of (someone or **something)** causing harm loss, embarrassment, etc (*He got to the top of the mountain but at the expense of his health*).

---

expensive *adj* (*expensive clothes*) costly, high-priced, dear, overpriced, exorbitant, extortionate, (*inf*) steep.

experience *n* **1** (*a terrifying experience*) event, incident, occurrence, happening, affair, episode. **2** (*a job requiring experience as well as a university degree*) practical knowledge, skill, practice, training, (*inf*) know-how, (*inf*) hands-on experience.

experiment *n* (*medical experiments to find new drugs*) test, trial, investigation, research, pilot study.

expert *n* (*an expert on local history*) authority, specialist, professional, pundit, (*inf*) buff.

expert *adj* (*an expert chess player*) knowledgeable, specialist, experienced, professional, skilful, proficient, adept, (*inf*) crack.

expire *vb* **1** (*Her membership of the club has expired*) run out, be no longer valid, end, come to an end, finish, stop, cease, lapse. **2** (*people expiring from lack of food*) die, pass away, breathe one's last, decease.

explain *vb* **1** (*explain how to work the machine*) give an explanation of, describe, define, make clear, spell out, throw light on. **2** (*called upon to explain their actions*) give an explanation of, account for, give a reason for, justify, defend, vindicate.

explanation *n* **1** (*a clear explanation as to how the machine works*) description, definition, clarification, interpretation. **2** (*unable to accept their explanation for their absence*) account, reason, grounds, excuse, justification, defence, vindication

explode *vb* **1** (*The bomb exploded*) blow up, go of, detonate, burst. **2** (*The gas boiler exploded*) blow up, burst open, fly into pieces, erupt. **3** (*explode his theory*) disprove, discredit, refute, invalidate, debunk.

exploit *n* (*a book about the exploits of the knights of old*) deed, feat, adventure, stunt.

exploit *vb* **1** (*exploit the resources which they have*) make use of, use, utilize, put to good use, turn to one's advantage, profit by, make capital out of. **2** (*a mill-owner who exploited the workers/a man who exploited his friends*) make use of, take advantage of, abuse, impose upon.

explore *vb* **1** (*explore areas of jungle*) travel in, survey, reconnoitre. **2** (*explore every possibility*) examine, look into, investigate, inquire into, consider, research.

explosion *n* **1** (*There was a loud*

explosion and we discovered the boiler had blown up) bang, blast, boom, rumble, crash, crack, report. 2 (*an explosion in the population figures*) increase, escalation, mushrooming, rocketing.

expose *vb* **1** (*expose her skin to the sun*) bare, lay bare, uncover. **2** (*newspapers exposing the details of the scandal*) reveal, disclose, divulge, make known, uncover, unveil. **3** (*expose the baby to harsh weather*) lay open to, leave unprotected by, put at risk from.

express *vb* **1** (*express their gratitude in a short speech*) voice, state, put into words, articulate, utter, make known, communicate. **2** (*express their appreciation with a gift of money*) show, demonstrate, indicate, convey. **3** (*express juice from the oranges*) press, squeeze, force out, extract.

expression *n* **1** (*We could tell from her expression that she was angry*) face, countenance, look, appearance, air. **2** (*find the right expression to say what she means*) word, words, phrase, term, wording, language, turn of phrase, phraseology. **3** (*play the violin piece with expression*) feeling, emotion, passion, intensity, vividness.

extant *adj* (*a species of bird that is still extant*) still existing, in existence, living, alive, existent, surviving, remaining.

extend *vb* **1** (*extend the territory which he rules over*) expand, increase, enlarge, lengthen. **2** (*extend the ladder to its full length*) stretch out, draw out, lengthen, elongate. **3** (*extend the period of his employment*) increase, prolong, lengthen, stretch out, protract. **4** (*The lake extends for many miles*) continue, stretch, stretch out, carry on, run on. **5** (*extend a warm welcome to the guests*) offer, give, proffer, hold out.

extensive *adj* **1** (*a house with extensive grounds*) large, large-scale, sizeable, substantial, vast, immense. **2** (*have extensive knowledge of the Bible*) comprehensive, thorough, wide-ranging, wide, broad. **3** (*The storm caused extensive damage to the crops*) great, widespread, wholesale, universal.

extent *n* **1** (*the extent of her knowledge/the extent of the damage*) scope, range, coverage, degree. **2** (*the extent of the land around the house*) area, expanse, length, stretch.

exterior *adj* (*the exterior surface*) outside, outer, outermost, outward, external, surface.

extinct *adj* **1** (*a species of bird now extinct*) died out, wiped out, gone, defunct. **2** (*an extinct volcano*) inactive, extinguished, burnt out.

extinguish *vb* (*extinguish the candles*) put out, blow out, quench, snuff out.

extra *adj* **1** (*They need extra help to finish the job*) more, additional, added, further, supplementary, auxiliary, subsidiary. **2** (*We have extra food in our picnic—would you like some?*) surplus, spare, left over, superfluous, excess, reserve.

extract *vb* (*extract a tooth*) pull out, draw out, take out, remove.

extract *n* (*read extracts from her novel on the radio*) excerpt, passage, selection, quotation, citation.

extraordinary *adj* **1** (*have an extraordinary memory*) exceptional, unusual, uncommon, rare, striking, remarkable. phenomenal. **2** (*It was extraordinary that* *she survived*) amazing, astonishing, remarkable, astounding, surprising, strange.

extravagant *adj* **1** (*an extravagant way of life/It was extravagant to buy such an expensive dress*) spendthrift, thriftless, improvident, profligate, wasteful. **2** (*He tried to flatter her by paying her extravagant compliments*) exaggerated, excessive, outrageous, absurd, (*inf*) over the top.

extreme *adj* **1** (*in the extreme north of the country*) farthest, furthest, outermost, most remote. **2** (*in extreme danger*) very great, greatest, maximum, utmost, severe. **3** (*people who hold extreme political views*) immoderate, fanatical, exaggerated, intemperate.

extremely *adv* (*She is extremely beautiful*) very, exceedingly, exceptionally, extraordinarily, markedly, uncommonly.

eye *n* **1** (*have sharp eyes*) eyesight, sight, vision. **2** (*The police are keeping an eye on her/She is under the eagle eye of the head teacher*) watch, observation, notice, surveillance. ▼

---

be one in the eye for (someone) to be something unpleasant that happens to someone who deserves it. **have an eye for (something)** to be a good judge of (something), to be able to spot (something) as a good example (*She has an eye for a bargain in the housing market*).

F

fabric *n* **1** (*curtains made of a brightly coloured fabric*) cloth, material, textile, stuff. **2** (*the fabric of the building/the fabric of society*) framework, frame, structure, constitution.

fabulous *adj* **1** (*stories about fabulous creatures such as dragons*) mythical, imaginary, fictitious, fictional, legendary. **2** (*an emperor of fabulous wealth*) incredible, unbelievable, unimaginable, inconceivable, astonishing. **3** (*They had a fabulous time on holiday*) marvellous, wonderful, superb, great, (*inf*) fab, (*inf*) super.

face *n* **1** (*She had a beautiful face*) countenance, features. **2** (*She came rushing out with an angry face*) expression, look, air. **3** (*the faces of a cube*) front, side, surface. **4** (*She was afraid of losing face in the firm*) prestige, status, standing, dignity. **5** (*She had the face to call us liars*) impudence, impertinence, audacity, effrontery, cheek, (*inf*) nerve, (*inf*) brass neck.▼

---

on the face of it judging from what one can see or find out from first impressions, especially when this turns out to be wrong (*On the face of it he seemed ideal for the job but he turned out to be hopeless*).
take (someone or something) at face value to judge (someone or something) on outward appearance only without bothering to get any more information (*He seemed genuine and she took him at face value but he turned out to be a crook*).

---

face *vb* **1** (*a block of flats facing the sea*) look on to, overlook, be opposite to, front on to. **2** (*They are facing many difficulties*) meet, encounter, confront.

facetious *adj* (*Please don't make facetious remarks—it is a serious situation*) flippant, frivolous, lighthearted, joking, jocular, funny, amusing.

fact *n* **1** (*difficult to separate fact from fiction*) reality, actuality, truth. **2** (*wish to have all the facts of the case*) detail, particular, factor, piece of information, piece of data, circumstance.

factor *n* (*consider all the factors connected with the situation*) element, point, detail, feature, item, circumstance.

fade *vb* **1** (*The curtains had faded in the sunlight*) lose colour, become bleached, become pale, become washed out, dull, dim. **2** (*fresh flowers that had faded*) wilt, wither, droop, die. **3** (*Hope had faded/Memories of the occasion had faded*) dim, grow less, die away, dwindle, grow faint, vanish, die.

fail *vb* **1** (*Their attempt to climb the mountain failed*) be unsuccessful, fall through, be in vain, come to nothing, come to grief, (*inf*) flop. **2** (*They failed the exam*) not pass, (*inf*) flunk. **3** (*The engine failed*) break down, stop working, cut out, (*inf*) conk out. **4** (*He failed to keep us informed*) omit, neglect, forget. **5** (*Her health is failing*) decline, deteriorate, diminish, dwindle, wane. **6** (*His business has failed*) collapse, crash, go under, go bankrupt, go to the wall, fold, (*inf*) go bust, (*inf*) flop.

failing *n* (*Untidiness is his main failing*) fault, shortcoming, weakness, flaw, imperfection, defect, foible.

failure *n* (*Our attempt was a complete failure*) non-success, disaster, fiasco, (*inf*) flop.

faint *adj* **1** (*faint traces of paint on the table*) indistinct, unclear, dim, faded, obscure. **2** (*hear a faint sound of laughter*) indistinct, soft, low, muted, feeble. **3** (*a faint smell of violets*) slight, indistinct, delicate. **4** (*have a faint chance of winning the match*) slight, small, remote, vague. **5** (*feel faint*) dizzy, giddy, light-headed, (*inf*) muzzy. ▼

---

faint heart never won fair lady if you want to achieve what you desire you must be bold and determined. **not have the faintest** (*inf*) not to know at all, to know absolutely nothing about something (*She thought that I knew where he had gone but I didn't have the faintest*) <Short for not to have the faintest idea>.

---

faint *vb* (*She fainted in the heat*) pass out, collapse, black out, lose consciousness, swoon, (*inf*) conk out.

fair *adj* **1** (*She had fair hair*) blond, yellow, flaxen, pale, light brown. **2** (*the accused was given a fair trial*) just, impartial, unprejudiced, unbiased, objective. **3** (*a fair judge*) fair-minded, just, impartial, unprejudiced, unbiased, open-minded, honest. **4** (*the weather was fair for the picnic*) fine, dry, bright. **5** (*The standard of his work is just fair*) satisfactory, all right, middling, so-so, average, adequate. ▼

---

by fair means or foul in any way possible, whether just or unjust (*He intends to get that by fair means or foul*).

---

fairly *adv* (*She was fairly good at playing the piano*) quite, rather, somewhat, reasonably, passably, tolerably, (*inf*) pretty.

faith *n* **1** (*they have faith in their doctor*) trust, confidence, belief, reliance. **2** (*they are of the Christian faith*) religion, creed, belief, persuasion. ▼

---

keep faith with (someone) be loyal to (someone or something (*They tried to get her to betray her leader but she kept faith with him*).

---

faithful *adj* **1** (*the leader's faithful followers*) loyal, constant, true, devoted, dependable, reliable, trustworthy, staunch. **2** (*a faithful account of the event/a faithful copy of the picture*) accurate, true, exact, precise, close.

fake *adj* **1** (*fake ten pound notes*) counterfeit, forged, fraudulent, false, imitation, (*inf*) phoney. **2** (*wearing a string of fake pearls*) imitation, artificial, synthetic, simulated, mock, sham, ersatz.

fall *vb* **1** (*The leaves fall in autumn*) drop, descend. **2** (*The child fell as she left the bus*) fall down, trip over, stumble, topple over, go head over heels, (*inf*) take a spill. **3** (*The level of the water in the river was falling in the drought*) sink, subside, abate. **4** (*The price of houses has fallen*) decrease, decline, go down, grow less, plummet, slump. **5** (*a memorial to the soldiers who fell in battle*) die, be killed, be slain, perish, be a fatality, be a casualty. **6** (*Her birthday falls on a Monday this year*) be, take place, occur, happen. ▼

---

fall flat to have no effect, to fail to have the expected or desired effect, to fail (*The comedian was supposed to be very funny but his jokes fell flat*). **fall over oneself to (do something)** to set about (doing something) with great willingness and eagerness (*They were all falling over themselves to be charming to the wealthy man*).

---

false *adj* **1** (*They gave a false account of their movements to the police*) untrue, wrong, incorrect, inaccurate, erroneous. **2** (*He gave a false name*) assumed, made-up, invented, fictitious, (*inf*) phoney. **3** (*false friends*) disloyal, unfaithful, faithless, treacherous, untrustworthy. ▼

---

under false pretences by being deceitful (*The burglars got into the house under false pretences by pretending to be workmen*).

---

falsehood *n* (*accuse him of telling falsehoods*) lie, untruth, fib, story, (*inf*) porky.

falter *vb* **1** (*The young boxer faltered when he saw the size of his opponent*) hesitate, waver, flinch, stumble. **2** (*The speaker was nervous and faltered over his speech*) stumble, stutter, stammer.

fame *n* (*His fame as an artist has spread/seek fame in Hollywood*) renown, eminence, distinction, notability, greatness, glory, honour.

familiar *adj* **1** (*The old man was a familiar sight in the village shop*) well-known, common, customary, accustomed, regular, commonplace, everyday. **2** (*workers who were familiar with the computing system*) acquainted with, conversant with, versed in, experienced in, with knowledge of. ▼

---

familiarity breeds contempt people do not appreciate people or things that they know very well or see frequently.

---

family *n* **1** (*people of noble family*) ancestry, parentage, descent, extraction, blood, line. **2** (*The poor old woman has no family*) relatives, relations, people, one's own flesh and blood, next of kin. **3** (*The couple have no family*) children, offspring, progeny, (*inf*) kids.▼

---

run in the family to be a characteristic found in many members of the same family (*Red hair runs in the family*).

---

fan *n* (*a football fan/a fan of the pop star*) admirer, follower, enthusiast, devotee, fanatic, addict, aficionado, (*inf*) buff, (*inf*) freak.

fancy *n* **1** (*the fancy of the poet*) imagination, creativity. **2** (*The person from Mars was just a fancy on the child's part*) figment of the imagination, hallucination, illusion, delusion, fantasy. **3** (*have *a fancy for some chocolate*) desire, urge, notion, wish, want, hankering, longing, yearning, (*inf*) yen. ▼

---

footloose and fancy free to be not married, engaged or in love with someone (*He said that he was engaged once but he is now footloose and fancy free*).

---

fancy *vb* **1** (*He fancied he saw a ghostly figure*) imagine, think, believe. **2** (*He said that he fancied a drink*) would like, wish, want, desire, hanker after, long for, yearn for, (*inf*) have a yen for. ▼

---

fancy one's chances to think that one is highly likely to be successful (*He is the youngest player in the tennis tournament but he certainly fancies his chances*).

---

fancy *adj* (*fancy patterns/fancy decorations*) ornate, elaborate, ornamental, decorated, adorned, embellished, showy, (*inf*) jazzy.

fantastic *adj* **1** (*He had fantastic notions about seeing aliens from Mars*) fanciful, imaginary, wild, strange. **2** (*fantastic figures and shapes in his painting*) strange, weird, bizarre, outlandish, fanciful, whimsical. **3** (*He earns a fantastic amount of money*) huge, enormous, tremendous. **4** (*He thought the concert was fantastic*) marvellous, wonderful, sensational, superb, excellent.

fantasy *n* **1** (*a children's book which is full of fantasy*) fancy, imagination, creativity, originality, vision. **2** (*She is always having fantasies about winning a lot of money*) flight of fancy, dream, daydream, pipe-dream, reverie, illusion.

far *adv* **1** (*it is not far to the next village*) a long way, a great distance. **2** (*It is far too soon to know*) by a long way, to a great extent, very much. ▼

---

go far to be very successful, especially in one's career (*The schoolmaster said that the boy would go far*). **go too far** to do or say something that is beyond the limits of what is acceptable (*He has always had a hot temper but he went too far when he bit a policeman*).

---

far *adj* (*the far places of the world*) far-away, far-off, distant, remote, far-flung.

fare *n* (*Train fares have gone up*) ticket, charge, cost, price.

far-fetched *adj* (*They found his story rather far-fetched*) unlikely, improbable, implausible, incredible, unbelievable, unconvincing .

farm *vb* (*farm land in the north*) cultivate, till, work.

fascinate *vb* (*The children were fascinated by the mime artist*) captivate, enchant, enthral, entrance, hold spellbound, charm, absorb, engross.

fashion *n* **1** (*the fashions of the nineteenth century*) style, trend, taste, craze, vogue. **2** (*She has a job in fashion*) clothes, the clothes industry, couture, (*inf*) the rag trade. **3** (*She arranged things in an organized fashion*) way, manner, method, style, system.

fashionable *adj* (*fashionable clothes/furniture that is no longer fashionable*) in fashion, stylish, up-to-date, in vogue, modern, contemporary, (*inf*) trendy.

fast *adj* **1** (*at a fast pace*) quick, rapid, swift, brisk, speedy, hurried. **2** (*fast colours*) fixed, indelible, permanent. ▼

---

pull a fast one on (someone) to succeed in tricking or deceiving (someone) (*She pulled a fast one on her friend by selling him her old car, which she knew was in bad condition*) <From bowling a fast ball in cricket>.

---

fast *adv* **1** (*walk fast*) quickly, rapidly, swiftly, briskly, speedily, hurriedly, like the wind. **2** (*a lorry stuck fast in the mud*) firmly, tightly, securely, immovably. **3** (*children who were fast asleep*) sound, deeply.

fast *vb* (*people who fast during certain religious holidays/fasting in aid of a famine charity*) go without food, eat nothing, go hungry, starve oneself, deny oneself food.

fasten *vb* **1** (*She fastened a brooch to her dress*) attach, fix, clip, pin. **2** (*fasten the dog to the gatepost*) attach, tie, bind, tether. **3** (*The links of the chain are fastened to each other*) join, connect, couple, unite, link.

fat *adj* **1** (*fat people trying to lose weight*) plump, obese, stout, overweight, portly, chubby, tubby, podgy, flabby. **2** (*fat reference books*) thick, big, substantial. **3** (*people told to avoid fat substances for the sake of their health*) fatty, greasy, oily.

fat *n* **1** (*require some form of fat to make a cake*) animal fat, vegetable fat, lard, butter, margarine. **2** (*She was embarrassed by her fat*) fatness, plumpness, obesity, stoutness, portliness, chubbiness, tubbiness, flab. ▼

---

the fat is in the fire trouble has been started and nothing can be done to stop it (*The fat was in the fire when his boss discovered that he was at a football match instead of being at work*) <From the fact that fat causes a fire to flare up>.

---

fatal *adj* (*a fatal blow/a fatal illness*) mortal, deadly, lethal, killing, terminal.

fatality *n* (*There were several fatalities in the motorway crash*) death, dead, casualty, mortality.

fate *n* (*She wondered what fate had in store for him*) destiny, providence, chance, luck, fortune, the stars, nemesis. ▼

---

seal (someone's) fate to ensure that something, usually something unpleasant, happens to someone (*Her fate was sealed when the teachers discovered that she had been cheating in the exam*).

---

fateful *adj* (*a fateful meeting*) critical, crucial, decisive, momentous, important.

father *n* **1** (*Her father left her a lot of money*) male parent, (*inf*) dad, (*inf*) daddy, (*inf*) pa, (*inf*) old man. **2** (*the father of modern medicine*) founder, originator, initiator, creator, architect.

fatigue *n* (*He was suffering from fatigue after climbing the mountain*) tiredness, overtiredness, weariness, exhaustion.

fatty *adj* (*fatty foods*) fat, greasy, oily.

fault *n* **1** (*discover a fault in the material*) flaw, defect, imperfection. **2** (*one of the main faults in her character*) flaw, defect, failing, shortcoming, weakness, weak point, deficiency. **3** (*The accident was her fault*) blame, responsibility.

faulty *adj* **1** (*a faulty lock*) broken, damaged, defective, unsound. **2**

(*take the faulty goods back to the shop*) flawed, defective, imperfect.

favour *n* **1** (*He did her a favour by giving her a lift*) good turn, good deed, service, kindness. **2** (*He looked on the new scheme with favour*) approval, approbation, goodwill, friendliness. ▼

---

curry favour with (someone) to try to win the approval or friendship of (someone) by the use of insincere flattery or by being extremely agreeable to (him or her) (*She is currying favour with the teacher to try to get into the school play*).

---

favourable *adj* **1** (*in less favourable circumstances/favourable winds*) advantageous, beneficial, helpful, promising, auspicious. **2** (*She hoped to make a favourable impression on her friend's parents*) good, pleasing, agreeable. **3** (*He received a favourable report from his teacher*) good, approving, praising, commendatory, enthusiastic.

favourite *adj* (*the child's favourite toy*) best-loved, dearest, favoured, chosen, preferred.

favourite *n* (*The youngest child is her grandfather's favourite*) pet, darling, idol, (*inf*) blue-eyed boy/girl.

fear *n* (*filled with fear at the sight of the strange man*) fright, terror, alarm, panic, apprehensiveness, dread, horror, nervousness. ▼

---

there is no fear of (something) it is not at all likely that (something) will happen (*There is no fear of our getting any extra money*).

---

fear *vb* **1** (*They fear their grandfather*) be afraid of, be scared of, be apprehensive of, dread. **2** (*We fear for their safety*) worry, be anxious, feel concerned. **3** (*We fear that they could be right*) be afraid, suspect, have a suspicion.

fearful *adj* **1** (*They were fearful of disturbing the guard dogs*) afraid, frightened, terrified, alarmed, apprehensive. **2** (*The smashed cars were a fearful sight*) terrible, frightful, appalling, ghastly, horrific, horrible, shocking. **3** (*The house was in a fearful mess*) terrible, frightful, appalling, very great.

fearless *adj* (*fearless soldiers fighting the enemy/fearless explorers*) brave, courageous, gallant, valiant, intrepid, bold, heroic.

feasible *adj* (*It was not feasible to leave earlier*) possible, practicable, workable, reasonable, realistic, within reason.

feat *n* (*read about the daring feats of the knights of old*) deed, act, action, exploit, achievement.

feather *n* (*the bird's feathers*) plumage, plumes, down. ▼

---

a feather in one's cap something of which one can be justly proud (*Winning the tournament was a real feather in his cap as he was the youngest person taking part*) <Perhaps from the custom of American Indians who wore feathers on their head as a sign of their bravery in war>. **feather one's own nest** to make a profit for oneself, often at the expense of someone else, such as one's employer (*All the time he was storekeeper with the firm he was feathering his own nest*).

---

feature *n* (*the feature of the burglary*

that confused the police) aspect, characteristic, side, detail, quality, peculiarity.

features *npl* (*She had very regular features*) face, countenance.

fee *n* (*the fee for membership of the club*) charge, price, cost, payment, subscription.

feeble *adj* **1** (*people who have grown feeble with age*) weak, weakly, frail, infirm, delicate, failing, helpless, debilitated. **2** (*They made a feeble attempt to get there on time*) ineffective, ineffectual, weak, futile, inadequate.

feed *vb* (*not make enough money to feed the family*) give food to, nourish, provide for, cater for.

feel *vb* **1** (*feel faint at her father's words*) experience, undergo, know, be conscious of, be aware of, notice. **2** (*feel the silky cloth*) touch, stroke, caress, finger, handle, fondle. **3** (*He tried to feel his way to the house in the dark*) grope, fumble. **4** (*The weather feels warmer today*) seem, appear. **5** (*feel the temperature of the water before bathing the baby*) test, try out. **6** (*We feel that we ought to go*) believe, think, consider, be of the opinion, judge. ▼

feeling *n* **1** (*Blind people are able to identify objects by feeling*) feel, touch, sense of touch, **2** (*He could not describe his feelings when he lost his job*) emotion, sentiment, sensation. **3** (*There was a feeling of unhappiness about the place*) feel, atmosphere, mood, impression, air, aura. **4** (*My feeling is that we should go*) thoughts, opinion, view, way of thinking, instinct. **5** (*I had a feeling that he would win*) idea, suspicion, funny feeling, hunch.

feign *vb* **1** (*feign illness*) pretend, fake, simulate, sham, affect, give the appearance of. **2** (*We thought that he was sleeping but he was only feigning*) pretend, put on an act, put it on, fake, sham, act, play-act.

fellow *n* (*a suspicious-looking fellow over there*) man, boy, individual, (*inf*) chap, (*inf*) bloke, (*inf*) guy, (*inf*) character.

fellowship *n* (*Now that she has retired she misses the fellowship of her workmates*) companionship, company, friendship, comradeship.

female *n* (*a club just for females*) woman, lady, girl.

feminine *adj* **1** (*a very feminine young woman/feminine clothes*) womanly, ladylike, soft, delicate. **2** (*a rather feminine man*) effeminate, womanish, unmanly, (*inf*) sissyish, (*inf*).

fence *n* (*build a fence round the garden*) barrier, barricade, railing, paling, hedge, wall. ▼

---

mend fences to put things right after a quarrel or disagreement (*I quarrelled with my sister years ago and I would like to try and mend fences now*). **sit on the fence** to decline or refuse to take sides in a dispute or to commit oneself to a point of view (*Her two best friends are having a terrible argument but she is sitting on the fence because she does not want to offend either of them*).

---

fence *vb* **1** (*fence the garden*) enclose, surround, encircle. **2** (*fence in the cows*) shut in, confine, pen.

fend *vb* (*He tried to fend off his attacker's blows with his arm/a *speaker trying to fend off questions*) ward off, turn aside, deflect, avert, keep off.

ferment *vb* **1** (*beer fermenting in vats*) foam, froth, bubble, effervesce. **2** (*He set out to ferment trouble in the crowd*) cause, incite, excite, provoke, stir up, foment.

ferocious *adj* **1** (*ferocious animals*) fierce, savage, wild. **2** (*He was injured in a ferocious attack*) fierce, savage, brutal, vicious, violent, murderous, barbaric.

fertile *adj* **1** (*fertile soil*) fruitful, productive, rich, fecund. **2** (*a fertile imagination*) inventive, creative, resourceful, ingenious.

fertilizer *n* (*put fertilizer on the garden*) plant food, manure, compost.

fervent *adj* (*his fervent enthusiasm for football/a fervent supporter of animal rights*) passionate, ardent, zealous, devout, vehement, eager, earnest.

festival *n* (*the village's annual festival*) fête, carnival, gala day.

fetch *vb* **1** (*She sent her son to fetch the milk from the shop*) get, go for, bring, carry, collect, transport. **2** (*an antique table that fetched thousands of pounds at the auction*) sell for, go for, realize. ▼

---

fetch and carry for (someone) to run about doing a series of small jobs for (someone) as though one were a servant (*He expects his wife to fetch and carry for him*).

---

feud *n* (*There had been a bitter feud between the families for generations*) vendetta, quarrel, dispute, conflict.

fiasco *n* (*The picnic was a fiasco because of the weather*) disaster, catastrophe, failure, (*inf*) flop.

fickle *adj* (*so fickle that she is always changing boyfriends/fickle weather*) capricious, changeable, variable, unpredictable, unstable, unreliable.

fictitious *adj* **1** (*not a real person but a fictitious character*) fictional, made up, invented, imaginary, unreal, mythical. **2** (*He gave a fictitious address to the police*) false, invented, bogus, fake, sham.

fiddle *vb* **1** (*fiddling with his pencil instead of writing his essay*) play, fidget, toy, twiddle. **2** (*fiddle his accounts*) falsify, forge, (*inf*) cook. ▼

---

fiddle while Rome burns to do absolutely nothing while something important is being ruined, destroyed or damaged (*The government is being accused of fiddling while Rome burns as the rate of unemployment rises*) <The Roman emperor Nero was said to have played on a lyre, a musical instrument similar to a fiddle, while the city of Rome was burning>.

---

fidelity *n* (*a leader who looked for fidelity in his followers*) faithfulness, loyalty, devotion, allegiance, constancy, trustworthiness.

fidget *vb* (*children fidgeting with boredom*) to be restless, wriggle, squirm. **2** (*pupils fidgeting with their pencils*) fiddle, play, toy, twiddle.

field *n* **1** (*look at the cows in the field*) pasture, meadow, paddock. **2** (*He was working in the field of* *computing*) area, sphere, line, speciality. **3** (*the school games field*) ground, pitch, arena, stadium. ▼

---

fresh fields and pastures new new places, new activities (*She is tired of her current job and is seriously thinking about moving abroad to explore fresh fields and pastures new*) <A misquotation from 'Lycidas' by the poet John Milton, who actually wrote 'woods' instead of 'fields'>. **have a field day** to have a very busy, successful or enjoyable day (*The reporters had a field day when the scandal about the filmstar was announced*) <A field day is a day on which soldiers practise for battle in front of high-ranking officers and so is a special occasion>.

---

fierce *adj* **1** (*a fierce animal*) ferocious, savage, wild. **2** (*a fierce attack*) ferocious, savage, brutal, vicious, violent, murderous. **3** (*her fierce love of liberty*) passionate, ardent, intense, fervent. **4** (*a fierce wind*) strong, violent, stormy, blustery. **5** (*face fierce competition in the race*) keen, intense, strong, competitive.

fight *vb* **1** (*enemy armies fighting*) do battle, wage war, take up arms, meet in combat. **2** (*armies fighting a battle*) wage, carry on, be engaged in. **3** (*two men fighting in the street*) exchange blows, hit each other, punch each other, brawl. **4** (*The two sisters are always fighting with each other*) quarrel, argue, bicker, squabble, disagree, (*inf*) fall out, feud. **5** (*decide to fight the council's plans for a new road*) contest, take a stand against, oppose, object to, protest against. ▼

---

fight like Kilkenny cats to fight extremely fiercely (*The boys in the playground were fighting like Kilkenny cats*) <From a story about two cats in the Irish town of Kilkenny which were tied together by their tails and fought each other until only their tails were left>.

---

fight *n* **1** (*Our army lost the fight*) battle, encounter, engagement. **2** (*The champion lost the fight*) boxing match. **3** (*two men in a fight outside the pub*) brawl, fisticuffs, (*inf*) scrap, (*inf*) punch-up. **4** (*She has had a fight with her sister*) quarrel, argument, disagreement, difference of opinion, squabble, dispute, feud.

figure *n* **1** (*write down the figures from 1 to 10*) number, numeral, digit. **2** (*What figure did you have in mind as a salary?*) amount, sum. **3** (*fail to recognize the figures disappearing into the mist*) shape, form, outline, silhouette. **4** (*have rather a plump figure*) body, shape, build, physique. **5** (*a bronze figure of the saint*) likeness, image, statue, carving. **6** (*the figures in the text*) diagram, illustration, drawing, chart.

figure *vb* **1** (*figure out the cost of the holiday*) calculate, count, work out, reckon, add up. **2** (*try to figure out why he did it*) work out, make out, understand, comprehend, fathom. **3** (*His mother figures in his novel*) appear, feature, play a part, be mentioned.

fill *vb* **1** (*fill the supermarket shelves*) load, stock, supply. **2** (*food that will fill the children*) make full, satisfy, stuff. **3** (*The perfume of roses filled the air*) pervade, permeate, spread through. **4** (*They filled the hole with sand*) stop up, block up, bung up, plug. **5** (*fill in the form*) fill up, answer. ▼

---

fill the bill to be exactly what is required (*She was looking for a new hat for the wedding and finally found one that filled the bill*) <Originally referred to a handbill or public notice>.

---

film *n* **1** (*a film of oil on the road*) layer, coat, coating, covering, sheet. **2** (*see it through a film of tears*) haze, mist, blur. **3** (*a Walt Disney film*) movie, picture.

film *vb* (*film the wedding ceremony*) photograph, take photographs of, take pictures of, shoot, video, make a film of, televise.

filter *vb* (*filter the coffee*) strain, sieve, sift.

filth *n* **1** (*an old basement covered in filth*) dirt, grime, muck, mud, squalor, (*inf*) crud. **2** (*complaining about the filth in some magazines*) pornography, obscenity, smut, bawdiness.

filthy *adj* **1** (*filthy houses/filthy hands*) dirty, grimy, grubby, mucky, muddy, squalid, unwashed, unclean. **2** (*filthy literature*) pornographic, obscene, indecent, smutty, bawdy, (*inf*) blue.

final *adj* **1** (*the final minutes of the football match*) last, closing, concluding, finishing, terminal. **2** (*The decision of the judges is final*) conclusive, decisive, unalterable, indisputable, definitive, absolute.

finalize *vb* (*finalize our arrangements*) complete, conclude, settle, put the finishing touches to.

finance *n* **1** (*Once he had got his degree he looked for a job relating to finance*) money matters, money management, economics. **2** (*Our finances are low at this time of year*) money, cash, capital, funds, assets, resources.

finance *vb* (*look for someone to finance*) pay for, fund, provide capital for, provide backing for, subsidize.

find *vb* **1** (*We found a wallet in the street*) come across, stumble on, discover. **2** (*She lost her handbag and never found it*) get back, recover, retrieve. **3** (*doctors trying to find a cure for cancer*) discover, come upon, bring to light, uncover, unearth, hit upon. **4** (*He is trying to find a new job*) get, obtain, acquire, procure. **5** (*She found that the food did not agree with her*) discover, realize, become aware, learn. ▼

---

find one's feet to be in the process of becoming used to a situation (*He is not very experienced in the job yet—he's just finding his feet*). **find out the hard way** to find out something by one's own experience (*We told her that she would not enjoy the job but she had to find out the hard way*).

---

fine *adj* **1** (*hope for a fine day for their picnic*) dry, fair, clear, sunny. **2** (*ornaments made of fine china*) delicate, fragile, dainty. **3** (*summer dresses made of fine material*) light, lightweight, thin, delicate, filmy, flimsy. **4** (*a beach with fine sand*) powdery, fine-grained. **5** (*There is only a fine distinction between the two schemes*) tiny, minute, subtle. **6** (*The musician gave a fine performance*) splendid, excellent, first-class, first-rate, outstanding. **7** (*a wedding party wearing fine* *clothes*) elegant, stylish, expensive. **8** (*He was ill but he is fine now*) all right, well. **9** (*If you want to leave early that is fine with us*) all right, acceptable, suitable, (*inf*) OK. ▼

---

fine words butter no parsnips a proverb indicating that the use of fine-sounding elegant language will not necessarily get you what you want, any more so than plain language will (*He gave a very clever, persuasive speech saying why he should get the job but they gave it to someone who just said a few words. Fine words butter no parsnips*). **get (something) down to a fine art** to have learned to do something extremely skilfully and usually rapidly (*She has got dealing with unwelcome visitors down to a fine art*).

---

fine *n* (*a fine for speeding*) penalty, forfeit.

finger *vb* (*children told not to finger the fruit before buying it*) touch, handle, feel, fiddle with. ▼

---

be all fingers and thumbs to be clumsy or awkward when using one's hands (*She was so nervous about holding a dinner party that she was all fingers and thumbs and kept dropping things*). **let (something) slip through one's fingers** to lose (an opportunity or advantage) by one's own neglect or inactivity.

---

finish *vb* **1** (*workmen who did not finish the job in time*) complete, accomplish, carry out, get done, fulfil. **2** (*when the concert finished/when the work finished*) end, come to an end, conclude, cease, stop, terminate. **3** (*We finished the bread at breakfast*) use, use up, consume, exhaust, (*inf*) polish off. **4** (*They finish work at five o'clock*) stop, cease, end, discontinue, halt. ▼

---

the finishing touches the final details which complete something or make it very good or perfect (*She put the finishing touches to the dinner table by putting an arrangement of flowers on it*).

---

fire *n* **1** (*modern homes that do not have a fire*) fireplace, hearth, grate. **2** (*Fortunately no one was hurt in the fire*) blaze, flames, conflagration, inferno. **3** (*make a fire to burn the rubbish*) bonfire. **4** (*Her playing of the piece was without fire*) passion, ardour, inspiration.▼

---

get on like a house on fire to get on extremely well (*I didn't think my friends would like each other but they got on like a house on fire*). **play with fire** to take risks, to do something dangerous (*The child is playing with fire by teasing that dog. It will bite her*).

---

fire *vb* **1** (*He fired the gun*) shoot, let off, discharge. **2** (*They were found guilty of firing the farm buildings*) set fire to, set on fire, set alight, ignite. **3** (*His performance fired them with enthusiasm*) inspire, rouse, arouse, stir up, stimulate. **4** (*He was fired for always being late*) sack, dismiss, declare redundant, (*inf*) axe.

firm *adj* **1** (*The ice was not firm*

enough to skate on) hard, hardened, solid, set, rigid. **2** (*The poles for the fence must be firm in the ground*) fixed, secure, fast, stable, set, tight. **3** (*We have no firm plans/make a firm arrangement*) fixed, settled, agreed, definite, decided, established. **4** (*They were quite firm about refusing the invitation*) determined, resolute, resolved, decided, adamant, unwavering, obstinate, stubborn. **5** (*They have become firm friends*) devoted, faithful, loyal, dependable.

firm *n* (*he started his own publishing firm*) business, company, organization, establishment, concern.

first *adj* **1** (*the first stages of the manufacturing process*) early, earliest, opening, introductory. **2** (*the first aeroplane*) earliest, original. **3** (*the first people to arrive*) earliest, soonest. ▼

---

first thing early in the morning or early in the working day (*The pupil was told to go to see the headmaster first thing*). **not to know the first thing about (it/something)** to know nothing whatsoever about (something), to have no knowledge or experience of (something) (*He has opened a wine shop although he does not know the first thing about wine*).

---

first *n* (*We knew from the first that he was not suitable*) beginning, start, outset, commencement, (*inf*) the word go.

fit *adj* **1** (*Is the water fit to drink?*) suitable, good enough, satisfactory, appropriate. **2** (*She was not fit for the job*) suitable, good enough, satisfactory, able, capable, competent, adequate, trained, qualified. **3** (*The football player was injured but he is fit now*) well, healthy, in good health, strong, in good condition, in good shape.

fit *vb* **1** (*The shoes do not fit*) be the right size, be the correct size. **2** (*fit the parts of the doll's house together*) assemble, put together, join, connect. **3** (*fit the tiles to the floor*) lay, fix, put in place, put in position, position. **4** (*clothes that do not fit the occasion*) suit, be suitable for, be appropriate for, be apt for. **5** (*His account of the accident does not fit with hers*) agree, be in agreement, match, accord, concur, tally. ▼

---

fit like a glove to fit very well and comfortably (*She did not have to have the wedding dress altered. It fitted her like a glove*). **if the cap fits, wear it** if you think that what has been said might apply to you then you should take particular notice of it.

---

fit *n* **1** (*She had a coughing fit*) bout, attack, spell. **2** (*an epileptic fit*) convulsion, seizure, spasm, paroxysm.

fitting *adj* **1** (*The criminal should receive a fitting punishment*) suitable, appropriate, due, apt. **2** (*It was not fitting for her to wear those clothes to a funeral*) proper, right, seemly, decent, decorous, suitable, appropriate.

fix *vb* **1** (*fix the bookshelves to the study wall*) attach, fasten, secure, stick, screw, nail. **2** (*fix a date for the party*) set, decide on, settle, arrange, agree on, name. **3** (*He is trying to fix the car*) repair, mend, sort, put right, put to rights.

fizzy *adj* (*fizzy drinks*) sparkling, bubbly, effervescent.

flabbergasted *adj* (*He was flabbergasted at how much the new car was going to cost*) astounded, amazed, dumbfounded, stunned, staggered, nonplussed, (*inf*) gobsmacked.

flag *n* (*decorate the streets with flags for the coronation*) banner, pennant, streamer, standard. ▼

---

show the flag to attend an event only so that one can say that one has been present, or in order to make sure that one's firm, organization, etc. is represented (*I don't really want to go to the advertising firm's party but no-one else from our firm is going and someone really ought to go and show the flag*).

---

flag *vb* **1** (*Their interest in the subject matter is flagging*) fade, fail, decrease, decline, diminish. **2** (*The speeding motorist was flagged down by the police*) wave down, signal to stop.

flair *n* (*have a flair for languages*) talent, gift, ability, aptitude, bent, genius.

flake *n* (*flakes of paint*) *n* chip, shaving, sliver, fragment, bit.

flame *n* (*burn with a bright flame*) fire, glow, gleam, brightness. ▼

---

an old flame a former boyfriend or girlfriend (*His wife objected to the fact that he had lunch with an old flame*) <The suggestion is that the flame of love has died down>.

---

flame *vb* (*The dry wood flamed up*) burn, blaze, burst into flames, catch fire.

flap *vb* **1** (*The flags were flapping in the wind*) flutter, wave, swing. **2** (*birds with wings flapping*) beat, flail, vibrate, thresh. **3** (*The hostess started to flap when the oven broke down*) panic, go into a panic, become flustered, become agitated, (*inf*) be in a state.

flare *vb* **1** (*The fire suddenly flared up*) blaze, flame. **2** (*Trouble flared up when the army left*) break out, burst out, recur. **3** (*She flares up whenever anyone disagrees with her*) lose one's temper, go into a rage, get angry, fly off the handle.

flash *n* **1** (*a flash of light*) blaze, burst, flare, gleam, beam, streak. **2** (*She was there in a flash*) instant, moment, second, trice, twinkling of an eye. ▼

---

a flash in the pan a sudden and short-lived success (*Our team did unexpectedly well in the first round of the tournament but it turned out to be just a flash in the pan. We were knocked out in the next round*) <A reference to a flintlock gun in which the spark from the flint ignited the gunpowder in the priming pan, the flash then travelling to the main barrel. If this failed to go off there was only a flash in the pan instead of the gun firing>.

---

flashy *adj* (*wear flashy clothes*) showy, gaudy, ostentatious, flamboyant, loud, garish, tawdry, (*inf*) jazzy, (*inf*) tacky, (*inf*) glitzy.

flat *adj* **1** (*flat surfaces*) level, horizontal, even, smooth. **2** (*lying in a flat position*) spread out, stretched out, prone, supine, prostrate. **3** (*a flat tyre*) deflated, collapsed, burst, punctured. **4** (*The party was rather flat after* *she had left*) boring, dull, tedious, unexciting, lifeless, uninspired.▼

---

in a flat spin in a state of confused excitement, in a state of panic or agitation (*They were in a flat spin when they heard that their guests were going to arrive a day early*).

---

flat *n* (*She left home and rented a flat*) apartment, rooms.

flatten *vb* **1** (*flatten the surface to make the new road*) make flat, level, even out, smooth out, plane. **2** (*flatten the old buildings to make way for a new housing development*) pull down, knock down, tear down, demolish, raze to the ground. **3** (*gales which flattened the crops*) crush, squash, compress.

flatter *vb* **1** (*He flatters her whenever he wants to borrow her car*) pay compliments to, compliment, praise, sing the praises of, humour, (*inf*) sweet-talk. **2** (*The dress flatters her*) suit, become, show to advantage.

flavour *n* **1** (*people who dislike the flavour of garlic*) taste, savour. **2** (*a sauce in need of flavour*) flavouring, seasoning, spiciness, piquancy. **3** (*a book that captured the flavour of the times*) spirit, character, feel, feeling, tone, nature, essence, ambience. ▼

---

the flavour of the month a person or thing that is very popular only for a short time (*The new secretary is flavour of the month with the boss/Words that are flavour of the month with the media*) <From the practice of some ice-cream firms of trying to persuade customers to try out new flavours>.

---

flaw *n* **1** (*a flaw in the dress material*) defect, imperfection, fault. **2** (*a flaw in the china*) defect, imperfection, fault, crack, chip.

flee *vb* (*The villagers fled as the enemy army approached*) run away, run off, escape, take flight, make off, abscond, (*inf*) do a bunk, retreat.

fleeting *adj* (*a fleeting feeling of regret*) brief, short-lived, momentary, transient, transitory, ephemeral.

flesh *n* **1** (*the flesh and bones of the animals*) meat, brawn, muscle. **2** (*prefer the pleasures of the flesh to those of the spirit*) body, human body, physical nature.▼

---

get one's pound of flesh to obtain everything that one is entitled to, especially if this causes difficulties or suffering to those who have to give it (*He is well paid but he works such long hours that the company certainly get their pound of flesh*) <A reference to Shakespeare's *Merchant of Venice*, in which Shylock, the money-lender, tries to enforce an agreement by which he is allowed to cut a pound of flesh from Antonio>.

---

flexible *adj* **1** (*flexible materials*) pliable, pliant, elastic, springy, bendable. **2** (*Our holiday plans are flexible at the moment*) adaptable, adjustable, variable, changeable, open to change.

flight *n* **1** (*the flight of the refugees from the war zone*) fleeing, running away, escape, absconding, retreat. **2** (*write a book on the history of flight*) flying, aviation. **3** (*The flight to Australia from London is very long*) plane journey, plane trip.

flimsy *adj* **1** (*a summer dress made of a flimsy material*) thin, lightweight, light, delicate, sheer. **2** (*a flimsy hut to shelter the refugees*) insubstantial, frail, rickety, ramshackle, makeshift. **3** (*a flimsy excuse for being absent*) feeble, weak, poor, thin, inadequate, unconvincing.

flinch *vb* **1** (*The boy flinched as his father raised his fist*) draw back, recoil, shrink, quail, wince. **2** (*soldiers who do not flinch from their duty*) shrink from, shy away from, shirk, dodge, duck.

fling *vb* (*fling the rubbish into the tip*) throw, toss, hurl, cast, pitch, lob, heave, (*inf*) chuck.

flippant *adj* (*She gave a flippant reply to his serious question*) frivolous, shallow, glib, offhand, carefree.

float *vb* **1** (*things which can float on water*) stay afloat, be buoyant. **2** (*marker buoys floating along*) bob, drift. **3** (*balloons floating in the air*) drift, hover, hang.

flog *vb* (*people who think that wrongdoers should be flogged*) whip, lash, flay, birch, scourge, beat, thrash, cane. ▼

---

flog a dead horse to continue to try to arouse interest, enthusiasm, etc, in something which is obviously not, or no longer, of interest (*He's canvassing for votes but he's flogging a dead horse. His opponent is bound to win*).

---

flood *n* **1** (*property damaged in the flood*) deluge, torrent, spate, inundation. **2** (*After the article in the newspaper there was a flood of correspondence*) abundance, overabundance, profusion.

flood *vb* **1** (*houses damaged by rivers flooding*) overflow, break its banks. **2** (*water which flooded the town*) pour over, inundate, submerge, immerse.

floor *n* (*a house on three floors*) storey, level.▼

---

get in on the ground floor to be in at the very start of a project, business, etc (*He got in on the ground floor of the computer firm and made a lot of money*).

---

flop *vb* **1** (*His head flopped to one side and he fell asleep*) droop, sag, dangle. **2** (*She flopped into a chair after a hard day's work*) slump, drop, collapse, fall. **3** (*His first play flopped*) fail, be unsuccessful, be a disaster, (*inf*) bomb.

flourish *vb* **1** (*plants which flourish in a dry climate*) thrive, bloom, grow, do well, develop. **2** (*The company is flourishing now*) be in good condition, thrive, be successful, succeed, make progress. **3** (*He flourished the trophy which he had won*) brandish, wave, wield, swing, shake, twirl, hold aloft.

flow *vb* **1** (*rivers flowing*) run, glide, course, stream, ripple, surge. **2** (*a serious wound with blood flowing from it*) gush, well, spurt, spill, ooze.

flower *n* (*put the flowers in a vase*) bloom, blossom. ▼

---

the flower of (something) the best and finest of (something) (*The young men who were killed in the battle were the flower of the nation*).

---

flowery *adj* **1** (*curtains with a flowery pattern*) floral, flower-covered. **2** (*dislike the flowery *language of his writing*) high-flown, ornate, elaborate, bombastic.

fluent *adj* **1** (*a fluent lecturer*) eloquent, articulate, smooth-spoken. **2** (*We admired his fluent French*) smooth, flowing, effortless, unhesitating.

flurry *n* **1** (*a sudden flurry of snow*) shower, gust, squall. **2** (*in a flurry of excitement waiting for the visitors to arrive*) fluster, bustle, whirl, fuss, flap.

flush *vb* **1** (*flush the toilet*) rinse out, wash out, cleanse. **2** (*She flushed with embarrassment*) blush, redden, go red, turn red, crimson, colour. ▼

---

in the first flush of (something) in the early and strongest stages of (something) (*They raised a lot of money for the project in the first flush of their enthusiasm*).

---

fluster *vb* (*The guests flustered her by arriving early*) agitate, unsettle, upset, ruffle, panic, confuse, disconcert, (*inf*) rattle.

flutter *vb* **1** (*birds fluttering their wings*) flap, beat, quiver, vibrate. **2** (*streamers fluttering in the wind*) flap, wave, fly, ripple.

fly *vb* **1** (*We decided to fly to Paris rather than go by train*) go by air, go by plane, **2** (*He was flying the plane*) pilot, control, operate. **3** (*watch the birds flying overhead*) hover, flutter, soar. **4** (*flags flying to celebrate the victory*) wave, flap, flutter. **5** (*She flew to the window when she heard the car*) rush, race, run, dash, dart. **6** (*They decided to fly as the enemy army approached*) flee, run away, take flight, make one's escape, escape, retreat. ▼

---

be flying high to be extremely successful, to be in a position of power or influence (*He was flying high a few years ago but he was declared redundant and is now unemployed*). **pigs might fly** an expression used to show that one thinks that something is extremely unlikely to happen (*You seriously think that he will lend us his car. Pigs might fly!*).

---

foam *n* **1** (*the foam on the beer*) froth, head. **2** (*the foam on the soapy water*) froth, bubbles, lather, suds, spume.

foe *n* (*They easily defeated their foes*) enemy, opponent, adversary, rival, antagonist.

fog *n* (*The fog was making it difficult for motorists to see*) mist, haze, smog.▼

---

not to have the foggiest (*inf*) not to have the slightest idea or knowledge (*I haven't the foggiest where they have gone*).

---

foil *vb* (*The police foiled the thief's attempt to rob the bank*) thwart, frustrate, stop.

foist *vb* (*He tried to foist some of his work on to the junior employees*) force, unload, thrust, impose.

fold *vb* **1** (*fold the sheets*) double over, overlap, crease. **2** (*The firm lost money and folded*) fail, collapse, shut down, go bankrupt, (*inf*) go bust.

folder *n* (*The documents for the meeting were in a folder*) file, binder, cover.

follow *vb* **1** (*She followed her brother into the house*) walk behind, go behind, go after. **2** (*We asked the taxi to follow the car with the thieves in it*) go after, pursue, chase, (*inf*) tail. **3** (*He followed his father as king*) come after, succeed, replace, take the place of. **4** (*They were told to follow the instructions*) obey, observe, keep to, comply with, heed, take notice of. **5** (*The students could not follow what the lecturer was saying*) understand, comprehend, grasp, fathom. **6** (*He follows the local football team*) be a follower of, be a fan of, be an admirer of, be a supporter of. ▼

---

follow suit to do just as someone else has done (*She got up from the dinner table and everyone else followed suit*) <A reference to card-playing when a player plays a card of the same suit as the previous player>.

---

fond *adj* (*He is very fond of his grandchildren/She is fond of spicy food*) having love for, having a liking for, keen on, attached to, having a soft spot for.

food *n* **1** (*children with not enough food to survive on*) sustenance, nourishment, provisions. **2** (*The hostess served delicious food*) refreshment, fare, diet, (*inf*) grub, (*inf*) nosh. ▼

---

food for thought something which makes one think very carefully (*The manager's letter about the financial state of the firm gave all the workers food for thought*).

---

foolish *adj* **1** (*It was a foolish idea/They thought it was a foolish thing to do*) silly, absurd, senseless, unintelligent, unwise, ill-considered. **2** (*He is a foolish fellow*) stupid, silly, unintelligent, brainless, dense, ignorant, dull-witted, (*inf*) dumb.

foot *n* **1** (*the foot of the pillar*) base, bottom. **2** (*We met at the foot of the road*) bottom, end. ▼

---

put one's foot down to be firm about something, to forbid someone to do something (*She wanted to go hitch-hiking but her mother put her foot down and now she's going by bus*). **put one's foot in it** to do or say something tactless or something that will upset or embarrass someone or cause trouble (*You put your foot in it when you mentioned her husband. He has just left her*). **shoot oneself in the foot** to make a make a mistake or do something stupid which causes problems for oneself or harms one's chances of success (*Dave shot himself in the foot when he stole money from his grandmother; she was going to leave him all her money but she changed her will before she died*).

---

forbid *vb* (*They were forbidden to go on the farmer's land*) prohibit, ban, bar, debar, preclude.

force *n* **1** (*It required a great deal of force to open the door*) strength, power, might, energy, effort, exertion, pressure, vigour. **2** (*They were accused of using force to get him to confess*) pressure, compulsion, coercion, duress, constraint, violence. **3** (*recognize the force of his arguments*) persuasiveness, effectiveness, strength, power, cogency.

force *vb* **1** (*You cannot force them to go with you*) use force on, make, compel, coerce, bring pressure to bear on, pressurize. **2** (*We *lost the key and had to force the drawer*) break open, burst open.

forecast *vb* (*We could have forecast that they would win*) predict, foretell, prophesy, foresee, speculate.

foreign *adj* (*customs that were foreign to them*) alien, unfamiliar, strange, unknown, unfamiliar, exotic.

foresee *vb* (*We could not have foreseen those problems*) anticipate, envisage, predict, foretell, forecast, prophesy.

forfeit *vb* (*She had to forfeit her pocket money to pay for the damage*) give up, hand over, relinquish, surrender.

forge *vb* (*He forged his father's signature on the cheque*) falsify, fake, counterfeit, imitate, copy.

forget *vb* **1** (*I forget their address*) be unable to remember, be unable to recall. **2** (*He tried to forget the terrible event*) put out of one's mind, ignore, disregard. **3** (*She forgot her husband's birthday*) overlook, neglect, disregard. **4** (*She forgot her gloves*) leave behind, omit to take.

forgive *vb* (*Their mother forgave them for being late*) excuse, pardon, let off.

form *n* **1** (*describe the form of the crystals*) shape, formation, structure. **2** (*the human form*) body, figure, shape, build, frame, physique, anatomy **3** (*a form of entertainment*) kind, type, sort, variety. **4** (*She is in the fourth form at our school*) class, year. **5** (*fill in a form to apply for the job*) document, paper, application.

form *vb* **1** (*form clay into animal shapes*) shape, mould, fashion, model, make. **2** (*They formed a committee to raise money for charity*) set up, establish, found, institute. **3** (*begin to form plans to solve the problem*) put together, draw up, think up, devise, frame. **4** (*icicles began to form in the cold weather*) take shape, develop, appear, materialize. ▼

---

be bad form not to be in keeping with social customs or accepted manners (*It is bad form to smoke before the end of a meal*). **true to form** in keeping with someone's usual pattern of behaviour (*True to form, they arrived very late*).

---

forthcoming *adj* **1** (*forthcoming events in the town*) future, coming, approaching, imminent. **2** (*The children were not very forthcoming about where they had been*) communicative, talkative, informative, open.

forthright *adj* (*a very forthright person who told them the truth*) direct, frank, candid, blunt, plain-speaking.

fortunate *adj* **1** (*He was fortunate to survive the accident*) in luck. **2** (*They are in a fortunate position to have been offered jobs*) favourable, lucky, advantageous.

fortune *n* **1** (*It was only by good fortune that he found the book*) chance, luck, accident. **2** (*He amassed a great fortune*) wealth, riches, assets, possessions.

forward *adj* **1** (*the forward part of the army*) front, foremost, leading **2** (*They were annoyed at her forward behaviour*) bold, brash, brazen, impudent, impertinent, (*inf*) pushy.

foul *adj* **1** (*The rotting meat was a foul sight*) disgusting, revolting, repulsive, nauseating, nasty, dirty. **2** (*The air was foul/foul water*) polluted, contaminated, impure, dirty. **3** (*foul weather*) rainy, stormy, wild, rainy, wet, nasty, disagreeable. **4** (*foul language*) profane, blasphemous, vulgar, crude, coarse, rude, filthy. **5** (*What a foul thing to do*) horrible, nasty, hateful, disgraceful, low, wicked, evil. ▼

---

foul play a criminal act, especially one involving murder (*The police have found a body and they are suspecting foul play*).

---

found *vb* (*found a new company*) set up, establish, institute, start, create.

fracture *n* (*fractures in the outer wall*) break, crack, split.

fragile *adj* (*china that is very fragile*) delicate, fine, breakable, brittle, frail.

fragment *n* (*fragments of glass*) piece, bit, chip, sliver, splinter, particle.

frail *adj* **1** (*frail old ladies*) delicate, infirm, weak, slight. **2** (*frail model aeroplanes*) fragile, breakable, flimsy, insubstantial.

frame *n* **1** (*ships built on a frame of steel*) framework, foundation, shell, skeleton. **2** (*a photograph frame*) mounting, mount. **3** (*wrestlers with huge frames*) body, physique, figure,

frank *adj* (*He answered in a frank manner*) direct, candid, forthright, plain, open, outspoken, blunt.

fraud *n* **1** (*He was accused of fraud*) swindling, sharp practice, dishonesty, crookedness, deceit, deception. **2** (*The magician's act was a fraud*) swindle, hoax, deception, (*inf*) con, (*inf*) rip-off. **3** (*The bank-note was a fraud*) fake, counterfeit, sham, (*inf*) phoney.

frayed *adj* (*frayed shirt cuffs*) ragged, tattered, worn.

freak *adj* (*a freak storm*) abnormal, unusual, atypical, exceptional, odd, strange, bizarre.

free *adj* **1** (*We got free tickets for the concert*) free of charge, for nothing, without charge, at no cost, complimentary, gratis. **2** (*They were free of any worries*) without, devoid of, unaffected by, clear of. **3** (*We were free to go anywhere we wanted*) allowed, permitted, able. **4** (*They asked us to the party but we were not free*) available, unoccupied, not busy, at leisure. **5** (*We looked for a free table in the cafe*) unoccupied, empty, vacant, spare. **6** (*nations that wanted to be free*) independent, self-governing, emancipated. ▼

---

free and easy informal, casual, at ease (*He is the boss but he is always very free and easy with the employees*). **give (someone) a free hand** give (someone) permission to do as he or she wishes (*They gave their gardener a free hand to choose the plants*).

---

freedom *n* **1** (*prisoners longing for their freedom*) liberty, release. **2** (*nations seeking freedom*) independence, self-government, sovereignty.

freezing *adj* **1** (*freezing weather*) icy, frosty, chilly, arctic, wintry. **2** (*We were freezing waiting for the bus*) chilled through, chilled to the marrow, numb with cold.

frequent *adj* **1** (*They have frequent storms in that area*) many, numerous, repeated, recurrent, persistent. **2** (*a frequent visitor*) regular, habitual, common, usual, constant.

fresh *adj* **1** (*serve fresh fruit for dessert*) raw, unpreserved, unprocessed. **2** (*a supply of fresh water*) pure, unpolluted, uncontaminated, clean. **3** (*They are hoping for some fresh ideas*) new, modern, original. **4** (*We felt fresh after our holiday*) energetic, invigorated, lively, refreshed, revived.

friend *n* (*The children invited their friends to a party*) companions, (*inf*) pal, (*inf*) chum, (*inf*) mate. ▼

---

a friend in need is a friend indeed a friend who provides help when one is in trouble is truly a friend. **fair-weather friends** people who are friendly towards one only when one is not in trouble of any kind (*All his fair-weather friends deserted him when he lost his job*).

---

friendly *adj* (*friendly neighbours*) amiable, affable, sociable, hospitable, approachable, good-natured, kindly.

frighten *vb* (*The children were frightened when they heard the noise*) scare, alarm, startle, terrify.

front *n* **1** (*the front of the queue*) head, top, beginning. **2** (*They painted the front of the building red*) frontage, façade, face. **3** (*His business is just a front for drug-dealing*) cover, cover-up, disguise, blind, mask.

froth *n* **1** (*froth on the soapy water*) bubbles, lather, suds, spume. **2** (*froth on the beer*) bubbles, effervescence, head.

frown *vb* **1** (*She frowned in anger*) scowl, glower, glare. **2** (*They frowned upon casual clothes at the club*) disapprove of, take a dim view of, dislike.

fulfil *vb* **1** (*He failed to fulfil the tasks given to him*) carry out, perform, discharge, accomplish, complete, execute. **2** (*He was the only person who fulfilled the job requirements*) satisfy, meet, answer, obey.

full *adj* **1** (*Their glasses were full*) filled, brimming, brimful. **2** (*All the hotel rooms are full*) occupied, taken, in use. **3** (*The supermarket was full on Saturdays*) crowded, packed, crammed, chock-a-block. **4** (*She gave us a full list of the names of people present*) complete, whole, entire, comprehensive, detailed, thorough.

fumble *vb* **1** (*fumble for his keys in the dark*) grope, feel for. **2** (*fumble a catch at cricket*) miss, mishandle.

fumes *npl* (*the fumes from the car's exhaust pipe*) gases, smoke, vapour, smell.

fun *n* (*The children had fun at the party*) entertainment, amusement, enjoyment, pleasure, a good time. ▼

---

make fun of (someone or **something)** to laugh at or make mocking remarks about (someone or something) (*Her classmates made fun of her for wearing old-fashioned clothes*).

---

function *n* **1** (*his function in the firm*) role, job, duty, task, responsibility. **2** (*the function of the machine*) use, purpose. **3** (*invited to the firm's annual function*) party, reception, gathering, social occasion, social event.

fundamental *adj* (*learn fundamental cooking skills*) basic, rudimentary, elementary, essential, primary.

funny *adj* **1** (*They laughed at his funny stories*) amusing, comic, comical, humorous, hilarious, laughable, riotous. **2** (*There was something funny about the way he was behaving*) odd, peculiar, strange, queer, weird, bizarre, suspicious.

furious *adj* (*They were furious at being treated rudely*) enraged, infuriated, indignant, angry, wrathful.

furnish *vb* **1** (*furnish the room with modern furniture*) equip, fit out. **2** (*furnish the committee with the required information*) provide, supply, equip, present.

furniture *n* (*buy antique furniture for the house*) furnishings, appointments, effects.

further *adj* (*require further supplies*) additional, more, extra.

furtive *adj* (*The police were suspicious of his furtive behaviour*) secretive, stealthy, sneaky, surreptitious, sly.

fury *n* (*her parent's fury at the damage caused during the party*) anger, rage, wrath, ire.

future *n* **1** (*hope for better things in the future*) time to come, time ahead, time hereafter. **2** (*There is little future for that industry*) prospects, expectations, outlook, likely success.

future *adj* (*an advertisement for future events*) coming, approaching, to come.

G

gadget *n* (*a kitchen with a lot of labour-saving gadgets*) appliance, device, piece of apparatus, implement.

gag *n* (*The comedian told a series of old gags*) joke, jest, quip, witticism, wisecrack.

gain *vb* (*They tried to gain an advantage over the opposition*) get, obtain, acquire, procure, secure, achieve.

gain *n* (*their gains from the sale of the company*) profit, return, yield, proceeds, earnings, reward, benefit, (*inf*) pickings. ▼

---

gain ground to make progress, to become more generally acceptable or popular (*The campaign in favour of animal rights is gaining ground*). **nothing ventured, nothing gained** one cannot achieve anything worthwhile in life if one is not prepared to take any risks (*It's risky starting a new business without much capital, but there again nothing ventured, nothing gained*).

---

gale *n* (*ships damaged at sea in a gale*) storm, hurricane, squall, tempest, tornado, cyclone.

gallant *adj* (*gallant soldiers who died in battle*) brave, courageous, valiant, heroic, plucky, fearless, intrepid, stout-hearted.

gallop *vb* **1** (*horses galloping around the field*) canter, prance, frisk. **2** (*The children always gallop home for tea*) rush, run, dash, race, sprint, hurry.

gamble *vb* **1** (*He loves to gamble and loses a lot of money*) bet, place a bet, wager, lay a wager, (*inf*) punt. **2** (*He gambled when he invested in the company*) take a risk, take a chance, speculate, venture.

game *n* **1** (*the children's games*) amusement, entertainment, diversion, sport, pastime, hobby. **2** (*We are all going to the game tomorrow*) match, competition, contest, tournament, athletics event, sports meeting. ▼

---

beat (someone) at his or her own game to be more successful than (someone) at the kind of activity he or she usually takes part in, especially a cunning or dishonest one (*In previous years he won the cross-country race by taking a short cut but this year another competitor did the same and beat him at his own game*). **give the game away** to reveal a secret plan, trick, etc, usually accidentally. **play the game** to behave in a fair and honourable way (*He didn't play the game. He got his friend's job when she was off sick*).

---

gang *n* **1** (*A gang of people had gathered to listen to the speaker*) group, band, crowd, mob, horde. **2** (*The boys formed a gang*) club, clique, circle, set. **3** (*a gang of workmen*) squad, team, troop.

gap *n* **1** (*crawl through a gap in the*

wall) opening, hole, aperture, space, chink. 2 (*The police are trying to fill in a few gaps in the account of the accident*) omission, blank, void, lacuna.

gape *vb* 1 (*They gaped at the sheer size of the huge man*) stare, goggle, gaze. 2 (*The caves gaped before them*) open wide, yawn.

garden *n* (*He grows vegetables in his garden*) allotment, plot. ▼

---

everything in the garden is lovely everything is going very well (*The firm had a few problems last year but now everything in the garden is lovely*). **lead (someone) up the garden path** to mislead or deceive (someone) (*She thought that he was going to marry her but he was just leading her up the garden path*).

---

garish *adj* (*The holidaymakers were wearing garish clothes*) flashy, loud, gaudy, bold, flamboyant.

garland *n* (*wearing garlands of flowers round their necks*) wreath, festoon.

garment *n* (*wearing a strange black garment*) piece of clothing, item of clothing, article of clothing.

garments *npl* (*wearing mourning garments*) clothes, clothing, dress, attire, apparel, outfit, garb.

gash *n* (*He gashed his hand when carving the meat*) cut, slash, lacerate, wound, nick.

gasp *vb* (*He was gasping as he reached the top of the mountain*) pant, puff, puff and pant, blow, choke, wheeze. ▼

---

at one's last gasp just about to collapse, to be ruined, to die, etc (*She was at her last gasp when the ambulance arrived*).

---

gate *n* (*the gate at the end of the driveway to the house*) gateway, barrier, entrance.

gather *vb* 1 (*A crowd gathered to hear the speaker*) collect, come together, assemble, congregate, meet. 2 (*gather food for the fire*) collect, get together, accumulate, heap up, store, stockpile, hoard. 3 (*gather blackberries*) pick, pluck, harvest, collect. 4 (*We gather that she is ill*) understand, believe, be led to believe, hear, learn.

gathering *n* (*be invited to the firm's annual gathering*) party, function, get-together, social.

gaudy *adj* garish, bold, over-bright, loud, glaring, flashy, showy, lurid.

gauge *vb* 1 (*He was asked to gauge the length of the garden*) measure, calculate, determine, estimate. 2 (*It is difficult to gauge the extent of his interest in the project*) assess, estimate, judge, guess.

gaunt *adj* (*He looked gaunt after his long illness*) haggard, drawn, emaciated, skinny, bony, scrawny, scraggy, skeletal, cadaverous.

gay *adj* 1 (*people feeling gay on holiday*) merry, jolly, light-hearted, glad, happy, cheerful, in good spirits. 2 (*girls wearing summer dresses in gay colours*) bright, brightly coloured, vivid, brilliant, flamboyant. 3 (*a gay club*) homosexual, (*inf*) queer.

gaze *vb* (*tourists gazing at the beauty of the sunset*) stare, eye, contemplate, look fixedly.

gear *n* 1 (*the mountaineers and all their gear*) equipment, apparatus, kit, implements, tackle, things, possessions, belongings, (*inf*) stuff, paraphernalia. 2 (*young people who like to be dressed in* *the latest gear*) clothes, clothing, dress, garments, attire, apparel, (*inf*) togs.

gem *n* (*an engagement ring with sparkling gems*) jewel, precious stone, stone.

general *adj* **1** (*The general feeling is that he is guilty*) common, widespread, broad, wide, accepted, prevalent, universal. **2** (*The general rule is that people have to have three years' experience before getting a job there*) usual, customary, common, normal, standard, ordinary, typical. **3** (*He gave them a general idea of his plans for the business*) broad, non-detailed, vague, indefinite, inexact, rough.

generous *adj* **1** (*he was a generous contributor to the charity*) kind, liberal, magnanimous, benevolent, lavish, open-handed. **2** (*there was a generous supply of food and drinks at the party*) abundant, liberal, plentiful, ample, copious, rich.

genius *n* **1** (*He is a genius at mathematics*) master-mind, prodigy, intellectual, expert, (*inf*) Einstein. **2** (*people of genius*) brilliance, brains, intellect, intelligence. **3** (*have a genius for making delicious low-cost meals*) gift, talent, flair, bent, knack, aptitude, ability, forte.

gentle *adj* **1** (*She remembered with love her gentle mother*) kind, kindly, lenient, tender-hearted, sweet-tempered, mild, soft, peaceful. **2** (*her gentle touch*) soft, light, smooth, soothing. **3** (*a gentle breeze*) mild, light, soft, moderate, temperate. **4** (*children learning to ski on gentle slopes*) gradual, slight. **5** (*The dog was a very gentle animal*) tame. placid, docile. **6** (*She tried to give him a gentle hint about his bad manners*) indirect, subtle.

genuine *adj* **1** (*His excuse for being absent turned out to be genuine*) real, true, authentic, sound, legitimate, valid, (*inf*) kosher, (*inf*) the real McCoy. **2** (*They doubted if his feelings were genuine*) real, sincere, honest, truthful, true, unaffected.

gesture *n* (*He made a gesture to indicate that he agreed*) signal, sign, motion.

get *vb* **1** (*She wondered where she could get a book on antiques*) obtain, acquire, get hold of, come by, procure, buy, purchase. **2** (*He went upstairs to get a book for his mother*) fetch, bring, carry, go for, retrieve. **3** (*They get a high salary*) earn, be paid, bring in, make, clear, take home. **4** (*She got flu last winter*) catch, become infected by, contract. **5** (*The children were getting tired*) become, grow. **6** (*When do you expect to get there?*) arrive at, reach. **7** (*I didn't get what he was talking about*) understand, comprehend, follow, grasp. **8** (*We eventually got her to agree*) persuade, coax, induce, talk (someone) into. ▼

---

be getting on for (something) to be close to (a particular age, time, etc) (*It was getting on for midnight when we arrived/ Their grandmother is getting on for ninety*). **get nowhere** to make absolutely no progress (*The two sides have been having talks to try to find a solution but they are getting nowhere*). **tell (someone) where to get off** to tell (someone) that one will not tolerate his or her behaviour or actions anymore.

---

ghastly *adj* **1** (*There has been a ghastly motorway accident*) terrible, horrible, dreadful, frightful, shocking, grim, horrifying. **2** (*She looked ghastly when she went to hospital*) white, white as a sheet, pale, pallid, wan, colourless, drawn, ashen. **3** (*He is an absolutely ghastly man*) dreadful, nasty, unpleasant, disagreeable, hateful, loathsome, foul, contemptible.

ghost *n* (*She imagined that she saw a ghost in the graveyard*) apparition, spectre, phantom, spirit, wraith, (*inf*) spook. ▼

---

give up the ghost to die, to stop working, to stop trying, etc (*Our old car has finally given up the ghost*) <Ghost refers to a person's spirit—a biblical reference to Job 14:10>. **not to have the ghost of a chance** not to have the slightest possibility of success (*He has decided to enter the race but he doesn't have the ghost of a chance*).

---

gibberish *n* (*They accused him of talking gibberish*) nonsense, rubbish, twaddle, drivel, balderdash, (*inf*) poppycock, (*inf*) piffle.

gibe *n* (*She was upset at the gibes of her classmates*) sneer, jeer, taunt, mocking, scorn.

giddy *adj* **1** (*feel giddy at the top of the ladder*) dizzy, light-headed, faint, (*inf*) woozy. **2** (*giddy girls who had no interest in having a career*) silly, flighty, frivolous, irresponsible, thoughtless, unstable.

gift *n* **1** (*birthday gifts*) present. **2** (*He was thanked for his gift to the charity*) present, donation, contribution, offering. **3** (*The pupil has a gift for foreign languages*) talent, flair, aptitude, knack, ability, expertise, genius. ▼

---

a Greek gift a gift that is disadvantageous or dangerous to the person given it (*My uncle gave us his old car but it turned out to be a Greek gift. The steering was faulty and we were nearly killed*). **look a gift horse in the mouth** to criticize something that has been given to one (*She was complaining about flaws in the antique table which he gave her. She really shouldn't look a gift horse in the mouth*) <Looking at a horse's teeth is a way of telling its age and of estimating its value>.

---

gigantic *adj* (*They caught sight of a gigantic mountain through the mist*) huge, enormous, colossal, immense, vast, mammoth, gargantuan.

giggle *vb* (*pupils giggling at the back of the class*) titter, snigger, snicker, laugh, (*inf*) tee-hee.

girl *n* **1** (*She lived in the village as a girl*) young woman, (*inf*) lass. **2** (*The couple have a boy and a girl*) daughter. **3** (*He went to the pictures with his girl*) girlfriend, sweetheart, fiancée.

gist *n* (*Some of his lecture was a bit difficult for the audience but most of them got the gist of it*) drift, substance, essence, sense.

give *vb* **1** (*She lifted the book and gave it to him*) hand, hand over, pass. **2** (*The old lady gave a very large sum of money to the local hospital*) donate, contribute, present, bestow, make over. **3** (*The charity worker was giving out soup and bread to homeless people*) hand out, distribute, allot, allocate, dole out. **4** (*They were *given some bad advice*) provide, supply, furnish, offer. **5** (*She gives the impression of being very efficient*) show, display, demonstrate, manifest, indicate. **6** (*The chair gave and the child fell to the floor*) give way, collapse, break, come apart, fall apart. ▼

---

give and take willingness to compromise (*There has to be some give and take in a friendship but she wanted to get her own way all the time*). **give as good as one gets** to be as successful as one's opponent in an argument, quarrel, contest, etc (*He tries to bully his wife but she gives as good as she gets*).

---

giver *n* (*the giver of the money to the hospital*) donor, contributor.

glad *adj* **1** (*We were very glad to see our visitors*) happy, pleased, delighted, (*inf*) chuffed. **2** (*hear the glad news*) happy, delightful, joyful, welcome, cheerful. ▼

---

glad rags (*inf*) one's best clothes worn on special occasions (*They put on their glad rags and went to the most expensive restaurant in town*).

---

glamorous *adj* **1** (*glamorous filmstars*) beautiful, lovely, attractive, elegant, smart, dazzling, alluring. **2** (*She has a glamorous career in advertising*) exciting, fascinating, dazzling, high-profile, (*inf*) glitzy.

glance *vb* **1** (*He only glanced at the stranger*) take a quick look at, look briefly at, glimpse, peep. **2** (*glance through the newspapers at breakfast*) skim through, leaf through, flick through, flip through, thumb through, scan. **3** (*The bullet glanced off the tree*) bounce, rebound, ricochet. **4** (*The car glanced the wall as he drove it into the garage*) graze, brush, touch, skim.

glare *n* **1** (*He was unaware of her angry glares*) scowl, frown, glower, black look, (*inf*) dirty look. **2** (*the glare from the headlights of oncoming cars*) flare, blaze, dazzle.

glass *n* (*a glass of cold water*) tumbler, beaker, goblet. ▼

---

people who live in glass houses should not throw stones people who have certain faults or disadvantages themselves should not criticize similar faults or disadvantages in others (*He complains about his neighbours playing music loudly but he does the same. Somebody should tell him that people in glass houses should not throw stones*).

---

gleam *n* **1** (*a gleam of light*) beam, glow, ray, shimmer, sparkle. **2** (*the gleam of the polished tables*) glow, shine, gloss, sheen, lustre. **3** (*There is still a gleam of hope*) glimmer, ray, trace, suggestion, hint, flicker.

glib *adj* (*She was persuaded into buying the goods by a glib salesman*) smooth, plausible, smooth-talking, fluent, suave.

glide *vb* (*They watched the yachts gliding by*) sail, slide, slip, skim, float, drift.

glimpse *n* (*She thought that she glimpsed a stranger through the trees*) catch sight of, spot, make out, notice, espy.

glitter *vb* (*The diamonds glittered in the candlelight*) sparkle, flash, twinkle, flicker, blink, wink, shimmer, gleam, glint.

gloat *vb* (*She was gloating over her rival's misfortunes*) relish, delight in, take pleasure in, revel in, rejoice in, glory in, crow about.

global *adj* **1** (*the possibility of global war*) world, world-wide, universal, international. **2** (*The government tried to impose a global wage settlement on all public service employees*) general, universal, across-the-board, comprehensive.

gloomy *adj* **1** (*a gloomy November day*) dark, overcast, cloudy, dull, dismal, dreary. **2** (*an old house full of gloomy rooms*) dark, sombre, dingy, dismal, dreary, depressing. **3** (*He is in a gloomy mood today*) in low spirits, depressed, sad, unhappy, miserable, dejected, downcast, down-hearted, glum, melancholy.

glorious *adj* **1** (*It was a glorious day*) bright, beautiful, lovely, sunny. **2** (*The royal procession was a glorious sight*) splendid, magnificent, wonderful, marvellous. **3** (*celebrate a glorious victory*) famous, celebrated, renowned, noble, distinguished.

glossy *adj* (*the glossy surfaces of the polished tables*) gleaming, shining, shiny, bright, sparkling, shimmering, polished, burnished.

glow *vb* (*The lights glowed*) gleam, shine, glimmer.

glow *n* **1** (*the glow from the table lights*) gleam, brightness, glimmer, luminosity. **2** (*the glow from the fire*) warmth, heat, redness. **3** (*She felt a warm glow when she thought of her friends*) warmth, happiness, contentment, satisfaction.

glower *vb* (*She glowered at her rival*) scowl, frown, look daggers at.

glue *vb* (*glue the broken pieces together*) stick, gum, paste, cement.

glum *adj* (*in a glum mood*) gloomy, depressed, sad, unhappy, miserable, dejected, downcast, downhearted, melancholy.

glut *n* (*a glut of soft fruit on the market*) surplus, excess, surfeit, superfluity, overabundance, oversupply.

gnaw *vb* **1** (*The dog was gnawing on a bone*) chew, munch, crunch, bite, nibble, worry. **2** (*The metal had been gnawed away by rust*) erode, corrode, wear away, eat away.

go *vb* **1** (*go carefully on the icy roads*) move, proceed, walk, travel. **2** (*It is time to go*) go away, leave, depart, withdraw, set off, set out. **3** (*The pain has gone*) stop, cease, vanish, disappear, fade, be no more. **4** (*The machine has stopped going*) work, be in working order, function, operate, run. **5** (*His beard has gone white*) become, grow, turn, get, come to be. **6** (*This road goes to the next town*) extend, stretch, reach, lead to. **7** (*Time went slowly while they were waiting for the train*) pass, elapse, slip by. **8** (*How did the party go?*) turn out, work out, progress, fare. **9** (*curtains and carpets that don't go*) go together, match, blend, harmonize. ▼

---

from the word go right from the very start (*We knew from the word go that he was not the right person for the job*). **make a go of (something)** to make a success of (something) (*They tried very hard to make a go of their restaurant*). **on the go** always very active or busy (*She has three small children and is on the go all day*).

---

goal *n* (*Making a lot of money was his one goal in life/He read out a statement of the goals of the organization*) aim, objective, end, purpose, object, target, ambition. ▼

---

move the goalposts to change the rules or conditions after a project of some kind is in progress, especially in order to prevent someone else from achieving success. **score an own goal** to be the cause of one's own misfortune, ruin, etc (*He scored an own goal when he suggested to the boss that they employed too many people. He was among the people who got the sack*).

---

gobble *vb* (*children told not to gobble their food*) wolf, bolt, gulp, guzzle, (*inf*) scoff.

god *n* (*the gods of ancient Greece*) deity, divinity, divine being, idol.▼

---

a little tin god a person who has much too high an opinion of himself or herself and tries to order others around (*The workers thoroughly dislike the deputy manager who is a little tin god*). **in the lap of the gods** uncertain, left to chance or fate (*There's nothing else we can do. Whether we get the job or not is in the lap of the gods*).

God *n* (*the biblical story about God and Moses*) God Almighty, the Almighty, God the Father, Our Maker. ▼

---

there but for the grace of God go I if I had not been fortunate then that piece of misfortune could easily have happened to me (*There were a lot of redundancies in the firm and as I said goodbye to some of my colleagues I thought 'There but for the grace of God go I'*). **think that one is God's gift to (someone)** to have a very conceited opinion of oneself (*He thinks that he is God's gift to women*).

---

golden *adj* **1** (*girls with golden hair*) gold-coloured, blond, yellow, fair, flaxen. **2** (*a golden opportunity*) splendid, superb, excellent, favourable, fortunate, advantageous, profitable.▼

---

a golden handshake a large amount of money given to someone who is leaving a job, usually because he or she is retiring. **the golden rule** a rule or practice that it is vital to remember if things are to run smoothly (*The golden rule when baking a sponge cake is never to open the oven door when it is cooking*) <Originally the golden rule was that one should do to others as one would wish them to do to oneself>.

---

good *adj* **1** (*The children were told to be good*) well-behaved, well-mannered, obedient, manageable. **2** (*She is such a good person who never treats anyone badly*) honourable, virtuous, righteous, upright, honest, decent, moral, ethical. **3** (*She is noted for her good deeds*) helpful, kind, thoughtful, virtuous, admirable, creditable. **4** (*He is not a very good driver*) competent, capable, able, skilful, adept, proficient, expert, first-class, (*inf*) A1. **5** (*The car does not have very good brakes*) efficient, reliable, dependable, trustworthy. **6** (*athletes in good condition*) fine, healthy, sound, strong, robust, vigorous. **7** (*The party was very good*) enjoyable, agreeable, entertaining, pleasant, lovely, nice. **8** (*We had good weather on holiday*) fine, sunny, pleasant. ▼

---

be up to no good be planning to do something wrong or illegal (*The policeman thought that the boys standing by the cars were up to no good*). **make good** be successful in one's career or business (*He comes from a very poor background but he made good at an early age in the advertising business*). **take (something) in good part** accept (something) without being angry or offended (*The children were teasing him but he took it in good part*).

---

gossip *n* **1** (*I heard that he had been in prison but it turned out to be just gossip*) rumour, tittle-tattle, scandal, hearsay, (*inf*) mud-slinging. **2** (*She was having a good gossip with her neighbour*) chat, blether, tête à tête, (*inf*) chin-wag.

govern *vb* (*the party that is governing the country*) rule, manage, lead, be in power over, be in charge of, preside over, control.

government *n* (*He is a member of the government*) administration, parliament, congress, ministry, council, (*inf*) the powers that be.

grab *vb* **1** (*He was told to grab the end of the rope*) catch hold of, take hold of, grasp, clutch, grip. **2** (*He grabbed the money and ran*) seize, snatch. ▼

---

up for grabs ready to be taken, bought, etc (*There are several jobs up for grabs in the firm*).

---

grace *n* **1** (*admire the grace of the dancers*) gracefulness, elegance. **2** (*He did not to have the grace to apologize*) manners, courtesy, decency, decorum. **3** (*He was at one time the king's favourite courtier but he fell from grace*) favour, goodwill. **4** (*pray for God's grace*) forgiveness, mercy, pardon, clemency. **5** (*say grace before dinner*) blessing, benediction, thanksgiving. ▼

---

saving grace a good quality that prevents someone or something from being completely bad, unpleasant, useless, etc (*She is not very bright but her saving grace is that she is a very hard worker*). **with a bad** *or* **good grace** in an unwilling or willing way (*She acknowledged her defeat with a good grace*).

---

graceful *adj* **1** (*They admired the gymnasts' graceful movements*) smooth, flowing, supple, agile, easy, elegant. **2** (*He gave a graceful speech of thanks*) elegant, polished, suave, refined.

gracious *adj* **1** (*The old duchess was a very gracious lady*) kind, kindly, benevolent, friendly, amiable, pleasant, cordial, courteous, polite, civil. **2** (*their gracious lifestyle*) elegant, tasteful, comfortable, luxurious. **3** (*believe in a gracious God*) merciful, compassionate, lenient, gentle.

grade *n* **1** (*What grade has he reached in the firm?*) level, stage, position, rank, standard. **2** (*grades of eggs*) category, class, classification.

gradual *adj* (*There has been a gradual improvement*) slow, steady, gentle, moderate, step-by-step, systematic.

grain *n* **1** (*have grains of sand in her shoes*) particle, granule, bit, piece, fragment, speck. **2** (*the farmer grows grain*) cereal crop, corn. **3** (*We found that there was not a grain of truth in his statement*) particle, scrap, iota, trace, hint, suggestion. **4** (*the grain of the wood*) texture, surface. ▼

---

go against the grain to be against someone's inclinations, feelings or wishes (*It goes against the grain for him to lie but he did not want to tell the truth and hurt her feelings*) <Refers to the direction of the grain in wood, it being easier to cut or smooth wood with the grain rather than across or against it>.

---

grand *adj* **1** (*the grand houses of the rich*) great, impressive, magnificent, splendid, imposing, majestic, stately, palatial. **2** (*a grand occasion*) important, great, splendid, magnificent, (*inf*) posh.

grant *vb* **1** (*The president granted the journalist an interview*) agree to, consent to, give one's assent to, allow, permit. **2** (*I grant that you may be right*) acknowledge, admit, concede, allow.

grant *n* (*get a grant to study at college*) allowance, award, subsidy, bursary.

grapple *vb* **1** (*The policeman grappled with the burglar*) struggle, wrestle, fight, tussle, clash. **2** (*He is still grappling with the problem of how to get there*) struggle, tackle, handle, deal with, cope with, attend to.

grasp *vb* **1** (*He grasped the handrail to prevent himself from falling*) grip, clutch, grab, take hold of, hold on to, clench. **2** (*He seemed unable to grasp the situation*) understand, follow, comprehend, take in, get the drift of. ▼

---

grasp the nettle to set about an unpleasant or difficult task in a firm and determined manner (*I know that you do not wish to hurt her but you must grasp the nettle and tell her that her work is not up to standard*).

---

grateful *adj* **1** (*They were grateful to him for his help*) thankful, filled with gratitude, indebted, obliged, appreciative. **2** (*We received a grateful letter for our contribution*) appreciative, thankful.

grave *n* (*the grave of the unknown soldier*) burial place, tomb, sepulchre.

grave *adj* **1** (*He was in a grave mood when he came back from the hospital*) solemn, serious, earnest, sober, sombre, grim, severe, unsmiling. **2** (*There were grave matters to discuss at the meeting*) serious, important, significant, weighty, pressing, urgent, vital, crucial.

graveyard *n* (*The funeral procession arrived at the graveyard*) cemetery, burial ground, churchyard.

graze *vb* **1** (*He grazed his knee*) scrape, skin, scratch, wound, bruise, abrade. **2** (*The car grazed the garage wall*) brush, touch, glance off, shave, skim.

greasy *adj* **1** (*dislike greasy foods*) fatty, fat, oily. **2** (*The car skidded on the greasy roads*) slippery, slippy, slimy.

great *adj* **1** (*a great stretch of water*) large, big, extensive, vast, immense, huge. **2** (*The invalid was in great pain*) extreme, severe, intense, acute. **3** (*They have travelled to all the great cities of the world*) major, main, chief, principal, leading. **4** (*the great people of the country*) important, prominent, leading, top, eminent, distinguished, notable, famous. **5** (*He was a great tennis player*) expert, skilful, adept, proficient, masterly, (*inf*) ace, (*inf*) crack. **6** (*They had a great time at the party*) enjoyable, splendid, wonderful, marvellous, (*inf*) fabulous. ▼

---

go great guns to be performing very well (*The runner got off to a slow start but he is going great guns now*). **great minds think alike** an expression used humorously when someone else shares one's opinion or has had the same idea as oneself (*John came up with the same solution to the problem as I did—great minds think alike*).

---

greedy *adj* **1** (*greedy children who ate all the cakes before some people arrived*) gluttonous, gannet-like, (*inf*) gutsy. **2** (*people greedy for information*) avid, eager, hungry, desirous of, craving. **3** (*a greedy miser hoarding gold*) grasping, avaricious, acquisitive, miserly, tight-fisted.

greet *vb* **1** (*He greeted his neighbour as he walked down the street*) say 'hello' to, address, hail. **2** (*The hostess greeted her guests*) receive, welcome, meet.

grief *n* (*her grief at the death of her husband*) sorrow, sadness, misery, distress, heartbreak, dejection, mourning. ▼

---

come to grief to suffer misfortune, to be unsuccessful (*All their schemes for making money came to grief*).

---

grievance *n* (*Management refused to listen to the workers' grievances*) complaint, protest, charge, grumble, (*inf*) gripe, (*inf*) grouse.

grieve *vb* **1** (*The widow is still grieving*) mourn, be in mourning, lament, be sorrowful, sorrow, be sad, be distressed, fret. **2** (*She was grieved by her son's behaviour*) hurt, upset, distress, sadden, wound.

grim *adj* **1** (*She held on with grim determination*) determined, resolute, obstinate, unwavering, relentless. **2** (*The teacher was wearing a grim expression*) stern, severe, fierce, forbidding, formidable, sombre. **3** (*The murdered corpse was a grim sight*) horrible, dreadful, terrible, frightful, shocking, ghastly, gruesome.

grime *n* (*trying to clean the grime from the old house*) dirt, filth, dust, (*inf*) muck, (*inf*) grunge, (*inf*) crud.

grin *vb* smile, smile broadly, smile from ear to ear. ▼

---

grin like a Cheshire cat to smile very broadly, often with self-satisfaction (*She was grinning like a Cheshire cat as she was handed the prize*) <Refers to *Alice's Adventures in Wonderland* by Lewis Carroll, in which the Cheshire cat gradually disappears, leaving his smile behind>.

---

grind *vb* **1** (*grind coffee beans*) crush, pound, pulverize, powder, mill. **2** (*grind knives*) sharpen, whet, file, polish. **3** (*She had a habit of grinding her teeth*) gnash, grate, rasp.

grip *vb* **1** (*She gripped the handrail of the ship*) grasp, clutch, clasp, clench, grab, take hold of, seize. **2** (*The audience was gripped by the exciting play*) absorb, rivet, engross, fascinate, enthral, hold spellbound.

grit *n* **1** (*put grit on icy roads*) gravel, pebbles, dirt, sand, dust. **2** (*He did not have the grit to tell her himself that he was breaking off the engagement*) courage, bravery, pluck, nerve, backbone. ▼

---

grit one's teeth to make every effort not to show one's feelings of pain, distress, disappointment, anger, etc (*He had to grit his teeth when his boss read out a list of his faults*).

---

groan *vb* **1** (*The accident victim groaned in pain*) moan, whimper, wail, cry. **2** (*The workers were groaning about their low wages*) grumble, complain, moan, (*inf*) grouse, (*inf*) gripe.

grope *vb* **1** (*They had to grope their way in the pitch dark*) fumble, feel. **2** (*She groped for her keys in her handbag*) fumble, feel for, fish for, scrabble for.

ground *n* **1** (*The ground is very wet after all the rain*) earth, soil, dirt, land, loam. **2** (*She became ill and fell to the ground*) earth, floor, (*inf*) deck. **3** (*They would like a new sports ground for their school*) stadium, pitch, field, arena, park. ▼

---

get (something) off the ground to get (a project) started and under way (*It sounds like a good idea but I think the scheme is too expensive ever to get off the ground*). **hit the ground running** to start a new activity immediately with a great deal of energy and enthusiasm (*We expected the new manager to hit the ground running and introduce new ideas immediately, but she said that she would rather wait and see how things were done*). *<From soldiers leaving a helicopter or getting up from being dropped by parachute and immediately running into battle>*. **shift one's ground** to change one's opinions, attitudes, ideas, etc (*We thought that we were going to lose the vote but several members of the opposition have shifted their ground*)

---

grounds *npl* **1** (*They have grounds for concern about their missing son*) reason, cause, basis, foundation, justification. **2** (*The house was set in beautiful grounds*) land, surroundings, property, estate, lawns, gardens, park. **3** (*coffee grounds*) dregs, lees, deposit, sediment.

group *n* **1** (*We divided the books into groups*) category, class, set, lot, batch. **2** (*She has joined a cookery group*) society, association, club, circle. **3** (*A group of people gathered to watch the fight*) band, gathering, cluster, crowd, flock, bunch.

grow *vb* **1** (*The farmers grow wheat*) cultivate, produce, raise, farm. **2** (*The plants will not grow in this very dry soil*) shoot up, spring up, sprout, germinate, thrive, flourish. **3** (*The boy is growing rapidly*) become taller, get bigger, grow larger, stretch, lengthen, expand, fill out. **4** (*The situation is growing serious*) become, come to be, get, get to be, turn, turn out to be.

grudge *vb* (*She grudges them their success*) begrudge, resent, be jealous of, envy, mind.

grumble *vb* (*The passengers were grumbling about the train being late*) complain, protest, object, moan, (*inf*) grouse, (*inf*) gripe, (*inf*) beef.

guarantee *vb* **1** (*He guaranteed that he would attend the meeting*) promise, pledge, give one's word, give an assurance, vow, swear. **2** (*This ticket guarantees you a seat at the match*) ensure, secure. **3** (*He guaranteed his daughter's car loan*) act as guarantor, provide security for, provide surety for, underwrite, vouch for.

guard *n* **1** (*prison guards*) warder, jailer, gaoler, keeper, (*inf*) screw. **2** (*the castle guards*) sentry, sentinel, custodian, watchman, lookout, garrison. **3** (*put a new guard on the machine*) safety guard, safety device, shield. ▼

---

be off one's guard to be unprepared for a difficult or dangerous situation (*He was very tired and so the thieves stole his watch when he was off his guard*) <Refers to fencing>.

---

guard *vb* **1** (*the people who were guarding the jewels*) stand guard over, watch over, protect, safeguard, defend, shield, look after, preserve. **2** (*the people guarding the prisoners*) keep under guard, keep watch over, keep under surveillance, mind, supervise. **3** (*Tourists are asked to guard against thieves*) beware of, be on the alert for, be on the look-out for, keep an eye out for.

guess *vb* **1** (*We were asked to guess the weight of the cake*) estimate, predict, (*inf*) guesstimate. **2** (*We guessed that they would take the shortest route*) surmise, conjecture, suppose, assume, reckon.

guest *n* (*The hostess welcomed her guests*) visitor, company, caller.

guide *vb* **1** (*He guided them down the mountain*) lead, conduct, show, usher, direct, show the way to, escort. **2** (*They asked for someone to guide them in their choice of career*) advise, give advice to, counsel, direct.

guide *n* **1** (*They hired a guide to show them round the city sights*) escort, leader, advisor. **2** (*buy a guide to Rome*) guidebook, handbook, directory, manual. **3** (*The lights acted as a guide to shipping*) landmark, marker, signal, beacon. **4** (*The pupils were given an essay as a guide*) model, pattern, standard, example, yardstick.

guilt *n* **1** (*It was impossible to prove his guilt*) guiltiness, blame, blameworthiness, culpability, fault, responsibility. **2** (*feelings of guilt at their treatment of her*) guiltiness, guilty conscience, remorse, penitence, shame.

guilty *adj* **1** (*He was tried and found guilty*) to blame, blameworthy, culpable, at fault, responsible. **2** (*they felt guilty about not inviting her*) conscience-stricken, remorseful, repentant, penitent, ashamed, shamefaced, sheepish.

gulf *n* **1** (*They were asked to find the Gulf of Mexico on the map*) bay, cove, inlet. **2** (*They had a quarrel and there is now a gulf between* *the two families*) chasm, rift, split, division, divide.

gullible *adj* (*The old lady was not gullible enough to be taken in by his story*) naive, ingenuous, over-trustful, foolish, credulous.

gulp *vb* **1** (*The children were told not to gulp their food*) bolt, wolf, gobble, devour. **2** (*She tried to gulp back her tears*) fight back, choke back, suppress, stifle, smother.

gush *vb* **1** (*Water gushed from the burst pipe*) pour, steam, rush, spout, spurt, flood, cascade. **2** (*She embarrassed the little girls by gushing about their prettiness*) enthuse, be effusive, babble, fuss.

gust *n* (*a gust of wind*) puff, rush, flurry, blast, squall.

gutter *n* (*flood water running down the gutter*) drain, sewer, sluice, ditch.

H

habit *n* **1** (*It was their habit to eat late in the evening*) custom, practice, routine, convention. **2** (*smoking and other harmful habits*) addiction, dependence, compulsion, obsession.

habitat *n* (*the animal's usual habitat*) environment, background, home.

habitual *n* **1** (*They went home by their habitual route*) usual, customary, accustomed, regular, routine. **2** (*He is a habitual smoker*) addicted, confirmed, hardened.

hack *vb* (*They hacked down the trees*) chop down, cut down, fell, hew.

hackneyed *adj* (*The writer is too apt to use hackneyed phrases*) overused, stale, stereotyped, unoriginal, run-of-the-mill, stock.

haggard *adj* (*She looked haggard with tiredness*) drawn, gaunt, hollow-cheeked.

haggle *vb* (*haggle over the price of a shawl in the market*) bargain.

hail *vb* (*She hailed her friend in the street*) greet, salute, wave to, say 'hello' to.

hair *n* **1** (*She has beautiful hair*) locks, tresses. **2** (*the animal's hair*) fur, coat. ▼

---

let one's hair down to behave in an informal, relaxed manner (*She always seemed reserved but she let her hair down at the party and danced on the table*). **split hairs** to argue about small, unimportant details, to quibble (*She is leaving the job. There is no point in splitting hairs as to whether she was bored with it or tired*). **keep one's hair on** (*inf*) to remain calm and not get angry (*Keep your hair on. We didn't mean to scratch your car*).

---

half-hearted *adj* (*They made a half-hearted attempt at saving the business*) lukewarm, unenthusiastic, apathetic, indifferent.

hall *n* **1** (*The guests left their coats in the hall*) entrance hall, hallway, lobby, vestibule. **2** (*The crowds surged into the hall*) concert hall, auditorium, theatre.

hallucination *n* (*She thought that she had seen a ghost but it was only a hallucination*) illusion, figment of the imagination, vision, fantasy, apparition.

halt *vb* **1** (*The traffic has to halt at the end of the road*) come to a halt, stop, come to a stop, pull up, draw up. **2** (*Work halted when the heating system broke down*) stop, finish, end, break off, discontinue. **3** (*The strike halted progress on the export order*) stop, put a stop to, put an end to, arrest, interrupt, obstruct, impede.

halve *vb* (*halve the orange for the two children*) cut in half, divide in two. ▼

---

go halves with (someone) to share costs with (someone) (*When they go to the cinema they go halves on the tickets*).

---

hamper *vb* (*The bad weather hampered progress on the building*) hinder, impede, obstruct, hold up.

hand *n* **1** (*the hand of a clock*) pointer, indicator, needle. **2** (*They had to sack some of the hands*) worker, employee, helper. ▼

---

be hand in glove with (someone) to be closely associated with (someone) for a bad or illegal purpose (*The police discovered that one of the assistants in the jewellery shop had been hand in glove with the jewel thieves*). **have a hand in (something)** to be involved in (something), to have contributed to the cause of (something) (*She had a hand in the surprise birthday party for her friend*).

---

hand *vb* (*hand the prize to the winner*) hand over, give, pass, transfer, transmit. ▼

---

keep one's hand in to retain one's skill at (something) by doing it occasionally (*The ex-champion does not play tennis very often but he keeps his hand in by playing with his son occasionally*).

---

handbook *n* (*read the instructions in the handbook*) manual, directions, instructions, guide, guidebook.

handicap *vb* (*Her lack of qualifications was a handicap to her in her career*) disadvantage, impediment, obstruction, hindrance, block.

handle *vb* (*the handle of the tool/the handle of the pan*) shaft, grip, hilt. ▼

---

fly off the handle to lose one's temper (*She flies off the handle whenever anyone disagrees with her*) <A reference to an axe head which flies off the handle when it is being used>.

---

handle *vb* **1** (*They were asked not to handle the goods before they bought them*) touch, finger, feel, pick up, lift. **2** (*He cannot handle the more difficult pupils*) cope with, deal with, manage, control.

handsome *n* **1** (*Her husband is a very handsome man*) attractive, good-looking. **2** (*The antique table was a handsome piece of furniture*) attractive, fine, elegant, tasteful. **3** (*Her parents gave them a handsome gift as a wedding present*) generous, magnanimous, lavish, sizeable.

handy *adj* **1** (*Do you have the book handy?*) to hand, available, within reach, accessible, nearby. **2** (*That is a handy kitchen utensil*) useful, helpful, convenient, practical. **3** (*It is useful to have someone handy to do repairs around the house*) good with one's hands, practical, capable.

hang *vb* **1** (*There were mobiles hanging from the ceiling in the nursery*) hang down, be suspended, dangle, swing. **2** (*She hung the picture from the picture rail*) suspend, put up. **3** (*She employed him to hang wallpaper*) put up, stick on. **4** (*They used to hang murderers in Britain*) send to the gallows, put a noose on, send to the gibbet, execute, (*inf*) string up. ▼

---

a hanging matter a very serious deed, often one which receives a harsh punishment (*I was surprised that he was expelled* *from the school. I would not have thought that his action was a hanging matter*) <A reference to a crime that was punishable by execution or hanging>. **get the hang of (something)** to learn how to do (something) or to begin to understand (something) (*I think the learner driver has finally got the hang of changing gears*).

---

hanker *vb* (*She hankers after a cottage in the country*) desire, long for, yearn for, crave, covet, fancy, (*inf*) have a yen for.

haphazard *adj* (*The books were arranged in a haphazard way*) random, unsystematic, unmethodical, disorganized, slapdash, careless.

happen *vb* **1** (*The accident happened on icy roads*) occur, take place, come about. **2** (*We happened to meet her in the supermarket*) chance. **3** (*Whatever happened to them?*) become of, befall. **4** (*They happened upon some valuable old books*) find, come upon, chance upon, stumble upon.

happening *n* (*There has been a series of sad happenings in her life*) event, incident, occurrence, experience.

happy *adj* **1** (*The children were happy playing in the sunshine*) cheerful, merry, light-hearted, joyful, carefree. **2** (*They were happy to see their grandparents*) pleased, glad, delighted. **3** (*By a happy chance we found the lost necklace*) fortunate, lucky. ▼

---

a happy event the birth of a baby (*The young couple are expecting a happy event*). **a happy hunting ground** a place where someone finds what he or she desires or where he or she is successful (*That boutique is a happy hunting ground for her. She has bought all her nicest clothes there*).

---

harass *vb* (*The children were bored and were harassing their mother*) pester, disturb, bother, annoy, badger, torment, (*inf*) hassle.

harbour *n* (*The ships were tied up in the harbour*) quay, jetty, pier, wharf, dock.

harbour *vb* **1** (*She was accused of harbouring an escaped prisoner*) shelter, give protection to, give asylum to. **2** (*They still harbour resentment against their mother for abandoning them*) nurse, retain, maintain, cling to.

hard *adj* **1** (*The ground was hard*) solid, solidified, stony, rocky. **2** (*a hard substance*) solid, rigid, stiff, inflexible, tough. **3** (*The work was very hard*) arduous, strenuous, heavy, laborious, tiring, demanding, taxing, exacting. **4** (*The problem was a hard one*) difficult, complicated, complex, involved, intricate. **5** (*They are hard workers*) industrious, diligent, energetic, keen. **6** (*Their father was a hard man*) harsh, stern, severe, ruthless. **7** (*He was wounded by a hard blow to the head*) strong, forceful, powerful, violent. **8** (*She had a hard life*) difficult, uncomfortable, harsh, grim, unpleasant, distressing. ▼

---

be hard put to it to have great difficulty (*You would be hard put to it to find a more comfortable hotel than the one in the village*). **hard lines** bad luck (*It was hard lines that it rained during the children's picnic*)

<Perhaps a reference to a ship's ropes being made hard by ice>.

---

hardship *n* (*The refugees are suffering hardship*) adversity, deprivation, want, need, distress.

harm *n vb* **1** (*The kidnappers did not harm the child*) hurt, injure, wound, abuse, maltreat. **2** (*The incident harmed his reputation*) damage, mar, spoil.

harm *n* **1** (*No harm came to the child*) injury, hurt, pain, suffering, abuse. **2** (*Some harm was done to his reputation*) damage, detriment, loss.

harmful *adj* (*The drug is not thought to have any harmful effects*) hurtful, injurious, disadvantageous, detrimental, deleterious.

harmless *adj* **1** (*a weed-killer that is thought to be harmless to pets*) safe, innocuous, non-toxic. **2** (*He was just a harmless old man*) innocuous, inoffensive, blameless, innocent.

harmony *n* (*The different nationalities lived in harmony in the country*) peace, peacefulness, agreement, accord, concord, friendship.

harsh *adj* **1** (*The harsh noise grated on their ears*) grating, jarring, rasping, strident, discordant. **2** (*The colours of the walls were a bit harsh*) gaudy, garish, loud, bold. **3** (*It had been a harsh winter*) hard, severe, cold. **4** (*She had been brought up under harsh conditions*) severe, grim, rough, austere. **5** (*He was a harsh ruler*) cruel, brutal, merciless, ruthless, tyrannical. **6** (*The school rules used to be very harsh*) severe, stern, stringent, inflexible.

haste *n* (*Haste is required to get the order delivered on time*) speed, swiftness, rapidity, fastness. ▼

---

more haste less speed if one attempts to do something in too much of a hurry one makes careless mistakes and ends up taking longer to do it (*If you ask them to type faster they just make mistakes. It is a case of more haste less speed*).

---

hasty *adj* **1** (*You should avoid making hasty decisions*) hurried, rushed, impetuous, impulsive. **2** (*She gave a hasty look at her notes before she spoke*) quick, rapid, swift, brief, fleeting, cursory, superficial. **3** (*She has a hasty temper*) hot, fiery, quick, irritable.

hat *n* (*He wore a hat to protect his head from the sun*) cap, bonnet. ▼

---

hat trick any action done three times in a row (*He scored a third goal to make a hat trick*) <A reference to a cricketer who received a hat from his club for putting out three batsmen with three balls in a row>. **hats off to (someone)** (someone) should be praised and congratulated (*Hats off to the new boy for standing up to the school bully*). **pass the hat round** to ask for contributions of money (*We passed the hat round the office for a wedding gift for her*).

---

hate *vb* **1** (*He hates his rival/She hates football*) loathe, detest, dislike, abhor, have an aversion to. **2** (*I would hate to upset her*) be reluctant, be loath, be unwilling.

hateful *adj* (*She thinks that he is a hateful person*) loathsome, detestable, abhorrent, revolting, offensive, horrible, nasty.

hatred *n* (*He is full of hatred towards his rivals*) hate, loathing, abhorrence, dislike, aversion, ill-will.

haughty *adj* (*She looks at everyone in a very haughty way*) arrogant, proud, disdainful, condescending, snobbish.

haul *vb* (*They hauled the dead body from the river*) pull, tug, drag, draw, heave. ▼

---

haul (someone) over the coals to scold severely (*The salesgirl was hauled over the coals for being rude to the customer*) <A reference to an old practice of burning people alive because of their religious beliefs>.

---

have *vb* **1** (*They have two cats*) own, possess, keep. **2** (*The house has five rooms*) contain, comprise, include. **3** (*She had a lot of trouble with her eldest son*) experience, undergo, go through, endure. **4** (*She will not have such behaviour in her house*) permit, allow, tolerate, stand for. ▼

---

have had it to have no hope of survival, success, etc (*The owners of the corner shop will have had it when the new supermarket opens*). **have (someone) on** to try to deceive (someone), often for a joke (*The police don't want to see you. Your brother was having you on when he said that they did*). **let (someone) have it** suddenly to attack (someone) either physically or verbally (*The boy was tired of being beaten and turned round and let the bully have it*).

---

hay *n* (*They gave hay to the horses*) fodder, straw. ▼

---

make hay while the sun shines to take advantage of an opportunity while one has the chance (*He has been offered some overtime and he needs the money. He might as well make hay while the sun shines*).

---

hazard *n* (*one of the hazards of being a soldier*) danger, risk, peril, menace.

hazy *adj* **1** (*It was rather a hazy day*) misty, foggy. **2** (*Her memory of the event is a bit hazy*) unclear, vague, blurred, fuzzy, muddled.

head *n* **1** (*He has a good head for business*) mind, brain, intellect. **2** (*He was the head of the whole organization*) chief, leader, director, manager, principal, boss. **3** (*She is at the head of the company*) top, control, command, charge, leadership. **4** (*at the head of the hill*) top, summit, crest, brow, apex. **5** (*She was at the head of the queue*) top, front. ▼

---

bring (something) to a head to bring (something) to a state where something must be done about it (*There has been hostility between them for some time but his public criticism of her brought matters to a head*) <A reference to a boil, etc coming to a head>. **go to (someone's) head 1** to make (someone) conceited or arrogant (*Winning first prize went to his head and he goes around boasting all the time*). **2** to make (someone) slightly drunk (*One glass of wine goes to her head*).

---

head *vb* **1** (*He was heading the expedition*) be in charge of, lead, be in control of, direct. **2** (*They *headed for town*) make for, set out for, go to.

heal *vb* **1** (*The ointment will heal the wound*) cure, make better, remedy, treat. **2** (*The wound began to heal*) get better, mend, improve.

health *n* (*The children are full of health*) healthiness, fitness, strength, vigour.

healthy *adj* **1** (*healthy young men playing football*) well, fit, robust, strong, vigorous. **2** (*They live in a healthy climate*) health-giving, invigorating, bracing. **3** (*They eat a healthy diet*) health-giving, healthful, nutritious, nourishing, wholesome.

heap *n* (*heaps of leaves in the garden*) pile, mound, stack, mass, stockpile.

heap *vb* (*The children heaped up the leaves in the garden*) pile, stack, stockpile, accumulate.

hear *vb* **1** (*I could not hear what she said*) catch, take in. **2** (*We heard that they had gone abroad*) find out, discover, gather, learn.

heart *n* **1** (*He loves her with all his heart*) love, passion, affection, emotion. **2** (*She thinks he has no heart*) tenderness, compassion, sympathy, humanity, kindness. **3** (*The discussion did not get to the heart of the matter*) centre, core, nucleus, hub, crux. ▼

---

his, her, etc, **heart is in the right place** he, she, etc, is basically kind, sympathetic, etc, although sometimes not appearing to be so (*Our neighbour seems very stern towards the children but her heart is in the right place*). **take (something) to heart 1** to be upset by (something) (*He was only teasing but she took his remarks to heart*). **2** to be influenced by and take notice of (something) (*She took the doctor's advice to heart and tried to get more rest*).

---

hearten *vb* (*The team were heartened by their success*) cheer, cheer up, uplift, encourage, elate, buoy up.

hearty *adj* **1** (*They were given a hearty welcome*) enthusiastic, eager, warm, friendly. **2** (*He has a hearty dislike of deceit*) wholehearted, great, complete, thorough. **3** (*They ate a hearty breakfast*) substantial, solid, filling, ample.

heat *n* (*The heat melted the ice*) hotness, warmth. ▼

---

in the heat of the moment while influenced by the excitement or emotion of the occasion (*They were having a quarrel and in the heat of the moment she threatened to kill him*). **take the heat out of (something)** to make (a situation) less emotional, tense, etc (*They were just about to hit each other but their friend suggested that they sit down and discuss their differences to take the heat of the situation*).

---

heave *vb* **1** (*He hurt his back heaving heavy weights*) lift, raise, haul, pull, tug. **2** (*They heaved a sigh of relief*) utter, give, let out.

heaven *n* **1** (*Bible stories about heaven*) paradise. **2** (*She thought that lying on a beach in the sun was heaven*) bliss, ecstasy, rapture, supreme happiness. ▼

---

be in seventh heaven to be extremely happy (*She was in seventh heaven when her twins* *were born*) <In Jewish literature the seventh heaven is the highest of all heavens where God lives>. **pennies from heaven** a sudden and unexpected sum of money or piece of good fortune (*They were poverty-stricken and so the prize money was pennies from heaven*).

---

heavy *adj* **1** (*He had to carry heavy weights in his job*) weighty, hefty, substantial, burdensome. **2** (*It proved a heavy task*) hard, difficult, arduous, laborious, demanding, exacting. **3** (*He received a heavy blow to the head*) hard, strong, powerful, forceful, violent. **4** (*He was a heavy man*) large, bulky, hefty, stout, overweight, fat, obese. **5** (*a heavy mist*) dense, thick, solid. **6** (*with heavy heart*) depressed, gloomy, downcast, despondent. ▼

---

make heavy weather of (something) to make more effort to do (something) than should be necessary (*The pupils made heavy weather of the exam although it was quite easy*) <Refers originally to a ship which does not handle well in difficult conditions>.

---

hectic *adj* (*They had a hectic day at the office*) busy, frantic, bustling, frenzied.

hedge *vb* **1** (*The trees hedged in the garden*) surround, enclose, encircle, fence in. **2** (*She simply hedged when they asked her a direct question*) prevaricate, equivocate, hum and haw, beat about the bush.▼

---

look as though one has been dragged through a hedge backwards to look extremely untidy (*The little boy always looks as though he has been dragged through a hedge backwards at the end of the school day*).

---

heed *n* (*They pay no heed to what anyone says*) attention, notice, note, consideration.

hefty *adj* (*He is a hefty young man*) heavy, bulky, stout, brawny, muscular, powerfully built.

height *n* **1** (*measure the height*) tallness, altitude. **2** (*He died at the height of his career*) culmination, peak, zenith.

heir/heiress *ns* (*He was heir to his father's estate*) inheritor, beneficiary, legate.

help *vb* **1** (*She did it to help her parents*) assist, aid, support, lend a hand to. **2** (*They gave her something to help the pain*) ease, soothe, relieve, alleviate, cure.

help *n* **1** (*The old lady is in need of some help*) assistance, aid, support. **2** (*There was no help for the condition*) ease, relief, alleviation, cure.

helpful *adj* **1** (*He made some helpful suggestions*) useful, of use, beneficial, advantageous, valuable. **2** (*Their neighbours are very helpful people*) supportive, obliging, cooperative, caring, charitable, friendly.

hereditary *adj* **1** (*The disease is hereditary*) inherited, genetic, congenital. **2** (*hereditary property*) inherited, bequeathed.

hero *n* **1** (*He was the hero of the battle*) victor, champion, celebrity. **2** (*The pop singer is the girl's hero*) idol, ideal. **3** (*the hero in the play*) male lead.

heroic *adj* (*It was a heroic act to try and save his friend's life*) brave, courageous, valiant, gallant, intrepid, fearless, bold.

hesitate *vb* **1** (*She hesitated before making such an important decision*) pause, delay, hang back, wait, vacillate, waver, shilly-shally. **2** (*They hesitate to interfere in their daughter's life*) be reluctant, be unwilling, be disinclined, shrink from. **3** (*He hesitates a bit when he gets nervous*) stammer, stutter, stumble, falter.

hide *vb* **1** (*The thieves hid the jewels in the garden*) conceal, secrete. **2** (*The escaped prisoners were hiding in the cellar*) take cover, lie low, conceal oneself, go to ground. **3** (*clouds hiding the sun*) obscure, block, eclipse, obstruct. **4** (*She tried to hide her motives*) conceal, keep secret, suppress, hush up.

hide *n* (*the animal's hide*) skin, pelt, coat, fur. ▼

---

neither hide nor hair of (someone *or* **something)** no trace at all of (someone or something) (*The police are searching for the missing prisoner but so far they have found neither hide nor hair of him*) <'Hide' here means skin>. **tan (someone's) hide** to beat or thrash (someone) (*The boy's father threatened to tan his hide if he got into trouble at school again*) <A reference to leather-making>.

---

hideous *adj* **1** (*The new curtains are hideous*) ugly, unsightly, gruesome, grim, repulsive, revolting. **2** (*It was a hideous crime*) horrible, horrific, shocking, outrageous, dreadful, appalling.

high *adj* **1** (*a street with high buildings*) tall, lofty, towering. **2** (*He has a high rank in the organization*) top, leading, prominent, important, powerful. **3** (*They have a high opinion of his work*) favourable, good, approving, admiring. **4** (*She has a very high voice*) high-pitched, shrill, sharp, piercing. **5** (*The ship was in difficulties in the high winds*) strong, intense, forceful, violent. ▼

---

a high flier a person who is bound to be very successful or who has achieved great success (*She was one of the high fliers in our year at university*). **high and mighty** arrogant (*Since he has become so rich he is so high and mighty that he won't speak to his former neighbours*). **leave (someone) high and dry** to leave (someone) in a difficult or helpless state (*His secretary walked out and left him high and dry in the middle of the busiest time of the year*) <A reference to a ship left stranded>.

---

highbrow *adj* (*Her taste in books is rather highbrow*) intellectual, scholarly, educated, bookish.

highlight *n* (*The trip to the theatre was one of the highlights of our trip*) high spot, feature, peak, climax.

hijack *vb* (*The thieves hijacked the lorry*) seize, take over, commandeer, expropriate.

hike *vb* (*They hiked over the hills*) tramp, march, walk, ramble, trek, trudge.

hilarious *adj* (*The comedian's jokes were hilarious*) uproarious, hysterical, side-splitting, funny, amusing, humorous, comic, entertaining.

hill *n* **1** (*The hills behind the town*) heights, highland, rising ground, mountain, peak. **2** (*The cars went *slowly up the steep hill*) slope, rise, incline, gradient. ▼

as old as the hills extremely old (*Some of the village traditions are as old as the hills*). **over the hill** past one's best or past one's prime (*In that firm you are considered over the hill at thirty*).

hinder *vb* (*The bad weather hindered their efforts to get the bridge built*) hamper, impede, hold up, obstruct, delay, curb, block.

hindrance *n* (*Their long tight skirts were a hindrance to them when they tried to hurry*) impediment, obstacle, obstruction, handicap, drawback.

hint *n* **1** (*She gave no hint that she was planning to leave*) inkling, clue, suggestion, indication, mention. **2** (*He writes a column in the newspaper giving gardening hints*) tip, suggestion, pointer. **3** (*There was just a hint of ginger in the sauce*) trace, touch, dash, suggestion, soupçon.

hire *vb* **1** (*They hired a boat*) rent, lease, charter. **2** (*The firm is hiring more staff*) engage, take on, sign on, appoint, employ.

hiss *vb* **1** (*The kettle was hissing*) whistle, wheeze. **2** (*The audience hissed at the comic's bad jokes*) boo, jeer.

historic *n* (*It was a historic battle/It was a historic event when the country gained its independence*) famous, notable, celebrated, memorable, important, significant, outstanding.

hit *vb* **1** (*The bully hit the little boy*) strike, slap, smack, punch, bang, thump. **2** (*The car was out of control and hit the lorry*) bang into, crash into, knock into, smash into. ▼

hit it off to get on well, to become friendly immediately (*I knew those two would hit it off. They have so much in common*). **hit the hay** (*inf*) to go to bed (*He was so tired that he decided to hit the hay immediately after dinner*) <Beds were formerly filled with hay>.

hitch *n* (*Our travel arrangements were going well but then there was a sud- den hitch*) snag, hindrance, hold-up, obstacle, difficulty, stumbling-block, (*inf*) glitch.

hoard *vb* (*They hoarded food in the summer in case of bad weather in the winter/misers hoarding gold*) store, stock up, save, accumulate, pile up, gather, collect.

hoarse *adj* (*She had a cold and her voice was hoarse*) harsh, gruff, husky, croaking, grating, rasping, raucous.

hoax *n* (*The bomb threat was a hoax*) practical joke, joke, prank, trick, (*inf*) spoof.

hobble *vb* (*Her feet were sore and she had to hobble down to the shops*) limp, shuffle, totter.

hobby *n* (*They work so hard that they have little time for hobbies*) pastime, diversion, amusement, sport.

hold *vb* **1** (*They held their luggage tightly*) hold on to, clutch, grip, grasp, cling to. **2** (*They held each other close*) embrace, cuddle, hug, clasp. **3** (*The bank holds all their private documents*) have, keep, retain, own, possess. **4** (*He holds a position of responsibility*) hold down, have, be in, occupy, fill. **5** (*One suitcase will not* *hold all these clothes*) contain, take, carry, include. **6** (*The bridge will not hold his weight*) bear, carry, support, sustain. **7** (*Police are holding him to help with their inquiries*) detain, hold in custody, confine, keep, imprison. **8** (*It is difficult to hold the interest of the children*) keep, retain, occupy, engage. **9** (*I wonder if the warm weather will hold*) last, continue, go on, remain, stay. **10** (*The old rule does not hold anymore*) be valid, be in force, apply. **11** (*They hold him responsible for the accident*) consider, think, regard, view. **12** (*The club holds meetings every month*) have, conduct, run. ▼

---

have a hold over (someone) to have power or influence over (someone), often because one knows something bad about him or her (*We thought that he had a hold over her and then we discovered that he had found out that she had been in prison*). **hold forth** to talk for a long time forcefully or pompously about (something) (*He bored everyone by holding forth about his opinion of the government*). **hold good** to be valid, to still apply (*The rule about no smoking still holds good*).

---

hole *n* **1** (*There was a hole in the hedge/The material was full of holes*) opening, aperture, gap, breach, break, crack, rent, slit, perforation, orifice. **2** (*There was a huge hole in the ground after the explosion*) crater, cavity, chasm, hollow, depression, dip. 3 (*the animal's hole*) lair, burrow, earth. ▼

---

make a hole in (something) use a large part of (somethin (*Going on holiday left a huge hole in our savings*). **pick holes in (something)** to find faults in (something) (*They spent their time picking holes in her theory*).

---

holiday *n* (*Today is a school holiday/They usually take their holidays in the late spring*) vacation, time off, day off, leave.

hollow *adj* **1** (*a hollow space*) hollowed out, empty, vacant. **2** (*She has hollow cheeks*) sunken, concave. **3** (*We heard a hollow sound*) dull, low, muffled, deep.

hollow *vb* (*They hollowed out a tree trunk to make a canoe*) scoop out, gouge out, excavate.

holy *adj* **1** (*The saint's grave was a holy place*) blessed, consecrated, sacred, hallowed. **2** (*They are holy people*) God-fearing, religious, pious, devout.▼

---

the holy of holies a private or special place inside a building (*That's her father's study. It's the holy of holies in the house*) <A literal translation of the Hebrew name of the inner sanctuary in the Jewish Temple where the Ark of the Covenant was kept>.

---

home *n* **1** (*I know where he works but not where his home is*) house, residence, abode, domicile, dwelling place. **2** (*the home of the chimpanzee*) habitat, environment, abode. **3** (*The old lady is in a home*) residential home, institution.▼

---

a home from home a place where one feels comfortable

and relaxed (*Her friend's house is a home from home for her*). **home truth** a plain, direct statement of something that is true but unpleasant or difficult for someone to accept (*I told her a few home truths about how her behaviour was affecting everyone else*).

---

honest *adj* **1** (*honest people who do not steal other people's goods*) honourable, upright, good, decent, righteous, moral, virtuous, trustworthy, law-abiding. **2** (*She gave honest replies to the questions*) true, truthful, sincere, genuine, direct, frank, candid. **3** (*He gave an honest judgement*) fair, just, impartial, objective, unbiased.

honour *n* **1** (*He was a man of honour and handed in the money which he had found*) honesty, integrity, uprightness, decency, principle, righteousness, morals, virtue. **2** (*His honour was at stake*) reputation, good name. **3** (*He did not care about the honour of winning*) glory, prestige, fame, renown, distinction.

honourable *adj* **1** (*honourable people who tell the truth*) honest, upright, good, decent, righteous, moral, virtuous, trustworthy, admirable. **2** (*It was an honourable victory for the army*) famous, renowned, prestigious, notable, distinguished.

hook *n* **1** (*a hook used for cutting corn*) scythe, sickle. **2** (*hooks for the children's coats*) peg. **3** (*the hook of the dress*) fastener, catch.

hook *vb* **1** (*They hooked a fish*) catch, take. **2** (*hook the trailer on to the car*) fasten, secure. ▼

---

get (someone) off the hook to free (someone) from some difficulty, problem, etc, or from something that he or she does not want to do (*I did not want to go to the party and my friends got me of the hook by asking me to babysit*) <A reference to angling>.

---

hooked *adj* **1** (*She has a hooked nose*) hook-shaped, aquiline, curved, bent. **2** (*He is hooked on cigarettes*) addicted, dependent, obsessed by.

hooligan *n* (*The police are looking for the hooligans who damaged the cars*) ruffian, thug, vandal, (*inf*) yobbo.

hoop *n* (*hoops of steel*) ring, band, circle, circlet. ▼

---

put (someone) through the hoop to cause (someone) to experience something unpleasant or difficult (*The interviewers certainly put the candidates for the job through the hoop*) <A reference to circus performers who jump through hoops set on fire or to circus animals which are made to jump through hoops>.

---

hop *vb* (*The frogs were hopping everywhere*) jump, leap, bound, spring, skip.

hope *n* **1** (*We were full of hope for a victory*) hopefulness, optimism, confidence, expectation, faith. **2** (*Is there any hope of success?*) likelihood, prospect.

hope *vb* (*We are hoping for victory*) have hopes of, be hopeful of, expect, anticipate, look forward to, have confidence in.

hopeful *adj* **1** (*We are hopeful of winning*) expectant, optimistic, confident. **2** (*The news is hopeful*) optimistic, promising, encouraging, favourable. ▼

hope against hope to continue to hope although there is very little reason to be hopeful (*She is seriously ill but they are hoping against hope that she will recover*).

horizontal *adj* (*both the horizontal and vertical supports of the frame/an invalid lying horizontal*) flat, level, prone, supine.

horrible *adj* **1** (*It was a horrible sight*) dreadful, awful, horrid, terrible, frightful, shocking, appalling, grim, hideous, ghastly, gruesome, disgusting, revolting. **2** (*She was a horrible old woman*) disagreeable, nasty, unpleasant, mean, obnoxious.

horrify *vb* (*We were horrified at her behaviour*) shock, appall, outrage, scandalize, disgust.

horror *n* (*They looked at the dead body with horror*) terror, fear, alarm, shock.

horse *n* (*She rode a brown horse*) mount, hack, pony, steed, stallion, mare, racehorse. ▼

horse sense common sense (*She has no specialist business knowledge but she has horse sense*). **horses for courses** certain people are better suited to certain tasks or situations than others <A reference to the fact that some horses run better on certain types of ground>.

hospitable *adj* (*The people we stayed with were most hospitable*) generous, kind, cordial, sociable, friendly.

hostage *n* (*They kept the child hostage*) captive, prisoner, pawn, surety.

hostile *adj* **1** (*The crowd grew hostile*) belligerent, aggressive, antagonistic, angry, unfriendly. **2** (*were quite hostile to the idea*) opposed, averse, antagonistic.

hot *adj* **1** (*There was no hot food left in the restaurant/hot food straight from the oven*) warm, piping hot, boiling, sizzling, scalding. **2** (*It was a very hot day*) boiling, sweltering, scorching, baking, blistering, sultry, torrid. **3** (*The sauce was too hot for their taste*) spicy, peppery, pungent, sharp. **4** (*She had a hot temper*) fiery, fierce, furious, violent.▼

a hot potato something which it is difficult or dangerous to deal with (*The complaint about bad food is a hot potato. You had better pass it on to the restaurant manager*). **be hot under the collar** to be very angry or agitated (*He got hot under the collar when she refused to believe him*). **make things hot for (someone)** to make a situation unpleasant or impossible for (someone) (*She might as well leave if the boss does not like her. He'll just make things hot for her if she stays*).

hotel *n* (*book in at the local hotel*) inn, tavern, guest-house, boarding house.

house *n* **1** (*The house they live in is very old*) abode, residence, dwelling, home. **2** (*They own a publishing house*) firm, company, business, establishment, concern. ▼

bring the house down cause great amusement or applause (*The comedian's jokes brought the house down*). **on the house** paid by the owner of the shop, restaurant or pub rather than by the customer (*The owner's wife has just had a baby and the drinks are on the house*).

---

house *vb* (*The flats house about thirty people*) accommodate, lodge, have room for.

hover *vb* **1** (*children's kites hovering in the air*) hang, flutter, fly, drift, float. **2** (*She was hovering behind them hoping to hear what they were talking about*) linger, hang about, wait.

howl *vb* **1** (*hear the dogs howling*) bay, yowl, yelp. **2** (*children howling for their mothers*) cry, weep, scream, bawl, wail.

huddle *vb* **1** (*The children huddled together to keep warm*) cuddle up, snuggle, nestle, curl up. **2** (*The sheep huddled in the corner of the field*) crowd, cluster, squeeze, pack.

hue *n* (*ribbons of many hues*) colour, shade, tone, tint. ▼

---

a hue and cry a loud protest, an outcry (*There was a real hue and cry when they threatened to close the local school*) <An old legal term meaning a summons for people to join in a hunt for a wanted criminal>.

---

hug *vb* (*The children hugged their mother*) embrace, cuddle, hold close.

huge *adj* (*a story about huge monsters*) enormous, massive, vast, immense, colossal, gigantic.

hum *vb* **1** (*machines humming in the factory*) drone, vibrate, throb, whirr, buzz. **2** (*She was humming a happy tune*) croon, murmur, mumble, sing.

human *n* (*animals and humans/fairies and humans*) human being, mortal.

humane *adj* (*It is humane to put animals down when they are in pain*) kind, compassionate, sympathetic, merciful, charitable.

humble *adj* **1** (*He has achieved much fame but is very humble*) modest, unassuming, self-effacing, unpretentious. **2** (*The humble people of the village*) common, ordinary, low-born, lowly, poor, unimportant. **3** (*She hates his humble attitude to his employer*) servile, subservient, submissive, obsequious, sycophantic. ▼

---

eat humble pie to be forced to admit that one has been wrong (*He said that his wife would never pass her driving test and had to eat humble pie when she passed it first time*) <A reference to a dish made from the 'umble' or offal of a deer once eaten by the lower classes>.

---

humid *adj* (*a humid atmosphere*) damp, moist, muggy, sticky, steamy, clammy.

humiliate *vb* (*She humiliated her husband by criticizing him in public*) mortify, make ashamed, humble, disgrace, embarrass.

humility *n* (*He showed humility even when he won*) humbleness, modesty, self-effacement.

humorous *adj* (*He told a very humorous story*) funny, amusing, comic, hilarious, facetious, entertaining.

humour *n* **1** (*He could not see the humour in the situation*) funny side, comedy, farce, absurdity. **2** (*his own particular brand of humour*) comedy, jokes, jests, wit. **3** (*He is not in a very good humour*) mood, temper, temperament, frame of mind, disposition.

hunch *n* **1** (*He has a hunch on his

back) hump, swelling, bump, bulge. 2 (*The police have a hunch that he is guilty*) feeling, intuition, sixth sense, inkling, suspicion.

hunger *n* 1 (*The children died of hunger*) starvation, famine. 2 (*He has a hunger for knowledge*) desire, longing, yearning, craving, thirst.

hungry *adj* 1 (*hungry children with nothing to eat*) starving, famished, ravenous. 2 (*They are hungry for knowledge*) eager, anxious, avid, craving, longing for.

hunk *n* (*a hunk of cheese*) lump, block, chunk, wedge, mass.

hunt *vb* 1 (*They are hunting stags*) chase, pursue, stalk, track. 2 (*She was hunting for her glasses*) look for, search for, seek, rummage for, scrabble for.

hurdle *n* 1 (*The runner failed to clear the first hurdle*) fence, rail, railing, barrier. 2 (*There were several hurdles in the way of progress*) obstacle, obstruction, impediment, barrier, stumbling block.

hurl *vb* (*The crowd hurled stones at the police*) throw, fling, cast, pitch, toss.

hurricane *n* (*lives lost in the hurricane*) tornado, cyclone, typhoon, storm, tempest.

hurry *vb* (*You must hurry if you want to catch the train*) hurry up, hasten, make haste, speed up, run, dash, (*inf*) get a move on.

hurt *vb* 1 (*His leg was hurt in the accident*) injure, wound, bruise, maim. 2 (*Her leg hurts*) be sore, be painful, ache, throb. 3 (*She was hurt by his unkind remarks*) upset, wound, grieve, sadden, offend.

hurtle *vb* (*The runner hurtled towards the finishing post*) race, dash, sprint, rush.

hush *vb* 1 (*Try to hush the children*) quieten, silence, (*inf*) shut up. 2 (*The crowd suddenly hushed*) fall silent, quieten down, (*inf*) shut up. 3 (*They tried to hush up the scandal but the press found out*) conceal, suppress, cover up.

hut *n* (*a garden hut*) shed, lean-to, shack, cabin.

hygienic *adj* (*Hospitals must be hygienic*) sanitary, clean, sterile, germ-free.

hymn *n* (*sing hymns in church*) psalm, religious song.

hypnotic *adj* (*hypnotic effects*) mesmerizing, mesmeric.

hypocritical *adj* (*It is hypocritical of him to go to church as he is a very evil person*) insincere, false, deceitful, dishonest, dissembling.

hypothetical *adj* (*Let us take a hypothetical case*) supposed, assumed, theoretical, imagined.

hysterical *adj* 1 (*She became hysterical at the news of his death*) frantic, frenzied, in a frenzy, out of control, berserk, beside oneself, distracted, overwrought, demented, crazed. 2 (*She told us a hysterical story about her travels*) hilarious, uproarious, side-splitting, comical, funny, amusing.

I

idea *n* **1** (*The idea of death terrifies him*) concept, notion. **2** (*We asked for their ideas on the subject*) thought, view, opinion, feeling. **3** (*I had an idea that he was dead*) thought, impression, belief, suspicion. **4** (*Their idea is to sail round the world*) plan, aim, intention, objective. **5** (*We need some idea of the cost*) estimation, approximation, guess.

ideal *adj* (*The conditions were ideal*) perfect, faultless, excellent.

identify *vb* **1** (*She was able to identify her attacker*) recognize, name, distinguish, pinpoint. **2** (*They were able to identify the cause of the problem*) establish, find out, ascertain, diagnose. **3** (*She identifies her mother with security*) associate, connect. **4** (*She identifies with homeless people*) empathize, relate.

identical *adj* **1** (*The twins wear identical clothes*) like, similar, matching. **2** (*That is the identical dress that her sister wore last week*) same.

idiot *n* (*He was an idiot to behave in that way*) fool, dolt, ass, dunce.

idiotic *adj* (*It was an idiotic thing to do*) stupid, foolish, senseless.

idle *adj* **1** (*He was an idle fellow who did not want to work*) lazy, indolent, slothful. **2** (*The workers are idle through no fault of their own*) unemployed, jobless.

idol *n* **1** (*The heathens were worshipping idols*) god, icon, image, effigy. **2** (*He is a pop idol to the teenagers*) hero/heroine, favourite, darling.

idolize *vb* (*The children idolize their grandfather*) adore, love, worship.

ignite *vb* **1** (*ignite the fire*) set alight, set fire to, kindle. **2** (*The dry material ignited easily*) catch fire, burn, burst into flames.

ignorant *adj* **1** (*They had never gone to school and were quite ignorant*) uneducated, illiterate. **2** (*They were ignorant of the legal facts*) unaware, unconscious, uninformed.

ignore *vb* **1** (*The child was told to ignore their insulting remarks*) disregard, take no notice of. **2** (*The pupils were told to ignore the last question in the exam paper*) disregard, omit, (*inf*) skip.

ill *adj* **1** (*She has been ill and off work for some time*) unwell, sick, poorly, indisposed, unhealthy, (*inf*) under the weather. **2** (*The medicine has no ill effects*) harmful, detrimental. **3** (*There is ill feeling between the two families*) hostile, antagonistic, unfriendly. ▼

---

it's an ill wind in almost every kind of misfortune there is something of benefit to someone (*There was an accident on the road and we might have been involved in it if our car had not broken down. It's an ill wind*) <Short for 'it's an ill wind that blows nobody any good'>. **take (something) ill that** to be offended or annoyed at (something) (*She took it ill that we hadn't invited her to the party*).

---

illegal *adj* (*They were imprisoned for their illegal deeds*) unlawful, illicit, criminal.
illegible *adj* (*Her handwriting was illegible*) unreadable, indecipherable, unintelligible.
illiterate *adj* (*people who never went to school and so are illiterate*) uneducated, unschooled, ignorant.
illness *n* (*She is suffering from a mysterious illness*) complaint, ailment, disease, disorder, affliction, (*inf*) bug.
illogical *vb* (*His behaviour was illogical*) irrational, unreasonable, unsound.
illusion *n* **1** (*The magician did not really do that—it was just an illusion*) deception. **2** (*The supposed ghost was just an illusion*) hallucination, dream, fantasy **3** (*She was under the illusion the he was unmarried*) delusion, misapprehension, misconception.
illustrate *vb* **1** (*She illustrated the children's book*) decorate, ornament. **2** (*He illustrated his theory with examples*) demonstrate, exemplify.
illustration *n* **1** (*the coloured illustrations in the book*) picture, drawing, sketch, diagram. **2** (*the illustrations which he used to prove his point*) example, case, instance.
image *adj* **1** (*There were images of famous saints in the churchyard*) likeness, effigy, statue, figure, representation. **2** (*You can see your image in the mirror*) reflection, likeness. ▼

---

be the spitting image of (someone *or* something) to be extremely like (someone or something) (*The child is the spitting image of his father*).

---

imaginary *adj* (*The child has an imaginary friend*) fictitious, invented, made up, legendary, mythical, unreal, fanciful.
imagination *n* **1** (*The poem shows imagination*) creativity, vision, inspiration, fancifulness . **2** (*She thought she saw her father but it was only her imagination*) illusion, fancy, hallucination, dream, figment of the imagination.
imagine *vb* **1** (*Can you imagine what life will be like in fifty years?*) picture, visualize, envisage, conceive. **2** (*He imagined that the meeting would last an hour*) presume, assume, suppose, think, believe.
imitate *vb* **1** (*She imitated the style used by the writer*) copy, emulate, follow. **2** (*The cruel children imitated the boy with the limp*) mimic, impersonate, mock, parody.
imitation *n* (*The portrait is not genuine but an imitation*) copy, reproduction, counterfeit, forgery, fake.
immature *adj* **1** (*It was immature of the young man to behave like that*) childish, juvenile, infantile. **2** (*The fruit was picked when it was immature*) unripe, green.
immediate *adj* **1** (*There was an immediate reaction to his speech*) instant, instantaneous, prompt, swift, sudden. **2** (*He turned to his immediate neighbour in the hall*) next, near, nearest, adjacent. **3** (*We have no immediate plans to go*) existing, current.
immediately *adv* **1** (*He plans to leave immediately*) right away, straight away, at once, without

delay. **2** (*They were sitting immediately behind us*) directly, right.

immense *adj* **1** (*an immense figure of a man*) huge, enormous, vast, colossal, gigantic, giant. **2** (*There has been an immense improvement*) huge, immense, vast.

immerse *vb* **1** (*She immersed the dress in the soapy water*) submerge, plunge, dip, lower. **2** (*They immersed themselves in their work before the exam*) absorb, engross, occupy, preoccupy.

immoral *adj* (*Everyone disapproved of his immoral acts*) bad, wrong, evil, wicked, sinful, unethical.

immortal *adj* (*Human beings are not immortal*) everlasting, endless, eternal, undying.

impact *n* **1** (*Both cars were damaged in the impact*) collision, crash, bump, smash, clash. **2** (*His speech had a powerful impact on the crowd*) effect, influence, impression. **3** (*His nose took the full impact of the blow*) force, shock, impetus, brunt.

impartial *adj* (*We had to make sure that the judge was impartial*) unbiased, unprejudiced, disinterested, objective, detached.

impatient *adj* **1** (*The children were impatient to get out to play*) eager, anxious, keen, avid. **2** (*The show was late starting and the audience was growing impatient*) restless, restive, agitated, edgy, fidgety.

impeccable *adj* (*His performance was impeccable*) faultless, flawless, perfect, exemplary.

impede *vb* (*The weather impeded their progress*) hinder, obstruct, hamper, block, check, delay, deter.

impediment *n* **1** (*The weather was an impediment to their plans*) hindrance, obstruction, obstacle, handicap, block, check, bar, barrier. **2** (*She has an impediment and has to speak slowly*) stammer, stutter.

imperative *adj* (*It is imperative that we leave now*) essential, necessary, urgent, vital, important, crucial.

imperceptible *adj* (*The difference between the two vases was imperceptible*) undetectable, unnoticeable, slight, small, minute.

impersonal *adj* (*The nurse had a very impersonal manner*) cold, cool, aloof, distant, stiff, formal, detached.

impersonate *vb* (*The pupil began to impersonate the teacher*) imitate, copy, mimic, mock, ape.

impertinent *adj* (*It was impertinent to speak to the old lady like that*) insolent, impudent, cheeky, rude, impolite, ill-mannered.

imperturbable *adj* (*She is imperturbable even in an emergency*) calm, cool, composed, unruffled.

impetuous *adj* (*He is given to impetuous actions*) hasty, impulsive, spontaneous, rash, foolhardy.

implement *n* (*The garden implements have been stolen/buy new kitchen implements*) tool, utensil, appliance, instrument, device, gadget.

implore *vb* (*She implored him to help*) beg, plead with, appeal to, entreat, beseech.

imply *vb* (*He implied that she was not telling the truth*) insinuate, hint, suggest, indicate.

important *adj* **1** (*It is important to arrive on time*) necessary, essential, vital, crucial, urgent. **2** (*The two countries are having important talks*) significant, critical, crucial, serious, momentous, of great import. **3** (*She noted the *important points in the lecture*) chief, main, principal, salient, significant. **4** (*All the important people in the town were invited to the reception*) prominent, notable, leading, distinguished, eminent.

impose *vb* **1** (*The judge imposed a heavy fine on him*) exact, charge, levy, inflict, enforce. **2** (*She tries to impose her views on all her colleagues*) force, foist, inflict, thrust. **3** (*They felt she was imposing on their mother's generosity*) take advantage, exploit, abuse.

impossible *adj* **1** (*It was obviously an impossible task*) unimaginable, inconceivable, impracticable, impractical, hopeless. **2** (*Life became impossible for them in the damp conditions*) unbearable, intolerable.

impostor, imposter *ns* (*They thought that he was a doctor but he was an impostor*) fake, fraud, charlatan, swindler, cheat, (*inf*) con man.

impotent *adj* (*The small army was impotent in the face of the enemy*) powerless, helpless, weak, feeble.

impoverished *adj* (*impoverished people with no homes*) poor, poverty-stricken, penniless, impecunious, destitute, indigent.

impracticable *adj* (*The task was totally impracticable*) impossible, out of the question.

impractical *adj* **1** (*The proposed solution was totally impractical*) impossible, non-viable, hopeless, ineffective, useless. **2** (*They are impractical people*) unrealistic, idealistic.

impress *vb* **1** (*The crowd was impressed by his speech*) make an impression on, affect, influence, sway, move, stir. **2** (*You must impress on them the need for silence*) stress, emphasize, inculcate.

impression *n* **1** (*His speech made a powerful impression on his audience*) effect, influence, impact. **2** (*We had the impression that he disliked us*) feeling, idea, notion, sensation, suspicion, hunch. **3** (*He does impressions of the prime minister*) impersonation, imitation, mimicry, parody, (*inf*) send-up.

impressive *adj* **1** (*It was an impressive building*) imposing, grand, splendid, magnificent. **2** (*He made an impressive speech*) moving, stirring, powerful.

imprison *vb* (*The criminals were imprisoned*) put in prison, jail, lock up, take into custody, incarcerate, confine, detain.

impromptu *adj* (*He made an impromptu speech at the wedding reception*) unrehearsed, unprepared, spontaneous, improvised, extempore, off the cuff, ad lib.

improve *vb* **1** (*They tried to improve conditions for the poor*) better, make better. **2** (*The standard of her work has improved*) get better, advance, progress, move on.

improvise *vb* **1** (*They had to improvise a shelter when they lost their tent*) put together, devise, rig up, concoct. **2** (*He has not prepared a speech and so he will have to improvise*) make do, extemporise, ad lib.

impudent *adj* (*The girl was impudent enough to swear at the teacher*) impertinent, insolent, cheeky, bold, forward, brazen, presumptuous.

impulsive *adj* (*He was given to impulsive decisions*) impetuous, impromptu, spontaneous, hasty, rash, thoughtless.

in *adj* **1** (*Short skirts are in*) fashionable, stylish, (*inf*) trendy. **2** (*She is in with the boss*) in favour, favoured. ▼

---

be in for (something) likely to experience (something, often something unpleasant) (*The sky is so dark that I think we are in for a storm*). **be in on (something)** to be involved in (something), to know about (something) (*Not many people were in on the scheme*). **have it in for (someone)** to try to cause trouble for (someone) (*They have had it in for the boy since he reported them to the teacher*). **the ins and outs of (something)** the details of (something) (*I know that they had a disagreement but I don't know the ins and outs of it*).

---

inadequate *adj* **1** (*Their supplies of fuel are inadequate*) insufficient, deficient, scanty, meagre. **2** (*She feels that she is an inadequate mother*) incompetent, inefficient, inept.

inadvertent *adj* (*There were a few inadvertent omissions from the list of guests*) accidental, unintentional.

inane *adj* (*It was an inane thing to do*) foolish, stupid, idiotic, absurd, ridiculous.

inanimate *adj* (*inanimate objects*) lifeless, without life.

inapt *adj* (*her inapt remarks*) inappropriate, unsuitable, inapposite.

inaugurate *vb* (*They are inaugurating a new club*) launch, initiate, begin, commence, found, establish.

inborn *adj* (*his inborn pessimism*) inherent, innate, inbred, inherited.

incense *vb* (*He was incensed at the children's behaviour*) enrage, annoy, anger, infuriate, exasperate.

incentive *n* (*They gave the workers more money as an incentive*) inducement, incitement, encouragement, motivation, spur.

inception *n* (*She has been a member of the club since its inception*) start, beginning, launch, opening.

incessant *adj* (*They were tired of their neighbour's incessant noise*) never-ending, unending, endless, unceasing, continuous, continual, unremitting.

incident *n* (*various sad incidents in her life*) event, happening, occurrence, episode, occasion.

incite *vb* **1** (*The speaker tried to incite the crowd to rebellion*) egg on, urge, goad, spur on, excite, rouse, stimulate. **2** (*They incited a rebellion*) provoke, instigate, stir up.

inclination *n* **1** (*He has an inclination to put on weight*) tendency, propensity, predisposition, habit. **2** (*flat ground with a slight inclination*) slope, gradient, rise. **3** (*with a slight inclination of his head*) bow, bending, nod.

incline *vb* **1** (*The land inclines towards the shore*) slope, slant, tilt, bend. **2** (*He inclines towards the left on politics*) tend, lean, veer.

incline, be inclined to *vbs* (*They are inclined to tell lies*) be apt to, have a tendency to, have a habit of, be liable to, be likely to.

include *vb* **1** (*The menu includes all their favourite dishes*) contain, take in, incorporate, comprise. **2** (*Remember to include their names on the list*) put in, add, insert, enter.

inclusive *adj* **1** (*The hotel quoted an inclusive price*) all-in. **2** (*the total bill inclusive of service charge*) including.

incognito *adj/adv* (*He travelled incognito*) in disguise, disguised.

incoherent *adj* (*She was badly shaken and gave a very incoherent account of the accident*) confused, muddled, jumbled, disjointed, garbled.

income *n* (*his income after tax*) salary, wages, pay, earnings, profits.

incompatible *adj* **1** (*Their two statements are incompatible*) conflicting, contradictory, inconsistent. **2** (*It was obvious before they married that they were incompatible*) unsuited, mismatched, ill-assorted.

incongruous *adj* (*The modern steel furniture looked incongruous with the old style of decoration*) out of keeping, unsuitable, unsuited, inappropriate, discordant, strange, odd.

increase *vb* **1** (*Demand for the product has increased*) grow, go up, rise, multiply, mushroom, escalate. **2** (*They have increased the number of college places*) add to, augment, enlarge, extend, expand, raise, (*inf*) step up.

incredible *adj* **1** (*His story seemed quite incredible*) unbelievable, far-fetched, unconvincing, unlikely. **2** (*The gymnast's performance was quite incredible*) extraordinary, marvellous, amazing.

incriminate *vb* (*He was found guilty of the crime and tried to incriminate his friend*) accuse, charge, blame, implicate, involve.

indecent *adj* (*The comic told indecent jokes*) vulgar, crude, coarse, rude, bawdy, smutty, dirty, blue.

indefinite *adj* **1** (*He gave us rather an indefinite answer*) vague, unclear, confused, ambiguous. **2** (*She was rather indefinite about whether to go or not*) undecided, indecisive, uncertain, irresolute. **3** (*The date for the meeting is indefinite as yet*) undecided, unsettled, uncertain. **4** (*an indefinite shape in the mist*) indistinct, blurred, vague, dim.

indent *vb* (*They have indented for more textbooks*) order, request, ask for.

independent *adj* **1** (*It is an independent state*) self-governing, autonomous, free. **2** (*The children are grown up and independent*) self-supporting, self-sufficient. **3** (*The firms are independent of each other*) unattached, unconnected, unrelated, separate.

indicate *vb* **1** (*His ragged clothes indicated his poverty*) show, demonstrate, point to, be a sign of, suggest, mean. **2** (*He indicated which direction he was turning*) show, point out, make known.

indication *n* **1** (*Her paleness is an indication of her illness*) sign, symptom, mark, signal. **2** (*He frowned as an indication of his anger*) demonstration, display, show.

indifferent *adj* **1** (*He seemed indifferent about the result of his trial*) apathetic, unconcerned, detached, unemotional. **2** (*He gave an indifferent performance*) mediocre, run-of-the-mill, commonplace, uninspired, undistinguished.

indignant *adj* (*They were indignant at being ignored*) angry, annoyed, irate, furious.

indispensable *adj* (*employees who were considered indispensable*) essential, necessary, crucial, imperative.

indisposed *adj* ill, unwell, poorly, (*inf*) under the weather.

indistinct *adj* **1** (*indistinct noises*) muffled, low. **2** (*The picture was rather indistinct*) blurred, fuzzy, hazy, misty.

individual *adj* **1** (*the individual petals of the flower*) single, separate, particular, specific. **2** (*The writer has a very individual style*) characteristic, distinctive, peculiar, original, idiosyncratic.

indolent *vb* (*He was too indolent to look for a job*) lazy, idle, slothful.

induce *vb* **1** (*The salesman tried to induce them to buy a new car*) persuade, prevail upon, get, press. **2** (*The drug induced a skin reaction*) produce, cause, give rise to, bring about.

indulgent *adj* (*The children's grandparents are too indulgent*) permissive, easygoing, doting.

industrial *adj* (*an industrial area of the country*) manufacturing.

industrious *adj* (*industrious pupils*) hard-working, diligent, conscientious, assiduous.

inert *adj* (*people lying inert after the previous night's party*) inactive, motionless, still.

inevitable *adj* (*A guilty verdict seemed inevitable*) unavoidable, unpreventable, inescapable, irrevocable.

infallible *adj* (*She claims that it is an infallible cure*) unfailing, foolproof, reliable, sure, certain.

infamous *adj* **1** (*He is an infamous criminal*) notorious, villainous, wicked. **2** (*It was an infamous crime*) notorious, scandalous, disgraceful, shocking, outrageous.

infant *n* (*She was very ill as an infant*) baby, young child.

infatuation *n* (*his infatuation with one of his female colleagues*) love, fancy, obsession, fixation, (*inf*) crush.

infect *vb* **1** (*waste material that infected the town's water supply*) contaminate, pollute, taint. **2** (*The wound was infected*) poison, make septic. **3** (*He infected others with his enthusiasm*) influence, affect.

infectious *adj* (*an infectious disease*), communicable, transmittable, catching.

infer *vb* (*From the evidence the jury inferred that he was guilty*) deduce, reason, conclude, gather.

inferior *adj* **1** (*She occupies an inferior position in the firm)* subordinate, lower, lesser, junior, minor, low, humble. **2** (*The firm produces inferior goods*) imperfect, faulty, defective, substandard, shoddy. **3** (*They do not employ inferior workers*) incompetent, second-rate.

infest *vb* (*houses infested with rats*) overrun, pervade, invade, plague.

infidelity *n* **1** (*accused of infidelity to their king*) disloyalty, unfaithfulness, treachery, perfidy. **2** (*his wife's infidelity*) unfaithfulness, adultery.

infinite *adj* **1** (*Space is infinite*) boundless, unbounded, limitless, unlimited, endless. **2** (*She has infinite patience*) unlimited, endless, unending, inexhaustible.

infirm *adj* (*The old people are becoming infirm*) frail, failing, feeble, weak.

inflamed *adj* **1** (*a badly inflamed arm*) red, reddened, sore, infected, festering, septic. **2** (*inflamed passions*) aroused, roused, excited.

inflammable *adj* (*nightdresses made of inflammable material*) flammable, combustible.

inflammation *n* (*He was given some ointment to cure the inflammation*) redness, sore, swelling.

inflate *vb* **1** (*He had to stop and inflate his bicycle tyres*) blow up, pump up. **2** (*a decision that might inflate prices*) increase, raise, boost, escalate.

inflexible *adj* **1** (*inflexible substances*) rigid, stiff, hard. **2** (*an inflexible work schedule*) fixed, rigid, unalterable. **3** (*their inflexible attitudes*) stubborn, obstinate, adamant, firm, unaccommodating, unbending.

inflict *vb* (*inflict distress on his parents*) administer, deal out, mete out, impose, give.

influence *vb* **1** (*Her state of health influenced her decision*) affect, have an effect on, have an impact on, sway, control, determine. **2** (*They would like to influence the jury*) sway, bias, prejudice, bribe.

influence *n* **1** (*She had a great deal of influence on her colleagues*) effect, impact, sway, control, power. **2** (*He was under the influence of alcohol*) effect.

influential *adj* (*He is an influential figure in the government*) powerful, important, leading.

inform *vb* **1** (*We had to inform her that he was dead*) tell, advise, notify, communicate to, impart to. **2** (*He informed on his friends to the police*) betray, (*inf*) grass on, (*inf*) blow the whistle on.

informal *adj* **1** (*wear informal clothes at weekends*) casual, comfortable. **2** (*an informal party*) casual, unceremonious, unofficial, simple, relaxed.

information *n* **1** (*collect information on all of the countries of the world*) data, facts, statistics. **2** (*When will we receive information about the next meeting?*) news, word, communication, advice, instruction.

infringe *vb* **1** (*infringe the rules*) break, disobey, violate, contravene, disregard. **2** (*He infringed on his neighbour's land*) encroach, intrude, trespass.

infuriate *vb* (*They were infuriated at being overcharged in the restaurant*) enrage, incense, annoy, anger, exasperate.

ingenious *adj* (*They thought up an ingenious plan*) clever, shrewd, cunning, inventive, resourceful.

ingenuous *adj* (*She was too ingenuous to try to deceive them*) open, sincere, honest, frank, artless, simple, guileless.

inhabit *vb* (*They inhabit a remote area of the country*) live in, dwell in, reside in, occupy.

inherent *adj* **1** (*There is an inherent tendency to heart disease in the family*) inborn, inbred, hereditary, congenital. **2** (*It was an inherent part of the design of the building*) intrinsic, innate, essential, basic, fundamental.

inherit *vb* **1** (*She inherited a great deal of money from her grandmother*) be left, be bequeathed. **2** (*He inherited the title on his father's death*) succeed to, accede to, assume.

inheritance *n* (*He has already spent his inheritance from his father*) legacy, bequest, estate.

inhibited *adj* (*She feels inhibited in the presence of her parents*) shy, reticent, reserved, self-conscious, subdued.

initial *adj* (*He was involved right from the initial stages of the company*) first, beginning, commencing, opening, early, introductory.

initiate *vb* **1** (*They asked him to initiate the proceedings*) begin, start off, commence, open, institute, launch. **2** (*The boys initiated a new member into their gang*) admit, introduce, induct, install, enrol.

initiative *n* **1** (*He took the initiative and made the opening speech*) first move, first step, lead, start, beginning. **2** (*There will be promotion prospects for workers with *initiative*) enterprise, resourcefulness, inventiveness, drive.

injection *n* (*He was given an injection against tetanus*) inoculation, vaccination, shot, (*inf*) jab.

injure *vb* **1** (*He injured his leg in the accident*) hurt, damage, wound. **2** (*His behaviour has injured his reputation*) damage, ruin, spoil, mar.

inkling *n* (*The workers had no inkling that the firm was going to shut down*) hint, clue, indication, suspicion.

inlet *n* (*They tied the boat up in a sandy inlet*) cove, bay.

inn *n* (*They had a meal at the local inn*) pub, tavern.

inner *adj* (*the inner layer*) inside, interior.

innocent *adj* **1** (*The accused was found innocent*) not guilty, guiltless, blameless. **2** (*innocent young girls*) simple, naive, artless, trusting, inexperienced, gullible, virtuous, pure. **3** (*It was just innocent fun*) harmless, safe, inoffensive.

innocuous *adj* (*The substance was found to be innocuous*) harmless, safe, non-toxic.

innovation *n* (*The new owner introduced some innovations*) new measure, change, alteration.

innuendo *n* (*She made an innuendo about his lack of honesty*) insinuation, suggestion, hint.

innumerable *adj* (*He has been late on innumerable occasions*) numerous, countless, many.

inordinate *n* (*They caused an inordinate amount of trouble*) excessive, undue, unreasonable, uncalled-for.

inquire *vb* **1** (*The police are inquiring into the cause of the fire*) make inquiries, investigate, look into, probe, query. **2** (*We inquired about her mother's health*) ask, make inquiries.

inquiry *n* **1** (*The police are conducting a murder inquiry*) investigation, inquest, interrogation, examination. **2** (*She is employed to answer customers' inquiries*) query, question.

inquisitive *adj* (*She is inquisitive about other people's business*) curious, prying, snooping, (*inf*) nosy.

insane *adj* **1** (*The murderer has been declared insane*) mad, deranged, demented, unhinged, out of one's mind. **2** (*It was insane to take such risks*) mad, crazy, idiotic, foolish, stupid, absurd.

insanitary *adj* (*The toilet facilities are insanitary*) dirty, filthy, unhygienic, unhealthy, contaminated, polluted.

insatiable *adj* (*He has an insatiable appetite/insatiable for knowledge*) hungry, greedy, voracious.

inscription *n* **1** (*the inscription on the gravestone*) writing, engraving, epitaph. **2** (*the inscription in the front of the book*) dedication, message.

insert *vb* **1** (*She inserted the letter in the envelope*) put in, push in, thrust in, slip in. **2** (*He decided to insert a few more lines into his report*) put in, introduce, enter, interpolate.

inside *adv* (*She decided to stay inside in the cold weather*) indoors.

insignificant *adj* (*concentrate on the main points in the report and ignore the insignificant details*) unimportant, minor, trivial, trifling, negligible.

insinuate *vb* **1** (*She insinuated that she did not trust him*) hint, suggest, imply, indicate. **2** (*She succeeded in insinuating herself into the old lady's affections*) worm one's way, work one's way, ingratiate oneself.

insipid *adj* (*She is a very insipid person*) colourless, dull, drab, vapid, uninteresting.

insist *vb* **1** (*At first they refused to go but their parents insisted*) stand firm, be firm, stand one's ground, be determined, not to take no for an answer. **2** (*She insisted that they go immediately*) demand, command, urge. **3** (*He insists that he is innocent*) maintain, assert, declare, swear.

insolent *adj* (*The pupil was accused of being insolent*) impertinent, impudent, cheeky, rude.

inspect *vb* (*The police inspected the stolen car*) examine, check, scrutinize, study.

inspiration *n* **1** (*His wife acts as an inspiration to the artist*) stimulus, stimulation, encouragement, motivation, spur. **2** (*His poetry lacks inspiration*) creativity, originality, inventiveness, imagination. **3** (*They were completely puzzled but then he had a sudden inspiration*) bright idea.

install *vb* **1** (*They have installed a new bathroom*) put in, insert, fix, establish. **2** (*They installed themselves in comfortable chairs*) settle.

instalment *n* **1** (*They are paying for the goods by instalment*) part payment, hire purchase, HP. **2** (*They published the novel in instalments*) part, portion, section.

instance *n* (*That was just one instance of his impertinence*) case, example, illustration.

instant *adj* (*She demanded an instant reply*) instantaneous, immediate, on-the-spot, rapid, prompt.

instant *n* (*He was gone in an instant*) moment, minute, second, trice, (*inf*) jiffy.

instinct *n* **1** (*Some birds migrate by instinct*) intuition, sixth sense. **2** (*She has an instinct for doing the right thing*) ability, knack, aptitude, gift, talent.

institution *n* **1** (*He has been living in an institution since he was very young*) home, hospital, detention centre. **2** (*It was one of the village's institutions*) custom, tradition, practice.

instruct *vb* **1** (*He instructs the pupils in gymnastics*) teach, train, coach, educate. **2** (*She instructed the bank to close her account*) tell, order, command, direct, bid.

instructor *n* (*a sports instructor*) teacher, coach, trainer, tutor.

instrument *n* **1** (*instruments used by dentists*) implement, tool, appliance, apparatus, utensil, gadget. **2** (*She plays several instruments*) musical instrument.

insult *n* (*His insults were quite unjustified*) slur, abuse, affront, slight, gibe.

insult *vb* (*She was deeply insulted by his accusations*) affront, give offence to, abuse, slight, hurt. ▼

---

add insult to injury to make matters worse (*Having given his first play a bad review the critic added insult to injury by ignoring his second one*).

---

intact *adj* (*They were pleased to find all their furniture intact after they moved house*) whole, in one piece, sound, unbroken, complete, undamaged.

integrate *vb* (*They integrated the various parts into a whole*) combine, unite, join, amalgamate, merge, fuse.

integrity *n* (*No person of integrity would have got involved in the scheme*) honour, honesty, uprightness, righteousness. decency.

intellect *n* (*people of limited intellect*) brain, mind, intelligence.

intellectual *adj* (*They are an intellectual family*) academic. well-educated, well-read, scholarly, bookish, clever.

intelligent *adj* (*the more intelligent pupils*) clever, bright, sharp, quick, smart, (*inf*) brainy.

intend *vb* (*She intends to leave soon*) aim, mean, plan.

intense *adj* **1** (*She could not stand the intense heat*) severe, acute, fierce, extreme, strong, powerful. **2** (*She has an intense desire to travel*) deep, profound, passionate, fervent, burning, eager, ardent.

intent *adj* **1** (*They were intent on getting there on time*) set on, bent on, determined to. **2** (*The child wore an intent expression as he worked*) absorbed, engrossed, attentive, concentrating.

intention *n* (*It is his intention to go to university*) aim, purpose, intent, goal, objective, design.

intentional *adj* (*It was not an accident that he hurt her—it was intentional*) deliberate, meant, purposeful, planned, calculated.

interest *n* **1** (*He showed no interest in the project*) concern, heed, regard, notice, attention, curiosity. **2** (*Stamp-collecting is one of his interests*) hobby, pastime, diversion. **3** (*This is a matter of interest to us all*) concern, importance, import, consequence. ▼

---

a vested interest in (something) a personal and biased interest in (something) (*She has a vested interest in campaigning against the proposed new hotel. It would be competition for hers*). **with interest** to an even greater extent than something has been done, etc, to someone (*He issued a stream of insults at her and she returned them with interest*).

---

interested *adj* **1** (*The children were not interested*) attentive, absorbed, curious. **2** (*the interested parties*) concerned, involved. **3** (*No interested person is allowed to be a judge in the competition*) involved, biased, prejudiced, partial, partisan.

interesting *adj* (*It was an interesting book*) absorbing, engrossing, fascinating, riveting, gripping, amusing, entertaining.

interfere *vb* **1** (*He is always interfering in other people's business*) meddle with, pry into, intrude into, (*inf*) poke one's nose into, (*inf*) stick one's oar into. **2** (*He lets his sports training interfere with his school work*) hinder, impede, hamper, obstruct, get in the way of.

interior *n* **1** (*They are painting the interior of the building*) inside. **2** (*They travelled to the interior of the country*) centre, middle, heart.

interlude *n* (*during the interlude at the theatre*) interval, intermission, break, lull, pause.

intermediate *adj* (*The team is in an intermediate position in the league*) middle, midway, halfway.

interminable *adj* **1** (*The journey seemed interminable*) endless, never-ending, everlasting. **2** (*She was tired of his interminable questions*) endless, everlasting, ceaseless, incessant, continuous, continual, constant, persistent.

intermittent *adj* (*Their telephone has an intermittent fault*) occasional, irregular, sporadic, fitful, recurrent.

internal *adj* **1** (*They knocked down

an internal wall) interior, inside, inner, inward. 2 (*the country's internal affairs*) home, domestic,.

international *adj* (*international issues*) global, universal, worldwide.

interpret *vb* 1 (*The pupils need someone to interpret the difficult text*) explain, clarify, expound, elucidate. 2 (*They interpreted her silence as agreement*) take, construe, read, understand. 3 (*She is employed to interpret for foreign businessmen*) translate.

interrogate *vb* (*The police are interrogating the accused*) question, ask questions, examine, cross-examine, quiz, give the third degree to, (*inf*) grill.

interrupt *vb* 1 (*People in the audience kept interrupting his speech*) cut in on, break in on, butt in on, intrude on, disturb. 2 (*They interrupted the meeting to make an important announcement*) discontinue, break off, suspend, leave off, delay.

intersection *n* (*There was a bad road accident at the intersection*) junction, interchange, crossroads, roundabout.

interval *n* 1 (*There was quite an interval between the two meetings*) gap, wait, space, period. 2 (*during the interval in the theatre*) intermission, interlude, break, pause, lull.

intervene *n* 1 (*The quarrel between the children was so bad that their parents had to intervene*) intercede, mediate, step in, interfere. 2 (*A period of several years intervened before they met again*) occur, pass, happen, take place, ensue.

interview *n* 1 (*The candidates for the job had to attend an interview*) meeting, discussion, dialogue, evaluation. 2 (*The president was giving an interview to the press*) audience, press conference, dialogue, question and answer session.

intimate *adj* 1 (*They were intimate friends*) close, dear, near, loving, friendly, amicable. 2 (*the intimate details of her life as noted in her diary*) personal, private, confidential, secret.

intimidate *vb* (*They felt intimidated by the three huge men*) frighten, scare, alarm, terrify, terrorize, threaten.

intolerable *adj* (*an intolerable level of pain*) unbearable, unendurable, insufferable, insupportable.

intolerant *adj* (*intolerant members of the community who objected to the activities of young people*) bigoted, illiberal, narrow-minded, biased, prejudiced, provincial, parochial.

intoxicated *adj* (*They were so intoxicated that they could not walk straight*) drunk, tipsy, under the influence, (*inf*) one over the eight, (*inf*) tight.

intrepid *adj* (*intrepid explorers who went into the heart of the jungle*) fearless, bold, daring, brave, courageous.

intricate *adj* 1 (*an intricate pattern*) elaborate, fancy, ornate. 2 (*intricate problems*) complex, complicated, involved, difficult.

intriguing *adj* (*an intriguing story*) fascinating, riveting, absorbing, interesting, captivating.

introduce *vb* 1 (*She introduced the speaker*) present, announce. 2 (*She introduced her friends to each other*) present, make known. 3 (*They introduced new business methods*) bring in, initiate, launch, institute, establish, start.

introduction *n* (*the introduction to

the book) preface, foreword, front matter, prologue.

introverted *adj* (*Her sister is very outgoing but she is introverted*) inward-looking, introspective, withdrawn.

intrude *vb* (*Although they had been invited to the party they felt as though they were intruding*) interrupt, barge in, interfere, butt in.

intruder *n* (*The police arrested the intruder*) burglar, housebreaker, thief.

intuition *n* (*She seemed to know by intuition where her child was*) instinct, sixth sense.

inundate *vb* **1** (*The river burst its banks and inundated the town*) flood, overflow, swamp, deluge, engulf. **2** (*They were inundated with complaints*) overwhelm, swamp, bog down.

invade *vb* (*The enemy army invaded the city*) overrun, storm, take over, attack, raid.

invalid *adj* (*The doctor visited their invalid mother*) ill, sick, ailing, unwell, infirm.

invaluable *adj* (*We thanked them for their invaluable help*) useful, helpful, precious, inestimable.

invariable *adj* (*an invariable temperature/Her style of dress was quite invariable*) unchanging, constant, unvarying, fixed, regular, uniform.

invasion *n* (*the enemy's invasion of the city*) attack, assault, raid, onslaught.

invent *n* **1** (*the person who invented television*) originate, create, discover, design, devise, think up. **2** (*He invented an excuse for not being present*) make up, concoct, fabricate, hatch, (*inf*) cook up.

investigate *vb* (*investigate a murder case*) research, examine, explore, inquire into, study.

invincible *adj* **1** (*Their army seemed invincible*) unbeatable, unconquerable. **2** (*The obstacles to progress seem invincible*) insuperable, insurmountable, overwhelming.

invisible *adj* **1** (*The high hedge made the cottage invisible to passers-by*) unseen, unnoticed, out of sight, hidden, concealed. **2** (*an invisible repair*) inconspicuous, unnoticeable, imperceptible.

invite *vb* **1** (*We invited them to dinner*) ask, send an invitation to. **2** (*The company is inviting applications for sales assistants*) ask, request, seek, call for.

involuntary *adj* (*Blinking is usually an involuntary reaction*) reflex, automatic, instinctive, unthinking, mechanical.

involve *vb* **1** (*His new job involves working with computers*) entail, include, necessitate, require. **2** (*They hoped to involve all the children in the scheme*) include, take in, incorporate, concern, interest. **3** (*He tried to involve his friends in his plans for the robbery*) implicate, associate, mix up. **4** (*find a hobby that involves them*) interest, absorb, occupy, grip, engross.

involved *adj* (*Her excuse seemed very involved*) complicated, complex, intricate, elaborate, confused, muddled.

irate *adj* (*They tried to calm the irate old man*) angry, furious, indignant, infuriated.

iron *vb* (*They had to iron their creased shirts*) press, smooth.

iron, iron out *vbs* (*They had talks to try to iron out their problems*) sort out, clear up, straighten out, settle, solve. ▼

---

have several irons in the fire to be involved in several projects, schemes, etc, at the same time

(One of his businesses has gone bankrupt but he still has several irons in the fire) <A reference to a blacksmith who heats pieces of iron before shaping them>. **strike while the iron is hot** to act at a point at which things are favourable to one *(Your father seems to be in a good mood. Why don't you strike while the iron is hot and ask him for an increase in pocket money?)* **the iron hand in the velvet glove** sternness or ruthlessness *(Her father looks a very nice man but he frequently beats his children. It is a case of the iron hand in the velvet glove)*.

---

ironic *adj* (*He has a tendency to make ironic remarks*) satirical, mocking, scoffing, scornful, sneering, sarcastic.

irritable *adj* (*He gets irritable when he is tired*) bad-tempered, ill-tempered, cross, touchy, crabbed, grumpy, cantankerous.

irritate *vb* **1** (*His constant stream of jokes irritates her*) annoy, get on one's nerves, try one's patience, exasperate, infuriate. **2** (*The material irritated her skin*) inflame, redden, chafe, cause discomfort to.

isolated *adj* **1** (*They live in an isolated place*) remote, out-of the way, outlying, secluded, desolate, inaccessible. **2** (*She felt isolated living far away from her family and friends*) lonely, solitary, alone, forsaken. **3** (*The doctors do not think it is an epidemic but just an isolated example of the disease*) single, solitary, abnormal, unusual, atypical.

issue *vb* **1** (*Smoke issued from the factory chimney*) pour forth, discharge. **2** (*A steady stream of people issued from the building*) come out, emerge, leave, appear from. **3** (*New stamps have been issued to mark the occasion/They issued a press release*) put out, distribute, circulate, release, disseminate.

issue *n* **1** (*They argue over political issues*) matter, subject, topic, affair, problem. **2** (*They plan to buy the next issue of the magazine*) edition, number, instalment. **3** (*They have been having talks about peace but the issue is still in doubt*) result, outcome, decision, conclusion.

itch *n* **1** (*She has an itch in her head*) tingling, prickling, irritation. **2** (*She has an itch to travel*) desire, longing, yearning, craving, hankering, (*inf*) yen.

item *n* **1** (*make a list of items for sale*) object, article, thing. **2** (*There are several items to be discussed at the meeting*) point, matter, issue, thing. ▼

---

be an item to be regarded as having a romantic relationship *(I didn't realize that Ralph and Carol are an item; I thought they were just good friends)*.

---

itinerant *adj* (*an itinerant salesman*) travelling, peripatetic.

itinerary *n* (*Our itinerary takes us through Belgium*) route, journey, travels.

J

jab *vb* (*She jabbed him in the ribs to wake him*) prod, poke, nudge, dig.

jagged *adj* (*the jagged edge of the bread knife*) rough, uneven, pointed, notched, serrated.

jail *n* (*The prisoners have escaped from jail*) gaol, prison, lock-up, (*inf*) nick, (*inf*) clink, (*inf*) slammer, (*inf*) cooler, (*inf*) jug.

jail *vb* (*The judge jailed him for life*) gaol, imprison, send to prison, lock up, put away, confine, incarcerate.

jam *vb* **1** (*They tried to jam too many people into the hall*) crowd, pack, cram, squeeze, crush. **2** (*roads jammed by the sheer volume of traffic*) block, obstruct, congest, clog. **3** (*They jammed a piece of paper under the door to keep it open*) wedge, stick, force, push, stuff.

jam *n* (*bread, butter and jam*) preserves, jelly. ▼

---

jam tomorrow the promise of better things in the future (*Governments often promise jam tomorrow but many people would prefer to have improvements now*) <From a statement by the White Queen in *Through the Looking Glass* by Lewis Carroll>.

want jam on it to want an even better situation than one already has even though one is already well off, comfortable, etc.

---

jar *vb* **1** (*The knife jarred against the metal surface of the box*) grate, rasp, scratch, squeak. **2** (*He jarred his shoulder in the car crash*) jolt, jerk, shake.

jealous *adj* **1** (*She was jealous because her sister won the race*) envious, grudging, resentful, covetous, green with envy. **2** (*He had a jealous wife*) suspicious, distrustful, mistrustful, possessive.

jeer *vb* (*When the politician tried to speak the crowd jeered*) mock, scoff, ridicule, taunt, sneer.

jerk *vb* **1** (*His leg was jerking uncontrollably*) twitch, shake, tremble. **2** (*She jerked the child out of his seat*) pull, yank, tug, wrench. **3** (*The old bus jerked along the country roads*) jolt, bump, lurch, jar.

jewel *n* (*She kept her jewels in a safe*) gem, precious stone. ▼

---

the jewel in the crown the best or most valued part of something (*The cathedral is the jewel in the city's crown*).

---

jewellery *n* (*She wore silver jewellery on her black dress*) jewels, gems, trinkets, ornament.

jittery *adj* (*He was jittery before the exam*) nervous, nervy, jumpy, uneasy, anxious.

job *n* **1** (*He took days to finish a simple job*) task, piece of work, chore, assignment, undertaking. **2** (*What is her job?*) occupation, profession, employment, career, trade. **3** (*It was his job to look after the garden*) task, chore, responsibility, concern, function, role. ▼

---

a job lot a mixed collection (*The furniture in the students' flats is a real job lot*). **give (something) up as a bad job** to stop doing (something) because one has so little hope of success (*We tried to persuade her to stay but we finally gave it up as a bad job*).

---

jog *vb* **1** (*They jogged round the park*) go jogging, run, trot, lope. **2** (*We tried to jog her memory but she had forgotten all about the incident*) prompt, stir, stimulate, refresh.

join *vb* **1** (*We had to join the two pieces of string*) fasten, attach, put together, link, connect, tie. **2** (*We joined in the search party to look for the dog*) take part in, participate in, contribute to. **3** (*We were asked to join the tennis club*) become a member of, take up membership of, enrol in, sign up for. **4** (*The two clubs have joined together*) join forces, amalgamate, merge, combine, ally. **5** (*Their garden joins ours*) adjoin, abut on, border, border on, meet. ▼

---

if you can't beat 'em, join 'em if you cannot persuade other people to think and act as you do, then often the easiest thing to do is to begin to think and act like them (*We tried to keep the flat tidy but they always left a mess. Finally we decided that if you can't beat 'em, join 'em*).

---

joint *n* (*the joints in the water pipes*) join, junction, coupling, seam.

joint *adj* (*The organization of the party was a joint effort*) common, shared, mutual, combined, collective, cooperative, united.

joke *n* **1** (*Her uncle tells very funny jokes*) jest, gag, witticism, (*inf*) funny. **2** (*We took his bike for a joke*) practical joke, prank, hoax, piece of fun, trick, (*inf*) lark. ▼

---

be beyond a joke be no longer amusing, to be rather serious or annoying (*We were a bit amused by the child's smart remarks at first but they are now beyond a joke*).

---

joke *vb* **1** (*She was hurt by his remark but he was only joking*) tease, fool, pull (someone's) leg. **2** (*He can be rather annoying as he jokes all the time*) tell jokes, crack jokes, jest.

jolly *adj* (*The party was a very jolly occasion*) merry, happy, gay, joyful, cheerful, light-hearted.

jolt *vb* **1** (*The old car jolted along the bumpy roads*) jerk, lurch, bump, bounce. **2** (*The little boy kept getting jolted in the crowd*) bump, jostle, push, shove, nudge. **3** (*His unexpected failure in the exam jolted him*) upset, disturb, perturb, shake, disconcert, stun.

jostle *vb* (*people in the crowd jostling each other to the front*) push, shove, elbow, nudge, bump, knock, jolt.

jot *vb* (*jot down the names of the pupil*) note, make a note of, take down, write down, mark down, list.

journalist *n* (*The local artist was interviewed by a journalist*) reporter, newsman/newswoman, member of the press.

journey *n* (*They were tired after

their long train journey) trip, excursion, expedition, travels.

joy *n* (*their joy at the birth of their daughter*) delight, pleasure, happiness, gladness, rapture. ▼

---

have no joy (*inf*) to have no success or luck (*We looked for the lost watch but we had no joy*). **wish (someone) joy of (someone** or **something)** to say that one wishes that (someone or something) will be a pleasure or benefit to (someone) although one does not really believe that it will.

---

joyful *adj* (*It was a joyful occasion*) happy, cheerful, merry, gay, jolly, light-hearted.

judge *vb* **1** (*A senior member of the legal profession judged the case*) try, pronounce a verdict. **2** (*The local mayor judged the pets' competition*) adjudicate, arbitrate, evaluate, assess. **3** (*He is too ready to judge others*) pass judgement on, criticize, find fault with. **4** (*We judge that the meat would take an hour to cook*) estimate, guess, surmise, reckon, suppose, consider, think, believe.

judgement *n* **1** (*The magistrate will give his judgement tomorrow*) verdict, ruling, decision, finding, conclusion. **2** (*He is not a good businessman as he is lacking in judgement*) good sense, sense, shrewdness, wisdom, judiciousness, acumen.

juicy *adj* (*juicy fruit*) succulent, moist, ripe.

jump *vb* **1** (*The dog escaped by jumping over the fence*) leap over, vault, clear, hurdle. **2** (*The game involved the children jumping*) leap, spring, bound, bounce. **3** (*The sudden noise made everyone jump*) start, flinch, jerk.

jumper *n* (*wear a warm jumper*) sweater, jersey, pullover, knit, top.

junction *n* (*The cars collided at the junction*) intersection, interchange, cross-roads.

jungle *n* (*wild animals in the jungle*) forest, tropical forest, undergrowth. ▼

---

the law of the jungle the unofficial rules for survival or success in a dangerous or difficult situation where the usual civilized laws do not apply or are not effective.

---

junior *adj* **1** (*the junior members of the family*) younger. **2** (*the junior posts in the company*) subordinate, lower, lesser, minor.

just *adj* (*We felt it was a just decision*) fair, honest, impartial, unprejudiced, unbiased, objective.

just *adv* **1** (*He's just a boy*) only, merely. **2** (*I just met them*) now, a moment ago, recently. **3** (*we just caught the bus*) only just, barely, scarcely, (*inf*) by the skin of our teeth. **4** (*The house was just right for them*) exactly, absolutely, precisely, entirely. ▼

---

just the job exactly what is required or desired (*A cool drink after our long walk would be just the job*).

---

justice *n* (*He expects justice from the British courts*) justness, fairness, fair-mindedness, impartiality, lack of bias, objectivity.

justify *vb* **1** (*He was asked to justify his absence*) account for, give reasons for, give grounds for, explain, defend, excuse. **2** (*His *behaviour justified our concern for his health*) support, warrant, bear out, confirm.

jut *vb* (*The cliff juts out over the road*) stick out, project, protrude, overhang.

juvenile *adj* **1** (*the juvenile section of the musical competition*) junior, young, youthful. **2** (*We were amazed at their juvenile attitude to losing the game*) childish, immature, infantile.

K

keen *adj* **1** (*The keen pupils asked for extra practice*) enthusiastic, eager, willing, avid, zealous, conscientious. **2** (*people who are keen on football*) fond of, devoted to, having a liking for, being a fan of. **3** (*people who are keen to get more education*) eager, anxious, avid. **4** (*a keen edge on the sword*) sharp, sharp-edged. **5** (*a keen sense of smell*) sharp, acute, sensitive. **6** (*admire her keen mind*) sharp, astute, shrewd, quick, clever, bright, intelligent. **7** (*a keen frost*) intense, extreme, severe. ▼

---

as keen as mustard extremely keen or enthusiastic (*The young football players are as keen as mustard*).

---

keep *vb* **1** (*She kept the ring which he had given her*) hold on to, retain, (*inf*) hang on to. **2** (*The child keeps all his old magazines*) save up, store, accumulate, hoard, collect. **3** (*The firm tried to keep going*) continue, carry on, persist, persevere. **4** (*The local shop keeps a wide range of goods*) stock, sell, stock, carry. **5** (*He does not earn enough to keep a wife and children*) provide, support, maintain, feed. **6** (*Everyone should keep to the rules*) obey, comply with, observe, abide by, carry out. **7** (*Try to keep the news of his accident from his mother*) keep back, keep secret, hide, conceal, withhold, suppress. **8** (*He is late—something must have kept him*) keep back, delay, hold back, detain, hinder. ▼

---

keep oneself to oneself not to seek the company of others, to tell others very little about oneself (*We do not know our new neighbours—they keep themselves very much to themselves*).
keep up with the Joneses to make an effort to remain on the same social level as one's neighbours or friends by buying everything that they buy, etc (*She insists that they change their car every time one of her friends gets a new one. She spends all her time keeping up with the Joneses*).

---

keep *n* (*She pays for her own keep*) board, food, maintenance, support.

keepsake *n* (*be given a keepsake of her holiday*) memento, souvenir, reminder, remembrance.

keg *n* (*kegs of beer*) barrel, cask, vat, tun, butt.

kernel *n* **1** (*hazelnut kernels*) nut, stone, seed. **2** (*try to get to the kernel of the problem*) nub, core, centre, heart, (*inf*) nitty-gritty.

key *n* **1** (*musical keys*) tone, pitch, timbre. **2** (*find the key to the problem*) clue, guide, pointer, answer, solution, explanation.

kick *vb* **1** (*kick the ball*) boot, punt. **2** (*kick the man lying on the ground*) boot, take one's boot to, take one's feet to. **3** (*try to kick* *the smoking habit*) give up, stop, abandon, quit. ▼

---

kick oneself to be annoyed with oneself (*He could have kicked himself when he realized that he had been tactless*).

---

kidnap *vb* (*The president's son has been kidnapped*) abduct, snatch, seize, hold to ransom, take hostage.

kill *vb* **1** (*He was killed by a member of a rival gang*) take (someone's) life, slay, murder, do to death, put to death, execute, assassinate, (*inf*) bump off. **2** (*The news of his death killed all our hopes*) destroy, put an end to, ruin, extinguish, scotch. ▼

---

kill (someone) with kindness to spoil (someone) to the extent that it is a disadvantage to him or her (*The old lady is killing her dog with kindness by giving him too much food*). **kill two birds with one stone** to succeed in fulfilling two purposes with one act (*He was able to kill two birds withone stone when he went to a conference in New York. He gave a lecture and visited old friends*).

---

kind *adj* (*Kind people helped him/They appreciated his kind action*) kind-hearted, kindly, generous, charitable, benevolent, helpful, considerate, obliging, thoughtful, friendly, amiable.

kind *n* (*a kind of dog/a kind of car*) type, sort, variety, class, category, brand, make, species. ▼

---

two of a kind two people of a very similar type or character (*Don't worry about him treating her badly because she treats him just as badly. They're two of a kind*).

---

king *n* (*He was crowned king of Denmark*) monarch, ruler, sovereign. ▼

---

a king's ransom a very large sum of money (*They paid a king's ransom for that house*).

---

kingdom *n* (*The ruler's kingdom extended to the sea*) realm, domain, land, country, territory. ▼

---

till kingdom come for an extremely long time (*They will talk about the problem till kingdom come but they will not take any action*) <Refers to the Lord's Prayer>. **to kingdom come** to death (*The bomb is powerful enough to blow us all to kingdom come*).

---

kink *n* **1** (*There were some kinks in the rope*) twist, bend, coil, loop, tangle. **2** (*the kinks in her character*) quirk, eccentricity, idiosyncrasy.

kiosk *n* **1** (*buy a newspaper from a kiosk*) stall, stand, booth. **2** (*a telephone kiosk*) booth, box.

kit *n* (*He forgot his football kit*) equipment, gear, tackle, stuff, things, paraphernalia.

knack *n* (*He has the knack of getting people to tell him things*) talent, gift, aptitude, flair, ability, skill, expertise.

kneel *vb* (*He knelt to pick out some weeds*) get down on one's knees, bend, stoop, crouch.

knife *vb* (*He was knifed to death*) stab, pierce, run through, impale.▼

have one's knife in (someone) to wish to harm (someone) (*She has her knife in him because he got the job which she wanted*). **on a knife edge** in a very uncertain or risky state (*The peace talks between the countries are on a knife edge*).

knob *n* **1** (*turn the knob of the door*) handle. **2** (*turn the knob of the radio*) switch. **3** (*trees with knobs on the bark*) bump, bulge, lump, swelling, knot, nodule. **4** (*a knob of butter*) lump, piece, bit.

knock *vb* **1** (*They knocked at the door*) tap, rap, bang. **2** (*The child knocked into the table and hurt his head*) bang, bump, collide with, crash into. **3** (*He knocked his son on the head for being naughty*) strike, hit, slap, smack, box, thump, (*inf*) wallop. ▼

knock (someone) for six to take (someone) completely by surprise, to astonish (someone) (*The news of his redundancy knocked him for six*). **knock (something) on the head** to put an end to (something) (*Lack of money knocked his holiday plans on the head*).

know *vb* **1** (*We don't really know the other people in the street*) be acquainted with, have dealings with, socialize with. **2** (*We knew what they were saying about us*) realize, be aware of, be conscious of, notice, recognize. **3** (*He does not know any Spanish*) have knowledge of, understand, comprehend. **4** (*She has known great misfortune*) experience, go through, be familiar with. **5** (*He does not know one of the twins from the other*) distinguish, differentiate, tell. ▼

know one's onions to know all about a subject, one's job, etc. (*He is a very good teacher. He really knows his onions*). **not to know one is born** to lead a life that is free of trouble and worry (*She has enough money to do what she likes but she is always complaining. She does not know she is born*).

knowledge *n* **1** (*He showed his knowledge by doing well in the exam*) learning, education, scholarship, erudition. **2** (*admire the taxi driver's knowledge of the area*) familiarity, acquaintanceship. **3** (*He has little knowledge of the subject*) understanding, grasp, comprehension, expertise, skill, know-how.

knowledgeable *adj* (*She is very knowledgeable about local history*) informed, well-informed, educated, learned.

kudos *n* (*the kudos of being a famous writer*) prestige, fame, honour, glory, praise.

L

label *n* (*put a label on the luggage/the label on the article*) tag, tab, sticker, ticket.

laborious *adj* (*undertake a laborious task*) hard, difficult, arduous, strenuous, tiring.

labour *n* **1** (*They did not receive much money for their labour*) work, toil, effort, exertion, drudgery. **2** (*employ local labour in the new factory*) workers, employees, work force.▼

---

a labour of love a long or very difficult job done for one's own satisfaction or from affection for someone rather than for any form of payment or reward (*He hates gardening and so doing the weeding in his mother's garden is a real labour of love*).

---

laboured *adj* **1** (*the laboured breathing of the invalid*) heavy, strained, forced, difficult. **2** (*He has a laboured style of writing*) stilted, strained, stiff, unnatural.

labourer *n* (*labourers on the building site*) workman, worker, navvy.

labyrinth *n* **1** (*a labyrinth in the grounds of the stately home*) maze. **2** (*a labyrinth of cellars under the house/try to make their way through the labyrinth of rules and regulations*) maze, network, tangle, jungle.

lace *n* (*lose a lace from her shoe*) shoelace, cord, string.

lacerate *vb* (*He lacerated his hand on the cut glass*) cut, tear, gash, slash, rip.

lack *n* (*There is a lack of fresh water in the area*) shortage, dearth, insufficiency, scarcity, paucity, want.

lack *vb* (*She lacks training for the job*) be lacking, be without, have need of, be short of, be deficient in.

laconic *adj* (*She gave a laconic reply*) brief, concise, terse, succinct.

lad *n* (*They hired a lad to deliver the newspapers*) boy, youth, young man.

ladder *n* (*stand on a ladder to paint the ceiling*) stepladder, steps.

laden *adj* (*people laden with shopping*) loaded, burdened, weighed down, encumbered.

lag *vb* **1** (*He lagged behind the rest of the runners in the race*) fall behind, ail, linger, dawdle, dally. **2** (*They lagged their hot-water tank*) wrap up, insulate.

lair *n* (*the fox's lair*) den.

lake *n* (*The children paddled in the lake*) reservoir, loch.

lame *adj* **1** (*He has been lame since the accident*) limping, crippled. **2** (*She has a lame leg*) crippled, game, (*inf*) gammy. **3** (*He gave a lame excuse for being late*) weak, feeble, flimsy, inadequate. ▼

---

a lame duck a weak or inefficient person or organization (*You really should not invest in that firm. It is a bit of a lame duck and may soon go bankrupt*). **help a lame dog over a stile** to give assistance to someone in difficulties (*She is old and not well-off but she is always helping lame dogs over stiles*).

---

lamp *n* (*The lamps were still burning*) light.

land *n* **1** (*He went to live in a foreign land*) country, nation, state. **2** (*The land there will not grow much*) soil, earth, ground. **3** (*a large house with a great deal of land round it*) ground, estate, property. **4** (*prefer travelling on land to travelling by sea*) dry land, terra firma. ▼

---

a land of milk and honey a place where life is pleasant, with plenty of good things and possibilities of success (*The refugees saw the country to which they were sent as a land of milk and honey*) <A Biblical Reference to the Promised Land of the Israelites described in Exodus 3:8>. **see how the land lies** to look carefully at a situation before taking any action or decision (*She does not know how long she is going to stay with her friends. She is going to see how the land lies*) <A reference to sailors looking at the shore before landing>.

---

land *vb* **1** (*the plane landed*) touch down, come down, alight. **2** (*They met us as we landed at the dock*) dock, disembark.

landscape *n* (*a country with a flat landscape*) countryside.

lane *n* **1** (*take a walk down a country lane*) path, track. **2** (*motorway lanes*) track, course.

language *n* **1** (*the Spanish language*) tongue, speech, mother tongue. **2** (*Children acquire language at different rates*) speech, speaking, talking, words, vocabulary, communication.

lap *n* **1** (*The cat was sitting in its owner's lap*) knee, knees. **2** (*We are on our last lap of the journey*) round, section, stage. **3** (*The runners ran several laps of the track*) circuit, course. ▼

---

drop into (someone's) lap to happen to (someone) without any effort on his or her part (*The job just dropped into his lap. He didn't even apply for it—the employers contacted him*). **in the lap of luxury** in extremely comfortable or luxurious conditions (*She was a wealthy filmstar living in the lap of luxury*).

---

lap *vb* **1** (*The cats lapped up the milk*) drink, lick up. **2** (*The water lapped against the rocks*) wash, beat.

lapse *n* (*We saw him again after a lapse of time*) interval, break, gap, pause, passage.

large *adj* **1** (*They have a large garden/They are putting up large buildings*) big, sizeable, substantial, tall, high, huge, immense, enormous. **2** (*He is a very large man*) big, burly, heavy, strapping, hulking, hefty, fat. **3** (*We have large supplies of fuel*) big, ample, abundant, copious, liberal, plentiful. ▼

---

as large as life in person, actually present (*We thought he had drowned but he suddenly came into the room as large as life*).

---

lash *vb* **1** (*The master lashed the slave with a whip*) whip, flog, flail, birch, trash, beat. **2** (*They* *lashed the boat to the side of the ship*) tie, bind, fasten, tether, strap.

last *adj* **1** (*The last words of the speaker*) final, closing, concluding. **2** (*The last runners arrived exhausted*) hindmost, rearmost, final. ▼

---

as a last resort when all other methods have proved unsuccessful (*In the last resort we could walk to the next village although it is a long way*). **the last straw** an event which, added to everything that has already taken place, makes a situation impossible (*Everything had gone wrong that day and when she missed the last bus it was the last straw. She burst into tears*) <A shortened version of the saying 'it is the last straw that breaks the camel's back', indicating that, if a camel is carrying the absolute maximum load for its strength, even an extra straw might be too much for it and might break its back>.

---

last *vb* **1** (*How long is the meeting likely to last?*) continue, go on, carry on, remain, persist. **2** (*The climbers cannot last on the mountains in these blizzard conditions*) survive, live, endure. **3** (*People said that their marriage would not last*) survive, be permanent, hold out, last long. **4** (*buy shoes that will last*) wear well, last long, be durable.

late *adj* **1** (*Don't wait for her. She is always late*) unpunctual, overdue, behind schedule, slow. **2** (*She still misses her late husband*) dead, deceased. **3** (*Some late news has just arrived*) recent, new, fresh, up-to-the-minute. ▼

---

better late than never better for something to arrive, happen, etc, late than for it never to happen at all (*The letter offering him the job was a few days overdue but it was a case of better late than never*).

---

lather *n* (*The soap made a lot of lather*) suds, soapsuds, bubbles.

latter *adj* (*The latter is the more expensive*) last-named, second, the second of two.

laugh *vb* **1** (*The children laughed heartily at the antics of the clown*) chuckle, chortle, (*inf*) split one's sides, (*inf*) fall about, (*inf*) be rolling in the aisles. **2** (*The children laughed at the old-fashioned clothes which the little girl was wearing*) jeer, mock, ridicule, sneer, make fun of, poke fun at. ▼

---

have the last laugh be victorious or proved right in the end, especially after being scorned, criticized, etc (*His neighbours teased him for entering the best-kept garden competition but he had the last laugh when he won*) <A reference to the saying 'He who laughs last laughs longest'>. **laugh on the other side of one's face** suffer disappointment or misfortune after seeming to be successful or happy (*They were in good spirits because they thought their side had won the match but they laughed on the other side of their faces when the opposing side scored a late goal*).

---

launch *vb* **1** (*They launched the ship*) float, set afloat. **2** (*They *launched a missile*) fire, discharge, send forth. **3** (*We launch our new business tomorrow*) begin, start, embark upon, set up, establish.

laundry *n* (*She does the laundry on Mondays*) washing, wash.

lavatory *n* (*There is a bathroom and a separate lavatory in the flat*) toilet, WC, (*inf*) loo.

lavish *adj* (*a lavish supply of food*) generous, liberal, abundant, copious, plentiful.

law *n* **1** (*It was a new law issued by Parliament*) rule, regulation, statute, act, decree, edict. **2** (*All players must obey the laws of the game*) rule, regulation, instruction, guideline. ▼

---

be a law unto oneself behave as one wishes rather than obeying the usual rules and conventions (*He was the only person at the formal party who was not wearing evening dress but then he's always been a law unto himself*). **take the law into one's own hands** take action against a crime or injustice without involving the police or law courts (*When a child was murdered the villagers took the law into their own hands and nearly killed the person whom they thought had committed the murder*).

---

lawful *adj* **1** (*They are looking for the lawful owner of the car*) legal, legitimate, rightful. **2** (*It is not lawful to play football on the grass in the park*) legal, permitted, permissible, allowed, authorized.

lawyer *n* (*He hired a lawyer to sue his neighbour for damage to his property*) solicitor, legal practitioner, legal adviser.

lay *vb* **1** (*We were asked to lay our books on the table*) put down, set down, place, deposit. **2** (*lay the blame on his friend*) place, put, attribute, assign.

layer *n* (*a layer of ice on the road*) coat, sheet, skin, film.

lazy *adj* (*He is very lazy and does not want to work*) idle, indolent, slothful, inactive, work-shy.

lead *n* **1** (*They need a strong man to lead the country*) be in charge of, direct, govern, be in command of, manage, head. **2** (*The horse was leading but fell just before the finish*) be in the lead, be in front, be first, be winning. **3** (*He was asked to lead the visitors to their seats*) conduct, guide, direct, escort, usher. **4** (*We hope that they will lead a happy life*) have, live, pass, experience. ▼

---

lead (someone) by the nose get (someone) to do whatever one wants (*There is one pupil in the class who is very naughty and he seems to be able to lead all the other children by the nose*) <A reference to the ring on a bull's nose by which he can be led if necessary>.

---

lead *n* **1** (*the runners in the lead*) first place, leading position, forefront, vanguard. **2** (*She has the lead in the new play*) leading part, leading role, starring role, principal part. **3** (*We lost the dog's lead*) leash, chain, tether.

leader *n* **1** (*the leader of the team of climbers*) head, captain. **2** (*the leader of the country*) head, ruler, commander, chief. **3** (*a leader in the field of fashion/a leader in medical research*) front runner, trend-setter, pioneer, trail-blazer.

leading *adj* **1** (*They played a leading role in the peace talks*) chief, principal, foremost, important. **2** (*He was one of the leading artists of his day*) foremost, chief, most important, celebrated, eminent, outstanding.

leaf *vb* (*He leafed through the book to see if it was what he was looking for*) flick, skim, browse, glance. ▼

---

take a leaf out of (someone's) book to use (someone) as an example (*You should take a leaf out of your sister's book and start doing some studying for your exams*). **turn over a new leaf** to change one's behaviour, etc, for the better (*He was wild as a teenager but has turned over a new leaf now he is older*).

---

leaflet *n* (*an advertising leaflet*) pamphlet, booklet, brochure, circular handbill.

league *n* (*clubs forming a football league*) alliance, federation, association, union, group, society. ▼

---

be in league with (someone) to have joined together with (someone) usually for a bad purpose (*The police were sure that he was in league with the men who broke into the bank*).

---

leak *vb* **1** (*Water was leaking from the hole in the pipe*) escape, ooze, drip, seep, discharge, issue. **2** (*A member of the department leaked information to the press*) reveal, divulge, disclose, make known, pass on.

lean *vb* **1** (*lean the ladder against the wall*) rest, prop, support. **2** (*The ship leaned to one side*) incline, bend, slant, tilt, slope.

lean *adj* **1** (*He was tall and lean*) thin, slender, slim, spare, skinny **2** (*lean meat*) non-fat, low-fat.

leaning *n* (*He has a leaning towards scientific subjects*) tendency, inclination, bent, propensity.

leap *vb* **1** (*The dog leapt over the fence*) jump, spring, bound, vault. **2** (*The children were leaping around excitedly before the party*) jump, bound, bounce, skip, hop, dance. **3** (*House prices have leapt*) soar, rocket, mount, shoot up. ▼

---

a leap in the dark an action or decision the results of which cannot be foreseen (*It is too much of a leap in the dark to go to live abroad without having a permanent job to go to*).

---

learn *vb* **1** (*They had to learn a new method*) grasp, master, take in, pick up. **2** (*We go to school to learn*) be educated. **3** (*How did you learn that they had gone?*) find out, discover, gather, hear.

learned *adj* (*the learned men of the community*) erudite, educated, well-educated, well-read, scholarly, clever, intellectual.

learner *n* (*drivers who were learners*) trainee, pupil, apprentice.

lease *vb* (*They leased a car from an agency*) hire, rent, charter.

leash *n* (*a dog's leash*) lead, chain, cord. ▼

---

be straining at the leash to be very impatient or eager to do something (*It was a* lovely *afternoon and the children were straining at the leash to get out to play*) <A reference to a dog straining to get free from its leash>.

---

leather *n* (*jackets made of leather*) skin, hide.

leave *vb* **1** (*The guests left hurriedly*) depart, go away, take one's leave, set off. **2** (*He left his job and emigrated*) give up, quit, move from. **3** (*He left his wife and children*) abandon, desert, forsake, turn one's back on. **4** (*He left his gloves in the bus*) leave behind, forget, mislay. **5** (*They were asked to leave their boots by the front door*) place, put, deposit. **6** (*She plans to leave all her money to her nephew*) bequeath, will. ▼

---

leave (someone) in the lurch leave (someone) in a difficult or dangerous situation without any help (*She walked out and left her husband in the lurch with three young children*) <A lurch refers to a position at the end of certain games, such as cribbage, in which the loser has either lost by a huge margin or scored no points at all>.

---

leave *n* **1** (*The soldiers are taking some leave*) holiday, vacation, time off. **2** (*They were given leave to take some time off*) permission, consent, authorization. **3** (*They took their leave at midnight*) departure, leave-taking, farewell, goodbye. ▼

---

take French leave to stay away from work, without permission (*He might well be dismissed from his job for taking French leave to go and see the football match*) <A reference to an 18th century French custom of leaving a party without saying goodbye to one's host or hostess>.

---

lecture *n* (*The students attended a lecture on local history*) talk, speech, address.

leg *n* **1** (*She broke her leg*) lower limb. **2** (*The legs of the tripod for the telescope*) support, upright. **3** (*on the second leg of their journey*) stage, round, stretch, lap, part, portion. ▼

---

pull (someone's) leg to try as a joke to get (someone) to believe something that is not true (*There is not really a lion walking down the street. He was pulling your leg*). **not to have a leg to stand on** not to have any defence or justification for one's actions (*He was definitely speeding when the police stopped him. He does not have leg to stand on*).

---

legacy *n* (*He received a legacy in his aunt's will*) bequest, inheritance.

legal *adj* (*His action was not quite legal*) lawful, legitimate, law-abiding, permissible.

legend *n* (*legends about giants*) myth, saga, epic, folk-tale.

legendary *adj* **1** (*giants and other legendary figures*) mythical, fictitious, fictional, fabled. **2** (*legendary Hollywood actors*) famous, renowned, celebrated, illustrious.

legible *adj* (*writing that was scarcely legible*) readable, decipherable, clear.

leisure *n* (*hobbies he pursued in periods of leisure*) free time, spare time.

lend *vb* **1** (*She lent him a book on gardening*) loan, give (someone) a loan of, let (someone) have the use of. **2** (*The flowers lend a freshness to the room*) add, give, impart, supply.

length *n* **1** (*What length is the

room?) distance. **2** (*The audience were bored by the sheer length of the speech*) longness, lengthiness, extensiveness, long-windedness.

lengthen *vb* **1** (*They lengthened the skirts*) make longer, elongate, let down **2** (*It will lengthen the time the job takes*) make longer, draw out, prolong, extend, protract. **3** (*It is early spring and the days are lengthening*) become longer, draw out.

lengthy *adj* **1** (*He gave a lengthy speech/The meeting was a lengthy affair*) long, long-lasting, prolonged, protracted, too long.

lenient *adj* **1** (*a lenient judge*) merciful, clement, forgiving, compassionate, tolerant, gentle. **2** (*The accused was given a lenient sentence*) mild, moderate.

lessen *vb* **1** (*They hoped that the storm would lessen*) grow less, get less, abate, subside, ease off, let up, dwindle, decrease. **2** (*He was given pills to lessen the pain*) reduce, decrease, ease, relieve, soothe, assuage.

lesson *n* **1** (*The children are having a French lesson*) class. **2** (*The Bible story is meant to teach a lesson*) moral, message, example, warning.

let *vb* **1** (*They let the children play in the garden*) allow, permit, give permission to, authorize. **2** (*He lets his flat to students*) let out, rent, rent out, lease, hire.

lethal *adj* (*The blow to his head proved lethal*) fatal, deadly, mortal, terminal, destructive.

lethargic *adj* (*They felt lethargic after a heavy lunch*) sluggish, inactive, listless, sleepy, lazy, languid.

letter *n* **1** (*the letters of the alphabet*) character, symbol. **2** (*We sent a letter of thanks*) message, note, epistle. ▼

---

the letter of the law the exact wording of a law, rule, agreement, etc (*According to the letter of the law he is responsible for repairs to the house but he refuses to carry them out*).

---

level *adj* **1** (*We need a level surface to build it on*) even, flat, smooth, flush, horizontal. **2** (*The scores were level at half-time*) equal, even, neck and neck. **3** (*We need to keep the room at a level temperature*) even, uniform, regular, consistent, stable, constant.

level *n* **1** (*At eye-level*) height, altitude. **2** (*The lift will take you to the second level*) floor, storey. **3** (*The two gymnasts are at about the same level of competence*) stage, standard, grade.

liable *adj* **1** (*The hotel is not liable for customers' lost goods*) responsible, accountable, answerable, at fault. **2** (*People who climb high buildings are liable to injury*) exposed, open to, in danger of, at risk of, subject to, vulnerable. **3** (*She is liable to burst into tears if you criticize her*) likely, apt, inclined, prone.

liberal *adj* **1** (*a liberal supply of food*) abundant, copious, ample, plentiful, generous, lavish. **2** (*Her parents have very liberal ideas*) tolerant, broad-minded, unprejudiced, enlightened.

liberty *n* **1** (*a country that values its liberty*) freedom, independence. **2** (*The prisoners were suddenly given their liberty*) freedom, release, discharge, emancipation. ▼

---

take liberties with (something) to treat (something) with too much freedom or with not enough respect (*The writer of the book thought that the publisher had taken liberties with her text and changed the plot totally*).

---

licence *n* (*He showed his driving licence as proof of identity*) permit, certificate, document, documentation.

license *vb* (*The shop is licensed to sell alcohol*) authorize, permit, allow.

lid *vb* (*He removed the lid from the jar*) cover, top, cork, stopper. ▼

---

blow the lid off (something), to take the lid off (something) (*inf*) to reveal the truth about (something) about which there has formerly been some secrecy (*When the worker was sacked he blew the lid off the firm's illegal methods of accountancy*). **put the tin lid on (something)** (*inf*) finish (something) off completely, usually in an unpleasant way, to be the last straw (*When he forgot her birthday it put the tin lid on their relationship which was already breaking up*).

---

lie *n* (*It was obvious that he was telling a lie*) untruth, falsehood, fib, white lie.

lie *vb* **1** (*The jury felt that the witness was lying*) tell a lie, tell a falsehood, fib, dissemble. **2** (*The doctor asked him to lie on the sofa*) recline, stretch out, be supine, be prone, be prostrate, be horizontal. **3** (*The village lies at the foot of a hill*) be situated, be located, be. **4** (*The volcano lies dormant*) be, continue, remain. ▼

---

take (something) lying down accept an unpleasant situation without protesting or taking action against it. **lie through one's teeth** tell lies in an obvious and unashamed way (*He was lying through his teeth when he told her that he had been working late at the office*).

---

life *n* **1** (*when life began on earth*) existence, being. **2** (*They worked hard all their lives*) lifetime, life span, existence. **3** (*The children were full of life*) liveliness, animation, vitality, vivacity. **4** (*He was the life of the party*) spirit, vital spark, moving force. **5** (*They published a life of Winston Churchill*) biography, autobiography. ▼

---

come to life become active or lively (*The restaurants there don't come to life until late in the evening*). **see life** have wide experience of varying conditions and situations (*As a social worker she certainly sees life*). **take one's life in one's hands** take the risk of being killed, injured or harmed (*So many cars speed along that road that you take your life in your hands when you cross it*).

---

lifeless *adj* **1** (*A lifeless figure lay on the shore*) dead, deceased. **2** (*He seems to prefer lifeless objects to people*) inanimate, without life. **3** (*lifeless stretches of the world*) infertile, barren, sterile, bare, desolate. **4** (*The actor gave rather a lifeless performance*) spiritless, colourless, uninspired, flat, lacklustre.

lift *vb* **1** (*They lifted the sacks on to the lorry*) hoist, pick up, raise, carry. **2** (*They lifted the ban*) raise, remove, withdraw, revoke, relax, end. **3** (*The mist soon lifted*) rise, disperse, disappear.

struck a light) flame, spark. **4** (*We would prefer to arrive in the light*) daylight, daytime, day. **5** (*He began to see things in a different light*) aspect, angle, slant, approach, viewpoint, point of view. ▼

---

hide one's light under a bushel be modest or silent about one's abilities or talents (*We discovered quite accidentally that she has a marvellous singing voice. She certainly had been hiding her light under a bushel*) <A biblical reference to Matthew 5:15, quoting a remark made by Christ>. **light at the end of the tunnel** the possibility of success, happiness, etc, after a long period of suffering, depression, misery, etc (*He has been depressed about being unemployed but now there is a possibility of some work coming up there may be light at the end of the tunnel for him*).

---

light *adj* **1** (*a light, airy room*) bright, well-lit **2** (*wearing light clothes*) light-coloured, pale, pastel. **3** (*She had very light hair*) light-coloured, fair, blond, pale. **4** (*The suitcases are quite light*) easy to carry, portable. **5** (*A suit of a light material*) lightweight, thin, flimsy, delicate. **6** (*The child is very light for her age*) slight, small, thin. **7** (*He is able to do only light tasks*) easy, simple, effortless, undemanding, unexacting. **8** (*She woke up with a light heart*) happy, merry, carefree, cheerful. **9** (*They were told that it was not a light matter*) frivolous, unimportant, insignificant, trivial, trifling. **10** (*There was a light wind blowing*) gentle, soft, slight. ▼

---

be light-fingered (*inf*) to be in the habit of stealing (*Some of the hotel staff must be light-fingered. Several guests have lost valuable property*).

---

light *vb* **1** (*They light the fire in the evenings*) ignite, kindle, set fire to, set alight. **2** (*The fireworks lit up the sky*) illuminate, brighten, lighten.

lighten *vb* **1** (*The sky lightened*) grow light, grow bright, grow brighter, brighten. **2** (*We had to lighten the donkey's load*) make lighter, lessen, reduce.

lightweight *adj* **1** (*wearing a lightweight suit in the heat*) light, thin, flimsy. **2** (*He is rather a lightweight writer*) insignificant, unimportant, trivial.

like *prep* **1** (*It was like her to lose her temper*) typical, characteristic, in keeping with. **2** (*She writes rather like Jane Austen*) in the manner of, in the same way as, resembling.

like *adj* (*They have like tastes*) similar, identical, corresponding, compatible.

like *vb* **1** (*They seemed to like each other right away*) have a liking for, be fond of, be attracted to, be keen on, love, admire, appreciate, approve of. **2** (*She does not like pop music*) enjoy, delight in, relish, be partial to, have a preference for. **3** (*We would like to go to the party but we have another engagement*) wish, want, desire, prefer.

likelihood *n* (*There is no likelihood of our arriving on time*) possibility, probability, chance, prospect.

likely *adj* **1** (*It is likely that she will fail*) probable, to be expected, possible. **2** (*It is likely to be wet there at that time of year*) liable, apt, inclined. **3** (*They gave a likely enough reason for being absent*) plausible, feasible, reasonable, credible. **4** (*She found a likely place to build a house*) suitable, appropriate, fitting, acceptable, reasonable.

likeness *n* (*There is a distinct likeness between the two faces*) similarity, resemblance, sameness.

limb *n* **1** (*He injured his limbs in the accident*) arm, leg, extremity. **2** (*They cut a limb from the tree because it was keeping out the light from the house*) branch, bough. ▼

---

be out on a limb to be in a risky and often solitary position, having ideas, opinions, etc, that are different from those of other people (*Most of the members of the research department said that the new drug was absolutely safe but the young scientist went out on a limb and said that it could have serious side effects*).

---

limelight *n* (*She was a film actress who enjoyed the limelight*) public eye, public notice.

limit *n* **1** (*They were fishing outside the agreed limits*) boundary, border, extremity, cut-off point. **2** (*They tried to impose some kind of limit on their expenditure*) limitation, ceiling, maximum, restriction, restraint. **3** (*The climb up the mountain pushed their powers of endurance to the limit*) utmost, maximum, extremity, end.

limit *vb* **1** (*They tried to limit their expenditure*) restrict, restrain, curb, hold in check, **2** (*She felt that having children would limit her freedom*) restrict, restrain, curb, impede, hinder, hamper. ▼

---

be the limit be as much as, or more than, one can put up with (*The boy who delivers the newspaper is the limit. He either forgets to deliver it or leaves it at the foot of the garden*).

---

limp *vb* (*He still limps after the accident to his leg*) be lame, hobble.

limp *adj* **1** (*a salad consisting of tomatoes and a few limp lettuce leaves*) drooping, floppy, wilting, sagging. **2** (*They felt limp in the heat*) drooping, wilting, lethargic, exhausted.

line *n* **1** (*The pupils were asked to draw a line*) stroke. **2** (*There was dirty line along the bath*) band, strip, stripe, seam. **3** (*The old woman had a face full of lines*) wrinkle, furrow, crease, groove. **3** (*A line of police kept back the crowd*) row, column, chain, cordon, procession, queue, file. **4** (*She is hanging the washing on a line in the back garden*) rope, string, cable, wire. **5** (*The police are taking a tough line against the wrongdoers*) course of action, policy, approach, position, procedure. **6** (*What line is he in?*) line of work, work, business, employment, job, occupation, profession, trade. ▼

---

step out of line behave differently from what is considered acceptable or expected (*Any pupil who steps out of line and *does not wear school uniform will be punished*) <A reference to a line of soldiers on parade>. **toe the line** obey rules or orders or act in a way that is considered to be acceptable (*The children have been used to being disobedient but the new head teacher will soon get them to toe the line*) <A reference to competitors having to stand with their toes to a line when starting a race, etc>. **lay it on the line** make the situation absolutely clear to someone (*His boss really laid it on the line to the workers. They had to arrive punctually or be sacked*).

---

line *vb* **1** (*Age had lined her face*) wrinkle, furrow, crease. **2** (*Beech trees lined the avenue*) border, edge. **3** (*The children were asked to line up outside their classroom*) form a line, queue up.

linger *n* **1** (*The smell of fried fish lingered in the hall*) stay, remain, persist, hang around. **2** (*Some of the students lingered to ask the lecturer questions*) stay behind, wait behind, hang around, loiter, delay, stay, remain.

link *n* **1** (*A link has been established between smoking and certain illnesses*) connection, association, relationship, tie-up. **2** (*They have strong family links*) bond, attachment, tie, **3** (*the links of the chain*) loop, ring, coupling.

link *vb* **1** (*Shex has lost the piece that links the two parts together*) join, connect, fasten together, attach, couple. **2** (*The police are linking the murder with a previous one*) connect, associate, relate, bracket together.

lip *n* (*the lip of the cup*) edge, rim, brim, border, brink. ▼

---

lick one's lips to look forward to something with great pleasure (*He was positively licking his lips at the thought of a holiday in the sun*) <A reference to literally licking one's lips at the thought or smell of appetizing food>.

---

liquid *adj* (*a liquid substance*) fluid, flowing, runny, watery.

liquidize *vb* (*She liquidized the mixture*) blend, crush, purée.

liquor *n* (*He drinks only fruit juice, not liquor*) spirits, alcohol, alcoholic drink, strong drink, (*inf*) the hard stuff.

list *n* (*make a list of the titles of the books*) record, catalogue, register, inventory, table.

list *vb* **1** (*Please list the articles which you bought*) make a list of, note down, write down, itemize, enumerate, enter, record, register. **2** (*The ship listed in the storm*) lean, tilt, tip, heel over.

listen *vb* (*They listened carefully to what the teacher was saying*) pay attention to, take heed, heed, take notice of, hear.

listless *adj* (*feeling listless in the heat*) lethargic, sluggish, weak, exhausted, inactive.

litter *n* **1** (*with litter lying all over the park*) rubbish, debris, refuse, waste, junk, (*Amer*) trash, (*Amer*) garbage. **2** (*a litter of pups*) family.

little *adj* **1** (*a little man/a little object*) small, slight, short, tiny, minute, diminutive, mini, infinitesimal, microscopic. **2** (*a little book*) small, concise, compact. **3** (*You will gain little advantage *from doing that*) hardly any, scant, slight, negligible. **4** (*They had a little argument about which of them should pay the bill*) small, minor, petty, trivial, trifling, unimportant, insignificant. **5** (*They have nasty little minds*) mean, narrow, small, shallow.

little *n* **1** (*He will take a little of the milk*) touch, trace, bit, dash, spot. **2** (*You will see him in a little*) short time, little while, minute, moment.

live *adj* (*live animals/live bodies*) alive, living, breathing, existing, animate. ▼

---

a live wire an energetic, enthusiastic person (*She's a real live wire who always makes parties very enjoyable*) <A reference to a live electrical wire>.

---

live *vb* **1** (*in the days when dinosaurs lived*) be alive, exist, have life, be. **2** (*The casualty was not expected to live*) survive, last, endure. **3** (*old customs that live on*) survive, stay, remain, continue, abide. **4** (*They live on fruit and vegetables*) eat, feed on. **5** (*They live by begging*) make a living, subsist, support oneself, maintain oneself. **6** (*They live in a flat in town*) dwell, inhabit, reside, lodge, occupy. ▼

---

live and let live to get on with one's own life and let other people get on with theirs without one interfering (*Everyone else complains about the noise made by the neighbours in the end house but we believe we should live and let live*). **live it up** to have an enjoyable and expensive time (*They really lived it up when they were on holiday and now they are faced with lots of debts*).

---

lively *adj* **1** (*They are very lively children*) active, energetic, spirited, sprightly, perky. **2** (*They had a lively discussion on local politics*) animated, spirited, stimulating, enthusiastic.

livid *adj* **1** (*Their father was livid when he saw the damage which they had done to the car*) furious, enraged, infuriated, fuming. **2** (*He had a livid mark on his forehead*) bruised, discoloured, black-and-white, purplish, bluish. **3** (*the livid faces of the dead*) ashen, pale, pallid, ghastly.

load *n* **1** (*The donkey had a heavy load*) burden, weight. **2** (*the lorry's load*) cargo, freight, contents.

load *vb* **1** (*They helped to load the lorry*) fill, fill up, pack, stack. **2** (*He loaded the gun*) prime, charge, fill. ▼

---

a loaded question a question intended to lead someone into admitting or agreeing with something when he or she does not wish to do so (*The accused was tricked into admitting his presence at the crime by a loaded question from the prosecuting barrister*) <A reference to a die loaded or weighted so that it tends always to show the same score>.

---

loaf *vb* (*loafing around the house instead of working*) laze, idle, lounge.

loan *vb* (*They loaned him money*) lend, give on loan.

loathe *vb* (*They used to be friends but now they loathe each other*) hate, detest, abhor, have an aversion to.

local *adj* (*They attend the local school*) nearby, near, neighbourhood.

locality *n* (*There are several hotels in the locality*) area, district, region, neighbourhood, vicinity.

locate *vb* **1** (*They plan to locate the hotel on the outside of the village*) place, position, situate, site, build, establish. **2** (*We finally located the cause of the trouble with the engine*) find, discover, detect, identify, pinpoint.

lock *vb* **1** (*They locked the door*) bolt, bar, fasten, secure. **2** (*The guards locked the prisoners up*) shut up, confine, imprison.

logical *adj* **1** (*His argument was not at all logical*) reasoned, rational, sound, coherent. **2** (*It seemed the logical thing to do*) rational, reasonable, sensible, intelligent.

loiter *vb* **1** (*There were gangs of youths loitering the street corners*) hang around, hang about, wait, skulk, lounge, loaf, idle. **2** (*They loitered along the road to school*) dawdle, dally, saunter, dilly-dally.

lone *adj* (*The sailors saw a lone yachtsman*) solitary, single, sole, unaccompanied, by oneself.

lonely *adj* **1** (*She lived by herself and sometime felt lonely*) friendless, lonesome, forlorn, neglected, desolate, isolated, unhappy, sad. **2** (*a lonely landscape*) desolate, isolated, remote, out-of-the-way, deserted.

long *adj* (*a piece of wood three metres long*) in length, lengthways, lengthwise. **2** (*It was a long journey*) lengthy, extended, slow, prolonged. **3** (*He gave a long speech*) lengthy, prolonged, protracted, long-drawn-out, wordy, long-winded.

long *vb* (*They longed for a long cool drink*) yearn for, wish for, desire, crave, pine for, hanker after.

longing *n* (*They had a longing for some sunshine*) yearning, wish, desire, craving.

long-winded *adj* (*a long-winded speech*) wordy, verbose, rambling, lengthy, long-drawn-out, prolonged, protracted.

look *vb* **1** (*We looked and saw a beautiful painting*) take a look, observe, view, contemplate, gaze, stare, examine, study. **2** (*She looks ill*) appear, seem. **3** (*The dining room looks south*) face, overlook.

loom *vb* **1** (*A dark figure loomed out of the shadows*) appear, emerge, materialise. **2** (*The exams are looming*) be imminent, be close, be ominously close.

loop *n* (*loops of ribbon*) coil, hoop, circle, curl.

loose *adj* **1** (*They wore loose clothes*) loose-fitting, slack, wide, baggy. **2** (*The table leg is loose*) not secure, insecure, movable, wobbly, unsteady, shaky. **3** (*The rope was loose*) slack, untied, unfastened. **4** (*The pigs were loose in the village street*) at large, at liberty, free, unconfined.

loose *vb* (*She loosed the dogs when she saw the strange man in the garden*) let loose, set free, release, unleash, untie.

loosen *vb* **1** (*He loosened his belt*) slacken, let out, undo, unfasten, unhook. **2** (*He loosened his grip on the rail*) relax, slacken, weaken.

loot *n* (*The police found the burglar's loot*) booty, haul, plunder, spoils.

loot *vb* (*Gangs looted the shops after the fire in the city centre*) plunder, pillage, ransack, rob, burgle.

lorry *n* (*They loaded the lorry*) truck, van, juggernaut.

lose *vb* **1** (*We lost our keys*) mislay, misplace, forget. **2** (*They lost their way in the dark*) stray from, wander from. **3** (*She lost a lot of blood*) be deprived of. **4** (*They lost several opportunities*) miss, pass, neglect, waste. **5** (*Our team lost*) be defeated, suffer defeat, be conquered.

loss *n* (*The firm made a loss that year*) deficit, non-profit.

lost *adj* **1** (*They eventually found the lost gloves*) missing, misplaced, mislaid, forgotten. **2** (*lost opportunities*) missed, passed, neglected, wasted.

lot *n* **1** (*A lot of people were present*) a great many, many, a good deal, a great deal, numerous, an abundance, plenty, masses. **2** (*She weeps a lot*) a good deal, much, many times. **3** (*The furniture was sold at auction as one lot*) collection, set, batch, quantity.

lotion *n* (*a lotion to soothe his sunburned skin*) cream, salve, ointment.

lottery *n* (*He hoped to gain a lot of money in the lottery*) draw, sweepstake, drawing of lots.

loud *adj* **1** (*The children were frightened by the loud noise*) noisy, blaring, booming, deafening, earsplitting. **2** (*She disliked the loud colours in the restaurant*) garish, gaudy, flamboyant, flashy, vulgar. **3** (*She disapproved of their loud behaviour*) noisy, rowdy, boisterous, rough.

loutish *adj* (*Because of their loutish behaviour he was asked to leave the bar*) boorish, oafish, doltish, churlish.

love *n* **1** (*He showed his love by sending her red roses*) affection, fondness, care, concern, attachment, devotion, adoration, passion. **2** (*The child has a great love of chocolates*) liking, weakness, partiality, relish.

love *vb* **1** (*It was obvious that she loved him*) be in love with, care for, be fond of, adore, (*inf*) have a crush on. **2** (*She loves fresh peaches*) like, have a weakness for, be partial to, enjoy.

lovely *adj* **1** (*She is a lovely girl*) beautiful, pretty, attractive, good-looking, charming, enchanting. **2** (*We had a lovely time at the party*) delightful, pleasant, nice, marvellous, wonderful.

low *adj* **1** (*a low table*) short. **2** (*a low position in the firm*) inferior, humble, subordinate, junior. **3** (*She spoke in a low voice*) soft, quiet, whispered, hushed. **4** (*She was feeling low after her defeat*) in low spirits, down, down-hearted, dejected, depressed, despondent. **5** (*They have a low opinion of him*) unfavourable, poor, bad, adverse, negative, hostile. **6** (*Our supplies of food are low*) sparse, meagre, scarce, scant, scanty, paltry, inadequate. **7** (*It was a low thing to do*) nasty, mean, foul, vile, base, dishonourable, despicable, wicked, evil.

lower *vb* **1** (*They lowered the flag*) let down, take down, haul down. **2** (*They have lowered the prices*) reduce, decrease, bring down, cut, slash. **3** (*She was asked to lower her voice/They lowered the volume of the radio*) quieten, soften, hush, turn down.

loyal *adj* (*They were loyal subjects of the king*) faithful, true, trusted, trustworthy, trusty, reliable, dependable, devoted, constant.

loyalty *n* (*They showed their loyalty to the king*) faith, faithfulness, fidelity, allegiance, trustworthiness, reliability, dependability, devotion, constancy.

lucid *adj* **1** (*Her explanation was extremely lucid*) clear, crystal clear, plain, intelligible, graphic. **2** (*an old man who was scarcely lucid*) sane, in one's right mind, rational, compos mentis, (*inf*) all there.

luck *n* **1** (*She found the perfect flat just by luck*) chance, fortune, destiny, fate, accident, serendipity. **2** (*We wished them luck*) good luck, good fortune, success, prosperity.

lucky *adj* **1** (*She seemed a very lucky person who always got what she wanted*) fortunate, favoured, advantaged. **2** (*She didn't know the answer—it was just a lucky guess*) fortunate, providential, opportune, timely, auspicious.

lucrative *adj* (*His firm is very lucrative*) profitable, profit-making, money-making, remunerative.

ludicrous *adj* (*It was a really ludicrous suggestion*) absurd, ridiculous, laughable, foolish, silly, crazy, preposterous.

luggage *n* (*They carried her luggage to the train*) bags, baggage, suitcases, things, belongings, gear.

lull *vb* **1** (*They lulled the child to sleep*) soothe, hush, quieten. **2** (*Their fears were lulled*) soothe, quieten, silence, calm, allay, ease.

lull *n* (*They left while there was a lull in the storm*) pause, respite, interval, break, let-up.

lumbering *adj* (*He was a great lumbering creature*) awkward, clumsy, bumbling, blundering, hulking, ungainly.

luminous *adj* (*a clock with a luminous dial*) lighted, lit, shining, phosphorescent.

lump *n* **1** (*She bought a lump of cheese*) chunk, hunk, wedge, piece, mass, (*inf*) wodge. **2** (*He got a lump on the head when he fell*) bump, swelling, bulge, knob, bruise.

lunatic *adj* (*It was a lunatic thing to do*) mad, insane, foolish, stupid, idiotic, senseless, absurd, ludicrous.

lunge *vb* **1** (*She lunged at her attacker with a knife*) stab, jab, thrust, poke. **2** (*He lunged towards the door when he saw his attacker*) charge, dive, spring, leap, bound.

lurch *vb* (*drunk men lurching home*) stagger, sway, reel, roll, weave, stumble, totter.

lure *vb* (*Evil men lured the children into their car*) entice, attract, induce, inveigle, decoy, tempt, cajole.

lurid *adj* **1** (*She hated the lurid colours on the walls of the restaurant*) overbright, gaudy, garish, flamboyant, loud. **2** (*The newspaper published the lurid details of the murder*) gory, gruesome, macabre, sensational, melodramatic, explicit.

lurk *vb* (*She saw a figure lurking in the shadows*) skulk, lie in wait, crouch, slink, prowl.

luscious *adj* (*luscious peaches*) juicy, delicious, succulent, mouthwatering.

lust *n* (*They needed to satisfy their lust for power*) greed, craving, desire, yearning, hunger.

luxurious *adj* (*They live in luxurious surroundings*) opulent, affluent, sumptuous, splendid, magnificent, wealthy, expensive, rich, costly, lavish, de luxe.

luxury *n* (*After they won the lottery they lived in luxury*) opulence, affluence, splendour, magnificence, wealth, ease.

lynch *vb* (*The townspeople lynched the man who had murdered the child*) put to death, execute, hang, kill, murder.

lyrics *npl* (*He wrote lyrics for pop songs*) words, libretto, book, text.

M

machine *n* apparatus, appliance, instrument, device, mechanism.

machinery *n* **1** (*the machinery in the factory*) apparatus, equipment, gear, plant. **2** (*the machinery of government*) workings, organization, system, agency.

mad *adj* **1** (*She went mad with grief*) insane, demented, deranged, of unsound mind, crazed, crazy, unbalanced, unhinged. **2** (*mothers who were mad with their children*) annoyed, angry, furious, enraged. (*He is always engaging in mad schemes*) insane, crazy, idiotic, foolish, absurd, foolhardy, rash. **4** (*They are mad about jazz*) passionate, enthusiastic, keen, fervent, fanatical. ▼

---

mad as a hatter utterly insane, extremely foolish or eccentric (*The villagers thought that the inventor of strange gadgets was as mad as a hatter*) <Hatmaking used to involve the use of nitrate of mercury, exposure to which could cause a nervous illness which people thought was a symptom of insanity>. **mad as a March hare** insane, very silly, extremely eccentric, weird (*His neighbours regard him as being as mad as a March hare because of the peculiar clothes which he always wears*) <Hares tend to leap around wildly in the fields during March, which is their breeding season>.

---

magazine *n* (*She was looking for a gardening magazine*) periodical, journal, paper, (*inf*) glossy.

magic *adj* **1** (*people who believe in magic*) witchcraft, sorcery, wizardry, enchantment, the occult, voodoo. **2** (*the magic performed by the entertainer*) conjuring tricks, illusion, sleight of hand.

magician *n* **1** (*rather a frightening story about a magician*) sorcerer, witch, wizard, warlock, enchanter. **2** (*They hired a magician for the children's party*) conjuror, illusionist.

magnificent *adj* **1** (*a magnificent royal procession/a magnificent feast*) splendid, grand, impressive, superb, glorious. **2** (*It was a magnificent game of tennis*) excellent, skilful, fine, impressive, outstanding.

magnitude *vb* **1** (*try to estimate the magnitude of the explosion*) extent, size, dimensions, volume, bulk. **2** (*We were surprised at the magnitude of the flu epidemic*) size, extent, vastness, extensiveness. **3** (*fail to appreciate the magnitude of the problem*) scale, importance, significance.

maid *n* (*the hotel maids*) domestic worker, domestic, servant. ▼

---

maiden speech the first speech made as a member of the House of Commons or House of Lords (*Our local MP made his maiden speech on law and order*). **maiden voyage** the first voyage undertaken by a ship

(The ship ran aground on its maiden voyage).

---

mail *n* **1** (*The postman delivered the morning mail*) post, letters, junk mail, email, snail mail. **2** (*She sent the package by mail*) post, postal service. **3** (*The knights of old wore mail*) chain, coat of mail, armour.

main *adj* (*the main points in the discussion/the main cities in the world*) chief, principal, leading, foremost, major, important. ▼

---

have an eye to the main chance to watch carefully for what will be advantageous or profitable to oneself (*He is learning to play golf because the boss plays it. He always has an eye to the main chance*).

---

mainly *adv* (*They mainly lived on fruit and vegetables*) for the most part, mostly, on the whole, largely.

maintain *vb* **1** (*He has always maintained that he is innocent*) declare, insist, assert, state, proclaim, claim. **2** (*He has a family to maintain*) keep, support, provide for, take care of, look after. **3** (*He maintained a steady speed throughout the journey*) keep, keep up, continue, sustain.

major *adj* **1** (*play a major part in the victory*) important, leading, principal, great, crucial. **2** (*the major part of his fortune*) larger, greater, bigger, main. **3** (*one of our major artists*) leading, chief, foremost, greatest, main, outstanding, notable, eminent.

majority *n* (*the majority of the people*) most, bulk, mass, main body.

make *vb* **1** (*make furniture at his woodwork class*) build, construct, assemble, fabricate, form, fashion. **2** (*try not to make a noise*) create, produce, bring about. **3** (*He made a bow to the queen*) perform, execute, carry out, effect. **4** (*They made him apologize*) force, compel. **5** (*The bride's father made a speech*) give, deliver, utter. **6** (*He made a fortune before he was thirty-five*) earn, gain, acquire, obtain, get. **7** (*She will make a wonderful mother*) become, grow into, turn into. **8** (*We made an appointment to see him*) arrange, fix, agree on, settle on, decide on. **9** (*6 and 2 make 8*) add up to, amount to, come to, total. **10** (*He made the* v *into a* y *by mistake*) alter, change, turn, transform. **11** (*He hoped to make his destination by nightfall*) reach, arrive at, get to, achieve. **12** (*We could not make out what he was saying*) understand, follow, work out, hear. **13** (*He made up an excuse for not being present*) invent, think up, concoct, fabricate. ▼

---

make it 1 to be successful, especially financially (*He said that if you don't make it by thirty-five you never do*). **2** to arrive somewhere, to succeed in reaching somewhere (*When the car broke down on the way to the wedding we thought we would not make it*). **make it up** to become friendly again after a quarrel (*The two families have not spoken to each other for years but they have now agreed to make it up*).

---

make *n* (*various makes of car*) brand, kind, variety, sort, type. ▼

---

on the make (*inf*) with the intention of making a profit for oneself (*She thought he was *trying to help her by giving her financial advice but he was really on the make*).

---

make-believe *n* (*She said that she saw a fairy but it was only make-believe*) fantasy, pretence, imagination.

make-believe *adj* (*the child's make-believe friend*) fantasy, made-up, pretended, feigned, imaginary, fictitious, unreal.

make-up *n* (*She put on her make-up in the cloakroom*) cosmetics.

male *adj* (*male creatures*) masculine, manly, virile, macho.

male *n* (*two males and a female*) man, boy, gentleman.

malicious *adj* (*She received an anonymous malicious letter*) spiteful, vindictive, vicious, venomous, nasty, bitter, evil.

malignant *adj* **1** (*The doctor discovered that she had a malignant growth*) cancerous. **2** (*a malignant disease/a malignant influence*) dangerous, destructive, fatal, deadly, harmful.

maltreat *vb* (*Her parents were accused of maltreating her*) abuse, ill-treat, harm, injure, molest.

mammoth *adj* (*They faced a mammoth task/a mammoth serving of ice cream*) huge, enormous, gigantic, vast, colossal, massive.

man *n* **1** (*three men and a woman*) male, gentleman, (*inf*) chap, (*inf*) guy, (*inf*) bloke. **2** (*man and animals*) mankind, humankind, the human race, humans. ▼

---

be one's own man to be independent with regard to one's opinions, attitudes, actions, etc (*He's not his own man. He just agrees with whatever his friends say*). **the man in the street** the ordinary, average person (*Politicians should pay more attention to the man in the street*). **to a man** everyone without exception (*The workers voted to a man to go on strike*).

---

manage *vb* **1** (*He manages the whole firm*) run, be in charge of, be head of, control, preside over, administer. **2** (*We don't know how they managed to survive/manage the work*) succeed in, contrive, achieve, accomplish, effect. **3** (*It is going to be a large dinner party. Will you manage?*) cope, get by. **4** (*She really cannot manage such a lively horse*) handle, cope with, deal with, control.

manager *vb* (*the workers and the departmental manager*) head, superintendent, supervisor, boss, chief, administrator.

mandatory *adj* (*Taking part in the conference was not mandatory*) compulsory, obligatory, imperative, essential.

manful *adj* (*make a manful attempt to get to the summit of the mountain*) brave, courageous, gallant, heroic, bold, determined.

manhandle *vb* **1** (*The removal men had to manhandle the piano upstairs*) manoeuvre, haul, heave, push. **2** (*The police were accused of manhandling the protesters*) knock about, maul, mistreat, ill-treat, abuse, (*inf*) beat up.

mania *n* **1** (*Sometimes he suffers from depression and sometimes from mania*) frenzy, hysteria, wildness, derangement, madness, insanity. **2** (*They have a mania for attending auction sales*) fixation, obsession, compulsion, fascination, passion, enthusiasm, fad.

manipulate *vb* **1** (*manipulate the controls of the aircraft*) handle, operate, use, manage, manoeuvre.

2 (*A clever lawyer can manipulate a jury*) influence, control, guide, exploit.

mankind *n* (*the history of mankind*) man, humankind, the human race, Homo sapiens.

manly *adj* 1 (*a manly figure*) masculine, virile. 2 (*showing manly characteristics*) manful, brave, courageous, gallant.

manner *n* 1 (*She does the work in an efficient manner*) way, means, fashion, style, method, system. 2 (*They dislike his bossy manner*) attitude, behaviour, conduct, bearing, look. ▼

---

in a manner of speaking in a way, in a sense (*I suppose you could call him her guardian in a manner of speaking*). **to the manner born** as if accustomed since birth to a particular way of behaviour, etc (*She comes from a very poor family but she attends royal functions to the manner born*).

---

manners *npl* (*The children should be taught manners*) polite behaviour, politeness, courtesy, social graces, etiquette.

mannish *adj* (*rather a mannish voice*) masculine, unfeminine, unwomanly, (*inf*) butch.

manoeuvre *vb* (*He manoeuvred the piece of metal into position*) guide, steer, ease, move, negotiate, manipulate.

manoeuvre *vb* 1 (*army manoeuvres*) movement, operation, exercise. 2 (*It was a clever manoeuvre to try and obtain promotion*) move, tactic, trick, stratagem, scheme, ploy, ruse.

mansion *n* (*The rich family live in a huge mansion*) manor house, stately home.

manual *adj* 1 (*a manual gear change*) by hand, hand-operated. 2 (*manual workers rather than desk workers*) physical, labouring.

manual *n* (*an instruction manual with the washing machine*) handbook, instructions, guide, guidebook.

manufacture *vb* (*a factory manufacturing computer parts*) make, produce, build, construct, turn out.

manure *n* (*farmers spreading manure on the ground*) dung, fertilizer.

many *adj* (*many people did not turn up*) numerous, a large number, innumerable, countless, (*inf*) a lot of, (*inf*) lots of, (*inf*) oodles of. ▼

---

many hands make light work a job is easier to do if there are several people involved in doing it (*It looks as though the weeding of the garden will take a long time. Still there are a lot of us and many hands make light work*).

---

map *n* (*a map of the city centre*) chart, plan, diagram, guide. ▼

---

put (somewhere) on the map to become well-known or important (*Building a theme park there really put the town on the map*).

---

march *vb* 1 (*The soldiers marched along*) walk, stride, tramp, parade, file. 2 (*Time marches on*) progress, advance, go on, continue. ▼

---

get one's marching orders to be told to leave, to be dismissed (*She was given her marching orders for always arriving at* *work late*) <Originally a military term>. **steal a march on (someone)** to gain an advantage over (someone) by doing something earlier than expected (*We succeeded in stealing a march on them by launching our new product before they could launch a similar one*).

---

margin *n* **1** (*They won by a narrow margin*) amount, difference. **2** (*We have so little money that there is little margin for error*) scope, room, allowance, latitude, leeway. **3** (*the margin of the lake*) edge, side, border, verge, boundary.

marginal *adj* (*There has been only a marginal improvement*) slight, minimal, small, tiny, minor, insignificant.

mark *n* **1** (*the dirty marks on the tablecloth*) stain, spot, speck, smear, streak, blotch, smudge. **2** (*a mark of respect*) sign, symbol, indication, token. **3** (*His war experiences had left their mark on him*) impression, effect, impact, influence, imprint. ▼

---

be up to the mark to reach the required or normal standard (*They sacked him on the grounds that his work was just not up to the mark*). **make one's mark** to make oneself well-known or famous, to make a lasting impression (*When he was a student his teachers were sure that he would make his mark on the art world*).

---

mark *vb* **1** (*The hot teacups marked the table*) stain, smear, streak, blotch, smudge. **2** (*mark the battle sites on the map*) indicate, label, flag, tag. **3** (*teachers marking exam papers*) correct, assess, evaluate, appraise. **4** (*They marked his birthday with a huge party*) celebrate, commemorate, observe. **5** (*You should mark what the headmaster says*) pay attention to, take heed of, heed, note, take notice of, mind.

market *n* (*tourists buying souvenirs in the market*) market place, bazaar. **2** (*There is no market for such expensive goods in this part of the city*) demand, call, need.

maroon *vb* (*He was marooned on a desert island*) abandon, forsake, desert, strand.

marriage *n* **1** (*the marriage of their daughter to the son of their best friends*) wedding. **2** (*Their marriage lasted twenty years*) matrimony, union.

marry *vb* **1** (*The couple will marry later in the year*) be married, wed, be wed, become man and wife, (*inf*) tie the knot, (*inf*) get hitched. **2** (*They decided to marry their skills and set up business together*) join, unite, combine, merge.

marsh *n* (*plants that grow in marshes*) marshland, bog, swamp, mire, quagmire.

martial *adj* **1** (*the martial arts*) warlike, militant, combative, belligerent, pugnacious. **2** (*martial law*) military, army.

martyr *n* (*early martyrs killed because of their Christian faith*) victim, sufferer.

marvel *n* (*The pyramids are one of the marvels of the world*) wonder, sensation, phenomenon, miracle.

marvel *vb* (*We marvelled at the exploits of the acrobats*) be amazed, be astonished, stare, gape, wonder at.

marvellous *adj* **1** (*admire the marvellous exploits of the acrobats*) amazing, astonishing, astounding, sensational, breathtaking, spectacular, remarkable, extraordinary. 2 (*We had a marvellous evening at the theatre*) splendid, wonderful, glorious, excellent, enjoyable.

masculine *adj* 1 (*That tends to be a masculine habit*) male, manlike. 2 (*She says she likes really masculine men*) manly, virile, (*inf*) macho.

mash *vb* (*mash the potatoes*) pulp, purée, crush, pound.

mask *vb* (*We planted trees at the bottom of the garden to mask the view of the factory*) screen, camouflage, hide, conceal, cover up, blot out.

mass *n* 1 (*a mass of wood*) block, lump, hunk, chunk, piece, (*inf*) wodge. 2 (*measure the mass of the body*) size, dimension, bulk, capacity. 3 (*A mass of people attended the meeting*) many, crowd, throng, multiplexity, mob, crowd, host.

massacre *vb* (*The world was shocked at the massacre of civilians*) slaughter, carnage, mass murder, butchery, pogrom.

massage *vb* (*She massaged their stiff limbs*) knead, rub, pummel.

masses *npl* (*The leader did not care what the masses thought*) the people, the common people, the public, the populace, the mob.

massive *adj* (*They built a massive wall round their estate*) huge, enormous, immense, vast, colossal, gigantic, mammoth.

master *n* 1 (*In earlier time a master would have many servants*) lord, owner, employer. 2 (*He likes to think that he is master in the household*) chief, head, boss. 3 (*He is master of the ship*) captain, skipper. 4 (*Several golf masters took part in the tournament*) expert, professional, virtuoso, genius, (*inf*) ace. 5 (*pupils being taught by the French master*) schoolmaster, schoolteacher, tutor. ▼

---

past master someone extremely talented or skilful (*He is a past master in the art of charming women*). **old master** any great painter, or a work painted by any of them, who painted before the nineteenth century, especially a painter of the fifteenth and sixteenth centuries.

---

master *vb* 1 (*unable to master his horse/He must try to master his emotions*) control, subdue, check, curb, quell. 2 (*She seems unable to master the techniques of driving*) learn, grasp, understand, (*inf*) get the hang of.

match *n* 1 (*Take bets on who will win the football match*) contest, competition, game, tournament, trial, bout. 2 (*She was no match for the stronger player*) equal, equivalent, counterpart, rival. 3 (*Their parents tried to arrange a match*) marriage, union. ▼

---

meet one's match to find oneself opposing someone who has the ability to defeat one in a contest, argument, or activity (*She has been winning the annual tennis match for years but she has met her match in this new young player*).

---

mate *n* 1 (*He goes to the pub with his mates every week*) friend, companion, comrade, workman, classmate, (*inf*) chum, (*inf*) pal, (*inf*) buddy. 2 (*a plumber's mate*) apprentice, assistant. 3 (*the mate* *of this glove*) fellow, pair, match. **4** (*Her friends think she is looking for a mate*) spouse, partner, husband/wife.

material *n* **1** (*dresses made of a silky material*) cloth, fabric, stuff, textile. **2** (*organic material*) matter, substance, stuff. **3** (*research material for his novel*) information, facts, details, data, (*inf*) gen.

materialize *vb* **1** (*We had very elaborate plans but they did not materialize*) happen, come into being, come about, occur. **2** (*Suddenly figures materialized out of the fog*) appear, come into view, become visible, emerge.

maternal *adj* (*maternal feelings*) motherly.

matrimony *adj* (*She feels she is not ready for matrimony*) marriage, wedlock.

matted *adj* (*The child's hair was dirty and matted*) tangled, knotted, tousled, unkempt.

matter *n* **1** (*There are important matters to discuss*) topic, issue, subject. **2** (*It was no laughing matter*) affair, business, situation, circumstance. **3** (*waste matter*) material, substance, stuff. **4** (*What is the matter with the car?*) problem, trouble, difficulty. **5** (*matter oozing from the wound*) pus, discharge. ▼

---

a matter of life and death something of great urgency that may involve loss of life or some kind of other disaster (*Send for an ambulance and tell the driver that it is a matter of life and death/Please give me a lift to town. It's a matter of life and death—I'm late for work*).

---

matter *vb* (*Will it matter if we arrive a bit late?*) be of importance, be important, make any difference, count, be relevant.

mature *adj* **1** (*mature human beings*) adult, grown-up, grown, fully grown. **2** (*mature fruit/mature cheese*) ripe, ripened, ready, mellow.

maul *vb* **1** (*The zoo keeper was mauled by a lion*) tear to pieces, lacerate, mutilate, mangle. **2** (*He was accused of mauling the female employees*) paw, molest.

maximum *adj* (*the maximum number*) highest, greatest, utmost.

maybe perhaps, possibly.

maze *n* (*get lost in the maze of corridors in the hospital*) labyrinth, network, mesh, confusion.

meadow *n* (*cows grazing in the meadow*) field, grassland, pasture.

meagre *adj* (*unable to feed themselves on their meagre supply of money*) sparse, scarce, scanty, paltry, inadequate, insufficient, (*inf*) measly.

mean *vb* **1** (*What did his words mean?*) signify, indicate, convey, denote, stand for, suggest, imply. **2** (*We did not mean to hurt her*) intend, plan, set out, aim, propose. **3** (*I am afraid that this will mean war*) lead to, involve, result in, give rise to.

mean *adj* **1** (*He's too mean to buy anyone a Christmas present*) miserly, niggardly, parsimonious, penny-pinching, grasping, greedy. **2** (*It was a mean thing to take the child's sweets*) nasty, disagreeable, foul, vile, contemptible, hateful, cruel.

meaning *n* **1** (*He does not know the meaning of the word*) sense, significance, drift, gist, implication. **2** (*His life seems to have no meaning anymore*) point, value, worth.

3 (*She gave him a look full of meaning*) significance, eloquence.

means *n* **1** (*We have no means of getting there*) way, method, manner, course. **2** (*His father is a man of means*) wealth, riches, money, property, substance. **3** (*They have not the means to buy the car*) money, capital, finance, funds, resources.

measure *n* **1** (*use a linear measure*) standard, scale, system. **2** (*They had to take drastic measures to stop the truancy in the school*) action, act, course of action, step, means. ▼

---

for good measure something in addition to what is necessary (*She locked the door and for good measure put a table in front of it*). **have (someone's) measure** to have formed an impression or judgement of (someone) (*He thought that he would easily deceive the old woman but she soon had his measure*).

---

measure *vb* (*measure the length of the room*) calculate, estimate, compute.

measurement *n* (*take the measurements of the room*) size, dimensions, proportions, extent, capacity.

mechanism *n* (*the mechanism that drives the machine*) machinery, workings, apparatus, device.

meddle *vb* (*His neighbours tried to meddle in his affairs*) interfere, intrude, pry, butt in.

media *npl* (*The politician blamed his unpopularity on the media*) the press, journalists, radio and television.

medicine *n* (*The doctor gave the patient some medicine*) medication, drug, medicament. ▼

---

a dose of one's own medicine something unpleasant done to a person who is in the habit of doing similar things to other people (*He is always bullying the younger boys but he got a dose of his own medicine when their brothers beat him up*). **take one's medicine like a man** to accept bravely and without complaint any punishment or retribution that is due to one (*There is no point in complaining about having to write a punishment exercise. You were late for school and will just have to take your punishment like a man*).

---

mediocre *adj* (*She used to be at the top of the class but her work this term has been mediocre*) average, ordinary, indifferent, middling, passable, adequate, uninspired.

meditate *vb* (*take time to meditate on the gravity of the matter*) think about, contemplate, reflect on, consider, deliberate on.

medium *adj* (*of medium height*) average, middling.

meek *adj* (*meek people being bullied by the others*) docile, gentle, humble, patient, long-suffering.

meet *vb* **1** (*I met an old friend by chance in the high street*) encounter, come across, run into, bump into. **2** (*The committee meet on Thursday afternoons*) gather, assemble, congregate. **3** (*They met the demands of the job*) satisfy, fulfil, comply with. **4** (*meet one's responsibilities*) carry out, perform, execute. **5** (*He met death bravely*) face, encounter, confront. **6** (*where the two roads meet*) join, connect, unite, adjoin. ▼

meet one's Waterloo to be finally defeated, ruined, etc, often after a period of success (*He had been tennis champion at the club for years but met his Waterloo when the new member beat him*) <Napoleon Bonaparte was finally defeated at the battle of Waterloo>.

meeting *n* **1** (*A politician addressed the meeting*) gathering, assembly, conference. **2** (*a happy meeting between the two old friends*) encounter.

melancholy *adj* (*in a melancholy mood*) depressed, dejected, gloomy.

melancholy *n* depression, gloom, blues, low spirits.

mellow *adj* **1** (*mellow fruit*) ripe, mature, juicy, luscious. **2** (*She spoke in mellow tones*) sweet, tuneful, melodious, dulcet. **3** (*in a mellow mood after a good dinner*) cheerful, happy, genial, jovial.

melodious *adj* (*melodious sounds*) tuneful, musical, harmonious, dulcet.

melodramatic *adj* (*Her reaction to the news was rather melodramatic*) theatrical, overdone, extravagant.

melt *vb* **1** (*The sun had melted the snow*) thaw, soften. **2** (*solids melting rapidly*) dissolve, thaw, defrost, soften. ▼

be in the melting pot to be in the process of changing, to be subject to change (*There has been a change of government and so the educational system is in the melting pot again*).

memento *n* (*He gave her a memento of their holiday*) souvenir, keepsake, token, remembrance.

memorable *adj* (*a memorable occasion*) unforgettable, momentous, significant, notable,.

memory *n* **1** (*Her memory of the event is rather hazy*) recollection, recall. **2** (*They built a statue in memory of the soldiers killed in the war*) remembrance, commemoration, honour.

menacing *adj* (*He gave them a menacing look*) threatening, ominous, frightening, sinister.

mend *vb* **1** (*He mended the broken table*) repair, fix, renovate, restore. **2** (*She mended the children's socks*) darn, sew, patch. ▼

be on the mend to be getting better after an illness or injury (*He was badly injured in a road accident but he is now on the mend*).

mention *vb* **1** (*She mentioned your name as someone who might be interested in the job*) refer to, allude to, touch on. **2** (*She did mention that she was thinking of leaving*) remark, comment, observe.

mercenary *adj* (*She is very mercenary and wants to marry a rich man*) grasping, greedy, avaricious, (*inf*) gold-digging.

merciful *adj* (*a merciful judge*) lenient, compassionate, forgiving, sympathetic, humane.

mercy *n* (*The judge showed mercy to the man who had stolen money to feed his children*) leniency, clemency, pity, compassion, forgiveness. ▼

at the mercy of (someone) wholly in the power or control of (someone) (*The villagers are at the mercy of the cruel tyrant who owns the land* *which they rent*). **be thankful for small mercies** to be grateful for advantages in an otherwise difficult situation (*We have no meat or vegetables but we do have some bread. We should be thankful for small mercies*).

---

merge *vb* **1** (*The two firms have merged and staff have been made redundant*) amalgamate, combine, unite, join forces. **2** (*The colours in the picture seemed to merge*) blend, fuse, mingle.

merit *n* **1** (*He put forward the merits of the scheme*) advantage, asset, plus, good point. **2** (*She received a certificate of merit*) distinction, credit. **3** (*The artist's work is thought to have little merit*) worth, value.

merry *adj* (*merry children*) cheerful, gay, happy, light-hearted, joyful.

mess *n* **1** (*their mother asked them to clear up the mess in the kitchen*) clutter, litter, shambles, disorder, untidiness.

message *n* (*They were out and so we left a message for them*) note, memo, word, information, news, communication. ▼

---

get the message (*inf*) to understand something, especially something that is not directly referred to (*His guests stayed so late that he offered them some cocoa hoping that they would get the message*).

---

method *n* (*teaching methods*) system, technique, procedure, routine. ▼

---

there is method in his or her madness someone has a good, logical reason for acting as he or she does, although his or her actions seem strange or unreasonable (*We thought that he was a fool to resign but he got his redundancy money and the firm went bankrupt a few months later—there was method in his madness*). <From Shakespeare's *Hamlet*, Act II, Scene ii, 'Polonius: Though this be madness, yet there is method in't.'>

---

microscopic *adj* (*microscopic insects*) tiny, minute, minuscule.

middle *n* (*The children formed a circle and the little girl was in the middle/right in the middle of the city*) centre, heart.

might *n* (*unable to overcome the might of the enemy*) power, force, strength.

mighty *n* **1** (*a mighty blow*) powerful, strong, forceful, hefty. **2** (*mighty mountains*) huge, massive, vast, enormous, colossal.

migrate *vb* (*swallow migrating to the south in the summer/people migrating to find work*) move, relocate.

mild *adj* **1** (*mild climate/mild weather*) moderate, warm, soft, balmy. **2** (*She is usually of a mild disposition but she really lost her temper at the children*) gentle, tender, soft-hearted, warm-hearted, compassionate, lenient, calm. **3** (*a mild sauce*) subtle, bland, non-spicy.

militant *adj* (*in a militant mood*) belligerent, aggressive, pugnacious, combative, warlike.

mimic *vb* (*The pupil was caught mimicking the teacher*) impersonate, give an impersonation of, imitate, copy, parody, (*inf*) take off.

mind *vb* **1** (*Tell him to mind the low ceiling—he might bump his head*) be careful of, watch out for, look out for, beware of. **2** (*I am sure that they won't mind if you use the phone*) object, care, bother, be upset, complain, disapprove. **3** (*You should mind your own business*) attend to, pay attention to, concentrate on.

mind *n* **1** (*She failed her exams although she has a good mind*) brain, intellect, powers of reasoning. **2** (*It brought thoughts of her father to mind*) memory, recollection, remembrance. ▼

---

have a mind of one's own to be in the habit of forming one's own opinions, to be independent (*Her parents try to get her to do what they want but she has a mind of her own*). **put (someone) in mind of (someone or something)** to remind (someone) of (someone or something) because of some kind of similarity (*He puts me in mind of his father at that age*).

---

mingle *vb* **1** (*the colours mingled*) mix, blend. **2** (*She was too shy to mingle with the other guests at the party*) mix, socialize, circulate.

miniature *adj* (*a miniature railway*) small-scale, mini, diminutive, minute, tiny.

minimum *adj* (*the minimum price*) lowest, smallest, least, bottom.

minute *adj* **1** (*insects which are minute creatures*) tiny, diminutive, microscopic, minuscule. **2** (*There is just a minute difference between the two*) tiny, insignificant, infinitesimal, negligible.

miracle *n* (*miracles described in the Bible*) wonder, marvel.

miraculous *adj* (*She made a miraculous recovery from the accident*) amazing, remarkable, extraordinary, incredible.

mirage *n* (*The travellers thought they saw an oasis in the desert but it was a mirage*) hallucination, illusion, vision.

mirror *n* (*She looked in the mirror to apply her make-up*) looking-glass, glass.

mirth *n* (*There was a lot of mirth at the party*) laughter, merriment, hilarity, revelry.

misadventure *n* (*The verdict was death by misadventure*) accident, misfortune, mischance.

misbehave *vb* (*The children misbehaved when their mother was away*) behave badly, be naughty, be disobedient, (*inf*) act up.

miscellaneous *adj* (*a miscellaneous collection of old clothes for the jumble sale*) assorted, mixed, varied, motley.

mischief *n* (*children who are bored and getting up to mischief*) mischievousness, naughtiness, bad behaviour, misbehaviour, misconduct, wrongdoing, trouble.

mischievous *adj* **1** (*mischievous children*) naughty, badly behaved, disobedient, rascally, roguish. **2** (*They were upset by the mischievous rumours their neighbours spread about them*) malicious, spiteful.

miser *n* (*The old miser would not give any money to charity*) Scrooge, skinflint, niggard,(*inf*) cheapskate.

miserly *adj* (*They were too miserly to give any money to charity*) mean, niggardly, parsimonious, tight-fisted, Scrooge-like, (*inf*) stingy.

misery *n* (*the misery of being homeless and hungry*) wretchedness, hardship, suffering, unhappiness, distress, sorrow. ▼

put (someone) out of his or her misery to end a time of anxiety or suspense (for someone) (*Finally the teachers put the pupils out of their misery by giving them their exam results*).

misfortune *n* **1** (*He endured many misfortunes before becoming a successful businessman*) trouble, setback, adversity, calamity, disaster. **2** (*By misfortune we missed the last bus*) bad luck, ill luck, accident.

misgiving *n* (*We had misgivings about lending them the car*) qualm, doubt, reservation, suspicion.

mislay *n* (*Grandfather has mislaid his glasses again*) lose, misplace.

mislead *vb* (*She deliberately tried to mislead her parents*) misinform, deceive, hoodwink.

miss *vb* **1** (*He missed a great opportunity*) pass up, let go, **2** (*The children are missing their mother*) long for, pine for. **3** (*He missed the shot*) bungle, botch, muff. **4** (*We tried to miss heavy traffic by leaving early*) avoid, evade, escape, dodge. **5** (*Try not to miss anything out when you give an account of the accident*) leave out, omit, forget, overlook. ▼

a miss is as good as a mile if something fails to happen that is what is important and how close it came to happening does not matter (*He failed the exam by only two marks but unfortunately a miss is as good as a mile*).

missile *n* (*guided missiles*) projectile, rocket.

mist *n* (*There was a morning mist but it soon lifted*) haze, fog.

mistake *n* **1** (*His homework was full of mistakes*) error, inaccuracy, fault, blunder, (*inf*) slip-up, (*inf*) howler. ▼

and no mistake without any doubt (*We were extremely nervous and no mistake*).

misty *adj* **1** (*a misty morning*) hazy, foggy. **2** (*only a misty idea of what we are supposed to be doing*) vague, hazy, nebulous. **3** (*My eyesight is a bit misty just now*) blurred, fuzzy.

mix *vb* (*mix the ingredients for the cake*) blend, combine, put together. **2** (*She never mixes with the rest of the people in the street*) socialize, associate with, have dealings with. **3** (*The demands of her job and looking after children just don't mix*) be compatible. **4** (*She mixed up the two parcels and sent us the wrong one*) muddle, jumble, confuse. **5** (*I think that he is mixed up in the crime*) involve, implicate.

mixed *adj* (*a mixed lot of old clothes for the jumble sale*) miscellaneous, assorted, varied, motley. ▼

a mixed bag a very varied mixture (*The new class of pupils were a mixed bag*). **a mixed blessing** something that has disadvantages as well as advantages (*Having a lodger was a mixed blessing. The extra income was useful but she interfered with their privacy*).

mixture *n* **1** (*Pour the cake mixture into a bowl*) mix, blend, compound, concoction. **2** (*There was quite a mixture of people on the* *jury*) miscellany, assortment, variety, mix, collection.

moan *vb* **1** (*The injured woman moaned in pain*) groan. **2** (*She was always moaning about how poor she was although she spent a lot of money on clothes*) complain, grumble, whinge, (*inf*) grouse, (*inf*) gripe.

mob *n* **1** (*an angry mob of protesters*) crowd, horde, throng, multitude. **2** (*She thinks she is too aristocratic to mix with the mob*) the common people, the masses, the populace, the rabble.

mobile *adj* **1** (*a mobile caravan/a mobile shop*) movable, transportable, travelling. **2** (*The patients are mobile*) moving, walking.

mock *vb* (*The children mocked the new girl because she was wearing very thick glasses*) ridicule, jeer at, sneer at, laugh at, tease, mimic.

model *n* **1** (*a model of an old aeroplane*) replica, copy, imitation. **2** (*What model of car would you like?*) design, style, variety, type. **3** (*The architects showed us the model of the new housing estate*) prototype, design, pattern. **4** (*She wants to be a model*) fashion model, mannequin. **5** (*The art teacher used one of the pupils as a model*) artist's model, subject, sitter.

moderate *adj* **1** (*moderate winds*) mild, gentle, light. **2** (*We had moderate success*) reasonable, acceptable, tolerable, adequate, middling, average. **3** (*The prisoners' demands seemed moderate*) reasonable, within reason, fair. **4** (*a moderate lifestyle*) restrained, controlled, sober, steady.

modern *adj* **1** (*politicians in modern times*) present-day, present, contemporary, current. **2** (*Her ideas on education are very modern/modern styles of clothes*) up to date, new, advanced, progressive, state-of-the-art, fashionable, (*inf*) trendy.

modest *adj* **1** (*He had accomplished a great deal in life but was very modest*) unassuming, self-effacing, humble. **2** (*She was asked to wear modest clothes for the occasion*) demure, seemly, decent, decorous. **3** (*They are rich but live in a modest house*) humble, plain, simple, inexpensive. **4** (*Their demands seemed very modest*) small, slight, limited, reasonable, moderate.

modify *vb* (*They may have to modify the design of the new plane slightly*) alter, change, adjust, vary.

moist *adj* **1** (*moist weather*) wet, damp, dank, rainy, humid, clammy. **2** (*soil moist after the rain*) wet, damp. **3** (*a moist fruit cake*) juicy, soft.

moisture *n* (*moisture running down the walls of the damp house*) water, liquid, wetness, wet, dampness.

mole *n* (*a small mole on her back*) blemish, blotch, discoloration.

moment *n* **1** (*The peculiar noise lasted only a moment*) short time, instant, second, flash, (*inf*) jiffy. **2** (*It was a moment of great importance when the leaders first met*) time, occasion, point in time. **3** (*discuss matters of great moment*) importance, significance, note, seriousness. ▼

---

have had one's moments to have experienced times of success, happiness, excitement (*The old lady seems to lead a very boring life now but she has certainly had her moments*). **on the spur of the moment** suddenly, without previous planning (*On the spur of the moment they decided to go away for the weekend*).

---

momentous *adj* (*a momentous event in history*) crucial, important, significant, serious.

monarch *n* (*French monarchs*) ruler, sovereign, king/queen.

money *n* (*They have enough money to buy a new car*) cash, capital, finance, (*inf*) wherewithal. ▼

---

have money to burn to have so much money that one can afford to spend it in ways considered over-extravagant or foolish (*That child has more toys than she knows what to do with. Her parents have money to burn*). **throw good money after bad** to spend money in an unsuccessful attempt to get back money which one has already lost (*He is trying to borrow thousands of pounds from the bank to invest in a firm that is losing money rapidly. He is simply trying to throw good money after bad*).

---

monitor *vb* (*doctors monitoring the patient's condition*) watch, observe, check, keep an eye on.

monotonous *adj* **1** (*people who have to do monotonous jobs*) without variety, repetitious, routine, humdrum, boring, dull, tedious. **2** (*He has a very monotonous job*) flat, droning.

monstrous *adj* **1** (*They serve monstrous helpings of food/monstrous lorries speeding down the motorways*) huge, immense, vast, colossal. **2** (*Sacking them for asking for more money was a monstrous thing to do*) shocking, outrageous, disgraceful, scandalous, terrible, dreadful, foul, vile, despicable.

monument *n* (*a monument to soldiers who died in the war*) memorial, statue, shrine.

mood *n* **1** (*They were in a happy mood*) humour, temper, state of mind, disposition. **2** (*She is in a mood*) bad mood, bad temper, sulks.

moody *adj* (*Teenagers are often accused of being moody*) temperamental, unpredictable, irritable, short-tempered, bad-tempered, touchy, sulky.

moon *vb* (*mooning around complaining of boredom*) mope, idle, languish. ▼

---

ask for the moon *or* **cry for the moon** to ask for something that is impossible, or virtually impossible, to obtain (*She keeps asking to go to Disneyland but she is crying for the moon. Her parents have scarcely enough to live on*).

---

moor *vb* (*moor the boat in the harbour*) secure, tie up, fasten, anchor.

mope *vb* (*Since her boyfriend went away she has been moping around the house*) be miserable, be unhappy, brood, fret, sulk, idle, languish.

moral *adj* (*They are far too moral to break the law*) upright, honourable, virtuous, righteous, law-abiding, pure. ▼

---

moral support encouragement without actual physical, financial, etc, help (*Her parents could not afford to help her out financially when she was at university but they gave her moral support*).

---

morale *n* (*The team's morale was low after their third defeat in a row*) spirit, confidence, self-confidence, heart.

morsel *n* (*a morsel of cheese*) mouthful, bite, piece, bit, crumb, little.

mortal *adj* **1** (*a mortal blow*) deadly, fatal, lethal, destructive. **2** (*All of us are mortal*) human, earthly.

mostly *adv* (*The people in the group were mostly quite young*) for the most part, mainly, in the main, on the whole, largely, chiefly.

mother *n* (*her mother and father*) female parent, (*inf*) mum, (*inf*) mummy.

motherly *adj* (*The school matron is a very motherly person*) maternal, kind, loving, warm.

motion *adj* (*sickness caused by the motion of the boat*) movement, moving. ▼

---

go through the motions to make a show of doing something, to pretend to do something (*He was bored stiff at the concert to which she took him but, to be polite, he had to go through the motions of enjoying himself*).

---

motivate *vb* (*trying to motivate the children into reading novels*) stimulate, inspire, stir, persuade.

motive *n* (*She seems to have had no motive for the murder*) reason, cause, grounds, basis.

mottled *adj* (*skin with rather a mottled appearance*) blotchy, speckled, flecked, spotted, marbled.

motto *n* (*'Service with a smile' is the shop's motto*) slogan, saying, watchword.

mould *n* **1** (*cheese covered in mould/old wood with a layer of mould*) fungus, mildew, must. **2** (*put the jelly in a mould to set/hot metal left to set in a mould*) shape, cast. ▼

---

cast in the same mould as (someone) very similar to (someone) (*She's cast in the same mould as her mother. They both have very hot tempers*).

---

mouldy *adj* (*food having gone mouldy in the cupboard*) mildewed, musty.

mound *n* (*mounds of leaves in the garden*) heap, pile, stack, bank.

mount *vb* **1** (*mount the stairs to go to bed*) climb, ascend, go up. **2** (*mount the bus*) get on, board. **3** (*He mounted the picture*) frame. **4** (*mount a book exhibition*) put on, set up, stage, organize, arrange. **5** (*If you save a little each week your savings will soon mount up*) grow, increase, accumulate, pile up. **6** (*House prices are mounting*) rise, go up, increase, soar, escalate.

mountain *n* **1** (*A climber was injured on the mountain*) peak, hill. **2** (*They received mountains of mail complaining about the programme*) pile, mound, heap, stack. ▼

---

make a mountain out of a molehill greatly to exaggerate the extent of a problem, etc (*She is talking of going to the hospital casualty department with a small cut on her finger. She is really making a mountain out of a molehill*).

---

mourn *vb* (*She is still mourning after the death of her husband last year*) grieve, sorrow, be sad.

mournful *adj* (*wearing a mournful*

expression) sad, sorrowful, dejected, gloomy.

mouth *n* **1** (*the mouth of the river*) outlet, estuary. **2** (*the mouth of the cave*) opening, entry, entrance. ▼

---

be down in the mouth to be depressed, to be in low spirits (*I am not surprised that he looks down in the mouth. He cannot find a job*). **foam at the mouth** to be very angry (*He was foaming at the mouth at getting a parking ticket*) <Mad dogs foam at the mouth>.

---

move *vb* **1** (*They moved slowly round the room*) walk, go, proceed, progress. **2** (*We moved the furniture from one room to another*) carry, transport, transfer, convey, shift. **3** (*He is moving because he has a new job*) move house, relocate, leave, go away. **4** (*She was moved by the sight of the orphan children*) affect, touch, upset, disturb. **5** (*The sight moved her to tears/They finally felt moved to act*) rouse, stir, influence, induce, prompt. **6** (*At the meeting she moved that the chairman resign*) propose, put forward, suggest.

move n (It is difficult to predict what our opponent's next move will be) act, action, step, deed. ▼

---

make the first move to be the person who acts first, especially in a situation where two people are romantically or sexually attracted to each other (*Sam and Laura have been sitting looking longingly at each other all night, but both of them are too shy to make the first move*).

---

moving *adj* **1** (*the moving parts of the machinery*) movable, mobile. **2** (*the moving force behind the scheme*) driving, stimulating, dynamic. **3** (*a moving story about two orphans*) touching, affecting, emotional, emotive.

mow *vb* (*mow the grass*) cut, clip, trim.

mud *n* dirt, slime, sludge, (*inf*) muck.

muddle *vb* **1** (*She accidentally muddled the books in the library*) confuse, mix up, jumble up, disorganize, mess up. **2** (*New faces tend to muddle the old woman*) confuse, bewilder, perplex, puzzle.

muffle *vb* **1** (*You must muffle yourself up against the cold*) wrap up, cover up. **2** (*try to muffle the loud noise*) stifle, suppress, deaden, quieten.

mug *n* (*a mug of cocoa*) beaker, cup.

mug *vb* (*They mugged an old man to get his wallet*) attack, assault, rob, (*inf*) beat up.

muggy *adj* (*muggy weather*) close, stuffy, sultry, oppressive, humid, clammy.

multiple *adj* (*She received multiple fractures in the accident*) many, several, numerous, various.

multiply *vb* **1** (*mice multiplying rapidly*) reproduce, breed. **2** (*Their troubles seem to be multiplying*) increase, grow, spread, accumulate.

multitude *n* (*They were surprised at the multitude of people who turned up for the meeting*) crowd, horde, mob.

mumble *vb* (*mumbling a few words*) mutter, whisper, murmur.

munch *vb* (*munching an apple*) chew, bite, gnaw.

mundane *adj* (*a meeting supposedly designed to discuss important* *church issues but ending up discussing mundane matters*) commonplace, common, ordinary, everyday, routine, normal, typical.

murder *n* (*He was charged with murder*) killing, slaying, homicide, slaughter.

murder *vb* (*convicted of murdering his father*) kill, slay, put to death, (*inf*) do in, (*inf*) bump off.

murky *adj* **1** (*murky water*) muddy, dirty, cloudy, opaque. **2** (*a murky time of day*) dark, dim, gloomy.

murmur *vb* (*She murmured that she wanted to leave*) whisper, mutter, mumble.

muscle *n* (*He strained the muscle while high-jumping*) tendon, sinew, ligament.

muscular *adj* (*muscular young men involved in body-building*) brawny, strapping, hefty, burly.

muse *vb* (*He mused over the situation*) think about, consider, contemplate, meditate on, reflect on.

mushroom *vb* (*housing estates mushrooming everywhere*) spring up, shoot up, sprout, boom, thrive.

music *n* (*people enjoying the music*) melody, tune, air, rhythm.

musical *adj* (*a musical sound*) tuneful, melodic, melodious, sweet-sounding, dulcet.

muss *vb* (*Climbing through the hedge had mussed her hair*) disarrange, tousle, dishevel, make untidy.

muster *vb* (*The general mustered the troops/He had to muster all his energy to climb the stairs*) gather, summon, rally.

musty *adj* (*a musty smell in the old house*) mouldy, stale, fusty, stuffy, airless, damp.

mute *adj* (*animals making a mute appeal for help*) silent, speechless, unspoken, dumb, wordless.

muted *adj* (*muted colours*) soft, subtle, subdued, discreet, understated.

mutilate *vb* (*soldiers horribly mutilated in the war*) cripple, maim, mangle, disfigure, dismember.

mutinous *adj* (*a mutinous crew on board ship*) rebellious, revolutionary, insubordinate, disobedient, unruly.

mutiny *n* (*mutiny on board ship*) rebellion, revolt, insurrection, revolution, riot.

mutter *vb* (*She muttered that she did not want to go*) mumble, murmur, whisper, complain.

mutual *adj* (*They have mutual friends*) common, shared, joint.

mysterious *adj* **1** (*There were mysterious noises coming from the room where they were getting ready for the party*) peculiar, strange, odd, weird, curious, puzzling. **2** (*They were being very mysterious about where they were going*) secretive, reticent, evasive.

mythical *adj* **1** (*The dragon is a mythical creature*) legendary, mythological, fabulous, imaginary, fictitious. **2** (*She is always talking about her rich uncle but we think that he is a mythical figure*) imaginary, fantasy, make-believe, invented, made up, (*inf*) pretend.

N

nag *vb* **1** (*She is always nagging her husband*) scold, carp at, find fault with, bully. **2** (*children nagging their mother to buy them sweets*) pester, badger, harass, (*inf*) hassle.

nail *n* (*the joiner's wood and nails*) pin, tack. ▼

---

hit the nail on the head to be extremely accurate in one's description, judgement, etc (*You certainly hit the nail on the head when you said that he was work-shy*). **pay (something) on the nail** to pay (something) right away (*My mother hates to receive a reminder about a bill. She always pays her bills on the nail*).

---

naive *adj* (*She was so naive that she believed every word he said*) gullible, trusting, innocent.

naked *adj* **1** (*She could not answer the door as she was naked after her shower*) nude, in the nude, undressed, unclothed, bare, stark naked. **2** (*a naked flame*) unprotected, uncovered, exposed. **3** (*the naked truth*) undisguised, unadorned, stark, plain, simple.

name *n* **1** (*We don't know the name of the book*) title. **2** (*He made his name in the theatre*) reputation, fame, renown, distinction. ▼

---

call (someone) names to use insulting or rude names to (someone) (*The other children called the poor boy names because he wore ragged clothes*). **name names** *vb* to give the names of people, especially people who have been involved in some form of crime or wrongdoing (*The children are being bullied at school but they are afraid of naming names in case they are attacked*).

---

nap *n* catnap, sleep, doze, (*inf*) snooze, (*inf*) forty winks.

narrate *vb* (*The old man narrated the story of his life*) tell, relate, recount, describe.

narrow *adj* **1** (*They have very narrow wrists*) slender, slim, thin. **2** (*They stock only a narrow range of goods*) limited, restricted, small. ▼

---

a narrow squeak a narrow escape (*It was a narrow squeak. The car nearly ran me down*).

---

narrow-minded *adj* (*She was too narrow-minded to listen to other people's points of view*) intolerant, prejudiced, bigoted, biased.

nasty *n* **1** (*The rotting meat was a nasty sight*) unpleasant, disagreeable, horrible, foul. **2** (*a nasty old woman*) disagreeable, bad-tempered, spiteful, mean. ▼

---

a nasty piece of work someone who is very unpleasant or behaves very unpleasantly (*Try not to argue with him. He's a very nasty piece of work who has been in prison for assault*).

---

nation *n* (*an organization consisting of the nations of the world*) country, land, state.

nationalistic *adj* (*He is nationalistic and does not like foreigners*) patriotic, chauvinistic.

native *adj* **1** (*the native plants of the region*) indigenous, original, local. **2** (*their native instincts*) natural, inborn.

natural *adj* **1** (*a shop selling natural produce*) organic, pure. **2** (*natural behaviour*) unaffected, simple, genuine, spontaneous. **3** (*their natural instincts*) inborn, native, instinctive. **4** (*The illness took its natural course*) usual, normal, regular, ordinary, common.

nature *n* **1** (*The children are interested in nature*) environment, Mother Nature, creation. **2** (*He has a warm nature*) temperament, disposition, character, personality. ▼

---

second nature a firmly established habit (*It was second nature to him to work as hard as he could*).

---

naughty *adj* (*The children were being naughty*) badly behaved, bad, mischievous, misbehaving, disobedient.

nauseate *vb* (*The sight of the rotting meat nauseated her*) sicken, make sick, turn one's stomach, disgust, revolt.

navigate *vb* (*He navigated the ship through the narrow straits*) steer, pilot, direct, guide.

near *adj* (*The station is very near*) nearby, close, at hand, handy. ▼

---

a near miss something unpleasant that very nearly happened, often the near collision of two planes in the sky (*The chimney fell to the ground just in front of me. It was certainly a near miss*). **one's nearest and dearest** one's close family (*Even her nearest and dearest think that she is bad-tempered in the morning*).

---

nearly *adv* **1** (*We nearly drowned*) almost, all but, as good as, practically. **2** (*They collected nearly £500*) almost, roughly, approximately.

neat *adj* **1** (*children looking neat going to school*) tidy, smart, spruce. **2** (*They made a mess of the neat room*) tidy, orderly.

necessary *adj* (*They took the necessary action in time*) essential, needful, indispensable, required, vital.

need *n* **1** (*There is no need to shout*) necessity, requirement, obligation, call. **2** (*Their needs are very few*) want, wish, demand, requirement. **3** (*The charity helps people in need*) want, poverty, deprivation. ▼

---

needs must when the devil drives if it is absolutely necessary for something to be done then one must do it (*I would like to take some time off but I have too much work to do. Needs must when the devil drives*).

---

neglect *vb* (*She went to the cinema and neglected her work*) pay no attention to, disregard, ignore, overlook, skip, shirk.

negligent *adj* (*He was found negligent for falling asleep on duty*) neglectful, careless, inattentive, sloppy.

negotiate *vb* **1** (*The two sides

succeeded in negotiating a settlement) work out, arrange, agree on. **2** (*The two sides are negotiating about a financial settlement*) bargain, hold talks, discuss.

neighbourhood *n* (*They are moving to a new neighbourhood*) district, area, region, locality. ▼

in the neighbourhood of (something) around, about, approximately, roughly.

nerve *n* **1** (*Climbing the outside of the tower requires nerve*) courage, bravery, daring, pluck, (*inf*) guts. **2** (*They had the nerve to ask us to pay more*) impertinence, impudence, cheek, brazenness, effrontery, temerity. ▼

a bag of nerves a very nervous, anxious person (*She was a bag of nerves waiting to hear the results of her exams*).

nervous *adj* **1** (*He was feeling nervous about his visit to the doctor*) edgy, on edge, tense, anxious, agitated. **2** (*They are very nervous people*) timid, anxious, edgy, tense, apprehensive.

network *n* **1** (*The pattern consisted of a network of lines*) latticework, mesh. **2** (*When looking for work she contacted her network of old friends*) system, organization.

neutral *n* **1** (*It is essential for referees to be neutral*) impartial, unbiased, unprejudiced, open-minded, detached, disinterested. **2** (*She was looking for curtains in neutral colours*) indefinite, colourless, beige, stone.

never *adv* (*She never lies*) not ever, not at all, under no circumstances. ▼

never-never land an imaginary land where conditions are absolutely ideal (*They are hoping for a never-never land in which they will have no money worries*) <A corruption of never-land in J.M. Barrie's play *Peter Pan*>.

new *adj* **1** (*They are buying a new car*) brand new, unused. **2** (*We need some new ideas*) fresh, original, imaginative. **3** (*They have introduced a new system of cataloguing books*) different, modern, up-to-date. ▼

a new broom someone who has just been appointed to a post and who is eager to show his or her efficiency by making changes, etc (*The present production system works perfectly well but the manager is a new broom who is intends to change it all around*) <From the saying 'A new broom sweeps clean', meaning that a brand new brush will be more effective than one which is worn>.
turn over a new leaf to make changes in one's behaviour, etc which are for the better (*The pupil always used to arrive at school late but he has turned over a new leaf*).

news *npl* (*There has been no news of the missing climbers*) information, facts, communication, word, data. ▼

no news is good news if one has not received any information about someone or something then one can probably assume that all is well, since, if something bad, such as an accident, had happened, one would have heard.

---

next *adj* **1** (*the next bus/the next prime minister*) following, subsequent, succeeding. **2** (*the next house in the avenue*) neighbouring, adjacent, adjoining, closest, nearest.

nibble *vb* (*mice nibbling on a piece of cheese*) bite, gnaw, munch.

nice *adj* **1** (*His father is a nice person*) pleasant, friendly, kind, agreeable, charming. **2** (*We had a nice time at the theatre*) pleasant, enjoyable, delightful. **3** (*It was a nice day for the wedding*) fine, sunny, dry. **4** (*There is a nice distinction in meaning between the two words*) fine, subtle, minute, precise.

night *n* (*when night fell*) night-time, darkness, dark. ▼

---

a night owl someone who is in the habit of staying up very late at night (*She is a real night owl. She rarely goes to bed before 2 a.m.*).

---

nimble *adj* **1** (*The old lady was still very nimble*) agile, lithe, quick-moving, spry. **2** (*The knitters had very nimble fingers*) supple, deft.

nip *vb* **1** (*The little boy cried out when his friend nipped him*) pinch, tweak, squeeze. **2** (*The dog nipped her ankle*) bite, snap at. **3** (*He's just nipped out to the bank*) dash, rush, dart, hurry. ▼

---

nip (something) in the bud to put a stop or end to (something) at an early stage in the development of (something) (*Her father tried to nip her new romance in the bud by finding her a job overseas*).

---

noble *adj* **1** (*the king and the noble people of the land*) aristocratic, high-born, titled, blue-blooded. **2** (*a knight noted for his noble deeds*) brave, courageous, gallant, heroic, honourable, chivalrous. **3** (*The tourists admired the city's noble buildings*) impressive, imposing, magnificent, stately, grand.

nod *vb* **1** (*He nodded his head in agreement*) bow, incline, bob. **2** (*The audience began to nod*) nod off, drop off, fall asleep, doze. ▼

---

the land of Nod sleep (*It is time that you children were in the land of Nod*) <A reference to a place mentioned in the Bible in Genesis 4:16 and the fact that nodding is associated with falling asleep>.

---

noise *n* (*They were kept awake by the noise of traffic*) sound, loud sound, din, racket, clamour, row, commotion, hubbub, bedlam, pandemonium. ▼

---

a big noise an important person, especially one who acts in a very dominating way (*They are giving all the wards a special clean. Some big noise must be visiting the hospital*).

---

noisy *adj* **1** (*The teacher tried to quieten the noisy children*) rowdy, boisterous, loud. **2** (*noisy music*) loud, blaring, deafening, ear-splitting.

nondescript *adj* (*She was wearing nondescript clothes*) unremarkable, undistinguished, commonplace, ordinary.

nonsense *n* (*They told her that she was talking absolute nonsense*) rubbish, drivel, twaddle, gibberish, balderdash.

normal *adj* **1** (*temperatures that were normal for the time of year*) average, usual, common, standard, ordinary, typical. **2** (*He is of more than normal size*) average, standard.

nosey, nosy *adjs* (*They have nosey neighbours*) inquisitive, prying, curious, interfering, (*inf*) snooping.

notable *adj* **1** (*the notable achievements of the politician*) noteworthy, outstanding, remarkable, memorable, important, significant. **2** (*All the notable people in the town were present at the reception*) noted, of note, distinguished, well-known, eminent, prominent.

notch *n* (*make notches in the stick*) nick, dent, cut, indentation.

note *n* **1** (*It is wise to keep a note of how much you spend*) record, account. **2** (*I wrote her a note thanking her*) letter, line, message. **3** (*His advice is worthy of note*) notice, attention, heed, observation, **4** (*people of note in the community*) distinction, eminence, prestige, fame. **5** (*There was a note of sadness in her voice*) tone, sound. **6** (*He changed his notes into coins*) banknote, paper money. ▼

---

strike the right note to say or do something suitable for the occasion (*Her dark clothes struck just the right note at the funeral*) <A reference to the playing of a musical instrument>.

---

note *vb* **1** (*She noted the details in her diary*) write down, jot down, put down, enter. **2** (*The police noted that he seemed frightened*) notice, observe, perceive, detect.

notice *n* **1** (*Very little escapes the headmaster's notice*) attention, observation, heed. **2** (*We have received notice of a meeting to be held next week*) notification, information, news, announcement. **3** (*a notice on the board giving details of the meeting*) poster, handbill, information sheet, bulletin, circular. **4** (*Several workers have received their notice*) notice to quit, redundancy notice, the sack, (*inf*) marching orders.

notice *vb* (*We could not help noticing the bruise on her face*) see, observe, note, detect, spot, perceive, discern.

noticeable *adj* **1** (*The scar on her cheek was quite noticeable*) visible, obvious, plain, plain to see. **2** (*There had been a noticeable improvement in the pupil's work*) marked, obvious, evident, conspicuous, distinct.

notify *vb* (*They notified the police about the stranger in the garden*) inform, tell, advise, acquaint.

notion *n* (*They have some peculiar notions*) idea, belief, opinion, conviction, theory, thought.

notorious *adj* (*He is a notorious criminal*) infamous, well-known, scandalous.

nourishing *adj* (*give the children nourishing food*) nutritious, healthy, wholesome, beneficial.

novel *adj* (*He had a novel approach to the teaching of history*) new, fresh, different, original, unusual.

novelty *n* (*a stall at the seaside selling novelties*) knick-knack, trinket, bauble, souvenir, memento, gimmick.

novice *n* (*They are complete novices at the game*) beginner, learner, trainee, apprentice, newcomer, recruit.

nude *adj* (*They were sunbathing nude*) in the nude, naked, stark naked, bare, undressed, unclothed.

nudge *vb* (*She nudged him in the ribs to tell him to keep quiet*) prod, jab, poke, dig, elbow, push.

nuisance *n* (*She regards the cat next door as a nuisance*) pest, bother, irritant, problem, trial, bore.

numb *adj* (*Her fingers were numb with cold*) without feeling, immobilized, frozen, paralysed.

number *n* **1** (*write down all the numbers*) figure, numeral, digit. **2** (*A large number of people attended*) quantity, amount, collection. **3** (*This is last week's number of the magazine*) issue, edition, copy. ▼

---

a back number a person or thing that is no longer useful, important, popular, etc (*He was a famous pop star once but he is a bit of a back number now*). **(someone's) number is up** (*inf*) someone is about to suffer something unpleasant, such as dying, failing, being punished, etc (*He has been stealing from the firm for years but his number is up now. The manager has just begun to conduct an investigation*).

---

numerous *adj* (*He has numerous reasons for leaving*) many, very many, innumerable, several.

nurse *vb* **1** (*She nursed the sick child*) take care of, look after, tend, treat. **2** (*They still nurse feelings of resentment against their parents*) have, hold, harbour, entertain.

nutritious *adj* (*get the children to eat nutritious food instead of junk food*) nourishing, healthy, health-giving, wholesome, beneficial.

O

oath *n* **1** (*take an oath of loyalty to the king*) vow, promise, pledge, word. **2** (*She was offended by the oaths used by the drunk man*) swear word, curse, obscenity.

obedient *adj* (*obedient children/ obedient dogs*) biddable, well-behaved, well-trained, docile.

obey *vb* **1** (*obey the school rules*) observe, abide by, comply with, keep to. **2** (*soldiers obeying orders*) carry out, perform, fulfil, execute. **3** (*children taught to obey their parents*) be dutiful to, follow the orders of.

object *n* **1** (*pick up a wooden object lying on the pavement*) thing, article, item. **2** (*The object of the exercise was to collect money for charity*) aim, goal, purpose, point, objective. **3** (*the object of their abuse*) target, focus, recipient. ▼

---

money, distance, etc, **is no object** it does not matter how much money, distance etc is involved (*Money was obviously no object at the lavish wedding reception/The delivery service advertised the fact that distance was no object*) <Originally 'money is no object' meant money or profits were not the main aim of an exercise but the expression came to be misapplied>.

---

object *vb* (*We objected to the way they handled the situation*) raise objections to, protest against, complain, take exception to, grumble.

objection *n* (*There were several objections to the scheme*) protest, complaint, grumble.

objectionable *adj* (*He is a most objectionable young man/We found her manner objectionable*) offensive, obnoxious, unpleasant, disagreeable, nasty.

objective *adj* (*Referees have to be objective*) impartial, unbiased, unprejudiced, neutral, disinterested, detached.

objective *n* (*Our objective was to get there before nightfall*) object, aim, goal, target, intention.

obliged *adj* (*You are not obliged to say anything at this stage*) bound, compelled, forced, required.

obliging *adj* (*We have very obliging neighbours*) helpful, accommodating, willing, generous, cooperative.

oblivious *adj* (*They were oblivious to the danger they were in*) unaware, heedless, unheeding, unmindful, unconscious, ignorant.

obnoxious *adj* (*a most obnoxious sales assistant*) offensive, objectionable, unpleasant, disagreeable, nasty, horrible, odious.

obscene *adj* (*obscene videos*) pornographic, indecent, blue, bawdy, smutty, dirty.

obscure *adj* **1** (*For some obscure reason they suddenly decided to leave*) unclear, hidden, concealed, puzzling, mysterious. **2** (*a book by some obscure poet*) unheard of, unknown, little known, insignificant.

obscure *vb* **1** (*The new block of flats obscures our view of the lake*) hide, conceal, screen, block out. **2** (*His remarks simply obscured the issue*) confuse, muddle, complicate, cloud.

observant *adj* (*The observant lad was able to get the car's registration number*) sharp-eyed, eagle-eyed, attentive, heedful, vigilant.

observe *vb* **1** (*He observed a man watching his neighbour's house*) see, catch sight of, notice, perceive, witness. **2** (*All players must observe the rules of the game*) obey, keep, abide by, adhere to, comply with, follow, heed. **3** (*She observed that it was going to rain*) remark, comment, state, announce.

obsession *n* (*She has an obsession about having a spotlessly clean house*) fixation, preoccupation, compulsion, mania.

obsolete *adj* (*The factory uses obsolete machinery/The book has a great many obsolete words*) outworn, outmoded, antiquated, out of date, old-fashioned, archaic.

obstacle *n* (*the obstacles in the way of progress*) hindrance, impediment, obstruction, barrier, bar, hurdle.

obstinate *adj* (*The two sisters had a quarrel and were too obstinate to apologize*) stubborn, pig-headed, mulish, headstrong, unyielding.

obstreperous *adj* (*The police tried to control the obstreperous football crowd*) unruly, disorderly, rowdy, boisterous, rough, wild, turbulent, riotous.

obstruct *vb* **1** (*fallen trees obstructing the flow of traffic*) block, bar, check, halt. **2** (*The protesters tried to obstruct progress on the building of the new motorway*) hinder, delay, impede, hamper, block, interrupt, hold up.

obstruction *n* (*obstructions to progress*) obstacle, impediment, hindrance, hurdle, barrier, bar.

obtain *vb* (*We tried to obtain a copy of the book*) get, get hold of, acquire, come by, procure, gain.

obvious *adj* (*It was obvious that she was crying/The bruise on his face was very obvious*) clear, clear-cut, plain, noticeable, evident, apparent.

occasion *n* **1** (*They met on several occasions*) time, point. **2** (*The leaving party was a sad occasion*) event, incident, occurrence, happening. **3** (*She will go abroad if the occasion arises*) opportunity, chance, opening. **4** (*They met at a festive occasion*) function, gathering, party, (*inf*) do. ▼

---

rise to the occasion to be able to carry out whatever action is required in an important or urgent situation (*Her father was very nervous about speaking in public but he rose to the occasion at her wedding reception*).

---

occasional *adj* (*It will be a fine day with occasional showers*) infrequent, irregular, sporadic, rare, odd.

occupation *n* (*write down your occupation on the application form*) job, employment, profession, business, trade, career.

occupied *adj* **1** (*All the hotel rooms are occupied*) full, in use, engaged, taken. **2** (*The houses in the new estate are all occupied already*) inhabited. **3** (*The manager is occupied just now and cannot speak to you*) busy, engaged, (*inf*) tied up.

occupy *vb* **1** (*How many people occupy this flat?*) inhabit, live in, reside in, dwell in. **2** (*The enemy army occupied the city*) take possession of, seize, invade, capture. **3** (*How does she occupy her leisure hours?*) fill, use, utilize, take up. **4** (*They occupy junior posts*) hold, have, fill.

occur *vb* **1** (*The police think the murder occurred last night*) take place, happen, come about. **2** (*The same mistakes occur throughout the piece of work*) arise, be found, appear, be present. **3** (*It occurred to me that I had seen her before*) come to, enter one's head, strike.

occurrence *n* (*Car theft is a common occurrence these days*) event, incident, happening.

odd *adj* **1** (*We thought her behaviour was odd*) strange, peculiar, queer, weird, bizarre, outlandish, abnormal, curious. **2** (*She thinks of him at odd moments*) occasional, random, irregular. **3** (*He found an odd sock*) spare, left over, single, unmatched.

odious *adj* (*Our new neighbours are odious people*) horrible, nasty, loathsome, detestable, hateful, objectionable, offensive.

odour *n* (*the odour of frying onions*) smell, aroma, scent, fragrance, stink, stench. ▼

---

in bad odour in disfavour (*He is in bad odour with his teachers for playing truant*).

---

offence *n* **1** (*They were punished for the offence which they committed*) crime, misdeed, wrong. **2** (*His ungrateful behaviour caused offence*) upset, displeasure, annoyance, disapproval.

offend *vb* (*He offended her parents by not thanking them for the meal*) hurt, upset, displease, annoy.

offensive *adj* **1** (*He was forced to apologize for his offensive remarks*) hurtful, upsetting, distressful, abusive. **2** (*He is an offensive person/We noticed an offensive smell*) unpleasant, nasty, horrible, foul, vile, objectionable, odious.

offer *vb* **1** (*He offered several suggestions*) put forward, propose, submit, suggest. **2** (*We offered to babysit for them*) volunteer. **3** (*The job offers good career prospects*) give, present, afford, supply, furnish.

office *n* **1** (*His office is on the top floor*) place of business, workplace, room. **2** (*He has the office of company secretary*) post, position, appointment, job.

official *adj* **1** (*receive official permission/the official documents*) authorized, formal, licensed, certified, legal. **2** (*We had to wear evening dress to the official function*) formal, ceremonial.

officious *adj* (*the officious man at the counter in the unemployment office*) interfering, meddlesome, bumptious, self-important.

offspring *n* (*a couple with no offspring*) children, family, young.

oil *n* **1** (*fry the food in oil, not lard*) cooking oil. **2** (*oil to lubricate the hinges of the gate*) grease, lubrication. ▼

---

pour oil on troubled waters to attempt to bring a state of calm and peace to a situation of disagreement or dispute (*When the two sisters quarrel their mother always tries to pour oil on troubled waters*) <Since oil floats on water it has the effect

of making waves flat>. **strike oil** to obtain exactly what one wants, to be successful (*We have been looking for our ideal house for ages and now we've struck oil*).

---

oil *vb* (*oil the rusty hinges of the gate*) grease, lubricate. ▼

---

oil the wheels to make something easier to do or obtain (*She obtained a visa quite quickly. Knowing someone at the embassy oiled the wheels a bit*) <Wheels turn more easily if they are oiled>.

---

oily *adj* (*She dislikes oily food*) greasy, fat, fatty.

ointment *n* (*put ointment on his wound*) medication, cream, lotion. ▼

---

a fly in the ointment something that spoils something otherwise perfect, enjoyable, etc (*She really enjoyed her job. The only fly in the ointment is that she has to work on Saturdays*).

---

old *adj* **1** (*a ward in the hospital full of old people*) elderly, aged, (*inf*) long in the tooth. **2** (*She was wearing old clothes to garden in*) worn, shabby. **3** (*tired of his old ideas*) old-fashioned, outdated, out-of-date, outmoded, antiquated. **4** (*the old ruins in the centre of town*) dilapidated, run-down, ramshackle, crumbling. **5** (*He collects old cars*) antique, veteran, vintage. **6** (*in the old days*) past, bygone, earlier. **7** (*an old girlfriend*) former, ex-, previous. ▼

---

an old hand someone who is very experienced at doing something (*She's an old hand at looking after children*). **old hat** old-fashioned, no longer popular (*He used to be thought very modern but his ideas are considered old hat these days*).

---

old-fashioned *adj* (*old-fashioned clothes/old-fashioned ideas*) out of date, outdated, out of date, unfashionable, outmoded, (*inf*) past the sell-by date.

omen *n* (*They were superstitious and thought that walking under a ladder was a bad omen*) sign, portent forewarning, prophesy.

ominous *adj* (*We heard the ominous sound of gunfire*) threatening, menacing.

omit *vb* (*We omitted his name from the invitation list in error*) leave out, exclude, miss out, delete, eliminate.

onlooker *n* (*The police tried to move on the onlookers at the accident scene*) observer, witness, eyewitness, spectator, bystander.

ooze *vb* (*Pus was oozing from the wound*) flow, discharge, seep, exude, leak, drip.

opaque *adj* **1** (*opaque glass*) non-transparent, cloudy. **2** (*The waters were opaque with mud*) cloudy, dark, murky, hazy.

open *adj* **1** (*The door was open*) ajar, unlocked, unbolted, unfastened. **2** (*open boxes*) uncovered, unsealed. **3** (*find some open spaces for the children to run around in*) unfenced, unenclosed, extensive, broad, spacious. **4** (*maps lying open on the table*) spread out, unfolded. **5** (*She was quite open about her hatred of them*) frank, candid, forthright, honest, blunt, plain-spoken. **6** (*There was open hostility between *them*) obvious, evident, visible, unconcealed. ▼

---

an open-and-shut case something that is free from uncertainty, having an obvious outcome (*I do not think that the trial of the accused murderer will take long. It seems an open-and-shut case*). **lay oneself wide open to (something)** to put oneself in a position in which one is liable to be in receipt of (blame, criticism, accusations, attack, etc) (*If the personnel officer goes out to dinner with one of the applicants for the job he will be laying himself wide open to charges of prejudice*).

---

opening *n* **1** (*an opening in the hedge/an opening in the wall*) gap, space, aperture, hole, breach. **2** (*at the opening of the meeting*) beginning, start, commencement, outset. **3** (*There is an opening in the firm for a receptionist*) vacancy, position, post, place.

operate *vb* **1** (*The machine suddenly ceased to operate*) work, function, go, run. **2** (*Can you operate this machine?*) work, use, handle. **3** (*The surgeon had to operate on her leg*) perform surgery on.

operation *n* **1** (*She had to have an operation on her leg*) surgery. **2** (*The troops took part in a military operation*) manoeuvre, campaign, action.

opinion *n* (*We were asked to give our opinions on the state of the company*) view, point of view, viewpoint, thought, belief, idea.

opponent *n* (*his opponent in the snooker game*) rival, adversary, opposition, enemy, foe.

opportunity *n* **1** (*You should go abroad if the opportunity arises*) chance, occasion. **2** (*It was a good opportunity to spend some time with her family*) chance, occasion, time, moment.

oppose *vb* (*Some of the committee opposed the company's plans for expansion*) contest, take a stand against, argue against.

opposite *adj* **1** (*rows of houses opposite each other*) facing, face-to-face. **2** (*The two brothers were on opposite sides in the dispute*) opposing, rival, competitive, warring. **3** (*They hold opposite views*) differing, different, contrary, conflicting, contradictory, incompatible. ▼

(someone's) opposite number the person in another company, country, etc, whose job or role corresponds to someone's (*the editor of the daily newspaper and his opposite number on the evening paper*).

---

oppress *vb* (*The cruel tyrant oppressed the poor people of the villages*) crush, abuse, maltreat, persecute.

oppressive *adj* **1** (*the oppressive regimes in the world*) tyrannical, despotic, repressive, undemocratic, harsh, severe, brutal. **2** (*They were unable to sleep in that oppressive weather*) close, stifling, stuffy, suffocating, sultry.

opt *vb* (*He opted for a red car*) choose, select, pick, settle on, decide on.

optimistic *adj* **1** (*We were optimistic about our chances of success*) hopeful, confident. **2** (*He was in an optimistic mood*) hopeful, confident, cheerful, positive.

option *adj* (*We had only two*

options—to accept his offer or resign) choice, alternative. ▼

---

keep one's options open delay making a definite decision so that all possible choices remain available for as long as possible (*Avoid replying to the job offer until you hear from the other firms. It is best to keep your options open*).

---

optional *adj* (*Attendance at the meeting is optional*) voluntary, non-compulsory, discretionary.

oral *adj* (*He was asked to give an oral report of the events*) spoken, verbal, by word of mouth.

orator *n* (*The crowds gathered to hear the orator*) speaker, public speaker.

orbit *n* (*The spacecraft made an orbit of the earth*) revolution, circle.

ordeal *n* (*The climb up the mountain in blizzard conditions was a real ordeal*) test, trial, tribulation, suffering, torment, torture, nightmare.

order *n* **1** (*Soldiers must obey orders*) command, direction, instruction, decree. **2** (*The teacher restored order in the rowdy class*) calm, peace, control, discipline, good behaviour. **3** (*They restored the room to order after the party*) orderliness, neatness, tidiness. **4** (*Is the machine in working order?*) condition, state, shape. **5** (*arrange the words in alphabetical order*) arrangement, grouping, sequence, series, system, categorization. **6** (*place an order for his new novel*) request, booking, reservation. ▼

---

a tall order a very difficult or problematic task (*She said that she must receive the book by the next day but that was a tall order*). **in apple-pie order** with everything tidy and correctly arranged (*She always leaves the office files in apple-pie order*) <From French *nappe pliée*, literally 'folded linen', linen neatly laid out>.

---

order *vb* **1** (*the general ordered the soldiers to shoot*) command, direct, instruct, bid. **2** (*The shop did not have the book and so we ordered it*) place an order for, book, reserve.

orderly *adj* **1** (*an orderly piece of work*) organized, methodical, systematic. **2** (*an orderly crowd*) well-behaved, disciplined, quiet, peaceful, restrained.

ordinary *adj* **1** (*We followed our ordinary procedure*) usual, normal, standard, common, customary, regular, routine, typical. **2** (*lead ordinary lives/ordinary people*) unremarkable, unexceptional, average, run-of-the-mill, commonplace, humdrum.

organization *n* (*He is head of the organization*) company, firm, corporation, association, society, club, group.

organize *vb* **1** (*organize the books in alphabetical order by the name of the author*) arrange, group, sort, classify, categorize. **2** (*We organized a Christmas party for the children*) arrange, coordinate, set up, put together, run, see to.

origin *n* **1** (*discuss the origin of life*) source, basis, creation, start, commencement. **2** (*the origin of the word*) derivation, etymology, root.

original *adj* **1** (*the original owners of the house*) first, earliest, initial.

2 (*The judges are looking for original work*) innovative, inventive, creative, new, fresh, novel, unusual.

ornament *n* **1** (*There was a row of ornaments on the mantelpiece*) knick-knack, trinket, bauble, whatnot. **2** (*an outfit entirely without ornament*) decoration, adornment.

ornate *adj* **1** (*an ornate style of architecture*) decorated, elaborate, fancy, fussy, showy. **2** (*her ornate writing style*) elaborate, flowery, high-flown, pompous, pretentious.

orthodox *adj* (*people who question orthodox ideas*) conventional, accepted, established, traditional, standard.

ostentatious *adj* (*She was wearing a very ostentatious dress*) showy, conspicuous, obtrusive, loud, pretentious, over-elaborate.

other *adj* **1** (*We shall have to use other methods*) different, alternative. **2** (*give some other examples*) more, additional, further. ▼

---

look the other way deliberately to ignore or disregard something wrong, illegal, etc (*The local policeman would look the other way when the village pub was open after hours*).

---

outbreak *n* (*an outbreak of measles*) epidemic, flare-up.

outcast *n* (*He was an outcast from his native land*) exile, refugee, outlaw.

outcome *n* (*The outcome of the talks was that the workers went on strike*) result, consequence, upshot, conclusion, effect.

outcry *n* (*the outcry when the village post office was threatened with closure*) protest, commotion, outburst, uproar, clamour, hullabaloo.

outer *adj* (*the outer layer*) outside, exterior, external.

outfit *n* **1** (*her wedding outfit*) clothes, ensemble, costume, clothes, (*inf*) gear, (*inf*) rig-out. **2** (*a bicycle repair outfit*) kit, equipment, gear, apparatus.

outing *n* (*The children went on an outing to the seaside*) trip, excursion, jaunt, expedition.

outlaw *n* (*a book about outlaws who escaped from prison*) criminal, fugitive, outcast, bandit.

outlet *n* **1** (*water pouring through the outlet*) way out, exit, vent, opening. **2** (*an outlet for their farm produce*) market.

outline *n* **1** (*They saw the outline of someone against the wall*) silhouette, shadow, profile, shape. **2** (*They gave an outline of their plans*) summary, synopsis, rough idea.

outline *vb* (*We outlined our plans to the planning committee*) sketch out, rough out, summarize.

outlook *n* **1** (*The attic bedroom has a wonderful outlook*) view, prospect, aspect. **2** (*She is quite ill but the outlook is good*) future, prediction, forecast. **3** (*He has a depressed outlook on life*) view, opinion, attitude.

outlying *adj* (*outlying areas of the country*) remote, distant, far-flung.

outrageous *adj* **1** (*They objected to the drunk's outrageous behaviour*) disgraceful, shocking, scandalous, offensive, intolerable. **2** (*The invading army committed outrageous acts*) terrible, dreadful, abominable, foul, vile. **3** (*The prices in that restaurant are outrageous*) exorbitant, excessive, preposterous.

outside *n* **1** (*They painted the outside of the building white*) exterior, surface. **2** (*The fruit is dark green on the outside*) exterior, surface, skin, shell. ▼

---

at the outside at the most, at the absolute maximum (*The drive to the city will take two hours at the outside*).

---

outskirts *npl* (*a shopping complex on the outskirts of the town*) suburbs, outlying area.

outstanding *adj* **1** (*He is an outstanding artist*) excellent, exceptional, remarkable, eminent, noted, well-known. **2** (*His bill is still outstanding*) unpaid, owing, due.

outward *adj* **1** (*the outward layers*) outer, outside, external, exterior. **2** (*His outward cheerfulness hid his grief*) external, superficial, visible, discernible.

outwit *vb* (*He tried to cheat in order to win but the other player outwitted him*) outsmart, trick, fool, dupe.

oval *adj* (*an oval face*) egg-shaped, ovoid.

overcome *vb* **1** (*Our army succeeded in overcoming the enemy*) defeat, conquer, beat, vanquish, overthrow, crush. **2** (*He tried to overcome his disability*) conquer, master, triumph over.

overdue *adj* (*The train is overdue*) late, behind-hand, delayed, unpunctual.

overheads *npl* (*try to reduce the firm's overheads*) expenses, expenditure, outlay, running costs.

overjoyed *adj* (*They were overjoyed when their baby was born*) elated, thrilled, delighted, ecstatic.

overlook *vb* **1** (*Her bedroom window overlooks the lake*) face, have a view of, look out on. **2** (*He said he would overlook the error just this once*) disregard, ignore, pay no attention to, let pass, turn a blind eye to, condone. **3** (*He overlooked a note at the foot of the contract*) miss, fail to notice.

oversight *n* (*Omitting your name from the list was an oversight*) mistake, error, blunder, slip-up.

overtake *vb* (*The car overtook us on the motorway*) pass, overhaul, outdistance, catch up with.

overthrow *vb* (*overthrow the invading army*) overcome, defeat, conquer, vanquish, beat, overwhelm.

overwhelm *vb* **1** (*A tidal wave overwhelmed the village*) flood, swamp, inundate, deluge, engulf. **2** (*They overwhelmed the invading army*) overcome, defeat, conquer, vanquish, crush.

owing *adj* (*We had to pay the money owing right away*) outstanding, unpaid, due.

own *adj* (*Each of the girls had her own car*) individual, personal, particular, private. ▼

---

come into one's own to have the opportunity to show one's good qualities, talent, skill, etc (*She is a marvellous hostess and really comes into her own at parties*).

hold one's own 1 to perform as well as one's opponents in a contest, argument, etc (*The younger player succeeded in holding his own against the champion*). **2** to be surviving, to be holding on to life (*He was badly injured in the accident but he is holding his own*).

---

own *vb* **1** (*They own two cars*) have, possess, keep. **2** (*You have to own that he may be right*) admit, acknowledge, allow, concede. **3** (*The boy finally owned up to his crime*) confess, admit, acknowledge, (*inf*) come clean.

owner *n* **1** (*the owner of the car*) possessor, keeper, holder. **2** (*the owner of the business*) proprietor, boss.

P

pack *vb* **1** (*They packed their suitcases*) fill, load, stuff, cram. **2** (*They packed their old clothes in a trunk*) place, put, store, stow. **3** (*Protesters packed the hall*) fill, crowd, throng, mob, cram, jam, press into, squeeze into. ▼

---

send (someone) packing to send (someone) away firmly and frankly (*She never buys anything from door-to-door salesmen—she sends them packing immediately*). **packed like herring in a barrel** very tightly packed, very crowded (*The audience was packed like herring in a barrel at the pop concert*). **pack it in** (*inf*) to stop doing something, e.g. working on something (*He used to play football on Saturdays but he has packed it in*).

---

packet *n* **1** (*a packet of soap powder*) carton, pack, package, container. **2** (*The postman tried to deliver a packet*) package, parcel.

painful *adj* (*The leg that she injured is very painful*) sore, hurting, aching, throbbing, smarting, agonizing, excruciating.

paint *vb* **1** (*They are painting the walls*) apply paint to, decorate. **2** (*He painted the view from his bedroom window*) portray, depict, draw, sketch. ▼

---

paint the town red to go out and celebrate in a lively, noisy manner (*As soon as they finished their exams* the students went out to paint the town red). **like watching paint dry** used to describe something extremely boring: *Tim loves playing cricket, but his wife refuses to go and spectate because she says that it's like watching paint dry.*

---

painting *n* (*the paintings hanging in the gallery*) picture, portrait, sketch, drawing.

pale *adj* **1** (*She looks pale after her illness*) white, whitish, white-faced, colourless, wan, drained, pallid, pasty, peaky, ashen, as white as a sheet, as white as a ghost. **2** (*She always wears pale colours*) light, light-coloured, muted, subdued, pastel.

pan *n* (*the pans on the stove*) saucepan, pot, frying pan.

panic *n* (*They were filled with panic at the sight of the flames*) alarm, agitation, hysteria, fear, fright, terror, trepidation.

paper *n* **1** (*the paper that they take on a Sunday*) newspaper. **2** (*chose a paper for the living room*) wallpaper, wall-covering. **3** (*The students have to write a paper on Shakespeare's 'Hamlet'*) essay, report, dissertation, article, treatise, thesis. **4** (*get a photocopy of all the papers for today's meeting*) document, legal paper. ▼

---

paper over the cracks to try to hide faults, mistakes, difficulties, etc, in a hasty or careless way in order to pretend that there were no faults, mistakes, etc, in the first place (*There are many faults in their accounting system but they are desperately trying to paper over the cracks so that they can sell the firm*). **paper tiger** someone or something that has the outward appearance of being powerful and threatening but is in fact ineffective (*The president used to be feared by everyone but since the rebellion he is regarded as a paper tiger*).

---

paralyse *vb* **1** (*His legs were paralysed in the accident*) immobilize, make powerless, numb, deaden, cripple, disable. **2** (*The traffic system was paralysed in the snow storm*) immobilize, bring to a halt, bring to a stop, bring to a standstill.

parcel *n* (*The postman tried to deliver a parcel*) package, packet.

parcel *vb* (*parcel the Christmas presents*) parcel up, wrap, wrap up, pack, tie up.

pardon *vb* **1** (*The prisoner was pardoned by the king*) reprieve, let off, release, absolve, acquit, exonerate. **2** (*He asked her to pardon him for being so ill-tempered*) excuse, forgive, let off, condone.

part *n* **1** (*the last part of the book*) section, portion, segment, bit. **2** (*the parts of the machine*) component, bit, constituent. **3** (*She went to the northern part of the island*) section, area, district, quarter, sector. **4** (*Originally the book was issued in several parts*) section, bit, episode, volume. **5** (*He apologized for the part which he played in the hoax*) role, function, responsibility, job. **6** (*She plays the part of Joan of Arc in the play*) role, character. ▼

---

look the part to have the appearance appropriate to a particular kind of person (*If she wants to be a top executive she will have to look the part—at the moment she is too casually dressed*). **take (someone's) part** to support (someone) in an argument, debate, etc (*She always takes her mother's part when her parents disagree*).

---

part *vb* **1** (*They had to part when he went back to his own country*) separate, say 'goodbye'. **2** (*After three years of marriage they have decided to part*) separate, leave each other, split up, break up, divorce, go their separate ways. **3** (*The police parted the crowd to reach the troublemakers at the front*) divide, separate, break up.

partial *adj* **1** (*There was only a partial improvement in his work*) part, in part, incomplete, limited, imperfect. **2** (*The referee was accused of being partial*) biased, prejudiced, partisan, discriminatory, unfair, unjust.

partial:—be partial to *adj* (*She is partial to seafood*) like, have a liking for, love, be fond of, have a weakness for.

particular *adj* **1** (*You must pay particular attention to what he says*) special, exceptional, unusual. **2** (*In this particular case I think we should be generous*) specific, individual, single. **3** (*She is particular about who cuts her hair*) fussy, fastidious, selective, discriminating, (*inf*) pernickety, (*inf*) choosy.

partner *n* **1** (*They are business partners*) associate, colleague, co-owner. **2** (*the burglar and his partner in crime*) ally, confederate, accomplice. **3** (*All her friends *and their partners were invited to the wedding*) husband/wife, spouse, boyfriend/girlfriend.

party *n* **1** (*It was he who was host at the party*) social gathering, social function, function, reception, (*inf*) do, (*inf*) get-together **2** (*They were part of the hunting party*) group, band, company, contingent. **3** (*a certain party who shall remain nameless*) person, individual. ▼

---

the party's over a pleasant or happy time has come to an end (*This used to be a very free-and-easy department but I think the party's over. The new manager is said to be very strict*). **follow the party line** always to speak and act in line with the official opinions, ideas, attitudes, etc, as set down by the leaders of a particular group. **(someone's) party piece** an act, joke, speech, etc, that someone frequently performs in public (*Don't let Uncle Jim get started on his party piece. It is a very boring conjuring act*).

---

pass *vb* **1** (*The car passed us on a dangerous stretch of road*) overtake. **2** (*Lorries passed along the road all night*) go, proceed, drive, run, travel. **3** (*Time passed quickly*) go past, advance, roll by, flow by, slip by. **4** (*How does he pass the time now he has retired?*) spend, fill, occupy, take up, use, while away. **5** (*He passed her the papers for the meeting*) hand over, give, reach. **6** (*The estate passes to his eldest son on his death*) be passed on, be transferred, be signed over to. **7** (*All the students have passed the exams*) be successful, get through, gain a pass. **8** (*Parliament passed the new bill*) vote for, accept, prove, adopt, sanction. **9** (*The judge passed sentence*) pronounce, utter, deliver, declare. **10** (*Eventually the hurricane passed*) run its course, die out, fade, finish. **11** (*They were still friends after everything that had passed between them*) occur, happen, take place. ▼

---

make a pass at (someone) to try to start a romantic relationship with (someone) (*At the dinner he made a pass at the girl who was sitting next to him*) <Originally a fencing term>. **pass by on the other side** to ignore someone in trouble and not help him or her (*When he was made homeless he did not expect his friends to pass by on the other side*) <A biblical reference to the parable of the good Samaritan—Luke 10>. **pass for (someone *or* something)** to be mistaken for (someone or something) (*Her mother could easily pass for her sister*).

---

past *adj* **1** (*They were congratulated on their past successes*) former, previous, prior, foregoing. **2** (*He has become very ill in the past few days*) recent, preceding, last. **3** (*the history of past ages*) gone by, bygone, former. ▼

---

past it less good, effective, etc, than one used to be when one was young (*He used to be a good footballer but he is past it now*). **not put it past (someone)** to think that (someone) is quite capable of doing something bad (*I would not put it past him to tell a lie to get a job*).

pastime *n* (*He is going to have to take up a pastime in his retirement*) hobby, recreation, diversion, distraction, leisure activity, amusement, entertainment.

path *n* **1** (*a winding path up the mountain*) pathway, trail, track, way. **2** (*They are studying the moon's path*) course, route, circuit, orbit. ▼

---

beat a path to (someone's) door to visit (someone) very frequently or in large numbers (*The world's press beat a path to her door when she said that she had witnessed a miracle*).

---

pathetic *adj* **1** (*The starving children were a pathetic sight*) pitiful, pitiable, moving, touching, affecting, poignant, distressing, heart-breaking. **2** (*He could not play cricket and made only a few pathetic attempts to hit the ball*) feeble, inadequate, unsatisfactory, poor.

patient *adj* (*There is nothing to be done about the delayed flight—we shall have to be patient*) calm, composed, even-tempered, restrained, tolerant, forbearing, resigned, stoical, uncomplaining.

pause *n* (*There was a pause in the music while he changed the tape*) interval, lull, break, halt, gap.

pay *vb* **1** (*They had to pay a huge amount for that house*) pay out, spend, lay out, part with, (*inf*) shell out, (*inf*) fork out. **2** (*He will get paid at the end of the job*) give payment to, remunerate. **3** (*He enjoys the work but it doesn't really pay*) be profitable, make money, be remunerative. **4** (*He pays his bills right away*) settle, defray. **5** (*He likes to pay compliments to women*) bestow, offer, extend. ▼

---

pay the piper to provide the money for something and therefore be entitled to have a say in the organization of it (*Their parents feel that they should choose where the family goes on holiday since they are paying the piper*) <A reference to the saying 'he who pays the piper calls the tune'>. **put paid to (something)** to prevent (an action, plan, etc) from being carried out (*Having to move house put paid to our holiday plans. We didn't have any money left*).

---

peaceful *adj* **1** (*They were at war but conditions between the countries are now peaceful*) peaceable, at peace, friendly, amicable. **2** (*The old man looked peaceful lying asleep in his chair*) at peace, tranquil, serene, calm, composed, placid, undisturbed. **3** (*They longed for a house in a peaceful country setting*) quiet, restful, tranquil, calm, still.

peculiar *adj* **1** (*She wears such peculiar hats*) strange, odd, queer, funny, weird, bizarre, eccentric, outlandish, unconventional, offbeat. **2** (*There was a peculiar smell in the hall*) odd, unusual, strange, curious, abnormal. **3** (*a manner of walking that is peculiar to her*) characteristic, typical, individualistic, special, unique.

peel *vb* **1** (*peel the skin from the fruit*) pare, remove. **2** (*peel the fruit*) pare, skin. **3** (*Her skin was peeling after sunbathing*) flake off, scale off.

peg *n* (*They fastened the pieces of wood with a peg*) pin, nail, screw, bolt, spike, skewer.

penetrate *vb* **1** (*The knife of the attacker did not penetrate the skin*) pierce, bore, perforate, stab. **2**

(*unable to penetrate the dense jungle*) go through, get through, enter, infiltrate.

people *npl* **1** (*an issue that should be decided by the people*) the public, the general public, the common people, the populace, the electorate. **2** (*an area inhabited by a nomadic people*) population, tribe, race, nation. **3** (*A lot of people were expected to attend*) individuals, persons. **4** (*Her people should be looking after her*) relatives, relations, family, folk.

perfect *adj* **1** (*Her performance on the piano is perfect*) flawless, faultless, impeccable, consummate, ideal, supreme, excellent, marvellous. **2** (*a perfect set of the encyclopedia*) complete, full, whole, entire. **3** (*The boy is a perfect fool*) absolute, utter, complete, out-and-out, thoroughgoing.

perform *vb* (*They performed all the tasks which they were given*) carry out, do, execute, discharge, effect, fulfil.

perfume *n* (*a garden full of the perfume of roses*) scent, fragrance, aroma, smell, bouquet.

peril *n* (*animals in peril*) danger, risk, jeopardy, menace, threat.

period *n* **1** (*during the Tudor period of English history*) time, age, era, epoch. **2** (*Her condition worsened over a period of years*) time, space, interval, spell, stretch, span. ▼

---

period piece someone or something that is exceptionally typical of the time when he or she was born or when it was made (*She has a household full of Victorian furniture—real period pieces*).

---

perish *vb* **1** (*The food perished in the heat*) go bad, go off,decay, rot, decompose. **2** (*villagers who perished in the earthquake*) die, be killed, lose one's life.

permanent *adj* (*The accident left him with a permanent limp*) lasting, perpetual, persistent, enduring, abiding, eternal, endless, never-ending, unending.

permission *n* (*He took his father's car without permission*) authorization, leave, sanction, consent, assent, agreement, approval.

permit *vb* (*Her parents would not permit her to stay out late*) give permission to, allow, let, give leave, authorize, action, consent to, assent to, agree to,.

persecute *vb* (*people who were persecuted for their religious beliefs*) oppress, abuse, maltreat, torment, torture, victimize.

persevere *vb* (*You must persevere in your attempts to get a job*) persist, keep at, keep on, continue, carry on, be resolute, be determined, be insistent.

persistent *adj* **1** (*their persistent attempts to get planning permission*) determined, relentless, unrelenting, constant, continual, incessant, endless. **2** (*persistent people who will not give up trying*) persevering, determined, resolute, insistent, obstinate, tenacious.

personal *adj* **1** (*His reasons for being off work are purely personal*) private, confidential, individual, secret. **2** (*her personal interpretation of the piece of music*) individual, individualistic, idiosyncratic, peculiar.

personality *n* **1** (*She has a very pleasant personality*) nature, disposition, temperament, character. **2** (*It is a job for someone with personality*) character, charisma, magnetism, charm. **3** (*There were many sporting personalities at the dinner*) celebrity, dignitary, famous name, VIP.

personnel *n* (*the person in the firm in charge of personnel*) staff, employees, workers, work force.

persuade *vb* (*Could you try to persuade her to go?*) influence, induce, talk into, win over, prevail upon, cajole, wheedle.

pessimistic *adj* (*He has a pessimistic outlook on life*) gloomy, cynical, defeatist, fatalistic, resigned, distrustful.

pest *n* (*He thought the child was a pest*) nuisance, bother, irritant, trouble, worry, problem, inconvenience, trial.

pet *n* (*The boy is teased about being the teacher's pet*) favourite, darling, apple of one's eye.

petty *adj* (*have no time to discuss the petty details of the case*) trivial, trifling, minor, unimportant, inconsequential, slight.

phobia *n* (*She has a phobia about spiders*) aversion, fear, dread, horror, loathing, revulsion, (*inf*) thing, (*inf*) hang-up.

pick *vb* **1** (*They are picking fruit*) gather, collect, harvest, pull. **2** (*The little girls was asked to pick a toy*) choose, select, single out, opt for, plump for, decide upon, settle on. **3** (*The burglar picked the lock*) break open, force, prise open. ▼

---

pick and choose to choose very carefully from a range of things (*There is such a huge selection of dresses here that you can pick and choose*).

---

picture *n* **1** (*a picture painted by a famous artist*) painting, drawing, sketch, likeness, portrait, illustration. **2** (*He was paid to take pictures at the wedding*) photograph, photo, snapshot, snap. **3** (*The novel painted a distressing picture of Victorian England*) scene, view, vision, impression, description, portrayal, account, report. **4** (*a horror picture*) film, movie, motion picture. ▼

---

put (someone) in the picture to give (someone) all the information and detail about a situation (*Could you put me in the picture about what's been happening in the firm?*)

---

pie *n* (*a piece of apple pie*) tart, tartlet, pasty, quiche, pastry. ▼

---

pie in the sky something expected or promised in the future which is unlikely to come about (*He is planning a trip round the world but it's all pie in the sky. He'll never save that much money*) <A reference to a quotation from a poem by the American poet Joe Hills>.

---

pill *n* (*medicine in the form of pills*) tablet, capsule. ▼

---

sugar the pill to make something unpleasant more palatable.

---

piece *n* **1** (*put the pieces of the jigsaw together*) bit, part, section, segment, component, unit. **2** (*a quilt made of pieces of cloth*) length, bit, remnant, scrap. **3** (*a piece of pie*) bit, chunk, wedge, hunk, lump, (*inf*) wodge. **4** (*Each of his children will get a piece of his estate*) bit, share, slice, portion, percentage. **5** (*The valuable vase smashed to pieces*) bit, fragment, smithereens, shard. **6** (*an impressive piece *of antique furniture*) example, sample, specimen, instance, illustration. 7 (*a musical piece*) work, creation, composition, opus. **8** (*The journalist wrote a piece on the war*) article, item, story, report. ▼

---

go to pieces to be unable to continue coping with a situation, life, etc (*She goes to pieces in an emergency*).

---

pierce *vb* **1** (*Did the knife pierce the skin*) penetrate, puncture, prick, perforate, stab, pass through, enter. **2** (*pierce the piece of leather to make a leash for the dog*) perforate, bore, drill. **3** (*The cries of the bird pierced the air*) fill, pervade, penetrate.

pile *n* **1** (*dead leaves in piles around the garden*) heap, mound, stack, collection, stockpile, mountain. **2** (*We have a pile of homework*) great deal, abundance, (*inf*) lots, (*inf*) oodles. **3** (*He made his pile forging money*) fortune, wealth, money.

pillar *n* (*the pillars at the front of the temple*) column, post, upright, support, pilaster. ▼

---

from pillar to post from one place to another, often repeatedly (*The authorities sent us from pillar to post in search of a visa*) <From the game of real tennis>.

---

pin *n* **1** (*Can you pin the brooch to my dress?*) fasten, fix, secure, attach. **2** (*The man was pinned under the overturned tractor*) hold, press, pinion, restrain, immobilize. ▼

---

for two pins given the least encouragement or reason (*For two pins I would take the day off*). **you could have heard a pin drop** there was silence (*You could have heard a pin drop when she made the accusation*).

---

pinch *vb* **1** (*She pinched her friend's arm to wake her up*) nip, tweak, squeeze. **3** (*Her new shoes are pinching her toes*) hurt, crush, squeeze. **4** (*She pinched a cake from the baker's shop*) steal, take, thieve, rob, filch, pilfer, purloin, (*inf*) swipe.▼

---

at a pinch if it is absolutely necessary (*We do not have much space but at a pinch we could accommodate three of you*). **feel the pinch** (*inf*) to have financial problems (*They are feeling the pinch now that they have retired*).

---

pious *adj* (*pious members of the parish*) religious, godly, devout, God-fearing, righteous.

pitch *vb* **1** (*They pitched their tent in a field*) put up, set up, erect, raise. **2** (*The children began to pitch stones into the lake*) throw, cast, fling, hurl, toss, heave, (*inf*) chuck. **3** (*The ships were pitching in the high winds*) roll, rock, lurch, sway.

pity *n* **1** (*They felt pity for the poor orphans*) compassion, sympathy, commiseration, distress, sadness. **2** (*The tyrant showed the prisoners no pity*) mercy, leniency, kindness, clemency. **3** (*It was a pity that their bus was late*) shame, crying shame, misfortune.

placard *n* (*placards advertising the show*) poster, notice, bill, sticker.

place *n* **1** (*This is the place where she lost the ring/the place where he built the houses*) spot, location, site, setting, position, situation, area, region. **2** (*She won third place in the competition*) position, grade, level, rank. **3** (*It was not his place to sort out the dispute*) responsibility, job, task, function, role. **4** (*The pupil returned to her place*) seat, position.

plain *adj* **1** (*It was plain to all of us that she was in pain*) clear, crystal-clear, obvious, evident, apparent, manifest, unmistakable, noticeable, conspicuous. **2** (*We need a plain statement of what happened*) clear, straightforward, simple, intelligible, lucid. **3** (*The style of decoration is very plain*) simple, restrained, bare, austere, stark, basic, unadorned, spartan. **4** (*She is very beautiful now and yet she was rather plain as a child*) unattractive, unprepossessing, ugly. ▼

---

as plain as a pikestaff very obvious (*It was as plain as a pikestaff that she was jealous of her sister*) <'Pikestaff' was originally 'packstaff', a staff for holding a traveller's pack and lacking any decoration. Plain, meaning without decoration, has been confused with plain meaning clear>.

---

plan *n* **1** (*They have plans to expand the firm/The prisoners have an escape plan*) scheme, strategy, tactics, system, method, project. **2** (*Their holiday plans have been ruined*) arrangements, schedule, programme, procedure, method, system. **3** (*Their plan was to travel overnight*) aim, intention, objective, scheme, proposal. **4** (*The architect's plans for the new building are on show*) drawing, blueprint, representation, model.

play *vb* **1** (*Children need time to play*) amuse oneself, enjoy oneself, entertain oneself, have fun. **2** (*The children were playing in the garden with the dog*) play games, frolic, romp, frisk, gambol, cavort. **3** (*He likes to play football*) take part in, engage in, be involved in, participate in. **4** (*Our team is playing against strong opposition*) compete against, take on, oppose, challenge, vie with, contend with. **5** (*She plays the piano*) perform on. **6** (*The children played tricks on their grandfather*) perform, carry out, do, execute, discharge. **6** (*He played Hamlet in the National Theatre production*) play the part of, act the part of, perform, portray. ▼

---

make a play for (someone *or* **something)** to try to obtain (someone or something) (*He is not really qualified for the job but he is making a play for it*).

play possum to pretend to be asleep, unconscious or dead (*Their father played possum when the children went into his room early in the morning*) <The possum is an animal which pretends to be dead when it is under threat of attack from another animal>.

---

plead *vb* (*They pleaded for mercy*) beg, entreat, implore.

pleasant *adj* **1** (*It was a very pleasant occasion*) agreeable, enjoyable, pleasing, delightful, nice, good, lovely, entertaining, amusing **2** (*Our neighbours are very pleasant*) agreeable, friendly, amiable, affable, likeable, charming.

please *vb* **1** (*We were going to go to the theatre but it is difficult to find a show that will please everyone*) give pleasure to, satisfy, suit, delight, amuse, entertain. **2** (*Whatever advice you give her she will do as she pleases*) wish, want, like, choose, prefer, see fit.

pleasure *n* **1** (*a gift that will bring their mother a great deal of pleasure*) happiness, joy, delight, enjoyment, amusement, entertainment, satisfaction. **2** (*one of the old man's few pleasures*) joy, delight, enjoyment, recreation, diversion.

plentiful *adj* (*plentiful supplies of fuel*) abundant, copious, ample, profuse, generous, liberal, large.

plot *n* **1** (*They uncovered a plot to murder the king*) conspiracy, intrigue. **2** (*The novel has a complicated plot*) theme, action, story line, subject. **3** (*He grows potatoes on his vegetable plot*) allotment, patch. ▼

---

the plot thickens the situation is getting more complicated and more interesting (*He is trying to get her job but he doesn't know that she is trying to get him sacked. The plot thickens*).

---

plump *adj* (*She was plump as a little girl*) chubby, tubby, fat.

plunder *vb* (*They crossed the border and plundered the enemy villages*) rob, raid, loot, pillage, lay waste.

poetry *n* (*He writes poetry as a hobby*) poems, verse, verses.

point *n* **1** (*The spear had a very sharp point*) tip, end, top. **2** (*She reached a point where she could not go on*) stage, position, situation, circumstances, time. **3** (*at some point during the meeting*) time, juncture, stage. **4** (*They discussed the various points in the report*) detail, item, particular, issue, subject, topic. **5** (*The speaker spoke at length but few people got the point of his talk*) meaning, significance, import, substance, gist, drift. **6** (*He took ages to get to the point when he was declaring them redundant*) main point, salient point, crux of the matter, crux, heart of the matter, (*inf*) nitty-gritty. **7** (*What is the point of this discussion?*) aim, purpose, intention, object, objective, goal. **8** (*That is one of the weak points of the argument/He has many good points*) aspect, feature, attribute, quality, characteristic, trait. **9** (*the team that has most points*) mark. ▼

---

make a point of (doing something) to be exceptionally careful about (doing something) (*He makes a point of visiting his elderly parents once a week*). **up to a point** to some extent but not completely (*I agree with him up to a point but there are weaknesses in his argument*).

---

point:— point out *vb* (*We pointed out the benefits*) draw attention to, call attention to, identify, indicate, show, mention, specify.

pointless *adj* **1** (*It was pointless to continue the search after dark*) in vain, useless, futile, to no purpose, senseless, stupid **2** (*They made a few pointless comments*) worthless, meaningless, insignificant, irrelevant.

poisonous *adj* **1** (*an area with poisonous snakes*) venomous. **2** (*poisonous chemical substances*) toxic, deadly, lethal, fatal.

poke *vb* **1** (*The child tried to poke a pencil in the electric socket*) jab, push, thrust, shove, stick. **2** (*He* *poked his friend in the ribs to get him to stop laughing*) jab, prod, dig, nudge, elbow.

polish *vb* **1** (*She has to polish the furniture*) wax, shine, buff up, burnish. **2** (*She wants to polish up her French before she goes on holiday*) improve, revise, perfect, brush up.

polite *adj* **1** (*Children taught to be polite*) well-mannered, mannerly, courteous, civil, well-bred, well-behaved. **2** (*the way things are done in polite society*) well-bred, civilized, cultured, refined, genteel.

pollute *vb* (*chemicals that pollute the water*) contaminate, taint, infect, adulterate, poison, befoul, dirty.

pompous *adj* (*They were kept out of the building by a pompous official*) self-important, presumptuous, overbearing, egotistic.

poor *n* **1** (*poor people with not enough money to live on*) poverty-stricken, penniless, needy, in need, impoverished, deprived, destitute, hard up, badly off. **2** (*It was a poor attempt*) inadequate, unsatisfactory, inferior.

popular *adj* **1** (*The place is popular with young people*) liked, favoured, approved, in demand, in fashion. **2** (*ideas that were popular at the time*) current, accepted, widespread, common, general.

population *n* (*The population of the area is mainly elderly*) people, inhabitants, residents, community.

portion *n* **1** (*Each of his children got an equal portion of his fortune*) part, share, division, piece, bit, quota, percentage. **2** (*The restaurant serves children's portions on request*) serving, helping, quantity. **3** (*They bought four portions of the cake*) piece, bit, slice, section, segment, lump, chunk.

position *n* **1** (*He had been sitting in an uncomfortable position*) posture, attitude, pose. **2** (*try to find the position of the wrecked ship*) location, whereabouts. **3** (*These trees grow well in a shady position*) situation, location, place, spot, area, setting. **4** (*He is in a very fortunate position*) situation, state, circumstances, condition. **5** (*the position of the team in the league tables*) place, level, grade, status, rank, ranking. **6** (*The position of manager is vacant*) situation, post, job, role. **7** (*people of position in society*) rank, status, influence, standing, prestige.

positive *adj* **1** (*She is positive that she saw him*) sure, certain, confident, convinced. **2** (*try to give some positive criticism of the essays*) constructive, helpful, useful. **3** (*He should try to have a more positive attitude to life*) optimistic, hopeful, confident, determined. **4** (*The results of the medical tests were positive*) affirmative. **5** (*He is a positive fool*) absolute, utter, complete, total, out-and-out.

possess *vb* **1** (*They do not possess a car*) own, be the owner of, have. **2** (*He thought that he was possessed by devils*) control, dominate, influence, bewitch.

possessions *npl* (*Our flat is full of her possessions*) belongings, property, goods, things, personal effects.

possible *adj* **1** (*It is not possible to get there on time*) feasible, practicable, achievable. **2** (*one possible solution*) likely, potential, conceivable, imaginable.

post *n* **1** (*hammer in posts to make a*

fence) stake, pole, upright. **2** (*The post has been filled*) job, position, appointment, situation. ▼

---

pipped at the post beaten at the last moment (*I thought that we would get the house at a price we could afford but we were pipped at the post by someone who suddenly offered more*) <Refers originally to the finishing post in horse-racing. A horse is pipped at the post if another house passes it at the end of the race>.

---

postpone *vb* (*They have had to postpone the wedding*) put off, put back, defer, delay, put on ice.

pounce *vb* (*The cat pounced on the mouse*) swoop, spring, leap, jump.

pound *vb* **1** (*She pounded the seeds to a powder*) crush, smash, beat, pulverize, grind. **2** (*She pounded her father's chest with her fists*) beat, pummel, strike, hit, hammer. **3** (*Her heart was pounding*) beat heavily, throb, pulse, pulsate, palpitate. **4** (*They pounded the pavements looking for somewhere to live*) tramp, tread, trudge.

pour *vb* **1** (*Water began to pour from the burst pipe*) rush, gush, stream, spout, spurt, flow. **2** (*pour custard over the tart*) let flow, splash, spill. **3** (*It was pouring*) come down in torrents, rain cats and dogs, come down in sheets, (*inf*) be bucketing. ▼

---

it never rains but it pours when something goes wrong it goes wrong very badly or other things go wrong too (*I forgot where I had parked the car and then I got a parking ticket. It never rains but it pours*).

---

poverty *n* need, want, deprivation, hardship.

power *n* **1** (*the power of speech*) ability, capability, capacity, faculty. **2** (*The tyrant had her in his power*) control, command, rule, domination, mastery, authority. **3** (*people of power gaining victory over the weak*) powerfulness, strength, force, forcefulness, might, vigour, effectiveness. **4** (*electricity and other kinds of power*) energy. ▼

---

the power behind the throne the person who is really in control or makes all the decisions while giving the impression that someone else is (*He is the chairman of the company but his wife is the power behind the throne*). **the powers that be** the people who are in charge, the authorities. (*The powers that be have decided that all sales staff should wear uniform*).

---

powerful *adj* **1** (*weight-lifters of powerful build*) strong, sturdy, strapping, tough, mighty. **2** (*the most powerful members of the community*) dominant, controlling, influential, authoritative, strong, forceful, vigorous. **3** (*She drew up a powerful argument against the scheme*) strong, forceful, effective, convincing, persuasive, compelling.

practical *adj* **1** (*They want people with practical experience of the job*) applied, experienced, skilled, hands-on. **2** (*She is very bright academically but not at all practical*) sensible, down-to-earth, realistic, businesslike. **3** (*wear practical footwear for walking*) sensible, functional, useful, utilitarian.

practise *vb* **1** (*She has to practise her piano performances*) rehearse, go over, run through, work at, prepare, train for, study for, polish up. **2** (*She seems quite unable to practise self-control*) carry out, perform, execute, do. **3** (*They practise medicine*) work in, be engaged in. ▼

---

practise what one preaches to act in a way that one recommends to others (*The manager always reminds all the workers that they must get there on time but he is often very late himself. He really should practise what he preaches*).

---

praise *vb* **1** (*They praised her performance*) applaud, express admiration for, admire, compliment, pay tribute to, sing the praises of. **2** (*praise God*) worship, glorify, honour, exalt. ▼

---

praise (someone) to the skies to praise (someone) very highly (*The critics praise the new actor's performance to the skies*).
sing (somone's *or* **something's) praises** to praise (someone or something) with great enthusiasm (*She keeps singing the praises of her new car*).

---

precarious *adj* **1** (*It was rather a precarious journey through the jungle*) risky, dangerous, hazardous, perilous. **2** (*a precarious way to earn one's living*) risky, unreliable, uncertain, unsure, chancy, unpredictable.

precious *adj* **1** (*a necklace full of precious stones*) valuable, costly, expensive. **2** (*family photographs that are very precious to her/her precious memories*) valued, treasured, cherished, prized, beloved, dear.

precise *adj* **1** (*We need to know her precise words*) exact, actual, literal. **2** (*at that precise moment*) very, exact, actual, particular. **3** (*He is a very precise person*) exact, careful, accurate, meticulous.

predict *vb* (*She claimed to be able to predict the future*) foretell, forecast, foresee, prophesy.

predominant *adj* (*Red is the predominant colour in the pattern*) chief, main, principal, dominant.

prefer *vb* **1** (*She prefers the blue pattern to the yellow*) like better, favour, choose, select, pick, opt for, plump for. **2** (*They could drive but they prefer to go by train*) like better, would rather, would sooner, favour, choose.

prejudiced *adj* (*They have a prejudiced attitude towards people of a different race/prejudiced employers*) biased, discriminatory, partial, partisan, bigoted, intolerant, unfair, unjust.

premature *adj* (*the premature birth of the baby*) too soon, too early.

premonition *n* (*She had a premonition that something tragic was going to happen*) feeling, foreboding, presentiment, intuition, hunch.

prepare *vb* **1** (*They must prepare their proposal to present it to the committee*) get ready, arrange, assemble, draw up, put together. **2** (*prepare a meal*) make, cook, put together.

presence *n* **1** (*the presence of chemical waste in the drinking water*) existence. **2** (*They are asking for our presence at the meeting*) attendance. **3** (*They felt inadequate in the presence of the great man*) company, vicinity, proximity. ▼

presence of mind the ability to keep calm and think and act sensibly whatever the situation (*She had the presence of mind to throw a wet cloth over the pan when it caught fire*).

present *adj* **1** (*Pollutants were present in the water supply*) existing, existent. **2** (*There should be a nurse present*) in attendance, here, there, on hand. **3** (*in the present situation*) current, existing, present-day, contemporary.

present *n* **1** (*thinking about the present rather than the future*) now, today, the present moment. **2** (*a present on her birthday/a present for all their hard work*) gift, reward. ▼

there's no time like the present if one has decided on a course of action one should get started on it right away (*If you are going to sell the house, phone the estate agent. There's no time like the present*).

presentable *adj* (*make yourself presentable before you see the headmaster*) tidy, well-groomed, smart, spruce.

preserve *vb* **1** (*try to preserve the old village traditions*) keep, keep up, continue, maintain, uphold, conserve. **2** (*a substance to preserve wood*) protect, conserve. **3** (*They had to preserve the city from enemy attack*) protect, save, safeguard, keep, defend. **4** (*preserve some money for one's old age*) keep, put aside, save, retain.

press *vb* **1** (*You should press the door bell again*) push. **2** (*villagers pressing grapes to make wine*) crush, squeeze, compress. **3** (*need an iron to press her skirt*) iron, smooth. **3** (*The mother pressed the tired child against her*) clasp, hold, pull, squeeze, crush, hug. **4** (*They are pressing the planning committee for a decision*) urge, entreat, implore, pressure, put pressure on, pressurize. ▼

be pressed for (something) to be short of (something) such as time or money (*I can't stay and talk. I'm really pressed for time*). **press-gang (someone) into (doing something)** to force (someone) or persuade (someone) against his or her will to (do something) (*She's press-ganged us into being in charge of a stall at the local fete*) <The press gang was a group of sailors in the 18th century who seized men and forced them to join the navy>.

pressure *n* **1** (*They had to exert a great deal of pressure to get the door open*) force, strength, weight. **2** (*She tried to withstand the pressure of her parents to get her to stay at home*) force, compulsion, constraint, duress. **3** (*the pressures of modern living*) strain, stress, tension. ▼

pressure group a group of people formed to bring the attention of the authorities, etc, to certain issues, with a view to influencing them into making some changes (*They formed a pressure group to persuade the council to save the local school*).

prestige *n* (*He does not want to lose his prestige in the community*) status, kudos, standing, importance, reputation, esteem, influence.

pretence *n* **1** (*She did not really faint—it was just pretence*) dissembling, shamming, faking, make-believe. **2** (*They left on the pretence that they were going to a meeting*) pretext, excuse.

pretend *vb* (*He was not sleeping at all—he was just pretending*) put on an act, put it on, play-act, sham, fake, dissemble.

pretty *adj* (*She is a very pretty girl*) attractive, good-looking, lovely, nice-looking.

pretty *adv* (*She was feeling pretty annoyed*) rather, quite, very. ▼

---

be sitting pretty to be in a very comfortable or advantageous position (*She's the boss's daughter. While the rest of us are worrying about our jobs she is sitting pretty*). **come to a pretty pass** to get into a bad or unfortunate state (*Things have come to a pretty pass if the firm is making people redundant*).

---

prevent *vb* **1** (*Her parents tried to prevent her marrying him*) stop, halt, restrain, prohibit, bar, hinder, obstruct, impede, hamper. **2** (*try to prevent the spread of the infection*) stop, halt, arrest, check, block, check, hinder, obstruct, impede.

previous *adj* **1** (*the previous chairman*) former, preceding, ex-, foregoing. **2** (*We met on a previous occasion*) earlier, prior, former.

price *n* (*ask the price of the bookcase*) cost, charge. ▼

---

a price on (someone's) head a reward offered for the capture or killing (of someone), such as an outlaw (*The escaped prisoner was never caught although there was a price on his head*).

---

prick *vb* **1** (*The child pricked the balloon with a pin*) pierce, puncture, stab, gash. **2** (*She pricked her finger on the needle*) jab, jag, stab, wound. **3** (*Their eyes began to prick in the smoke from the fire*) smart, sting, tingle.

pride *n* **1** (*They take pride in their work*) satisfaction, gratification, pleasure. **2** (*Her pride was hurt when he left her for another girl*) self-esteem, self-respect, ego. **3** (*He is guilty of the sin of pride*) conceit, vanity, arrogance, egotism, self-importance, (*inf*) bigheadedness. ▼

---

pride goes before a fall being too conceited often leads to misfortune (*The player who was boasting about how good she was got beaten. It just shows you that pride goes before a fall*). **pride of place** the most important or privileged position (*His children's photograph took pride of place on his desk*). **swallow one's pride** to behave in a more humble way than one usually does or than one would wish to do (*When she could not pay the rent she swallowed her pride and asked her father for a loan*).

---

prim *adj* (*He is much too prim to join in the fun*) proper, demure, strait-laced, stuffy, starchy, prudish, (*inf*) goody-goody.

prime *adj* **1** (*meat of prime quality*) top, best, first-class, superior, choice, select. **2** (*His prime ambition was to make money*) chief, main, principal. **3** (*The prime *cause of the infection was the water*) basic, fundamental.

prime *n* (*in the prime of life*) peak, height, zenith, acme. ▼

---

be cut off in one's prime to die or be killed in one's youth or at the most successful part of one's life (*The townspeople mourned the soldiers cut off in their prime*). **prime mover** someone or something that gets something started (*She was the prime mover in the campaign against the new motorway*).

---

principal *adj* **1** (*the principal members of the organization*) chief, leading, foremost, dominant. **2** (*the principal issues to be discussed*) main, major, key, essential.

principle *n* **1** (*the principles of socialism*) idea, theory, philosophy, basis, code. **2** (*He is a man of principle*) morals, ethics, integrity, uprightness, honour.

prison *n* (*He was sent to prison for theft*) jail, gaol, lock-up, (*inf*) clink, (*inf*) nick.

private *adj* **1** (*a private discussion between cabinet ministers*) confidential, secret, privileged, (*inf*) hush-hush. **2** (*She wished to be private to think about things*) undisturbed, uninterrupted, alone, solitary. **3** (*She would not disclose her private thoughts*) personal, intimate, secret. **4** (*a private place in the large garden*) secluded, quiet, out-of-the-way.

privileged *adj* (*She comes from a privileged background*) advantaged, favoured, elite.

probable *adj* (*the probable outcome/It is probable that he will lose*) likely, expected.

problem *n* **1** (*an arithmetical problem*) question, puzzle, poser, brain-teaser. **2** (*They have had a few financial problems*) difficulty, trouble, complication, predicament. **3** (*Their teenage son is a real problem*) trouble, bother, nuisance, pest.

proceed *vb* **1** (*We were unsure as to how to proceed*) act, take action, move, progress. **2** (*We proceeded up the mountain as fast as we could*) make one's way, carry on, go on, advance, go forward, progress.

process: *n* **1** (*the manufacturing process*) operation, activity, stages. **2** (*a new process for cleaning carpets*) system, method, technique, procedure.

process: in the process of (something) (*They are in the process of moving house*) in the midst of, in the course of.

procession *n* (*a procession to celebrate the town's centenary*) parade, march, cavalcade.

produce *vb* **1** (*an agricultural area that produces a wide variety of crops*) yield, bear, give. **2** (*a cat that has just produced kittens*) give birth to, bear. **3** (*His article produced an angry response*) cause, give rise to, evoke, generate, start, spark off. **4** (*The country produces a great many goods for export*) make, manufacture, turn out. **5** (*The police have produced proof that he is guilty*) bring forward, present, advance.

product *n* (*a firm specializing in electronic products*) commodity, goods, wares, merchandise.

profit *n* (*They made little profit from the sale*) gain, return, yield, proceeds, income.

profitable *adj* (*The business is no longer profitable*) profit-making, money-making, commercial, lucrative.

programme *n* **1** (*watch the television programme*) production, show, performance, broadcast. **2** (*the programme of events for the fete*) schedule, plan, scheme, list, calendar, syllabus.

progress *n* **1** (*They have been discussing the matter for ages but they have made little progress*) headway, advancement. **2** (*Her work shows no sign of progress*) headway, advancement, improvement.

project *n* (*take part in a project to build a new swimming pool*) scheme, plan, undertaking, enterprise, venture, operation.

prominent *adj* **1** (*prominent members of the government*) leading, chief, foremost, eminent, top. **2** (*The palm trees are a prominent feature of the area*) striking, conspicuous, noticeable, obvious, eye-catching. **3** (*She has prominent cheekbones*) protruding, obvious.

promise *n* **1** (*She made a promise that she would be there*) pledge, vow, bond, assurance, commitment. **2** (*A young skater of promise*) potential, talent, flair. **3** (*There was a promise of good times to come*) indication, sign, suggestion, hint.

promote *vb* **1** (*They plan to promote him to manager*) upgrade, elevate. **2** (*The company is promoting a new line in perfume*) advertise, publicize, push, (*inf*) plug. **3** (*They need volunteers to promote the cause of animals' rights*) support, champion, further, advance, help, assist, boost.

prompt *adj* (*They will expect a prompt reply*) rapid, swift, quick, fast, speedy, immediate, instant.

proof *n* **1** (*The police had little proof of his guilt*) evidence, confirmation, corroboration. **2** (*The workmen had no proof of their identity*) evidence, verification, authentication, certification.

proper *adj* **1** (*the proper behaviour on such an occasion*) right, correct, suitable, fitting, appropriate, acceptable, conventional. **2** (*put the plates in their proper place in the kitchen*) right, correct, usual, own.

property *n* (*items that were his property*) belongings, possessions, things, goods, goods and chattels.

proportion *n* **1** (*an area with a high proportion of agricultural workers*) ratio, distribution. **2** (*He gives a large proportion of his earnings to the church*) part, share, percentage, measure. ▼

---

a sense of proportion the ability to decide what is important, etc, and what is not (*She went into hysterics just because she got a small stain on her dress. She has no sense of proportion*).

---

propose *vb* **1** (*We are proposing to go by train*) plan, intend, aim, suggest. **2** (*They proposed some alterations to the system*) put forward, submit, recommend, advocate. **3** (*They proposed him as chairman*) put forward, nominate, suggest.

prosper *vb* (*The family began to prosper*) thrive, do well, succeed, flourish, make good.

prosperous *adj* (*prosperous people with a great deal of money to spend*) well-off, wealthy, affluent, rich, successful.

protect *vb* (*They wished to protect*

the child from danger) safeguard, guard, keep, preserve, shield, defend.

protest *n* (*They lodged a protest against the closure of the school*) objection, opposition, complaint, disagreement, dissent, outcry.

proud *adj* **1** (*He is rich and now too proud to talk to his former neighbours*) conceited, vain, arrogant, egotistical, haughty, boastful, supercilious, (*inf*) snooty. **2** (*He was proud of his son's achievement*) gratified, appreciative, pleased, happy. ▼

---

do (someone) proud to treat (someone) exceptionally well or lavishly (*They did us proud at the Christmas party*).

---

prove *vb* (*evidence that proved his innocence*) establish, determine, confirm, corroborate.

provide *vb* **1** (*They provided the money for the trip*) give, supply, donate, contribute. **2** (*a job that provides opportunity for travel*) give, grant, offer, afford, present.

prowl *vb* (*burglars prowling round the house*) roam, skulk, slink, sneak.

pry *vb* (*She likes to pry into her neighbours' affairs*) interfere, meddle, snoop.

public *adj* **1** (*Public feeling is against the new road*) popular, general, common. **2** (*make their views public*) known, plain. **3** (*public figures*) well-known, prominent, eminent, influential.

publicity *n* **1** (*She only did it to get publicity in the press*) public attention, public interest. **2** (*The reception was part of the publicity for her book*) promotion, advertisement, advertising, (*inf*) hype.

pudding *n* (*have apple tart for pudding*) dessert, sweet, (*inf*) afters. ▼

---

the proof of the pudding is in the eating the real worth of something is found only when it has been put into practice or use (*The government's theories on education are all very well, but the proof of the pudding will be in the eating when they are tried out in schools*).

---

pull *vb* **1** (*He pulled the nail out of the wall*) pull out, draw out, take out, extract, remove. **2** (*They began to pull the rope*) haul, tug, (*inf*) yank. **3** (*The child was pulling a toy train behind him*) haul, drag, trail, tow, tug. **3** (*The athlete has pulled a muscle*) strain, sprain, wrench. ▼

---

pull (something) off to be successful in (something) (*We were all surprised when he pulled off a victory against the golf champion*). **pull through** to survive, to get better (*We thought that he was going to die after the operation but he pulled through*).

---

punch *vb* (*The boy punched him on the nose*) strike, hit, box. ▼

---

as pleased as Punch extremely pleased or happy (*The little girl was as pleased as Punch with her new bike*) <A reference to Punch, the puppet show character in *Punch and Judy*, who is usually portrayed as smiling gleefully>. **pull one's punches** to be less forceful or harsh in one's attack or criticism than one is capable of (*The manager rarely pulls his punches when he is criticizing the employees'* *work*) <A reference to striking blows in boxing without using one's full strength>.

---

punctual *adj* (*It is important to be punctual at meetings*) on time, prompt, in good time.

punish *vb* **1** (*She punished the children for being naughty*) discipline, chastise, smack, slap. **2** (*criminals punished for doing wrong*) discipline, penalize.

puny *adj* (*too puny to fight against such a strong opponent*) weak, weakly, frail, feeble, undersized, stunted, slight, small.

pure *adj* **1** (*breathing in the pure mountain air*) clean, clear, fresh, unpolluted, uncontaminated, untainted, wholesome. **2** (*dishes of pure gold*) unalloyed, unmixed, unadulterated, true, real. **3** (*people who are expected to be of pure character*) virtuous, honourable, moral, ethical, righteous, blameless, uncorrupted, impeccable, flawless, spotless. **4** (*It was pure folly to do that*) sheer, utter, absolute, downright, total, complete, out-and-out. **5** (*The students are studying pure science*) theoretical, abstract. ▼

---

as pure as the driven snow extremely virtuous or moral (*He will expect his bride to be as pure as the driven snow*) <A reference to snow that has been blown into heaps by the wind and has not yet become dirty>.

---

purpose *n* **1** (*What was the purpose of their inquiries?*) reason, point, motivation, cause, grounds, justification. **2** (*The young man should try to get a purpose in life*) aim, goal, objective, object, target, aspiration, ambition. **3** (*The search for the missing goods lacked purpose*) determination, resoluteness, resolve, firmness, perseverance. **4** (*The talks went on all night but to little purpose*) worth, use, usefulness, value, advantage, benefit, avail. ▼

---

be at cross purposes of two people or groups, to be involved in a misunderstanding because of talking or thinking about different things without the people involved realizing it (*No wonder I couldn't understand what she was talking about. We were talking at cross purposes*). **serve the purpose** to be useful in a particular situation, to fulfil a need (*I really need a screwdriver for this job but a knife will serve the purpose*).

---

pursue *vb* **1** (*The policeman pursued the bank robber*) go after, run after, follow, chase, give chase to, trail, stalk, shadow, (*inf*) tail. **2** (*The police are pursuing a line of inquiry in the murder case*) follow, proceed with, go on with, continue with. **3** (*She wishes to pursue a career in medicine*) follow, be engaged in, work in. **4** (*They are pursuing their goal of making a fortune*) strive towards, be intent on.

push *vb* **1** (*The little boy pushed his friend into the pool*) shove, thrust, propel, ram, drive. **2** (*She pushed her way to the front of the crowd*) force, shove, thrust, press, elbow, shoulder, jostle. **3** (*push the button to start the machine*) press. **4** (*He said that his parents pushed him into going to university*) force, coerce, press, dragoon, browbeat, prod, goad, urge. **5** (*The company held a reception *to push their new product*) promote, advertise, publicize, boost, (*inf*) plug. ▼

---

push off (*inf*) to go away (*It's very late. We had better be pushing off*). **push one's luck** to risk failure by trying to gain too much (*He is pushing his luck by asking for yet more time off*).

---

put *vb* **1** (*They were asked to put the books on the desk*) place, lay, set down, deposit. **2** (*They tried to put the blame on their friend*) place, lay, attach, attribute, assign. **3** (*She put the value of the antique vase at £4000*) assess, evaluate, calculate, reckon, guess, (*inf*) guesstimate. **4** (*You should put the idea to your parents*) put forward, propose, present, submit. **5** (*He put a large sum of money on the horse*) place, bet, wager, gamble. ▼

---

a put-up job (*inf*) something done to deceive or trick (someone) (*The police pretended to believe him but it was a put-up job. They were just trying to get him to confess*). **be put upon** to be made use of for someone else's benefit, to be taken advantage of (*She is really put upon by her daughter. She is expected to babysit every night*). **put it on** to pretend, to feign (*She said that she had sprained her ankle but she was just putting it on because she didn't want to walk any farther*).

---

puzzle *vb* (*Her parents were puzzled by the change in her behaviour*) perplex, mystify, baffle, bewilder, nonplus, stump.

Q

qualified *adj* **1** (*a qualified doctor/ She is qualified to teach*) trained, certificated, equipped. **2** (*They gave the plan qualified approval*) limited, conditional, modified, restricted.

quarrel *n* (*The sisters have had a quarrel*) disagreement, argument, row, fight, difference of opinion, dispute, wrangle, altercation, misunderstanding.

queer *adj* (*Their behaviour seemed very queer*) strange, odd, peculiar, funny, weird, bizarre. ▼

---

in queer street in financial difficulties (*If they both lose their jobs they'll be in queer street when it comes to paying the mortgage*). **queer (someone's) pitch** to upset (someone's) plans or arrangements (*He was going to ask her out but his best friend queered his pitch accidentally by telling her he already had a girlfriend*) <'Pitch' here refers to the site of a market stall. Originally 'to queer someone's pitch' was to set up a stall beside it selling the same kind of goods>.

---

question *n* **1** (*She was unable to answer his questions*) inquiry, query, interrogation. **2** (*We must consider the question of safety*) issue, matter, point, subject, topic. ▼

---

be out of the question not to be possible (*It is out of the question for you to take a holiday now—we are too busy*). **pop the question** to ask someone to marry one (*He popped the question on her birthday*). **rhetorical question** a question which does not require or expect an answer (*'What happened to the happy times of our youth?' is a rhetorical question*).

---

quick *adj* **1** (*You will have to be quick to catch the bus*) fast, swift, rapid, speedy. **2** (*She wants a quick reply to her letter*) prompt, without delay, immediate. **3** (*She took a quick look at the instructions*) hasty, brief, fleeting, cursory.

quiet *adj* (*It was very quiet in the church*) hushed, silent, soundless, noiseless. **2** (*He spoke in quiet tones*) soft, low, hushed, whispered, inaudible. **3** (*lead a quiet life in the country*) peaceful, tranquil, calm, serene, placid, untroubled, undisturbed. **4** (*They are both rather quiet people*) reserved, taciturn, uncommunicative, reticent, placid, unexcitable. **5** (*She dresses in quiet colours*) restrained, unobtrusive, muted, subdued, subtle, conservative, sober, dull. **6** (*They kept the news of their engagement quiet*) secret, confidential, private, (*inf*) hush hush.

quite *adj* **1** (*Has he quite recovered after his accident?*) completely, totally, entirely, fully, wholly. **2**

(*She is quite good at tennis but she will not win the match*) fairly, relatively, moderately, somewhat, rather. ▼

---

quite something something special or remarkable (*The house that he designed himself is quite something*).

R

race *vb* (*runners racing towards the finishing post*) run, sprint, dash, speed, bolt, dart. ▼

---

the rat race the fierce competitive struggle for success in business, etc (*He has given up the rat race of the advertising world and has gone off to live on a remote island*).

---

race *n* (*Humankind is divided into races*) ethnic group, racial division.

racial *adj* (*racial discrimination*) ethnic, race-related.

racism *n* racial discrimination, racial prejudice.

rack *n* (*a plate rack*) frame, framework, stand, support, holder. ▼

---

go to rack and ruin to fall into a state of disrepair or into a worthless condition (*The estate has gone to rack and ruin because the owner has no money*) <'Rack' here means destruction>. **on the rack** in distress, under a great deal of strain (*His employer has him on the rack making him wait to see if he has been made redundant*).

---

racket *n* **1** (*We couldn't sleep because of the racket from the party next door*) din, noise, commotion, row, hubbub, disturbance. **2** (*They think he was involved in a drugs racket*) fraud, criminal scheme.

radiant *adj* **1** (*They could not see properly in the radiant light*) brilliant, shining, bright, gleaming, irradiant. **2** (*The winners looked radiant*) joyful, elated, ecstatic, delighted.

radiate *vb* **1** (*The fire radiated a fierce heat*) send out, emit, disperse. **2** (*roads radiating out from the town centre*) branch out, spread out, diverge.

radical *adj* **1** (*There have been radical changes in their business methods*) thorough, complete, total, sweeping, exhaustive, drastic, violent. **2** (*She holds radical political views*) extremist, fundamental.

rage *n* **1** (*She went into a rage when they criticized her*) temper, tantrum. **2** (*She was filled with rage at the sight of her rival*) fury, anger, annoyance, exasperation. ▼

---

be all the rage to be extremely fashionable or popular (*Mini skirts were all the rage then*).

---

rags *npl* (*The homeless woman was dressed in rags*) tatters.

raid *n* **1** (*enemy raids on the town*) attack, assault, onslaught, invasion, foray, sortie. **2** (*a bank raid*) robbery, break-in.

railing *n* (*the railing round the balcony*) rail, paling, barrier, fence.

rain *vb* (*It was raining during the match*) pour, drizzle, (*inf*) rain cats and dogs, (*inf*) come down in stair rods. ▼

---

as right as rain perfectly all right, completely well (*The young girl* *was injured in the accident but she is as right as rain now*).

---

rainy *adj* (*We got a rainy day for the picnic*) wet, damp, showery, drizzly. ▼

---

keep (something) for a rainy day to keep (something, especially a sum of money) until one really has need of it (*The old lady does not have enough food to eat but she insists on keeping a large sum of money for a rainy day*) <Formerly many jobs, such as farm jobs, could not be carried out in wet weather and so no money was earned then>.

---

raise *vb* **1** (*They need a crane to raise the wrecked car*) lift, hoist, heave up, elevate. **2** (*They are going to raise a block of flats there*) put up, build, construct, erect. **3** (*The news raised our hopes*) increase, boost, build up, stimulate. **4** (*They had to raise the temperature in the greenhouse*) put up, increase, augment, intensify. **5** (*The local hotels raise their prices in the summer*) put up, increase, inflate, (*inf*) hike up. **6** (*They raise turkeys*) breed, rear. **7** (*He raises cereal crops*) grow, cultivate, produce, farm. **8** (*They have raised several children*) rear, bring up, nurture. ▼

---

raise the wind to get enough money to do something (*They are trying to raise the wind to buy a new car but the bank has refused them a loan*).

---

rake *vb* **1** (*rake up the dead leaves*) scrape up, collect, gather. **2** (*They raked the soil before planting the seeds*) smooth, level, flatten, even out. **3** (*The burglars raked through her things*) search, hunt, ransack, rummage, rifle.

rally *n* **1** (*They held a rally to demonstrate against the new parliamentary bill*) meeting, mass meeting, gathering, assembly, convention, demonstration, (*inf*) demo. **2** (*Stock market prices fell but then there was a sudden rally*) recovery, revival, improvement, comeback.

rally *vb* **1** (*The troops rallied to support the king*) assemble, gather, convene, unite. **2** (*The invalid was seriously ill but she has rallied*) recover, recuperate, revive, get better, improve, pull through, take a turn for the better.

ram *vb* **1** (*ram the clothes into the suitcase in a hurry*) force, cram, stuff, thrust. **2** (*His car rammed ours*) hit, strike, run into, collide with, bump. ▼

---

ram (something) down (someone's) throat to try forcefully to make (someone) accept ideas, opinions, course of action, etc.

---

ramble *vb* **1** (*They rambled over the hills for the afternoon*) walk, hike, wander, roam. **2** (*The lecturer rambled on without the students understanding a word*) babble, gibber, rattle on, (*inf*) rabbit on, (*inf*) witter.

rampage *vb* (*children rampaging around their neighbour's garden*) rush, charge, tear, run riot.

ramshackle *adj* (*They bought a ramshackle cottage and are going to rebuild it*) tumble-down, broken-down, run-down, dilapidated, derelict, crumbling.

random *adj* (*ask a random selection of the population how they were going to vote*) haphazard, chance, arbitrary, indiscriminate, unsystematic, unmethodical, unplanned, accidental.

range *n* **1** (*a range of mountains*) row, line, chain. **2** (*It was not within their range of vision*) scope, field, area, limit, reach. **3** (*The shop stocks a wide range of goods*) selection, assortment, variety.

range *vb* **1** (*Prices range from £10 to £200*) extend, stretch, go, vary. **2** (*The books are ranged according to subject*) classify, categorize, group, class. **3** (*sheep ranging over the hills*) roam, rove, ramble, wander, stray.

rank *n* **1** (*What is the soldier's rank?*) grade, position. **2** (*The salary in the organization is according to rank*) grade, level, position, status. **3** (*The people in the big house were people of rank*) nobility, aristocracy, eminence, power, influence. ▼

---

close ranks to act together and support each other as a defensive measure (*The dead patient's husband tried to enquire into the cause of her death but the doctors closed ranks and would tell him nothing*). **the rank and file** the ordinary people or the ordinary members of an organization, etc (*It was suggested that the union leaders should listen more to the opinions of the rank and file*) <Literally ranks and files were the horizontal and vertical lines in which ordinary soldiers were drawn up on parade>.

---

ransack *vb* **1** (*Raiders ransacked the shops after the explosion*) loot, plunder, rob, rifle, pillage. **2** (*We ransacked the house to try to find the lost passport*) search, rummage, scour, turn upside down.

rap *vb* **1** (*She rapped on the door*) knock, tap, bang. **2** (*The teacher rapped him over the knuckles with a ruler*) hit, strike, bang, whack.

rapid *adj* (*They set off at a rapid pace*) swift, fast, quick, speedy, hurried, hasty, brisk, lively.

rapture *n* (*their rapture at the birth of their child*) joy, ecstasy, bliss, euphoria, delight.

rare *adj* **1** (*The wild flower was a rare specimen*) unusual, uncommon, out of the ordinary, atypical, remarkable. **2** (*He made one of his rare appearances*) infrequent, few and far between, sparse, sporadic.

rascal *n* **1** (*The child was a little rascal*) imp, scamp, scallywag. **2** (*Her husband is a rascal who is always in trouble with the police*) scoundrel, villain, rogue, blackguard, ne'er-do-well, good-for-nothing.

rash *adj* (*Leaving her job to go round the world proved to be a rash decision*) impetuous, reckless, hasty, impulsive, unthinking, incautious, imprudent, foolhardy.

rash *n* **1** (*She woke up with a rash on her face*) spots, redness, eruption, hives. **2** (*There has been a rash of car thefts in the area*) spate, outbreak, wave, flood, series, run, plague, epidemic.

rasping *adj* (*She has a rasping voice/ the rasping noise of a knife on metal*) grating, discordant, jarring, harsh, rough, gruff, croaky.

rate *n* **1** (*They walked at a very fast rate*) pace, speed, tempo, velocity. **2** (*the bank's rate of interest*) ratio, proportion, scale, degree. **3** (*The hotel is charging its winter rates*) price, charge, cost, tariff, fee, payment.

rate *vb* **1** (*How would you rate the team's performance*) judge, assess, evaluate, measure, weigh up, rank, class. **2** (*She rates more respect from them*) deserve, merit, be entitled to.

rather *adv* **1** (*She would rather go than stay*) for preference, sooner, from choice. **2** (*She is pretty rather than beautiful*) more. **3** (*She tends to be rather blunt*) quite, fairly, somewhat, slightly.

ratify *vb* (*The two sides still have to ratify the agreement*) confirm, endorse, sign, approve, sanction.

ratio *n* (*the ratio of staff to pupils in the school*) proportion, percentage, fraction.

rational *adj* **1** (*It seemed a rational decision*) sensible, reasonable, logical, sound, intelligent, wise, judicious. **2** (*His mind has been affected but he has a few rational moments*) sane, balanced, lucid, coherent.

rattle *vb* **1** (*The windows rattled in the wind*) bang, clatter, clank, jangle. **2** (*She rattled the door knocker*) bang, knock, rap. **3** (*He was rattling on about his hobbies and boring everyone*) chatter, babble, prattle, jabber, gibber, blether, (*inf*) rabbit on, (*inf*) witter. **4** (*The speaker was obviously rattled by some of the questions from the audience*) agitate, disturb, fluster, upset, shake.

raucous *adj* (*the raucous singing of the drunk men*) strident, shrill, grating, jarring, discordant, piercing.

ravenous *adj* (*They were ravenous after walking all day*) famished, starving, hungry.

raw *adj* **1** (*She prefers to eat raw vegetables*) uncooked, fresh. **2** (*raw sugar*) unrefined, unprocessed, crude, natural. **3** (*It was a raw winter's day*) cold, chilly, bitter. **4** (*She has a raw place on her elbow from when she fell over*) red, sore, inflamed, tender, abraded, grazed. **5** (*raw recruits to the job*) inexperienced, untrained, unskilled, callow, green. ▼

---

touch (someone) on the raw to hurt or anger (someone) (*You touched him on the raw when you mentioned his wife—she left him last year*) <A raw place on the skin is sore to the touch>.

---

ray *n* **1** (*The rays of light showed up the dust on the furniture*) beam, shaft, streak, gleam, flash. **2** (*There did not seem to be a ray of hope left*) glimmer, flicker, trace, indication, suggestion.

reach *vb* **1** (*He reached his hand out for the book*) stretch, extend. **2** (*The child could not reach the door handle*) get hold of, grasp, touch. **3** (*We finally reached our destination*) get to, arrive at. **4** (*He has not reached the required standard*) get to, achieve, attain.

react *vb* **1** (*How did he react when he discovered that she had gone?*) behave, act, respond. **2** (*The teenagers are reacting against their parents' beliefs*) rebel against.

read *vb* **1** (*She read a book while she waited*) peruse, study, pore over, browse through. **2** (*Can you read his handwriting?*) decipher, make out. **3** (*They read his silence as consent*) interpret, take to mean. ▼

---

take (something) as read to assume (something) (*You can take it as read that all the candidates for the job are well qualified*).

---

ready *adj* **1** (*The meal is ready*) prepared, completed. **2** (*They are *ready for battle*) prepared, equipped, organized, all set. **3** (*Her neighbours are always ready to help*) willing, eager, keen, inclined, disposed. **4** (*She was ready to collapse when she got to the bottom of the mountain*) about to, on the point of, in danger of. **5** (*She always has a ready answer*) prompt, quick, rapid, swift, speedy. **6** (*Have you got your ticket ready for collection?*) available, to hand, accessible.

real *adj* **1** (*things connected with the real world*) actual, factual. **2** (*The coat was made of real leather*) genuine, authentic. **3** (*She showed signs of real emotion*) genuine, authentic, sincere, unfeigned, honest, truthful. **4** (*He has been a real friend*) true, sincere. ▼

---

the real McCoy something that is genuine and very good as opposed to something that is not (*This lasagne is the real McCoy, not something from the supermarket freezer*).

---

realistic *adj* **1** (*The model of the bear was very realistic*) lifelike, true-to-life, naturalistic, authentic. **2** (*He has to try to be realistic about his job prospects*) practical, down-to-earth, matter-of-fact, sensible, level-headed, unromantic, no-nonsense.

realize *vb* **1** (*We began to realize that she was ill*) understand, grasp, take in, become aware, appreciate, recognize. **2** (*I hope that she realizes her dreams*) fulfil, achieve, attain, accomplish.

really *adv* **1** (*It was a really beautiful day*) truly, genuinely, undoubtedly, unquestionably, indeed. **2** (*The performer is dressed as a woman but is really a man*) in fact, in actual fact, in truth.

rear *n* **1** (*They sat at the rear of the train*) back. **2** (*They were at the rear of the cinema queue*) back, tail, end.

rear *vb* **1** (*She reared three children on her own*) bring up, raise, care for. **2** (*The farmer rears turkeys*) breed, raise, keep.

reason *n* **1** (*There seemed no reason for his behaviour*) grounds, cause, basis, motive, justification. **2** (*The old man has lost his reason*) sanity, mind. ▼

---

it stands to reason that it is logical or obvious that (*It stands to reason that she would be in pain. She has broken her leg in two places*). **see reason** to be persuaded by someone's advice, etc, to act or think sensibly (*At first he refused to go to the doctor with his sore leg but he finally saw reason*). **within reason** within sensible limits (*She was told that she could have anything she wanted for her birthday—within reason*).

---

reasonable *adj* **1** (*It seemed a reasonable thing to do*) logical, rational, practical, sensible, intelligent, wise, sound. **2** (*I thought that he was quite a reasonable person*) fair, just, decent, unbiased. **3** (*The prices in the new restaurant were quite reasonable*) inexpensive, moderate, modest, cheap.

rebel *vb* **1** (*The crew are rebelling*) mutiny, riot, revolt, rise up. **2** (*teenagers rebelling against their parents' authority*) defy, disobey.

rebellion *n* (*They joined in a rebellion against the king*) revolt, revolution, insurrection, uprising, rising, riot.

rebellious *adj* (*the rebellious troops/ the rebellious schoolgirls*) defiant, disobedient, unruly, unmanageable, intractable, mutinous, insurgent.

rebuke *vb* (*Her teacher rebuked her for being late*) scold, chide, admonish, (*inf*) tell off.

recall *vb* **1** (*She was unable to recall his name*) call to mind, remember, recollect, think of. **2** (*The manufacturers have recalled a batch of cars with faulty brakes*) call back, withdraw.

recede *vb* **1** (*The flood water began to recede*) go back, retreat, subside, ebb. **2** (*The danger seems to have receded*) grow less, lessen, fade, diminish.

receive *vb* **1** (*She said that she posted the goods but we never received them*) get, be in receipt of. **2** (*She received many benefits from the scheme*) get, obtain, gain, acquire. **3** (*She received the best of treatment in the hospital*) get, experience, undergo, meet with. **4** (*She got ready to receive her dinner guests*) welcome, greet, entertain.

recent *adj* (*The doctor tries to keep up with recent medical developments*) new, fresh, latest, modern.

recite *vb* (*The little girl was asked to recite a poem*) say, repeat, speak, deliver.

reckless *adj* (*He later regretted his reckless action*) rash, careless, thoughtless, inattentive, incautious, irresponsible, negligent.

reclaim *vb* **1** (*They went to the police station to reclaim their property*) get back, recover, retrieve. **2** (*They reclaimed some land from the sea to build a bird sanctuary*) get back, recover, retrieve, regain, store, save, salvage, rescue.

recline *vb* (*The invalid reclined on a sofa*) lie down, lie, stretch out, lean back, be recumbent, rest, repose, lounge.

recognize *vb* **1** (*I failed to recognize my cousin after all these years*) know, know again, identify, recall, call to mind, recollect, remember. **2** (*The authorities are refusing to recognize his claim to the title*) acknowledge, accept, allow, grant, validate. **3** (*He recognized that he had been at fault*) realize, be aware, appreciate, admit, acknowledge. **4** (*His genius as a composer was not recognized in his lifetime*) appreciate, honour, pay homage to, reward.

recoil *vb* (*He recoiled when he realized that his fellow thief had a gun*) flinch, shrink, draw back, wince.

recollect *vb* (*I cannot recollect his name*) remember, recall, call to mind, think of.

recommend *vb* **1** (*He recommended a cure for a cold*) commend, advocate, speak favourably of, approve, vouch for. **2** (*They recommend caution in that case*) advise, urge.

reconcile *vb* **1** (*The couple separated for a time but have now been reconciled*) bring together, reunite. **2** (*They quarrelled but have now reconciled their differences*) settle, resolve, put to rights. **3** (*We have now reconciled ourselves to our misfortune*) resign oneself, accept, make the best of it.

record *n* **1** (*He is using parish records to write a history of the area*) register, documents, information, data, chronicles, annals. **2** (*She kept a diary of her holiday experiences*) account, note, description, report, diary, register. **3** (*She played a dance record*) gramophone record, disc, album, vinyl.

record *vb* **1** (*All births, marriages*

and deaths must be recorded) register, enter, note, document, minute, catalogue. **2** (*The group have recorded some folk songs*) make, cut, tape, videotape, video. ▼

---

break the record to do something better, faster, etc, than has been done before (*The sprinter has broken the world record*). **off the record** not to be made public (*Although the politician said that he had made the remark off the record the newspaper published it*). **set the record straight** to put right a mistake or misunderstanding (*People thought that he had got the sack but he was able to set the record straight*).

---

recount *vb* (*They recounted the tale of their holiday adventure*) tell, relate, narrate, unfold, repeat.

recover *vb* **1** (*She has been seriously ill but she is now recovering*) get well, get better, recuperate, improve, rally, pull through. **2** (*They recovered some of their stolen property*) get back, regain, recoup, retrieve, reclaim, repossess, redeem. **3** (*They recovered land from the sea*) reclaim, restore, salvage, save.

recreation *n* **1** (*His recreations include wind-surfing*) hobby, pastime, diversion, amusement, distraction. **2** (*What does he do for recreation?*) leisure, relaxation, amusement, entertainment, fun, pleasure, diversion, distraction.

recruit *vb* (*The club is hoping to recruit new members*) enrol, enlist, sign up, take on.

recur *vb* (*His illness has recurred*) come back, return, reappear.

recurrent *adj* (*a recurrent fault*) recurring, repeated, repetitive, periodic, frequent.

recycle *vb* (*recycle paper products*) reuse, use again, reprocess, salvage.

red *adj* **1** (*She was red with embarrassment*) flushed, blushing. **2** (*Her face goes red in the cold*) ruddy, florid. ▼

---

red tape the rules and regulations, official papers, etc that are thought to be typical of government departments (*With all the red tape it took a long time for us to get a work permit*) <From the reddish tape used by government offices to tie bundles of official papers>. **like a red rag to a bull** certain to make someone extremely anger (*Any criticism of the government is like a red rag to a bull to the old man*) <From the widespread belief that bulls are angered by the sight of the colour red although they are in fact colour-blind>. **see red** to get extremely angry (*She is usually very calm but she saw red when she witnessed him whipping the dog*).

---

reduce *vb* **1** (*reduce the amount of food they eat*) cut, curtail, decrease, lessen, diminish. **2** (*Drivers should reduce speed*) decrease, moderate, lessen, lower. **3** (*Prices have been reduced*) cut, lower, mark down, take down, slash, cheapen.

redundant *adj* **1** (*The introduction of the new technology in the firm made many of the workers redundant*) unemployed, jobless. **2** (*a piece of writing full of redundant words*) unnecessary, superfluous, surplus.

refer *vb* **1** (*He referred to the difficulty of the task in his speech*) mention, allude to, touch on, speak of. **2** (*She referred the complaint to the manager*) pass, hand on, direct, transfer. **3** (*If you do not know the meaning of the word you should refer to a dictionary*) consult, look up, turn to.

referee *n* (*select a referee for the match*) umpire, judge, adjudicator, arbiter, arbitrator, (*inf*) ref.

reference *n* **1** (*She made no reference to the previous day's quarrel*) mention, allusion. **2** (*His comments have no reference to the case being discussed*) relation, relevance, connection, bearing, application. **3** (*She asked her former teacher for a reference when she applied for a job*) character reference, testimonial, commendation.

refined *adj* **1** (*refined sugar*) processed, purified, treated. **2** (*She felt she was too refined to mix with them*) polished, cultivated, cultured, civilized, well-bred.

reflect *vb* **1** (*Glass reflects light*) send back, throw back, diffuse. **2** (*His expression reflected his mood*) show, indicate, reveal, communicate. **3** (*She needed time to reflect on her problems*) think about, consider, contemplate, mull over, ponder.

reflection *n* (*his reflection in the mirror*) image, likeness.

reform *vb* (*make efforts to reform the educational system*) improve, make better, better, amend, rectify, reorganize, revolutionize.

refreshing *adj* **1** (*a refreshing cool drink/ a refreshing cool breeze*) invigorating, reviving, bracing, exhilarating. **2** (*Some of his ideas seemed very refreshing*) fresh, new, novel, original, different.

refuge *n* **1** (*They sought refuge from their enemies/seek refuge from the storm*) asylum, sanctuary, protection, safety, shelter, cover. **2** (*The building was a refuge for the homeless*) safe house, sanctuary, shelter, retreat, haven.

refugee *n* (*refugees from the famine area*) fugitive, exile, displaced person, stateless person.

refuse *vb* (*She refused their invitation*) turn down, reject, decline.

refuse *n* (*dispose of household refuse*) rubbish, waste, debris, litter, (*esp Amer*) garbage.

regard *vb* **1** (*The policeman was regarding them closely as they tried to get into the car*) look at, watch, observe, study, eye. **2** (*He regards his job prospects with optimism*) look on, view, consider. **3** (*They regard him as rather a fool*) consider, judge, rate, assess.

regard *n* **1** (*They paid no regard to his advice*) heed, notice, attention. **2** (*He is looked upon with regard in the firm*) respect, esteem, admiration.

region *n* (*the cold regions of the world*) area, territory, section, tract, zone, part, place. ▼

---

in the region of (something) approximately, roughly (*The price will be in the region of £50,000*).

---

register *vb* **1** (*The hotel guests were asked to sign the register*) list, record, directory. **2** (*He used the parish registers for his research*) record, chronicle, annal. **3** (*the register of her voice*) range, scale, reach, gamut.

register *vb* **1** (*They registered the birth of their son/They had to register their arrival on the list*) record, put on record, enter, write down. **2** (*The thermostat *registered twenty degrees*) read, indicate, show, display. 3 (*Her face registered her surprise*) show, express, display, reveal.

regret *vb* (*She regrets that she did it*) feel sorry, feel repentant, feel remorse, repent, to be ashamed of.

regretful *adj* (*She gave a regretful smile*) apologetic, repentant, contrite, remorseful, penitent.

regular *adj* 1 (*The postman did not follow his regular route*) usual, customary, accustomed, habitual, normal. 2 (*The breathing of the patient is regular*) even, steady, rhythmic. 3 (*They planted the trees at regular intervals*) even, fixed, uniform. 4 (*You will have to apply through the regular channels*) usual, standard, official, conventional, orthodox.

regulation *n* (*traffic regulations*) rule, order, law, decree.

rehearse *vb* (*The actors were rehearsing the play*) practise, try out, go over, run through.

reject *vb* 1 (*She has rejected their invitation*) refuse, turn down, decline. 2 (*She rejected the baby at birth*) abandon, forsake, renounce, cast aside.

rejoice *vb* (*They rejoiced on hearing that they had won*) be joyful, be happy, be glad, be delighted, be overjoyed, celebrate.

relapse *n* (*The patient was improving but then suffered a relapse*) set-back, turn for the worse.

relate *vb* 1 (*He related the story of his misfortune*) tell, recount, describe, narrate, report. 2 (*information not relating to the matter*) apply, be relevant, concern, have a bearing on.

relations *npl* 1 (*She has no relations in the area*) family, kin. 2 (*They have business relations*) dealings, associations.

relationship *n* 1 (*I don't think there is any relationship between the two events*) connection, association, link. 2 (*Their relationship is over*) friendship, partnership, love affair.

relax *vb* 1 (*He relaxes by swimming*) rest, unwind, take it easy, be at leisure, amuse oneself. 2 (*He relaxed his grip on the dog's leash*) loosen, lose, slacken, weaken 3 (*The police will not relax their efforts to find the criminal*) reduce, lessen, decrease, diminish.

release *vb* 1 (*The police have released the accused*) free, set free, let out, set loose, liberate. 2 (*They were tied up by the burglars and could not release themselves*) set free, free, untie, undo. 3 (*They have released the news of the royal engagement*) make public, make known, issue, announce, disclose, put out, circulate, publish.

relentless *adj* 1 (*The judge was completely relentless*) ruthless, unmerciful, merciless, pitiless, unforgiving, harsh, cruel. 2 (*their relentless efforts to persuade him*) persistent, persevering, unremitting, non-stop, unceasing.

relevant *adj* (*the information was not relevant to the discussion*) applicable, pertinent, apposite, appropriate.

reliable *adj* 1 (*her most reliable friends*) dependable, trustworthy, true, loyal, devoted. 2 (*The evidence was not considered reliable*) dependable, trustworthy, well-founded, sound.

relieve *vb* 1 (*a drug to relieve the pain*) alleviate, soothe, assuage, ease, reduce. 2 (*collect money to relieve the distress of the famine victims*) help, assist, aid, bring aid to. **3** (*She was to relieve the nurse on duty*) take over from, take the place of, stand in for, substitute for. **4** (*look for something to relieve the monotony of her life*) break up, interrupt, vary, lighten.

religious *adj* **1** (*take part in a religious ceremony/a religious discussion*) church, holy, divine, theological. **2** (*She comes from a religious family*) church-going, pious, devout, God-fearing.

relinquish *vb* (*He relinquished his right to the title*) give up, renounce, surrender.

reluctant *adj* **1** (*a reluctant witness*) unwilling, unenthusiastic, grudging **2** (*She was reluctant to go*) unwilling, disinclined, loath, averse.

rely *vb* (*She was relying on her parents for help*) depend on, count on, bank on, trust, put one's faith in.

remain *vb* **1** (*She remained calm in the emergency*) stay, keep, continue. **2** (*Only a few of the original inhabitants remained*) be left, survive, last, endure. **3** (*He has to remain in hospital*) stay, wait.

remark *n* (*She made some critical remarks*) comment, statement, observation.

remarkable *adj* (*It was a remarkable achievement for one so young*) extraordinary, unusual, exceptional, outstanding, impressive.

remedy *n* (*a remedy for the common cold*) cure, treatment.

remember *vb* **1** (I *cannot remember his name*) recall, call to mind, recollect, think of. **2** (*Try to remember to post the letter*) keep in mind, bear in mind.

reminisce *vb* (*old people reminiscing about their youth*) call to mind, recall, remember, recollect, think back on.

remorse *n* (*She showed remorse for her wrongdoing*) regret, penitence, compunction, contriteness.

remote *adj* **1** (*They live in a remote mountain village*) distant, far-off, out-of-the way, isolated. **2** (*She is rather a remote person*) distant, aloof, reserved, unfriendly. **3** (*There is a remote possibility that he will win*) outside, unlikely, slender, slight.

remove *vb* **1** (*They removed their shoes*) take off. **2** (*She was asked to remove her books from the table*) move, shift, take away, carry away. **3** (*They tried to remove him from his post*) get rid of, throw out, dismiss, sack, expel, evict, oust. **4** (*She has had a tooth removed*) take out, pull out, extract.

renounce *vb* **1** (*He renounced his claim to the title*) give up, relinquish, surrender, waive. **2** (*He renounced the smoking habit*) give up, swear off, abstain from, desist from. **3** (*They renounced their religion*) give up, abandon, turn one's back on, forsake.

renovate *vb* (*They are renovating an old country cottage*) modernize, restore, recondition, overhaul.

renown *n* ((*Her renown as a singer spread*) fame, acclaim, reputation, eminence, prestige.

rent *vb* (*They rented a boat*) hire, lease, charter.

repair *vb* **1** (*The mechanic repaired the car*) mend, fix, put right. **2** (*They repaired the torn clothes*) mend, sew, darn, patch.

repeal *vb* (*They have repealed that law*) revoke, annul, declare null and void, cancel, retract.

repeat *vb* **1** (*He was asked to repeat his statement to the committee*) say again, iterate, restate, recapitulate. **2** (*The boy repeated his father's words*) say again, echo, quote, parrot. **3** (*They have to *repeat the task*) re-do, do again, duplicate.

repel *vb* **1** (*They succeed in repelling their attackers*) drive back, push back, repulse, fend off, ward off. **2** (*The sight of the rotting meat repelled them*) revolt, disgust, nauseate, sicken.

repent *vb* (*She committed a sin but she has repented*) feel regret, feel remorse, be sorry, be repentant, be penitent, be contrite.

repercussion *n* (*He could not have foretold the repercussions of his actions*) consequence, effect, result, reverberation.

repetitive *adj* (*His work consists of repetitive tasks*) repeated, unchanging, monotonous.

replica *n* (*The original of the necklace is in the bank—this is a replica*) copy, duplicate, reproduction, imitation, model.

reply *n* **1** (*She gave no reply to his question*) answer, response, retort, rejoinder. **2** (*He received a reply to his letter*) answer, response, acknowledgement.

report *n* **1** (*the firm's annual financial report*) statement, record, register. **2** (*a newspaper report of the accident*) account, article, piece, story, write-up. **3** (*They heard the report of a gun*) bang, explosion, blast, boom, crack.

report *vb* **1** (*They reported that they had been successful*) announce, communicate, tell, relate. **2** (*The soldiers were to report to the sergeant at noon*) present oneself, announce oneself, appear, arrive. **3** (*They reported him to the police*) inform on, accuse, tell on, complain about, (*inf*) rat on, (*inf*) grass on.

repose *n* (*enjoy some repose after his hard work*) rest, relaxation, respite, time off, sleep.

represent *vb* **1** (*A closed fist represents violence*) symbolize, stand for, epitomize, personify. **2** (*The queen was represented in the picture as a warrior*) depict, portray, picture, show. **3** (*His lawyer represented him*) appear for, act for, speak for, be the representative of.

repressive *adj* (*a repressive regime*) repressing, tyrannical, despotic, dictatorial, oppressive, harsh, stern.

reprieve *vb* (*The woman was reprieved because she had killed in self-defence*) pardon, let off, spare.

reprimand *vb* (*The pupils were reprimanded for being late*) scold, chide, reprove, admonish, reproach, (*inf*) tell off, (*inf*) tick off.

reprisal *n* (*When their village was attacked they took reprisals on the attackers*) retaliation, vengeance, revenge, retribution, redress, requital.

reproach *n* (*She was upset by his words of reproach*) criticism, censure, condemnation, reprimand, reproof.

reproduce *vb* **1** (*Can the photocopier reproduce coloured documents?*) copy, photocopy, duplicate. **2** (*We were unable to reproduce the lighting effect we produced last week*) repeat, recreate, emulate. **3** (*Rabbits reproduce quickly*) breed, bear young, procreate, multiply.

repulsive *adj* (*It was a repulsive sight*) revolting, repellent, disgusting, nauseating, offensive, objectionable, loathsome, nasty, horrible, foul.

reputable *adj* (*get a reputable firm to do the work*) respected, respectable, well-thought-of, esteemed, reliable, dependable.

reputation *n* **1** (*The firm has a bad

reputation for shoddy work) name, character. 2 (*The incident damaged their reputation*) good name, respectability, esteem. ▼

---

live up to one's reputation to behave in the way that one is reputed or expected to behave (*He lived up to his reputation for meanness by refusing to give a contribution to the charity*).

---

request *vb* (*They requested more help*) ask for, seek, apply for, demand, beg for, plead for, petition.

require *vb* **1** (*They require more money*) need, have need of, be short of, lack, want. **2** (*The job requires concentration*) need, involve, take, call for. **3** (*The police required him to go to the police station*) order, instruct, command.

rescue *vb* (*They rescued the drowning man from the river/They rescued the men from prison*) save, get out, extricate, free, liberate.

research *n* (*They were carrying out medical research into new drugs*) investigation, exploration, inquiry, study, analysis.

resemble *vb* (*She resembles her mother*) look like, be like, bear a semblance to, be similar to, take after, put one in mind of, remind one of.

resent *vb* (*She resents the fact that her sister earns more money than she does*) begrudge, grudge, be bitter, feel aggrieved, envy, be jealous.

reserve *vb* **1** (*We reserved seats for the play*) book, order. **2** (*You should reserve some fuel for the winter*) keep, put aside, conserve, save, store. **3** (*They should reserve judgement until they have heard all the facts*) postpone, delay, defer.

reserved *adj* (*She is very reserved and does not speak to many people*) shy, retiring, diffident, reticent, aloof, distant, unsociable, uncommunicative.

reside *vb* (*He resides in a large house in London now*) live in, stay in, occupy, inhabit, dwell in.

residence *n* **1** (*They have an impressive Georgian residence*) house, dwelling place, domicile. **2** (*They take up residence next week*) occupation, occupancy, tenancy.

resident *n* **1** (*the residents of the new block of flats*) occupant, occupier, inhabitant. **2** (*the hotel residents*) guest, visitor.

resign *vb* **1** (*He resigned yesterday*) give notice, hand in one's notice, leave. **2** (*He resigned from his job yesterday*) leave, quit, give up.

resist *vb* (*The troops resisted the invading army*) fight against, stand up to, withstand, hold out against, defy, oppose, repel.

resolve *vb* **1** (*She resolved to try harder*) decide, make up one's mind, determine, settle. **2** (*They seemed unable to resolve the problem*) solve, sort out, work out, clear up, answer.

resourceful *adj* (*resourceful people who made do with what they had*) ingenious, inventive, creative, imaginative, clever, capable.

respect *n* **1** (*They had great respect for him as a painter*) esteem, high regard, admiration, reverence, deference. **2** (*With respect to the matter under discussion*) reference, relevance, regard, relation. **3** (*The plan was not perfect in all respects*) aspect, facet, feature, way, sense, particular, point, detail.

respectable *adj* (*Her neighbours do not think that she is very respectable*) of good reputation, upright, honourable, honest, decent, worthy.

response *n* (*They asked several questions but received no response*) answer, reply, acknowledgement, reaction.

responsible *adj* **1** (*They said that he was responsible for the damage*) blameworthy, to blame, guilty, at fault, accountable, answerable. **2** (*They need a responsible person to look after the children*) mature, sensible, level-headed, stable, reliable, dependable, trustworthy.

rest *n* **1** (*a period of rest after work*) repose, relaxation, leisure, ease, inactivity, sleep. **2** (*She is going away for a rest*) break, holiday, vacation.

restless *adj* **1** (*The children got restless in the afternoon*) fidgety, restive, agitated. **2** (*They passed a restless night*) wakeful, fitful.

restrain *vb* **1** (*They tried to restrain him from jumping off the bus*) prevent, hold back, impede. **2** (*She tried to restrain her laughter*) suppress, curb, check, stifle, contain. **3** (*It was her job to restrain the dogs*) control, keep under control, subdue, curb.

restrict *vb* **1** (*The long tight skirt restricted her freedom of movement*) hinder, hamper, impede, obstruct. **2** (*He was told by the doctor to restrict his consumption of salt*) limit, regulate, control, moderate.

restricted *adj* **1** (*a restricted space*) cramped, confined. **2** (*There is a restricted area around the military camp*) out of bounds, off limits, private.

result *n* (*His illness was a result of overwork*) effect, consequence, upshot, outcome, repercussion.

retain *vb* **1** (*They were asked to retain their train tickets*) keep, hold on to, hang on to. **2** (*The village still retains some of the old traditions*) keep, maintain, continue, preserve.

retaliate *vb* (*They hit the new boy and he retaliated*) take revenge, seek retribution, take reprisals, get even, give tit for tat.

reticent *adj* (*He was very outgoing but his wife was very reticent*) reserved, diffident, uncommunicative, taciturn, unforthcoming, silent.

retiring *adj* (*Very few people know her as she is very retiring*) shy, diffident, bashful, self-effacing, unassertive.

retreat *vb* **1** (*The army retreated before the enemy*) withdraw, go back, fall back, take flight, flee, beat a retreat. **2** (*The tide retreated*) go back, recede, ebb.

retrieve *vb* (*He tried to retrieve his stolen property*) get back, recover, regain, recoup, reclaim.

return *vb* **1** (*Their parents will return tomorrow*) come back, go back, reappear. **2** (*She asked him to return the book which she had lent him*) give back, send back.

reveal *vb* **1** (*She took off her coat and revealed a white dress*) show, display, exhibit, expose, uncover. **2** (*The press revealed the truth about the affair*) disclose, divulge, tell, let out, make known.

revenge *n* (*He wanted revenge for his brother's murder*) vengeance, retribution, retaliation, reprisal.

reverse *vb* **1** (*They reversed their roles for the day*) change, exchange, swap, trade. **2** (*They have reversed their previous decision*) alter, change, overturn, repeal, revoke. **3** (*He reversed the car*) back. **4** (*reverse the coat*) turn round, put back to front.

revise *vb* **1** (*The pupils are revising the term's work*) go over, reread, (*inf*) swot up. **2** (*She had to revise the text of the manuscript*) amend, emend, correct, alter, edit. **3** (*We have had to revise our holiday plans*) reconsider, review, alter, change.

revolt *vb* **1** (*The sight of the dried blood revolted her*) disgust, repel, nauseate, sicken, (*inf*) turn one off. **2** (*The citizens are revolting against the tyrant*) rebel, rise up, take up arms, mutiny.

revolution *n* **1** (*There was a revolution against the king*) rebellion, revolt, uprising, insurrection, mutiny, riot. **2** (*There has been a revolution in the computer industry*) complete change, transformation, reformation, innovation. **3** (*one revolution of the wheel*) rotation, round, whirl, spin. **4** (*The satellite made a revolution of the sun*) orbit, circuit, turn.

revolve *vb* **1** (*The wheel revolved slowly*) go round, turn, rotate, spin, whirl. **2** (*The planet revolves round the sun*) orbit, circle. **3** (*His world revolves round his family*) centre on, focus on, concentrate on.

reward *n* (*He received a reward for bravery*) award, prize, recompense, gift, decoration, medal.

rhythm *n* (*The tune had a fast rhythm*) beat, pulse, throb, tempo, cadence.

rich *adj* (*rich people who owned several houses*) wealthy, affluent, well off, prosperous, well-to-do, moneyed. **2** (*a house with rich furnishings*) costly, expensive, opulent, luxurious, sumptuous, splendid, magnificent. **3** (*The area has a very rich soil*) fertile, fruitful, productive, fecund. **4** (*curtains of a very rich colour*) strong, deep, vivid, intense, brilliant. **5** (*The country has rich supplies of oil*) abundant, copious, ample, plentiful. ▼

---

as rich as Croesus extremely wealthy (*He can well afford to buy her diamonds. He is as rich as Croesus*) <Croesus was a ruler of the ancient kingdom of Lydia and was very wealthy>.

---

rid:—**get rid of** *vb* (*She should get rid of those old clothes*) dispose of, throw away, throw out, jettison, dump.

riddle *n* (*unable to solve the riddle*) puzzle, conundrum, poser, brainteaser.

ridiculous *adj* **1** (*It was a ridiculous thing to do*) absurd, pointless, senseless, foolish, inane. **2** (*He told us a ridiculous story about his holiday/She always wears ridiculous hats*) absurd, comical, funny, laughable, humorous, ludicrous. **3** (*It is ridiculous that he got away with the crime*) shocking, outrageous, monstrous, preposterous, incredible.

right *adj* **1** (*They all gave the right answer*) correct, accurate. **2** (*He was not the right person for the job*) suitable, appropriate, fitting, desirable. **3** (*He is not in his right mind*) sane, sound, rational, sensible. **4** (*They thought the judge did not make the right decision*) just, fair, impartial, good, honest, virtuous. ▼

---

put (someone) right to cause (someone) to realize his or her mistake, incorrect beliefs, etc

(*He thought that the house was still for sale but we were able to put him right*). **put (something) right** to repair, to rectify (*The machine was broken but it has been put right/There had been misunderstanding about money but it has been put right*). **serve (someone) right** to be something unpleasant that (someone) deserves (*It serves her right that she has lost her job as manager—she was responsible for getting rid of so many other workers*).

---

rigid *adj* **1** (*It was made of a rigid substance*) stiff, hard, taut, inflexible, unbending. **2** (*The headmaster was a rigid disciplinarian*) strict, severe, stern, stringent, harsh, inflexible.

ring *n* **1** (*She wore a gold ring*) band, hoop. **2** (*They saw a ring around the moon*) circle, loop. **3** (*He jumped into the boxing ring*) arena, area, enclosure. **4** (*The police have discovered a spy ring*) gang, organization, league, combine, syndicate.

ring *vb* **1** (*church bells ringing*) toll, sound, peal, chime. **2** (*The hall rang with music*) resound, reverberate, echo, resonate. **3** (*He said that he would ring back*) call, phone, telephone. ▼

---

have a ringside seat to be in a position to observe clearly what is happening (*We all had a ringside seat during the couple's constant quarrels*) <A reference to a boxing ring>. **ring down the curtain on (something)** to cause (something) to come to an end (*The government is ringing down the curtain on the new roads scheme because it is too expensive*) <A reference to curtains in a theatre being lowered at the end of a performance>. **ring the changes** to add variety by doing or arranging things in different ways (*He cannot afford new furniture but he rings the changes by shifting the furniture from room to room*).

---

riot *n* (*There was a riot in the crowd when their leader was arrested*) rebellion, revolt, uprising, insurrection, mutiny, uproar. ▼

---

read the riot act to (someone) to scold (someone) severely and warn him or her to behave better (*Their mother read the riot act to the children about their rooms*) <The Riot Act of 1715 was read to gatherings of people who were considered unlawful in order to break up the gatherings. If the people refused to disperse, action could be taken against them>.

---

ripe *adj* (*ripe fruit*) mature, ready to eat, ready, mellow.

rise *vb* **1** (*The balloon will rise into the air*) go up, climb, ascend. **2** (*the mountains rising behind the village*) rear up, tower, soar, loom. **3** (*She always rises early*) get up. **4** (*Prices are set to rise*) go up, increase, mount, escalate, rocket. **5** (*The dough for the bread failed to rise*) puff up, swell, expand. **6** (*The stream rises in the mountains*) originate, begin, start, flow from. ▼

---

rise and shine to get out of bed and be lively and cheerful (*Rise and shine! We have to leave in half-an-hour*).

---

risk *n* **1** (*There is a risk of flooding*) danger, chance, possibility, likelihood. **2** (*Their actions put lives at risk*) danger, peril, jeopardy.

rival *n* (*her rival in the competition*) opponent, opposition, adversary.

roar *vb* **1** (*The lion roared*) bellow. **2** (*He roared in rage*) bellow, yell, bawl, shout.

robbery *n* (*The criminals committed robbery*) burglary, theft, stealing, larceny. ▼

---

daylight robbery the charging of prices that are far too high (*Taxi fares in that city are daylight robbery*).

---

robust *adj* (*in robust health*) strong, vigorous, tough, rugged, sturdy, stalwart.

rock *vb* **1** (*The boat began to rock in the storm*) roll, lurch, pitch, swing, sway, wobble. **2** (*rock the cradle*) sway, swing.

rogue *n* (*He was a rogue who ended up in prison*) villain, scoundrel, rascal.

role *n* **1** (*her role in the play*) part, character. **2** (*He attended in his role as chairman*) capacity, position, function, post.

roll *vb* **1** (*The wheels began to roll*) turn, go round, rotate, revolve, spin. **2** (*roll up a newspaper to swat a fly*) furl, coil, fold. **3** (*roll the lawn*) flatten level, smooth, even out. **4** (*as time rolls on*) pass, go by. **5** (*as the ship rolled*) rock, lurch, pitch, toss, swing, sway. ▼

---

a rolling stone gathers no moss a person who does not stay very long in one place does not acquire much in the way of possessions, responsibilities, etc (*He has been a rolling stone all his life and has no furniture to put in the house he has been left*). **be rolling in the aisles** to laugh extremely heartily (*The comedian had the audience rolling in the aisles*).

---

romantic *adj* **1** (*She has a very romantic idea of what it is like to live in a remote village*) unrealistic, impractical, idealistic, starry-eyed. **2** (*romantic words on a greetings card*) loving, amorous, sentimental. **3** (*She seemed to them a romantic figure*) fascinating, glamorous, mysterious, exotic, exciting.

rope *n* (*tie the logs up with a rope*) string, cord, cable, line. ▼

---

give (someone) enough rope and he or she will hang himself *or* **herself** let (someone foolish) act as he or she pleases and he or she will bring about his or her own downfall, ruin, etc (*I know that he is running the department badly but don't say anything just now. Give him enough rope and he will hang himself*). **know the ropes** to know the details and methods associated with a business, procedure, activity, etc (*We need someone for the job who knows the ropes*).

---

rotate *vb* **1** (*The wheels rotate*) turn, go round, revolve, spin. **2** (*The two doctors rotate between the two wards*) alternate, take turns.

rotten *adj* **1** (*rotten food*) bad, mouldy, decaying, decomposed, putrid, rancid, stinking. **2** (*rotten wood*) decaying, crumbling, disintegrating, corroding. **3** (*What a rotten thing to do!*) nasty, mean, foul, despicable, contemptible.

rough *adj* **1** (*sand down the rough surface of the table*) uneven, bumpy, jaggy, rugged, irregular. **2** (*They have a dog with a rough coat*) shaggy, bushy, hairy, coarse, bristly. **3** (*people with rough voices*) gruff, hoarse, harsh, husky. **4** (*rough weather at sea*) stormy, squally, wild, inclement. **5** (*He goes around with a rough crowd*) rowdy, disorderly, wild, uncouth, coarse, loutish, boorish. **6** (*at a rough estimate*) approximate, inexact, imprecise. **7** (*He made a rough sketch of the house*) rough-and ready, hasty, quick, sketchy, rudimentary. ▼

---

give (someone) the rough edge of one's tongue to scold or criticize (someone) severely (*She said that she would give the child the rough edge of her tongue for letting the dog out*). **take the rough with the smooth** to accept the disadvantages as well as the advantages and benefits of a situation (*Shopping can be difficult if you live in the country. Still we live in a beautiful area and you have to take the rough with the smooth*).

---

round *adj* (*a round shape*) circular, ring-shaped, spherical. ▼

---

a round trip the journey to somewhere and the journey back (*The round trip to my parents' house takes about four hours*). **get round to (something)** to find the time and opportunity to do (something) (*I never seem to get round to writing letters*).

---

route *n* (*They went home by a different route*) way, road, course.

routine *n* (*He hates to have his routine upset*) custom, habit, practice, procedure.

row *n* **1** (*children standing in rows*) line, column, queue, series. **2** (*empty rows of seats in the theatre*) line, tier, rank.

row *n* **1** (*The two brothers had a row over money*) argument, disagreement, dispute, squabble, fight. **2** (*the row coming from the party*) noise, din, rumpus, uproar, commotion.

rowdy *adj* (*the rowdy drunks in the pub*) unruly, disorderly, noisy, boisterous, loud, wild.

rub *vb* **1** (*She rubbed his sore neck*) massage, knead. **2** (*The child began to rub the cat's back*) pat, caress, fondle. **3** (*rub off the dirty mark*) wipe off, remove, erase. **4** (*rub the ointment into the skin*) apply, work in, spread. ▼

---

rub (something) in to keep reminding someone about (something) (*I know that I made a fool of myself but there is no need to rub it in*). **rub (someone) up the wrong way** to irritate (someone) (*He tries to be friendly but he has a habit of rubbing people up the wrong way*).

---

rude *adj* **1** (*The children were very rude*) ill-mannered, bad-mannered, impolite, discourteous, impertinent, impudent, cheeky. **2** (*They told rude jokes*) vulgar, coarse, smutty, dirty, bawdy, blue. **3** (*The peasants had only a few rude tools*) crude, primitive, rough, rudimentary, simple.

ruffian *n* (*The old man was attacked by a gang of ruffians*) rogue, thug, villain, hooligan, scoundrel.

rugged *adj* **1** (*a rugged landscape*) rough, uneven, irregular, bumpy, rocky, jagged. **2** (*rugged men who do hard physical work*) tough, strong, stalwart, robust, sturdy, muscular, brawny.

rubbish *n* **1** (*They put the rubbish in sacks*) refuse, waste, litter, debris, junk. **2** (*She talks a lot of rubbish*) nonsense, drivel, balderdash, gibberish, twaddle.

ruin *vb* **1** (*The storm ruined the crops*) spoil, damage, wreck, wreack havoc on, destroy, lay waste. **2** (*The recession ruined many small businesses*) bring to ruin, bankrupt, make insolvent, impoverish.

rule *vb* **1** (*The emperor ruled over several countries*) govern, preside over, have control over, have authority over, be in command of. **2** (*The judge ruled that the accused be released*) order, command, direct, decide. ▼

---

rule the roost to be the person in charge whose orders or wishes are obeyed (*When his father is away his elder brother tries to rule the roost*) <A reference to a cockerel in the farmyard>. **rule of thumb** a rough or inexact guide used for calculations of some kind (*I did not have a tape measure but I estimated the length of the curtains by rule of thumb*).

---

rumour *n* (*Rumour has it that he has gone*) gossip, hearsay, the grapevine.

run *vb* **1** (*They had to run to catch the bus*) race, sprint, dash, rush, bolt, charge. **2** (*Do the trains run on Sundays?*) operate, go, travel. **3** (*water running down the walls*) flow, stream, pour, gush. **4** (*The dye from the black trousers ran on to the white shirt*) spread, mix with. **5** (*He runs a successful business*) operate, conduct, carry on, manage, administer, control, be in charge of, rule. **6** (*They left the engine running*) go, operate, function. ▼

---

run the gauntlet to be exposed or subjected to extreme criticism, blame or risk (*Before he married her he had to run the gauntlet of her family's disapproval*) <'Gauntlet' is a mistaken form of Swedish *gatlopp*. 'Running the gatlopp' was a Swedish military punishment in which the culprit had to run between two lines of men with whips who struck him as he passed>. **run the show** to be in charge of an organisation, etc: *I don't know what will happen to our jobs* (*There's a new man running the show now*). <Refers literally to the theatre>.

---

rural *adj* (*a house in a rural setting*) country, rustic, pastoral.

ruse *n* (*He gained entrance to the house by a ruse*) trick, stratagem, subterfuge, dodge, ploy, deception, hoax.

rush *vb* (*They rushed to switch off the water*) hurry, hasten, make haste, run, race, dash. ▼

---

the rush hour a period when there is a lot of traffic on the roads, usually when people are going to, or coming from, work.

---

ruthless *adj* (*He was a ruthless tyrant*) merciless, pitiless, relentless, unforgiving, harsh, severe, heartless, cruel.

S

sacred *adj* **1** (*playing sacred music*) religious, church, spiritual, devotional. **2** (*The temple was a sacred place*) holy, blessed, hallowed, consecrated, godly, divine. **3** (*In Hinduism the cow is a sacred animal*) sacrosanct, protected. ▼

a sacred cow something that is regarded with too much respect for people to be allowed to criticize it freely (*Don't let anyone hear you saying that the town hall is ugly. It is one of the community's sacred cows*).

sad *adj* **1** (*She felt sad when her friend went away*) unhappy, miserable, wretched, dejected, downcast, in low spirits, depressed, gloomy, melancholy. **2** (*She tried to forget the sad events of her childhood*) unhappy, unfortunate, distressing, tragic. **3** (*He thought that the country was in a sad state*) sorry, wretched, unfortunate, regrettable, deplorable, disgraceful.

safe *adj* **1** (*The children are safe indoors*) safe and sound, secure, protected, uninjured, unscathed, free from harm, free from danger, out of harm's way. **2** (*Is the building a safe place for the children to play?*) secure, sound, risk-free. **3** (*She is a safe person to look after the children*) reliable, dependable, trustworthy. **4** (*a safe driver*) careful, cautious, prudent. ▼

be on the safe side not to take any risks (*I don't think it will rain but to be on the safe side I'll take my umbrella*). **there's safety in numbers** it is safer to undertake a risky venture if there are several people involved (*He would not go on strike on his own in case he got the sack but his colleagues are joining him and there's safety in numbers*).

sail *vb* (*We sail at dawn*) set sail, embark, put to sea, put off. ▼

sail close to the wind to come close to breaking the law or a rule (*The second-hand car dealer is not a convicted criminal but he sails very close to the wind*).

salary *n* (*He earns a good salary*) wage, pay, earnings, remuneration.

same *adj* **1** (*That is the same dress which she wore yesterday*) identical, selfsame, the very. **2** (*The restaurant sells the same old food, week after week*) identical, similar, unchanging, unvarying. ▼

be all the same to (someone) to be a matter of no importance to (someone) (*It's all the same to us whether he goes or stays*). **not be in the same league as (someone)** not to be as able, talented, etc, as (someone) (*The new teacher is just not in the* *same league as the previous one*). **the same old story** a situation, etc, that recurs frequently (*It was the same old story. They said that he couldn't have the job because he had no experience but he couldn't find a job to gain the experience*).

---

sample *n* **1** (*The artist showed the advertising agency a sample of her work*) specimen, example, illustration, instance. **2** (*They gave the questionnaire to a sample of the population*) cross-section, sampling, random sample.

sane *adj* (*He said that he had not been sane when he committed the murder*) of sound mind, in one's right mind, rational, compos mentis, rational, lucid, (*inf*) all there.

sarcastic *adj* (*They were hurt by her sarcastic remarks*) caustic, acerbic, sardonic, sneering, mocking, scoffing, derisive.

satisfactory *adj* (*They did not find her work satisfactory*) adequate, good enough, all right, acceptable, passable, up to scratch, up to standard.

satisfied *adj* **1** (*They were satisfied with the results/satisfied customers*) pleased, happy, content. **2** (*The police were satisfied that he was innocent*) convinced, sure, certain, positive. **3** (*They felt satisfied after one course of the meal*) full.

satisfy *vb* **1** (*students who satisfy the university entrance requirements*) fulfil, meet, be sufficient for. **2** (*products that satisfy the demands of the customers*) fulfil, gratify. **3** (*find some cool water to satisfy their thirst*) quench, slake, satiate. **4** (*He was able to satisfy her parents that she was telling the truth*) convince, persuade, assure.

savage *adj* **1** (*attacked by a savage animal*) ferocious, fierce, wild. **2** (*During the attack she received a savage blow to the head*) vicious, brutal. **3** (*He was really savage to his family*) brutal, cruel, vicious, harsh, grim, barbarous, merciless. **4** (*The explorers were attacked by a savage tribe*) primitive, uncivilized, wild. ▼

---

noble savage a primitive person brought up in primitive surroundings who is thought of as being less corrupt, worthier, etc, than people brought up in ordinary modern circumstances (*The child whom they found living alone in the jungle was hailed as a noble savage*).

---

save *vb* **1** (*try to save some money for a holiday*) put aside, set aside, put by, keep, reserve, conserve, stockpile, hoard. **2** (*It will save a lot of inconvenience*) prevent, obviate, rule out. **3** (*He saved his friend from death*) rescue, deliver, snatch, free. ▼

---

saved by the bell rescued from an unpleasant situation by something suddenly bringing that situation to an end (*The teacher asked him for his homework which he had not done. He was saved by the bell when a parent arrived to see the teacher*) <A reference to a bell that marks the end of a round in boxing>.

---

say *vb* **1** (*say a few words*) speak, utter, voice, pronounce. **2** (*You should say what you are thinking*) express, tell, put into words, state, communicate, make known, articulate. **3** (*'It's snowing heavily,' she said*) state, remark, announce. ▼

---

say the word say what you want and your wishes will be carried out (*If you want some food just say the word*). **you can say that again** you are absolutely right (*I told her that I thought that the restaurant was very expensive. "You can say that again!" she said*).

---

scandalous *adj* **1** (*a politician who had to resign because of his scandalous behaviour*) disgraceful, dishonourable, shocking, outrageous, disreputable, improper. **2** (*scandalous rumours circulating about the family*) slanderous, defamatory. libellous, scurrilous.

scant *adj* (*take scant notice of what her mother said*) little, slight, minimal, inadequate, insufficient.

scar *n* (*The accident left him with a scar on his face*) blemish, mark, blotch, disfigurement.

scarce *adj* (*Copies of the book are scarce now*) rare, few, few and far between, in short supply, scant, uncommon, unusual.

scare *vb* (*The sight of the man scared the children*) frighten, make afraid, alarm, startle, terrify, terrorize.

scatter *vb* **1** (*scatter the breadcrumbs for the birds*) spread, disseminate, sow, sprinkle. **2** (*The crowd scattered when the police arrived*) disperse, break up, separate, disband.

scene *n* **1** (*They visited the scene of the battle*) site, location, position, spot. **2** (*The photographs were taken against a winter scene*) background, setting, landscape, view, vista, outlook. **3** (*It was a moving scene when child and mother were reunited*) event, incident, happening, situation. **4** (*The child made a scene when she did not get her own way*) fuss, outburst, commotion, exhibition, to-do, upset, row. ▼

---

behind the scenes out of sight of the public, etc (*Our hostess took all the credit for the successful dinner party but she had a team of caterers behind the scenes*) <A reference to people in a theatrical production who work behind the scenery offstage>. **come on the scene** to arrive or appear (*They were happily married until that young woman came on the scene*). **not (someone's) scene** not the kind of thing that (someone) likes (*Opera is not his scene*).

---

scenery *n* (*tourists admiring the scenery*) view, outlook, prospect, vista, landscape.

scent *n* **1** (*He bought her an expensive scent for her* birthday) perfume, fragrance. **2** (*the scent of roses in the room*) perfume, fragrance, smell. **3** (*the scent of newly baked bread*) aroma, smell, bouquet, odour. **4** (*dogs following the scent of the fox*) trail, track, spoor. ▼

---

throw (someone) off the scent to distract (someone) from a search for someone or something, e.g. by giving him or her wrong information (*The police were put off the scent of the real killer when someone made a false confession*) <Refers literally to distracting dogs from

the scent of someone or something which they are following>.

---

sceptical *adj* (*She was sceptical about her chances of success*) doubtful, dubious, distrustful, mistrustful, unconvinced.

scheme *n* **1** (*They have developed a new training scheme for young people*) plan, programme, project, system, procedure, strategy, design, tactics. **2** (*a modern colour scheme*) arrangement, system. ▼

---

the best-laid schemes of mice and men gang aft agley the most carefully arranged plans often go wrong (*We had checked our holiday itinerary very carefully but everything seemed to go wrong at the last minute. Ah well, the best-laid schemes of mice and men gang aft agley*) <A reference to Robert Burns' poem, 'To a Mouse'>.

---

scoff *vb* (*They began to scoff at his efforts to bake a cake*) jeer at, mock at, laugh at, ridicule.

scold *vb* (*Her parents scolded her for being late*) rebuke, reprimand, chide, upbraid.

score *n* **1** (*What was the score at half-time?*) result, outcome. **2** (*She noticed a deep score on the table*) scrape, scratch, groove, cut, mark. ▼

---

know the score (*inf*) to know exactly what is involved, to know all the facts of a situation (*She knew the score when she married him. He has been in and out of jail all his life*). **settle old scores** to get revenge for wrongs committed in the past (*He has just met the man who killed his brother in a fight years ago and wants to settle old scores*).

---

scorn *n* (*He treated everyone else's ideas with scorn*) contempt, disdain, mockery, derision.

scowl *vb* (*He scowled when they disagreed with him*) frown, glower, glare, look daggers.

scrap *n* **1** (*use scraps of material to make a patchwork quilt*) remnant, fragment, bit, piece, snippet. **2** (*feed the dog scraps of food*) piece, bit, morsel, particle. **3** (*He is a scrap merchant*) waste, junk. **4** (*There was not a scrap of sincerity in what she said*) bit, grain, iota, trace, whit.

scrape *vb* **1** (*scrape the surface of the table*) scratch. **2** (*The child fell and scraped her knee*) graze, scratch, abrade, cut.

scratch *vb* **1** (*try to scratch an itchy spot on her back*) rub, tear at. **2** (*She scratched her hand on a rusty nail*) graze, cut, abrade, skin, lacerate, wound. ▼

---

be up to scratch to be up to the required standard (*The pupil will have to repeat the year if his work is not up to scratch*) <Refers originally to the starting line, formerly scratched on the ground, from which runners start unless their handicap allows them to start farther down the track>. **start from scratch** to start from the very beginning without any advantages (*She had absolutely no educational qualifications. She had to start from scratch with her studying*).

---

scream *vb* (*He screamed when the*

heavy weight fell on him) shriek, shout, yell, howl, squeal, yelp, wail.

screen *n* **1** (*a screen at the window to stop people looking in*) curtain, blind. **2** (*trees to act as a screen from the wind*) shelter, shield, protection, guard. **3** (*The business was a screen for his drug-dealing*) front, façade, blind, disguise, camouflage, cover, cloak.

scruffy *adj* (*He was told to tidy up, that he was too scruffy to go to school*) untidy, unkempt, dishevelled, messy, slovenly.

scurry *vb* (*The children were late and scurried home*) hurry, hasten, rush, run, race, dash, scamper.

seal *vb* **1** (*They sealed the parcel before posting it*) fasten, secure, close up, shut. **2** (*They filled the jars with fruit and sealed them*) make airtight, close, shut, cork. **3** (*The police sealed off the area*) cordon off, shut off, close off. **4** (*They have sealed a bargain*) settle, secure, clinch. ▼

---

set one's seal of approval on (something) to give one's agreement or approval to (something) (*The council has set its seal of approval on the new leisure centre*).

---

search *vb* **1** (*The police are searching for clues to the crime*) look for, seek, hunt for, ferret out. **2** (*They searched the building for the missing jewels*) look through, hunt through, rifle through, scour. ▼

---

search high and low for (someone *or* **something)** to search absolutely everywhere for (someone or something) (*We searched high and low for the missing ring but did not find it*).

---

secluded *adj* (*a secluded part of the large garden*) sheltered, private, remote, out-of-the way.

secret *adj* **1** (*They were told to keep the matter secret*) confidential, private, under wraps, (*inf*) hush-hush. **2** (*a desk with a secret drawer*) hidden, concealed.

secretive *adj* (*She is very secretive about where she is going*) reticent, uncommunicative, unforthcoming, taciturn, silent.

section *n* **1** (*He bought the wood in sections*) part, segment, piece, portion, bit. **2** (*a book divided into sections*) part, division, chapter. **3** (*the children's section of the bookshop*) part, department.

secure *adj* **1** (*The children feel secure at their grandparents' house*) safe, protected, free from danger, out of harm's way. **2** (*They can no longer look forward to a secure future*) safe, settled, solid, dependable, reliable. **3** (*The stepladder is not very secure*) steady, stable, sturdy, sold.

see *vb* **1** (*They could not see the cottage through the mists*) make out, catch sight of, spot, glimpse, look at, discern, perceive, notice, observe, view. **2** (*I see what he means*) understand, grasp, get, comprehend, follow, take in. **3** (*I will go and see where he is*) find out, discover, learn, ascertain. **4** (*We asked her to see that the children went to bed early*) make sure, be sure, ensure, mind, see to it, take care. **5** (*When she asked if she could go on holiday her parents said that they would have to see*) think, have a think, give it some thought, consider, reflect. **6** (*The two friends see each other once a week*) meet, arrange to meet. **7** (*He saw his mother to her door*) escort, accompany, usher, guide, lead. **8** (*Did you see the documentary on TV last night?*) watch, look at, view. ▼

---

see daylight to be coming to the end of a long task (*I have been working for months on this research project but I'm beginning to see daylight*). **see stars** to see flashes of light as a result of a bang on the head (*When he bumped his head on the wooden beam he saw stars*).

---

seek *vb* **1** (*The police are seeking more information*) search for, look for, hunt for. **2** (*After the accident she was advised that she should seek help from a counsellor*) request, ask for, solicit.

seem *vb* (*They seem rather pleasant people*) appear to be, look to be, give the impression of being.

seemly *adj* (*They thought that her behaviour was far from seemly*) decent, proper, decorous, fitting, suitable, appropriate, becoming.

seize *vb* **1** (*He seized a hanging branch to pull himself out of the water*) grab, grab hold of, take hold of, grasp, grip, clutch at. **2** (*Kidnappers seized the children*) snatch, kidnap, abduct.

seldom *adv* (*We seldom see them*) rarely, hardly ever, infrequently.

select *vb* (*The little boy was asked to select a toy as a present*) choose, pick, opt for, decide on, settle on, plump for.

selfish *adj* (*The child is selfish and will not share anything with his friends*) self-centred, self-seeking, egotistic, egocentric.

sell *vb* **1** (*They plan to sell their house soon*) put on sale, put up for sale. **2** (*shops selling foodstuffs*) offer for sale, stock, carry, deal in, market. ▼

---

sell (someone) a pup to deceive (someone), often to sell or recommend something to (someone) that turns out not to be as good as he or she thought (*This computer keeps breaking down. I think we've been sold a pup*). **sell (someone) down the river** to betray or be disloyal to (someone) (*He sold his friend down the river by telling the police that she had been present at the crime*) <Refers historically to selling slaves in America from the upper Mississippi states to buyers in Louisiana where working and living conditions were much harsher>.

---

send *vb* **1** (*send a parcel by airmail*) dispatch, convey, transport, remit, post, mail. **2** (*She sent her parents a message that she was well*) communicate, convey, transmit.

sensational *adj* (*tabloid newspapers with a sensational story about a politician*) spectacular, exciting, dramatic, startling, shocking, scandalous.

sense *n* **1** (*a sense of smell*) sensation, faculty, feeling. **2** (*They have no sense of honour*) awareness, understanding, appreciation. **3** (*He now has a sense of shame*) feeling. **4** (*The child had the sense to wait for her mother*) common sense, intelligence, cleverness, wisdom, practicality. **5** (*a word with more than one sense*) meaning, definition. ▼

come to one's senses to begin to behave or think sensibly (*He was going to leave his job and go round the world but he came to his senses when he counted up the cost*). **sixth sense** intuition, an ability to feel or realize something not perceived by the five senses of sight, hearing, smell, taste, and touch (*He could not see anyone but a sixth sense told him that he was not alone*). **take leave of one's senses** to become deranged or very foolish (*I think that she's taken leave of her senses. She has left her husband and children to go off with an absolutely horrible man*).

sensitive *adj* **1** (*She has very sensitive skin*) delicate, fine, soft. **2** (*She is very sensitive to noise*) easily affected by, susceptible to. **3** (*She is a very sensitive person*) responsive, perceptive, sympathetic, understanding. **4** (*She is too sensitive to work in such a competitive firm*) over-sensitive, thin-skinned, touchy. **5** (*The two sides were discussing a very sensitive issue*) delicate, difficult, problematic, thorny.

sentence *n* **1** (*The judge delivered his sentence*) judgement, verdict, ruling, decision. **2** (*Her attacker is serving a ten-year sentence*) prison sentence, prison term, (*inf*) porridge.

sentimental *adj* **1** (*The vase is not valuable but she has a sentimental attachment to it*) emotional, nostalgic. **2** (*The group were singing sentimental love songs*) emotional, overemotional, romantic, mawkish, maudlin, (*inf*) soppy, (*inf*) schmaltzy.

separate *adj* **1** (*The two issues are quite separate*) unconnected, unrelated, divorced, distinct, different. **2** (*They have separate flats*) individual, independent, different. ▼

separate the sheep from the goats to distinguish the good, useful, talented, etc, people from the bad, useless, stupid, etc, ones (*The teacher said that the exam would separate the sheep from the goats*) <A Biblical reference to Matthew 25:32>.

series *n* (*a series of sporting events/a series of misfortunes*) succession, progression, sequence, chain, train, run, cycle, order.

serious *adj* **1** (*The headmaster was looking very serious*) solemn, grave, earnest, unsmiling, sombre, sober. **2** (*The accident victim has serious injuries*) bad, grave, critical, acute, dangerous. **3** (*They have several serious matters to discuss*) grave, important, weighty, of consequence, urgent, pressing, crucial, vital. **4** (*make a serious attempt at the championship*) earnest, determined, resolute, honest, sincere.

serve *vb* **1** (*He has served his master loyally for many years*) be in the service of, work for, be employed by. **2** (*people who have served the community*) be of service to, be of use to, help, assist, benefit, support. **3** (*He served three years as a plumber's apprentice*) spend, carry out, fulfil, complete. **4** (*a sofa that will also serve as a bed*) function, act as, do duty as. **5** (*The hostess is just about to serve the first course*) dish up, give out, deal out. **6** (*She *is trying to find a salesperson to serve her*) attend to, assist.

service *n* **1** (*She retired after forty years' service with the firm*) work, employment. **2** (*We did him a service by telling him the truth about his friends*) good turn, benefit, advantage, help, assistance. **3** (*His car is due for a service*) overhaul, check-up, repair, maintenance. **4** (*guests at the wedding service*) ceremony, rite, ritual. ▼

---

at (someone's) service ready to be of assistance to (someone) (*He said that his chauffeur was at our service for the day*).

---

session *n* (*old friends having a good gossip session*) time, period, spell.

set *vb* **1** (*set their suitcases down on the pavement*) put, put down, lay down, place, deposit. **2** (*set the jewel in a gold ring*) fix, embed, arrange, mount. **3** (*set the thermostat*) regulate, adjust. **4** (*set the house on fire*) put, cause to be, start. **5** (*The jelly will not set*) solidify, thicken, harden, gel. **6** (*At what time does the sun set?*) go down, sink, subside. **7** (*The runner set a new record for the course*) set up, establish, create, institute. **8** (*We must set a date for the annual dinner*) fix, establish, settle, agree on, decide on, select. **9** (*His behaviour set them talking*) start, cause. **10** (*The teacher set the children an exam*) assign, allot. ▼

---

set about (someone *or* **something) 1** to begin (something or doing something) (*How will you set about finding your father after all these years?*). **2** to attack (someone or something) (*The thug set about the old man with an iron bar*).

---

settle *vb* **1** (*We must settle on a date for the annual dance*) set, decide on, agree on, fix, arrange, choose, select. **2** (*I hope they settle the dispute soon*) clear up, resolve, bring to an end, conclude. **3** (*He wants to settle his financial affairs before he dies*) set to rights, put in order, arrange, clear out, straighten up. **4** (*enough money to settle their bills*) pay, meet. **5** (*The coffee dregs had settled at the foot of the cup*) sink, subside, fall. **6** (*She was so upset that the doctor had to give her something to settle her*) calm, calm down, quieten, sedate, compose, tranquillize. **7** (*The family emigrated from Ireland to settle in America*) make one's home, take up residence, go to live, move to. **8** (*a part of America settled by Scots*) establish, colonize, occupy, inhabit, populate.

sever *vb* **1** (*In the accident he severed his leg at the knee*) cut off, chop off, lop off. **2** (*He had to sever the logs in two*) divide, split. **3** (*The two families quarrelled and severed relations with each other*) break off, suspend, end, terminate.

several *adj* **1** (*She has invited several people to dinner*) some, a number of, a few. **2** (*Eventually we all went our several ways*) separate, different, respective, individual, particular.

severe *adj* **1** (*He wore a very severe expression*) stern, grim, forbidding, disapproving, sombre, serious. **2** (*The tyrant ruled over a severe regime*) harsh, hard, strict, cruel, brutal, savage, merciless. **3**

(*She always wore severe clothes*) plain, simple, unadorned, austere. **4** (*We have had a severe winter*) harsh, hard, extreme. **5** (*She suffers from severe pain in her legs*) extreme, intense, fierce, strong, violent, very bad.

shabby *adj* **1** (*She wore shabby clothes*) worn, threadbare, scruffy. **2** (*The house is looking rather shabby*) dilapidated, run-down, broken-down, tumbledown, ramshackle, dingy, seedy, squalid, slum-like. **3** (*The way he treated her was shabby*) despicable, dishonourable, mean, shoddy.

shade *n* **1** (*They sat in the shade of a tree*) shadow, cover. **2** (*a shade of blue*) colour, tint, tone, hue. **3** (*a shade against the light*) screen, shield, cover, blind. ▼

---

put (someone *or* something) in the shade to be much better than (someone or something) (*Her singing puts the rest of the choir in the shade*) <Refers to making someone seem dark by being so much brighter oneself>. **shades of (someone *or* something)** that reminds me of (someone or something) (*The food at the conference reminded me of school dinners. Shades of childhood!*) <It is as though the shade or ghost of someone or something was present>.

---

shadow *n* **1** (*in the shadow of the tree*) shade, cover. **2** (*the shadow of the children on the wall*) silhouette, outline, shape. ▼

---

be worn to a shadow to be made exhausted and thin by overworking (*She is worn to a shadow looking after six young children*). **cast a shadow over (something)** to lessen the happiness or joy of (something) (*Knowing that he was going away cast a shadow over her last meeting with him*).

---

shady *adj* **1** (*sit in a shady part of the garden on a hot day*) shaded, shadowy, sheltered, screened, dark, dim. **2** (*The shop is run by rather a shady character*) suspicious, suspect, questionable, devious, underhand, dishonest, dishonourable.

shake *vb* **1** (*The child shook her piggy bank to hear the coins jingling*) rattle, jolt, jerk. **2** (*The car shook as we drove over the stony roads*) bump, jolt, bounce, rock, roll. **3** (*The child was feverish and was shaking*) shiver, quiver, tremble, quake, shudder. **4** (*Her failure had shaken her confidence for future tournaments*) undermine, lessen, weaken. **5** (*She was obviously shaken by the news of the accident*) disturb, upset, shock, agitate, perturb, disquiet, disconcert. ▼

---

in two shakes of a lamb's tail in an extremely short time (*Your mother will be back in two shakes of a lamb's tail*). **no great shakes** not very good or important (*I think our team is bound to win. The opposition is no great shakes*).

---

shame *n* **1** (*He seemed to feel no shame at his crime*) guilt, remorse, compunction, discomfiture, humiliation. **2** (*It was a shame that it rained on the picnic*) pity, misfortune, bad luck, ill-luck. **3** (*She felt that he had brought shame to the school by* *his action*) disgrace, dishonour, scandal, discredit, disrepute, ignominy.

shape *n* **1** (*children playing with pieces of cardboard of different shapes*) form, formation, outline. **2** (*Help came in the shape of a passing motorist*) form, guise, appearance. **3** (*Put the jelly in shapes*) mould. **4** (*The players must be in good shape for tomorrow's game*) condition, state, fettle, trim. ▼

---

knock (someone *or* **something) into shape** to get (someone or something) into the desired or good condition (*The present office system is chaotic but we will soon knock it into shape*). **shape up** to be developing into the desired state or form (*The new player was not very good to start with but he is shaping up now*).

---

share *n* (*Each of them will receive a share of the profits*) portion, part, quota, percentage, division, allocation.

sharp *adj* **1** (*need a sharp knife to carve the meat*) keen, razor-edged. **2** (*The child was injured by a sharp length of metal*) pointed, spiky. **3** (*She felt a sharp pain in her side*) acute, intense, keen, piercing, stabbing, severe. **4** (*The sauce had rather a sharp taste*) pungent, sour, tart, bitter, biting. **5** (*There is a sharp drop to the sea just there*) steep, sheer, abrupt, precipitous. **6** (*He was sharp enough to realize that they were trying to swindle him*) clever, shrewd, bright, smart, intelligent. **7** (*She sounded rather sharp on the phone*) abrupt, brusque, curt, short. ▼

---

look sharp to be quick (*You had better look sharp if you want to catch that train*). **sharp practice** dishonest dealing (*Their accounts department has been found guilty of sharp practice*).

---

sheer *adj* **1** (*It was sheer stupidity to behave like that*) utter, downright, total, complete, out-and-out. **2** (*It was a sheer drop to the sea*) steep, abrupt, sharp, precipitous.

sheet *n* **1** (*sheet of glass*) piece, length, panel. **2** (*a sheet of ice on the roadway*) layer, coat, coating, cover, covering, film, blanket, carpet. **3** (*sheets of water left after the flood*) expanse, stretch.

shelf *n* (*build a shelf for the books*) ledge. ▼

---

be on the shelf to be unmarried and unlikely to get married because of being old, unattractive, etc (*She has no sense. She thinks that she is on the shelf at 23!*) <A reference to goods that are not sold and so are left on the shelf in a shop>.

---

shield *vb* (*try to shield her eyes from the sun/shield the children from danger*) protect, screen, guard, safeguard.

shine *vb* (*The street lights were shining*) gleam, glow, glint, sparkle, flash, glitter, shimmer.

shiver *vb* (*They began to shiver with cold*) shake, quiver, tremble, shudder, quake.

shock *vb* **1** (*She was shocked by the state of the slum housing*) appal, horrify, outrage, disturb, amaze, astound, traumatize.

short *adj* **1** (*He is too short to reach the branch*) small, tiny, diminutive. **2** (*short holiday/a short relationship*) brief, short-lived, short-term, fleeting, transitory, transient, ephemeral. **3** (*She was asked to write a short account of the incident*) brief, concise, succinct, terse. **4** (*She was rather short on the phone*) sharp, brusque, abrupt, curt. **5** (*Their supply of money is getting a bit short*) deficient, insufficient, scarce, scanty, sparse, meagre, tight. ▼

---

give (someone or something) short shrift to spend very little time or thought on (someone or something) (*She resigned and then asked for her job back but she was given short shrift*). **go short** not to have or take enough of something that one needs (*The mother goes short herself in order to give her children enough food to eat*). **short and sweet** to the point, short and to the point (*When he left the firm his farewell speech was short and sweet*).

---

shot *n* **1** (*hear a shot*) gun-fire, report of a gun, bang, blast, explosion. **2** (*have a shot at winning*) try, attempt, effort, (*inf*) go, (*inf*) stab. **3** (*take shots at trying to hit the target*) turn, opportunity. **4** (*tourists taking shots of the beauty spot*) photograph, photo, snapshot, snap, film. **5** (*have to have several shots before going on a trip to the tropics*) vaccination, inoculation, injection, (*inf*) jab. ▼

---

like a shot very quickly (*They were out of the office like a shot at five o'clock*).

---

shout *vb* (*They shouted to attract his attention/He shouted out in pain*) cry, call, yell, howl, roar, scream, bellow.

show *vb* **1** (*show the new products to the customers*) display, exhibit, present, demonstrate, set forth. **2** (*show them how to use the machine*) demonstrate, point out, explain, teach, instruct. **3** (*He showed his displeasure by leaving the meeting early*) indicate, demonstrate, express, manifest, make known, reveal. **4** (*The effects of his illness are beginning to show*) be visible, be seen, be obvious, appear. **5** (*ushers to show them to their seats at the wedding service*) escort, accompany, guide, usher, conduct. ▼

---

for show for appearance, in order to impress people (*The country's annual military procession is just for show*). **show off** to behave in such a way as to try to impress others with one's possessions, abilities, etc (*The child has just learned to dance and is showing off*).

---

shrewd *adj* (*a shrewd businessman*) astute, clever, smart, sharp.

shrill *adj* (*a shrill voice*) high-pitched, high, sharp, piercing, penetrating, screeching, shrieking.

shrink *vb* **1** (*That blouse might shrink in the wash*) get smaller. **2** (*The market for goods like that will shrink*) grow less, become smaller, contract, diminish, fall off, drop off. **3** (*They shrank from him in fear*) draw back, coil, flinch, cringe.

shut *vb* (*Please shut the door when everyone is here*) close, fasten, secure, lock.

shy *adj* (*She is too shy to say much in public*) bashful, diffident, reserved, reticent, retiring, withdrawn, self-effacing, self-conscious, timid.

sick *adj* **1** (*She has been sick and is off work*) ill, unwell, indisposed, poorly, ailing, below par, (*inf*) under the weather. **2** (*She felt sick on the sea voyage*) nauseated, queasy, bilious. **3** (*He is sick of his present job*) tired, weary, bored, jaded, (*inf*) fed up. **4** (*That was rather a sick joke*) morbid, macabre, ghoulish, gruesome. ▼

---

as sick as a parrot extremely disappointed (*She was as sick as a parrot when she lost the match*).

---

side *n* **1** (*flowers growing by the side of the river*) edge, border, verge. **2** (*the upper side of the desk*) surface, part. **3** (*They live on the north side of the town*) part, area, region, district, quarter, section, neighbourhood. **4** (*discuss all sides of the problem*) aspect, angle, facet, point of view, viewpoint, standpoint. **5** (*on his side in the dispute*) camp, faction, party, group, wing. **6** (*the side that is playing against them tomorrow*) team, squad. ▼

---

on the side in a way other than by means of one's ordinary occupation (*He has a full-time job as a teacher but he earns a bit on the side as a barman*). **side by side** beside one another (*They climbed the hill side by side*). **take sides** to support a particular person, group, etc, against another (*Two of the workers quarrelled and the whole office took sides*).

---

sight *n* **1** (*It was her first sight of the old family house*) view, glimpse. **2** (*The child was told to stay within sight of her parents*) view, range of vision, field of vision. **3** (*Her sight is now poor*) eyesight, vision, eyes, power of sight. **4** (*visitors going on a tour of the town's sights*) spectacle. **5** (*What a sight she was in that hat*) spectacle, eyesore, mess, (*inf*) fright. ▼

---

have one's sights on (something) to try to obtain (something) (*She has set her sights on that big house at the edge of the village*) <A reference to the sight of a gun>.

---

sign *n* **1** (*Her thinness was a sign of her illness*) indication, symptom, evidence, clue. **2** (*a sign indicating the way to the museum*) signpost, notice, placard. **3** (*He gave them a sign to stay still*) signal, gesture, motion, movement, gesticulation. **4** (*mathematical signs*) symbol. **5** (*They believed that they would be given a sign of forthcoming tragedy*) omen, portent, warning, presage.

silent *adj* **1** (*It was very silent on the hills at night*) quiet, hushed, peaceful, tranquil. **2** (*They were completely silent as he told them the news*) speechless, wordless, unspeaking, without speaking, mute, taciturn, mum, uncommunicative. **3** (*She was upset by their silent reproach*) unspoken, wordless, unsaid, unexpressed, tacit, implicit. ▼

---

the silent majority the people who make up most of the population but who rarely make their views known although these are thought to be moderate and reasonable (*The politicians stated that it was time that the silent majority had an influence on the running of the country*).

---

silly *adj* **1** (*She is a very silly person*) foolish, stupid, irresponsible, giddy, frivolous, immature. **2** (*It was a very silly thing to do*) foolish, stupid, senseless, idiotic, unwise, foolhardy, irresponsible, ridiculous, absurd. ▼

---

the silly season a period of the year, usually late summer, when the newspapers carry a great deal of unimportant stories in the absence of important news (*There's a story here about a funny-shaped potato. It must be the silly season*).

---

simple *adj* **1** (*It was a very simple task*) easy, uncomplicated, elementary, straightforward, effortless. **2** (*You will have to explain it to them in simple language*) plain, uncomplicated, clear, straightforward, direct, intelligible. **3** (*They are wealthy but lead a very simple life*) ordinary, modest, unpretentious, humble. **4** (*She was a simple peasant girl*) unsophisticated, innocent, naive, ingenuous, inexperienced. **5** (*The boy is a bit simple*) simple-minded, feeble-minded, backward, retarded.

sin *n* (*They will be punished for their sin*) wrong, wrongdoing, evil, evildoing, badness, crime, offence, immorality.

sincere *adj* **1** (*Her apology was obviously sincere*) genuine, real, true, honest, wholehearted, heartfelt.

single *adj* **1** (*Only a single flower was left blooming*) sole, solitary, one, lone, isolated, by itself. **2** (*He is still single*) unmarried, unwed, unattached, free.

sink *vb* **1** (*The ship began to sink*) go under, submerge, founder, capsize. **2** (*He sank to his knees to ask forgiveness*) fall, drop, slump. **3** (*The invalid is thought to be sinking rapidly*) decline, deteriorate, fail, fade.

sit *vb* **1** (*The audience were asked to sit*) sit down, take a seat, be seated. **2** (*Their suitcases were sitting on the pavement*) be placed, be situated. **3** (*Parliament was sitting all night*) be in session, meet, assemble. **4** (*We require a table that sits twelve people*) seat, accommodate, hold, have room for.

situation *n* **1** (*a cottage in a picturesque situation*) place, position, location, setting, site. **2** (*The firm is in an unstable financial situation*) circumstances, state, state of affairs, condition, predicament. **3** (*There is a vacant situation in the accounts department*) post, position, job, place.

size *n* (*measure the size of the room*) dimensions, measurements, proportions, area, extent. ▼

---

size up (someone *or* **something)** to consider carefully and form an opinion of the worth, nature, etc, of (someone or something) (*You should size up the employment position before you leave your job*).

---

skilful *adj* (*He is a very skilful carpenter*) skilled, able, good, competent, adept, accomplished, expert, deft, masterly.

slack *adj* **1** (*She has lost a lot of weight and her clothes are now slack*) loose, baggy. **2** (*Since he stopped exercising his muscles have got slack*) limp, flabby, flaccid. **3** (*Business is slack just now*) slow, quiet, inactive, sluggish. **4** (*The pupils have got rather slack about their work*) negligent, neglectful, remiss, careless, slapdash, slipshod.

slap *vb* (*She slapped his face*) strike, hit, whack, cuff (*inf*) wallop. ▼

---

a slap on the wrist a reprimand (*She will get a slap on the wrist for forgetting to give the boss the message*).

---

sleep *n* (*have a short sleep after lunch*) nap, doze, rest, (*inf*) snooze, (*inf*) forty winks. ▼

---

sleep like a log to sleep extremely soundly (*I didn't hear a noise in the night. I slept like a log*). **put (something) to sleep** to kill (an animal) painlessly because it is incurably ill, etc (*The vet put the dog to sleep when it lost the use of its legs*).

---

sleepy *adj* **1** (*She had not had much rest and was feeling sleepy*) tired, drowsy, lethargic, sluggish. **2** (*a sleepy little village*) quiet, peaceful, inactive.

slight *adj* **1** (*There had been a slight improvement*) small, little, minute, subtle, modest. **2** (*slight matters*) unimportant, minor, insignificant, trifling, trivial. **3** (*She was very slight*) slightly built, slender, slim, small, delicate.

slip *vb* **1** (*The old lady slipped on the ice and broke her leg*) slide, skid, slither, lose one's footing. **2** (*The cup slipped from her grasp*) fall, slide, drop. **3** (*She became upset and slipped from the room*) steal, creep, sneak. **4** (*She just had time to slip on some clothes*) put on, pull on. **5** (*Some people think that educational standards have slipped*) drop, fall, decline, deteriorate, degenerate. ▼

---

give (someone) the slip to succeed in escaping from or evading (someone) (*The escaped prisoner gave the police the slip*). **let (something) slip** to say or reveal (something) accidentally (*I'm sorry that I let slip that you're leaving*).

---

slope *n* **1** (*The floors of the building are on a slight slope*) slant, angle, inclination, tilt, dip. **2** (*They had picnic on a grassy slope*) hill, hillock, bank, rise.

slow *adj* **1** (*They moved along at a very slow pace*) slow-moving, leisurely, unhurried, dawdling, snail-like. **2** (*Getting planning permission can be a slow process*) slow-moving, drawn-out, long-drawn-out, prolonged, protracted, time-consuming. **3** (*pupils who are rather slow*) slow-witted, backward, retarded, stupid, unintelligent. **4** (*Business is rather slow*) slack, quiet, sluggish.

sly *adj* (*It is difficult to know what he is doing—he is very sly*) cunning, crafty, wily, artful, sneaky, devious, underhand, scheming, shifty, furtive.

small *adj* **1** (*The child is very small for her age*) little, tiny, slight, short, diminutive, under-sized, (*inf*) pint-sized. **2** (*It was just a small mistake*) slight, minor, unimportant, insignificant, trifling, trivial. **3** (*He is rich and powerful* *but came from small beginnings*) humble, low, lowly, modest, poor, inferior. ▼

---

make (someone) look small to make (someone) seem foolish or insignificant (*He made her look small by criticizing her in front of the whole school*).
small talk light conversation about unimportant or light-hearted matters (*He always talks about his work. He has absolutely no small talk*).

---

smart *adj* **1** (*You must try to look smart for your job interview*) well-dressed, elegant, neat, spruce, (*inf*) natty. **2** (*The child is smart for her age*) clever, bright, intelligent, sharp. ▼

---

a smart aleck someone who thinks that he or she is very clever and acts as though this were the case (*He is such a smart aleck that he tried to teach us our jobs when we have been doing them for years*).
look smart to be quick, to act swiftly (*You will have to look smart if you are to catch the last bus*).

---

smash *vb* **1** (*She smashed several plates when washing up*) break, shatter. **2** (*He smashed his father's car*) crash, wreck, collide. **3** (*Our hopes of success were smashed*) shatter, ruin, wreck.
smell *n* **1** (*the smell of roses*) scent, perfume, fragrance. **2** (*The smell of freshly baked bread*) aroma, odour. **3** (*The smell of rotting meat*) stink, stench. ▼

---

smell a rat to have a suspicion that something is wrong or that one is being deceived (*I smelled a rat when she did not ask me into the house*) <A reference to a terrier hunting rats>.

---

smooth *adj* **1** (*smooth surfaces*) even, level, flat, plane. **2** (*The sea was very smooth*) calm, still, flat, tranquil. **3** (*He is responsible for the smooth running of the firm*) trouble-free, steady, regular, effortless. **4** (*young men with smooth faces*) clean-shaven, hairless. **5** (*She was approached in the shop by a smooth salesman*) smooth-tongued, suave, glib, urbane, courteous, gracious.
smother *vb* **1** (*She was accused of trying to smother the old lady with a pillow*) suffocate, stifle, asphyxiate. **2** (*She tried to smother a giggle*) suppress, stifle, muffle.
snag *n* (*He did not see the possible snags in his plans*) drawback, hitch, catch, obstacle, stumbling-block.
snap *vb* **1** (*The branch suddenly snapped*) break, splinter, fracture, crack. **2** (*She snapped her fingers*) click, crack. **3** (*The dog snapped at our ankles*) bite, snarl, growl. **4** (*She was tired and began to snap at the children*) speak irritably, shout, growl, snarl. **5** (*She was behaving very calmly and then she suddenly snapped*) collapse, break down.
snatch *vb* **1** (*She was late and had to snatch a piece of toast from the table and run for the bus*) grab, seize, take hold of. **2** (*The thief snatched my handbag at the airport*) rob, steal, make off with. **3** (*They snatched the millionaire's child and demanded a ransom*) kidnap, abduct, seize, grab.
sneer *vb* (*sneering at her attempts*)

smirk, snicker, snigger, scoff, scorn, mock, jeer.

snobbish *adj* (*She has a very snobbish attitude towards people who are badly off*) arrogant, haughty, proud, disdainful, condescending, supercilious, (*inf*) snooty, (*inf*) uppity.

soak *vb* **1** (*They got soaked in the storm*) drench, wet through, saturate. **2** (*soak the dress in cold water to remove the stain*) steep, immerse. **3** (*blood soaking through the bandage*) penetrate, permeate.

sob *vb* (*She began to sob as her mother left*) weep, cry, wail.

sociable *adj* **1** (*Our neighbours are very sociable people*) friendly, affable, social, gregarious, communicative, outgoing.

soft *adj* **1** (*The car got stuck in soft mud*) spongy, mushy. **2** (*The ground by the river was very soft*) swampy, spongy, boggy. **3** (*soft substances such as plasticine*) pliable, pliant, flexible, malleable. **4** (*a dress of a soft material*) smooth, silky, velvety. **5** (*dresses in soft colours*) pale, light, pastel, muted, subdued, restrained. **6** (*The lighting in the room was very soft*) low, dim, faint, muted, subdued. **7** (*She spoke in a soft voice so that the others would not hear*) quiet, hushed, low, faint, whispered. **8** (*parents accused of being too soft with their children*) lenient, indulgent, easygoing, permissive, liberal. ▼

---

a soft touch (*inf*) someone who is easily taken advantage of, deceived, etc (*He would lend money to anyone who asked him. He's a really soft touch*).

soft option a choice or alternative that is easier or more pleasant than the others on offer (*At school camp there was a choice of climbing the mountain or walking along the river bank and many of the children went for the soft option*).

---

soil *n* **1** (*The soil is very poor in that area*) earth, ground, dirt. **2** (*troops killed on foreign soil*) land, country.

solemn *adj* **1** (*She wore a solemn expression*) grave, serious, unsmiling, sombre. **2** (*It was a solemn occasion*) serious, grave, important, formal, grand, stately, dignified, ceremonious. **3** (*a solemn promise*) earnest, sincere, genuine, honest.

solid *adj* **1** (*a solid rather than a liquid substance*) firm, hard, dense, thick. **2** (*jewellery made of solid gold*) pure, unalloyed, complete. **3** (*solid houses made of stone and built to last*) substantial, strong, sturdy.

solitary *adj* (*He leads a solitary life with no family or friends*) lonely, lonesome, friendless, unsociable. **2** (*A solitary tree in the barren landscape*) single, lone, sole, by oneself/itself.

solution *n* **1** (*unable to find the solution to the mathematical problem*) answer, result, resolution. **2** (*a solution of salt and water*) suspension, mixture.

soothe *vb* **1** (*an ointment to soothe the painful sunburn*) ease, alleviate, assuage, lessen, reduce. **2** (*He tried to soothe the crying baby*) quieten, calm, pacify.

sophisticated *adj* **1** (*She regards herself as being a sophisticated city-dweller*) worldly, experienced, cultivated, cultured, urbane, suave, cosmopolitan. **2** (*an office equipped with sophisticated electronic *equipment*) advanced, complex, complicated, elaborate.

sore *adj* **1** (*She has a sore patch on her arm*) painful, in pain, aching, tender, raw, smarting, inflamed, bruised. **2** (*people in sore need of somewhere to live*) urgent, pressing, desperate, critical, dire.

sorry *adj* **1** (*He is not at all sorry for his misdeeds*) apologetic, regretful, ashamed, repentant, penitent, remorseful, contrite. **2** (*We were sorry to hear that she was ill*) sad, unhappy, distressed, regretful. **3** (*They felt sorry for the homeless people*) sympathetic, compassionate, full of pity, moved.

sort *n* (*several different sorts of vegetable/a new sort of computer*) kind, variety, type, class, category, make, brand. ▼

---

it takes all sorts to make a world a saying indicating that one should be tolerant of all people, whatever they are like (*The new neighbours seem a bit odd to us but I suppose it takes all sorts to make a world*). **out of sorts** not feeling very well, not in a very good mood (*He has been out of sorts since he has had the flu*).

---

sound *n* **1** (*There was not a sound from the children's room*) noise. **2** (*The sound of someone playing the recorder*) noise, music. **3** (*We did not like the sound of their plans for improvement*) impression, idea.

sour *adj* **1** (*a sauce that was rather sour*) tart, acid, bitter, sharp. **2** (*milk that had turned sour*) curdled, bad, rancid, off. **3** (*He is a sour old man*) ill-tempered, disagreeable, irritable, cross.

space *n* **1** (*travel in space*) outer space, infinity. **2** (*large pieces of furniture that take up a great deal of space*) room, expanse, area, scope. **3** (*There was only a narrow space between each house*) gap, interval, opening, break. **4** (*There is a space on the form to explain why you want the job*) blank space, blank, empty space, gap. **5** (*They both died within the space of two years*) time, period, span, interval, duration. **6** (*There are no spaces left on the course*) place, room.

spare *adj* **1** (*take a spare pair of socks*) extra, additional, reserve, supplementary, surplus. **2** (*She works long hours and has little spare time*) free, unoccupied, leisure.

sparse *adj* (*a sparse covering of grass*) scanty, meagre, slight.

spasm *n* **1** (*He is in agony with stomach spasms*) contraction, cramp. **2** (*limb spasms*) twitching, convulsion. **3** (*a sudden spasm of coughing*) fit, paroxysm, convulsion, bout, attack.

speak *vb* **1** (*Did he speak the truth?*) say, tell, state, utter, voice, express, pronounce. **2** (*The two sisters quarrelled and have not spoken to each other for years*) talk to, converse with, communicate with, chat. **3** (*The lecturer is to speak for an hour*) talk, lecture, deliver a speech.

special *adj* **1** (*We were asked to take special care of the book*) especial, particular, exceptional, extra special. **2** (*It was a special occasion for the old people*) unusual, exceptional, remarkable. out-of-the ordinary, notable, outstanding, memorable, significant, important, momentous.

spectacular *adj* (*a spectacular*

firework display) striking, remarkable, impressive, magnificent, splendid, sensational, breathtaking, dramatic.

speech *n* **1** (*the power of speech*) talk, communication. **2** (*He was drunk and his speech was slurred*) diction, enunciation, pronunciation. **3** (*He gave a speech thanking everyone*) talk, lecture, address.

speed *n* **1** (*the speed at which they were going*) rate. **2** (*They moved with amazing speed*) rapidity, swiftness, fastness, quickness, haste, hurry.

spend *vb* **1** (*They will have to spend a great deal of money on that house*) pay out, lay out, expend, (*inf*) fork out, (*inf*) shell out. **2** (*They spend hours on the beach*) pass, while away, fill, occupy. **3** (*A great deal of effort was spent on the task*) use, employ, apply, devote.

spill *vb* (*Water was spilling from the bucket as she walked*) flow, pour, overflow, brim over, run over, slop over.

spirit *n* **1** (*His spirit was troubled*) soul, psyche, inner self. **2** (*They were people of determined spirit*) character, temperament, disposition, quality. **2** (*He required spirit to undertake the journey*) courage, bravery, mettle, pluck, determination. **4** (*The children performed the play with spirit*) liveliness, animation, enthusiasm, energy, vivacity, verve.

spite *n* (*She damaged her friend's bike out of spite*) malice, maliciousness, ill-will, hostility, resentment, vindictiveness.

splendid *adj* **1** (*We had a splendid holiday*) excellent, fine, first-class, superb, marvellous, wonderful, great. **2** (*a splendid royal palace*) magnificent, sumptuous, imposing, impressive, glorious, luxurious.

split *vb* **1** (*split the logs for the fire*) break, chop, cut. **2** (*The plate seemed just to split in two*) break, snap, splinter. **3** (*The robbers split the profits from the burglary amongst themselves*) divide, share, apportion, distribute. **4** (*The argument over the local school split the village into two groups*) divide, separate. **5** (*The couple have split up*) separate, part, divorce, break up.

spoil *vb* **1** (*a substance that spoiled the surface of the table*) damage, mar, impair, blemish, deface, ruin, destroy. **2** (*She spoils her daughter*) over-indulge, indulge, pamper, cosset, coddle, mollycoddle.

spot *n* **1** (*spots of soot on the washing on the line*) mark, speck, fleck, dot, smudge, stain, blotch. **2** (*get ointment for the spots on her chin*) pimple, pustule, boil, blemish. **3** (*a pleasant spot for a country cottage*) place, area, location, site, situation, setting.

spread *vb* **1** (*They spread rumours*) circulate, disseminate, transmit, propagate, publicize. **2** (*Feeling against the new road is spreading*) extend, increase, proliferate, escalate, mushroom. **3** (*The farmer spread fertilizer on the fields*) lay, put, apply, cover. **4** (*The bird spread its wings and flew off*) stretch, extend, open out, unfurl.

squeeze *vb* **1** (*squeeze limes to make a cool drink*) squash, crush, compress. **2** (*She squeezed his arm to attract his attention*) pinch, press, grip. **3** (*She squeezed the water from the dress and hung it up*) wring, twist, press. **4** (*They squeezed the water from the wet* *sweaters*) extract, press, force, express. **5** (*The speaker was so popular that the audience was squeezed into the hall*) crush, squash, pack, crowd, cram, jam, wedge.

stage *n* **1** (*the stages in the production process*) point, step, period, level, phase. **2** (*the first stage of the journey*) lap, leg, phase. **3** (*She was too nervous to go on the stage*) platform, dais, rostrum, podium.

stand *vb* **1** (*The audience was asked to stand*) rise, get to one's feet, get up, be upright, be erect, be vertical. **2** (*The block of flats that used to stand here*) be, be situated, be located. **3** (*stand the bookcase against the wall near the fireplace*) place, put, position, erect, set up. **4** (*They appealed against the judge's ruling but the sentence stood*) remain, stay, hold, hold good, prevail. **5** (*She cannot stand loud noise*) put up with, tolerate, bear, endure, abide.

start *vb* **1** (*before the war started*) begin, commence, get underway, come into being. **2** (*start the machine*) turn on, put on, set in motion, activate. **3** (*She started a new society*) begin, commence, set up, establish, found, launch.

state *n* **1** (*a system in a state of chaos*) condition, situation, circumstances, position, state of affairs, predicament. **2** (*She was in a tearful state*) condition, mood, humour, frame of mind. **3** (*His mother got into a state when he did not come home*) panic, fluster, (*inf*) flap. **4** (*occasions of state attended by the queen*) pomp, ceremony, majesty, grandeur. **5** (*the various states in the world*) country, nation, land.

state *vb* (*state their reasons for going*) express, voice, utter, say, declare, tell, announce.

stay *vb* **1** (*They left but we decided to stay*) remain, wait, linger. **2** (*She stayed angry a long time*) remain, continue. **3** (*They stayed at a small hotel*) put up, reside.

steady *adj* **1** (*drive at a steady pace*) uniform, even, regular, consistent. **2** (*try to keep the table steady on the moving ship*) stable, immovable, unmoving, motionless. **3** (*her steady love for him*) constant, unchanging, unfaltering, continuous, endless. **4** (*require a steady young person for the job*) sensible, level-headed, calm, reliable.

step *n* **1** (*take one step nearer the sea*) stride. **2** (*She listened for her father's steps on the stairs*) footstep, footfall, tread. **3** (*She took a rash step*) act, course of action, move, deed. **4** (*looking for the next step in his promotion*) stage, level, grade, rank, degree. **5** (*a rotten step on the ladder*) rung, tread.

stick *vb* **1** (*The child began to stick the pictures in a book*) glue, paste, gum, attach, fix, pin, tack. **2** (*She stuck a knife in the meat to see if it was cooked*) thrust, push, jab, poke, insert. **3** (*The machine has stuck*) jam, stop, halt, come to a halt.

stiff *adj* **1** (*a piece of stiff card*) rigid, hard, unyielding, inflexible. **2** (*Her muscles are stiff after the long climb*) tight, tense, taut. **3** (*The robbers received a stiff sentence*) severe, harsh, hard, heavy, drastic, stringent. **4** (*She was rather stiff when we arrived*) formal, cold, aloof.

still *adj* **1** (*It was a still day*) calm, windless. **2** (*They were asked to *stay completely still*) motionless, immobile, stationary. **3** (*The house was still*) quiet, peaceful, silent, hushed.

stop *vb* **1** (*They tried to stop the fight*) bring to a halt, halt, end, finish, terminate, bring to a standstill, wind up. **2** (*She could not stop shivering*) refrain from, desist, cease, leave, hinder, impede, obstruct.

story *n* **1** (*a story about dragons*) tale, fairy story, myth, legend, fable. **2** (*the story of how he got home*) account, report.

straight *adj* **1** (*The picture is not straight*) level, in line. **2** (*a straight line*) uncurving, unbent. **3** (*They would not give a straight answer*) direct, forthright, frank, candid, honest, sincere.

strange *adj* **1** (*It was a strange sight*) peculiar, odd, queer, bizarre, weird. **2** (*a market stocking strange fruits*) exotic, foreign, alien, unfamiliar.

strong *adj* **1** (*require someone strong to lift the heavy furniture*) powerful, muscular, well-built, burly, sturdy, strapping, robust. **2** (*strong doors at the castle entrance*) solid, heavy, sturdy. **3** (*They have a very strong argument against closing the station*) sound, powerful, cogent, compelling. **4** (*There is a strong similarity between the two styles*) marked, noticeable, pronounced, distinct, definite, striking. **5** (*They have strong feelings on the subject of education*) intense, fervent, passionate. **6** (*wearing strong colours*) bright, vivid, deep, intense. **7** (*strong coffee*) concentrated. **8** (*take strong measures*) active, firm, severe, drastic, extreme.

stupid *adj* **1** (*He is too stupid to follow the instructions*) unintelligent, thick, dense, dim, dull-witted, foolish. **2** (*It was a stupid thing to do*) foolish, absurd, silly, idiotic, unwise, unintelligent.

suggest *vb* **1** (*suggest a plan of action*) propose, put forward, recommend, advocate. **2** (*What are you suggesting?*) hint at, insinuate, imply.

suit *vb* **1** (*find a time for the meeting that suits both of them*) be suitable for, be convenient for. **2** (*a style of dress that does not suit her*) become. **3** (*You must try to suit your speech to the occasion*) fit, tailor, adapt, adjust. ▼

---

suit oneself to do as one wishes (*We have all decided to go to the meeting but you can suit yourself*).

---

suitable *adj* **1** (*The books are not suitable for the course*) suited, right, appropriate, apt, in keeping with. **2** (*come at a suitable time*) convenient, acceptable.

supply *n* (*have a supply of fuel for the winter*) store, stock, reserve, pile, mass, heap, hoard, stockpile.

supply *vb* (*They supply us with fuel*) give, provide, furnish, equip.

support *vb* **1** (*the uprights that support the bridge*) bear, prop up, hold up, shore up, underpin. **2** (*He supported the local candidate in the election*) back, champion, assist, aid, help, be on the side of, vote for. **3** (*support the cause of animal rights*) back, champion, promote, further, favour, defend. **4** (*evidence to support his point of view*) back, bear out, substantiate, corroborate, confirm. **5** (*She works long hours to support the family*) maintain, provide for, look after, sustain.

suppose *vb* (*I suppose he will get there as soon as he can*) assume, presume, think, believe, expect, imagine.

sure *adj* **1** (*The police have to be sure that he is guilty*) certain, definite, positive, convinced, confident. **2** (*He felt that the project was a sure winner*) certain, definite, guaranteed, inevitable, (*inf*) in the bag. **3** (*a sure remedy for warts*) certain, unfailing, infallible, reliable, dependable.

suspicious *adj* **1** (*We are a bit suspicious of his story*) doubtful, distrustful, mistrustful, sceptical, disbelieving. **2** (*The circumstances of the case are rather suspicious*) odd, strange, queer, questionable, (*inf*) fishy. **3** (*a house now occupied by a suspicious character*) shady, shifty.

sweet *adj* **1** (*children who love sweet foods*) sugary, syrupy. **2** (*the sweet smell of roses*) fragrant, perfumed, scented. **3** (*the sweet sound of the flute*) musical, tuneful, dulcet, melodious. **4** (*What a sweet little girl*) delightful, charming, appealing, attractive. **5** (*She was always very sweet to us*) charming, pleasant, friendly, generous, kind, kindly, amiable.

sympathy *n* **1** (*They expressed their sympathy to the widow*) compassion, commiseration, pity, condolence, support, concern, consideration. **2** (*They have some sympathy for the cause of the protesters*) good will, approval, favour, support.

synthetic *adj* (*objects made of synthetic material*) man-made, manufactured, artificial, fake, mock.

system *n* **1** (*the public transport system*) structure, organization, arrangement, set-up. **2** (*a new system for filing information*) method, process, means, technique.

T

table *n* **1** (*pupils doing their homework at a table*) counter, bench, desk. **2** (*a book containing many tables*) diagram, chart, figure. **3** (*a table of contents at the front of the book*) list, catalogue, index. ▼

---

turn the tables on (someone) to change a situation so that one gains the advantage over (someone) after having been at a disadvantage (*Their team kept beating us but we soon turned the tables on them when we got two really good players*) <From the medieval game of tables, of which backgammon is a form, in which turning the board round would exactly reverse the position of the players>.

---

tablet *n* **1** (*take tablets for a headache*) pill, capsule. **2** (*The hotel provided tablets of soap*) bar, cake.

tackle *vb* (*He is going to tackle the job alone*) deal with, undertake, attempt, take on, apply oneself to.

tactful *adj* (*You will have to be tactful as she is very sensitive*) diplomatic, discreet, delicate, subtle, sensitive.

tactics *npl* (*They used dishonest tactics to win*) strategy, manoeuvres, scheme, plan, policy.

tail *n* **1** (*a fox's tail*) brush, scut. **2** (*We were at the tail of the queue*) end, rear, back. **3** (*The police were on his tail*) trail, scent.

tail *vb* **1** (*police tailing the crook*) follow, shadow, stalk. **2** (*Business tails off at the end of autumn*) dwindle, decrease, drop off, fall away, peter out, die away. ▼

---

with one's tail between one's legs in an ashamed, miserable or defeated state (*The children went home with their tails between their legs when the farmer scolded them for stealing apples*) <From the behaviour of an unhappy dog>.

---

take *vb* **1** (*The child took his mother's hand*) take hold of, grasp, seize, grip, grab, clutch, **2** (*The soldiers took several prisoners*) seize, catch, capture, arrest. **3** (*Someone has taken the teacher's pen*) remove, go off with, pick up, move, steal, (*inf*) pinch. **4** (*She took her sister to the pictures*) escort, accompany, conduct, guide. **5** (*The journey takes two hours*) take up, use, need, require, call for. **6** (*The bus will take you right there*) transport, carry, convey. **7** (*He took the books to school with him*) carry, bear, fetch, convey. **8** (*She decided to take the red dress*) choose, pick, select, buy, purchase. **9** (*She took the bad news well*) receive, accept, deal with, cope with. **10** (*She takes Latin at school*) study, learn, be taught. **11** (*I take it that you do not agree*) understand, gather, assume, believe. ▼

---

be taken with (someone *or* **something)** to find (someone or something) attractive or pleasing) (*They were quite taken with the unusual coffee table*). **take after (someone)** to resemble (someone) (*She takes after her father*). **take (someone) in** to deceive (someone) (*She really took the old lady in by pretending to be a social worker*).

---

tale *n* **1** (*a fairy tale*) story, anecdote, legend, fable, narrative. **2** (*We hear tales of his bad behaviour*) talk, rumour, gossip. ▼

---

tell its own tale to indicate clearly what had happened (*The charred remains of the house told their own tale*).

---

talented *adj* (*They are very talented musicians*) gifted, accomplished, able, capable, expert.

talk *vb* **1** (*The children were scolded for talking in class*) speak, express oneself, communicate, chatter, chat, gossip. **2** (*He was talking nonsense*) speak, say, utter, voice. **3** (*People are talking about her wild behaviour*) gossip, comment, spread rumours.

talk *n* **1** (*The lecturer gave an interesting talk*) lecture, speech, address. **2** (*She wanted to have a talk with him about her career*) chat, discussion, conversation, tête à tête, (*inf*) confab. ▼

---

the talk of the town someone or something that is the subject of general conversation or gossip (*His disgraceful behaviour is the talk of the town*).

---

talkative *adj* (*so talkative that no one else gets a chance to say anything*) garrulous, loquacious, voluble.

tall *adj* **1** (*Many good basketball players are tall*) big. **2** (*a town with many tall buildings*) high, lofty, towering. ▼

---

a tall story a story which is extremely unlikely to be true (*His latest tall story is that he saw a man from Mars*).

---

tame *adj* (*The animal is quite tame*) domesticated, gentle.

tamper *vb* (*Someone had tampered with the papers on her desk*) interfere with, meddle with, fiddle with.

tangled *adj* **1** (*tangled hair/tangled wool*) entangled, twisted, knotted, matted. **2** (*tangled financial affairs*) confused, muddled, jumbled, complicated, involved.

tap *vb* **1** (*tap on the door*) knock, rap, bang. **2** (*Someone tapped me on the shoulder*) touch, pat.

target *n* **1** (*The archer failed to hit the target*) mark, bull's eye. **2** (*The target for the appeal is £50, 000*) goal, aim, objective. **3** (*The new girl is the target of all their teasing*) butt, victim, scapegoat.

task *n* (*tasks to be done around the house*) job, chore, duty, assignment.

take (someone) to task to reprimand or criticize (someone) (*The teacher took the student to task for his untidy homework*).

taste *n* **1** (*The pudding had an odd taste*) flavour, tang. **2** (*her taste in literature*) like, liking, preference, inclination, predilection. **3** (*a house furnished with great taste*) stylishness, elegance, refinement, discrimination.

tasteless *adj* **1** (*The soup was tasteless*) flavourless, bland, insipid, watery. **2** (*tasteless Christmas decorations*) vulgar, tawdry, flashy, garish. **3** (*She made a few tasteless remarks*) unseemly, indelicate, vulgar.

teach *vb* **1** (*She teaches the younger children*) educate, give lessons to, instruct, coach, train. **2** (*He teaches history*) give lessons in, give instruction in. **3** (*His father taught him how to ride a bike*) instruct, train, show.

tease *vb* **1** (*The cat will scratch you if you tease it*) torment, annoy, bother, provoke. **2** (*She was upset by his remark but he was only teasing*) joke, fool.

technique *n* **1** (*The tennis player is trying out a new technique*) method, system, approach, way, strategy. **2** (*We admired the technique of the sculptor*) skill, expertise, artistry, proficiency, knack.

tedious *adj* (*The work is tedious*) boring, monotonous, dull, wearisome.

tell *vb* **1** (*We told them the news*) inform, make known, impart, communicate, announce, disclose, declare. **2** (*He told the children a story*) recount, relate, narrate. **3** (*The children were told to go home*) instruct, order, command, direct. **4** (*They know her secret but promised not to tell*) tell tales, blab, give the game away, let the cat out of the bag, (*inf*) spill the beans, (*inf*) grass. **5** (*We could not tell which twin was which*) distinguish, differentiate. ▼

---

tell tales to report someone's wrongdoing to someone in authority (*Don't mention to her that I've torn my jacket. She'll tell tales to my mother*). **you're telling me!** that is definitely the case (*You're telling me it is a difficult job!*).

---

temper *n* **1** (*She is in a temper*) bad mood, ill humour, rage, fury, tantrum. **2** (*He is of uncertain temper*) temperament, disposition, nature, character, mood. **3** (*She lost her temper*) composure, self-control, coolness, calm, good humour.

temperamental *adj* (*She is a good worker but she is very temperamental*) excitable, emotional, volatile, moody.

temporary *adj* **1** (*They have got temporary jobs*) short-term, provisional, impermanent. **2** (*His interest in golf was only temporary*) short-lived, brief, fleeting, ephemeral, transient.

tempt *vb* (*She was on a diet but was tempted by the sight of the chocolates*) entice, lure, attract, seduce.

tendency *n* **1** (*They have a tendency to tell lies*) inclination, leaning, propensity. **2** (*The upward tendency of the temperature graph*) movement, direction, trend, bias.

tender *adj* **1** (*The meat was tender*) not tough, juicy, succulent, soft. **2** (*She has a tender area on her head*) sore, painful, aching, irritated, inflamed. **3** (*The old man seems fierce but has a tender heart*) compassionate, soft-hearted, kind, sympathetic, caring, gentle. ▼

---

leave (someone *or* **something) to (someone's) tender mercies** to leave (someone or something) in the care of someone who is inefficient, careless, nasty, etc (*I wouldn't leave my car to his tender mercies. He is a terrible driver*).

---

tense *adj* **1** (*They are feeling tense as they wait for the results of the* *exam*) strained, under a strain, under pressure, overwrought, distraught, worked up, anxious, uneasy. **2** (*You have to keep the rope tense*) tight, taut, rigid, stretched, strained.

tentative *adj* **1** (*The toddler took a few tentative steps*) hesitant, hesitating, faltering, uncertain, cautious. **2** (*She asked if she could make a tentative suggestion*) speculative, exploratory, experimental, trial, untried.

term *n* **1** (*a document full of technical terms*) word, expression, phrase, name, title. **2** (*the mayor's term of office*) period, time, spell, interval, duration. ▼

---

come to terms with (something) to accept (something) as inevitable and try to cope with it as well as one can.

---

terrible *adj* **1** (*refugees who endured terrible hardship*) dreadful, appalling, shocking, horrible, horrific, grim. **2** (*the terrible heat from the fire*) extreme, severe, intolerable. **3** (*There was a terrible smell from the drains*) nasty, foul, vile, offensive, obnoxious. **4** (*He is a terrible dancer*) very bad, poor, incompetent, useless, dreadful, (*inf*) rotten.

terrify *vb* (*Walking through the churchyard at night would terrify her*) frighten, scare, alarm, petrify, terrorize.

terror *n* **1** (*She was gripped with terror when she heard noise*) fear, dread, alarm, panic. **2** (*That boy's a little terror*) rascal, rogue, imp, hooligan.

test *n* **1** (*The children are having an English test*) exam, examination. **2** (*a hearing test*) examination, check, assessment, appraisal, investigation, exploration. **3** (*the test of a successful film*) criterion, touchstone, yardstick, standard, measure.

test *vb* **1** (*test the child's hearing*) examine, check, assess, appraise, investigate, explore, analyse. **2** (*The children's behaviour really tested his patience*) try, tax, strain. **3** (*test the car*) try out, try.

text *n* **1** (*The text of his speech was world poverty*) topic, subject, subject matter, theme. **2** (*in the introduction, not in the text of the book*) body, main part. **3** (*He is responsible for the text but not the illustrations of the book*) words.

thankful *adj* (*Her parents were thankful that she was safe*) grateful, full of gratitude, appreciative, relieved.

thaw *vb* (*The ice began to thaw*) melt, defrost, liquefy.

theft *n* (*There have been a series of thefts from shops*) stealing, robbery, thieving, burglary, larceny, pilfering, (*inf*) pinching.

theoretical *adj* (*He was describing a theoretical situation rather than an actual one*) hypothetical, speculative, assumed.

thick *adj* **1** (*Thick snow lay on the roads*) deep. **2** (*She was reading a very thick book*) fat, substantial. **3** (*She thinks that she has thick legs*) broad, wide, fat, large, solid. **4** (*a thick rope to tie up the logs*) strong, stout, sturdy. **5** (*A thick mist descended*) dense, heavy, sold. **6** (*a voice thick with emotion*) husky, gruff, hoarse, rough, guttural, throaty. **7** (*He is too thick to understand the instructions*) stupid, dense, unintelligent, dim, dull-witted. ▼

---

thick and fast in great quantities and at a fast rate (*Entries *for the competition are coming in thick and fast*). **through thick and thin** no matter what difficulties or dangers arise (*He has vowed to support his leader through thick and thin*).

---

thief *n* (*The thief got away with his watch*) robber, pickpocket, burglar, housebreaker, larcenist.

thin *adj* **1** (*She is thin and ill-looking*) underweight, skinny, scrawny, emaciated, gaunt, skeletal, anorexic. **2** (*She is on a diet to try to get thin*) slim, slender, svelte, light. **3** (*a design formed of thin lines*) fine, narrow, delicate. **4** (*a dress made of a very thin material*) light, lightweight, delicate, flimsy, sheer, filmy. **5** (*She is worried about having thin hair*) sparse, scanty, wispy. **6** (*The custard was too thin*) dilute, watery, runny. **7** (*They had hoped for a large crowd but the audience was rather thin*) sparse, scarce, scanty, meagre. **8** (*rather a thin voice*) weak, low, feeble, faint. **9** (*It was rather a thin excuse*) flimsy, weak, feeble, poor, unconvincing, inadequate. ▼

---

be as thin as a rake to be extremely thin (*She keeps dieting but she is already as thin as a rake*). **be thin on top** to be going bald (*He often wears a hat to hide the fact that he is thin on top*).

---

thing *n* **1** (*There was a huge pile of things on the table*) article, item, object. **2** (*It was a sensible thing to do*) action, act, deed, undertaking. **3** (*It was a dreadful thing to happen*) incident, event, occurrence, happening. **4** (*Calmness is a useful thing to have in a crisis*) quality, characteristic, attribute, trait. **5** (*There are a few things which we should discuss*) fact, point, detail, particular. **6** (*The poor thing had nowhere to go*) wretch, creature. **7** (*She has a thing about spiders*) phobia, fear, aversion, dislike, horror. ▼

---

just one of those things something that just has to be accepted (*Our flight has been delayed but that is just one of those things*). **see things** to imagine that one sees something or someone that is not there (*She must be seeing things. She says there was a woman dressed in black in her bedroom*). **the thing is** the most important point or question is (*It would be good to expand the business but the thing is where will we get the money?*).

---

think *vb* **1** (*You must think before you act*) reflect, deliberate, concentrate, contemplate, ponder, ruminate. **2** (*The old lady was thinking about the past*) remember, recall, call to mind, reminisce. **3** (*We think that they will arrive tomorrow*) believe, expect, suppose, imagine, assume. **4** (*He is thought to be brilliant*) consider, regard, hold, deem.

thirst *adj* **1** (*They nearly died of thirst in the desert*) thirstiness, dehydration. **2** (*They had a great thirst for knowledge*) desire, craving, longing, yearning, avidity, eagerness, keenness.

thorough *adj* **1** (*The police conducted a thorough investigation*) exhaustive, in depth, comprehensive, intensive, extensive. **2** (*He is a slow worker but he is thorough*) meticulous, painstaking, punctilious, assiduous, careful. **3** (*He is a thorough villain*) thoroughgoing, utter, out and out, absolute, sheer, complete.

thought *n* **1** (*He is now incapable of rational thought*) thinking, powers of reasoning. **2** (*She was deep in thought*) thinking, reflection, contemplation, deliberation, musing. **3** (*I had a sudden thought as to what we should do*) idea, line of thought, notion. **4** (*We shall give the matter some thought*) consideration, attention, heed, regard. **5** (*We asked her for her thoughts on the subject*) idea, opinion, view, feeling. **6** (*In giving gifts it is the thought that counts*) thoughtfulness, consideration, care, kindness, compassion.

thoughtful *adj* **1** (*He seemed in a thoughtful mood*) reflective, contemplative, meditative, introspective, absorbed, in a brown study. **2** (*She is a thoughtful daughter*) considerate, attentive, caring, solicitous, helpful, kind, kindly.

threaten *vb* **1** (*The bully threatened the younger children*) make threats, menace, intimidate, browbeat, bully, pressurize. **2** (*Pollution threatens the environment*) be a threat to, menace, be a danger to, endanger, put at risk, jeopardize, put in jeopardy, imperil. **3** (*Rain was threatening*) be imminent, loom, be impending.

thrifty *adj* (*They have to be thrifty as they do not have much money*) economical, careful, frugal, sparing.

thrill *vb* (*The children were thrilled by the display of acrobatics*) excite, stimulate, arouse, stir, electrify, give joy to, (*inf*) get a kick out of.

thrive *vb* **1** (*The house plants thrive in that room*) flourish, do well, burgeon. **2** (*The firm is now thriving*) flourish, proper, do well, boom.

throb *vb* (*His pulse throbbed normally/Her heart throbbed*) beat, pulse, palpitate, pound, vibrate, thump. ▼

---

have another think coming to be quite mistaken (*If you think he will lend you the car you have another think coming*).
not to think much of (someone *or* **something)** to have a low opinion of (someone or something) (*We didn't think much of the play*).

---

throw *vb* **1** (*He threw a brick through the window*) hurl, fling, toss, cast, lob, sling, (*inf*) chuck. **2** (*She threw him a warning glance*) cast, send, give, bestow on. **3** (*She threw away all her old clothes*) throw out, discard, dispose of, get rid of, dispense with, (*inf*) dump. **4** (*The question completely threw him*) baffle, bamboozle, dumbfound, disconcert, astonish. ▼

---

throw in the towel to give up, to admit defeat (*He started a university course but he threw in the towel in his second year*) <From a method of conceding defeat in boxing>.

---

thrust *vb* **1** (*He thrust the present into her hands*) push, shove, ram. **2** (*They thrust the door open*) push, shove, drive, press, propel. **3** (*They thrust their way to the front of the queue*) push, shove, press, force, shoulder, elbow, jostle.

thud *n* (*The box fell with a loud thud*) thump, bang, crash, wham.

thug *n* (*The thug attacked the old man*) ruffian, villain, hoodlum, rogue, rough, tough.

thump *vb* **1** (*He turned round and thumped his attacker*) strike, hit, punch, wallop, smack, slap, batter. **2** (*Her heart was thumping in terror*) thud, pulse, pulsate, throb, palpitate. **3** (*He thumped on the table*) bang, batter, beat, crash, knock.

thwart *vb* (*Their plans for expansion were thwarted*) frustrate, foil, baulk, check, block, obstruct, impede, hamper, stop.

tidy *adj* **1** (*The room was very tidy*) neat, orderly, in order, in good order, clean, shipshape, spick and span, spruce. **2** (*Everyone had to be tidy for the school photograph*) neat, well-groomed, spruce. **3** (*He is not a tidy person*) neat, orderly, organized, methodical, systematic.

tie *vb* **1** (*He tied the string*) knot, make a bow in. **2** (*They tied the parcel with string*) bind. **3** (*They had to tie the dog to the gate*) tie up, tether, fasten, secure, attach, fix. **4** (*The two teams tied for first place*) draw, be equal, be even, be neck and neck.

tight *adj* **1** (*She wore a tight skirt instead of a full one*) tight-fitting, close-fitting, figure-hugging, narrow. **2** (*You must keep the rope tight*) taut, rigid, stiff, tense, stretched, strained. **3** (*She kept a tight grip on her mother's hand*) fast, secure. **4** (*We need a jar with a tight lid*) airtight, watertight, sealed, hermetically sealed. **5** (*make sure that the screws are tight*) secure, fast, fixed. **6** (*a tight mass of fibres*) compact, compressed. **7** (*Space was tight in the small house*) cramped, restricted, limited. **8** (*Security was tight at the meeting of the presidents*) strict, rigorous, stringent. **9** (*Money was tight*) scarce, scant, in short supply, limited, inadequate, insufficient. ▼

---

in a tight corner in a difficult or dangerous situation (*The troops were in a tight corner completely surrounded by the enemy*). **run a tight ship** to run an efficient, well-organized firm, etc (*During a recession it is exceptionally important to run a tight ship*).

---

time *n* **1** (*in the time of the cavemen*) period, age, era, epoch. **2** (*He seemed fine the last time I saw him*) occasion, point, juncture. **3** (*He felt that it was time to leave*) moment, point, stage. **4** (*I worked in Spain for a time*) while, period, spell. **5** (*It was a tune in waltz time*) rhythm, measure, tempo, beat. ▼

---

have no time for (someone *or* **something)** to have a very low opinion of (someone or something) and to wish not to associate with him/her/it (*I have no time for people who tell lies*). **have time on one's hands** to have more free time than one can usefully fill with work, hobbies, etc (*If you have time on your hands you should do some voluntary work*). **have the time of one's life** to have a very enjoyable time (*The child had the time of her life at the fair*).

---

timetable *n* (*give out copies of the conference timetable*) schedule, programme, list, agenda.

timid *adj* **1** (*The pupils were too

timid to stand up to the bullies) timorous, fearful, afraid, apprehensive, frightened, scared, cowardly. **2** (*She was too timid to ask the pop star for his autograph*) timorous, shy, bashful, diffident, reticent, retiring.

tingle *vb* (*Her fingers were tingling*) prickle, tickle, itch, sting, quiver, tremble.

tint *n* **1** (*The artist had several tints to chose from*) colour, shade, tone. **2** (*an auburn hair tint*) dye, colorant, colouring.

tiny *adj* **1** (*a tiny insect*) minute, diminutive, miniature, microscopic, infinitesimal, minuscule. **2** (*a tiny amount of water*) small, trifling, negligible, minor, insignificant.

tip *vb* **1** (*The dog tipped over the rubbish bin*) upset, overturn, topple, capsize. **2** (*She tipped the water into the bucket*) pour, empty. **3** (*The wardrobe tends to tip*) tilt, lean, list, cant. **4** (*He tipped the horse to win*) back, put one's money on, recommend. **5** (*tip the waiter*) give a tip to, reward.

tip *n* **1** (*the tip of the iceberg*) point, peak, top, apex. **2** (*the tips of his fingers*) end, extremity. **3** (*give the waiter a tip*) gratuity, reward, remuneration. **4** (*She gave him a few tips on cooking*) hint, suggestion, advice. **5** (*a racing tip*) recommendation. ▼

---

be on the tip of one's tongue to be about to be said (*It was on the tip of my tongue to tell her that he was married but I decided not to mention it*). **tip (someone) off** to give (someone) some private or secret information.

---

tired *adj* **1** (*They were tired after their long walk*) weary, fatigued, worn out, exhausted. **2** (*The comic told a series of tired jokes*) stale, hackneyed, outworn, trite, banal. **3** (*They were tired of her endless complaints*) bored, weary.

tiresome *adj* (*She finds the work tiresome*) wearisome, tedious, boring, dull, monotonous, unexciting, uninteresting.

title *n* **1** (*the title of the book*) name. **2** (*What title does the king's nephew have?*) form of address, name, designation.

toilet *n* (*public toilets*) lavatory, WC, (*inf*) loo.

tolerate *vb* **1** (*We could not tolerate the noise from next door*) put up with, stand, bear, endure. **2** (*People should be able to tolerate views that are different from theirs*) permit, allow, recognize, sanction, brook.

tone *n* **1** (*He enjoys the sweet tone of the flute*) sound, pitch, timbre. **2** (*He spoke in a whispered tone*) voice, intonation, inflection. **3** (*The tone of his letter was threatening*) mood, spirit, manner, tenor, vein, gist. **4** (*She was dressed in tones of blue*) tint, shade, tinge.

tool *n* (*The workman forgot one of his tools*) implement, instrument, utensil, gadget, appliance.

top *n* **1** (*They reached the top of the mountain*) peak, summit, crest, apex. **2** (*They are at the top of their careers*) height, peak, pinnacle, zenith, acme, culmination, climax. **3** (*replace the top on the bottle*) lid, cap, stopper, cork. **4** (*They were at the top of the queue*) head, front, **5** (*The child wore a white summer top*) sweater, jumper, jersey, blouse, shirt, T-shirt. ▼

be over the top to be excessive, to be extreme (*She went completely over the top with the catering for the party*). **the top of the ladder** *or* **tree** the highest point in a profession (*He is at the top of the tree in the legal profession*).

topical *adj* (*The pupils were asked to write about something topical*) newsworthy, in the news, current, contemporary, up to date.

toss *vb* **1** (*She tossed the book on the sofa*) throw, fling, hurl. **2** (*ships tossing on the waves*) rock, roll, sway, lurch, pitch, heave. **3** (*The horse tossed its head*) throw back, jerk. **4** (*They tossed and turned unable to sleep*) thrash, writhe, tumble. ▼

argue the toss to dispute a decision (*There is no point in arguing the toss. The judge's decision is final*) <A reference to an argument about the tossing of a coin>.

total *adj* **1** (*the total amount of money*) complete, entire, whole, full. **2** (*He's a total fool*) complete, thorough, utter, absolute, downright.

touch *vb* **1** (*The two wires should touch*) be in contact, come together, meet. **2** (*She touched his arm*) put her hand on, tap, pat. **3** (*You shouldn't touch his private things*) handle, pick up, hold, fiddle with, interfere with. **4** (*They were touched by the orphan's sad story*) affect, move, upset, disturb. **5** (*Some firms were not touched by the recession*) affect, have an effect on, concern, have a bearing on. ▼

be in touch with (someone) to be in communication with (someone) (*She tried to get in touch with an old friend*). **it's touch and go** it is a very uncertain or precarious situation (*It's touch and go whether he lives or dies*) <Perhaps a reference to a ship that touches rocks or the ground but goes on past the hazard without being damaged>. **touch (something) off** to give rise to (something) (*The leader's speech sparked off a rebellion*).

tough *adj* **1** (*objects made of a tough substance*) strong, durable, solid, sturdy, rigid, stiff. **2** (*The meat was tough*) chewy, leathery, gristly, sinewy. **3** (*They had to be tough to survive the weather conditions*) hardy, rugged, robust, sturdy, strong. **4** (*The job was very tough*) difficult, hard, arduous, strenuous, laborious. **5** (*They had a tough life*) hard, harsh, austere, rugged, rough, grim, difficult. **6** (*the tough kids of the district*) rough, rowdy, unruly, disorderly, wild, violent, law-breaking.

tourist *n* (*foreign tourists visiting the city*) visitor, traveller, sightseer, holiday-maker.

tower *n* (*a church tower*) spire, steeple, belfry, turret. ▼

a tower of strength someone who is very helpful, and supportive (*He was a tower of strength when her husband died*). **live in an ivory tower** to have a way of life that is protected from difficulty or unpleasantness (*The writer lives in an ivory tower. He doesn't realize the struggle that his wife has to keep the family*).

trace *n* **1** (*We could find no trace of where they had camped*) mark, sign, remains, vestige, indication, evidence. **2** (*There was not a trace of shame in his expression*) bit, hint, suggestion, suspicion, shadow, jot, iota. **3** (*follow the animal's traces*) track, trail, spoor, scent.

trace *vb* (*They were unable to trace their lost son/We tried to trace the missing letter*) find, discover, detect, track down, unearth, ferret out.

track *n* **1** (*The hunters were following the tracks of the bear*) marks, traces, prints, trail, spoor, scent. **2** (*They followed the track up the mountain*) path, road, trail, **3** (*The train suddenly left the track*) rail, line. **4** (*The runners had to run ten times round the track*) course, running track, racetrack. ▼

---

cover one's tracks to conceal one's activities or movements (*The bank raiders tried to cover their tracks by changing cars*). **make tracks** (*inf*) to leave or set out (*If we are to get there before night we had better be making tracks*).

---

trade *n* (*He is in the export trade*) commerce, business.

tradition *n* (*keep up the old village traditions*) custom, habit, belief, practice, convention, institution.

traffic *n* (*The noise of traffic kept him awake*) vehicles, cars.

tragedy *n* (*She was sad because of some tragedy in her life*) disaster, calamity, misfortune, adversity.

tragic *adj* **1** (*appalled at her tragic story about her childhood*) sad, unhappy, pathetic, moving, distressing, pitiful. **2** (*She was killed in a tragic accident*) disastrous, calamitous, catastrophic, terrible, dreadful, appalling, dire.

trail *vb* **1** (*They trailed the fallen trees behind them*) tow, pull, drag, haul, draw. **2** (*They trailed the fox to its earth*) follow, pursue, track, trace, tail, shadow.

train *vb* **1** (*She is training the pupils in cooking techniques*) teach, coach, instruct, educate, give lessons to. **2** (*She is training to be a vet*) study, learn. **3** (*The football players have to train every evening*) work out, do exercises, practise.

tramp *n* **1** (*tramps sleeping rough*) vagrant, derelict, down-and-out. **2** (*go for a tramp over the moors*) hike, trek, march, ramble, wander, roam, walk.

tranquil *adj* **1** (*a tranquil country scene*) peaceful, restful. quiet, still, serene. **2** (*a very tranquil person*) calm, serene, placid, composed.

transfer *vb* (*He transferred the furniture from one house to another*) move, shift, take, carry, convey, transport.

transform *vb* (*The new furnishings transformed the room*) change, alter, transfigure, revolutionize.

transmit *vb* (*transmit the information electronically*) pass on, transfer, communicate, spread, send, carry.

transparent *adj* **1** (*things made of a transparent material*) clear, see-through. **2** (*They were impressed by his transparent honesty*) obvious, clear, unmistakable, evident, noticeable, apparent.

travel *vb* **1** (*They travel a lot in the course of their work*) journey, move around, take a trip. **2** (*the speed at which sound travels*) be transmitted, proceed, progress. **3**

(*They travel the country begging*) journey, cross, traverse, roam, wander.

treacherous *adj* (*He was betrayed by a treacherous friend*) traitorous, disloyal, faithless, double-dealing, untrustworthy.

treasure *n* (*They looked for buried treasure*) riches, valuables, wealth, fortune.

treat *vb* **1** (*He treated his children badly*) act towards, behave towards, deal with, cope with, use. **2** (*They treated his remarks as a joke*) regard, consider, view. **3** (*The doctor treated the patient*) attend to, cure, heal, give treatment to, give medication to. **5** (*treat the wood with something to preserve it*) apply to, put on. **6** (*They treated us to dinner*) pay for, stand, entertain, take out. **7** (*She treats the subject in an original way*) deal with, discuss, consider, write about, speak about.

tremble *vb* (*They were trembling with fear*) shake, quiver, quake, shudder.

tremendous *adj* **1** (*It made a tremendous difference to their lives*) huge, enormous, great, immense, vast, colossal. **2** (*She is a tremendous cook*) excellent, exceptional, remarkable, wonderful, fabulous.

trend *n* **1** (*witness an upward trend in prices*) tendency, drift, swing, course. **2** (*She always follows fashion trends*) fashion, style, fad.

trial *n* **1** (*She was a witness at a murder trial*) court case, case, hearing. **2** (*He is giving the young man a trial as a trainee mechanic*) trial period, probation. **3** (*cars having passed safety trials*) test, try-out, check. **4** (*facing the trials of life*) trouble, worry, burden, hardship, suffering. ▼

---

trial and error the trying out of various approaches or methods of doing something until one finds out the right one (*The doctor found a cure for his skin rash by trial and error*). **trials and tribulations** difficulties and hardships (*She was complaining about the trials and tribulations of being a single parent*).

---

trick *n* **1** (*He gained entry to her house by a trick*) deception, hoax, ruse, stratagem, subterfuge. **2** (*The children played tricks on each other*) practical joke, joke, hoax, prank.

trick *vb* (*He was tricked into giving her his life's savings*) cheat, deceive, delude, mislead, hoodwink, dupe, swindle, defraud.

trip *vb* (*She tripped over her shoe laces*) stumble, lose one's footing, lose one's balance, slip, fall, tumble.

trip *n* (*They went on a trip to the seaside*) excursion, outing, jaunt, expedition.

triumphant *adj* **1** (*He gave a triumphant shout when he won*) exultant, joyful, jubilant. **2** (*the triumphant team*) winning, victorious, successful.

trivial *adj* (*They quarrelled over something trivial*) unimportant, insignificant, inconsequential, petty, minor, negligible.

trouble *n* **1** (*Their teenage children are causing them some trouble*) worry, bother, anxiety, disquiet, unease, inconvenience, difficulty, problems. **2** (*There has been a great deal of trouble in her life*) misfortune, difficulty, hardship, distress, suffering, unhappiness, sadness. **3** (*Our hosts went to a great deal of trouble*) bother, inconvenience, disturbance, fuss, effort. **4** (*There was a bit of trouble in the restaurant last night*) disturbance, disorder, strife, fighting, commotion. **5** (*He has chest trouble*) disorder, disease, illness.

trust *vb* **1** (*We do not trust his judgement*) place one's trust in, have confidence in, have faith in, believe in, be convinced by. **2** (*You can trust them to help if they offer*) rely on, bank on, depend on, count on, be sure of. **3** (*We trust that you will be there*) hope, assume, presume, expect, suppose.

true *adj* **1** (*What she said is true*) truthful, accurate, right, correct, genuine, reliable. **2** (*They are true friends*) real, genuine, loyal, faithful, trustworthy, reliable, dependable. **3** (*The book gives a true account of the war*) accurate, correct, exact, precise, faithful, close.

trustworthy *adj* (*He thinks that all his employees are trustworthy*) reliable, dependable, loyal, staunch, faithful, trusty, honest, honourable.

truth *n* **1** (*There seemed little truth in what he said*) truthfulness, accuracy, correctness, rightness, validity, veracity. **2** (*Truth is often stranger than fiction*) reality, actuality.

try *vb* **1** (*You must try to do well*) attempt, aim, endeavour, make an effort, exert oneself, strive, struggle. **2** (*We tried a new kind of cereal*) try out, test, evaluate. **3** (*The children are trying her patience*) tax, strain, exhaust. **4** (*He was the judge who tried the case*) hear, judge, adjudicate. ▼

---

try it on to act in a bold way in order to find out to what extent such behaviour will be tolerated (*He did not really expect his parents to let him go to the all-night party. He was just trying it on*).

---

trying *adj* **1** (*They had had a trying day*) taxing, demanding, difficult, stressful, hard, tough, arduous. **2** (*The children were particularly trying that day*) troublesome, tiresome, annoying, irritating, exasperating.

tuck *vb* **1** (*She tucked her blouse into her skirt*) push, ease, insert, stuff. **2** (*tuck the child up in bed*) cover up, wrap up. **3** (*They tucked into a hearty meal*) eat, devour, wolf down, gobble up.

tug *vb* **1** (*She tugged at the rope*) pull, jerk, yank. **2** (*The child tugged a toy cart behind him*) drag, draw, tow, lug. ▼

---

tug of love a struggle involving the custody of a child <A variation on a tug-of-war, which involves two teams pulling on a rope>.

---

tumble *vb* **1** (*Watch that the child does not tumble*) fall over, fall headlong, topple, stumble, trip. **2** (*Prices have tumbled*) fall, drop, plummet, plunge, slump. **3** (*acrobats tumbling*) turn somersaults, go head over heels.

tune *n* (*a group playing a folk tune*) melody, air, song. ▼

---

call the tune to be the person in control who gives the orders (*It is his deputy who has been calling the tune while he is ill*) <A reference to the saying 'He who pays the piper calls the tune'>.
in tune with (something) in agreement with (something), compatible with (something) (*Their ideas on the new scheme are very much in tune*).

---

turn *vb* **1** (*The wheel began to turn*) go round, rotate, revolve, spin, whirl, twirl. **2** (*He turned the car in the driveway*) turn round, reverse, make a U-turn. **3** (*He turned the steaks over on the grill*) turn over, flip over, invert, reverse. **4** (*The weather turned stormy*) become, grow, get. **5** (*Tadpoles turn into frogs*) become, change into. **6** (*The car turned the corner*) go round, round. **7** (*He turned the attic into a bedroom*) convert, change, transform, alter, modify. ▼

---

give (someone) quite a turn to give (someone) a sudden shock or surprise (*You gave me quite a turn coming up so quietly behind me*). **turn turtle** to turn upside down, to capsize (*We were afraid that the boat would turn turtle in the rough seas*) <A turtle is helpless and easy to kill if it is turned over on its back>. **turn up trumps** to do the right or required thing in a difficult situation, especially unexpectedly (*I didn't think that our team had a chance against the champions but they turned up trumps*).

---

tussle *n* (*The two boys had a tussle to gain possession of the bag*) struggle, fight, scuffle, skirmish.

tweak *vb* (*The boy tweaked his friend's ear*) twist, pinch, nip, pull, jerk.

twilight *n* (*They walked home at twilight*) dusk, half-light.

twinkle *vb* (*The stars twinkled*) sparkle, glitter, glint, flicker, shimmer.

twist *vb* **1** (*The extreme heat had twisted the metal*) bend, warp, distort, buckle. **2** (*He twisted the string round his finger*) wind, coil, curl, twine, twirl, loop. **3** (*The road twists up the mountain*) curve, wind, zigzag, snake, meander. **4** (*The ropes became twisted*) entangle, tangle, entwine. **5** (*They twisted his words*) distort, garble, misrepresent, falsify. **6** (*She twisted her head round to look at him*) turn, swivel, screw.

type *n* **1** (*a type of plant/a type of person*) kind, variety, sort, form, class. **2** (*in italic type*) print, face, fount.

twitch *n* **1** (*Her arm gave a twitch*) spasm, jerk, jump, quiver, tremor. **2** (*He has a twitch in his eye*) blink, flutter, tic.

U

ugly *adj* **1** (*an ugly monster/ugly buildings*) hideous, unattractive, unprepossessing, horrible, frightful. **2** (*The war situation grew more ugly*) dangerous, threatening, menacing, ominous, hostile, nasty. ▼

---

ugly duckling an unattractive or uninteresting person or thing that develops in time into something or someone very attractive, interesting, successful, etc (*She is now a beautiful filmstar but as a child she was a real ugly duckling*) <A reference to a story by Hans Andersen about a baby swan that is brought up by two ducks who consider it ugly by their standards until it grows into a beautiful swan>.

---

umpire *n* (*The umpire in the tournament*) referee, judge, adjudicator, arbitrator, (*inf*) ref.

unanimous *adj* (*The committee was unanimous in its decision to close down the club*) agreed, united, like-minded, at one, in harmony, with one voice.

unaware *adj* (*They were unaware of what people were saying about them*) unconscious, ignorant, oblivious, heedless, (*inf*) in the dark.

uncanny *adj* **1** (*There were uncanny happenings in the graveyard at night*) strange, odd, queer, mysterious, eerie, weird, unnatural, supernatural. **2** (*She bore an uncanny resemblance to her grandmother*) remarkable, striking, extraordinary, astonishing, incredible.

uncertain *adj* **1** (*The result of the talks is still uncertain*) unknown, undetermined, unsettled, up in the air. **2** (*We are uncertain about whether to go or stay*) unsure, doubtful, undecided, dubious, unresolved, indecisive, wavering, in two minds. **3** (*The future is uncertain*) unpredictable, risky, chancy.

uncouth *adj* (*uncouth table manners*) rough, coarse, uncivilized, unrefined, unpolished, boorish, ill-bred.

under *prep* **1** (*She sat under the tree*) below, underneath, beneath. **2** (*prices under £10*) below, less than, lower than. **3** (*army ranks under major*) low, lower than, inferior to, subordinate to, junior to. ▼

---

under one's very nose 1 right in front of one and so very easily seen (*She could not find her book although it was under her very nose*). **2** while one is actually present (*The thief stole my luggage from the train under my very nose*). **under one's own steam** entirely through one's own efforts (*There is no transport laid on to the picnic site and so everyone will have to get there under their own steam*) <A reference to steam engines>. **under the influence** under the influence of alcohol, drunk (*It is an offence to drive while you are under the influence*).

---

underclothes *npl* (*wear warm underclothes in the winter*) underwear, underclothing, undergarments, lingerie, (*inf*) smalls.

undergo *vb* (*undergo a terrible experience*) go through, experience, be subjected to, endure.

underground *adj* **1** (*an underground shelter*) subterranean, sunken. **2** (*an underground organization*) secret, clandestine, undercover, surreptitious.

undergrowth *n* (*The animals emerged from the undergrowth*) thicket, brushwood.

underhand *adj* (*She got the job by underhand methods*) deceitful, devious, crafty, cunning, sneaky, furtive, dishonest.

underline *vb* (*The burglary underlined the need for security staff*) emphasize, stress, highlight.

undermine *vb* (*They tried to undermine the authority of the manager*) weaken, impair, damage, destroy.

understand *vb* **1** (*We did not understand his instructions*) comprehend, grasp, take in, follow, fathom, interpret. **2** (*She failed to understand how the homeless people felt*) appreciate, sympathize with. **3** (*We understand that he has left*) gather, hear, be informed, learn, believe.

understanding *n* **1** (*have a poor understanding of the facts*) comprehension, grasp, knowledge, awareness. **2** (*His powers of understanding are poor*) reasoning, brain power, (*inf*) grey matter. **3** (*The two businessmen did not sign a contract but they had an unofficial understanding*) agreement, gentleman's agreement, arrangement, deal, pact. **4** (*She treated the difficult situation with great understanding*) sensitivity, consideration, insight, compassion, sympathy. **5** (*It was our understanding that he was leaving*) belief, opinion, feeling.

undertake *vb* (*They agreed to undertake the difficult task*) take on, assume, tackle, set about, enter upon.

underwear *n* (*wear warm underwear in winter*) underclothes, underclothing, undergarments, lingerie, (*inf*) smalls.

undo *vb* **1** (*She undid the hook on her dress*) unfasten, unhook, unbutton, untie, loosen, open. **2** (*They undid all his good work*) destroy, ruin, wreck, upset. **3** (*She rang to undo the arrangements for the meeting*) cancel, annul, revoke, set aside.

unearth *vb* **1** (*The police have unearthed new information about the murder*) uncover, discover, find, come across, bring to light, expose, turn up. **2** (*The dog unearthed an old bone*) dig up, excavate, exhume.

unearthly *adj* (*They heard an unearthly shriek*) eerie, uncanny, supernatural, ghostly, weird.

uneasy *adj* (*They felt uneasy when their son did not arrive home*) anxious, worried, concerned, troubled, nervous.

unemployed *adj* (*He has been unemployed for a year*) jobless, out of work, (*inf*) on the dole.

unfasten *vb* (*unfasten the gate/unfasten the knot*) undo, open, loose, untie, unlock.

unfortunate *adj* **1** (*in unfortunate circumstances*) adverse, disadvantageous, unfavourable. **2** (*The* *unfortunate girl lost all her money*) unlucky, out of luck, luckless, wretched, unhappy. **3** (*It was a most unfortunate remark*) regrettable, inappropriate, tactless.

unhappy *adj* (*She was unhappy when her dog died*) sad, miserable, sorrowful, dejected, gloomy.

uniform *adj* **1** (*pieces of cloth of uniform length*) same, alike, like, equal, identical. **2** (*keep the room at a uniform temperature*) constant, unvarying, unchanging, regular, even.

union *n* (*a union of youth clubs*) association, alliance, league, federation.

unique *adj* **1** (*a unique specimen*) one and only, single, sole, solitary, exclusive. **2** (*The salesmen pointed out the unique features of the dishwasher*) distinctive, unequalled, unparalleled.

unit *n* **1** (*The English course is divided into units*) component, part, section, portion, element. **2** (*The metre is a unit of length*) measurement, measure, quantity.

unite *vb* **1** (*The two sides united to fight their common enemy*) join, join together, get together, join forces, amalgamate, combine, merge. **2** (*They decided to unite the two teams*) join, combine, amalgamate, merge, link, fuse.

universal *adj* (*Poverty is a universal problem*) general, widespread, common, global, international, world-wide.

universe *n* (*the wonders of the universe*) world, cosmos.

unlikely *adv* (*It is unlikely that they will arrive on time*) improbable, doubtful.

unlucky *adj* **1** (*He was unlucky not to win/a most unlucky young man*) out of luck, luckless, down on one's luck, unfortunate, hapless. **2** (*By an unlucky set of circumstances they failed to arrive on time*) unfortunate, adverse, disadvantageous, unfavourable.

unmarried *adj* (*She is unmarried and lives with her parents*) single, unwed, unattached.

unpleasant *adj* (*an unpleasant experience/an unpleasant person*) disagreeable, nasty, horrible.

unreal *adj* (*a story about an unreal world*) imaginary, fictitious, make-believe, mythical.

unruly *adj* (*The teacher could not control the unruly children*) rowdy, wild, disorderly, noisy, uncontrollable, unmanageable.

unsightly *adj* (*unsightly modern blocks of flats in a historical area*) ugly, unattractive, hideous, horrible.

unsuccessful *adj* (*Their attempt to save the firm was unsuccessful*) without success, in vain, failed, futile, useless, ineffective.

untangle *vb* (*untangle the knots*) disentangle, unravel, straighten out.

untidy *adj* **1** (*The room where the children were playing was very untidy*) in disorder, disordered, disarranged, chaotic, disorganized. **2** (*The children were scolded for being untidy*) dishevelled, unkempt, rumpled, messy.

untie *vb* (*untie the gate/untie the string*) undo, unfasten, loosen.

untrue *adj* (*We felt that his account of the accident was untrue*) false, fallacious, erroneous, wrong, inaccurate.

unusual *adj* (*His behaviour was unusual*) uncommon, out of the ordinary, abnormal, odd, different, irregular.

unwell *adj* (*She is unwell and is off work*) ill, sick, ailing, unhealthy, (*inf*) under the weather.

unwilling *adj* (*They were unwilling to set off so late*) reluctant, disinclined, loath, averse.

up:— ▼

---

be on the up-and-up to be making successful progress (*The firm was doing badly but it is on the up-and-up now*). **be up to (something) 1** to be involved in something mischievous or dishonest (*Their mother could tell by the children's faces that they were up to something*). **2** to be good enough, competent enough, strong enough, etc, to do something (*She was under a lot of stress at work as she was not really up to the job*). **up-and-coming** likely to be successful, rising in importance or popularity (*She is an up-and-coming young musician*).

---

upbringing *n* (*They had a very strict upbringing*) rearing, training.

upheaval *n* (*Moving house caused a terrible upheaval*) disturbance, disruption, disorder, turmoil, chaos, confusion.

upkeep *n* (*pay for the upkeep of the house*) maintenance, running, support.

upper *adj* **1** (*the upper shelf*) higher. **2** (*the upper ranks in the army*) higher, superior, senior. ▼

---

have the upper hand to be in control or have the advantage (*The two flatmates are quarrelling but she has the upper hand as the flat belongs to her mother*). **on one's uppers** (*inf*) extremely poor (*We are on our uppers and cannot pay the rent*) <Literally with no soles to one's shoes>. **upper-crust** (*inf*) belonging to the upper class or aristocracy (*She has an upper-crust accent*) <Refers literally to the upper part of the pastry of a pie above the filling>.

---

upright *adj* **1** (*the upright posts in the fence*) erect, vertical, perpendicular. **2** (*He is an upright member of the community*) honest, honourable, decent, respectable, law-abiding, upstanding.

uproar *n* (*There was uproar when the football player kicked the ball into his own goal*) disturbance, turmoil, tumult, commotion, pandemonium, bedlam, riot, rumpus

upset *vb* **1** (*His remarks upset her*) hurt, distress, worry, bother. **2** (*The animals were upset by the thunderstorm*) agitate, alarm, frighten. **3** (*He got a new job and upset our holiday plans*) disorganize, disarrange, (*inf*) mess up. **4** (*The child upset the pail of water*) overturn, knock over, upend, capsize, tip over.

upshot *n* (*The upshot of the quarrel was that he left*) result, outcome, end, conclusion.

up-to-date *adj* (*His ideas are very up-to-date*) modern, current, contemporary, fashionable.

urban *n* (*urban areas*) city, town, metropolitan, inner-city.

urbane *adj* (*an urbane man whom women found charming*) suave, smooth, sophisticated, elegant, cultivated, polished, refined, gracious, courteous.

urge *vb* **1** (*urge the cattle to the milking shed*) drive, propel, force, push, hurry. **2** (*We urged her to accept the invitation*) advise, encourage, prompt, entreat, exhort. **3** (*The applause of the crowd urged the players on to greater effort*) spur, incite, stimulate, prod, goad, encourage, egg on.

urge *n* (*She had a sudden urge to laugh*) desire, compulsion, need, wish, impulse, longing.

urgent *adj* **1** (*It is urgent that we get him to hospital*) imperative, a matter of life or death, vital, crucial, critical, essential. **2** (*We have urgent matters to discuss*) important, crucial, vital, serious, grave, pressing.

use *n* **1** (*The lotion we bought at the chemist is for external use only*) application, utilization, employment. **2** (*What use is this old chair?*) usefulness, good, benefit, service. **3** (*We have no use for this old bike*) need, purpose. ▼

---

have no use for (someone) to wish not to be associated with (someone) (*I have no use for people who are disloyal to their friends*). **make use of (someone)** to take advantage of and exploit (someone), to use (someone) for one's own gain or benefit (*They just make use of her kind mother. They expect her to look after their children all day and every day*).

---

use *vb* **1** (*Do you know how to use this machine?*) make use of, utilize, work, operate, employ, wield. **2** (*You will have to use tact*) exercise, employ, apply. **3** (*Have you used all the flour?*) consume, get through.

used *adj* (*a shop selling used clothing*) second-hand, nearly new, cast-off.

useful *adj* (*This is a useful kitchen gadget*) of use, practical, of service, handy, convenient. ▼

---

come in useful to be useful at some time in the future (*She keeps a lot of old boxes in her garage in case they come in useful but they never do*).

---

usual *adj* **1** (*the postman's usual route*) regular, accustomed, customary, habitual, normal, routine, set, established. **2** (*The weather was usual for the time of year*) common, typical, standard, normal, average, run-of-the-mill.

usually *adv* (*We usually go out to lunch on Saturday*) generally, as a rule, normally, mostly, for the most part.

utter *vb* (*We heard him utter threats*) say, speak, voice, pronounce, express.

utter *adj* (*They are utter fools*) complete, absolute, total, thorough, out-and-out, perfect.

utterly *adv* (*We were utterly delighted at the news*) absolutely, completely, totally, thoroughly, perfectly.

V

vacant *adj* **1** (*The house is vacant*) empty, unoccupied, uninhabited, to let, deserted. **2** (*several vacant posts in the firm*) free, available, unfilled, unoccupied, empty. **3** (*look for a vacant seat*) empty, free, unoccupied, unused. **4** (*He wore a vacant look*) expressionless, blank, inexpressive, deadpan.

vagrant *n* (*vagrants begging for money for food*) tramp, homeless person, person of no fixed abode, itinerant.

vague *adj* **1** (*She has only a vague idea about her duties in her new job*) hazy, imprecise, ill-defined, uncertain, nebulous. **2** (*Our holiday plans are still rather vague*) hazy, uncertain, undecided, indefinite, (*inf*) up in the air, doubtful. **3** (*He gave rather a vague description of the person who attacked him*) imprecise, inexact, loose, hazy, woolly. **4** (*A vague shape loomed out of the mist*) indistinct, indeterminate, shadowy, unclear, hazy, dim, fuzzy. **5** (*She is rather a vague person*) absent-minded, dreamy, with one's head in the clouds.

vain *adj* **1** (*They made a vain attempt to save the drowning man*) unsuccessful, futile, useless, ineffective, abortive, unprofitable. **2** (*He is a very vain young man*) conceited, proud, arrogant, egotistical, narcissistic, cocky, (*inf*) big-headed. ▼

---

take (someone's) name in vain to use (someone's) name disrespectfully, especially to swear using God's name (*They were punished for taking the Lord's name in vain*) <A Biblical reference to Exodus 20:7>.

---

valiant *adj* (*make a valiant attempt to save his friend's life*) brave, courageous, gallant, heroic, bold.

valid *adj* **1** (*The school regulation is still valid*) in force, effective, in effect, legal, lawful. **2** (*He has valid reasons for lodging an objection*) sound, well-founded, reasonable, justifiable, authentic.

valuable *adj* **1** (*The burglars took some valuable jewellery*) expensive, costly, high-priced, precious, priceless. **2** (*The old man gave them some valuable advice*) useful, helpful, beneficial, worthwhile.

value *n* **1** (*It is difficult to place a value on the antique table*) price, market price, cost. **2** (*She tried to convince the children of the value of a balanced diet*) worth, benefit, merit, advantage, gain, importance.

value *vb* **1** (*They asked him to value their house*) set a price on, price, place a value on. **2** (*She values the contribution that parents make to sports events*) appreciate, think highly of, rate highly, set store by.

vanish *vb* **1** (*The figure seemed to vanish into the mist*) disappear, fade, melt. **2** (*They were talking about a way of life that has now vanished*) go, die out, disappear, end, come to an end.

vanquish *vb* (*They vanquished the*

enemy army) conquer, defeat, triumph over, overcome, crush, trounce.

varied *adj* (*a varied selection of magazines*) assorted, mixed, miscellaneous, diversified.

variety *n* **1** (*They tried to introduce some variety into the diet*) variation, diversity, diversification, change. **2** (*A huge variety of flowers were on display*) assortment, miscellany, mixture, range, collection. ▼

---

variety is the spice of life the opportunity to do different things, experience different things, etc, is what makes life interesting (*I am going to the pop concert although I am really a classical music fan. Variety is the spice of life*).

---

various *adj* **1** (*The dress comes in various colours*) varying, diverse, different, many, assorted. **2** (*For various reasons we are unable to attend the meeting*) numerous, several, many, varied.

vary *vb* **1** (*They tend to vary slightly in size*) differ, be different, be unlike, be dissimilar. **2** (*The temperature varies throughout the day*) change, alter. **3** (*try to vary your speed on a long journey*) change, alter, modify.

vast *adj* **1** (*the vast plains covered in ripe corn*) extensive, immense, expansive, wide, sweeping. **2** (*A vast shape suddenly loomed out of the fog*) huge, enormous, massive, colossal, gigantic.

vegetation *n* (*an area of the world with little vegetation*) plant life, plants, greenery, flora.

vehement *adj* (*a vehement denial*) emphatic, vigorous, forceful, strong, fervent, passionate.

vehicle *n* **1** (*no parking for unauthorized vehicles*) conveyance, car, bus, lorry, means of transport. **2** (*They use the magazine simply as a vehicle for spreading their political views*) medium, means of expression, agency, instrument.

veil *n* (*The mountain peaks were hidden under a veil of mist/They moved the body under a veil of secrecy*) cover, covering, screen, curtain, blanket, cloak, mantle, mask, shroud, cloud. ▼

---

draw a veil over (something) not to discuss (something), to keep (something) hidden or secret (*She obviously had a very unhappy childhood but she seems to prefer to draw a veil over it*).

---

vein *n* **1** (*Blood gushed from the vein*) blood vessel. **2** (*a vein of ore in the rocks*) seam, lode, stratum. **3** (*The marble fireplace had a pink vein in it*) streak, stripe, strip, line, thread. **4** (*There was a vein of humour in her criticism*) streak, strain, dash, hint. **5** (*The poem was in a serious vein*) mood, tone, tenor.

vengeance *n* (*They sought vengeance for the murder of their brother*) revenge, retaliation, reprisal, retribution, tit for tat. ▼

---

with a vengeance very strongly, very much, etc (*It began to snow with a vengeance*).

---

venom *n* **1** (*find an antidote for the snake's venom*) poison, toxin. **2** (*She spoke with venom about her fellow competitor*) spite, malice, ill will, animosity.

venture *n* (*a business venture*) enterprise, undertaking, project.

verbal *adj* (*asked to give a verbal account of the accident*) oral, spoken, in speech.

verdict *n* (*The jury delivered its verdict*) decision, findings, conclusion, judgement, ruling, opinion.

verge *n* (*the grass verge by the road*) edge, border, boundary. ▼

---

be on the verge of (something) to be about to experience something (*The research scientist thought that he was on the verge of a major medical discovery*).

---

verify *vb* (*He was asked to verify that he had been present*) confirm, corroborate, endorse, ratify.

versatile *adj* **1** (*a versatile kitchen gadget*) adaptable, multipurpose. **2** (*She is a very versatile musician*) adaptable, adjustable, flexible, resourceful.

version *n* **1** (*She gave us her version of what happened*) account, story, report, side, interpretation. **2** (*There are several versions of that song around*) variant, variation, form.

vertical *n* (*hammer vertical posts into the ground to make a fence*) upright, erect, perpendicular.

very *adj* **1** (*Those were her very words*) actual, exact, precise. **2** (*The beauty of the dress lay in its very simplicity*) sheer, utter, pure. **3** (*He has been a member from the very beginning*) absolute. ▼

---

the very thing exactly what is required (*That scarf is the very thing to complete her outfit*).

---

vessel *n* **1** (*There was a foreign flag flying from the vessel*) ship, boat, craft. **2** (*We need some kind of vessel to give the dog a drink*) container, receptacle.

veto *vb* (*Some members vetoed his membership of the club*) ban, bar, place an embargo on, forbid, disallow, reject, turn down, give the thumbs down to.

vex *vb* (*Her mother was vexed by her refusal to come home for Christmas*) annoy, irritate, upset, put out, distress, (*inf*) peeve, (*inf*) miff. ▼

---

a vexed question a difficult issue or problem that is much discussed without being resolved.

---

vibrate *vb* **1** (*The music vibrated throughout the hall*) throb, pulsate, resonate, reverberate, ring, echo. **2** (*The whole bus vibrated as the driver tried to start the engine*) shudder, tremble, shake, quiver, shiver.

vice *n* **1** (*Vice seems to be on the increase in the modern world*) sin, sinfulness, evil, wickedness, badness, wrongdoing, iniquity. **2** (*one of his many vices*) sin, offence, misdeed, failing, flaw, defect.

vicious *adj* **1** (*The postman was attacked by a vicious dog*) fierce, ferocious, savage, dangerous. **2** (*The attack on the old man was a particularly vicious one*) violent, savage, brutal, fierce, ferocious, inhuman. ▼

---

a vicious circle an unfortunate or bad situation, the result of which produces the original cause of the situation or something similar (*It is a vicious circle. They are so much in debt that they have to borrow money to pay their debts and end up even deeper in debt*).

---

victim *n* **1** (*They were victims of a vicious attack*) casualty, sufferer. **2** (*tracking down their victims*) prey, quarry.

victorious *adj* (*the victorious army/ the victorious team*) conquering, winning, triumphant, champion.

victory *n* (*We celebrated our victory*) win, success, conquest, triumph, achievement. ▼

---

landslide victory a victory in an election by a very large number of votes (*Early on in the counting of the votes it was obvious that the government was heading for a landslide victory*). **Pyrrhic victory** a success of some kind in which what one achieves is not worth the effort or sacrifice which one has had to make in the process of attaining it (*She won her case against her employers for unfair dismissal but it was a Pyrrhic victory. All her compensation money went on meeting the cost of the legal fees*) <From the costly victory of Pyrrhus, King of Epirus, over the Romans at Heracles in 280 bc>.

---

view *n* **1** (*The view from our balcony was beautiful*) outlook, prospect, panorama, vista. **2** (*A strange figure came into view*) sight, range of vision, eyeshot. **3** (*Our view is that he is dishonest*) opinion, point of view, viewpoint, belief, feeling, idea. ▼

---

a bird's-eye view of (something) **1** a view of (something) seen from high above (*We got a marvellous bird's-eye view of the town from the top of the tower*). **2** a brief description or account of (something) (*The book gives a bird's-eye view of the use of herbs in cooking*). **in view of (something)** taking (something) into consideration, because of (*In view of the rain we had to cancel our picnic*).

---

vigorous *adj* (*a vigorous attempt at winning the game*) strong, powerful, forceful, determined, enthusiastic, lively, energetic, strenuous.

vile *adj* (*What a vile thing to do*) nasty, foul, unpleasant, disagreeable, horrible, dreadful, disgusting, hateful, shocking.

villain *n* (*The police have caught the villains*) rogue, scoundrel, wrongdoer, ruffian, (*inf*) crook. ▼

---

the villain of the piece the person responsible for a crime, misdeed, etc (*We wondered who had broken the window and discovered that the boy next door was the villain of the piece*).

---

violent *adj* **1** (*a violent attack*) brutal, ferocious, cruel, savage, vicious. **2** (*He has a violent temper*) uncontrollable, unrestrained, wild, passionate, forceful. **3** (*He took a violent dislike to her at first sight*) strong, great, intense, extreme, vehement.

virtually *adv* (*Traffic was virtually at a standstill*) more or less, nearly, practically, as good as, effectively, in effect, in essence, for all practical purposes.

virtue *n* **1** (*The church admires virtue and discourages vice*) goodness, righteousness, morality, integrity, uprightness, honesty, decency.

visible *adj* **1** (*The hilltops were

scarcely visible in the mist) in view, discernible, perceptible. **2** (*His unhappiness was visible to us all*) obvious, evident, apparent, noticeable, plain, clear, unmistakable.

vision *n* **1** (*Certain jobs call for good vision*) eyesight, sight. **2** (*He claims to have seen a vision in the graveyard*) apparition, ghost, spectre. **3** (*He saw his dead brother in a vision*) dream, hallucination. **4** (*men of vision*) insight, perception, discernment, intuition.

visit *vb* (*He visits his aunt once a year*) pay a visit to, go to see, pay a call on, call on, (*inf*) drop in on.

vital *adj* **1** (*It is vital that you attend the meeting*) imperative, essential, necessary, crucial. **2** (*hold vital discussions*) indispensable, urgent, essential, necessary, key. **3** (*She was a very vital person*) lively, energetic, vivacious. ▼

---

vital statistics one's chest, waist and hip measurements (*The announcer in the beauty contest gave the vital statistics of all the contestants*).

---

vitality *n* (*well-nourished children full of vitality*) energy, liveliness, vigour, zest, vivacity.

vivacious *adj* (*She is so vivacious that everyone else seems dull beside her*) lively, animated, sparkling, scintillating, dynamic, vibrant.

vivid *adj* **1** (*vivid colours*) bright, brilliant, strong, intense. **2** (*a vivid description*) clear, graphic, powerful, dramatic.

vocabulary *n* (*the difficult vocabulary in the piece*) language, words.

voice *n* **1** (*She lost her voice when she had a cold*) speech. **2** (*They finally gave voice to their feelings*) expression, utterance. **3** (*governments refusing to listen to the voice of the people*) opinion, view, comment. ▼

---

a voice crying in the wilderness someone expressing an opinion or warning to which no one pays any attention (*She told them that the suggested new range of goods would not sell but she was a voice crying in the wilderness*). **the still small voice of reason** the expression of a calm, sensible point of view of the kind often given by one's conscience. <A Biblical reference to John the Baptist in Matthew 3:3>.

---

volume *n* **1** (*an encyclopedia in several volumes*) book. **2** (*measure the volume*) capacity, bulk. **3** (*the sheer volume of water pouring out*) amount, quantity, mass. **4** (*We asked them to turn down the volume of their radio*) loudness, sound.

voluntary *n* **1** (*Attendance at the meeting is entirely voluntary*) of one's own free will, optional, non-compulsory. **2** (*She is unemployed but does voluntary work*) unpaid, without payment, volunteer.

vote *vb* (*They are voting to elect a new president*) cast one's vote, go to the polls. **2** (*She voted for the woman candidate*) elect, opt for, select. ▼

---

vote with one's feet to show one's disapproval, dissatisfaction, etc, by leaving (*The workers have no confidence in the firm's management and are voting with their feet*).

---

vote *n* (*have a vote on who should lead the team*) ballot, poll, election. ▼

---

a vote of no confidence a vote taken to find out whether the government, a person, group of people, etc, is still trusted and supported.

---

voucher *n* (*lunch vouchers*) token, ticket, slip.

vow *n* (*marriage vows*) oath, promise, pledge.

vow *vb* (*He vowed to be true*) swear, promise, pledge, give one's word.

vulgar *adj* **1** (*They objected to his vulgar language*) rude, indecent, obscene, bawdy, smutty. **2** (*vulgar table manners*) rude, impolite, unmannerly, ill-mannered. **3** (*They thought her clothes were vulgar*) tasteless, flashy, gaudy, tawdry.

vulnerable *adj* (*They felt vulnerable camping out in that area*) exposed, unprotected, defenceless.

W

wad *n* **1** (*use a wad of cotton wool to clean the wound*) lump, chunk, plug. **2** (*wads of banknotes*) bundle, roll.

wadding *n* (*use cotton-wool wadding to pack the jewellery*) filling, packing, padding, lining, stuffing.

waddle *vb* (*The very fat lady waddled down the street*) wiggle, sway, totter.

wade *vb* **1** (*The children were wading in the pool in the park*) paddle, splash. **2** (*There was no bridge and they had to wade across the stream*) ford, cross.

waffle *vb* (*She did not have much to say about the subject but she waffled on*) ramble, babble, prattle, (*inf*) witter, (*inf*) rabbit.

wag *vb* **1** (*The dog's tail was wagging*) swing, sway, shake, twitch, quiver. **2** (*The teacher wagged her finger angrily at the children*) waggle, wiggle.

wage *vb* (*wage war*) carry on, conduct, engage in, undertake.

wager *n* (*He laid a wager that she would not win*) bet, gamble, stake, (*inf*) flutter.

wager *vb* (*She wagered that the horse would come first in the race*) bet, place a bet, lay a bet, lay odds, put money on, gamble.

wages *npl* (*She has asked for a rise in her wages*) pay, salary, earnings, income, remuneration.

wail *vb* (*The children were wailing because their mother would not give them sweets*) cry, weep, sob, lament, howl, whine.

wait *vb* **1** (*The children were told to wait at the side of the road*) stay, remain, stop, halt. **2** (*She does not know if she has got the job—she will just have to wait and see*) be patient, stand by, hang fire, mark time, (*inf*) sit tight. **3** (*They asked us to wait for them*) await, watch out for, expect. **4** (*They are employed to wait at table*) serve, be a waiter/waitress. ▼

---

lie in wait (for someone) to be on the watch (for someone), to ambush (someone) (*The soldier was attacked by terrorists who were lying in wait for him/The reporters were lying in wait for the filmstar as she left the studio*). **be waiting in the wings** to be in a state of readiness to do something, especially to take over someone else's job (*She is afraid to be away from the office for long because she feels that her assistant is just waiting in the wings*).

---

wake *vb* **1** (*He asked us to wake him early*) wake up, waken, rouse. **2** (*We woke at dawn*) awake, waken, wake up, get up, arise.

walk *vb* **1** (*We were able to walk to the shops*) go by foot, go on foot, take shanks's pony, (*inf*) hoof it. **2** (*The children were told to walk and not to run*) stroll, saunter, amble, march.

walk *n* **1** (*They went for a walk after lunch*) stroll, saunter, amble, ramble, hike. **2** (*I recognized him by his walk*) gait, step, stride. ▼

walk of life occupation or profession, one's way of earning a living (*People from all walks of life attended the funeral of the mayor*).

walker *n* (*We passed a few walkers as we drove to the village*) pedestrian, hiker, rambler.

wall *n* **1** (*The garden had a wall around it*) enclosure, barrier. **2** (*We tore down a wall of the house to knock two rooms into one*) partition. **3** (*tourists who went to visit the old city walls*) fortifications, ramparts, barricade, bulwark. ▼

go to the wall to fail, to suffer bankruptcy or ruin (*The firm went to the wall, when it lost the export order*). <Origin uncertain>. **walls have ears** someone unnoticed or unseen may be listening (*I asked him not to discuss our private business in the restaurant. It was not busy but walls have ears*).

wallet *n* (*His wallet was stolen and he now has no money*) pocketbook, note case, purse.

wallow *vb* **1** (*The animals were wallowing in mud*) roll, splash, tumble. **2** (*She was wallowing in self-pity*) bask, luxuriate, revel, delight.

wan *adj* (*She looked wan after having bad flu*) pale, white, pallid, (*inf*) peaky.

wand *n* (*The fairy godmother waved her wand*) stick, baton, rod.

wander *vb* **1** (*The child wandered off while his mother was shopping*) go off, get lost, stray, lose one's way. **2** (*They loved to wander over the hills when they were on holiday*) roam, ramble, rove, range. **3** (*The old man does not recognize his family and has started to wander*) ramble, rave, babble.

wane *vb* **1** (*The moon is waning*) decrease, diminish, dwindle. **2** (*The power of ancient Greece waned*) decrease, decline, diminish, dwindle, fade, subside, dim, vanish, die out.

want *vb* **1** (*The children wanted some sweets*) wish for, desire, demand, long for, crave, yearn for, hanker after. **2** (*poor people wanting food*) lack, be lacking in, be without, be devoid of, be short of.

war *n* **1** (*The war between the neighbouring countries lasted many years*) warfare, fighting, conflict, struggle, hostilities, battles. **2** (*There was a state of war between the two nations*) conflict, strife, hostility, enmity, ill-will. **3** (*She took part in the war against poverty in the area*) battle, fight, crusade, campaign. ▼

be on the warpath to be extremely angry and out for revenge (*Their father has discovered the broken window and is now on the warpath*) <An American Indian expression>. **have been in the wars** to have received a slight injury (*'You have been in the wars,' said the doctor to the little boy as he stitched his injured arm*).

ward *n* **1** (*The hospital ward holds four beds*) room, cubicle, compartment. **2** (*Which ward does the councillor represent?*) district, division. **3** (*Her parents are dead and she is a ward of her uncle*) charge, dependant.

ward *vb* **1** (*She succeeded in warding off his attack*) fend off, stave off, deflect, avert, rebuff. 2 (*They warded off the intruders*) drive back, repel, beat back.

warden *n* 1 (*She is employed as traffic warden*) supervisor, superintendent, overseer. 2 (*He is a game warden in Africa*) keeper, custodian, guardian, guard. 3 (*The prisoners attacked a warden*) warder, prison officer, guard, jailer, gaoler, (*inf*) screw.

wardrobe *n* 1 (*She hung her clothes up in the wardrobe*) cupboard. 2 (*She is buying a new wardrobe for her holiday*) clothes, trousseau.

warehouse *n* (*They collected the books from the warehouse*) store, depot, stockroom.

wares *npl* (*There were many people selling their wares in the market*) goods, products, merchandise, stock, commodities.

warlike *adj* (*They encountered warlike tribes in the jungle*) belligerent, aggressive, pugnacious, hostile.

warlock *n* (*a story about a warlock*) wizard, sorcerer, magician, witch.

warm *adj* 1 (*She bathed the wound in warm water*) heated, tepid, lukewarm. 2 (*go for a swim on a warm day*) sunny, hot, close, sultry. 3 (*She has a warm heart*) kind, kindly, sympathetic, tender, loving, affectionate. 4 (*We received a warm welcome*) hearty, cordial, friendly, enthusiastic. ▼

---

be as warm as toast to be very warm and cosy (*The children were as warm as toast under their duvets*). **get warm** to get close to the correct solution (*The quiz master said that her answer was not right but that she was getting warm*).

---

warm *vb* 1 (*The mother warmed the food for the baby*) heat, heat up. 2 (*The competitors warmed up for the race*) loosen up, limber up, exercise. ▼

---

warm the cockles of the heart to make one feel happy and contented (*It warmed the cockles of her heart to watch her children looking after the old woman*).

---

warn *vb* (*They were warned that they were entering a dangerous area*) advise, caution, make aware, notify, inform, (*inf*) tip off.

warning *n* 1 (*They had no warning of the terrible storm*) forewarning, notification, notice, information, indication, hint. 2 (*He was superstitious and regarded his experience as a warning of things to come*) omen, signal, threat.

warrior *n* (*a book about the deeds of ancient warriors*) fighter, combatant, champion, soldier, knight.

wary *adj* (*The children were taught to be wary of strangers*) cautious, careful, on one's guard, watchful, chary, suspicious, distrustful.

wash *vb* 1 (*They washed their hands before dinner*) clean, cleanse, scrub. 2 (*The children washed before going to bed*) have a wash, wash oneself, clean oneself, sponge oneself down. 3 (*They washed their clothes and hung them out to dry*) launder, clean. 4 (*waves washing against the boats*) splash, dash, beat. ▼

---

wash one's dirty linen in public to discuss personal or private matters or problems in public (*We hear all the details of their financial problems when they quarrel. I wish they wouldn't wash their dirty* *linen in public*). **wash one's hands of (someone or something)** to refuse to be held responsible for (someone or something) or to be involved any longer in (something) (*He has tried to help the pupil to get through her exams but since she refuses to work he has washed his hands of her*).

---

waste *vb* **1** (*They waste a lot of money/Try not to waste time*) squander, fritter, misuse, misspend. **2** (*Because of his illness his limbs are wasting away*) grow weak, grow thin, wither, atrophy. ▼

---

waste not, want not if one is thrifty and is careful not to waste anything, it is likely that one will never be in want (*Don't throw out the remains of the meat. We can use it tomorrow. Waste not, want not*).

---

waste *n* **1** (*find a way of getting rid of the waste*) rubbish, refuse, debris, (*esp Amer*) garbage. **2** (*doing research in the wastes of the Antarctic*) wasteland, wilderness, desert, vastness.

wasteful *adj* (*a wasteful use of money*) thriftless, extravagant, spendthrift, profligate, prodigal.

watch *vb* **1** (*We watched the sun going down*) look at, observe, view, contemplate, survey, stare at, gaze at. **2** (*If you watch what the teacher does you will be able to do the experiment yourself*) pay attention to, take notice of, to heed, concentrate on. **3** (*The police are watching him*) keep watch on, keep an eye on, keep under surveillance, follow, spy on. **4** (*Watch and don't get attacked in that area of the town*) take care, look out, take heed, beware, be alert. **5** (*She asked her mother to watch the children*) mind, take care of, look after, keep an eye on, tend. ▼

---

the watched pot never boils when one is waiting for something to happen the time taken seems much longer if one is constantly thinking about it. **watch (someone) like a hawk** to watch (someone) very carefully (*The teacher has to watch the boy like a hawk as he always tries to bully the other children*) <Birds of prey are thought to have particularly sharp eyesight>.

---

watchman *n* security guard, guard, caretaker, custodian, sentry.

water *n* **1** (*have a glass of water with the meal*) tap water, bottled water, mineral water. **2** (*children playing by the water*) pond, pool, lake, river, sea. ▼

---

be water off a duck's back to be totally ineffective or unsuccessful (*We tried to warn him that his journey would be dangerous but our warnings were like water off a duck's back*) <Refers to the fact that water runs straight off the oily feathers on a duck's back>. **hold water** to be able to be proved to be true, to be accurate (*The scientist's theory seemed interesting but when we put it to the test it did not hold water*) <A reference to a container of some kind that is not broken and so can hold liquids>.

---

watery *adj* **1** (*The gravy was wa-

tery/The soup was watery) thin, weak, dilute, runny, tasteless, flavourless. **2** (*watery eyes*) wet, moist, damp, tearful, weepy.

wave *vb* **1** (*flags waving in the breeze*) flutter, flap, ripple, shake, undulate. **2** (*He waved his sword angrily*) shake, swing, brandish. **3** (*He waved his hand to his friends*) flutter, waggle. **4** (*He waved to the driver*) gesture. **5** (*Her hair waves*) curl, kink, undulate.

wave *n* **1** (*The children were splashing in the waves*) breaker, swell, surf, billow. **2** (*the waves in her hair*) curl, kink, undulation, **3** (*a town hit by a crime wave*) upsurge, surge, rash, outbreak.

waver *vb* **1** (*His courage did not waver*) falter, vary, change. **2** (*We had been determined to go but then we began to waver*) hesitate, think twice, vacillate, shilly-shally. **3** (*lights wavering*) flicker, tremble, quiver.

wax *vb* (*The moon was waxing*) increase, enlarge.

way *n* **1** (*They asked which was the way to London*) road, route, direction. **2** (*She said that it was a long way to London from there*) distance, journey. **3** (*They were taught the correct way to change the wheel of a car*) method, procedure, technique, system, manner, means. **4** (*The children laughed at the way the old lady dressed*) manner, fashion, style, mode. **5** (*They have old-fashioned ways*) habit, custom, practice, conduct, behaviour. **6** (*His business affairs are in a bad way*) state, condition, situation. **7** (*In some ways I will miss them although mostly I am glad that they've gone*) respect, aspect, feature, detail, point. ▼

---

go out of one's way to make a special effort, to do more than is really necessary (*Our hosts went out of their way to make us feel welcome*). **have a way with (someone** *or* **something)** to have a special knack when dealing with (someone or something), to be good at dealing with (someone or something) (*She wants to become a nanny and she certainly has a way with children*).

---

weak *adj* **1** (*She felt very weak after her long illness*) weakly, frail, delicate, feeble, shaky, debilitated, tired. **2** (*Their leader was too weak to stand up to the enemy*) cowardly, timid, soft, spineless, powerless. **3** (*She made a weak excuse for being late*) feeble, lame, pathetic, unconvincing, unsatisfactory. **4** (*The tea was too weak*) dilute, watery, tasteless, wishy-washy. ▼

---

in a weak moment at a time when one is feeling unusually generous, sympathetic, etc (*In a weak moment I offered to lend them my car and then regretted it*).

---

weaken *vb* **1** (*The illness had obviously weakened her*) make weak, debilitate, tire, wear out. **2** (*Our chances of winning were weakened*) lessen, decrease, reduce, diminish, undermine. **3** (*Our parents refused to let us go but then they weakened*) relent, come round, give in.

weakness *n* **1** (*A tendency to lie is her major weakness*) fault, failing, flaw, defect, shortcoming, imperfection, foible. **2** (*She has a weakness for chocolate*) fondness, liking, love, soft spot, preference, penchant.

wealth *n* (*He shared his great wealth among his family*) riches, fortune, money, capital, assets.

wealthy *adj* (*an area of the town where wealthy people live*) affluent, rich, well-off, well-to-do, moneyed, (*inf*) well-heeled.

wear *vb* **1** (*The children were wearing warm coats*) be dressed in, be clothed in, have on. **2** (*She wore a gloomy expression*) have, show, display. **3** (*rocks worn away by water*) erode, eat away, rub away. **4** (*She was worn out by the long walk*) tire, fatigue, exhaust. ▼

---

wear one's heart on one's sleeve to let one's feelings be very obvious (*She is not one to wear her heart on her sleeve and so people did not realize that she was in love with him*).

---

weary *adj* **1** (*The children were weary at the end of the long school day*) tired, fatigued, exhausted, worn out, (*inf*) deadbeat. **2** (*She is weary of her present job*) bored, discontented, jaded, (*inf*) fed up.

weather *n* (*What is the weather like there in August?*) climate. ▼

---

be under the weather to be slightly unwell (*She left work early because she was under the weather*). **keep a weather eye open** to keep a close watch, to be alert (*He was keeping a weather eye open for the boys who were stealing his apples*) <A nautical term for watching for changes in the weather>.

---

web *n* (*a spider's web*) mesh, net, network, lattice.

wedding *n* wedding ceremony, marriage, marriage ceremony.

wedge *vb* **1** (*Since it was very hot they wedged the door open*) jam, secure. **2** (*Four of them were wedged in the back seat*) squeeze, jam, cram, pack.

wedge *n* (*a wedge of cheese*) chunk, hunk, lump, (*inf*) wodge. ▼

---

the thin end of the wedge a minor event or action which could be the first stage of something major and serious or harmful (*Letting her stay for a week could be the thin end of the wedge—she will want to stay permanently*) <A wedge is tapered at one end>.

---

weep *vb* (*The child wept when her mother went away*) cry, sob, shed tears.

weight *n* **1** (*estimate the weight of the cake*) heaviness. **2** (*A weight fell on his toe*) heavy object. **3** (*When their daughter returned it was a weight off their minds*) burden, load, onus, worry, trouble. **4** (*They attach a great deal of weight to his opinion*) importance, significance, value, substance. ▼

---

pull one's weight to do one's fair share of work, etc (*They were all supposed to help with the housework but she did not pull her weight*). **throw one's weight around** to use one's power or influence in a domineering, bullying way (*When her father is away her elder brother says that he is head of the house and throws his weight around*).

---

weird *adj* **1** (*We heard weird noises in the cellar*) eerie, strange, queer, uncanny, creepy, ghostly, unearthly, (*inf*) spooky. **2** (*She always wears weird clothes*) strange, queer, odd, bizarre, eccentric, outlandish, off-beat.

welcome *vb* **1** (*They welcomed their guests at the door*) greet, receive, meet. **2** (*We welcomed the news*) be pleased with, be glad at.

welfare *n* (*She was worried about her children's welfare*) well-being, health, happiness.

well *adj* **1** (*She has been ill but is now quite well*) in good health, healthy, fit, strong. **2** (*They found that all was well*) all right, satisfactory, fine, (*inf*) OK.

well *adv* **1** (*He plays the piano well*) competently, skilfully, expertly. **2** (*The children behaved well*) properly, correctly, suitably, satisfactorily. **3** (*They speak well of him*) highly, admiringly, approvingly, favourably. **4** (*They may well be right*) probably, likely, possibly.

wet *adj* **1** (*The ground was wet after the rain/Her clothes were wet*) damp, moist, soaked, drenched, saturated, sopping. **2** (*We had wet weather on holiday*) rainy, damp, showery.

wet *vb* **1** (*She wet the shirts before ironing them*) dampen, moisten, sprinkle, spray. **2** (*The rain really wet them*) soak, drench, saturate. ▼

---

a wet blanket a dull, uninteresting person who make s other people feel depressed (*We were enjoying the party until he arrived but he is such a wet blanket*). **be wet behind the ears** to be young and inexperienced (*Don't let the young salesman deal with that difficult customer. He's still wet behind the ears*).

---

wharf *vb* (*ships being unloaded at the wharf*) dock, quay, pier, jetty, landing stage.

wheeze *vb* (*She had a bad cold and was wheezing*) pant, puff, gasp.

whimper *vb* (*The dog was sitting whimpering on the doorstep*) whine, cry.

whine *vb* (*The children were bored and began to whine*) wail, cry, whimper, complain, (*inf*) grizzle.

whip *n* (*The jockey used his whip on the horse*) switch, crop, scourge, lash, horsewhip, cat o' nine tails.

whip *vb* **1** (*They used to whip people who had done wrong*) lash, flog, scourge, birch, beat, thrash. **2** (*She whipped the cream*) beat, whisk, mix, blend. **3** (*He whipped his handkerchief from his pocket*) pull, yank, jerk, snatch, whisk. ▼

---

have the whip hand to have control or an advantage (*He has the whip hand in that partnership. He makes all the decisions*) <A reference to driving a coach>. **whipping boy** someone who is blamed and punished for someone else's mistakes (*The young clerk is the whipping boy for the whole department*) <Refers historically to a boy who was punished by a tutor for any misdeeds a royal prince made, since the tutor was not allowed to strike a member of the royal family>.

---

whirl *vb* (*They watched the dancers whirling round the floor*) turn, spin, rotate, revolve, wheel, circle, twirl.

whisper *vb* (*She whispered to her friend at the back of the classroom*) murmur, mutter, breathe.

white *adj* **1** (*She was white with

fear) pale, wan, pallid, ashen, peaky. 2 (*Her hair is white with age*) grey, silver, snowy white. ▼

---

show the white feather to show signs of cowardice (*His fellow workers accused him of showing the white feather when he refused to ask the boss for a wage increase*) <A white feather in the tail of a fighting cock was a sign of inferior breeding>. **white elephant** something which is useless and often troublesome to look after (*The vase which my aunt gave me is a real white elephant. It's large and ugly and difficult to dust*) <White elephants were formerly given by the Kings of Siam to followers who had displeased them since the cost of keeping such an elephant was so great that it might well ruin the followers>. **white lie a** not very serious lie (*I told a white lie when she asked me if I liked her dress. I didn't want to upset her*).

---

whole *adj* **1** (*We asked her to tell us the whole story*) full, entire, complete, unabridged. **2** (*Not a single wine glass was left whole*) intact, in one piece, undamaged, unbroken. ▼

---

go the whole hog to do something completely and thoroughly (*We decorated one room and then decided to go the whole hog and paint the entire house*) <Perhaps refers to buying a whole pig at market instead of just parts of it for meat>.

---

wholesome *adj* (*wholesome food*) health-giving, healthy, nutritious, nourishing.

wholly *adv* **1** (*We are not wholly against the scheme*) entirely, completely, fully, thoroughly, utterly. **2** (*The responsibility lies wholly with him*) only, solely, purely, exclusively.

wicked *adj* (*the wicked people who attacked and robbed the old man*) evil, bad, sinful, vicious, immoral, unethical, villainous, criminal.

wide *adj* **1** (*a city with wide streets*) broad, spacious. **2** (*A wide range of subjects is available at the school*) broad, large, extensive, comprehensive, wide-ranging. **3** (*He always wears very wide trousers*) loose, baggy, roomy.

widespread *adj* (*There were widespread rumours of war*) general, common, universal, extensive, prevalent, rife.

width *n* **1** (*measure the width of the material*) wideness, breadth, broadness, span. **2** (*We admired the width of his knowledge*) wideness, breadth, scope, range, comprehensiveness.

wield *vb* **1** (*a knight wielding a sword*) brandish, flourish, wave, swing. **2** (*It is the deputy president who wields the power*) have, hold, exercise, exert.

wife *n* spouse, partner, (*inf*) better half.

wild *adj* **1** (*an area where wild animals roamed*) untamed, undomesticated, fierce, savage, ferocious. **2** (*the wild flowers of the area*) uncultivated, native, indigenous. **3** (*The ship sank in wild weather*) stormy, rough, blustery, turbulent, windy. **4** (*They had to travel across wild country*) rough, rugged, desolate, waste. **5** (*the wild behaviour of the* *football crowd*) rowdy, disorderly, unruly, violent, turbulent, uncontrolled. ▼

---

spread like wildfire to spread extremely rapidly (*The disease spread like wildfire in the overcrowded community*) <Wildfire was probably a kind of fire started by lightning>. **a wild goose chase** a search or hunt that is unlikely to end in success (*I knew it was a wild goose chase to look for a restaurant that was open at that time in the morning*). **wild horses would not drag (someone) to something** *or* **somewhere** nothing would persuade (someone) to attend something or go somewhere (*Wild horses would not drag me to the city centre on a Saturday afternoon. I hate crowds*).

---

wilful *adj* **1** (*a nanny finding it difficult to cope with such wilful children*) headstrong, strong-willed, obstinate, stubborn, determined, disobedient, contrary. **2** (*The jury decided that it was a case of wilful murder*) deliberate, intentional, planned, premeditated, calculated.

will *n* **1** (*He seems to have lost the will to live*) desire, wish, inclination, determination. **2** (*He died without making a will*) last will and testament, testament. ▼

---

with the best will in the world no matter how much one wants to do something or make something happen (*With the best will in the world we could not get there in time*).

---

willing *adj* **1** (*They had a lot of willing helpers at the church fête*) eager, keen, enthusiastic, avid. **2** (*There was no one willing to take responsibility for the organization of the event*) ready, prepared, disposed, agreeable, amenable. ▼

---

willing horse someone who is keen to work or help and for that reason usually ends up doing more than his or her fair share (*She is president of the committee but it is the willing horses who do all the work*).

---

wilt *vb* (*The flowers in the vase were wilting*) droop, wither, shrivel, dry up.

wily *adj* (*He was wily enough to convince the old lady that he was a representative of the church*) cunning, crafty, artful, scheming, sly, sharp.

win *vb* **1** (*We were not surprised when their team won*) be victorious, be the victor, come first, triumph, carry the day. **2** (*She won first prize*) gain, get, achieve, attain, acquire.

wince *vb* (*She winced when they reminded her of her tactless remark*) grimace, flinch, cringe, recoil.

wind *n* (*The wind blew the papers all around the room*) breeze, gale, gust, blast, draught. ▼

---

get wind of (something) to receive information about (something) usually indirectly or secretly (*They were planning to steal our bicycles but fortunately we got wind of their plans*) <A reference to the scent of an animal carried by the wind>. **get the wind up** (*inf*) to become frightened or nervous (*They got the wind up when they saw the strange men* *following them*). **take the wind out of (someone's) sails** to reduce (someone's) pride in his or her cleverness, abilities, achievements, etc (*She was boasting about how many exams she had passed when we took the wind out of her sails by telling her that everyone else had passed more*) <A reference to the fact that a ship takes the wind out of another ship's sails if it passes too close to it on the windward side>.

---

wind *vb* **1** (*Her grandmother asked her to wind her wool*) twist, twine, coil, roll. **2** (*The road winds up the mountain*) twist, twist and turn, curve, loop, zigzag, spiral, snake, meander.

wing *n* **1** (*The family occupy just the west wing of the castle*) side, annex. **2** (*They are on the right wing of the party*) section, side, group, segment. ▼

---

take (someone) under one's wing to take (someone) under one's protection and guidance (*The girl has been neglected. She needs an older woman to take her under her wing*).

---

wink *vb* **1** (*He winked an eye*) blink, flutter, bat. **2** (*lights winking on the water*) twinkle, flash, sparkle, glitter, gleam.

winner *n* (*They were the winners in the battle/the winner in the tennis tournament*) victor, champion, conqueror, vanquisher.

wipe *vb* (*wipe the kitchen surfaces*) clean, sponge, mop, rub, brush. ▼

---

wipe the floor with (someone) to defeat (someone), to scold (someone) very severely (*The visiting team wiped the floor with us/Mum wiped the floor with us when we arrived home late*).

---

wisdom *n* **1** (*admire their wisdom in getting out of the industry at the right time*) sense, common sense, prudence, good judgement, shrewdness, astuteness, smartness. **2** (*The young people benefited from the wisdom of their grandparents*) knowledge.

wise *adj* **1** (*We thought it wise to leave early when it began to snow*) sensible, well-advised, prudent, shrewd, astute, smart. **2** (*They asked the wise old men of the village for advice*) knowledgeable, learned, well-informed, enlightened, sage.

wish *vb* (*They could not have wished for friendlier neighbours*) want, desire, long for, yearn for, covet, (*inf*) have a yen for.

wish *n* **1** (*They were supposed to obey the king's every wish*) want, desire, demand, request. **2** (*At last she was able to satisfy her wish to travel*) desire, longing, yearning, fancy, inclination, craving, (*inf*) yen. ▼

---

wishful thinking believing that, or hoping that, something unlikely is true or will happen just because one wishes that it would (*We hoped our team would win but it was just wishful thinking. They were not very good*).

---

wistful *adj* (*She had a wistful expression as she watched them leave on holiday*) yearning, longing, forlorn, sad, pathetic.

wit *n* **1** (*He did not have the wit to realize that she was teasing him*) intelligence, brains, sense, common sense, shrewdness. 2 (*We had to admire his wit as he kept us all amused*) wittiness, humour. ▼

---

at one's wits' end extremely worried and desperate (*We were at our wits' end when all our money was stolen*). **live by one's wits** to make a living from cunning schemes rather than from working.

---

witch *n* (*a story about a witch and her broomstick*) enchantress, sorceress. ▼

---

witch-hunt a search for people who are thought to have done something wrong, hold opinions which are considered dangerous, etc, in order to persecute them (*There was a witch-hunt to remove people from the club who held different political opinions from the majority*) <Formerly there were organized searches for people thought to be witches in order that they might be punished>.

---

withdraw *vb* **1** (*She withdrew from the tennis match because of ill health*) pull out, come out, retire. **2** (*They withdrew their son from the school*) remove, take away, pull out. **3** (*The troops withdrew when they were defeated*) pull back, fall back, move back, retreat, retire, depart.

wither *vb* (*The flowers in the vase had withered*) fade, dry up, dry out, shrivel, die.

witness *vb* (*They witnessed a terrible accident*) see, observe, look on at, watch, view, be present at.

witness *n* (*The police asked for witnesses at the scene of the accident*) eye-witness, onlooker, observer, spectator, bystander.

witty *adj* (*witty stories/witty people*) amusing, funny, humorous, comic, clever.

wizard *n* (*a fairy story about wizards*) warlock, sorcerer, magician, enchanter.

wobble *vb* **1** (*This table wobbles*) rock, teeter, shake. **2** (*wobble down the street on stiletto heels*) totter, teeter, sway, stagger, waddle. **3** (*Her voice wobbled and she began to cry*) shake, tremble, quiver.

woe *n* (*We listened to her tale of woe*) misfortune, distress, suffering, trouble, misery, unhappiness.

wonder *n* **1** (*watched with wonder as the acrobats performed*) amazement, astonishment, awe, bewilderment, curosity. **2** (*The acrobats are a wonder*) marvel, miracle, prodigy, surprise. ▼

---

a nine days' wonder something that has aroused interest or talk for a short time only (*It was in all the papers when he was sent to prison but it was a nine days' wonder*).

---

wonder *vb* **1** (*wondering at the immensity of the sky*) admire, gape, marvel. **2** (*I wonder if they will marry*) conjecture, ponder, query, question, speculate.

wonderful *adj* **1** (*The church ceiling was a wonderful sight*) marvellous, remarkable, extraordinary, amazing, astonishing, fantastic. **2** (*She was a wonderful pianist*) superb, marvellous, brilliant, excellent, first-rate, outstanding.

wood *n* **1** (*houses made of wood*) timber. **2** (*go for a walk in the wood*) woods, forest, copse, thicket. ▼

be out of the woods to be free from danger or difficulty (*She was very ill and nearly died but she is out of the woods now*). **touch wood** to touch something made of wood supposedly in an effort to keep away bad luck or misfortune <A reference to a well-known superstition>.

woolly *adj* **1** (*buy the child a woolly toy*) fluffy, fleecy, furry. **2** (*woolly thoughts*) hazy, vague, muddled, confused, indefinite, uncertain.

word *n* **1** (*She was trying to think of another word for 'work'*) term, expression. **2** (*She gave him her word that she would be there*) promise, pledge, assurance, guarantee, undertaking. **3** (*They have had no word about their missing son*) news, information, communication. ▼

have words to quarrel or argue (*From the expressions on their faces I would say that they have had words*). **take (someone) at his or her word** to believe (someone) without question and act accordingly (*He said we could borrow the car any time and we took him at his word*).

work *n* **1** (*Making a doll's house for his daughter involved a lot of work*) effort, exertion, labour, toil, trouble, elbow grease. **2** (*Her work involves meeting a great many people*) job, employment, occupation, profession, trade. ▼

have one's work cut out to face a very difficult task (*You will have your work cut out to persuade him to stay*) <Literally to have a lot of work ready for one to do>. **throw a spanner in the works** to hinder or spoil (a plan, project, etc) (*We were going away for the weekend but my boss threw a spanner in the works by asking me to work on Saturday*).

work *vb* **1** (*He works in banking*) be employed, have a job. **2** (*The pupils will have to work at their studies to pass the exams*) exert oneself, apply oneself, make an effort, labour, toil. **3** (*Can you work this machine?*) operate, use, control, handle. **4** (*This machine does not work*) go, operate, function, run. **5** (*That idea will not work*) succeed, be successful, go well, be effective.

world *n* **1** (*the peoples of the world*) earth, globe, planet. **2** (*The world was shocked by the terrorist attack*) people, everyone, the public. **3** (*the medical world*) society, sector, section, group. ▼

out of this world remarkably good (*the food in the new restaurant is out of this world*). **think the world of (someone** *or* **something)** to be extremely fond of (someone or something) (*She thinks the world of her dog*).

worry *n* **1** (*His behaviour caused her a lot of worry*) anxiety, trouble, bother, distress, disturbance, upset, uneasiness. **2** (*She was a real worry to her parents*) trouble, nuisance, pest, problem, trial, thorn in the flesh.

worsen *vb* **1** (*The situation between workers and management has worsened*) get worse, take a turn for the worsen, deteriorate, degenerate. **2** (*His efforts to help *simply worsened the situation*) make worse, aggravate, exacerbate, increase.

worship *vb* **1** (*go to church to worship God*) pray to, praise, glorify, pay homage to. **2** (*He simply worships his wife*) idolize, adore, be devoted to, cherish, dote on.

worth *n* **1** (*The jewellery is of little financial worth but is of sentimental value*) value. **2** (*We regarded his advice as being of little worth*) value, use, advantage, benefit, gain. ▼

---

for all one is worth using maximum effort (*We tried for all we were worth to finish the job in time*). **make (something) worth (someone's) while** to make (something) worth (someone's) time and effort, to give (someone) sufficient reward or recompense (*If you want a workman to do repairs on a Sunday you will have to make it worth his while*).

---

worthy *adj* **1** (*They were not worthy of respect*) deserving, meriting. **2** (*the worthy people in the community*) good, decent, honourable, upright, virtuous, admirable, commendable, deserving.

wound *n* **1** (*He got his wound dressed in hospital*) injury, sore, cut, laceration, lesion. **2** (*Her remark was a wound to his pride*) blow, injury, hurt, damage, slight.

wrap *vb* **1** (*Wrap the child in a blanket and take him to a hospital*) cover, bundle up, swathe, enfold. **2** (*She wrapped the Christmas presents*) wrap up, parcel up, package, tie up, gift-wrap. ▼

---

be wrapped up in (someone *or* **something)** to give (someone or something) all one's attention (*She complains about the fact that her husband is completely wrapped up in his work*). **keep (something) under wraps** to keep (something) secret or confidential (*We are keeping our plans for the firm under wraps at the moment so that our rivals don't find out about them*).

---

wrath *n* (*They had to face the wrath of the teacher when they played truant*) anger, rage, fury, indignation, annoyance.

wreck *vb* **1** (*He wrecked his father's car*), smash, demolish, ruin, damage, (*inf*) write off. **2** (*His illness wrecked their holiday plans*) ruin, destroy, spoil, shatter.

wrench *vb* (*He wrenched the lid from the container*) twist, pull, tug, jerk, force.

wretched *adj* **1** (*She was feeling wretched about being away from home*) miserable, depressed, unhappy, sad. **2** (*He felt wretched when he had flu*) ill, unwell, sick, (*inf*) under the weather. **3** (*He has a wretched cold*) nasty, unpleasant, disagreeable.

wriggle *vb* **1** (*children wriggling with impatience in their seats*) twist, squirm, writhe. **2** (*She tried to wriggle out of helping with the housework*) dodge, evade, avoid, duck out of.

wring *vb* **1** (*wring the clothes out*) squeeze, twist. **2** (*His enemies wrung the information from him*) extract, force, wrench.

wrinkle *n* (*She ironed her blouse to remove the wrinkles*) crease, pucker, fold, furrow.

write *vb* **1** (*write an essay*) compose, pen. **2** (*She wrote down the names of the people present*) put down, take down, note, list, record. ▼

be nothing to write home about to be unremarkable, to be nothing special (*The meal in the new restaurant was all right but it was nothing to write home about*).

writer *n* (*He is a professional writer*) author, novelist, journalist.

writing *n* **1** (*She teaches children writing*) handwriting, penmanship, script. **2** (*a list of his writings*) work, book, publication. ▼

the writing on the wall something which indicates that something unpleasant, such as failure, unhappiness, disaster, etc, will happen (*She should have seen the writing on the wall when her boss kept complaining about her work*) <A Biblical reference to Daniel 5:5-31, in which the coming destruction of the Babylonian empire is made known to Belshazzar at a feast through mysterious writing on a wall>.

wrong *adj* **1** (*It is wrong to steal*) bad, wicked, sinful, illegal, unlawful, criminal, crooked. **2** (*There is something wrong with the computer*) broken, faulty, defective, out of order. **3** (*It was the wrong way to deal with the problem*) incorrect, improper, inappropriate, unsuitable. **4** (*She gave the wrong answer to the mathematical question*) incorrect, inaccurate, erroneous, mistaken. ▼

get on the wrong side of (someone) to cause (someone) to dislike or be hostile to one (*She seemed to get on the wrong side of the boss from her first day in the firm*). **not to put a foot wrong** not to make a mistake of any kind (*It was not surprising that he won the tennis match. He did not put a foot wrong throughout the game*).

wrong *n* **1** (*be taught right from wrong*) badness, evil, sin, sinfulness, unlawfulness. **2** (*He committed several wrongs*) misdeed, offence, crime. ▼

be in the wrong to be to blame, to be guilty of some kind of error (*The accident was his fault but he refused to admit that he had been in the wrong*).

Y

yearn *vb* (*They yearned for some sunshine*) long, pine, crave, desire, covet, fancy, hanker after, (*inf*) have a yen for.

yield *vb* **1** (*They refuse to yield to the invading army*) submit, give in, surrender, concede defeat. **2** (*They finally yielded to his demands*) give in, comply with, consent to, grant. **3** (*investments which yield a good return*) bring in, earn, return, produce. **4** (*an area which yields heavy crops*) produce, give, bear, grow, supply.

young *adj* (*young people*) youthful, juvenile, adolescent.

Z

zealous *adj* (*zealous followers of the sport/zealous in their efforts to gain support*) eager, keen, enthusiastic, passionate, fervent, earnest, fanatical.

zenith *n* (*when the Roman empire was at the zenith of its power*) peak, height, top, pinnacle, acme, apex.

zero *n* **1** (*How many zeroes are there when you write a million in figures?*) nought, nothing. **2** (*We won absolutely zero*) nothing, naught, nil, (inf) zilch.

zest *n* (*the old lady's zest for life*) enthusiasm, eagerness, relish, energy.

zone *n* (*a traffic-free zone*) area, sector, region.

Letter-writing

Introduction

Though some may question the need to write letters nowadays, to use the telephone, fax and email is not necessarily as effective—nor is it as lasting—as a letter. Phone calls may, on the face of it, be quick and easy, but who has not been kept on hold for extended periods listening to a maddening tinny tune, until they can stand it no longer and ring off in disgust. Neither a phone call nor an email message provides the formal documentation you may need to substantiate facts or follow something up at a later date. And in other situations, such as thanking someone or offering your sympathy, there really is no substitute for a note or letter written in your own hand.

Therefore, most of us will need to write letters at some time, whether we are making a complaint, writing to our bank or building society, accepting or rejecting a job offer, or offering condolences. Writing a letter allows you to consider carefully what you want to say, to express your feelings, to put things in a logical order, to revise and fine tune, and so produce an impressive and effective result.

The aim of this section is to set you firmly on the path of being a confident letter-writer.

First there is a brief history of letter-writing, then some guidance on the tools and equipment you may need, followed by some advice on presentation and layout, and pointers on how to make best use of the new technologies of word processing, emailing and text messaging.

A Potted History of Letters and Their Delivery

A letter—according to the *Shorter Oxford English Dictionary*—is 'a written, typed or printed communication, addressed to a person, organization, etc., and usually sent by post or messenger.' Expanding this definition a little, a letter is a written message delivered—by a variety of means—to an addressee located at some distance geographically from its sender.

Letters were, and still are, written for a variety of reasons: people may be too distant from each other to allow face-to-face discussion; they may not be able to communicate by any other means; one person may wish to communicate private or sensitive information to another; or it may be desirable to have a written record of an exchange which can be retained for future reference.

The communication boom

In ancient Egypt, Persia and Greece, the earliest recorded letters were written by the political and military elite, the only section of society able to write themselves, or to pay for the services of a scribe, and also with the means to organize, in a reliable and consistent way, the delivery of their messages.

In the Hellenistic period after the death of Alexander the Great, personal letter-writing seems to have become almost commonplace. Letters were being written by a wide range of people in many different situations for a variety of purposes. These purposes included maintaining contact during long separations, reporting news, expressing thanks or condolences, and making requests or giving advice. Certain conventions in letters of this period—especially the formulaic greetings and endings used—seem to suggest that basic letter-writing, or at least the basic structure of a letter, was taught in schools.

Because letters are often essentially substitutes for conversations between friends and acquaintances and because human beings are insatiably curious and social animals, the habit of letter-writing between private individuals became more and more popular and widespread. It was not even absolutely essential to be literate; those without the skill to write could dictate to a scribe, who, for a fee, would write the letter for the sender.

Once people began to write to each other regularly, they also started to put some time and effort into what they had to say and how it was said. The conventional greetings and endings of letters evolved and polite wishes for good health, etc., were included. Correspondents often vied to outdo each other in witty written exchanges. Especially amongst the educated classes and literati, letter-writing was elevated to an art form and began to be used as a literary device.

It is widely known that some of the New Testament of the Bible is in the form of letters, such as 'the Epistles of St Paul'. Some novels are also written in the form of letters, early examples being *Pamela* (1749) by Samuel Richardson and *The Expedition of Humphrey Clinker* (1771) by Tobias Smollett. Fiction in this style, known as the 'epistolary novel'—though comparatively rare—is classed as a literary genre. Poetry has also been written in epistolary verses; a notable example is 'An Epistle to Dr Arbuthnot' (1735) by Alexander Pope.

Delivery methods down the ages

News and information travelled very slowly between communities before letters. When it was absolutely necessary to convey information over a distance, the message would have to be communicated orally and carried by a messenger or courier. The most frequent senders of messages were the powerful: rulers, government officials and military commanders. Their messengers were usually a trusted servant or slave, or a soldier of their army.

A Persian queen, Atossa, is credited with being the person who 'invented' the letter. Whether this is historical fact or myth, it is known that one of the earliest known postal systems was set up in the ancient Persian Empire. Royal dispatches and other official documents were carried to the furthest points of the empire by a relay system of riders. A rider carried the message to a given point on the road where a fresh rider was stationed, waiting to carry the messages over the next stage to the next rider. This fast and efficient method of communication allowed the Persian rulers to maintain power and control over their empire. Similar relay systems were used in ancient Greece and Rome, mainly for military and official purposes. Letters written by private citizens were generally not carried by these early carrier systems.

As education brought literacy to greater numbers, letter-writing gave private citizens new opportunities to communicate over long distances. Although more and more people took to letter-writing, the difficulties of travel meant that delivery remained, for many centuries, very expensive or uncertain, with correspondents dependent, not on the cheap and reliable international postal system we have today, but on paid messengers, or any ships, traders, and merchants who might be travelling in the right direction and who reached their destination safely.

Even in more modern times (but before the establishment of a railway network) the delivery of letters was a slow and expensive business. It was not until the early sixteenth century that the faster and more efficient post-horse system (a relay system of horsemen similar to that first used in the ancient Persian Empire) replaced the personal messenger.

In the United States, too, there was the famous Pony Express relay system over some 2,000 miles from St Joseph, Missouri to Sacramento, California. An advertisement for riders in a Californian newspaper of the time read: 'Wanted. Young, skinny, wiry fellows. Not over 18. Must be expert riders. Willing to risk death daily. Orphans preferred.' Set up in part as a publicity stunt to try to secure a lucrative government mail contract, it operated for only 18 months between 1860 and 1861, before the first telegraph link was made with California. Despite its short life, the Pony Express is firmly fixed in the history of the American West; it provided the fastest communication between east and west before the telegraph, and captured the imagination of people all around the world.

Establishing the modern system of postal delivery

In Britain in 1626, the postal service which up until that time had been used only for royal dispatches and official messages was extended to run between London and Plymouth. Soon, a more extensive postal network grew up between the main cities of the United Kingdom. On 31 July 1635, King Charles I issued a proclamation extending the use of the Royal Mail to the public.

The British Post Office was reorganized in 1660; Henry Bishop was made Postmaster General, and, in 1661, he introduced the first postmark. This so-called 'Bishop mark' showed only the day and month of the posting, its principal purpose being to ensure that the letter carriers did not delay the mail. Also around this time, all letters were distributed around the country via one of the main post roads, to the cities of London, Edinburgh and Dublin, before being sent on to their specific destinations. Each of these three cities had individual Bishop marks. Similar postmarks were being used in America, notably in Philadelphia and New York. These early American postmarks are often referred to as 'Franklin marks', after Benjamin Franklin, who at one time was Deputy Postmaster General.

The network of post roads around London and the roads to Edinburgh and Dublin were soon added to with a series of additional routes: cross posts ran between two post roads and by-posts ran between a post road and a town some distance from it. A way-letter went between two towns on the same post road. Instructions for delivery were put on the bottom left corner of letters.

Before the invention of the prepaid penny postal system, the addressee—not the sender—usually had to pay the carrier. The letter carrier received payment on delivery, with the amount of the delivery charge calculated according to the distance travelled and the number of sheets of paper included in the letter. The whole process was very time-consuming and expensive, so that only the wealthy could afford to send letters regularly.

A special local penny-post was introduced in London in 1680 by William Dockwra. This cheap local post was soon used in other major cities and later adopted in many provincial towns.

Rowland Hill (1795–1879) was probably the greatest reformer of the postal service in Britain. He advocated a cheap and efficient postal system that everybody could afford to use, and a convenient method of prepaying the postage. He demonstrated that it was better to charge by the weight of a letter rather than by the number of sheets, suggesting a uniform charge of one penny per half ounce on all letters delivered within the United Kingdom, and recommending that postage should be prepaid using a stamp or special stationary. These innovations were eventually approved and a uniform penny post was introduced on 10 January 1840.

Stamps

On 6 May 1840, the famous Penny Black stamps went on sale at post offices. After the issue of these first stamps, many countries, which at that time were British colonies, wanted to have their own stamps. However, the General Post Office (GPO) in London would permit only a red-coloured hand-stamp to be applied to letters from countries within the British Empire. This stamp showed a crown on top of a circle with the words 'paid at' and the name of the city or country. The GPO's justification for refusing to allow country-specific stamps within the British Empire was that a plethora of designs might confuse the people whose job it was to sort the mail, and so lead to delays and errors.

Beyond the power and influence of Britain's General Post Office, other countries started to introduce their own postage stamps. Brazil introduced its famous Bull's Eye stamps on 1 August 1843, followed in 1843 and 1845 by the first issue of stamps from the cantons of Switzerland. In 1847, stamps were issued by the United States and Mauritius and, in 1849, by France, Belgium and Bavaria.

Postcodes

The earliest form of postcode was introduced in London in 1857. Sir Rowland Hill, the inventor of the penny post, divided London into districts using compass points, 'N' for north, 'SW' for south-west and so on. In 1916, numbers were added to the London postal districts to divide them up more specifically into NW1, SW2, etc. In 1864, Liverpool was the first provincial city to be divided into postal districts.

The modern British postcode, with its mixture of six letters and digits, was first used in Norwich in October 1959. Designed to facilitate sorting of the mail by machine, this was the world's first use of alphanumerical postal address codes. By 1974, the postcode system had been adopted throughout Britain.

In the United States, the ZIP code system using a five-digit code was introduced in 1963. The first digit designated a broad geographical area of the United States, from zero to nine. This was followed by two digits that pinpointed more closely population concentrations and those centres accessible to transportation networks. The final two digits designated small post offices or postal zones in larger cities.

An expanded ZIP Code was introduced in 1983. This ZIP + 4 code added a hyphen and four digits to the existing five-digit ZIP code. The first five numbers continue to identify an area of the country and delivery office. The sixth and seventh numbers denote a delivery sector, which might be several blocks, a group of streets or Post Office boxes, several office buildings or a single high-rise office building, a large apartment building or a small geographic area. The last two numbers denote a delivery segment, which might be a single floor of an office building, one side of a street between intersecting streets, specific departments in a firm, or specific Post Office boxes.

Writing surfaces

The earliest letters were written on tablets made of clay or wood, or, more rarely, metal or ivory. Often the writing surface would have a layer of wax into which the message was inscribed using a sharp pointed writing instrument, or stylus. Writing in a layer of wax meant that the message in the wax could be easily erased using the blunt end of the stylus, the wax surface made smooth again, and the tablet reused for another message.

Later, the materials on which letters were written were papyrus, followed by parchment, and then paper.

Paper was comparatively expensive until fairly recently. In the 18th and 19th centuries, writers sometimes tried to make a single sheet work overtime by writing on both sides of the sheet of paper, then turning the sheet sideways and writing across what they had already written. This was known as 'crossing' and made their letters messy and difficult to read. Irritation with the practice is expressed in many novels and journals of the time and is dealt with in one of the rules of Lewis Carroll's light-hearted 'Eight or Nine Wise Words About Letter Writing' (written under his real name of Charles Dodgson):

> *My ninth Rule. When you get to the end of a notesheet, and find you have more to say, take another piece of paper—a whole sheet, or a scrap, as the case may demand: but whatever you do, don't cross!*

Remember the old proverb 'Cross-writing makes cross reading.' 'The old proverb?' you say, inquiringly. 'How old?' Well, not so very ancient, I must confess. In fact, I'm afraid I invented it while writing this paragraph!

Writing instruments

Using a quill pen and inkwell too often must have made writing a laborious and messy business, and had very little to recommend it. Considerable practice and skill was needed for a good standard of penmanship. The continual trimming of nibs, filling of inkwells, blotting and sealing of letters made, all in all, for a time-consuming and bothersome process which most modern writers couldn't imagine having time for. An innovation that swept away the quill pen, and at the same time encouraged more people to write, was the modern fountain pen, invented by Lewis Edson Waterman around 1883. Waterman's version perfected earlier fountain pens—so-called from having a reservoir of ink attached—by adding a device that slowed down the rate at which the ink got to the nib, and so stopped the pen leaking.

Next came the ballpoint pen, invented and named after Hungarian-born Laszlo Biro, who patented the design in 1943. His design had a tiny ball that rotated inside the tip of the pen and delivered quick-drying ink to the writing surface, further reducing the risk of leaking.

Where next for letter-writing? Have the gains we have made in the last thirty years in convenience and efficiency been worth the cost? Should it be a cause for regret that skills, and aesthetic and decorative qualities, evolved over the whole history of letter-writing before the introduction of the computer, may quickly disappear? Does it matter that fewer and fewer people will want to learn and use the beautiful copperplate handwriting so often seen in old letters; and that collections of letters written on handmade paper and tied with ribbon may be seen only in museums?

Now and Into the Future

People of an older generation, who remember the pleasure of writing and reading long, newsy letters sent to, and received from, friends and family, may lament the fact that letter-writing seems to be something of a dying art. However, on a more positive note, it could be argued that we communicate much more now than we ever did in the past. It is the means of communication that has changed, not the inclination to communicate. But it is certainly true that, for most of us, for most of the time, the pen is far from being mightier than the phone, and when we do write it is more and more likely to be via electronic mail or text message than by the traditional method of letter-writing.

It is undisputedly the case that there has been a steep decline in the number of personal letters written in the traditional way, with pen on paper. Pace of life and lack of time have conspired with rapider methods of communication—telephone, fax, email and text messaging—against personal letter-writing. Or looked at another way, the rapider methods of communication have freed up time, time which people are now less inclined to fill by writing personal letters.

Whether this is also true of all types of formal and business correspondence is not quite so clear. Certainly there is a marked increase in certain types of letter; we all receive piles of letters—junk mail—from companies who are trying to drum up business, and shredders and paper-recycling plants are kept busy disposing of it all. But a fair amount of business correspondence is generated as a result of increasing affluence: think of all those letters from credit card and insurance companies, and the sometimes protracted exchanges associated with buying and selling property. Despite predictions of the 'paperless office' that computers were supposed to bring about, the opposite seems to have happened. The very ease with which written material can be produced with word processing software has meant the overall amount of printed material—which includes letters—has increased enormously.

There will be some fairly predictable consequences of the changes brought about by the new technologies, which will have an impact on certain types of research. In future, the decrease in social letter-writing may well deprive family historians and social historians of a valuable source of information. The content of personal letters is often an accurate record of events at the time of writing, within a family and in a wider social context. Amateur and professional genealogists hold great store by old family letters, which can be extremely informative and illuminating. The more ephemeral nature of communication via the new technologies will leave very little material for such research: telephone calls are routinely recorded only by big financial institutions and government agencies; faxes fade; not many people take the trouble to save, archive or print emails; and text messages are deleted to make room for more.

Biographers too are likely to have cause to regret the falling from favour of letter-writing; letters, both from and to the subject of a biography, can give an extremely valuable insight into the individual's character, temperament, relationships and circumstances. In the past, letters were often kept as precious mementoes by the recipient, or even returned to the sender where he or she had some inkling that the content might be of historical interest. In these ways, much was preserved for posterity.

Telephone

By the second part of the twentieth century most households in Britain had a telephone. Those who did not have a telephone in the home usually had access to a public telephone.

The telephone—and the more recent innovations of fax, email and texting—are in many ways more convenient forms of communication than letter-writing, because information is transferred almost instantaneously. With letters, time has to be allowed for the letter to reach the addressee, and for a reply to return.

The telephone has a further advantage over the letter in that you can be absolutely certain that your message has reached the person for whom it is intended. The telephone has a more informal, personal advantage too. If the person at the other end of the telephone line is a lover, good friend or family member, there is the pleasure of hearing his or her voice—a pleasure that is particularly welcome when the person is far away. If a face-to-face chat is not possible, the next best thing is a phone-to-phone one.

What was, and still is, appreciated about the telephone is that it saves a good deal of time and effort, even when some time has to be spent thinking out what we are going to say. It is, of course, an invaluable business tool.

Fax

Fax machines can send and receive handwritten notes, printed text, drawings, diagrams and photographs quickly along a telephone line from anywhere in the world. The fax machine gives the speed of delivery of the telephone while allowing the sender to consider and then write the information that they wish to convey. A fax has the immediacy of the telephone but also some of the permanence of the letter.

Most fax machines can store incoming faxes in their memory and print them out later. Many machines are now multi-functional, combining printer, scanner, photocopier, and fax machine. Other multi-function fax machines have mobile handsets and even offer SMS text messaging.

Faxes should always get to the person to whom they are directed, but lack of confidentiality can be a problem because the fax machine in an office is often shared. The basic message is: if you want to keep information confidential, avoid the fax machine.

Faxes have some other disadvantages. Fax is a shortened version of the word 'facsimile' and faxes are sent using a system called 'facsimile transmission'. The document with the printed text or image to be faxed is scanned and converted into digital code by the fax machine at the sending end and then transmitted down a telephone line to the fax machine at the receiving end. The receiving machine reconstitutes the information and produces a copy of the original. Very often the information comes out as clear at the receiving end as it went in at the sending end, but this is not always the case, especially where the document includes fine detail. Although it is usually possible to change the resolution to improve the readability and clarity of the image, high resolution faxes take much longer to transmit.

Many individuals and businesses—especially before emailing became widespread in the 1990s—abandoned all other forms of communication in favour of the fax. Now that more and more information is stored on computer and can be sent via a broadband Internet connection between computers, the fax is being used less and less.

Word processing

The word processor has probably had a greater effect on the production of letters and other documents than any technological advance since the invention of paper.

Before the word processor, if someone needed a letter typed, they usually had to write out what they wanted to say, hand this to a secretary, check it, check it again if there were any mistakes the first time round, and sign it. Or, letters would be dictated to a secretary, taken down in shorthand, typed, and finally presented for checking, correcting and signing. All this took up a great deal of time and effort and used a great many man and woman hours. Nor was it a very satisfactory way of dealing with highly confidential or personal information.

Now that there is a word processor in every office (and most homes too), gone are the shorthand notebooks, the heavy typewriters, the serried ranks of typists in typing pools, the tedious process of checking and rechecking, the correcting fluid . . . the boss has even learned to type his or her own letters!

The keyboard on the average word processor is relatively easy to use even by those who have never had a typing lesson. Using a word processor, it is a matter of a moment to correct an error or reword a sentence, and nearly all word processing programs will check your spelling, and even your grammar. If you suddenly realize you have used the words 'good' and 'nice' fifteen times in the same paragraph, your word processing program will almost certainly have an inbuilt thesaurus to offer suggestions for synonyms that will add a bit of variety and interest to leaden prose!

You can create documents that contain formatted text, columns, tables, and graphics.

You can add links to websites, and import and export data from your electronic files, the Web, and other programs.

If you want to send out a standard letter to a thousand different people, but you want to personalize each one, word processing packages have a facility called mail merge, which will print, from a database or electronic address book, each individual's details onto a copy of the standard letter.

Is there anything negative that can be said about this modern wonder? Well, yes, and it is mostly about the personal letters produced on word processors.

They may be personal letters but all that print with only the signature in handwriting doesn't seem very personal, does it? Was that word processed letter you got from your friend at Christmas also sent to all her other friends and relations, as you suspect it might have been? Can your grandson write with that nice fountain pen you gave him last year? You're pretty sure you haven't seen anything he's written using a pen on paper since he was eleven years old.

You found out the hard and embarrassing way when you wrote that letter to Mr Nolan, the bank manager, that the spellchecker on your word processor has to be configured not to 'correct' automatically the spellings of words it thinks might be wrong, especially when the words are proper names! You may also have found out the hard way that the spellchecker couldn't tell that there was something wrong when you typed 'the affect of this change' instead of 'the effect of this change'. You have stubbornly resisted taking a course in word processing and have thus spent a frightening percentage of your spare time trying to discover how to create columns and increase from the size of a pinhead the piece of clipart you've added to your document!

Email

No sooner had people come to grips with the fax and the word processor, when along came electronic mail (more usually known by its abbreviated name email, or e-mail). The advantages of email over fax and the traditional postal system, or 'snail mail', are its ease of use, its cheapness, and its speed of transmission from one computer to another. You can even keep or print out copies. In the first few years of its use, many people found email so convenient it encouraged them to communicate much more that they would otherwise have done. More recently, broadband Internet services have increased the speed of transmission even further, but unfortunately, it is also now fairly commonplace to get huge volumes of unsolicited email or 'spam', and emails can carry viruses that will damage your computer. They can also be the means by which identity thieves gain access to your personal details. However, as long as you are aware of the precautions that are necessary to guard against these nuisance and criminal activities by reviewing and updating your security systems regularly, email is a great way to communicate!

The business community has embraced email with enthusiasm because of its speed and convenience and because it made it possible to send any type of computer file over the Internet: pictures, sounds, video clips and text files. An email can be sent to hundreds, even thousands, of email addresses simultaneously and very cheaply.

Email addresses are made up of two parts:

everest@highestmountain.co.uk.

The first part of the address—the part before the @ symbol—is the user name (often a personal name or any nickname the user chooses to be known by); and the second part—the part after the @ symbol—is the domain name or host name (the Internet server through which the mail is sent and received). The domain name is often further subdivided into the subdomain (immediately after the @ sign), followed by the domain type (the type of organization, such as a business company, a government department, or an academic institution), followed by a country code (this last is omitted for many of the larger host names, like AOL). Elements in the domain name are separated by dots.

An email message is also made up of two parts: the header information and the message you type. The header information, written by the email software when the message is sent, includes the sender's name or email address, and the date and time of sending and receipt.

Although email is a fairly informal medium, there is a code of conduct (sometimes called 'Netiquette') designed to ensure that users do not give offence. It is bad form to SHOUT by typing whole words in capital letters; don't show anger or be intentionally rude in emails (this is called 'flaming'); always try to put something in the Subject line to give the recipient some idea of what your email is about; check email addresses have been typed correctly; and don't send anything confidential via email.

Messaging

With the introduction of mobile phones came text messaging which has also proved to be an extremely popular method of communication, especially among young people. The younger people are, the more likely they are to text. One study in the UK showed that 80% of those under the age of 25 are more likely to send a text message than make a phone call, while only 14% of people over 55 preferred texting to making a phone call. Other studies list the most popular reasons for social messaging: sending someone a birthday greeting, cancelling or arranging a meeting, receiving news updates and sporting news, contacting a partner, and flirting.

Of course, texting also has less frivolous purposes; increasingly businesses are using it as a standard method of sending messages to their clients or customers.

Texting has many advantages: it can be relatively cheap compared to a phone call; a text message can be sent in situations where it is not practical to talk or when the recipient is not able to answer a normal phone call; information can be sent to someone's phone which they would otherwise have to write down; and, like email, the same message can be sent to a large number of people.

With increasing technological sophistication, mobile phones are now becoming a one-stop communication tool, incorporating digital cameras and lots of other features. But texting doesn't have to be limited to mobile phones. Special software programs are available which allow you to send text messages from your PC to a mobile phone, and get replies via your email program. Also, with a text-compatible handset, you can send and receive texts from your traditional phone or landline.

At the time of writing, there are three main messaging technologies: SMS (Short Message Service); (EMS) Enhanced Message Service; and MMS (Multimedia Messaging Service).

SMS (Short Message Service)

SMS was the first messaging system to appear. It began as a fairly basic person-to-person text messaging system, using the GSM communication system.

GSM (Global System for Mobile Communications) is a digital mobile phone system and is one of the world's main second generation (2G) wireless standards used on mobile phone networks. GSM is very well established in Europe and many other countries of the world, and operates in three frequency bands: 900 megahertz, 1800 megahertz, and 1900 megahertz. The United States equivalent of GSM is PCS (Personal Communication Service), operating in the 1900 megahertz frequency band.

SMS allows alphanumeric text messages of up to 160 characters to be sent and received on a digital mobile phone. The SMS system works in a similar way to a paging service, with messages routed through the network's SMSC (Short Message Service Centre). This is a computer which stores the message until it can be delivered to the recipient. SMS text messages can be sent from a mobile phone, or via a dial-up connection using a modem and a computer.

The SMSC will store messages when the recipient's mobile phone is turned off. When their phone comes back into service, stored messages will then be delivered automatically. Messages can have an expiry time set, with the message being deleted if not delivered at the end of the expiry period.

When a message is received, it is stored in the SIM (Subscriber Identity Module) smart card chip, where it will be available to be read whenever needed, and saved until deleted. The SIM card, when inserted into a mobile phone handset, creates a mobile station. Without the SIM card, the mobile phone cannot make or receive calls (except emergency calls). Information stored on the SIM card includes the International Mobile Subscriber Identity (IMSI), the number used by the mobile phone network to track calls made and assign call charges.

Most mobile phones can be set to beep when a message is received, or have an indicator light on the display panel for situations where the sound of a beep would be inappropriate. Depending upon the phone and the SIM card, you can store between 5 and 15 messages.

Because SMS limits each message to 160 characters, a whole new language of abbreviations and shortened forms has developed. People, especially young people, are communicating by shortening words, using phonetic spellings, missing out letters, or using symbols to represent words, letter combinations, and syllables (*see* 'Texting hints' below and on the next page).

Messaging, with its informal style and abbreviated forms, is now so ubiquitous that some parents and educators are worried that text talk is affecting children's ability to spell and use English correctly. However, children and young people seem to be just as literate as they were before the texting boom. Concerns about standards of literacy have been around for decades, even centuries, and there was a move towards greater informality long before chat rooms, email or texting existed. It's a moot point whether loss of formality is a bad thing, but the reality is that things are changing and will go on changing. Our language is always in a state of subtle change. New words find their way into English all the time: coming from other languages; giving names to scientific, technical, and technological discoveries and innovations; reflecting social change; or adopted from street slang.

The spelling and shortening system used in texting is very unlikely to be used much outside the specific context for which it evolved. And, anyway, texting does have its own rules, however loose and informal. To shorten words and expressions in a meaningful way you first have to know something of the basic rules of English usage. In other words, you have to know the rules before you can break them. The anxious observers may just be anxious because they aren't particularly comfortable with the new technology, or perhaps it's because young people are busy with something that they haven't had to learn from their 'elders and betters'.

Many mobile phones now include a software application called Predictive Text Messaging, designed to make writing SMS text messages quicker and easier. Instead of the message writer having to perform multiple key strokes to scroll laboriously through letters, predictive text systems make the most of the limited number of keys found on phone keypads. Each key (usually one of nine) is allocated 3 or 4 letters of the alphabet. A dictionary database with the most commonly used words, abbreviations, emoticons, and punctuation comes as part of the predictive text messaging package. As the writer begins to key words in, the software reads the keystrokes and scans the dictionary for matching words. Where it finds a match, it will 'predict' what the word being typed is going to be and complete it. Where its prediction is wrong, changes can be made manually. Words that the software does not recognize can be entered into the dictionary and stored for future use. Like the spellcheckers used with word processing software, predictive text can sometimes get it very wrong, causing, at best, amusement and, at worst, irritation.

EMS (Enhanced Messaging Service)

EMS (Enhanced Messaging Service) adds a few more bells and whistles to SMS. It is what it says it is—an improved message system, which allows you to send and receive formatted text messages, simple pictures, sounds and animations. An EMS message may contain one or all of these elements. If messages exceed the length of a single SMS message then they will be made up of a number of concatenated (linked) SMS messages. However, the phone receiving an EMS message must also have EMS capability; otherwise the received message will be displayed without formatting, like a plain SMS text message.

MMS (Multimedia Messaging Service)

MMS (Multimedia Messaging Service) represents a significant advance from the fairly basic SMS. With MMS a message can include images, graphics, text and audio clips. Photo messaging is a popular use of MMS, with an inbuilt camera in the mobile photo used to take a photograph and the photograph then being sent as a message or an email. MMS offers unlimited text with formatting. Where a full third generation (3G) network is available, video clips can also added to messages. MMS will support graphs, tables, charts, diagrams, animated GIFs, image editing and sound streaming.

MMS messages can sent via web sites. For receiving MMS messages, if the device does not support MMS, the user gets an SMS message pointing to a URL where the message is stored. MMS messages can also be sent to an email address.

The steps in the delivery of MMS messages are slightly different from SMS. An MMS message is sent to a MMSC (Multi-Media Service Centre). When the MMSC receives the message, this is indicated on the sender's phone by 'Message Sent'. The MMSC sends the receiver a notification that a new message is waiting. The receiver can then download the message immediately, or download it later. When the receiver has successfully downloaded the message, the sender gets a 'Message Delivered' message.

For MMS to become fully functional network operators need to upgrade their infrastructure to the 3G standard. If change in the last 30 years is matched, MMS will very soon be the norm before being overtaken by the next generation of message systems!

Texting hints

Here are a few suggestions to make your text life more exciting.

- Shorten words by missing out vowels, eg:

  weekend wknd
  message msg

- Use numbers if they sound like a word, eg:

  wonder 1der
  to 2
  for 4
  ate 8

- Why use more than one letter when one will do?

  see C
  tea T
  you U

- You can substitute a single letter for combinations of letters when they sound the same, eg:

  phone fone
  some sum
  night nite

- A capital letter can be used as a substitute for a double letter that comes in the middle or at the end of a word, eg:

  middle miDle
  tell teL

- A capital letter can be used as a substitute for a long vowel, eg:

  phone fOn
  broke brOk

- A capital letter in a string of text can mean a new word starts here, eg:

  Jenny broke my phone JenyBrokMyFon

- The dollar sign ($) can be used for 'double S', eg:

  Tell me some gossip! TeLMeSumGo$ip!

- The percentage symbol (%) can mean 'double O' or the 'oo' sound, eg:

  could c%d
  would w%d
  wood w%d

Smileys

Why type 'I'm happy today' when you can use a smiley or :-)? Have you ever sent a text or email to someone and they took it completely the wrong way? Sometimes it's hard to tell whether someone is serious, joking, sarcastic, or boiling with rage, because you can't get any verbal cues from the words alone.

That's where smileys come in (also known as emoticons because they represent emotions). Adding a smiley to a statement can qualify it and indicate to the reader your feelings and mood.

In Internet folklore, the person supposed to have produced the first online smiley was Scott Fahlman of the Carnegie-Mellon University, Pittsburgh, Pennsylvania on the university's bulletin board in the early 1980s. There are, of course, rival claims!

Most smileys are viewed sideways and some are a lot more obvious than others. A selection of emoticons or smileys used in email and text messaging (viewed sideways) is shown below.

<table>
<tr><td>:,-(</td><td>crying</td><td>:x</td><td>silent</td></tr>
<tr><td>:-(</td><td>sad</td><td>|-o</td><td>bored, snoring</td></tr>
<tr><td>:-)</td><td>happy</td><td>:></td><td>cheeky</td></tr>
<tr><td>:-D</td><td>wide smile</td><td>:"></td><td>embarrassed</td></tr>
<tr><td>:-/)</td><td>not funny</td><td>:-e</td><td>disappointed</td></tr>
<tr><td>:-0</td><td>yelling</td><td>%-)</td><td>confused</td></tr>
<tr><td>:-@</td><td>screaming</td><td>:-/</td><td>sceptical</td></tr>
<tr><td>:-0</td><td>shocked</td><td>#:-o</td><td>shocked</td></tr>
<tr><td>:-y</td><td>said with a smile</td><td>{}</td><td>no comment</td></tr>
<tr><td>(:-&</td><td>angry</td><td>':-)</td><td>raised eyebrow</td></tr>
<tr><td>}:-[</td><td>angry, frustrated</td><td>:-&</td><td>tongue-tied</td></tr>
<tr><td>:-|</td><td>serious</td><td>:-) . . .</td><td>drooling</td></tr>
<tr><td>|:-|</td><td>frowning</td><td>8)</td><td>wearing sunglasses</td></tr>
<tr><td>;-)</td><td>winking</td><td></td><td></td></tr>
<tr><td>:-x</td><td>kiss</td><td></td><td></td></tr>
</table>

Getting Organized

While nowadays there may be many new effective ways of communicating and some of these may be quicker and more convenient than writing a letter, none has, so far, wholly or satisfactorily replaced letter-writing.

The traditional method of writing/typing and posting a letter will have a place for the foreseeable future, and there are still many situations when nothing else will serve your purpose so well as to write a letter.

But—and especially if you are a novice letter-writer—how do you decide when it is appropriate to write a letter and, once the decision to write is made, what do you need to make a start? Here are some pointers that might help you decide whether or not to write a letter:

1. What is your purpose? If your purpose can be fitted into one of the following broad categories, you should consider writing a letter:

- requesting information or action
- providing information or a detailed description
- acknowledging information or an event
- persuading someone to take action or demanding they take action
- giving someone bad news or saying 'no'.

2. Do you and the person with whom you want to communicate have a professional/business relationship? If the relationship is, or will be, a professional/business one, it is usually better to write a letter, at least for the first contact.

3. If this is the first contact, how can you be sure that the person you want to get in touch will be free to talk on the phone, or that they read faxes and pick up emails? A letter gives the recipient—especially someone who is busy and stressed—the opportunity to read your letter, digest the contents, and answer in their own way, and in their own time.

4. Does the person or organization require a letter or form with your signature before they will take action to deal with an issue? If this is the case, there is very little point in phoning or emailing them.

5. Is the matter-in-hand important, but not particularly urgent? If there is enough time to put it in a letter and send it by post, this is often the best way to ensure it is properly dealt with.

6. Is the information complicated and lengthy? If you don't spend the time considering layout and marshalling the information in a letter, is there a risk it may be misunderstood? Could it be communicated satisfactorily and in its entirety in a single phone call? If not, write it down in a letter.

7. Is the information confidential? Confidential material should be sent in a sealed envelope. Fax and email are not guaranteed to be secure.

8. Do you want to convey seriousness, formality or great depth of feeling? A well-written letter allows you to express yourself with the care and clarity, and in the tone, which best achieves these aims. Can this be done adequately in a phone call or by dashing off an email or fax? Probably not.

Social letters

For social correspondence, be guided by the context, the attitudes and personality of your reader, and your relationship (if any) with them. Remember that despite society's increasing tendency to informality, and the convenience of the telephone, fax and email, there are still situations where courtesy demands a more 'old-fashioned' approach. For example, many people would consider it impolite to receive a 'thank you' message by any other means than a letter or card, and unless you are very close to a bereaved person, condolences are best conveyed in writing.

Before making the decision to write a social letter ask yourself these questions:

- What is generally considered to be good manners in these particular circumstances?
- Is the matter to be dealt with one that you and/or the recipient are more comfortable writing/reading about than talking about? A letter is a good way of dealing with things that you find hard to talk about.
- Are you sure you want to leave a permanent record of your feelings, whatever they may be? It is not really a very good idea to write a letter when you are angry or in a state of high emotion. You may live to regret it! On the other hand, a written message of love, thanks, congratulation or sympathy is often appreciated much more than an ephemeral phone call, and may be treasured for a long time to come.
- Does the individual concerned enjoy receiving, reading and writing letters? Will he or she value the effort you have made and see that your letter of several pages is a labour of love and a work of art? Or, will the pearls of your composition be cast before indifferent or unappreciative swine? Know your audience and try to communicate in a way that does not cause embarrassment or feelings of inadequacy.
- Consider the recipient's physical and mental state. There is no point in writing a letter to a sight-impaired person unless you would be happy about someone else reading your letter to him or her, and this can be easily arranged. Remember that a very elderly person may find it a struggle to get through a long-winded letter.

Business and personal business letters

In the business and professional world, letter-writing plays a crucial role in communication with clients, negotiations, administration, marketing, recruitment and employment, and many other everyday situations.

On a personal level, legal, financial and insurance matters, complaints, requests for service, and job applications are just some of the business matters you will probably have to deal with by letter at some time in your life.

A well-crafted business letter makes a strong impression, so the ability to produce such a letter is an important skill.

Here are a few examples of circumstances in which it is recommended you write a letter—and keep a copy—rather than communicate by any of the other available means:

- when you need to keep a permanent record of an exchange (writing the information down and keeping a copy means you can refer to it later if necessary, and track any subsequent correspondence on the subject)

- when giving or confirming information, especially to institutions like banks and building societies, and government departments like the Inland Revenue
- when sending several documents in a single envelope (it is good practice to include a covering letter listing the documents being sent)
- when the information is confidential
- when applying for a job
- when making or responding to a complaint
- when a written reply is requested.

Handwritten or typed/word processed?

You have now decided to write a letter. The next decision is whether the letter should be handwritten or typed/word processed.

In the past, most letters were handwritten because not many people could type and few had access to a typewriter. Nowadays, the widespread ownership of personal computers with their word processing software and printers has made the decision rather more difficult.

If this choice is available to you, first take into consideration the likely reaction and attitude of the letter's recipient. Despite the fact that word processing skills are something that nearly everyone aims to acquire, there is a lingering feeling, especially among older people, that a handwritten letter is more personal and somehow more caring. So unless you are certain that the other person will not object to a typed letter, it is still advisable to write your most personal letters.

There are some specific situations where one method or the other is strongly recommended. Letters (or cards) that should, ideally, be handwritten include:

- love letters
- thank you letters
- letters of congratulation
- messages of condolence.

Letters that should, ideally, be typed or word processed include:

- all professional and business letters
- CV and covering letter (unless handwriting is specified by the prospective employer).

It is not only desirable, but increasingly necessary, to type all business letters. Handwritten ones create a less professional image and are therefore likely to receive less serious attention than those laid out and printed in the standard printed business format. If a letter is of particular importance and you cannot type it yourself, it is worthwhile getting someone to type it for you.

Before the word processor, most job applicants would have submitted a handwritten application. Nowadays, a letter of application should always be typed, as should the CV and its covering letter.

Very occasionally, a job advert will stipulate that applicants should apply only in their own handwriting. Reasons for making such a stipulation vary. It may be that the job is one in which legible handwriting matters, or the employer may feel that the neatness or otherwise of the handwriting gives a clue to the applicant's likely approach to the job. Amongst larger firms with human resources departments to vet and analyse applications, a handwritten application may even be scrutinized by a trained graphologist. Recruiting new staff is a time-consuming and costly business and appointing the wrong person to a job is even more costly. By using graphological analysis, the firm can get some insight into applicants' characters, personalities and suitability for the job.

Handwriting

Another important consideration when making the choice to write or type your letter is the legibility or otherwise of your handwriting. Most of us tend to be view our own handwriting through somewhat rose-tinted glasses. Because we can (usually) read our own handwriting we tend to assume that others will be able to read it too! Be self-critical and, above all, realistic. Is your handwriting really a thing of beauty, with clear well-formed letters that any child can read without the least difficulty? People whose handwriting is impossible to read should think about typing even their most personal letters. In another extract from his 'Eight or Nine Wise Words About Letter Writing', Lewis Carroll writes:

> *Here is a golden rule to begin with. Write legibly. The average temper of the human race would be perceptibly sweetened, if everybody obeyed this rule! A great deal of the bad writing in the world comes simply from writing too quickly. Of course you reply, 'I do it to save time.' A very good object, no doubt: but what right have you to do it at your friend's expense? Isn't his time as valuable as yours? Years ago, I used to receive letters from a friend—and very interesting letters too—written in one of the most atrocious hands ever invented. It generally took me about a week to read one of his letters. I used to carry it about in my pocket, and take it out at leisure times, to puzzle over the riddles which composed it—holding it in different positions, and at different distances, till at last the meaning of some hopeless scrawl would flash upon me, when I at once wrote down the English under it; and, when several had been thus guessed, the context would help with the others, till at last the whole series of hieroglyphics was deciphered. If all one's friends wrote like that, Life would be entirely spent in reading their letters!*

When your handwriting is an execrable, illegible, spidery, blotchy scrawl you cannot expect plaudits from your readers. They are likely to display the same sort of impatience as Lewis Carroll does here. But even if your handwriting is difficult to decipher, there are times when you should make a real effort to write neatly and when the recipient will probably exercise a little tolerance if your effort doesn't quite come off. Letters of condolence to the bereaved, love letters, and other letters of a particularly personal nature should be handwritten, however illegible your handwriting.

Remember that the overall appearance of your letter is almost as important as the content. A neat, well-laid-out letter is a courtesy to the person you are writing to and will create a good impression.

Writing tools

It is important to choose a pen that will make your handwriting as neat and attractive-looking as possible.

Some people derive great pleasure from using a good fountain pen and feel that their handwriting is at its best when they use one. There are very handsome fountain pens around, ranging from the modestly priced to the extremely expensive. Disadvantages of the fountain pen are that it is less forgiving and requires more skill to use than a ballpoint pen, it needs to be refilled with ink, and it can sometimes leak.

The ballpoint pen, or biro, is considerably cheaper and on the whole is easier and quicker to use. Check before writing your letter that the pen you intend to use does not leak and ink flows smoothly from the ballpoint. Otherwise, your writing may end up being blotchy, messy and difficult to read.

Other modern pen options which produce good results include fibre-tip pens, some of which have very fine points, and rollerball pens. The use of thicker felt-tip pens should be confined to marking uneven surfaces, such as the outside of bulky envelopes or packages.

Next give some thought to ink colour. As a general rule, stick to dark blue or black ink. They are unobtrusive and contrast best with white or pale cream paper. Vermilion or violet ink with silvery flecks are all very well if you are writing a very informal letter to a close friend but should always be avoided in more formal letters.

Never write a business letter in pencil.

Writing paper

The process of writing can be made more pleasurable if you use good quality paper that doesn't crease or tear and takes ink without smudging or blotching.

It is not a good idea to tear a piece of paper from one of your child's school exercise books and start writing. This is going to look both scrappy and sloppy—and will be treated as such!

It really is worth investing in good quality writing paper. As a rule it is best to opt for plain paper, white or off-white without ornament or fussy edgings. Avoid coloured paper unless you are absolutely certain that the recipient shares your taste for luminous violet or turquoise. Pale cream, pale blue or pale grey may look rather tasteful and will usually do very well for social letters, but for formal business letters it really is best to stick to white.

Because letters that are sent by airmail cost more in postage, there is nothing wrong with writing personal letters on the special thin (and light) writing paper produced for this purpose or you can use airmail letters (specially printed sheets that function as both writing paper and envelope, with the postage pre-paid and guide lines printed on the sheet indicating how it should be folded before sealing). Formal business letters should still be written on normal white writing paper.

Never use lined paper, even if your handwriting is of the kind that slopes ever more upwards or ever more downwards with every word you write. Lined paper tends to carry memories of the schoolroom with it. If you find it difficult to write in even-spaced horizontal lines, try using a ruled backing sheet under your unlined paper.

Anything in the way of fancy illustration should not appear on a business letter or on a formal personal letter. Writing paper dappled with tea roses, or with whistling bluebirds and cute cavorting teddy bears round the edges should be kept for your closest and most intimate friends.

If you are thinking about having your address and telephone number pre-printed or engraved on your personal writing paper, it is important to avoid anything too fancy. Better instead to have something simple and understated if you want to make a serious impression. If you are starting up your own business, and are not of an artistic bent, it is worth consulting a good designer to help you select something that is eye-catching and memorable but not too overwhelming. Ideally, your headed notepaper should be printed by a professional printer. Even if you have the most advanced design software on your computer and are practised in its use, for the smartest results it is usually still best to leave the printing of your design to a professional.

These days in the UK, Europe and many other places, nearly all commercially produced paper for writing, printing and photocopying is supplied in one of the 'A' sizes. The A sizing system is an international standard for paper. The main advantage of this standardization—from the paper manufacturers' and their customers' points of view—is that each A size is half the area of the previous one, in a descending scale from A0 to A7. Thus, an A1 sheet folded and cut in half will produce two A2 sheets, an A2 sheet will produce two A3 sheets, and so on. The dimensions of each A size are:

A0 = 841 mm × 1189 mm
A1 = 594 mm × 841 mm
A2 = 420 mm × 594 mm
A3 = 297 mm × 420 mm
A4 = 210 mm × 297 mm
A5 = 148 mm × 210 mm
A6 = 105 mm × 148 mm
A7 = 74 mm × 105 mm.

In the United States and Asia, imperial paper sizes may also be used. Their names and dimensions are:

Executive = 7.25 in × 10.5 in (184 mm × 267 mm)
Folio = 8.25 in × 13 in (210 mm × 330 mm)

Foolscap = 8 in × 13 in (203 mm × 330 mm)
Index card = 5 in × 8 in (127 mm × 203 mm)
Ledger = 17 in × 11 in (432 mm × 279 mm)
Legal = 8.5 in × 14 in (216 mm × 356 mm)
Letter = 8.5 in × 11 in (216 mm × 356 mm)
Photo = 4 in × 6 in (102 mm × 152 mm)
Quarto = 8.5 in × 1013/16 in (216 mm × 275 mm)
Statement/Halfletter = 5.5 in × 8.5 in (140 mm × 216 mm)
Tabloid= 11 in × 17 in (279 mm × 432 mm).

In the A series, the most frequently used paper sizes are A3, A4 and A5. A3 is too large for letters, and is used principally for spreadsheets and large printouts. A4 is the standard size used in business. It will fit into a standard file and filing system, and into the hoppers of printers and photocopying machines. A5 is mostly used for memos or shorter personal letters.

If your letter is to a business or other organization you should always use A4 paper. However, for personal letters you do not need to stick to the A4 size. Your main consideration here should be the likely length of your letter and the size of your handwriting. If you are planning to write a very long newsy letter and your handwriting is large and sprawling, then it is clearly sensible to choose a larger page size.

On the other hand, if you know that you have very little to say, it would be best to opt for a smaller page size, especially if you also have rather small, cramped writing. A few lines surrounded by huge area of blank paper will simply draw attention to the fact that you don't have much to say.

It is probably best to avoid notelets, especially highly colourful or fancy ones, unless you are writing to a close friend or a family member. They are not appropriate for formal letters.

The traditional advice was to avoid writing or printing on both sides of a piece of paper, though conservationists will point out that using both sides of the sheet saves paper and we should all be making an effort to avoid wasting precious resources. However, it is probably best to restrict this practice to your personal correspondence.

Business and formal letters should be typed or written on one side only, using continuation sheets for the second and subsequent pages.

Before sending a letter with writing on both sides of the paper, be sure that both sides are legible. If the pen has been pressed down heavily and dark ink has been used, the writing may be very difficult to read on both sides. If your handwritten letter stretches to more than three sides, it is a good idea to number the second and subsequent sheets. This avoids any muddle on the reader's part, should the individual sheets get out of order.

Cards

Those who do not really like writing letters, or who find them too difficult to write, often send a card instead. The main effort involved is in selecting a card that is suitable to the occasion and to the taste of the sender and intended recipient. There are many occasions for which greetings cards are perfectly acceptable, whether you choose to send a card with pre-printed message suitable for the occasion, or a 'blank' one in which you write your own greeting.

Christmas and birthdays generate the greatest volume of card-writing. It is quite usual to send a card rather than write a letter when someone passes an exam or a driving test or graduates from university. Likewise, if someone is ill we will send a 'get well' card, and for this and other occasions when people may appreciate a little humour, there are dozens of cards on sale, with humorous illustrations or messages.

Some occasions, on the other hand, can be trickier. If you have been a guest in someone's house, for example, and want to thank your host and hostess, it may be tempting to send a quick card. However, your host or hostess, especially if they are of an older generation, may be sticklers for formality and expect a letter (the kind of letter that used to be called a 'bread and butter letter'), thanking them for their hospitality and saying a few words about how pleasant your stay with them was.

Another difficult choice is whether to send a 'sympathy' card when someone dies. You will probably be able to gauge what is most appropriate in the circumstances, and a card at least lets the bereaved person know that you are thinking of them. However, a card with a short printed message followed by your signature may give the impression that you are just going through the motions. Though they are very difficult letters to write, ask yourself if the bereaved might not be more comforted by a letter which expresses more fully how you feel and offers them your support.

Postcards, unlike greetings cards, usually don't have to be put in an envelope and can be popped into the post-box with a minimum of fuss. However, they obviously shouldn't be used to send private or confidential information.

Here are some situations in which a blank postcard is useful:

- when you are moving house and want to let people know your new address
- when sending information about an appointment
- when sending non-personal information suitable for the eyes of the world
- when entering some competitions.

Some people find it worthwhile to have some postcards pre-printed with their address and phone number, for use on appropriate occasions.

Of course, the most familiar kind of postcard has a picture on one side and is bought principally by people who are on holiday or on a day trip somewhere to send to friends and family members at home. Their use in this context is absolutely standard and part of convention. At the end of the nineteenth and beginning of the twentieth century, picture postcards were used much more widely, with the pictures printed on them being more typically of some local event or activity or of a national or international event that was in the news. Postcards from that era are historical documents, and are now collectors' items.

Envelopes

When it comes to choosing an envelope it is best to select a good quality one that matches the colour and weight of your writing paper. Use a size that allows you to insert the letter into the envelope with the minimum of folds. Standard envelope sizes are:

DL = 110 mm × 220 mm
C3 = 324 mm × 458 mm
C4 = 324 mm × 229 mm
C5 = 229 mm × 162 mm
C6 = 162 mm × 114 mm.

If you don't want to fold an A4 sheet, use a C4 size envelope. The C5 size will take an A4 sheet folded once, or an A5 sheet unfolded; the C6 size will take an A4 sheet folded three times, an A5 sheet folded once, or an A6 sheet unfolded.

Many business letters are sent in DL envelopes measuring 110 mm × 220 mm. These take an A4 sheet folded neatly twice, ie into thirds. When using this size of envelope, make sure the corners of the sheet of paper are precisely aligned before making the folds. Any refolding or an extra small fold will spoil the appearance of your letter.

Window and aperture envelopes are occasionally used for business letters. A window envelope has a square or oblong panel cut out and covered with a transparent material through which the addressee's name and address on the letter can be seen. In an aperture envelope, there is no transparent protective covering over the cut-out section. For both of these types of envelope, the letter inside must be folded and inserted correctly so that the address appears in the correct position under the cut-out panel.

When the letter is a business communication or a fairly formal letter, especially to someone whose tastes you do not know, avoid decorated envelopes. Some business letters are routinely sent in brown, or manila, envelopes, because it is supposed to be less easy to detect an enclosure in a brown envelope. In the past, small brown envelopes were used for sending out bills. However, this practice is not so widespread now, and many bills today come through the letterbox in plain white envelopes. Airmail envelopes are available for letters going overseas.

If you are going to take the trouble to write a letter you should aim for as professional a final product as possible. It is worthwhile spending money on good paper, a good quality writing instrument, and putting a little thought into the layout. This will help you to create a good impression.

Presentation and Layout

The layout and design of a letter will have an impact on the reader before he or she gets around to considering its content. A high standard of presentation is very important, especially in today's highly competitive business and employment environments. (Of course, this applies not just to letters, but to all the communications that may affect an individual's, a company's or an organization's image: emails, faxes, reports, sales literature, advertisements, and brochures.)

You don't want any letter you write to give the impression that it has been produced hastily and carelessly. It should be well designed, properly spaced, and well organized. A well-laid-out letter can also help to highlight any important points you want to make.

Much of this chapter gives advice on how formal and business correspondence is laid out. For personal and social letters, you don't have to stick to a rigid structure, though some of the tips in this and the next chapter should nonetheless be useful for personal and less formal social letters.

If you use a word processor, a good deal of the formatting can be done automatically. You can also make use of the extra features that word-processing programs provide such as bullets and numbering, columns, tables and boxes. Most programs include letter templates of various designs and layouts from which to choose.

Blocked, indented and semi-blocked style

There are two main styles for presenting typed letters in the English-speaking world: blocked style and indented style. There is also an intermediate style, semi-blocked style. While all these styles can be individualized in some of their elements they are broadly as described in the pages that follow.

Fully blocked style

The most popular format for typed or printed formal and business letters is the fully blocked style with open punctuation, ie minimum punctuation.

An example of a letter laid out in fully blocked style is given on page 346. This sample letter also illustrates some of the standard elements of a letter, which are more fully described later in this chapter. The fully blocked format is easy to set out using a typewriter or personal computer and extremely convenient for the increasing numbers of people who word process their own correspondence, but do not necessarily have traditional secretarial skill.

Fully indented style

The fully indented style is the most traditional format, nowadays regarded in business and professional circles as being extremely old-fashioned. It is still occasionally used for personal and handwritten letters, but its popularity is steadily declining as more and more people use word processors at home. The stepped indents for each element of the fully indented format are time-consuming to set up on a word processor. (See the sample fully indented letter on page 347)

Hall Office Management Ltd
47 Yarn Street
LIVERPOOL
M100 XYZ
Telephone: +44 (0)1234 5678910
Facsimile: +44 (0)1234 5678911

Your ref: AA/Corr01
Our ref: VH/NDEC

7 July 2008

Mr Albert Appleby
Manager
Havestock Mill
101 Walpole Street
LIVERPOOL
M100 XXZ

Dear Mr Appleby

FULLY BLOCKED STYLE

This is an example of the style my company uses to present our business letters. It is nowadays the standard layout for nearly all business correspondence.

Blocked style's most obvious feature is that all the elements of the letter are aligned to the left. In the main body of the letter, the first line of each paragraph and all subsequent lines within a paragraph are also aligned to the left.

There is no punctuation in addresses or after the salutation or complimentary closing. Headings are in block capitals without underlining.

Notice that, in this layout, there is a single line space between the paragraphs and between all the other elements. This is the usual method of spacing in blocked style.

I enclose further examples of reports, faxes and memos in blocked style.

Yours sincerely

Victoria Hall

Victoria Hall
Director

ENC x 3

45 Yarn Street,
LIVERPOOL,
M100 XYZ.

7 July 2008

Messrs. Smith & Gemmell,
101 Walpole Street,
LIVERPOOL,
Merseyside,
M100 XXZ.

Dear Sirs,

FULLY INDENTED STYLE

I have pleasure in providing you with an example of a letter written in fully indented style, and a description of the main characteristics of this style.

The sender's address is on the right hand side of the sheet with the second and subsequent lines of the address beginning one or two characters to the right of the first letter or number on the preceding line. The date is to the right below the sender's address.

If the recipient's address is included the first line is aligned to the left with the second and subsequent lines beginning one or two characters to the right of the first letter on the preceding line.

There is a full stop following the last line of the address. Commas follow all other address lines, and the salutation and complimentary close. Generally, there is more punctuation in indented style than in fully blocked style.

The salutation or opening greeting is aligned to the left-hand margin, any heading following the salutation is centred above the main text of the letter and may be underlined, and the first line of each paragraph of the main text is indented.

Line spaces between the paragraphs of the main text are optional in indented style. While the indent is often sufficient to distinguish the paragraphs, no line spacing between paragraphs can give a dense appearance to the page.

The complimentary close and signature can be indented from the left margin, centred under the main text, or (as here) placed near the right hand margin of the page.

Yours sincerely,

Alicia Amberhurst

Alicia Amberhurst

Semi-blocked style

The semi-blocked style has some fully blocked elements and some indented elements. Though this format is thought by some people to be a little old-fashioned, it is quite easy to type on a word processor. It is therefore a useful way of ringing the changes from the seemingly ubiquitous fully blocked style. (See the sample semi-blocked letter below.)

45 Yarn Street,
LIVERPOOL,
M100 XYZ

7 July 2005

Messrs. Smith & Gemmell,
101 Walpole Street,
LIVERPOOL,
Merseyside,
M100 XXZ

Dear Sirs,

SEMI-BLOCKED STYLE

I have pleasure in providing you with an example of a letter written in semi-blocked style, which illustrates how blocking and indentation can be combined to vary the layout.

The sender's address is on the right hand side of the sheet with the second and subsequent lines of the address aligned with the first letter of the first line. The date is under, and aligned with, the sender's address. All lines of the recipient's address are aligned to the left of the page, as is the salutation.

Commas and full stops have been used in the addresses, with a comma following the salutation and complimentary close.

The salutation or opening greeting is aligned to the left hand margin, and the heading is centred and may be underlined. The first line of each paragraph of the main text is indented, and there are line spaces between the paragraphs.

The complimentary close and signature are centred under the main text.

Yours sincerely,

Alicia Amberhurst

Alicia Amberhurst

None of these styles needs to be rigidly adhered to and where the stationery has been pre-printed with the sender's name, address and other details, it is obviously not necessary to duplicate these details.

Pre-printed stationery

All letters should include the sender's address. Some people choose to avoid the trouble of laying out their address by having their address pre-printed on their personal notepaper. This is, of course, standard practice for business stationery; most large companies spend quite a lot of time and money on a design that will create the sort of image they want to project.

The pre-printed stationery of businesses, institutions and government agencies will usually include logo, name, full postal address, telephone number, fax number, and often also an email address and URL or website address. These elements usually appear at the top of the page. Private limited companies are legally obliged to show the company's registered number, registered address, and directors' names. This information is often printed along the bottom of the page. Businesses registered for VAT (value added tax) must print their VAT number somewhere on their stationery; often this is under or next to the company name and address.

The pre-printed stationery of a private individual will usually include their name, postal address, telephone number, fax number, and email address.

Graphics and text design tools come as part of nearly all modern word processing and desktop-publishing programs. It is perfectly possible to design your stationery on your personal computer using these tools. However, you should seriously consider paying a professional to print the stationery that will incorporate the design you decide on. Unless you have a very sophisticated printing machine, producing the stationery yourself may be a false economy.

If you do have your stationery printed by a professional printer, it is also a good idea to get a supply of continuation paper, ie sheets used for typing second and subsequent pages of a letter. These should match the colour and weight of your letterhead. Continuation sheets are often pre-printed with some element from the main letterhead, such as a company name and logo.

Formatting continuation sheets

When typing continuation sheets, it is usual to include a page number, the date, a reference, and/or the name of the addressee. One method of formatting these elements is shown in the sample below. Alternatively, you might prefer to have the page number, the date and the reference on the same line. A word processor can be set up to include automatically page number, date and various other types of references which will be printed as a header or footer on each page of the letter.

You should always leave 3–4 lines blank at the top of the continuation sheet before going on with the body of your letter.

Page 2 of 2

7 July 2005

Mr Albert Appleby

Notice that, in this layout, there is a single line space between the paragraphs and between all the other elements. This is the usual method of spacing in blocked style, though line spacing is sometimes varied to suit the extent of the letter.

I enclose further examples of reports, faxes and memos in blocked style.

I hope you will agree that this style has a pleasing and business-like appearance.

Yours sincerely

Victoria Hall

Victoria Hall
Director

ENC x 3

Overall Appearance

Use design and formatting to help the reader of your letter.

A good start

Make sure there is enough contrast between the colour of the ink and the paper. For preference, use black or dark blue ink on a white background.

Whether you are writing by hand or using a word processor, it is a good idea to take the time to make a first draft. A draft set out in paragraphs will give an idea of the length, and therefore how the lines ought to be spaced on the page. A draft will also make it easier to refine and correct the content. Aim to make the final version of the letter as professional-looking and free of corrections and errors as possible.

Spacing and line length

Leave generous margins. Try to allow a margin of about 25 mm at the top and bottom, and at both sides, of each page.

For the main body of the letter, the space between lines should always be greater than the space between words. Otherwise, the reader's eye can jump down the lines.

The usual (default) line spacing in a word processing program for 10–12 point type size will be 12 point, or about 120% of the type size.

Very long and very short lines make people read more slowly. A full line of body text should have about 10 to 12 words. The size of the type you use depends on the length of the line. Longer lines need larger type.

If your letter is short, the text should not be pushed up to the top of the sheet with a large area left blank at the bottom.

It does not look good if the first page is densely printed and closely spaced with only one or two lines appearing on a second page. Try to alter the spacing so that more text appears on the second page, or try to fit the letter into a single page. A second page, or continuation sheet, should have at least three or four lines of text, excluding the complimentary close and signature.

Alignment

Using a word processor, text can be aligned in various ways: justified, with the column of text aligned on both left and right; ranged left, also called ragged right; ranged right, also called ragged left; and centred. Examples of each are shown below.

This is an example of *justified* text. The spaces between the words are different lengths so that full lines of text align to the left and to the right.

This is an example of text *ranged left*. The spaces between the words
are the same length. The text is aligned at the left side of the page
but not at the right side, hence the informal name 'ragged right'.

This is an example of text *ranged right*. The spaces between the words
are the same length. The text is aligned at the right side of the page
but not at the left side, hence the informal name 'ragged left'.

This text is *centred* and has equal spaces between words.

It is best to avoid justifying the body text of your letter. Though it gives a neat appearance some people find it more difficult to read than body text aligned on the left side.

To avoid the long spaces between words that justified text can create, it may be a temptation to try to fit more into a gappy line by splitting a word at the end of a line and inserting a hyphen at the split. While this is a common technique in newspaper, magazine and reference-book publishing, it is not recommended for letter-writing, simply because anything that might inhibit the recipient's reading should be avoided. End of line splits can make the reader hesitate.

In any event, there is not absolute agreement about where words should be split, and it is quite likely you will irritate your reader by using a method of splitting that he or she does not agree with.

The standard alignment for letter-writing is to range the text to the left. Text ranged to the right is only used for specialist purposes or in certain languages. Centring the text can sometimes be useful for making some part of the letter stand out, but it is not used routinely.

Which typeface should be used when word processing a letter?

Fonts can be divided into two groups: serif fonts, which have little curls (serifs) on the letters, and sans serif (meaning 'without serif') fonts, which are plain.

There are many different fonts available to users of word processing and email programs and more are being designed every day. You may imagine having so many different font styles available to you gives you a great opportunity to express your individuality. Up to a point this is true, but don't get carried away.

For formal letters, business letters, and especially for job applications, care should be taken when selecting a font. Always consider readability and the appropriateness of the font for the task. After all, you would probably be rather taken aback to receive a letter from the tax office or the bank manager in a font that communicates a sense of playfulness or light-hearted simplicity.

Researchers in the field of CV-writing have found that the font can be an important factor in determining if a CV and its covering letter is rejected early in the vetting process, or given further attention. Keep in mind that an employer is likely to receive many CVs in response to a job advertisement, and while making the first selection of suitable candidates he or she may spend no more that a minute or so on each CV. If your CV and its covering letter are badly presented or difficult to read, your application is quite likely to fall at this first hurdle.

For typed CVs and covering letters, and formal correspondence in general, it is probably advisable to stick to more conservative fonts, such as the serif fonts:

Palatino
Times New Roman

or, a clear, elegant and readable sans serif fonts, such as:

Arial
Trebuchet MS

Avoid using more than two fonts in a letter. With so many different fonts available, you may be tempted to use more than two, but too many changes in font will almost certainly make your letter look cluttered and so reduce its readability. One font for headings and another for the text is usually enough. Alternatively, you could use a single font throughout, and use bold or a larger font size to make headings, reference lines or other elements stand out.

Type size is measured in units called 'points'. The type size most often used for letters is 12 point, though you can go down to 10 point if this is necessary to fit your letter onto a single sheet. Don't go below 10 point because smaller sized type will make your letter difficult to read. Headings are usually 2 point sizes larger than the text size, so if the main text of your letter is in 12 point, you might use 14 point or larger for headings.

Paragraphs

Keep paragraphs short. For formal and business letters, this usually means no more than six to eight lines per paragraph.

Don't leave one line of a paragraph at the bottom of the previous page or at the top of the next page. Try, wherever possible, to start a new page with a new paragraph.

Ideally, a formal letter or business letter should consist of a beginning, a middle and an end. There will usually be a short introductory paragraph, whose purpose is to acknowledge any previous letter received and/or state briefly the purpose or subject of the letter. This is followed by a longer paragraph, or series of paragraphs, making and expanding on various points. The letter should ideally end with a short final paragraph (the conclusion). Each paragraph should deal with only one main point or idea. The information should be laid out in a logical sequence, providing relevant details where required, and making sure the information flows smoothly from point to point.

Highlighting and structure

When formatting a letter, take care to get the balance right between style and content. As was mentioned in the previous chapter, take care about the font you use, and don't use more than 2 or 3 different fonts or sizes within the same letter.

The most effective way to highlight a word or phrase is to use bold. Avoid using block capital letters for emphasis in the body of the letter and try not to use underlining in the body of the letter. Italic should be used sparingly and not for long stretches of text, as this can be difficult to read, especially in a smaller font size.

It is becoming increasingly common to find 'bullet points' in business letters. These can give a professional and attractive appearance to a letter or report and allows the reader to extract each point easily. Bullet points, when used within the body of a long letter, can make the letter appear less dense and daunting. A cautionary note: because bullet points are designed to stand out they may be the only thing the reader focuses on, with the surrounding text getting little or no attention, for example:

We require separate estimates for:

- Re-roofing the house with traditional slates.
- Thatching the barn
- Clearing the old farm equipment and debris from the yard.
- Replacing any missing granite setts in the yard.
- Rebuilding any damaged boundary walls and fences.

The Individual Elements of a Formal or Business Letter

The sample given below shows all the elements likely to be used in a formal or business letter. This sample is intended to show the order in which these elements usually appear in blocked style. It is not necessary to include all of them in every letter. The obligatory elements are shown in bold in the sample. More information on each element is given in the pages that follow.

Return address (sender's address) including postcode

Sender's contact information

Reference

Date

Special instructions/type of dispatch

Attention line (1)
Inside address (recipient's address) including postcode
Attention line (2)

Salutation (opening greeting)

Subject heading

Body of letter

Complimentary close

Signature

Sender's name
Sender's position and/or personal contact details

Postscript

Enclosures

Copies

Return address (sender's address)

Where this is not already in place on pre-printed letterhead (often centred at the top of the page), the sender's address must be written or typed on every letter. When typing or keying the address, it should be placed at the top right-hand corner of the sheet of paper. The address must include all the information that will be needed for the fast and safe delivery of any reply. Make sure you include the post town and postcode (or ZIP code). The post town and postcode should be typed in capital letters.

23 Park Drive
SEAFIELD
RA14 2TY

If a county name is included only its first letter should be in capitals.

23 Park Drive
SEAFIELD
Blackshire
RA14 2TY

Inside the letter, the post town and postcode can be typed on the same line, but on the envelope the post town and postcode should always be on separate lines.

In the UK, postcodes are made up of a mixture of letters and numbers—a total of five, six or seven characters. The postcode should be typed with a single space before the group of three numbers/letters at the end of the code.

RA14 2TY

In the US, the Zip code is on the last line with the municipality and the state abbreviation, as shown below:

CHICAGO IL 85672-4332

Each country has its own formula for postcodes. For international mail, you should refer to your correspondent's letters to ensure you use the correct layout for their address and postcode. Also for international mail, the country name should be on a separate line after the postcode or Zip code and should be written in English.

Hermann Gottlieb
Hertzstrasse 12
16935 Leipzig
GERMANY

Punctuation in addresses has now largely been dispensed with but you can opt to use a more conventional level of punctuation, with commas after the street number and at the end of each line of the address—in the UK, it's really a matter of choice.

Sender's contact information

Nowadays, many individuals, and nearly all businesses, include contact information in their letters (telephone and fax number, email address and website address). This is likely to include telephone number and fax number, and sometimes also a mobile phone number, email address and website address. The positioning of this information is to some extent a matter of taste, though it is most often placed on the right-hand side below the sender's address.

For telephone and fax numbers, it is now standard practice to include the international dialling code. This comes at the beginning of the number and is preceded by a plus sign (+). For example, the international dialling code for the United Kingdom is 44, so a telephone number including this code will look like this:

+44 (0)141 000 1000

Note that the first digit of the area code is bracketed. This is because it is not used when dialling from abroad.

Ideally, and for clarity, there should be a line space between the contact information and the last line of the sender's address.

Contact information is often presented like this:

Tel: +44 (0)141 000 1000
Fax: +44 (0)141 000 1001
Email: heman@superrepairs.co.uk
Website: www.superrepairs.co.uk

Or, the words 'telephone' and 'facsimile' can be written out in full. This is, again, a matter of personal preference.

Reference line

Personal letters do not typically include reference lines. In business letters, the reference line is usually placed at the top left side of the page with a line space between it and the return address above it to the right, and a line space between it and the date below.

Reference lines usually include the word 'Reference' or the abbreviation 'Ref'. The abbreviation may or may not have a full stop, nowadays more often not. Conventionally, 'Reference' or 'Ref' is followed by a colon, thus:

Reference: MMM/BR
Ref: MMM/BR
Our ref: MMM/BR

However, those who prefer everything, except the body text, to be punctuation-free may use tab spaces instead of colons, thus:

Reference MMM/BR
Ref MMM/BR
Our ref MMM/BR

References may include the sender's initials followed by the initials of the person who typed the letter. As a rule both the sender's and the typist's initials are in capital letters and separated from each other by a forward slash, for example MMC/CMM. Sometimes the sender's initials are in capitals and the typist's initials are in lower case letters, for example MMC/cmm.

Reference lines frequently show other information, such as a customer account number, or it may include information relating to a company's internal filing system. This information is included in the reference line so that all correspondence on a specific topic or for a specified time period can be easily identified and filed together. A typical formula for such a reference line is:

Our ref: MMC/CMM/05projectX

If you are replying to a letter that has a reference line, you should always quote the other person's or company's reference in your reply. This will speed things up at the other end because the reference will help link your reply to previous correspondence. In business letters, the usual formula for the reference line is as follows:

Your ref ABC/DR/Accts

If you want to include your own reference as well, the usual formula is:

Your ref ABC/DR/Accts
Our ref MMC/CMM/05projectX

Date

The date used to be placed under the postcode (or the contact information) on the right side of the page with a line space between the address and the date. Nowadays, the date is almost invariably placed on the left hand side of the page above the inside address.

Here is another quote from Lewis Carroll's advice on letter-writing which deals with dates in letters. The advice is just as relevant now as it was when it was written:

> *. . . put the date in full. It is an aggravating thing, when you wish, years afterwards, to arrange a series of letters, to find them dated 'Feb. 17', 'Aug. 2', without any year to guide you as to which comes first. And never, never . . . put 'Wednesday', simply, as the date! That way madness lies.*

There are various ways to write the date:

14 August 2005
or
14th August 2005
or
August 14, 2005

The first and second reflect the usual ordering used in the UK: day, month, and year. The third is the ordering used in the US: month, day, and year. These styles have been variously adopted in other English-speaking countries.

The first style with a cardinal number for the day (for example 1, 2, 3, 14, 31) is now more common than the second with an ordinal number for the day (for example 1st, 2nd, 3rd, 14th, 31st).

In formal and business letters it is better not to use abbreviations for the month names.

In many other contexts, dates are written entirely in numbers, ie 14/8/05 or 14/08/2005. However, this is not recommended for letter-writing. Naming the month makes for speed of reference, especially when back correspondence is being consulted. Furthermore, in US style, the month number comes first in dates consisting entirely of numbers, thus the fourteenth of August 2005 is written 08/14/05 in the US. The same date is written 14/08/05 in the UK. This difference in style can cause bewilderment, particularly if the day of the month is in the range 1–12. The potential for confusion adds further weight to the argument that the month should always be written out in full.

Special instructions/dispatch type

These are usually typed in capital letters, below the date and above the inside address. However, some special instructions like CONFIDENTIAL and PERSONAL can be typed above the date and reference lines. When a letter is marked PERSONAL, it means that only the addressee should open it; when it is marked CONFIDENTIAL, it means someone deputizing for the addressee can open and read the letter, but that the information should not be made available outside the office or firm to which it is addressed; and PRIVATE & CONFIDENTIAL means no one but the addressee should open or read the letter.

Special instructions like CONFIDENTIAL are not used in personal letters.

Some examples of despatch instructions are RECORDED DELIVERY or CERTIFIED MAIL, SPECIAL DELIVERY, REGISTERED POST, BY COURIER, BY HAND, AIRMAIL and FIRST CLASS.

Special instructions and dispatch type should also be printed clearly on the envelope.

Attention line

Attention lines are not used in personal letters. In business letters, an attention line can be in one of two positions on the letter. It is usually duplicated on the envelope.

Where the letter is to be addressed to a company, organization or government department, but you expect the matter to be dealt with by a known individual within the company, the attention line (1) will usually be placed above the inside address, sometimes with a line space between, thus:

For attention of: Jeremy Anderson, Credit Controller

MMM Confectionery Ltd
276 Westwind Avenue
YORK
MM6 6MM

An attention line can also appear at the end of the inside address (2). This is done when there is a possibility that the person to whom the letter is addressed may not be available to attend to it. This second type of attention line usually names the person, or department, that the letter should be dealt with in the absence of the named addressee.

Jeremy Anderson, Credit Controller
MMM Confectionery Ltd
276 Westwind Avenue
YORK
MM6 6MM
For attention of: Accounts Department

There is often a line space between the inside address and the attention line. The wording and format of the attention line can vary, as in the following examples:

Attention: Jeremy Anderson, Credit Controller
Attention Jeremy Anderson, Credit Controller
Fao: Jeremy Anderson, Credit Controller
<u>For attention of</u> Jeremy Anderson, Credit Controller

Inside address (recipient's address)

You should always include the inside (recipient's) address in a formal or business letter. When you are writing a personal or social letter there is no need to include it. The inside address has the same elements as the return address, with the possible addition of a job title, and/or the department in which the recipient works.

Mrs Angelina Hobson, Principal Librarian
Special Collections
The University of Middle England
100-146 University Avenue
Hopehill
SEAFIELD
Blackshire
MM3 3MM

As with the return address, the building number and street name appear on one line; the next line may be used for a locality name, ie the name of a village or hamlet or a district of a larger town or city; the next line will be the post town; the next line may be used for a county name, and the last line (provided the letter is not to be sent abroad) for the postcode.

Courtesy titles

The usual courtesy titles are Mr, Miss, Mrs and Ms. It used to be quite common to address a gentleman as Esq. (short for 'Esquire'). However this is becoming more rare. Unlike the other courtesy titles, Esq. or Esq is placed after the surname and is obviously only used when the first name or initial is known. If Esq. is used, the courtesy title Mr is not used before the first name, so the name can be written:

James Barrington-Hume, Esq.
J. Barrington-Hume, Esq.
or
Mr James Barrington-Hume
Mr J Barrington-Hume
Mr Barrington-Hume
but never
Mr James Barrington-Hume, Esq.
Mr J Barrington-Hume, Esq.
Mr Barrington-Hume, Esq.

In common practice, it is now more and more usual to omit the courtesy titles Mr, Mrs, Miss and Ms. Only the name is used, thus:

James Black
Angus Foggert
Hermione Duval

While omitting the gender-specific title may seem somewhat radical, it is a neat way of avoiding faux pas that may arise from not being absolutely certain about the sex or marital status of the recipient. Even if it clear from the name that the correspondent is a woman, there remains the problem of how she should be addressed. People will very often find themselves asking the questions, 'How should I address this woman, whose marital status I do not know? Even if I know her marital status, I don't know how she prefers to be addressed. Does she use her husband's name and the title Mrs, or has she kept her maiden name for business purposes and prefers to be known as Miss or Mrs? Is she divorced, and if she is, has she kept the title Mrs?'

It can all be a bit of a minefield. More and more people, especially in business and the professions, ask why a woman's marital status should be important anyway, and why on earth there should be a different title for each state (Miss and Mrs), with an invented title (the dreadful Ms) for women whose marital status is not known? When addressing a letter to a man, no one would give a moment's thought to whether he was married or not. Doing away with titles altogether in addresses is one way of ensuring there is equality of treatment between the sexes.

While gender-specific titles may be becoming less popular in addresses, professional and academic titles (for example Prof, Dr), hereditary and aristocratic titles (for example Her Royal Highness, His Grace), honorary titles (for example Sir/Dame), and armed forces ranks (for example General, Rear Admiral) are usually still used. If first names are reduced to initials in the address, it used to be the case that each initial was followed by a full stop. Nowadays, full stops and commas in addresses are considered to be unnecessary, so the name in the inside address is more likely to appear in one of the following forms:

Mr J A Black
or
J A Black
or
James Black

In the UK and elsewhere, a company name may be followed by Ltd, short for 'limited' and indicating that it is a limited liability company. Other business names may be followed by plc or PLC, short for 'public limited company'. Again, it is not necessary to use full stops in these abbreviations.

In the US, corporations often have Inc. (short for 'incorporated') after the name. US style is to favour full stops in these and other abbreviations used in addresses.

Salutation (opening greeting)

The opening greeting should align with the inside address on the left-hand side of the page, under the last line of the inside address and with a line left blank, thus:

The Manager
Cosmo Furniture Store
12–15 King Street
SEAFIELD
RA11 6DR

Dear Sir

For personal letters where there is no inside address the opening greeting should go at the left-hand side after the date, usually with a line left blank, thus:

24 May 1966

Dear Mary

The way in which you address the recipient in the opening greeting depends on who the person is and your relationship to that person.

If you know you are writing to a man but you do not know his name, use the opening greeting 'Dear Sir'.

If you know you are writing to a woman but you do not know her name, then the opening greeting is 'Dear Madam'.

If you know you are writing to an individual but you do not know the person's sex or their name, the standard greeting is 'Dear Sir or Madam'.

If you are writing to a firm and you know very little about their set-up, it is common practice to use the opening greeting 'Dear Sirs'.

If you are on first-name terms with the person you are writing to, the greeting is straightforward, for example 'Dear Anwar' or 'Dear Matilda'. Correspondents whose names are known may be addressed as 'Dear Mr Brown' or 'Dear Miss Lee'. Otherwise the opening greeting will be 'Dear Sirs', 'Dear Sir/Madam' or 'Dear Sir or Madam'.

For formal and business correspondence, it used to be that the wording of the salutation dictated the wording of the complimentary close, as follows:

Salutation	**Complimentary close**
Dear Sir	Yours faithfully
Dear Sirs	Yours faithfully
Dear Sir or Madam	Yours faithfully
Dear Madam	Yours faithfully
Dear Mr Black	Yours sincerely
Dear Miss Green	Yours sincerely
Dear Mrs White	Yours sincerely
Dear Ms Brown	Yours sincerely
Dear John	Yours sincerely
Dear Mary	Yours sincerely

In other words, when the addressee was not named, the complimentary close was always 'Yours faithfully', and when the addressee was named, the complimentary close was always 'Yours sincerely'. This is no longer so much the case, as is more fully described below in the section on complimentary close.

Subject line

The subject line, if there is one, is typed after the salutation, with a line space between them. A subject line can be useful in letting the recipient of your letter know what it is about at a glance. Subject lines should be typed or written in capital letters to make them stand out. If you are using a word processor, you can also make the subject line bold to make it stand out even more.

Complimentary close

This is placed under the last paragraph of the body of the letter—there is often a blank line between the two—and above the signature. The positioning of the complimentary close will depend on the format of the letter: more usually, and always in fully blocked style, it must be aligned to the left; otherwise it may be centred or nearer the right-hand side of the page.

For formal and business correspondence, as mentioned under the heading 'Salutation', it used to be that the wording of the salutation dictated the wording of the complimentary close.

When the addressee was not named, the complimentary close was always 'Yours faithfully', and when the addressee was named, then the complimentary close was always 'Yours sincerely'. This rule, while still used today, is now not so widely and rigidly adhered to.

The closing greeting can now take various forms. Some feel it is peculiar and rather too obsequious to bring the concept of faithfulness into a letter to someone whom one does not know, and have come to regard 'Yours faithfully' in much the same way as 'Your obedient servant' and other phrases used in letters in the past. We now live in a much less formal, egalitarian age, and like everything else, the conventions used in letter-writing are being affected by this.

If you don't like 'Yours faithfully' but want to keep a slightly formal feel, it is nowadays perfectly acceptable to use 'Yours sincerely' with the salutations 'Dear Sir', 'Dear Sirs', 'Dear Madam' and 'Dear Sir or Madam'. As shown in the previous column, when you begin a letter 'Dear Mr Black' or 'Dear Ms Brown' you should close the letter with 'Yours sincerely'. Similarly, with a fairly personal salutation like 'Dear John' or 'Dear Mary' you can use 'Yours sincerely' where you want to maintain a measure of distance between you and the addressee.

Remember that not everyone likes the familiarity conveyed by some of the complimentary closes that are creeping into letters nowadays, probably influenced by email and text messaging.

Of course, there are situations where you may want to use a warmer, less impersonal close, such as 'With best wishes', 'Kind regards', 'Yours affectionately', 'Yours ever', or 'Yours'.

Closing phrases expressing love should be reserved for family members, lovers and very close personal friends, although certain people use these lavishly and loosely, particularly on postcards or greetings cards.

Complimentary closes suitable for business letters

Yours faithfully	formal
Yours sincerely	less formal
Sincerely,	mainly US
Sincerely yours,	mainly US
Cordially,	mainly US
Yours respectfully	very formal
Respectfully yours,	mainly US
Respectfully,	mainly US
Yours truly,	mainly US; informal
Best regards	informal
With kind regards	informal

Kind regards	informal
Warmest regards	informal
Regards	informal

Complimentary closes suitable for personal and social letters

With best wishes
Best wishes
All the best
Fondly
Yours affectionately
Affectionately
Love
Much love
With all my love

Never use 'Yours very faithfully' (you are either faithful or you are not). However, there is no technical reason for not using 'Yours very sincerely', though it is perhaps a little inelegant.

Only the first word in the closing greeting should be given a capital letter; do not write 'Yours Sincerely' or 'Yours Truly'. A comma at the end of the closing greeting is no longer obligatory.

Signature

As has been mentioned above, the signature is placed under the closing greeting, usually with a blank line between them. Since not everyone's signature is legible—indeed some people seem to pride themselves on the illegibility of their signatures—it is important to type or print your name underneath your signature so that people are in no doubt about the identity of the writer and their exact name, thus:

Yours sincerely

JBrown

James Brown

In business letters it is also a good idea to include your position in an organization or firm where this is relevant. This is usually typed on the line immediately following the name, thus:

Yours sincerely

JBrown

James Brown

Club Secretary

Sometimes a letter is signed on behalf of someone else. This usually happens when the person who has dictated the letter is not available to sign it after it has been typed or printed. The signature will then appear something like this:

Yours sincerely

Jane Green

p.p. (or pp) James Brown
Chief Executive Officer

The abbreviation p.p. does not stand for 'on behalf of', as is generally assumed, but is an abbreviation of the Latin phrase *per procurationem*, meaning 'by proxy'. Strictly speaking then, p.p. should precede the name of the person signing the letter and not the name of the person on whose behalf the letter is being signed. However, this is widely ignored.

It is important to remember to sign your letters. If you are in a hurry it is all too easy to type a letter on the word processor, print it out and put it in an envelope without signing it. Provided you have typed your name there will be no problem for the recipient in identifying the sender, but unsigned letters can cause offence because they send a message that you didn't care enough to take the time to check the letter before hastily stuffing it in the envelope.

Personal contact information

An individual writing on behalf of a company or organization may give their personal contact information in addition to the more general company contacts shown at the top of the letter. For example, they may give their individual email address, mobile phone number or telephone extension number. This information is often typed under or near their signature.

Yours sincerely

JBrown

James Brown
Sales Executive
Extn: 2073

Enclosures

When other documents are being sent with a letter, the convention is to note this on the covering letter, using the abbreviations Enc and Encs (Enclosure and Enclosures).

The abbreviation Enc (or Encs) is often followed by a number corresponding to the number of items to be enclosed, for example Encs x 3.

This is helpful for checking that you have gathered all the documents before putting them into the envelope and the recipient can see how many documents ought to be enclosed.

If there are enclosures, this is indicated below the signature, thus:

Yours sincerely

JBrown

James Brown

ENCLS x 3

There may be one or two line spaces between the printed signature and the enclosure line.

Copies

When a letter is being copied to others, this is also usually indicated. The standard formula is:

Copies to: Kenneth Barrett
Delia Jackson
Sam Trudeau

Notice that the names are in alphabetical order.

Another way of prefixing the names of the people to receive copies is to use the abbreviation CC or cc, meaning 'carbon copies'. This term is inherited from the days when all correspondence was typed and copies were made using carbon paper.

Postscripts

Postscripts are 'afterthoughts' printed or written after the signature. They are preceded by the abbreviation PS (or P.S.). Try to avoid them in business correspondence as they give the impression you have not formulated your thoughts sufficiently to make all the points you needed to make in the body of the letter.

Addressing Envelopes

Modern style is to align all the lines of the address with no indentation and no punctuation, as in the following example:

Mr James Brown
Flat 3
23 Whitehill Street
SEAFIELD
Blackshire
RA9 5JX

For standard-sized envelopes, the address should be aligned with the longer sides of the envelope, and placed slightly to the left of the mid point between the two shortest sides. The first line of the address should be about two thirds of the way down from the top edge of the envelope. This allows plenty of room for the stamp and postmark.

Legibility is the most important consideration when addressing an envelope. If the mail sorters or reading devices at sorting offices cannot read the address the letter cannot be delivered. Similarly, if there are errors or omissions in the address it may cause delays in delivery.

The conventions for addressing envelopes used to be the same as those for writing addresses within the letter, but nowadays more attention needs to be paid to the increasing automation of postal sorting, and, for international mail, to the conventions of the destination country.

The old style of indenting each line of the address with commas at the end of each line is now more or less obsolete.

The sender should write or print his or her own name and address on the back of the envelope so that the letter can be returned if it cannot be delivered. Alternatively, the sender's name and address can be printed on the front of the envelope at the top left hand side, provided it is sufficiently distinct and separate from the recipient's address, and is outside the 'reading zone' of mail sorting machines.

Automated Mail Sorting

The optical character reading (OCR) cameras used in many automated systems have a predetermined 'reading zone'. The camera will not read accurately anything that is written or printed outside this zone. To assist automatic sorting the advice is to write or print the address leaving at least 15 mm margins to left and right, with a 40 mm margin at the top edge of the envelope (where the postage information is sited). Address lines should be no longer than 100 mm.

The higher the contrast between ink colour and paper colour, the higher the accurate read rate of the OCR system will be. Black ink on white or cream paper is recommended.

Envelopes should not be too flimsy—the recommended paper weight is 75g/sqm. The paper should also have a high opacity so that the contents cannot be seen through the paper and interfere with reading the address.

For window envelopes, the material covering the address window should be shiny not matt and nothing other than the address should appear in the window.

To assist legibility there should be at least one character gap between words; and there should be uniform spacing between address lines, with a recommended gap between lines of 0. 5 mm to 12 mm.

While OCR can read most typed upper and lower case characters and numerals, fonts chosen should be clear and sharp, not script, artistic or italic. Some recommended fonts are Arial, Courier, Times New Roman and Century.

Printed addresses should be aligned at the left hand side and parallel to the top edge of the envelope. Adhesive address labels should be at least

80 mm×25 mm and placed in the 'reading zone' of the envelope. In handwritten addresses, the lines should be horizontal, the individual characters of even size, and characters should not overlap or touch each other.

Addressing guidance for different countries

The conventions for addressing envelopes vary from country to country.

United Kingdom

For the UK, addresses should include the information as set out in the table below.

Information	Is this information required?	Address line
Addressee's name	Yes, when applicable	**Mr James Brown**
Company name or Organization's name	Yes, when applicable	**Farington plc**
Flat or Apartment number	Yes, when applicable	**Flat 3/1**
Building name	Yes, except if the building also has a number	**Farington House**
Number of house, flat, building and name of street, road, etc	Yes	**23 Whitehill Street**
Name of locality	Yes, but only if there is a similar street or road name within the same post town area	**Greenhill**
Post town *(PRINT IN CAPITAL LETTERS)*	Yes	**SEAFIELD**
Postal county, historical county or administrative county/region	No longer necessary provided the post town and postcode are used	**Blackshire**
Postcode *(PRINT IN CAPITAL LETTERS)*	Yes	**RA9 5JX**
Country Name *(PRINT IN CAPITAL LETTERS)*	Only for international mail	**UNITED KINGDOM**

The Royal Mail advises that it is essential to include the post town name in every UK address. To leave it out when addressing an envelope risks a delay in delivery. Although the post town name does not provide any information that is not already contained in the postcode, it is sometimes used to check that the postcode is correct and to aid manual sorting where the postcode is missing or incorrect.

Post towns rarely correspond to political or administrative boundaries. Instead, each post town corresponds to one or more postcodes, and a single post town can cover many individual towns and villages. Thus, for mail sorting purposes, the Isle of Man is a post town, while Douglas, the island's main town, is categorized as a locality within the post town of Isle of Man. A post town may also cover a very large densely populated geographical area, such as Greater London. In large cities or conurbations it is quite usual to give more specific directions by giving a locality name on an additional line above the post town, for example Hampstead or Bethnal Green. However, including a locality is only really necessary where there are two or more similar addresses within the post town area.

It is no longer necessary to include a county name, provided the post town and postcode are used. Using the correct post town and postcode and omitting the county name may even avoid the confusion that can arise about county names. Postal counties—used by the Royal Mail internally for organizational purposes—do not necessarily correspond to historical or administrative boundaries.

Furthermore, with successive reorganizations of local government, boundaries for administrative counties, districts and regions have been redrawn many times, and areas renamed. Nonetheless, counties—historical, administrative, or otherwise—may still be included in addresses. To check the correct spelling of a city name and/or find a postcode and post town visit the Postcode Finder on the Royal Mail's information and service portal at:

www.royalmail.com/portal/rm

United States

The US Postal Service guidance is broadly that the address should have the recipient's name on the first line, the apartment or building number and street name on the second line, and the municipality, state symbol and ZIP code on the third line. When the letter is to a company or organization this basic structure obviously has to be adapted to take in other elements such as the recipient's title, the relevant department and the company name.

Use the two character state abbreviation instead of the full state name and separate the state abbreviation from the municipality by a single space. The ZIP code should be separated from the state abbreviation by two spaces, and if it is a nine digit ZIP code (Zip + 4) there should be a hyphen between the fifth and sixth digits.

Arthur M. Holbrook, Vice President
Public Affairs Department
Ardley, Blackley and Chatley, Inc
756 Juniper Rd
CHICAGO IL 47657-5675

To check the correct spelling of a city name or to find a ZIP code, visit the United States Postal Service website at:

www.usps.com.

Canada

Canada Post's addressing guide suggests addresses should be written entirely in upper case; postcodes should be in upper case with a space between the first three and the last three elements; and the municipality, province or territory, and the postal code should appear on the same line. For bilingual addressing (French is the first language in some parts of Canada) a solid black line should be drawn between the English and French versions of the address, with a clear space on each side of the black line.

Australia

In Australia, addresses are typically written on three lines, with the recipient's name on the top line, the number and name of the street on the next line, and the place name or post office of delivery + state or territory abbreviation + postcode on the last line. The information on the last line should be printed all in capitals without punctuation or underlining. One or two character spaces should be left between the place name and the state or territory name and the postcode. Some envelopes have pre-printed postcode squares; these are used only when the address is to be written by hand.

France

Madame Bouvier (recipient's name)
36, Rue Olivier (house/building number, street name)
17682 LYONS (postal code + city)
FRANCE (include the country only if posting the letter outside France)

Italy

Sig. Antonio Alberti (recipient's name)
Via Francesco 37 (street name, house/building number)
10000-ROMA RM (postal code-city/ province)
ITALY (include the country only if posting the letter outside Italy)

Spain

Sra. D. Garcia (recipient's name)
Avda de la Libertad 10, 3° B (street name,
house/building number, floor number)
28300 MADRID (postal code + city/town/locality)
SPAIN (include the country only if posting the letter outside Spain)

Germany

Herrn (form of address)
Hermann Gottlieb (name)
Hertzstrasse 12 (street name + street number)
16935 Leipzig (postal code + city)
GERMANY (include the country only if posting the letter outside Germany)

Faxes and Their Cover Pages/Sheets

Some points to remember when sending a fax:

- Always include a cover sheet (handwritten or typed) which shows, at a minimum, the name of the sender, the name of the recipient, fax number of the sender, date of transmission, and the number of pages sent.
- It is very important to include the number of pages on the cover sheet, and always number the individual pages. It is quite common for pages to become separated during or after transmission.
- Give your message a heading.
- Quote any reference for filing purposes and so that the fax can be linked to previous correspondence.
- There is no necessity to include an opening greeting, such as 'Dear Mr Singh' or 'Dear Britney'.
- Neither do you need to include one of the formal complimentary closes, such as 'Yours sincerely' or 'Yours faithfully'. However, some people do include a closing phrase, such as 'Kind regards' or 'Best wishes'.

The sample below gives a general idea of the different elements that are included in a fax cover page/sheet.

FAX

To: Peter Murray Company
Peter Murray Garden Structures Ltd
Fax Number: 07754 3067 8293
From: Rani Shavir
Date: 5 March 2004
No. of Pages: 3 (including cover page)

LANDSCAPING AT 275 LIME CRESCENT HEMEL HEMPSTEAD

As we discussed on the phone earlier this afternoon, I'm sending the approved drawings and plans for the rear garden, showing the location of the new conservatory and garage block. I'd appreciate if you would let me have your estimate within the next few days.

Regards

Rani Shavir

Letter Content and Style

This section looks at the content of a letter and deals with matters of style.

Your letter should be easy to read and easy to understand. If it is a business letter it should be obvious what it is about, and all the information the reader needs should be easy to find.

If your letter is not well constructed and clearly written, the point or points you are trying to make will probably be lost. It is not only essential to lay out and present your letter well, but also to consider carefully what you say and how you say it.

This means that the language you use should be easy to understand and grammar, punctuation and spelling should be correct. For certain categories of business correspondence, such as applying for a job or making a formal complaint, you will do yourself no favours at all if your letter is misspelled, ungrammatical and badly punctuated. Such a letter is very likely to be cast aside as not worthy of the reader's attention.

The tone of the letter should be pitched in an appropriate way—not too informal where a degree of formality is expected, and not too formal where it will be better appreciated if you express yourself in a more conversational style.

Before you start

Decide what you want to say before you begin to write. Marshal all the facts and information you need to include, and discard all that is irrelevant. Here are a few useful questions, which may help you to get your letter into shape:

- What is the purpose of this letter?
- Is it a personal or a business letter?
- Is it a formal or informal letter?
- Who is going to read the letter and in what circumstances will they be reading it?
- Do I have a clear idea of my aims? What do I hope to get out of writing this letter or what do I hope the recipient will get out of it? (It is sometimes a good idea to jot down your most important aims beforehand.)
- What specific information do I need to provide in this letter? Facts should be mustered and presented in a clear and accessible way.

It is always worth doing a rough draft of the letter so that you can check it for errors, or—if you are not confident that you have a complete grasp of grammar, usage and punctuation—ask someone to check it for you.

Vary the length of sentences

Short sentences coming one after the other are fine for special sections of the letter in which you want to list and highlight a number of points (perhaps also using bullets or numbering), but having every sentence short in the body of the letter can produce a rather severe staccato effect.

Long complex sentences should also be avoided, because it is all too easy to get lost, both when you are writing and when you are reading.

Don't pack sentences with too many ideas

If there are too many points or ideas in a single sentence, the reader may very well lose track. The usual advice is that a sentence should contain a single point or idea. Another good rule of thumb is to have only one subordinate clause with each main clause. Too many subordinate clauses in the sentence will reduce readability. A business letter usually has a fairly mundane purpose which will not sit well with complicated structures and rhetorical flourishes.

Paragraphs

Ideally, a paragraph should consist of two or more sentences. Start each paragraph with a topic sentence and use further sentences, as required, to amplify or expand your point.

Avoid very long paragraphs. If a paragraph is too long, it can look daunting and the reader may skip over important details to get through it. It is better to try to divide your ideas and points up and go for shorter paragraphs. This is especially important in letters.

Writers in general are advised to avoid one-sentence paragraphs. Letter-writers who are aiming for a degree of style in their prose should also follow this advice. However, for a letter whose purpose is simply to provide information, this is probably not worth agonizing over. There is nothing to be gained by padding the letter out just to avoid one-sentence paragraphs.

Register

Register is the name given by linguists to the varieties of language that people use when they interact in speech and writing. Language can vary from the extremely formal to extremely informal, with each variety displaying differences in vocabulary and syntax (ie the ways in which words are arranged).

In letter-writing, cues about the necessary level of formality can be taken from previous correspondence, but there will also be times when you will have to make an independent judgement about how formal or informal your letter should be. This is quite often a matter of common sense, keeping in mind that the tone you ought to use when writing a letter to a prospective employer is very unlikely to be the tone you are in the habit of using when texting or emailing your friends.

People who are nervous of writing are frequently told to write as they speak. This is probably quite good advice when the letter is to a friend or family member; the letter will then reflect the writer's personality and be recognizable to the recipient. Any small errors, or idiosyncrasies of style, will almost certainly be overlooked or forgiven by the recipient.

'Write as you speak' is not such good advice for a formal business letter, unless you are adept at changing your tone to suit your audience. In business contexts, too conversational a tone is not likely to suit your purpose or produce the desired effect.

Nonetheless, you should not attempt to use a high-flown formal style because you imagine it is what is expected or it is the only way to impress. When a letter is full of long, pretentious words and outdated expressions, the impression made is much more likely to be a negative one.

Furthermore, if you use language that you aren't familiar with and don't properly understand, you risk making yourself look ridiculous, like Mrs Malaprop in Sheridan's play *The Rivals*. Mrs Malaprop peppered her conversation with polysyllabic words so as to sound grand but, having no idea of their meaning, she invariably used them in the wrong context, with laughable results, for example 'He is the very pineapple of politeness.'

Even if these embarrassing extremes are avoided, where the writing style is too formal, the letter may be stiff, stilted and unnatural. The best advice is to try and be yourself as much as possible, without being overly conversational.

Try reading the letter aloud to make sure that it sounds unaffected, flows well, and is a true record of what you want to say.

Don't begin every sentence with the same word

It makes for smoother flowing prose if sentences begin in different ways. In particular, avoid beginning every sentence with the first person singular pronoun 'I' or the first person plural pronoun 'we'. One good way to vary sentences is to change the order of main clause and subordinate clause so that the subordinate clause comes before the main clause, for example, the sentence that follows:

> He won't be able to buy the property unless he can raise a big enough loan.
>
> *can be changed to*
>
> Unless he can raise a big enough loan, he won't be able to buy the property.

Brevity not verbosity

For some writers, the urge to use fourteen words when two or three will do seems to be quite irresistible. Although you may be tempted to try to thrill your correspondent with your wide vocabulary and impressive grasp of important-sounding terms, take care! There is a real danger your reader may view your writing style as pompous, or, more seriously, they may not understand what you are trying to say. It is wise to avoid long-windedness and high-falutin' language, and instead stick to clear plain English.

Simplicity and clarity should always be the watchwords for business correspondence. This usual also means aiming for brevity. Nowadays, people do not have the time, inclination or concentration span to read great screeds. When faced with a very long letter they will probably not read it closely, and some may not even begin to read it. A page and a half of A4 paper is about the extent that will be tolerated. While aiming for brevity, though, do ensure that you have included all the points you want to make and all the information that is required.

Various tests have been devised by linguists to assess the readability of texts. One such test is a lexical density test. Here, the number of different words used in the text is divided by the total number of words and the result is multiplied by 100 to give the lexical density. Texts with a lower lexical density are easier to read and understand.

Other tests base readability results on average sentence length and average number of syllables per word. Many modern word processors now provide statistics on readability based on such tests. For example, in Microsoft's® popular word processing program, Word, you are able to select 'readability statistics' in a tick box on the Spelling and Grammar tab (first select Tools, then Options to find the Spelling and Grammar tab). Information on the readability of the document will then be displayed each time a spelling and grammar check is completed on your document.

Avoid humour in formal and business letters

Keep things business-like. Don't try to funny. There is a time and a place for humour and irony—it's fine in personal letters, but not in a letter to your bank manager.

Watch what you say

Take care not to be abusive or libellous, and never tell lies or misrepresent yourself in a letter.

Don't rush to the post with a letter of complaint you have dashed off while upset or angry. Give yourself a bit of time to calm down and then decide if the letter should be sent as written, if it should be revised and toned down, or if it shouldn't be sent at all.

Political correctness aims to remove all forms of prejudice in language: sexism, racism, ageism, discrimination against the disabled, religious intolerance, etc. While the motives for promoting political correctness may be wholly admirable (ie to achieve a more equal society in which everyone respects each other), some people do carry it to extreme lengths.

It is really a matter of choice whether you observe the politically correct rules of language, but even if you don't you should always consider the likely effect of what you write on the feelings of the recipient. Will anything you have written cause irritation or offence?

Remember it costs nothing to be polite.

Avoid saying the same thing twice

Repetition is commonly used in speech for emphasis, or as a means of re-engaging listeners whose attention has momentarily been diverted elsewhere. However, when communication is in writing, the way information is transferred from one person to another is wholly different. In letter-writing, if points are to be emphasized this is usually done by highlighting in some way (for example by underlining, or using italic or bold lettering) not by repeating the point again and again.

Where a reader may have suffered a lapse in concentration or had an interruption, he or she can always go back over the text. In any event, if your point is made well enough in the first place, the reader will understand it and will be looking to move on. Repetition can sometimes be interpreted as patronizing, it may irritate or antagonize the reader, or it may even communicate a sense of desperation.

There is another style fault, of a slightly less obvious kind, that involves repetition. This saying in different words something that has been said already, otherwise known as tautology. While using tautological expressions in spoken language is no great sin, they can cause intense irritation to some readers and should be avoided.

Here are some examples of tautology, with the relevant word or phrase in bold and the duplicated meaning in italics:

Three *additional* sections **have been added** to this year's brochure.

Our *mutual* respect **for each other** made for an extremely cordial meeting.

Is a vegan diet **adequate** *enough* for a growing child?

He lived in *lonely* **isolation**.

Several letters of complaint arrived **one after the other** *in succession*.

The heavier particles sink *down* **to the bottom**.

The convoy **progressed** *forward* slowly.

I refer you to the documents **enclosed** *herewith*.

This *new* **innovation** will revolutionize office procedures.

I am *personally* not aware of any such instruction.

Personally, **I** wouldn't want to be in his position.

the *former* manners of **an earlier time**

The *past* **history** of the village is contained in these dusty volumes.

At this moment *in time*, there seems to be no obvious solution.

The building was **razed** *to the ground*.

Different Categories of Letters: Employment

Many of the formal letters we write relate to employment. Here, as with most kinds of business letter, you should, in general, aim for brevity. Letters of application generally take two forms—letters applying for advertised posts and speculative letters written to investigate possible job opportunities.

Speculative letters are mostly written by younger people who are just leaving school or further education and looking for their first job. Young job-seekers should be prepared to bombard the firms operating in the areas in which they are most interested. They should also be prepared for disappointment: there may be no job available and they may get a letter of rejection; or, more discouragingly, they may not even receive any acknowledgement at all of their letters. It can be extremely depressing for job-seekers to send off multiple letters and be met with complete silence. The most likely reason is that the employer receives so many speculative job applications they cannot reply to all of them and so getting no reply is seldom a reflection of the employer's opinion of the applicant.

If you are writing a letter that is not in reply to an advertisement and you don't know to whom the letter should be addressed, a quick phone call to the firm should provide you with the relevant name, or at the very least, the department. Reasonably large firms will have a Personnel or Human Resources manager.

If your letter is a reply to an advertisement you should obviously answer any questions or comply with any requirements made in the advertisement. Often a CV is asked for, in which case the cover letter should be a brief one stating why you are right for the job. Usually, you will need to send a CV and a brief typed letter which sells you and your skills to the firm.

Some useful phrases for job application letters

I wish to apply for the post of [*job title*] advertised in the [*publication*] on [*date*].

I am writing to enquire whether you have a suitable vacancy in your organization.

I am sending this letter and CV to apply for the position of [job title] with your company.

The advertised post calls for qualifications and experience that correspond to my professional background.

As an experienced [*job description*], I believe I am the candidate you are looking for.

I am confident my experience qualifies me for the position of [*job title*].

It is my aim to work for a company where my qualifications and working experience would make a positive contribution.

I look forward to hearing from you and to being granted the opportunity of an interview.

I hope you will consider my application favourably and grant me an interview.

The CV (Curriculum Vitae) and its covering letter

Because a CV (called 'the résumé' in the United States) can be such an important first step in gaining the attention of a potential employer, a great deal of care and attention should be devoted to how it is laid out, and, of course, to its content. Because presentation is so important, many people choose to have their CVs compiled by a professional agency.

Don't be tempted to use ornamental fonts or brightly coloured ink or paper, unless you are convinced the employer is looking for this sort of originality, and try to get all the information onto one sheet of paper. Both the CV and the covering letter should be typed unless otherwise stated but it is quite common for firms to ask for covering letters to be handwritten.

CVs often look remarkably similar so it can be a good idea to personalize either the CV or the covering letter, or both, to bring attention to your application. Many people nowadays choose to take advantage of the design features and templates offered in modern computer programs. However, don't make the design or layout too idiosyncratic just to attract attention.

Until quite recently it was the preferred practice to put in a CV just about everything the applicant had ever done or was ever interested in. For people in the middle of their career, this could make for a very long and crowded document which took a long time for prospective employers to digest. The preference nowadays is to keep the CV fairly brief, paring it down to a record of personal details, qualifications and employment (*see* the sample CV on the next page).

Many employers now rely more on the letter accompanying the CV to spark their interest. These covering letters are a good opportunity for applicants to sell themselves to prospective employers. The covering letter's main purpose is to accompany your CV, to introduce you and your credentials to the employer, to generate interest in you and to encourage the employer to grant you an interview.

Many firms and organizations also send out application forms. These can be quite challenging, especially if they include such questions as 'Why do you want this post?' or 'What qualities do you feel you could bring to this post?' There are many specialist courses and publications on how to tackle job applications and interviews to best effect, and it may be worthwhile considering some of these.

Employers are invariably dealing with many applications per vacancy and they are often also working to tight deadlines. They will make their first decision on your application by scanning your covering letter and your CV/résumé, and, while scanning, they will often be searching for a few keywords which will alert them to the fact that you fit the profile of the person they are looking for. The processing of job applications is very tedious task for most employers, so if you make their life easier they are more likely to take a positive attitude to you. And sadly any letter or CV/résumé that is difficult to read or navigate through will be discarded.

Note that in the US, it is usual practice to restrict a résumé to a single sheet of paper, headed with the applicant's name, and with his or her career objectives somewhere near the top of the page.

What a well-presented CV should do

- Attract the employer to read the CV immediately and before those of other applicants.
- Get across the sense that you have wider skills than the brief descriptions in your CV.

Name:

Address:

Tel:
Email:

Date of birth:

Nationality:

Marital status:

WORK EXPERIENCE
(*List with the most recent first and give date ranges*)

EDUCATION
(*List, giving the most recent first and including date ranges*)

OTHER RELEVANT SKILLS
(List only the most important: be concise)

INTERESTS
(List only the most interesting and relevant; be concise)

REFEREES
(Provide at least two names and addresses)

- Guide the employer to the key areas of your history.
- Give the employer a positive picture of you and your abilities.
- Get you an interview for the job.

What the covering letter accompanying a CV should/shouldn't do

The covering letter that accompanies your CV can be just as, or more, important than the CV. It should contain a brief account of all the features, qualifications and experience that make you ideal for the advertised post. A few 'dos' and 'don'ts' are suggested below:

Dos

- Do generate the reader's interest in the very first paragraph, and state your interest in the job.
- Do promote your potential value by focussing on the employer's needs and highlighting your strengths and abilities.
- Do provide a background summary of education and/or experience.
- Do try to include a statement that encourages a positive response.
- Do include a final statement of appreciation, such as 'Thank you' or 'Thank you for your consideration'.

Don'ts

Any or all of the following can contribute to lack of impact and efficacy and should be avoided in your covering letter.

- Don't ramble.
- Don't be pushy.
- Don't be self-deprecating—it can be irritating and professional interviewers are not usually convinced by an 'ever so humble' approach.
- Don't exaggerate or brag.
- Don't focus too much on your own needs, ignoring the needs of the employer.
- Avoid a characterless or uninteresting writing style, laced with overused expressions.
- Avoid bad grammar, spelling and punctuation.
- Avoid a messy, muddled or cluttered appearance.

Letters of appointment

Letters of appointment should detail the salary and other employment conditions. If a job description is being sent there will be no need to repeat the details from the job description in the letter offering the post.

Written warnings

Under employment or contract conditions, it is usually the case that an employee is entitled to receive a written warning before they can be dismissed. The warning letter will in most cases have been preceded by a verbal warning or discussion with the employee about their conduct. When writing warning letters it is usual to include details of the unsatisfactory conduct with dates, and to state the further steps that will be taken if the conduct is repeated.

Resignation letters

No matter how much you may have hated the job you are resigning from, or however badly you think you have been treated, you should resist the temptation to rant and rave or be abusive in a resignation letter.

Try to write a letter which will not sour your relations permanently with your ex-employer. You may find that your paths cross again later and, in any event, anger will almost certainly be tempered by time. If possible, you should always exercise restraint, be courteous, and try to include something positive about your period of employment with them.

Different Categories of Letters: Personal Business and Finance

There are many areas of personal business and finance that might conceivably require that you write a letter. If you think you may need to have written evidence of an offer, transaction or exchange, it is a good idea to conduct the business in writing and keep copies of all letters.

Complaints

We often write to complain or to ask for damaged things to be fixed. In order to be most effective, these letters should be brief and to the point, without going into too much detail. Letters of complaint should be factual rather than emotional, and calm and restrained rather than abusive. When writing letters of complaint, be firm. Set a reasonable timetable for things to be put right and stick to it and quote the relevant legislation where necessary.

Legislation relating to the supply of goods and services

The following acts and regulations deal with the supply of goods and services in the UK: the Sale of Goods Act 1979; Supply of Goods and Services Act 1982; Sale and Supply of Goods Act 1994; and the Sale and Supply of Goods to Consumers Regulations 2002.

It is the seller, not the manufacturer, who is responsible if goods do not conform to contract. This means they must be as described, fit for purpose and of satisfactory quality. Goods are deemed to be of satisfactory quality if they reach the standard that a 'reasonable' person would regard as satisfactory, taking into account the price and any description. Aspects of quality include fitness for purpose, freedom from minor defects, appearance and finish, durability and safety. If goods do not conform to contract at the time of sale, purchasers can request their money back within a 'reasonable' time.

Under the Supply of Goods and Services Act 1982 traders are required to provide services to a proper standard of workmanship. Any material used or goods supplied in providing the service must be of satisfactory quality. In addition, if a definite completion date or a price has not been fixed then the work must be completed within a 'reasonable' time and for a 'reasonable' charge. The law treats failure to meet these obligations as breach of contract and consumers would be entitled to seek redress, if necessary through the civil courts.

Finance

If you are unfortunate enough to experience difficulties in paying bills or loans, the golden rule is to contact the lender or creditor as soon as possible, preferably in writing. Remember also that any arrangement you come to should be a realistic one which you are confident you will be able to maintain.

More wide-ranging advice on money matters is available through local advice centres, such as CAB (the Citizens Advice Bureau).

Different Categories of Letters: Special Occasions

There are some circumstances in which there is a need for a rather more formulaic personal letter. These letters are often sent to mark the most joyous and the most solemn occasions in a life.

Formal wedding invitations

Formal wedding invitations are always written in the third person and are usually printed on cards with no opening greeting or complimentary close. The letters RSVP at the end of an invitation are an abbreviation for the French phrase *'Répondez s'il vouz plaît'* meaning, in English, 'Please reply'. When receiving a formal invitation in the third person, you should also reply in the third person.

Letters expressing sympathy

The tone and content of a letter expressing sympathy for an illness or injury will depend very much on whether the illness is serious or not. If the person is very likely to recover and is also someone you know reasonably well, the letter can be lighter in tone.

If the illness is a serious one, be careful about using the 'Get well soon' formula, because this may cause distress to the patient and their close relatives.

Letters of condolence

Even those people most practised in the art of letter-writing find letters of condolence amongst the most challenging to write. It can be very hard to find the right words, and many people shrink from the task for fear of intruding on the bereaved person's unhappiness. Obviously the person who is going to receive a letter of condolence is going to be in a distressed state and it is hard to think of anything to say that will bring any kind of comfort. In fact because it is impossible to give real comfort, the bereaved often appreciate very much the fact that people have remembered their relative and thought highly enough of him or her to write. A simple and natural acknowledgement of the loss suffered will always be appreciated and be a positive comfort.

Try to use straightforward everyday words and phrases. Be as sensitive as you can to the feelings of the person who will read the letter. Avoid expressions like 'a blessed release' and 'good innings'. Only refer to religious matters if you know the recipient is a believer.

It is difficult to avoid clichés in letters of sympathy and condolence, but bereavement is not an area in which striving for originality is especially appropriate. In the circumstances, a few clichés can be quite acceptable. One more thing—it is as well to set aside your word processor. Unless your handwriting is completely illegible it is much better to write, rather than type, letters of sympathy. This makes them personal in a way that a word-processed document can never be.

Often people opt to send a card with a short personal message written inside. It is probably better to go for a plain card with no pre-printed message. A message that is not in your own words can often seem a little impersonal. It is nearly always better to avoid those cards that include flowery or sentimental poems.

Thank-you letters

You should always write to thank someone—especially someone of the older generation—for a gift. Of course, it is often quite appropriate to telephone your thanks. You have to try and judge the preference of the person to whom you owe thanks and act accordingly.

Just as letters of condolence require a marked degree of sensitivity, so to do letters of thanks, especially those in response to presents.

The problem is often one of knowing what to say about an unwanted gift without being excessively enthusiastic and so risk getting a similar gift again!

It is often difficult to decide how to fill space in a thank-you letter. You can keep the message brief, but you have to do better than a couple of lines. However much or little you choose to write you might think of writing the letter by hand instead of dashing it off on your word processor. Most people prefer the more personal touch of a handwritten note.

A

abandon *vb* **1** (*abandon his wife and children*) desert, leave, forsake, depart from. **2** (*abandon the attempt*) give up, drop, discard, (*inf*) scrap.

abate *vb* (*The storm abated*) die down, lessen, ease, decrease, diminish, moderate, wane.

abbreviate *vb* (*abbreviate a word or phrase*) shorten, reduce, cut, cut short, cut down, contract. ▼

---

abbreviations include **BBC** = British Broadcasting Corporation, **CIA** = Central Intelligence Agency, **DIY** = do-it-yourself, **EC** = European Community, **FO** = Foreign Office, **GCE** = General Certificate of Education, **HGV** = heavy goods vehicle, **MEP** = Member of the European Parliament, **NHS** = National Health Service, **OAP** = old age pensioner, **PR** = public relations or proportional representation, **SF** = science fiction, **YHA** = Youth Hostels Association.

---

abdicate *vb* **1** (*The king abdicated in 1936*) give up, resign, stand down, retire, quit. **2** (*abdicate responsibilities*) give up, renounce, relinquish.

abdomen *n* (*a pain in the abdomen*) stomach, belly, (*inf*) tummy, (*inf*) insides, intestines.

abduct *vb* (*abduct someone else's child*) kidnap, carry off, seize, hold as hostage, (*inf*) snatch.

ability *n* (*a performer of great ability*) talent, skill, expertise, cleverness, competence.

able *adj* (*an able pupil*) clever, talented, capable, competent.

abnormal *adj* (*an abnormal thing to do*) unusual, strange, odd, peculiar, queer, extraordinary.

abolish *vb* (*abolish smoking in public*) do away with, put an end to, end, stop, eliminate.

abridge *vb* (*abridge the book for children*) shorten, cut down, condense, compress.

abroad *adv* (*go abroad on holiday*) overseas, to a foreign country, to a foreign land, out of the country.

abrupt *adj* **1** (*come to an abrupt end*) sudden, quick, hurried, hasty, swift, rapid, unexpected, unforeseen. **2** (*an abrupt reply*) curt, blunt, brusque, short, rude. **3** (*an abrupt slope*) steep, sheer, sudden, precipitous.

absent *adj* (*absent from school*) not present, away, off, missing, truant.

absent-minded *adj* (*so absent-minded that she didn't hear what people were saying to her*) distracted, preoccupied, absorbed, vague, inattentive.

absolute *adj* (*absolute trust*) complete, total, utter, out and out, outright, perfect, unqualified, sheer.

abstain *vb* (*abstain from voting/abstain from drinking*) refrain, desist, hold back, keep from.

absurd *adj* (*absurd plan*) ridiculous, foolish, silly, idiotic, stupid, nonsensical, senseless, crazy, ludicrous, hare-brained.

abundance *n* (*there was food in abundance*) plenty, plentifulness, profusion, (*inf*) heaps, (*inf*) bags, (*inf*) oodles.

abundant *adj* (*an abundant supply of fresh food*) plentiful, ample, large, great, copious, lavish, profuse.

abuse *vb* **1** (*abuse children*) mistreat, maltreat, ill-treat, ill-use, injure, hurt, harm. **2** (*abuse power*) misuse, misapply, misemploy, mishandle. **3** (*abuse the person who ran into his car*) swear at, curse, insult, rebuke.

abuse *n* **1** (*child abuse*) mistreatment, maltreatment, ill-treatment, ill-use, injury, hurting, harming. **2** (*the abuse of power/the abuse of alcohol*) misuse, misapplication, misapplying, mishandling.

abysmal *adj* **1** (*abysmal ignorance*) utter, extreme, complete, thorough, profound. **2** (*an abysmal performance*) dreadful, appalling, very bad, worthless.

accelerate *vb* **1** (*The car accelerated*) speed up, go faster, go quicker, pick up speed. **2** (*accelerate the process of change*) speed up, hasten, hurry along, expedite, spur on.

accent *n* **1** (*a Birmingham accent*) way of speaking, pronunciation, inflection, enunciation. **2** (*The accent is on the first syllable*) stress, emphasis, force, accentuation. **3** (*the accent must be on efficiency*) emphasis, stress, importance.

accept *vb* **1** (*accept the gift*) receive, take, take receipt of. **2** (*accept their decision*) agree to, consent to, comply with, acquiesce in, concur with, endorse.

acceptable *adj* **1** (*a very acceptable gift*) welcome, agreeable, delightful, pleasing, pleasant, desirable, (*inf*) cool. **2** (*work that is not acceptable*) satisfactory, good enough, adequate, passable, tolerable.

access *n* (*no direct access to the building from the main road*) entry, entrance, way in, admittance, approach.

accessible *adj* (*accessible sources of information*) attainable, available, reachable, obtainable.

accessory *n* **1** (*accessories for an electric drill*) attachment, fitment, extra, addition, adjunct. **2** (*accessories to the crime*) accomplice, associate, confederate, abettor.

accident *n* **1** (*people injured in the mining accident*) casualty, disaster, catastrophe, calamity, mishap. **2** (*old friends who met by accident*) chance, fate, good fortune, luck, (*inf*) fluke. ▼

---

a chapter of accidents a whole series of misfortunes, one after the other (*Their foreign holiday was a chapter of accidents—it rained all the time, the food was terrible and the hotel was next to a building site*).

---

accidental *adj* (*accidental death/an accidental meeting*) chance, unintentional, unintended, unexpected, unforeseen, unplanned, unpremeditated.

accommodation *n* (*find accommodation for the homeless*) housing, lodging, shelter, board, quarters, (*inf*) digs.

accompany *vb* (*accompany her to the dance*) partner, escort, go with, go along with.

accomplice *n* (*an accomplice in crime*) confederate, accessory, collaborator, abettor, ally, helper, henchman, (*inf*) sidekick.

accomplish *vb* (*accomplish a task*) finish, complete, do, perform, execute.

accomplished *adj* (*an accomplished*

pianist) skilled, skilful, expert, gifted, talented, masterly.

accomplishment *n* (*person of many accomplishments*) talent, gift, ability, skill, attainment, achievement.

account *n* **1** (*give a full account of the accident*) statement, report, description, record, story, tale. **2** (*send in the account for the work done*) bill, invoice, charges.

accumulate *vb* **1** (*rubbish accumulating in the streets*) gather, collect, pile up, build up. **2** (*accumulate many books over the years*) gather, collect, amass, stockpile, hoard.

accredited *adj* (*an accredited representative of the firm*) official, authorized, legal, approved, certified.

accurate *adj* **1** (*accurate measurements*) correct, precise, exact, right, errorless. **2** (*an accurate description*) correct, exact, close, true, faithful, strict.

accusation *n* (*deny the accusations*) charge, allegation, imputation, incrimination.

accuse *vb* **1** (*accuse her of murder*) charge, indict, ar-raign. **2** (*accuse the boys of breaking windows*) blame, put the blame on, lay the blame on, hold responsible for, hold accountable for, lay at the door of.

accustom *vb* (*accustom herself to her new surroundings*) adapt, adjust, acclimatize, get used to.

accustomed *adj* **1** (*our accustomed route home*) usual, normal, customary, regular, habitual, routine. **2** (*accustomed to public speaking*) used to, in the habit of, familiar with, acquainted with.

ache *vb* (*My head aches*) hurt, be sore, be painful, throb.

ache *n* (*an ache in his back*) pain, soreness, throbbing, twinge, pang.

achieve *vb* (*achieve one's aim*) accomplish, reach, attain, gain, obtain, acquire.

achievement *n* (*proud of his achievements on the sports field*) accomplishment, attainment, deed, act, effort, feat.

acid *adj* **1** (*an acid taste*) sour, tart, sharp, bitter, vinegary. **2** (*acid remarks*) sharp, sarcastic, caustic, trenchant, acerbic.

acknowledge *vb* **1** (*acknowledge a letter*) answer, reply to, respond to. **2** (*acknowledge defeat*) admit, accept, recognize, grant, concede.

acquire *vb* (*acquire enough money*) obtain, get, come by, gain, procure.

acquit *vb* (*the judge will acquit the accused*) clear, set free, release, discharge, pardon, absolve, exonerate.

act *vb* **1** (*act like a fool*) behave, do, operate. **2** (*act quickly to put out the fire*) take action, move, be active, perform. **3** (*act the part of Peter Pan*) play, perform, enact. **4** (*act in a new play*) be an actor, play a part, perform.

act *n* **1** (*a brave act*) action, deed, undertaking, feat, exploit. **2** (*enjoy the magician's act*) performance, show, turn, routine. **3** (*an act to forbid smoking*) law, ruling, rule, regulation, order, bill, decree, statute. ▼

---

catch someone in the act to find someone actually doing something wrong or bad (*The thief was breaking into the car and was caught in the act by the police*).

---

acting *adj* (*the acting head teacher*) temporary, interim, substitute.

action *n* **1** (*His action saved their*

lives) act, deed, move, behaviour, undertaking, feat, exploit. **2** (*a film full of action*) activity, movement, liveliness, energy, vitality.

active *adj* **1** (*active children tiring their mothers/lead active lives*) energetic, full of energy, lively, busy, nimble, (*inf*) on the go. **2** (*sports clubs which are still active*) in action, working, operating, in operation, functioning.

activity *n* **1** (*city streets full of activity*) movement, bustle, hustle and bustle, liveliness. **2** (*activities enjoyed after school*) pastime, interest, hobby, pursuit, project.

actual *adj* **1** (*The actual cost was far less than the newspapers reported*) real, true, genuine, authentic. **2** (*no actual evidence of burglary*) existing, definite, certain, positive, concrete.

actually *adv* (*The boy seems unhealthy but he is actually quite well*) really, in fact, in reality, in truth, truly.

adapt *vb* **1** (*adapt the scheme to suit younger children*) adjust, alter, change, convert, modify, vary, reshape, remodel. **2** (*find it difficult to adapt to a new way of life*) adjust, fit in, accustom oneself, become accustomed to, acclimatize.

add *vb* **1** (*add some more details to the report*) put in, include, append. **2** (*add the rows of figures*) add up, count, count up, (*inf*) tot up, total. **3** (*Money problems added to his worry*) increase, augment, amplify, intensify, aggravate.

addicted *adj* (*be addicted to alcohol*) dependent on, (*inf*) hooked on.

addiction *n* (*try to cure his drug addiction*) dependence, dependency, craving, habit.

additional *adj* (*require additional supplies*) more, extra, further, supplementary.

additive *n* (*additives listed on food labels*) supplement, preservative.

address *n* **1** (*find out his address*) where one lives, home, house, residence. **2** (*the address of the company's head office*) location, place, whereabouts. **3** (*unable to read the address on the parcel*) label, directions, inscription. **4** (*the head teacher's end-of-term address*) speech, talk, lecture.

address *vb* **1** (*address a parcel*) write the address on, label, write the directions on, direct, inscribe. **2** (*How do you address a bishop?*) name, call, speak to, write to, describe. **3** (*address one's remarks to the manager*) direct, communicate, convey, send.

adequate *adj* **1** (*adequate supplies for the week*) enough, sufficient, ample. **2** (*workers who are not adequate*) fit, able, competent, qualified, (*inf*) up to scratch.

adhesive *n* (*an adhesive to stick the tiles to the wall*) glue, cement, gum, fixative.

adjacent *adj* (*living in the adjacent house*) adjoining, next, next door, neighbouring, bordering.

adjourn *vb* (*adjourn the meeting till the next day*) break off, discontinue, defer, postpone, put off, shelve.

adjudicate *vb* (*adjudicate at the singing contest*) judge, arbitrate, referee, umpire.

adjust *vb* **1** (*unable to adjust to the new situation*) adapt, become accustomed to, accustom oneself to, get used to, acclimatize. **2** (*I tried to adjust the saddle of the bike*) alter, change, modify, rearrange.

administration *n* (*in hospital administration*) management, direction, government.